Colorado

THIS EDITION WRITTEN AND RESEARCHED BY

Carolyn McCarthy,
Greg Benchwick, Christopher Pitts

PLAN YOUR TRIP

DENVER P62

'I SEE WHAT YOU MEAN' BY LAWRENCE ARGENT; AN ORIGINAL WORK OWNED AND COMMISSIONED BY THE CITY AND COUNTY OF DENVER. IMAGE: WITOLD SKRYPCZAK/GETTY IMAGES ©

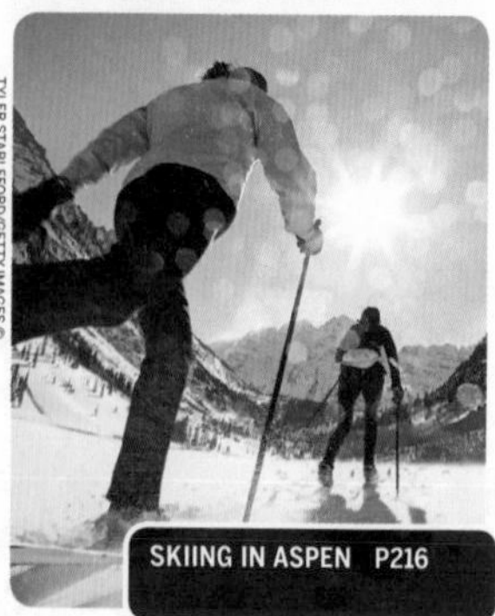

SKIING IN ASPEN P216

TYLER STABLEFORD/GETTY IMAGES ©

ON THE ROAD

Contents

Welcome to Colorado

Spectacular vistas, endless powder runs and mountain towns with echoes of the Old West. Colorado is a place that has forever beckoned people to adventure.

Mountain Bliss

The best known of the Rocky Mountain states, with the highest concentration of peaks above 14,000ft, Colorado owes its public adoration to the mountainous backbone that rises and rolls from the Front Range westward. But there are also mesas, desert canyons and sagebrush hills. Some 300-plus sunny days per year contribute to hiking, biking, river running and rock climbing that's unrivaled anywhere in the US West. Even during the peak summer season, when millions of tourists flood the state, visitors can still find solitude at a remote mountain lake or meadow, or atop a craggy summit. In Rocky Mountain National Park, the state's premier attraction, there are dozens of backcountry hikes and campsites that see few visitors – unless you count that moose or family of foxes that wandered by.

Ski Country USA

With heavy snowfalls and light powder, the long winters of the Colorado high country are the stuff of legend. Hares and mountain lions leave white tracks, boarders and skiers weave through pine forests and open bowls, and hearth fires roar in mountain lodges. With the longest ski run in the USA (Vail), some of the highest snowfall (Wolf Creek), and legendary ski-parking-lot BBQs (Arapahoe Basin), Colorado may have the best downhill skiing on earth. Remarkable cross-country and backcountry terrain bring a whole other dimension to winter – one where lift lines don't exist. If you're among the hard core, you can make turns from Halloween until early June. Iconic resorts like Aspen, Vail and Telluride attract visitors in droves, and after the last lift, parties kick into gear.

Beyond the Great Outdoors

In the shadow of the Rockies, Colorado's urban culture is vibrant and progressive. Industries like high tech, communications and education propel a robust economy. Former cow town Denver boasts iconic sports arenas, a revitalized downtown and plenty of bike routes, breweries and hipster hangouts. Nearby university towns of Boulder and Fort Collins pair stunning natural settings with progressive vibes. Even Aspen is known almost as much for its summer music festival and think-tank intellect as its adventure opportunities. South of the Arkansas River, Colorado was once Mexico, and pockets of Hispanic culture still thrive. Native American culture persists in the Ute Mountain and Southern Ute Indian Reservations in southwest Colorado.

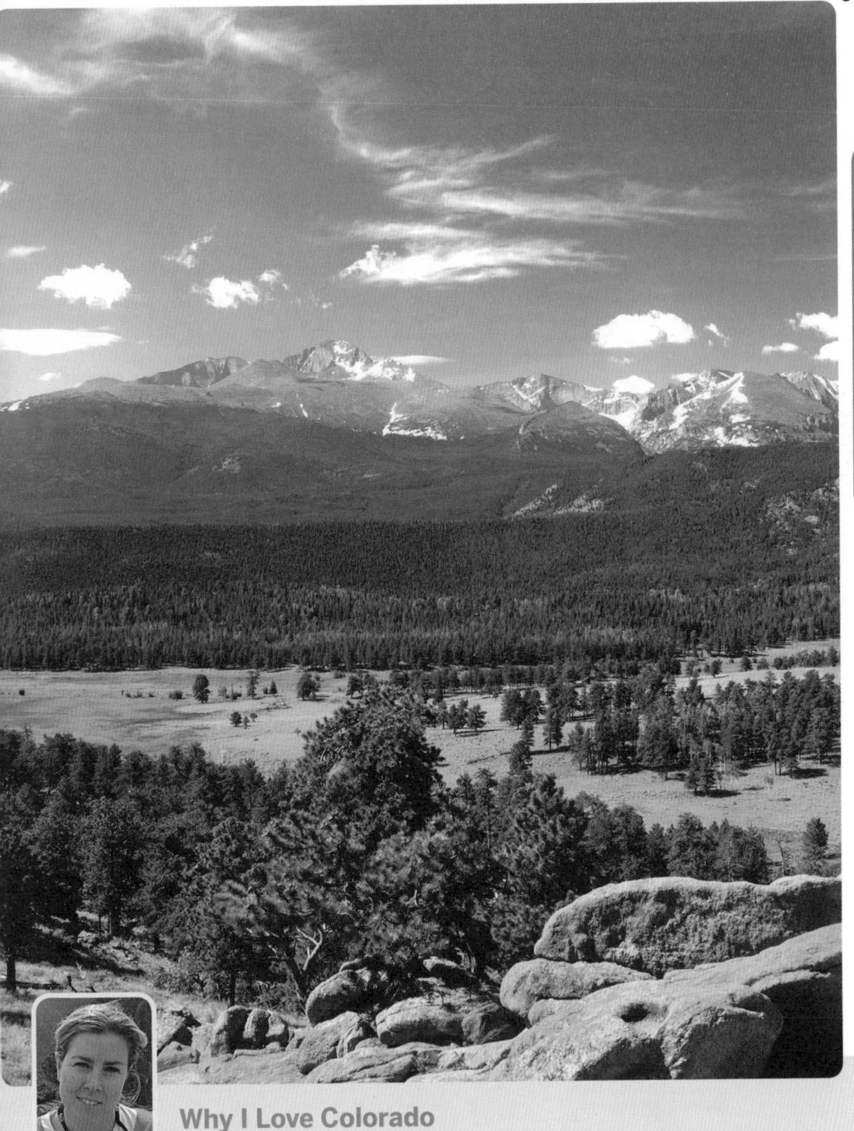

Why I Love Colorado

By Carolyn McCarthy, Author

At 17 I went to college in Colorado and spent my first break stuck in a blizzard with a dozen other classmates, our tents pitched at 12,000ft. We never did summit Crestone Peak, but later hiked out under banner blue skies and outrageous alpine scenery. I stayed for over a decade and keep returning. You could say Colorado was my education – in hiking, river running and just plain living well. With so many sunny days and the Rockies as your backyard, it takes all of us one step closer to the natural world.

For more about our authors, see page 384

Above: Long's Peak, Rocky Mountain National Park (p130)

Colorado

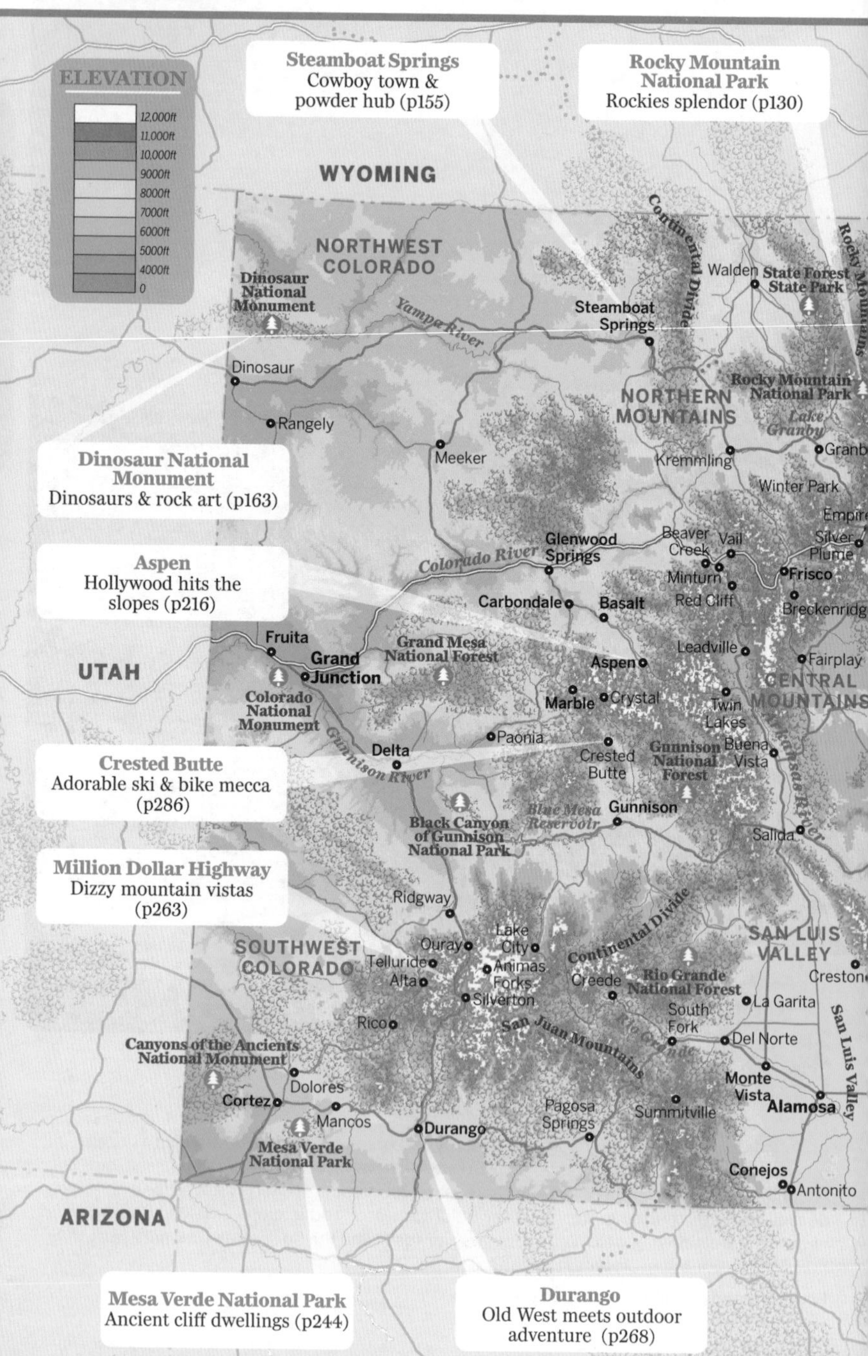

ELEVATION
12,000ft
11,000ft
10,000ft
9000ft
8000ft
7000ft
6000ft
5000ft
4000ft
0
Steamboat Springs
Cowboy town & powder hub (p155)
Rocky Mountain National Park
Rockies splendor (p130)
Dinosaur National Monument
Dinosaurs & rock art (p163)
Aspen
Hollywood hits the slopes (p216)
Crested Butte
Adorable ski & bike mecca (p286)
Million Dollar Highway
Dizzy mountain vistas (p263)
Mesa Verde National Park
Ancient cliff dwellings (p244)
Durango
Old West meets outdoor adventure (p268)
WYOMING
UTAH
ARIZONA
NORTHWEST COLORADO
NORTHERN MOUNTAINS
CENTRAL MOUNTAINS
SOUTHWEST COLORADO
SAN LUIS VALLEY
Continental Divide
Rocky Mountains
Yampa River
Colorado River
Gunnison River
Arkansas River
Rio Grande
San Juan Mountains
San Luis Valley
Blue Mesa Reservoir
Lake Granby
Dinosaur National Monument
Colorado National Monument
Grand Mesa National Forest
Black Canyon of Gunnison National Park
Gunnison National Forest
Rio Grande National Forest
Canyons of the Ancients National Monument
Mesa Verde National Park
State Forest State Park
Rocky Mountain National Park
Walden
Steamboat Springs
Dinosaur
Rangely
Meeker
Kremmling
Granby
Winter Park
Empire
Silver Plume
Glenwood Springs
Beaver Creek
Vail
Minturn
Red Cliff
Frisco
Breckenridge
Carbondale
Basalt
Fruita
Grand Junction
Leadville
Aspen
Fairplay
Marble
Crystal
Twin Lakes
Paonia
Delta
Crested Butte
Buena Vista
Gunnison
Salida
Ridgway
Ouray
Lake City
Telluride
Alta
Animas Forks
Silverton
Creede
Crestone
La Garita
Rico
South Fork
Del Norte
Monte Vista
Alamosa
Dolores
Cortez
Mancos
Durango
Pagosa Springs
Summitville
Conejos
Antonito

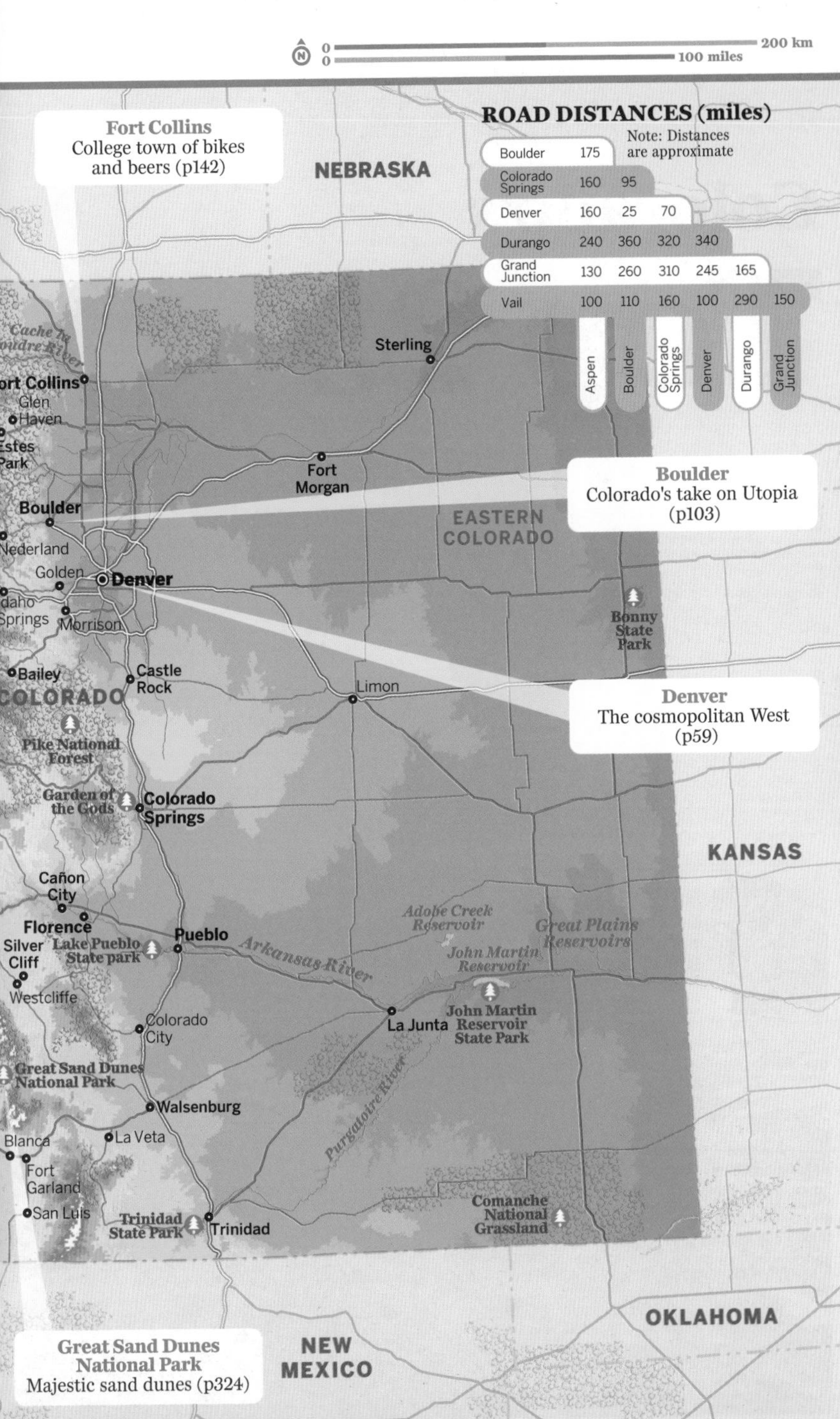

	Aspen	Boulder	Colorado Springs	Denver	Durango	Grand Junction
Boulder	175					
Colorado Springs	160	95				
Denver	160	25	70			
Durango	240	360	320	340		
Grand Junction	130	260	310	245	165	
Vail	100	110	160	100	290	150

Colorado's Top 25

1

Rocky Mountain National Park

1 With elk grazing under granite walls, alpine meadows rife with wildflowers and a winding road inching over the Continental Divide, the natural splendor of Rocky Mountain National Park (p130) packs a wallop. Don't get stuck behind a row of RVs on Trail Ridge Rd. Lace up your hiking boots instead. Trails cater to every ability and ambition, from epic outings on the Continental Divide National Scenic Trail to family-friendly romps in the Bear Lake area. And with a little effort, you can have the place all to yourself.

Boulder

2 Tucked up against its signature Flatirons, Boulder (p103) has a sweet location and a progressive soul, which has attracted a groovy bag of entrepreneurs, hippies and hardbodies. Packs of cyclists ride the Boulder Creek Bike Path, which links an abundance of city and county parks purchased through a popular Open Space tax. The lively epicenter is the pedestrian-only Pearl St Mall, ideal for people-watching, pub crawling and fine dining. In many ways Boulder, not Denver, is the region's tourist hub.

ETHAN WELTY/GETTY IMAGES ©

2

IAN DAGNALL/ALAMY ©

FRANZ MARC FREI/GETTY IMAGES ©

Mesa Verde National Park

3 You don't just walk into the past at Mesa Verde (p244), the site of 600 ancient cliff dwellings. You scramble up 10ft ladders, scale rock faces and crawl through tunnels. Yes, it's interactive exploring at its most low-tech, but it also makes for one of the most exhilarating adventures in the West. It's also a place to puzzle out the archaeological and cultural clues left by its former inhabitants – Ancestral Puebloans who vacated the site in AD 1300 for reasons still not fully understood.

Above: Cliff Palace

Aspen

4 Aspen (p216) is a town, unlike any other place in the US West. A cocktail of cowboy grit, Euro panache, Hollywood glam, Ivy League brains, fresh powder, live music and old money, where you can drop into an extreme vertical double-diamond run or stomp to the crest of a Continental Divide pass. There are ice walls to climb, superpipes to ride and exquisite concerts to absorb. Oh, and did we mention the frothing hot tubs, the fit baristas, multimillion-dollar estates and well-read barflies?

Colorado National Monument

5 Witness the sinking sun set fire to otherworldly red-rock formations, hike stark and beautiful high-desert trails and camp beneath frequent lightning storms as they roll across the distant plains. These canyon walls rise from the Uncompahgre Uplift of the Colorado Plateau, 2000ft above the Grand Valley of the Colorado River to reveal the twinkling lights of Grand Junction, the green river and tree-lined fields of the Grand Valley – all of it a landscape that was once patrolled by dinosaurs.

Microbreweries

6 Colorado has more microbreweries per capita than any other US state, and craft brewing has been elevated to a high art. Each September or October Denver hosts the Great American Beer Festival (p74), which draws 500-odd brewers and countless tasters. Best-of-show awards are judged across categories such as best chocolate- or coffee-flavored beer. Handcrafted brews are produced with passion in long-established and start-up operations. The Colorado Brewers Guild (www.coloradobeer.org) is the peak body, and a font of information. Right: Wynkoop Brewing Co (p84)

BLOOMBERG VIA GETTY IMAGES/GETTY IMAGES ©

Denver

7 Denver's neighborhoods have taken on a life of their own with the Mile High City's youth-oriented focus on urban living. Highlands has one of Denver's best collections of start-up restaurants and a handful of luminary bars. Lower Downtown (LoDo) has higher-end restaurants and jock bars, while the central Santa Fe, Five Points and River North (RiNo) arts districts have street art and a palpable and studied hipster-grunge vibe. Tonier neighborhoods with highly strollable shopping and restaurant areas include Washington Park, Cherry Creek and South Pearl Street.

Dude Ranches

8 With wide-open ranges, wildflower meadows and snow-kissed peaks, seeing Colorado from the saddle is a whole other world. Experiences range from the rustic and real charm of herding cattle on a bona fide ranch (p191) in South Park to venturing to a remote bison ranch (p327) with green credentials, or riding horses in the luxuriant Rocky Mountain retreat of Devil's Thumb (p175). Digs range from five-star refurbished log cabins to starlit camps with an eye on the Milky Way.

CONNOR WALBERG/GETTY IMAGES ©

BRYAN MULLENNIX/GETTY IMAGES ©

Silverton & Old West Towns

9 A rediscovered vintage gem, Silverton (p266) – like Leadville, Cripple Creek and Old Colorado City – was launched by rugged pioneer types seeking mineral riches. Hollywood shot its share of Westerns here in the 1950s, but when the last mine closed in 1991 it seemed destined to become another atmospheric ghost town like abandoned St Elmo and Ashcroft. Then came Durango & Silverton Narrow Gauge Railroad and the experts-only Silverton Mountain Ski Area and the town sprang back to life. Above: Silverton

Vail

10 Darling of the rich and famous, Vail (p195) resembles an elaborate amusement park for grown-ups, where every activity has been designed to send a tingle down your spine – in maximum comfort, of course. Indeed, no serious skier would dispute its status as Colorado's best and most varied resort, with 5000-plus acres of powdery back bowls, chutes and wickedly fun terrain. Whether it's your first time on a snowboard or you're flashing perfect telemark turns in the Outer Mongolia Bowl, this might very well be the ski trip of your dreams.

Dinosaur National Monument

11 One of the few places on Earth where you can literally get your hands on a dinosaur skeleton, Dinosaur National Monument (p163) is tucked into the far northwest corner of Colorado, and partly in Utah. Among the largest dinosaur fossil beds in North America, it was discovered in 1909. Explore desert trails, examine ancient rock art or raft the Yampa River through the serene landscape of its twisting red-rock canyons. The visitor center overlooks thousands of bones in the Dinosaur Quarry. Above: Petroglyphs

12

RICHARD NOWITZ/GETTY IMAGES ©

13

Rafting the Arkansas River

12 Running from Leadville down the eastern flank of Buena Vista and rocketing through the spectacular Royal Gorge at Class V speeds, the Arkansas River is the most diverse, longest and, arguably, the wildest river in the state. White-water outfitters tend to gather south of Buena Vista in Salida, where you'll also find the office for the Arkansas Headwaters Recreation Area (at the northern end of the wildest 99-mile stretch) and downriver near the Royal Gorge Bridge turn-off in Cañon City. Above left: Rafting beneath Royal Gorge Bridge

Mountain Biking the Southwest

13 Although singletrack enthusiasm is ubiquitous in Colorado, the trails zigzagging the red-rock landscape around Fruita (p297) are truly world-class. Sure, it's in the middle of nowhere, but the fanatical riders here wouldn't have it any other way. Other hot spots for mountain biking are the sagebrush hills and aspens around Crested Butte (p286) and the lesser-known desert trails near Cortez (p250). There are opportunities for every class of rider, and local bike shops are usually generous with fat-tire tips. Above right: Mountain biking, Fruita

Steam Trains

14 You don't have to be a train-spotter to appreciate a good puff of vintage coal-powered steam, the whine of iron on iron and the jolting grind of a narrow-gauge train balancing and rolling slowly through dynamited tunnels and along ridges blessed with some of the most stunning mountain vistas and canyon drop-offs imaginable. The best of the bunch is the impossibly scenic 45-mile Durango & Silverton Narrow Gauge Railroad (p269), but the Georgetown Loop (p172) and Cumbres & Toltec Scenic Railroad (p334) are other worthwhile rides. Above far right: Steam train crosses the Animas River, near Silverton

Million Dollar Highway

15 This is one amazing stretch of road. Driving this asphalt sliver south from Ouray towards Silverton positions drivers on the outside edge, a heartbeat from free-fall. Much of it is cut into the mountains and gains elevation by switching back in tight hairpins and S-bends. The brooding mountains loom large and close, snow clinging to their lofty mist-shrouded peaks even in high summer. In good weather the road is formidable. In drizzle or rain, fog or snow, it can be downright scary.

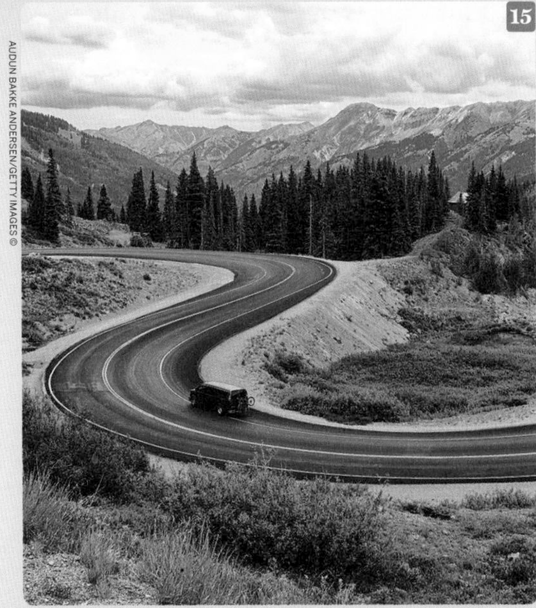

AUDUN BAKKE ANDERSEN/GETTY IMAGES ©

PETER PTSCHELINZEW/GETTY IMAGES ©

Hiking Colorado's 14ers

16 Colorado is home to 54 peaks over 14,000ft. That's well over half the the peaks of 14,000ft or more in the continental US. Two are accessible by road, one by rail. The rest you'll have to work for. Whether you decide to hike the shortest trail – just 3 miles to Quandary Peak (p186) near Breckenridge – tackle a multiday route to Longs Peak in Rocky Mountain National Park or make a run at the tallest of them all, Mt Elbert (p238), in the Mt Massive Wilderness Area, one adage holds true: no pain, no gain.

Above: Quandary Peak Trail

Farm-to-Table Dining

17 Colorado takes great pride in sustainable dining, and it is not uncommon here to sit down to grass-fed beef burgers at a local pub that also brews its own organic wheat ale. The abundance is apparent at city farmers markets, immense natural food stores and gourmet food trucks. From handcrafted ice cream sold from bike carts to the auteur restaurant with an *amuse-bouche* like a first kiss, Colorado dares to feature quality local ingredients as the new gold.

Durango

18 The cultural capital of southwest Colorado, Durango (p268) is a lovely town, rich in history yet elegantly modernized. The historic central precinct dates back to the 1880s, when the town was founded by the Denver & Rio Grande Railroad. Still tastefully authentic, it's a great base for exploring the San Juan mountains and Mesa Verde National Park. Think of it as artsy, rootsy and every day more quirky. The Durango & Silverton Narrow Gauge Railroad toots and puffs up to Silverton several times daily.

Great Sand Dunes National Park

19 Sculpted by wind and seemingly straight out of Arabia, these 55 sq miles of sand dunes seem to appear out of nowhere. Ringed by mountain peaks and glassy wetlands, Great Sand Dunes National Park (p324) is both eerie and amazing. Watch as sunlight forms shifting shadows and the wind wipes clean your footprints. Distance is an elusive concept in this monochromatic, misplaced sea of sand. The most dramatic time is day's end, when sunset puts the dunes in high contrast.

Denver Arts

20 Start at the new Clyfford Still Museum (p63), a showstopper of 20th-century abstract expressionism. The Denver Art Museum (p63), with the modern masterpiece Hamilton wing, shows cunning in its shape-shifting turns and tricks of natural light. It is home to one of the largest Native American art collections in the US. Still thinking of bronze bronco busts as Colorado arts? We didn't think so. But don't trust us, ask your kids, who will dive into interactive exhibits and not be heard from again until hunger strikes. Bottom: Denver Art Museum

19

20

ARCHITECT: DANIEL LIBESKIND, HAMILTON BUILDING; IMAGE: WITOLD SKRYPCZAK/GETTY IMAGES ©

Telluride

21 Let Aspen and Vail grab the headlines; Telluride (p255) is Colorado's most remote ski destination, where tourism has developed at an easygoing pace. Unless you arrive by plane, it's no easy feat to get here, but you're also unlikely to want to leave. Situated in the heart of the rugged San Juans, the village is snuggled into an isolated box canyon and surrounded by peaks unspoiled by over development. Out of season, Telluride also throws some of Colorado's best festivals, with banner events celebrating film and bluegrass.

Pikes Peak & Garden of the Gods

22 'Pikes Peak or bust!' The rallying cry of the Colorado gold rush put Pikes Peak (p304) on the map in 1859, and the *capitán* of Colorado Springs continues to lure adventurers with its cog railway, highway to the summit and even a lung-crushing marathon. The easternmost 14er in Colorado, it's the de facto symbol of the southern Rockies. Drive it, hike it or admire it from beneath the exquisitely thin red-rock spires of the Garden of the Gods (p306). Bottom: Garden of the Gods

21

22

RONDA KIMBROW PHOTOGRAPHY/GETTY IMAGES ©

DAVID EPPERSON/GETTY IMAGES ©

DAVID H. LEWIS/GETTY IMAGES ©

Black Canyon of the Gunnison National Park

23 A massive cleft in the landscape, the arresting Black Canyon of the Gunnison is a deep, narrow abyss that unexpectedly opens from the subdued undulations of the surrounding tablelands. The sheer walls of the Black Canyon – so called because daylight only briefly illuminates the narrow canyon floor – are dizzying in height, scored with eerie crevices and pinnacles, and veined with multicolored mineral deposits. It's one of the deepest, narrowest and longest canyons in North America.

Steamboat Springs

24 No Colorado ski town is more down-to-earth than this cow town that's turned out more Olympians than any other US city, and still greets visitors with a tip of the Stetson. The magnetism of Steamboat Springs (p155) holds true in all seasons: in summer visitors rumble down the hills on two wheels, raft rushing white-water and soak off long hikes at the sweet Strawberry Park Hot Springs. In winter, its epic skiing is a bit too far for city day trippers, leaving the delicious open glade and aspen skiing all for you.

Fort Collins

25 Here's a perfect day. Check out a free fat-tire cruiser and roll through one of America's most bike-friendly cities. When you get warm, point it towards the shady river path along the Poudre and spend the afternoon tubing along the trickling water. Cap things off by spending the afternoon sampling craft beer from a handful of Colorado's finest breweries. Forget about Fort Collins (p142) as Colorado's underdog college town: this small city on the edge of the Front Range is a delightful destination in its own right.

Need to Know

For more information, see Survival Guide (p361)

Currency
US dollars ($)

Language
English

Visas
All foreign visitors will need a visa to enter the USA unless they are Canadian citizens or part of the Visa Waiver Program.

Money
ATMs are widely available. Most businesses accept credit cards.

Cell Phones
Coverage is unreliable in mountain regions. GSM multiband models are the only phones that work in the USA.

Time
Mountain Standard Time (MST) is seven hours behind GMT/UTC and observes daylight savings in summer.

When to Go

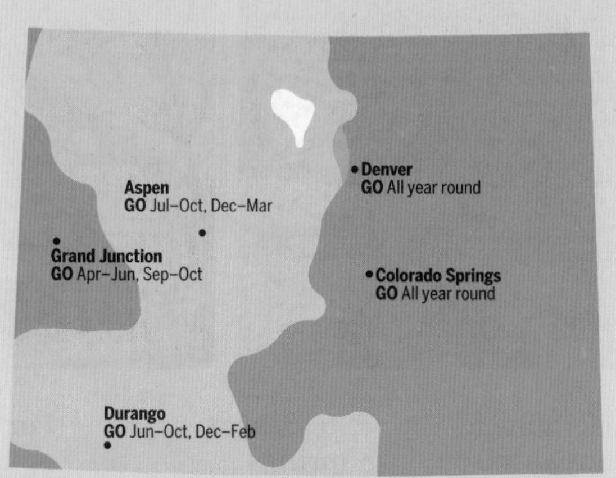

High Season
(late Nov–Apr)

- Ski and ride bums arrive in droves.
- Vacancies are at a premium and ski resorts capitalize big time, charging three times more than their summer rates, and even more between Christmas and New Year's Day.

Shoulder
(Jun–Sep)

- Summer is a shoulder season because in some spots you can get tremendous room rates while others enjoy a second high season. Crowds can be thick in places.

Low Season
(Oct–Nov & Apr–May)

- Bemoaned locally as 'mud season'; many businesses close shop to get ready for the winter crush.
- Hotels slash room rates and restaurants offer deals, too.

Websites

Colorado Tourism Board (www.colorado.com) All things Colorado.

Denver Post (www.denverpost.com) The state's top newspaper.

5280 (www.5280.com) Denver's best monthly magazine.

Westword (www.westword.com) Denver and Boulder nightlife.

Elephant Journal (www.elephantjournal.com) Boulder mindful-living publication.

14ers (www.14ers.com) Info on Colorado's 14,000ft-plus peaks.

Opensnow (www.opensnow.com) Powder forecasts for your location.

Lonely Planet (www.lonelyplanet.com) Destination info, hotel bookings, traveler forum.

Important Numbers

All phone numbers have a three-digit area code followed by a seven-digit local number. For long-distance and toll-free calls, dial 1 plus all 10 digits.

Country code	☎1
International dialing code	☎011
Operator	☎0
Emergency	☎911
Directory assistance (local)	☎411

Exchange Rates

Australia	A$1	$0.91
Canada	C$1	$0.94
Euro zone	€1	$1.37
Japan	¥100	$0.97
Mexico	MXN10	$0.78
New Zealand	NZ$1	$0.83
UK	£1	$1.64

For current exchange rates, see www.xe.com.

Daily Costs

Budget: Less than $100

- Campsites: $14–$20
- Dorm bed: $25–$40
- Self-cater, food trucks, cafes: $35
- Take advantage of backcountry hiking and skiing: free

Midrange: $100–$200

- Rooms in summer: $100–$150
- Mixing cafes and restaurants: $50

Top End: More than $200

- Rooms in summer: up to $200
- Rooms in ski season: up to $500

Opening Hours

High-season hours follow. In rural areas, many businesses close on Sunday.

Businesses 9am–5pm Monday to Friday

Banks 8:30am–5pm Monday to Friday, 9am–noon on Saturday

Stores 10am–6pm Monday to Saturday, noon–5pm Sunday; malls may extend to 8pm or 9pm

Supermarkets 8am–8pm; most cities have 24-hour supermarkets

Restaurants Breakfast 7am–10:30am, weekend brunch 9am–2pm; lunch 11:30am–2:30pm; and dinner 5–9:30pm, later on weekends

Bars & Pubs 5pm–midnight, to 2am on Friday and Saturday

Arriving in Colorado

Denver International Airport (DIA; p94).

Taxi Multiple companies queue outside Ground Transportation area (downtown $60).

Bus RTD operates SkyRide buses with frequent service between 3:30am and 1:10am to downtown Denver ($11, 55 minutes) and Boulder ($13, 70 minutes).

Shuttle SuperShuttle and others (rates from $33 per person) go to Denver, Boulder, Fort Collins, surrounding suburbs and parts of Wyoming. Some ski areas have shuttle services that are reasonably priced to and from Denver International Airport.

Getting Around

Car Essential for exploring the state, unless you stay on the Front Range or in a ski town. Rentals in every town or city. Drive on the right.

Bus Limited service, but good within Boulder and Denver.

Bicycle Join locals in loving the bike-sharing programs in Denver, Boulder and Fort Collins. Bikepaths in ski resort areas and cities help facilitate it.

Train Amtrak's *California Zephyr* stops here between San Francisco and Chicago. There are a few steam-train routes.

For much more on **getting around**, see p369

If You Like...

Hiking

To try and pin down the best hikes in the Rocky Mountains is kind of like ranking the world's greatest sunsets. But in a mountain range this huge, there are some variations in what you can see.

Rocky Mountain National Park Longs Peak gets all the buzz but there are several loop trails best done in two or three nights; wildlife sightings are the norm. (p130)

San Juan Skyway The hikes here wander between classic alpine country, aspen meadows, red-rock escarpments and bubbling hot springs.

Maroon Bells Pristine wilderness with epic Continental Divide views from spectacular mountain passes. (p230)

Spanish Peaks Stark granite walls rising from mountain meadows, two looming peaks, ample wildlife and thin crowds. (p318)

Old West Sites

Everyone from Harvard-educated blue bloods to pioneering entrepreneurs and desperate Civil War–scorched Southern families came west lured by gold, searching for a fresh start and a raw, new America.

Bent's Old Fort This melting pot of Mexican, American and Native American culture sustained the Santa Fe Trail, the overland lifeline of western expansion. (p322)

Leadville Colorado's highest incorporated city has plenty of boom-and-bust lore. (p237)

Ashcroft These mining-town ruins are 10 minutes from Aspen, and are accessible by cross-country trail in winter. (p218)

St Elmo Drive, snowmobile or horse trek to this atmospheric Collegiate Peaks ghost town. (p240)

Breckenridge This A-list and historic ski town sprouted in 1859 when the Colorado gold rush first took hold. (p182)

IF YOU LIKE...MOUNTAIN BIKING

Fruita offers the best mountain biking in the state. Its 128-mile Kokopelli Trail leads to Moab, Utah's mountain-biking hot spot. (p297)

Snow Sports

Colorado has a ski town to fit every personality, ranging from chic to cheap, from resort to quick Front Range getaway. Check websites for deals; discount tickets are sometimes sold at grocery stores.

Vail Known for its spectacular back-bowl terrain, it's Colorado's largest resort and one of its glitziest. (p195)

Aspen Star-studded Aspen's four mountains host the Winter X Games with epic terrain. (p216)

Winter Park Notable for tree runs and big moguls at Mary Jane. (p172)

Breckenridge With Victorian charm and the powder-bowl excitement of brand new Peak 6. (p182)

Arapahoe Basin Ski Area Stripped down, day-use, no frills, big air and big parties. (p181)

Telluride An old mining town reinvented as a top resort, and the slopes don't disappoint. (p255)

Steamboat Mountain Resort Excellent runs and an authentic Western small town; great for families. (p157)

(Top) St Elmo
(Bottom) Male Elk

Beer & Microbreweries

Although Colorado's long-established craft breweries have outgrown their 'micro' status, there's always another backyard hobbyist to challenge the status quo.

New Belgium Brewery Famous for Fat Tire, it runs a riot of a tour that could end with you in costume. (p143)

Wynkoop Brewing Company Denver's perennial favorite lists a dozen-odd award-winning brews. (p84)

Great Divide Brewing Company Produces a delicious array of seasonal brews alongside its perennial list. (p84)

Ska Brewing Company Live music, top-notch brews and BBQs. (p273)

Mountain Sun Pub & Brewery Boulder's fave brewpub produces a beer list as eclectic as its clientele. (p118)

Odell Brewing Company All about personality; arguably the best craft brewer in the state. (p146)

Scenic Railways

These narrow-gauge railways provide views, thrills and a bit of oral history.

Durango & Silverton Narrow Gauge Railroad Forty-five miles long and impossibly scenic, this is the longest and best of the bunch, landing you in historic Silverton. (p269)

Georgetown Loop Railroad The closest to Denver, this steep corkscrew track winds between the old mining towns of Georgetown and Silver Plume. (p172)

Pikes Peak Cog Railway Travels to the summit of Pikes Peak, a journey that helped inspire the song 'America the Beautiful.' (p307)

Cumbres & Toltec Scenic Railroad A chance to mount the Cumbres Pass by the power of steam; the depot is in Antonito. (p334)

Geology

From hidden 2000ft gorges to rock gardens and mind-bending arches, Colorado is home to some geologic masterworks.

Royal Gorge A deep and spectacular rift holding the Arkansas River, with a landmark bridge and scenic railway. (p313)

Garden of the Gods This odd formation of boulders and pinnacles is part of a red-rock vein that runs through Colorado Springs. (p306)

Great Dikes of the Spanish Peaks These sheer rock walls rise out of mountain meadows like a primordial fenceline hemming the Spanish Peaks. (p319)

Black Canyon of the Gunnison National Park A deep, narrow abyss with sheer, multicolored walls scored with eerie crevices and pinnacles. (p283)

Distilleries

Colorado's microdistillery movement follows in the tracks of craft breweries. These tipples are no moonshine – many distilleries are award-winning.

Stranahans Colorado Whiskey The most widely celebrated of Colorado's local liquors, this Denver craft whiskey is a staple of high-end cocktail menus. (p72)

Peach Street Distillers Palisade producer with a suite of fine spirits; the brightest star on the shelves is vodka infused with local peaches. (p300)

Mancos Valley Distillery Small-town visionary Ian James crafts the delicate Ian's Alley Rum and opens his brewing space to live blues and bluegrass. (p250)

Montanya Distillers Award-winning rum spun into stunning cocktails, with its production in Crested Butte and drinking in Silverton. (p288)

IF YOU LIKE... OTHERWORLDLY LANDSCAPES

If you like otherworldly landscapes, check out the Great Sand Dunes National Park: a hunk of Arabia plunked into the San Luis Valley. Its surreal, wind-swept forms are awesome to behold. (p324)

Wildlife

Colorado is home to a wealth of wildlife, from moose, elk, deer and antelope to fox, wolf, black bear, mountain lion and the bald eagle.

Rocky Mountain National Park With moose wading through wetlands and elk herds grazing by the park entrance, sightings are frequent and satisfying. (p130)

San Juan Mountains Backcountry treks can bump you into elk herds, black bears, mountain goats, beavers, river otters and golden eagles. (p255)

Black Canyon of the Gunnison National Park The stomping ground of mule deer, bighorn sheep, black bears and mountain lions. (p283)

Alamosa National Wildlife Refuge Bald eagles, coyotes, elk and migrating sandhill cranes flank the banks of the Rio Grande at dawn and dusk. (p328)

Food

No longer about steak and potatoes, Colorado flaunts an abundance of creative chefs, and farm-to-table kitchens are blooming across the state. You have some eating to do.

Matsuhisa World-class sushi with a South American influence; outlets in Aspen and Vail. (p226)

Root Down Denver's best restaurant has an 'eat local' ethos and high design. (p81)

Salt The liveliest of the new Boulder kitchens, with local and organic ingredients and tailored cocktails. (p118)

La Cocina de Luz Tart, organic lime margaritas, a chip bar with self-serve homemade salsas and authentic south-of-the-border classics in Telluride. (p259)

Month by Month

TOP EVENTS

Aspen Music Festival, July

Boulder Creek Festival, May

Telluride Film Festival, September

Breckenridge Spring Massive, April

Great American Beer Festival, September

January

Crowds are at their thickest around New Year, and are present through to Martin Luther King's birthday. This is also when the snow is as abundant as après-ski parties.

Winter X Games

ESPN's annual extreme winter sports competition takes place at Aspen's Buttermilk Mountain, with night and day events.

National Western Stock Show

Saddle up for the state's biggest stock show (www.nationalwestern.com), a Denver tradition since 1906. We're talking rodeos, cattle, cowboys, Wild West shows, hundreds of vendors and more.

February

It's the height of the ski season. Carnival is celebrated, and resorts fill for Presidents Day weekend. Advance reservations are crucial, with discounts midweek.

Carnival

Vail's jovial spin on Mardi Gras includes a parade and a king and queen. Breckenridge hosts a masquerade ball and a Fat Tuesday parade. (p188)

March

Coloradans swear the sun is always out – and it often is – but March is the beginning of the real sunshine, and spring break attracts families for the start of spring skiing.

Frozen Dead Guy Days

Irreverent and a little creepy, this festival suits Nederland. The town welcomes spring by rallying around its cryogenically frozen mascot, 'Grandpa Bredo,' with a snowshoe race, a dead-guy look-alike contest and beer drinking. (p126)

April

Spring skiing! Even as room rates dip slightly, midweek deals aren't hard to find, unless it's Easter week. The Colorado Rockies baseball team start knocking it out of the park at Coors Field.

Breckenridge Spring Massive

A two-week celebration (www.townofbreckenridge.com) made up of a range of festivals dedicated to food, microbrews and music. Oh, and there's the longest ski-mountaineering race found in North America.

May

'Mud season' hits the high country, while Boulder and Denver start to warm up. Summer unofficially begins on Memorial Day weekend – time for paddling.

Boulder Creek Festival

One of Colorado's biggest festivals comes to town. Boulder's traditional summer starter is all about food, drink, music and, above all, glorious summer sunshine. It all comes to a close with Bolder Boulder, a 10km race celebrated by screaming crowds. (p111)

Cinco de Mayo

Denver embraces this traditional celebration, hosting hundreds of exhibitors and food merchants and a good dose of margaritas. It's one of the biggest of its kind in the country. (p73)

June

Summer festivals start, river runoffs peak and Arapahoe Basin finally closes for the season. All mountain passes are open, and vacationing families start to hit the major parks and landmarks.

Telluride Bluegrass Festival

Thousands of fans descend on Telluride for a weekend-long homage to bluegrass. Camping out is popular at this well-organized outdoor festival. Along with bluegrass, a few straight-up rockers can be found here. (p257)

Pikes Peak International Hill Climb

When the first road to Pikes Peak was complete, this car race was born. Different classes of vehicle (pro trucks, motorbikes, stock cars…) hammer up 12 miles of road and a climb of 4700ft. (p308)

July

July ushers in 10 weeks of prime time for backcountry hikes and kayaking, now that the snow has melted and water is filtering through streams and meadows.

Aspen Music Festival

Classical musicians come from around the globe to play, teach and learn at this famous festival. Top-tier performers put on spectacular shows, while street corners burst into life with smaller groups. (p222)

August

A great time of year to get into the backcountry. Down the mountain, bulls and bronco busters square off at dozens of rodeos and country fairs.

Biking

Ski resorts become fat-tire havens, hosting fun amateur events, many compatible with beer drinking. The US Pro Cycling Challenge also pounds through Colorado, bringing Tour de France–style excitement to the Rockies.

September

With crisp fall air and golden aspens, the high country is paradise. It's still a good time for biking and hiking, with some off-season deals at resorts.

Great American Beer Festival

Craft brews are big business in Colorado. It's no surprise, then, that this Denver celebration with over 500 breweries participating sells out well in advance. (p74)

Telluride Film Festival

Holding its own against the likes of Utah's Sundance, Telluride debuts plenty of celebrated films. It's helped launch the careers of Michael Moore and Robert Rodriguez, among others. (p257)

Jazz Aspen Snowmass

This Labor Day festival leans away from jazz and more towards popular rock (the June version satisfies jazz fans). Big-name acts hit the outdoor stage in Snowmass Town Park. (p222)

December

Early ski seasons start in the first half of December. Once school lets out airports are jammed, rooms are booked and reservations become a must.

Snow Daze

Vail lets loose with one of the biggest early-season celebrations, a week-long festival with myriad competitions and activities and plenty of live performances from big-name musical stars. (p200)

Lights of December

Boulder's Pearl Street Mall hosts the city's traditional Christmas Parade with floats, costumed children and old St Nick himself. (p111)

Itineraries

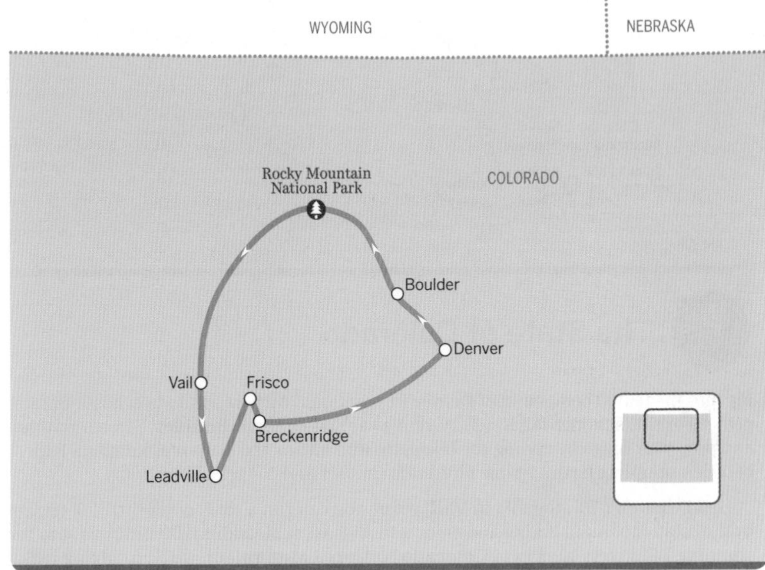

Denver & the Northern Rockies

Combining urban-infused energy with mountain escape, this is one unforgettable road trip from late spring to fall. Spend a couple of days in **Denver**, riding the bikepaths, sampling the upstart restaurants and luminary bars of the Highlands and taking in a ball game. Head north through fun and funky **Boulder** to **Rocky Mountain National Park** to spend a few days in massive wilderness.

Hit the road south on Hwy 40 through Winter Park then west on I-70 to **Vail**, where there's technical downhill mountain biking and access to a network of bikepaths that lead all the way to Breckenridge. Consider a river trip or perhaps a paraglide, and take the gondola up to Eagle's Nest.

From Vail drive the back roads through Minturn into **Leadville**, where you can stroll through history before taking Hwy 91 through lonely mountain towns, back to Hwy 6, into **Frisco** and onto **Breckenridge**. Luxuriate in your last days here, exploring the quaint historical district in the evenings and cycling and hiking during long summer days. Get in a river trip before heading back to Denver.

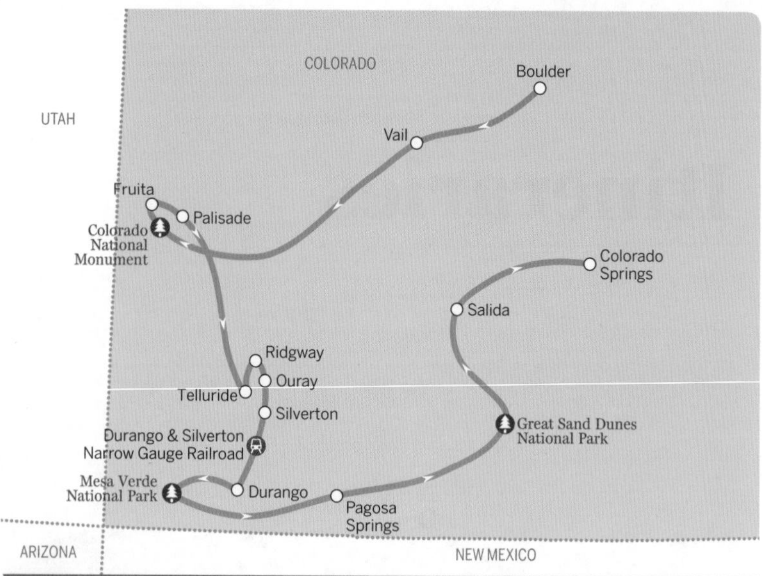

The State of Colorado

Fly into the tented compound of Denver International Airport, made to echo mountain peaks. For this summer-fall itinerary, rent a car and motor to **Boulder**. Stretch your legs and prep your lungs by cycling the bikepaths and hitting the trails of Chatauqua Park between sampling farm-to-table fare, coffee houses and congenial brewpubs.

Head west on I-70, stopping in **Vail**, where you can run a river, cover thrilling terrain by downhill mountain biking and enjoy a sushi feast at Matsuhisa. Continue west to the stunning Wild West scenery of **Colorado National Monument**, with crumbling red-rock mesas and deep canyons. Camp overnight and hit **Fruita** for extraordinary desert singletrack or **Palisade** for a day-long wine-tasting meander through the vineyards. Head south to the enchanted San Juan Mountains.

Climb back into the high country and dead-end in historic **Telluride**, in a stunning box canyon surrounded by steep peaks. Here you can take in a festival, ride the free gondola and soak in the chic mountain vibe. Head out through scenic ranch country, hitting the hot springs outside **Ridgway**. If you're here in middle to late summer, consider a two-day backpacking trip in the nearby San Juan high country. Explore funky **Ouray** and link to **Silverton** via the wild Million Dollar Hwy, a sinuous and steep journey through three mountain passes. If you need a break from being behind the wheel, drop into good-vibe **Durango** via the **Durango & Silverton Narrow Gauge Railroad**.

Detour to **Mesa Verde National Park** to explore stunning cliff dwellings. Camp here or enjoy a B&B in nearby Mancos. On your way east, take a soak in **Pagosa Springs**. Take Hwy 160 east to the **Great Sand Dunes National Park** on your way to **Salida** and the Collegiate Peaks Wilderness for world-class white-water rafting and hiking with grizzled mountain goats.

Take Hwy 24 west to **Colorado Springs**, where you can indulge with a night at the Broadmoor.

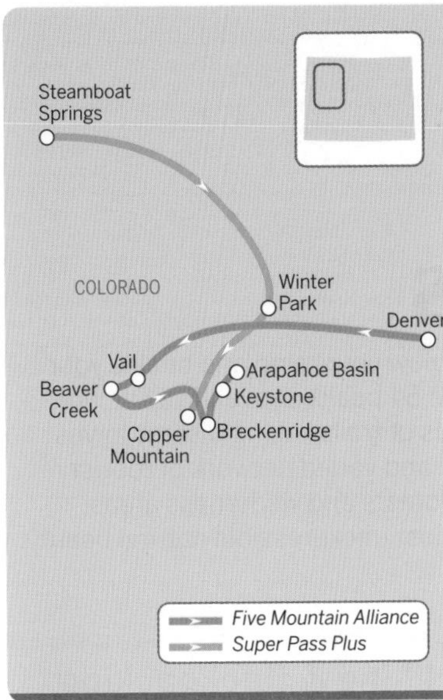

Ski Country

Vacationing skiers and boarders should take advantage of resort alliances. **Vail** has a five-mountain alliance that's hard to beat. Shuttle here from Denver, spending at least two days exploring the mother of all North American resorts. The vast back-bowl terrain is where you'll find the experts, unless they're at the terrain parks. Nearby **Beaver Creek** rings even more exclusive. Spend your next three days in Summit County. Base yourself in **Breckenridge**, which has plenty of beginner runs alongside some killer chutes and tree runs. Summit County's free public transportation can zip you to family-friendly **Keystone**, with ice skating and night skiing. Your lift ticket also serves funky **Arapahoe Basin** if you fancy a whiff of 'the Beach.'

Or hit the locals' faves. The Rocky Mountain Super Pass Plus covers Winter Park, Copper Mountain and Steamboat Springs. Start with two to three days at **Steamboat**, a real Western town with gorgeous glades and deep powder. Move on to **Winter Park**, hitting the Mary Jane's moguls. Zip out to I-70 and the easy charm of **Copper Mountain** before heading back to Denver.

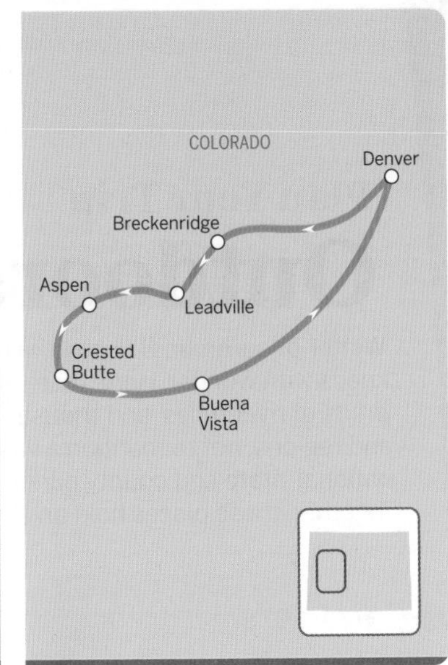

Rocky Mountain High

Fuel up with a great diner breakfast in Denver before jumping on 1-70 to begin this summer high-country trip. Veer off for **Breckenridge**, soaking up the Victorian ambience, stargazing from a hot tub and summiting your first 14er. Continue south to **Leadville**, a good lunch stop, then scoot south on Hwy 82 towards Twin Lakes. From here, climb to the heavens (with panoramas of the Continental Divide) on curvy Independence Pass, which plumbs you right into idyllic **Aspen**.

In Aspen, spend two nights hiking in the Maroon Bells Wilderness, cycling to Ashcroft and eating at the Pine Creek Cookhouse. Continue to nearby but remote **Crested Butte** via the summer-only Kebler Pass. The wildflower capital of Colorado, charming CB also boasts outstanding hiking, festivals and singletrack trails.

Next stop is the Arkansas River, the delight of anglers and rafters. Enjoy the cute Western ambience of **Buena Vista** and Salida. Take in the picturesque ghost town of St Elmo and soak in the healing waters of Mt Princeton Hot Springs. Meander back to Denver via the mountain route of Hwy 285.

Plan Your Trip

Outdoors

Winter or summer, Colorado will blow your mind and buckle your knees with wonder. Here, there are 54 peaks above 14,000ft, hundreds of river miles, and thousands of trails linking distant towns and regions, not to mention a vast and varied network of robust national, state and county parks, forests and wilderness areas. Together, these places hold an almost unexpressible natural beauty.

Top Ten 14ers

In Colorado 54 mountains top 14,000ft. Locals call them '14ers,' and many try to bag 'em all.

Rocky Mountain National Park
Longs Peak

Vail, Aspen & Central Colorado
Mt Elbert

Quandary Peak

Mt of the Holy Cross

Mt Princeton

Mt Massive

Uncompahgre Peak

Maroon Peak

Snowmass Mountain

Southeast Colorado
Pikes Peak

Hiking & Backpacking

Trails across the state beckon for day hikers and overnight backpackers between late May and early October. Many of these trails are accessible by county and forest service roads that are subject to closure. Contact the local ranger district if you plan on hiking early or late in the season. Trails are accessible year-round in lower-elevation destinations such as Boulder and Colorado National Monument.

Excellent long-distance trails for through hiking include the Colorado Trail and the Continental Divide Trail (www.continentaldividetrail.org).

Where to Hike

The Colorado Trail

The state's signature trail, also known as USFS Trail 1776, starts at Chatfield Reservoir near Denver before winding 500 miles to Durango through eight mountain ranges, seven national forests, six wilderness areas and five river systems. The Colorado Trail Foundation (www.coloradotrail.org) offers maps and books that describe the trail in detail.

Boulder

Boulder, a visionary small city, is surrounded by parkland paid for by a self-assessed tax that has been used to purchase vast swaths of city- and county-owned open space, including Chautauqua Park, which is precisely where you'll find the best hiking in the area. In the mountains above the city, past the town of Nederland (only a 30-minute drive west of downtown) is the Indian Peaks Wilderness Area, where you'll find miles of hiking trails and backcountry campsites. The hike up to 12,000ft Arapaho Pass, accessed from the Fourth of July campground, is an especially nice day hike.

Rocky Mountain National Park

One of the top draws in all of Colorado, **Rocky Mountain National Park** (☎970 586 1242; www.nps.gov/romo) is intersected by the Continental Divide, and offers some of the best wildlife viewing in the state. Its excellent hiking trails cross alpine meadows, skirt lakes and bring travelers into the wild and deeply beautiful backcountry. Just know that in the peak season (July and August) you will have to make reservations for backcountry campsites. This is especially true if you plan on climbing Longs Peak and staying overnight on the mountain.

Central Mountains

Breckenridge, Vail and Aspen are all tremendous resort areas with more hiking trails than can be explored in an entire season. Most ski areas have a summer lift to a ski lodge with trail access. Views can be excellent, particularly in Vail and Snowmass, and the groomed trails give you a taste of the high altitude with relatively smooth footing, but it ain't the wilderness.

One stunning hiking destination is the Maroon Bells. It's no secret, but if you start early and plan to hike all day, you can avoid the bussed-in crowds and head up and over Buckskin Pass, where solitude can be yours and the views are breathtaking. Other options in the Aspen area include a hike to the famous Grottos and a trail to Conundrum Hot Springs.

NATIONAL PARKS & MONUMENTS

Bent's Old Fort National Historic Site	In southeastern Colorado, on the north bank of the Arkansas River, this small site was an early prairie trading post for settlers.
Black Canyon of the Gunnison National Park	The Gunnison River cut this deep, narrow and scenic western Colorado gorge nearly 2500ft below the adjacent plateau. It also features forests of ancient piñon pines.
Colorado National Monument	Once dinosaur country, this 18,000-acre reserve near Grand Junction, in western Colorado, displays the most colorful, distinctive forms that only erosion can create.
Dinosaur National Monument	The Green and Yampa Rivers flow through this 298-sq-mile reserve in northeastern Utah and northwestern Colorado, where dinosaur fossils lie in impressive quarries. Native American petroglyphs embellish nearby scenic canyons.
Florissant Fossil Beds National Monument	Volcanic ash covered this former lake bed in the mountains west of Colorado Springs, preserving 6000 acres of fossil flora and fauna, including petrified sequoias.
Great Sand Dunes National Park	This spectacular dune field spreads for approximately 55 sq miles in the San Luis Valley, with the tallest dune rising, staggeringly, to almost 700ft.
Hovenweep National Monument	In southwestern Colorado and southeastern Utah, this 300-acre monument preserves the ruins of defensive fortifications that once protected a vital water supply for pre-Columbian inhabitants.
Mesa Verde National Park	In southwestern Colorado, covering 80 sq miles, this park is primarily an archaeological preserve. Its elaborate cliff dwellings are relics of Ancestral Puebloans.
Rocky Mountain National Park	Only a short hop from Denver, this park straddles the Continental Divide, offering 395 sq miles of alpine forests, lakes and tundra covered by summer wildflowers and grazed by bighorn sheep and elk.

The Collegiate Peaks Wilderness is a close second. Best accessed from Buena Vista on Hwy 24, it has eight peaks above 14,000ft. Vail or Minturn are the best departure points for Mt of the Holy Cross, while Quandary Peak holds the distinction of being the most accessible 14,000ft peak in the state, just outside Breckenridge.

If you want to sample the backcountry without having to rough it, look into the 10th Mountain Division Hut Association (p223). It manages 29 backcountry huts between Vail and Aspen stocked with firewood and some even with saunas, connected by 350 miles of trails.

Northwest Colorado

Dominated by the Routt National Forest, there are three wilderness areas in this region: Flattops Wilderness, Sarvis Creek Wilderness and Mt Zirkel Wilderness. All are laced with excellent hiking trails, but the Mt Zirkel Wilderness is especially magical. Untamed and roadless, it's dotted with icy glacial lakes and granite faces, and is intersected by the Continental Divide and two major rivers, the Elk and the Encampment, both of which are being considered for protection under the Wild & Scenic Rivers Act. In the center of it all is the 12,180ft Mt Zirkel.

Fans of canyon country will want to check out Colorado National Monument. Most of the trails are relatively short, but there's the rewarding 6-mile Monument Canyon Trail that skirts many of the park's most interesting natural features, including the Coke Ovens, the Kissing Couple and Independence Monument.

Southwest Colorado

Colorado's most diverse region features red-rock canyons, Mesa Verde National Park and spectacular high country – you may just want to head here directly. Black Canyon of the Gunnison National Park (p283) is a stunning place to stretch your legs. The easy 1.5-mile Oak Flat Trail offers good views of Black Canyon. At sunset take the 1.5-mile Warner Point Nature Trail to either High Point or Sunset View overlooks.

Telluride is a day hiker's dream town, with many trails accessible from downtown, including the 2.7-mile Jud Wiebe Trail. The Bear Creek Trail is slightly shorter – just over 2 miles – but includes a 1040ft climb to a waterfall. This trail also intersects the 12-mile Wasatch Trail. Backpackers should seek their solitude surrounded by the 14,000ft summits in the nearby Lizard Head and Mt Sneffels Wilderness Areas.

FIVE WAYS TO BE A GOOD BACKPACKER

- Leave only footprints, take only pictures. There's no garbage collection in the backcountry. Make sure that whatever you pack in, you pack out.
- Water. Water. Water. You should have water sanitation or a water-filtration system to enjoy the backcountry. The best way to eliminate potential bacteria is to boil the lake, creek or river water, but filters work well, too.
- Have the essentials: a map, extra layers of clothing, rain gear, extra food and water, flashlight, fire-starter kit (with waterproof matches and/or a lighter), camp stove, first-aid kit (with blister-care items), sunglasses, sunscreen, sleeping bag, tent and pocket knife.
- Only build fires where permitted, and only use dead and down wood, rather than breaking dead limbs from standing trees. Make sure you put out your fire completely before breaking camp.
- Due to high-density backcountry traffic, Colorado authorities are now suggesting that campers actually pack out their own personal solid waste, and are even offering free bags with which to do the trick. No joke. Human waste does impact the environment and the new guidelines are a response to that. At the very least, bury yours a minimum of 6in below the surface at least 200ft from any watercourses and pack out your toilet tissue.

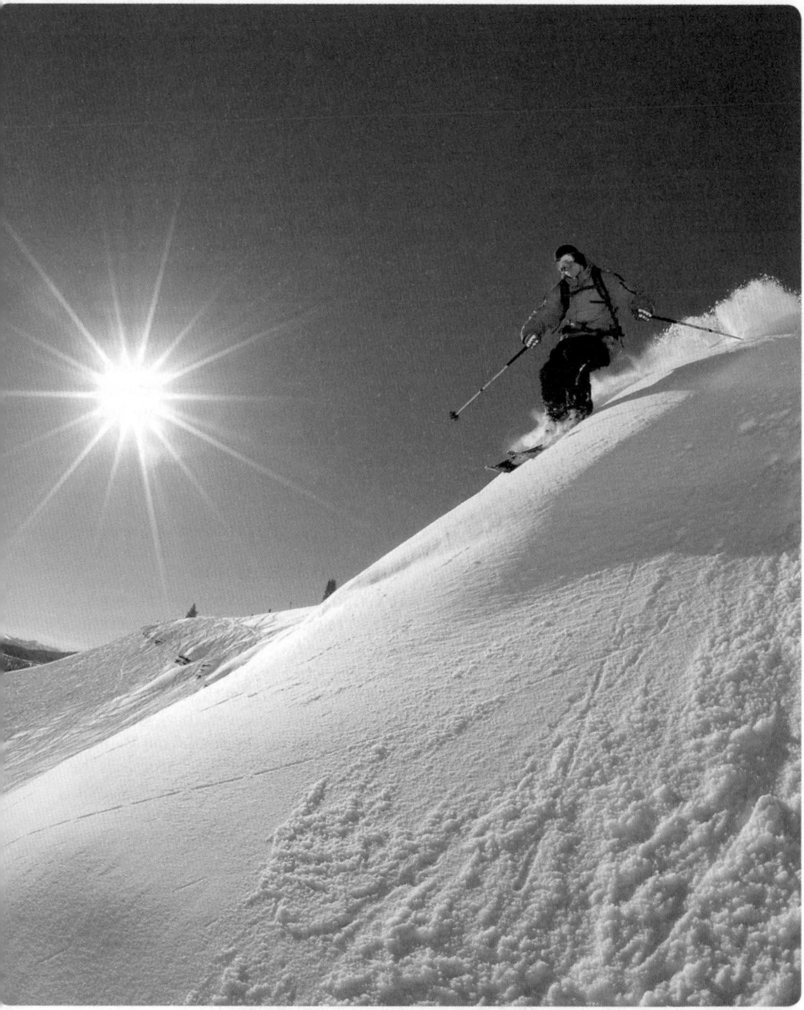

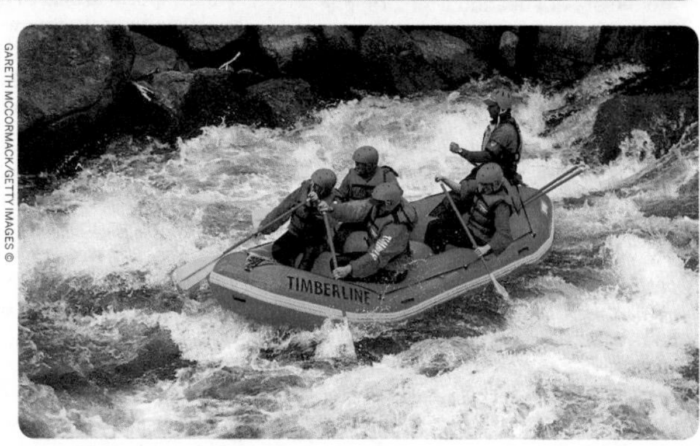

Above: Skier, Vail

Right: Rafting on the Arkansas River near Buena Vista

GARETH MCCORMACK/GETTY IMAGES ©

The region's jewel is the epic, craggy San Juan Range. There are more than 25 peaks over 11,000ft here, including 14 of Colorado's 54 14ers. Over the years the range has been explored by miners, skiers and mountaineers, but one look is enough to see that it's still untamed.

San Luis Valley & Southeastern Colorado

Pikes Peak gets all the press, and with good reason. After all, it is the most famous, but not nearly the tallest, of the 14ers. Some drive to the top, others take the train, but the 13-mile Barr Trail leads from the Cog Railway station through Barr Camp at the halfway point and finally through the scree fields to the summit. You can make it a very doable day hike by taking the train halfway up to a spur that leads into Barr Camp, where you can join the Barr Trail to the summit, then ride the rails back down.

While there is certainly something to be said for taking down a big-name mountain, backpackers seeking pristine nature, dramatic views and solitude will love the Spanish Peaks Wilderness. Extinct volcanoes that aren't part of the Continental Divide cordillera include East Spanish Peak at 12,683ft and West Spanish Peak at 13,625ft. There are trails to both summits and spectacular dikes that seem to erupt from the earth. All told there are three campgrounds and 65 miles of trails to explore.

> **SAFE HIKING**
>
> Hikers should always have their own maps. Adequate trail maps can be found at park headquarters, ranger district offices or outdoor clothing and supply stores such as REI. Weather conditions can change in a blink, so bring layers and rain gear. Mid-to-late-summer afternoon monsoon rains are frequent, and lightning is a real concern above the timberline. The catch-all rule is to stay off mountain peaks and passes after noon. Always carry more than enough food and water (and water-purification equipment). Dehydration will sap your energy and can provoke altitude sickness.

Skiing & Snowboarding

Colorado's wealth of ski and snowboarding terrain is well known. There are bunny slopes and moguls, tree runs and back bowls, terrain parks and superpipes. Winter recreation built this state's tourism industry, transforming places such as Aspen and Vail, and putting towns like Crested Butte and Telluride on the map. And powder is why those adrenaline-addled slackers are manning the reception desk, working the espresso machine, parking the cars and mixing your drinks. Colorado's resort-area service sector has a second life where all the people see and feel is powder and take orders only from the mountain. These people live to carve and ride, rocket downhill and perch on the edge of dramatic chutes. In Colorado, winter is bliss.

Where to Ski

Northern Mountains

Although this section of the state does have tremendous hiking and mountain biking – normally indicators of a nearby ski resort – much of the best mountain terrain is protected in the Rocky Mountain National Park. However, there is one day-use resort just up the road from Boulder. More convenient than epic (although the 1400ft vertical drop in Corona Bowl will get your attention), Eldora Mountain Resort, 4 miles west of Nederland, has around 500 skiable acres and 25-plus miles of well-groomed Nordic trails.

Central Mountains

Summit County has the world's highest concentration of ski, snowboard and winter-sports arenas. The resorts, it seems, are strung out like snow-white pearls off I-70 or the parallel Hwy 6. If you're trying to decide where to base your winter vacation, here are the basics:

➡ **Vail & Beaver Creek** Vail is the largest ski resort in the US, with 5289 skiable acres, 193 trails and three terrain parks. It lacks the downtown cohesion of an Aspen or Telluride, as this is classic plaza-style resort development, but for sheer variety and thrills Vail is top-notch. What makes it really special are the back bowls – more than 4000 of the acres are on the back side of Vail Mountain with postcard views. The drawback has always been expense. Historically, Vail has angled to be the most expensive lift

Ski Areas

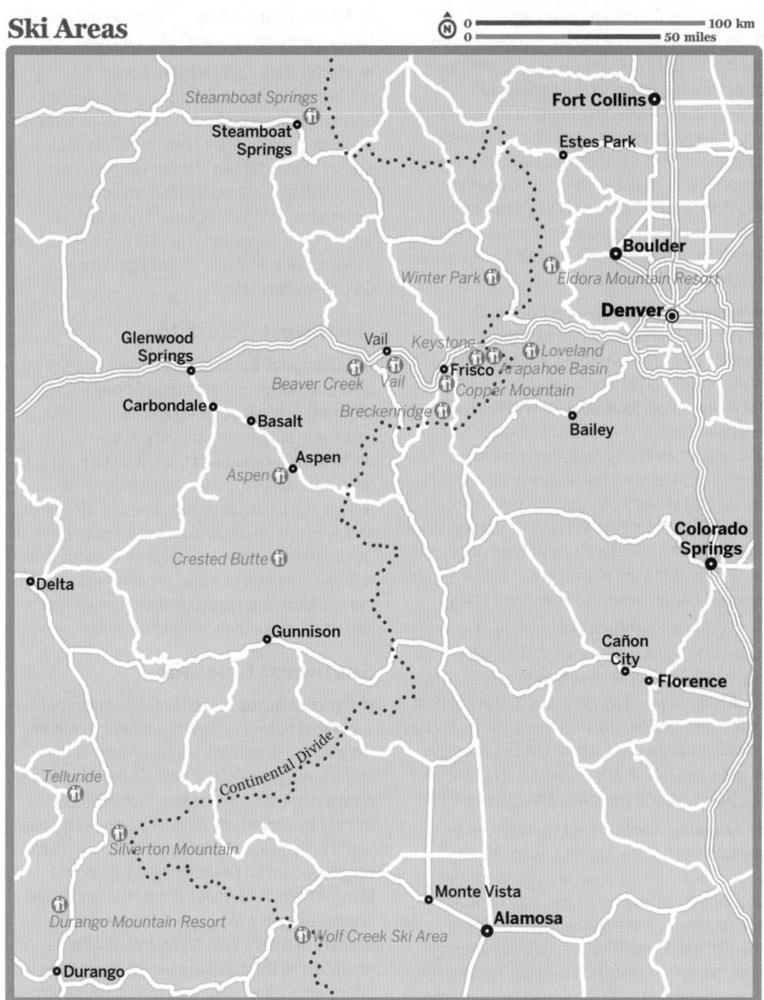

ticket in Colorado (often outpricing Aspen by $1), and lodging doesn't come cheap either, but at least your ticket is also good at four other resorts, including nearby Beaver Creek. Beginners love Beaver Creek because the mountain is upside down, with easier runs at the top of the mountain plus great views. But there's plenty of expert terrain, including a World Cup downhill course. Plus, this was the first Colorado resort to incorporate European-style village-to-village skiing.

➡ **Aspen & Around** With celebrity glitter, a historic downtown core and some of the best skiing in the state, Aspen is a terrific choice for those with a padded budget. One lift ticket grants access to the Four Mountains. Aspen and Aspen Highlands (the locals' under-the-radar choice) don't offer much for beginners, but there's plenty of green terrain here. Snowmass is the biggest, and some say the best, of the bunch, with over 3000 acres, three terrain parks and 60 miles of groomed Nordic trails. Buttermilk is the host to the Winter X Games, though this might change in the future. Cross-country skiers should also make their way to historic Ashcroft and the Pine Creek Cookhouse.

➡ **Breckenridge** Closer to Denver, with a jewel-box historic downtown and a ski resort spanning four luscious mountains covering 2900 acres. It will also be opening the anticipated Peak 6 during the 2013–14 ski season. Breckenridge offers great atmosphere. Beginner and intermediate skiers have some of the best runs in Colorado. Advanced skiers have plenty to rave about, too, and there's a state-of-the-art superpipe. A lift ticket here is also good at Keystone and A-Basin, plus Vail and Beaver Creek with a 3-day-plus pass. Also, it's on the free Summit County–wide public transportation system.

➡ **Keystone** Also in Summit County, the Keystone ski area encompasses three mountains of 3148 skiable acres laced with 135 trails, about half of which are expert runs. It's family-oriented, as almost 20% of the trails are beginner runs. The A51 Terrain Park is decked out with an array of jumps, jibs, rails and a superpipe. There's a fun and easy tubing area – perfect for young kids – on Dercum Mountain, and a CAT system that will take the daring above the lifts to the lips of a string of Black Diamond bowl runs at the top of the park. It's also the only Summit County resort to offer night skiing.

➡ **Copper Mountain** A self-contained resort area that's ideal for families, Copper Mountain has 2450 acres of skiable terrain accessed by 22 lifts and carved by 125 trails that are almost equally divided among beginners, intermediate, advanced and expert. There are 15-plus miles of groomed Nordic tracks, a tubing hill and free transportation to Keystone and Breckenridge.

➡ **Arapahoe Basin** One of two day-use ski areas in the Central Mountains; locals dig Arapahoe Basin because the lack of lodging and dining options keeps package tourists to a minimum. Put together by veterans of the 10th Mountain Division, this was among Colorado's first resorts. The top lift gets you to the summit (13,059ft), where you can drop into Montezuma Bowl on the back side. A-Basin, as it's affectionately known, is also famous for the Beach, which rages on Gaper Day. Summit County lift tickets are generally accepted here, too. A-Basin and Loveland have the longest ski seasons, and are usually open from October to June. The scene is at its peak April to May – when other resorts have tapered off, people are barbecuing and suntanning in the parking lot here, between slushy spring ski runs.

➡ **Loveland Ski Area** The oldest operating ski area in Colorado, Loveland opened in 1943 and is set against the Continental Divide, above the Eisenhower Tunnel on I-70. It's only 56 miles from Denver, lift tickets are reasonably priced, and it has plenty of intermediate and advanced terrain, with limited variety for newbies.

➡ **Winter Park** Connected to Denver by rail, Winter Park draws Denver and Colorado Springs locals, who flock here for down-to-earth weekend powder. It's a favorite of Coloradans, with awesome terrain without the pretension. The 3000 acres of skiable terrain occupy five mountains, with terrific mogul runs and hair-raising off-piste action. There are also six terrain parks serving all levels, from beginners to X Games–caliber talent.

Northwest Colorado

➡ **Steamboat Springs** One of the state's great all-around resorts, Steamboat Springs has 165 trails (3668ft vertical) and nearly 3000 acres with ample runs at every level. A great destination for multiday trips, it boasts a great town atmosphere alongside a whole lot of terrain. It's particularly renowned for tree skiing, and even intermediate skiers can weave through trees without the typical hazards. Serious skiers will also gravitate to a number of mogul runs on the hill. More than a few Olympic-caliber skiers and riders make their winter home here.

Southwest Colorado

➡ **Crested Butte** Tucked behind Aspen (but separated by impassable mountains in winter), Crested Butte isn't the biggest resort in the state, but it is one of the best. Come here if you want a more casual, Western feel, because the town is downright adorable. It also boasts some of the best scenery. Surrounded by forests and rugged mountain peaks in the West Elk and Maroon Bells Wilderness Areas, the landscape is mind-boggling. Way out of the way for day trippers, it doesn't get heavy traffic. The mountain's 1167 acres are mostly geared toward intermediate and advanced skiers, with a terrain park.

➡ **Telluride** Believe the stellar reviews – the quality of skiing at Telluride is truly world class. The steep, fast, north-facing runs are the main reason it has an experts-only reputation, but there are some moderate trails, too, particularly in the Goronno Basin. The best runs for non-experts are the aptly named See Forever and Lookout runs, both of which are graceful glides with panoramic views. For a bit more adrenaline, try the West Drain run. The Telluride Nordic Center can set up experienced cross-country skiers for a multiday backcountry trip between Telluride and Ouray along the San Juan Hut System.

ADVENTURE HIGHLIGHTS

ACTIVITY	LOCATION	DESCRIPTION	WEBSITE
Ski touring & mountain biking	San Juan Mountain Range	Linked by trails in the gorgeous San Juans, these mountain huts between Telluride and Moab, UT, are ideal for multi-day adventures	www.sanjuanhuts.com
Mountain biking	Buffalo Creek Mountain Biking Area	Some of the nation's best mountain-bike trails are just an hour from Denver near great roadside camping	www.frmbp.org
Rafting	Arkansas River	Colorado's top white-water river runs past Buena Vista, Salida and the Royal Gorge	www.buffalojoe.com
Horseback riding	South Park	Platte Ranch offers guests a bona fide cowboy experience with rides through open country on a working ranch	No website
Rock & ice climbing	Ridgway	Elite women climbers teach renowned climbing courses for women of all abilities, climbing ice in winter and rocks in summer	www.chickswithpicks.net
Hiking	Chautauqua Park	In Boulder, enjoy scenic foothills hikes or scramble up the Third Flatiron	http://bouldercolorado.gov/parks-rec/chautauqua-park
Backpacking	Mt Zirkel Wilderness	Trek peak to peak in this beautiful, lost wilderness area by Steamboat	www.fs.usda.gov
Fishing	Fryingpan River	A fly-fishing paradise upstream from Basalt	www.taylorcreek.com
Climbing	Rocky Mountain National Park	Break through the clouds on a guided alpine climbing adventure	www.totalclimbing.com
Ski touring	State Forest State Park	Head to this remote park that sports its own super-cool system of yurts and cabins	www.neversummernordic.com
Rafting	Colorado River	The upper reaches of the state's namesake river outside Glenwood Springs provide plenty of excitement	www.upthacreek.com
Fishing	Arkansas River	Downstream from Salida you'll find up to 5000 trout per mile and plenty of public access	www.arkanglers.com
Rafting	Cache la Poudre River	One of Colorado's most pristine river habitats also sports some kick-ass rapids	www.coloradorafting.org

➡ **Wolf Creek** Located 25 miles north of Pagosa Springs on US 160, this (really rich) family-owned ski area is one of Colorado's last and best-kept secrets – at least for now. In recent years major development has been proposed by Red McCombs, a founding father of Clear Channel Communications whose name often pops up on Forbes list of richest Americans. But for now it's still mostly a locals' place that isn't overrun with the out-of-state crowd and covered with high-end boutiques, and it can be an awesome place to ride with waist-high powder after a big storm. Seven lifts service 70 trails, from wide-open bowls to steep tree glades.

Slope Grades

Colorado ski and snowboard terrain is graded and signed with shapes and colors. Pay attention: don't get in over your head.

Green (circle) Beginner runs can be called 'greenies' or 'bunny slopes.' This is where you learn and build your skills.

Blue (square) Intermediate runs.

Blue/Black (blue square with a black diamond) Intermediate to advanced. Must be confident and experienced.

Black Diamond Advanced terrain.

Double Black Diamond Expert skiers and riders only. Don't be a hero unless you are one.

Yellow (oval) Freestyle. Used for terrain parks.

Cycling & Mountain Biking

There's a reason US Olympic cyclists train here. It would take a lifetime to ride every mile of Colorado's paved paths, fire roads and singletrack, with thin-air mountain passes a badge of honor. Ski resorts offer jumps and downhill riding with lift service.

Mountain cycling is so epic that you can ride on dedicated bikepaths from Glenwood Springs to Aspen, and from Vail to Breckenridge. Gondolas, buses and even Lake Dillon ferries are all outfitted to tote bikes. These mountains have inspired grueling 100-mile bike races in Leadville and summer racing seasons throughout the state. They've also prompted many business suits to ditch the car, shave their legs and go full-body spandex on their asses. The point is, in Colorado cycling is more than exercise. It's lifestyle.

In summer, annual bike tours such as **Bicycle Tour of Colorado** (☎303-985-1180; www.bicycletourcolorado.com) offer supported cycling through scenic routes for a week or more. It's ideal for cyclists who want a challenge but also the camaraderie of an enthusiastic group.

Mountain-biking enthusiasts should pick up a copy of *The Mountain Biker's Guide to Colorado* by Dan Hickstein.

Where to Cycle

It would take too long to list every worthy path and route in this bike-friendly state. Summer sees many ski resorts wave goodbye to the snow set and say hello to the two-wheelers. To get you oriented:

➡ **Around Grand Junction** The mix of flat roads and wineries is a tempting combination; some of the USA's best singletrack trails are near Fruita.

➡ **Crested Butte** Singletrack routes and amazing scenery? Check and check.

➡ **Salida** Epic rides year-round. Check out the Rainbow Trail, Monarch Crest Trail and 'S' mountain that bears down on town.

➡ **Central Mountains** This whole region is home to one of the state's best networks of bikepaths. Everything you could want is here: road, tracks and gravel.

➡ **Denver** A bike-lover's city, complete with bike-share program, bike-friendly public transportation and plenty of paths. In the process of building a bike route to Boulder.

➡ **Boulder** Possibly more bike crazed than Denver; paths and bike lanes lead to virtually everywhere in town and beyond.

➡ **Fort Collins** A bike museum is spread across the whole town; jumping on a fixie is the way to get around here.

Rock Climbing & Mountaineering

Despite a wealth of granite, sandstone and even limestone cliffs and outcrops, there are also many rock-climbing gyms, walls and outdoor bouldering parks – all the better to hone the skills for when you're ready to get serious. All the gyms offer instruction, and plenty of outfitters offer intensive multiday clinics for newbies and those wishing to refine their skills.

Where to Rock Climb

Around Boulder

Boulder's sticky Flatirons offer scores of classic routes. In fact there are 1145 rock-climbing routes in the Boulder area, with the majority found in the Flatirons (with walls up to 900ft high), Boulder Canyon and Eldorado Canyon (a spectacular site with dozens of 700ft climbs).

Northern Mountains

There are approximately 44 climbing routes in Rocky Mountain National Park. Buena Vista has great climbing at Elephant Rock and Bob's Rock off Tunnels Rd, and it has foam-core bouldering in its riverside park.

Central Mountains

Camp Hale offers 22 climbing routes graded from 5.9 to 5.11c, and Independence Pass has 60 routes, including the intense bulge that is Bulldog Balcony.

Southwest Colorado

Durango and Ouray are the stars of southwestern Colorado. Ouray Ice Park is a narrow slot canyon with 200ft walls and waterfalls frozen in thick sheets – perfect for ice climbing. Colorado National Monument near Grand Junction has superb climbing in Unaweep Canyon and Monument Canyon, and you can climb in Black Canyon of the Gunnison National Park.

Southeast Colorado

All the best climbing in southern Colorado can be found on the limestone cliffs and pinnacles along Shelf Rd, near where the state's best early dinosaur finds were discovered. The Gallery, the Bank and the North End are the best sites. Colorado Springs has a strict permit process for its top climbing destinations: Garden of the Gods and Red Rock Canyon.

Mountaineering

Unless you plan on tackling one of the estimated 161 technical high-altitude rock-climbing routes, mountaineering isn't necessary to bag peaks in Colorado. Intrepid mountaineers summit the 14ers in the winter, a highly technical pursuit that requires training and proper gear (usually ice axe, crampons, snowshoes or backcountry skis), and cold-weather clothing. Cold climes can exacerbate the effects of altitude sickness, and avalanches are a serious concern here.

Mt Elbert – Colorado's highest peak – is one of the least technical and avalanche prone in winter. Longs Peak and Pikes Peak are also popular and reasonably low-risk (though that can change in a blink) winter climbs. The Maroon Bells, on the other hand, are as risky and technical as Colorado mountaineering gets.

Summit Post (www.summitpost.org) is a solid online resource with basic climbing-route information, but proper maps and consultation with local ranger districts are a must, and guide services are always a good idea. Climbers should take a beacon and never go out alone.

Paddling & Tubing

Colorado is one of the great paddling destinations, with a long white-water season lasting from late May until September. Everything from class II float trips to a raging class V can be yours on five rivers. The Arkansas River is the most paddled body of water, with 150 miles of open water running from Leadville to the Royal Gorge. The best Arkansas paddling happens in June and early July. July is a good time to move from group rafting trips into your own kayak.

You can take lessons in Fort Collins or Denver, but the Rocky Mountain Outdoor Center (p231) in Salida has better scenery. The class III Blue River runs through Breckenridge in the heart of Summit County in the early season. Vail's Eagle River is a nice high-country early-season run, while the class V Gore Canyon is so big it's not even open to paddlers until late season. The Dolores River in southwest Colorado threads through the San Juan Mountains past Anasazi ruins and petroglyphs, with a short dam-controlled season. It makes a beautiful multiday trip.

White-water parks are de rigueur for municipalities throughout the state, including relatively new parks in Boulder, Denver, Fort Collins, Buena Vista and Cañon City. But you don't have to slip into a hull to get wet. Tubing is a popular summer pastime on Boulder Creek, on the Poudre River in Fort Collins, on the Yampa in Steamboat and in Pagosa Springs. You can run the Arkansas River in Cañon City in a tube or on a boogie board.

Plan Your Trip

Rocky Mountain Road Trips & Scenic Drives

Colorado has 25 nationally designated Scenic & Historic Byways, and a number of mind-blowing drives that didn't make the official list, but should definitely make yours. Some will take all day and have you discussing the blows of history and time; others are short hops to lonely mountain passes that are sure to leave you speechless and smiling. For road closures consult www.coloradodot.info.

Drive Safely!

Weather

In winter go slower than posted speed limits

Travel with chains, ice scraper and emergency kit in winter

Check for road closures and conditions at www.cotrip.org

Wildlife & Cyclists

Be careful driving at dawn and dusk, when wildlife is most active

Pull over to watch wildlife; don't stop in the road

Watch for cyclists, even on remote routes

The Law

Cell phones can only be used by drivers with a hands-free device

Seat belts are mandatory for drivers and front-seat passengers

Helmets are not required for adults on motorcycles, but still recommended

Cottonwood Pass

➡ Mileage: 60 miles

Why Go?

Passing through spectacular country, Cottonwood Pass Rd alternates between asphalt and graded gravel (those sections are few and far between) as it winds its way for 60 miles to the fly-fishing mecca of Almont from the quaint and, dare we say, damn cute prison town (and paddler paradise) of Buena Vista.

For a fresh-air fix, it would be hard to beat this lesser-known nook of Colorado. The fly-fishing is paradisiacal and the high-country trails are shared with mountain goat herds.

The Route

In Buena Vista, W Main St becomes Cottonwood Pass Rd. It swerves past beaver ponds along Cottonwood Creek, and skirts Cottonwood Hot Springs in the San Isabel National Forest. On the east side of the road is a turnoff to the Avalanche Trailhead, a spur of the Colorado Trail with access to spectacular Collegiate Peaks Wilderness.

The road goes from moderately sinuous to downright jagged as you approach the edge of the timberline. To the east the Collegiate Peaks fan out against the blue sky as you drive through boulder-field moonscapes.

Bring a picnic and take a long lunch at the pass before dropping into the Gunnison National Forest and down through the Taylor River Canyon to Almont, where the Taylor and East Rivers form the mighty Gunnison. And if you've forgotten your rod and reel, check into the Almont Resort, which is located on Co 135 at the headwaters of the Gunnison River. They'll sort you out.

When to Go

The road is usually open from June to October.

Worth a Stop

Before leaving Buena Vista, make sure you check out Tunnels Rd and Bob's Rock, a 75ft granite wall popular with climbers. It's located after the tunnels on the east side of the road.

Top of the Rockies

➡ Mileage: 115 miles

Why Go?

You'll cross three mountain passes, drop into four watersheds and glimpse Colorado's tallest peaks, as well as the headwaters of the Arkansas River. Not bad for a day's drive. Historic Leadville, the highest incorporated city in the US, which made its name and plenty of cash in the silver boom, is the hub of this drive, which can be done in two phases.

The Route

Start in Leadville. After a wander through the National Historic District (check out the Delaware Hotel), grab a slice at High Mountain Pies – the local favorite is usually packed. Head north from town on Hwy 91 over Fremont Pass before meeting up with I-70 west of Frisco.

Take the interstate past Vail to Hwy 24, where if you time it right you can have a stroll through a terrific farmers market in downtown Minturn, drive through tiny Red Cliff, pay homage to the 10th Mountain Division, and perhaps get some stellar rock climbing in at Camp Hale, before swerving up and over Tennessee Pass where Mt Massive looms supreme as you drive south through Leadville.

Further south, Mt Elbert dominates the horizon. Hang a right on Hwy 82 and head up to Twin Lakes, a historic mining town with some ruins on the lake shore, three inns, spectacular mountain and lake views and countless stars. Bed down here or drive up and over Independence Pass and into Aspen (summer only).

When to Go

Roads are open year-round, with the least advantageous time being 'mud season' (April to June), when ski resorts and some of their infrastructure closes and weather hovers between winter and warmth.

Detour

If you've had 14ers on the brain, why not top one of the state's two tallest peaks? Trailheads for both Mt Elbert and Mt Massive are easily accessible from this route.

Independence Pass

➡ Mileage: 27.2 miles

Why Go?

You'll see plenty of old mining ruins and blow-your-mind views. If you don't have time to drive the entire Top of the Rockies route, this stretch of Hwy 82 from Twin Lakes through Aspen's back gate will do just fine.

The Route

To call Twin Lakes a town is a bit of a stretch – this former mining camp was fed by steady stage-coach lines plying the trail between Leadville and Aspen – but it is a worthy destination in its own right. If you're here late in the season, you'll see camo-clad hunters, last-gasp family vacationers, Harley men and women and their

Rocky Mountain Driving Tours

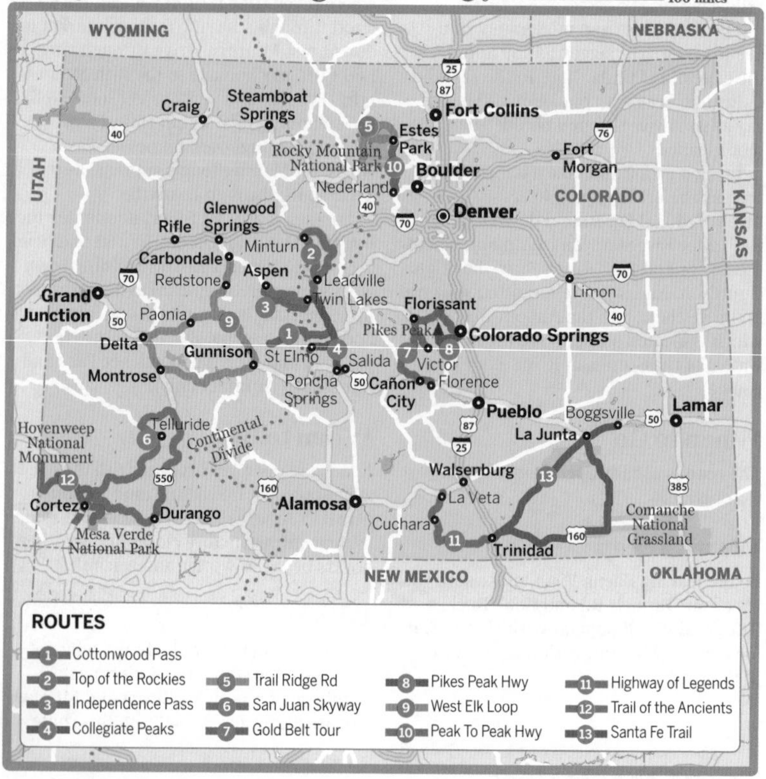

0 — 200 km
0 — 100 miles

ROUTES

1 Cottonwood Pass
2 Top of the Rockies
3 Independence Pass
4 Collegiate Peaks
5 Trail Ridge Rd
6 San Juan Skyway
7 Gold Belt Tour
8 Pikes Peak Hwy
9 West Elk Loop
10 Peak To Peak Hwy
11 Highway of Legends
12 Trail of the Ancients
13 Santa Fe Trail

hogs with bedrolls on the tailgate, and decked-out road cyclists with shaved legs and iPhones in their saddlebags.

Drive up a narrow ribbon of road above the tree line. Views are cinematic and spectacular – swatches of glacier are visible along the ridges of Twin Peaks. Tundra blooms at the top of the pass, where at 12,095ft you'll be on the edge of the Continental Divide. This, friends, is your own IMAX film.

As Hwy 82 continues over the pass the views are just as marvelous, and multi-million-dollar properties begin to dot the landscape as you edge toward Aspen. One of them belongs to Kevin Costner.

When to Go

Although the pass is closed in winter time (November to late May), you can still usually get up to the vast Twin Lakes, where the cross-country skiing, snowshoeing and ice-skating is magnificent.

Detour

If you have time, there's a terrific trail to the Interlaken, an old abandoned hotel fashionable in the 1890s. The trail leaves from the lower of the Twin Lakes.

Collegiate Peaks

➡ Mileage: 57 miles

Why Go?

This is the essence of Colorado: stark and soaring granite cliffs, multiple 14,000ft peaks, geothermal hot springs, the powerful Arkansas River and a bit of ghost town history, too.

The Route

The Collegiate Peaks Byway begins where the Top of the Rockies route ends, at Twin Lakes on Hwy 82, just below Independence Pass.

If you haven't yet explored the mining camp ruins at Twin Lakes, they're worth a look before you get on the road and head east on Hwy 82 to Hwy 24 South. Mt Yale will be the first of the Collegiate Peaks, part of the Sawatch Range, to reveal itself as you head into Buena Vista, a town that is absolutely worth your time. Ostensibly it's a prison town, but it's also recently become a magnet for groovy entrepreneurs who have opened restaurants, cafes, coffee roasters and even a yoga studio. Rock climbing and plenty of paddling are accessible from Main St, and even some spectacular free campsites on Tunnels Rd.

From here the official byway advises you to stay on Hwy 24 out of town. We beg to differ: instead, drive west on County Rd 306 from the center of town for 0.7 miles. Turn left on County Rd 321 and continue south for 7.2 miles. Turn right onto County Rd 322, then drive 0.8 miles to a fork in the road. Bear right and you'll be on Mt Princeton Rd, which will take you to the sprawling Mt Princeton Hot Springs Resort, at the base of magnificent Mt Princeton. Whether you choose to dip into the hot water by the river or scramble up to the peak is a question only you can answer.

You could also continue from the gates of the resort up County Rd 162 to St Elmo, an old abandoned gold-mining town. The road narrows as it runs further up the canyon, with the river flowing by and towering mountains laid out on both sides. The remaining buildings were built in and around 1881.

From St Elmo make your way south again toward Hwy 285, and the historic districts of Poncha Springs and Salida, which is also the gateway to the wild and scenic Arkansas River. From there, there is 99 miles of Arkansas River paddling all the way to the Royal Gorge. Salida is also a great place to slip into a kayak for the first time.

When to Go

You can do most of the drive, except for St Elmo, year-round, though springtime is mud season and not the best time to explore the trails.

Worth a Stop

On the way back to the Mt Princeton resort from St Elmo, you'll see the Love Meadow on your right. Once a pioneer homestead belonging to an impressive woman widowed in her youth, it's now a small and dramatically beautiful wildlife sanctuary.

Trail Ridge Rd

➡ Mileage: 47 miles

Why Go?

This is the highest continuously paved through road in North America, so expect outrageous views. Few roads that get up this high are in such good condition, and exploring tundra trails spotted with wildflowers without having to hike up to this altitude is a treat.

The Route

The signature drive in Rocky Mountain National Park, Trail Ridge Rd (US 34) ascends over the Continental Divide in a series of switchbacks. On the drive from Estes Park to Grand Lake, you'll see snowcapped peaks, meandering streams, high-country meadows dotted with wildflowers in midsummer and, with luck, some wildlife too. Archaeological evidence collected here suggests that humans transited this way for 6000 years. This former trade route was used by generations of Ute, Arapaho and Apache people to traverse Milner Pass. Trail Ridge Rd was originally surveyed in 1927 but not completed until 1932.

When to Go

Trail Ridge Rd opens in late May and is closed at Many Parks Curve on the east side by mid-October. You're more likely to see dramatic snowy scenery in May, when the pass first opens.

Worth a Stop

Before driving into the park, stop by the Stanley Hotel in Estes Park, the inspiration for Stephen King's *The Shining*.

NICOLAS RUSSELL/GETTY IMAGES ©

Above: Road to Independence Pass outside Aspen

Left: Main Street, Telluride

Detour

Consider a 9-mile detour up the original Fall River Rd, where you're likely to spot elk outside the Alpine Visitor Center.

San Juan Skyway

➡ Mileage: 236 miles

Why Go?

Among the USA's best drives, the San Juan Skyway is a 236-mile loop which includes the so-called Million Dollar Hwy, a handful of the region's coolest mountain towns and Mesa Verde National Park.

It's undoubtedly the best way to experience the drama of the San Juan range without strapping on your boots. Drive the Skyway and the tension of the daily grind gets lost somewhere among the towering peaks, picturesque towns and old mines around each bend, or evaporates in the bright sun of an intensely blue Colorado sky.

The Route

The climb on Hwys 62 and 145 skirts the biggest of the San Juans before you enter Telluride, preferably in time for some morning thrills on the slopes of the ski resort. If you're traveling in summer, climb on a mountain bike instead of the skis – just as fun and way cheaper. Grab lunch at The Butcher & The Baker and enjoy a bit more of the hills before pointing the car south for Cortez, where you should follow with dinner at lively Southwestern restaurant Pepperhead.

Take a ranger-guided tour of the Cliff Palace in Mesa Verde National Park, before you hit the road for Durango. Depart on the Durango & Silverton Narrow Gauge Railroad for a fascinating trip into the mineral-rich heart of the mountains.

Now you choose your own adventure: either continue north along the Million Dollar Hwy to Ouray to end the San Juan Skyway loop, or head east to catch a sunset over at Great Sand Dunes National Park.

When to Go

Aspen trees glow in late September or early October. The Million Dollar Hwy section between Silverton and Ouray may close in winter; chains are required and RVs (recreational vehicles) are not permitted at any time.

Gold Belt Tour

➡ Mileage: 131 miles

Why Go?

Explore old mining haunts, petrified tree stumps (they're cooler than you think), the Royal Gorge, dinosaur footprints and galleries. In between you'll glimpse a long and wide mountain plateau with all the country romance of a Willie Nelson tune.

The Route

From Colorado Springs, take Hwy 24 past Pikes Peak and Manitou Springs into the high country, where you'll find Florissant Fossil Beds National Monument. The entire area was once buried beneath ancient volcanic ash. A nature trail leads past sequoia-sized petrified stumps, and the surrounding countryside is special, too. While you're here consider stopping by the 1878 homestead, the Hornbeck House.

Between 1891 and 2005 more than 23.5 million ounces of gold were pulled from this mountain corridor. That's more gold than was ever found during the California and Alaska gold rushes combined! Most of the gold was mined in the twin cities of Cripple Creek and Victor. Both have seen better days. Cripple Creek is now a low-rent gambling destination with a strip mine still active above town, but the Cripple Creek & Victor Narrow Gauge Railroad is a treat. This 45-minute tour leads to Victor and back and includes many an old mining yarn. The views are marvelous. Cripple Creek also offers tours through an actual underground mine and a unique jailhouse museum.

From here you can travel south through the high-country meadows ringed with mountains along High Park Rd, which leads to Hwy 50, and the stunning Royal Gorge. The Royal Gorge Bridge & Park has historic kitsch and incredibly impressive views. Or you could take the slow journey along the graded Shelf Rd, a one-time stagecoach route. There is some fantastic rock climbing in the area, and

TOP TUNES FOR COLORADO ROAD-TRIPPING

Colorado's highways and back roads mix asphalt and gravel, and hairpin turns with fast flats and deep canyons – a sensory journey enhanced with just the right tunes.

Colorado natives DeVotchKa's symphonic alt-rock is reverent fuel for a road trip. Older acts include Big Head Todd & the Monsters and String Cheese Incident.

Aspen-inspired Bounce between violinist Sarah Chang, African banjo legend Béla Fleck, and fusion bands Pink Martini and Calexico, all recent performers at the Aspen Music Festival and Jazz Aspen Snowmass.

Willie Nelson The country legend wrote the songs on *Red Headed Stranger*, arguably his greatest record, while on a road trip through Colorado in 1975. It's as indigenous to this rugged country as the aspens themselves.

Bluegrass With multiple bluegrass festivals in the state, including the biggie in Telluride, you must have fiddler and singer-songwriter Alison Krauss, and guitarist and singer-songwriter Gillian Welch on the shortlist.

Hippie spillover From Boulder to Manitou Springs, earthy roots run deep. Channel your inner hippie with Edward Sharpe & the Magnetic Zeroes, who sell out in Denver, Boulder and Telluride's Bluegrass Festival.

it's also where you'll find the Garden Park Fossil Area, which once gave the world five new dinosaur species. Cañon City has some charm in its own right, along with easily arranged train and raft tours of the gorge.

When to Go

Summer is the best time to explore the high country and take in a rafting trip.

Detour

Not far from Cañon City, Florence blossoms with vintage, antique and found-art galleries, and the fabulous Florence Rose B&B is here, too. You can take the scenic Phantom Canyon Rd directly from Victor to Florence.

Pikes Peak Hwy

➡ Mileage: 38 miles

Why Go?

Climbing a 14er is a Colorado rite of passage, and who knows? Driving it might give you inspiration to take on the next one on your own two feet. On clear days you can look down on four states.

The Route

From Colorado Springs take US 24 west to the Pikes Peak Hwy/Toll Rd. First you'll skirt knife-edge drops into the valley below as Manitou Springs and Old Colorado City become scattered specks in the distance, then you'll roll through thick stands of pine and cedar and finally scree fields. You can thank eccentric tycoon Spencer Penrose for this luscious ribbon of surprisingly sound asphalt that winds up and up and up to the tippy (flat) top of Pikes Peak. After Penrose built the road, he christened it with the first ever Pikes Peak International Hill Climb, a car race that still runs each June.

Before you embark on your journey make sure your brakes and tires are sound, and remember that at altitude your car will have about half the horsepower it usually does. When driving back down, do so in a low gear. The Pikes Peak Hwy/Toll Rd is accessed via Manitou Springs, a fine place to have lunch, stroll and shop afterwards. It costs $40 per car (up to five people).

When to Go

The road is open most of the year, though it's sometimes closed during the winter.

Detour

After you get back into the flats, stop for a drink at the Broadmoor, where you can experience Penrose's game-changing resort and one of the earliest tourist draws to Colorado.

West Elk Loop

➡ Mileage: 205 miles

Why Go?

This gorgeous six- to eight-hour lasso loop is pinned down by the twin summits of Mt Sopris on one end and the spectacular Black Canyon of the Gunnison on the other. In between are historic gold-mining towns, two mountain passes, the mountain-bike mecca of Crested Butte and glamorous Aspen.

The Route

Redstone, on Hwy 133, is famous for its coke ovens used to process coal; the historic downtown is a pleasant stroll, too. From here you'll navigate McClure Pass through 35 miles of stunning mountain scenery before descending along the North Fork River into Paonia, a quirky town with the Grand Mesa on one side, Mt Lamborn on the other, a coal mine and a green streak. The Victorian buildings in downtown's 10-block historic district are as cool as the locals.

Head south on 92 West Hwy through Delta and you'll see the stark, spectacular Black Canyon of the Gunnison National Park, a 2000ft-deep gorge with outstanding hiking trails and rock climbing. From here the route follows Hwy 50 east to Gunnison from where you'll loop around on Hwy 135 into Crested Butte, the wildflower capital of Colorado with a restored Victorian core and looming Crested Butte Mountain, an awesome bike and ski destination. Next, take Hwy 12 over Kebler Pass and then head north on Hwy 133 to funky, progressive Carbondale.

> **QUIRKY COLORADO**
>
> America's tallest sand dune is found in Great Sand Dunes National Monument, a bizarre desertscape of 700ft sand peaks that was created over a million years ago by water and wind.

When to Go

In summer, exuberant wildflower patches around Crested Butte are second to none. Kebler Pass closes in winter.

Detour

If Crested Butte sucks you in, overnight at the Inn at Crested Butte and wake up early the next day for a hike into the nearby Maroon Bells-Snowmass Wilderness Area, one of the most dramatically beautiful wilderness areas in all of Colorado.

Peak to Peak Hwy

➡ Mileage: 55 miles

Why Go?

The Peak to Peak Hwy is one of Colorado's most scenic drives and an excellent option for the trip between Rocky Mountain National Park and Denver or Boulder. This north–south route takes you past a series of breathtaking mountains, including the 14,255ft Longs Peak, alpine valleys and open meadows, passing one-horse towns along the way.

The Route

You can start in Estes Park, near Rocky Mountain National Park, and head south to Nederland, just west of Boulder, or do the route in reverse. Along the way are little mountain hamlets. These include Ward, a former boom town and bohemian magnet that has settled into an artfully ramshackle state of disrepair; Peaceful Valley, notable for its little onion-domed church perched on a hillside; and several other tiny towns with expansive mountain vistas.

There are national forest campgrounds near Peaceful Valley and Allenspark, as well as the Longs Peak Campground, part of Rocky Mountain National Park. There are also places to stay in Peaceful Valley, Ferncliff, Allenspark and south of Estes Park, mostly in the form of lodges, cabins and B&Bs. Before arriving in Nederland there's access to excellent hiking in the Indian Peaks Wilderness via Brainard Lake.

At the southern end of the trip, the Peak to Peak Hwy starts from Nederland,

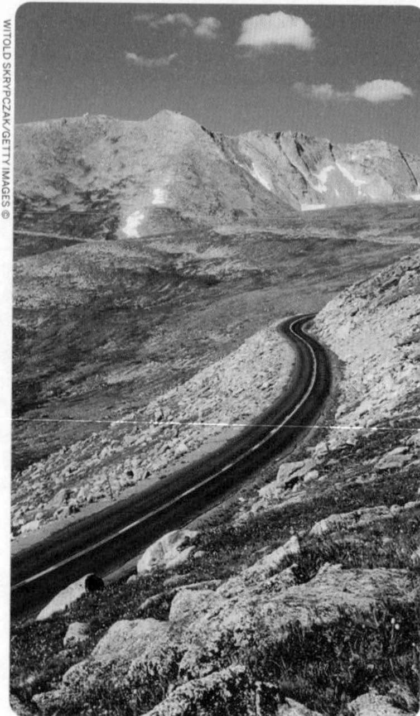

WITOLD SKRYPCZAK/GETTY IMAGES ©

Above: Mount Evans Road, Mt Evans

Boulder's hippie holdout with a few cool cafes. Although most of the route – everything north of Allenspark – follows Hwy 7, at Nederland it follows Hwy 72.

When to Go

Accessible year-round. In summer, watch big cumulus clouds rolling lazily over the green and granite peaks. In fall, the aspens turn the hillsides gold, while winter brings a stark white landscape.

Detour

To stretch your legs along the way, take the road opposite the turnoff for Ward that leads up to Brainard Lake. The lake itself is small but enjoys a gorgeous setting and several great trails. Stop in at the Millsite Inn, just north of the turnoff to Ward. The food is nothing special, but it's an interesting place for a bite and a beer, with plenty of local color, like local rock bands that channel 1971.

> **COLORADO EXTREME**
>
> North America's highest paved road reaches 14,258ft at the summit of Mt Evans. It's open summer only. Take exit I-70 from Idaho Springs.

Highway of Legends

➡ Mileage: 110 miles

Why Go?

This brief but epic detour liberates you from the interstate and escorts you through some of Colorado's most glorious countryside. It's a welcome detour from I-25 if you are headed north to Pueblo, Colorado Springs or Denver. If you're already privy to the majesty of the Spanish Peaks Wilderness, welcome home.

The Route

Your trip begins in Trinidad, where present-day Main St was once an important limb of the Santa Fe Trail. The Trinidad History Museum offers a primer, and while you're in town drop into Danielson Dry Goods for some road sustenance. Coal mining was also an important part of Trinidad's history. You'll see a 'canary in the coal mine' statue on Main St, which is where Mother Jones once marched with miners during the strike that led to the Ludlow Massacre, a turning point in US labor relations.

From Trinidad take Hwy 12 through Cokedale, where you'll see 350 coal ovens on the roadside (they look almost Roman), then head up and over majestic Cucharas Pass and into Cuchara.

Dominated by extinct volcanoes, the Spanish Peaks, and Great Dikes that jut from meadows to mountains, this place is magic. The rambling Cucharas River has terrific fishing, the Dog Bar & Grill serves tasty pizza and occasional live music, and the hiking in the Spanish Peaks Wilderness is some of the best in the state. You can extend the nature bliss by veering east on a recently added extension to the byway.

County Rd 46 weaves through the San Isabel National Forest for 35 miles to Aguilar on I-25, but we suggest staying on Hwy 12, which continues down the valley and into exceptionally cute La Veta, where there are more churches than paved roads, and the Spanish Peaks make for a spectacular backdrop as you check in to La Veta Inn.

When to Go

The route is open year-round but it's especially nice in spring; while winter still lingers in the high country it's warmer here.

Worth a Stop

On your way down Hwy 12 from La Veta toward the I-25, stop at the excellent mining museum in Walsenburg before heading north.

Trail of the Ancients

➡ Mileage: 135 miles

Why Go?

Explore the canyons, mountains and plains once inhabited by Ancestral Puebloans, with all of their mystery intact. This road trip connects Mesa Verde with Canyon of the Ancients and Hovenweep National Monuments, and also wanders down to the Four Corners state boundaries.

The Route

Start at Mesa Verde National Park, the true highlight of the itinerary with over 5000 archaeological sites within the 52,073-acre national park, including 600 Ancestral Puebloan cliff dwellings.

From Mesa Verde, take Hwy 145 north to Dolores through a windswept high desert landscape of cracked red earth, coyotes and sagebrush. Stop at the Anasazi Heritage Center, where you can peruse more ancient artifacts, including pottery from AD 400.

Leave Dolores via Hwy 184 West and take Hwy 491 south to Cortez, where County Road G takes you to McElmo Canyon (continue on the same county road for Hovenweep). In McElmo Canyon you can stay at Kelly Place, with kivas and private trails to ruins, and visit nearby Guy Drew Vineyard for a taster. Next stop, Canyon of the Ancients and Hovenweep National Monuments: both are Ancestral Puebloan treasures that have been largely left alone for hundreds of years. These trails are so solitary, you can almost hear spirit guide whispers on the wind.

Another branch of the byway leads southwest from Mesa Verde on Hwy 491 and then Hwy 160 to the actual Four Corners state boundaries.

When to Go

These roads are open year-round, but if you plan on doing a lot of hiking, they're best avoided in the hottest months, July and August.

Detour

To explore something more rugged, detour from Mesa Verde and head southwest of Cortez to Ute Mountain Tribal Park. It houses a number of lesser-known ruins. Access to the park is possible only with the accompaniment of a Ute guide. Half- and full-day tours can include visits to their adjacent reservation. In addition to the cliff dwellings, original pottery is prevalent; you may even see shards along the trails.

From the state line you can continue your journey on Utah's Trail of the Ancients Byway or head to other Ancestral Puebloan treasures such Chaco Canyon in New Mexico or Canyon de Chelly in Arizona.

Santa Fe Trail

➡ Mileage: 285 miles

Why Go?

History buffs will love this day-long spin through southeastern Colorado. Although the official byway follows the original trail for 188 miles from the Kansas border into Trinidad, you can cut the route down to its best bits and make it a fun four-hour journey.

The Route

An endless prairie unfurls on both sides of the open two-lane highway as you take Hwy 350 northeast of Trinidad to La Junta. The scenery is all grasslands and wheat fields, sugar-beet farms, horse corrals and railroad yards. One of the best parts of driving the Santa Fe Trail is this countryside.

The signature sight is Bent's Old Fort National Historic Site. Set just north of the Arkansas River – the natural and official border between the US and Old Mexico until 1846 – the fort was once a cultural crossroads. From 1833 to 1849 Native Americans, Mexicans and Americans with gold-rush dreams met, mingled, traded, danced and clashed here. The well-restored adobe fort has a blacksmith's shop, wood shop and fully stocked general store. The knowledgeable staff in period clothing lead tours, and a 1-mile trail runs around the fort to the edge of the Arkansas River and back to the parking lot.

Kit Carson frequented the fort, but his last base of operations and final resting place is about 16 miles east of here in Boggsville. If time is short, skip Boggsville, turn back at the fort, and head west again into more history.

You'll want to stop at Iron Spring, where you can see authentic Santa Fe Trail wagon ruts and, if daylight is on your side and you've made an advance reservation, you can drive to the famed Picketwire Dinosaur Tracksite, where dinosaur footprints are frozen in time. Both sites are in the Comanche National Grassland.

When the Santa Fe Trail brings you back to Main St in Trinidad, don't forget to stop at the fabulous Trinidad History Museum to round out the journey.

When to Go

You can take on this trip year-round.

Detour

If you have time there are two sites further east of Bent's Old Fort that shed light on

Above: Bent's Old Fort National Historic Site (p322)

America's dark side. Westward expansion made America, but it meant misery for many. The Sand Creek Massacre National Historic Site, just off the Santa Fe Trail north of Lamar, was a pivotal point in US–Native American relations – an estimated 163 of Chief Black Kettle's Cheyenne people were massacred here by Colorado Volunteers, after the Cheyenne encamped in this desolate land in compliance with a recently introduced American law. The event ended the Indian Wars and paved the way for further white settlement in Colorado and beyond.

South of Lamar are the ruins of Camp Amache, a World War II Japanese internment camp.

Plan Your Trip

Travel with Children

With amazing mountain trails, ghost towns, hands-on museum exhibits and interactive art spaces, river rafting and some of the country's best family-friendly skiing and cycling, traveling families are spoiled for options in Colorado. The endless blue skies, fresh air, archaeological ruins and wild country do wonders to detach kids from their gaming consoles, cell phones and iPods.

Colorado for Kids

In Colorado's main cities, junior travelers should head for the many hands-on science museums, playgrounds, theme parks and family-fun centers, as well as the main attraction of wide-open spaces.

Denver, despite being the state capital, sets the tone as a truly outdoorsy city, with miles of cycling and walking trails, riverside parks and gardens, and outdoor events and theme parks. Beyond the capital there are historic railroads to ride, canyons and peaks to climb, and old Western towns to explore.

Most national and state parks have some kid-oriented exhibits, trails and programs. Join organized wildlife-spotting tours in the parks and reserves, or hook a trout in a tumbling mountain river. Tubing and rafting on some of these rivers is as exhilarating for kids as it is for parents, and camping and hiking opportunities abound.

Throughout this book, the family-friendly icon denotes places that cater to families.

Best Regions for Kids

Denver

History Colorado Center, Denver Art Museum and Water World

Boulder

Pop jets on Pearl Street Mall, Boulder Creek bikepath and trails

Central Mountains

Vail's Adventure Ridge, Peak 8 Fun Park and Summit County bikepaths

Northern Mountains

Moose and elk herds at Rocky Mountain National Park

San Luis Valley

Great Sand Dunes National Park and Colorado Wolf & Wildlife Center

Southeast Colorado

Cheyenne Mountain Zoo and Garden of the Gods in Colorado Springs

Children's Highlights

Festivals & Events

Boulder Creek Hometown Fair A more manageable version of the Boulder Creek Fair. (p111)

Cherry Creek Arts Festival Three days of food, fun and arts. (p74)

Great Fruitcake Toss The cake that flies the furthest wins! (p308)

Lights of December A classic Christmas parade. (p111)

Strawberry Days Glenwood Springs' community festival. (p211)

Indoor Options

Buell Children's Museum Classic cars, bridges, jellyfish, fairy lands... (p317)

Buffalo Bill Museum & Grave For the young cowboys and cowgirls. (p96)

CU Wizards Monthly science shows at Boulder's university. (p108)

Children's Museum Engaging exhibits and activities. (p68)

Denver Firefighters Museum Interactive displays that make fire safety fun. (p59)

Denver Museum of Nature & Science The IMAX Theater and Planetarium are always a hit. (p67)

Rocky Mountain Dinosaur Center Watch lab techs assemble casts and clean fossils. (p312)

Dude Ranches

Drowsy Water Ranch Horseback riding and home cooking with accommodations in Western-themed cabins. (p153)

Echo Basin Ranch Basic, affordable and offers the whole gamut of ranch experiences. (p249)

Beaver Meadows Resort Ranch Horseback riding, rafting, fishing and hiking activities. (p151)

Vista Verde Guest Ranch The most luxurious experience. (p159)

Yellow Pine Guest Ranch Terrific accommodations in deluxe log cabins. (p319)

Kid-Friendly Hikes

Burly mountains (and altitude!) can be a challenge to little legs. Families with smaller children might stick to hikes under 3 miles. Some of our favorites:

St Mary's Glacier Tons of fun in winter. (p171)

Rocky Mountain National Park Try Wild Basin to Calypso Falls, or Lumpy Ridge. (p130)

Chautauqua Park Lots of fun rock scrambling. (p105)

Eldorado Canyon Combine hikes with visits to the public pool.

Planning

Perhaps the most difficult part of a family trip is avoiding the temptation to squeeze in too much. Distances are deceptive, and any single corner of Colorado could easily fill a two-week family vacation.

Choose a few primary destinations and connect them with a flexible driving plan with potential stops. Book rooms at the major destinations and make advance reservations for horseback rides, rafting trips, scenic train rides and educational programs or camps (particularly in peak season), but allow time between bookings to follow your fancy.

Don't forget about the small mountain towns. Their festivals, rodeos and state fairs can be excellent family entertainment.

Discounts for Kids

Child concessions often apply for tours, admission fees and transportation, with discounts as high as 50% off the adult rate. The definition of 'child' ranges from under 12 to under 16 years. Most sights also give free admission to children under two.

Websites

Family Travel Colorado (www.familytravelcolorado.com)

Kids Go Too (www.kidsgotootravel.com)

Kids.gov (www.kids.gov)

Regions at a Glance

With so many Rocky Mountain vistas, craggy canyons and homespun warmth, in addition to hip cities you can walk or ride around, Colorado may spoil you for all future road trips. The whole state moves outdoors in summer, when festivals and live music bring people together under the sun. The Front Range cities of Denver and Boulder offer all the urban pleasures, but you're still in Colorado folks, so these cities also satisfy outdoor ambitions. Vail, Aspen and central Colorado act as an adventure hub to the vast majority of those who want to hike, bike or ski the state's famed high country. To really get away from it all, head to the northern mountains or explore the backroads of southwestern Colorado.

Denver & Around

Outdoors
Food & Beer
Museums

Backyard Adventure

Denver's best feature is that it acts as a staging area for the majestic Rockies. In a short drive you can fly-fish Front Range streams, summit a 14er or ski deep powder. Welcome to Denver – now get out!

Eat + Drink = Merry

Foodies should hit adventuresome dining districts like the Highlands and South Broadway. And forget about watery Coors: Denver's inspired brewers have made the city a beer drinker's nirvana.

Culture

Though the Denver Art Museum and Denver Museum of Nature & Science please crowds, lesser-known gems include Black American West Museum and the new Clyfford Still Museum.

p56

Boulder & Around

Hiking
Cycling
Nightlife

Hit the Trail

From Chautauqua Park to Eldorado Canyon and the stunning alpine terrain of the Indian Peaks Wilderness Area, Boulder is a hoofer's haven. You might not even have to drive to the trailhead.

Two-Wheeling

Start with a rental or bike share. Pedal along the flat Boulder Creek bikepath and at Valmont Bike Park, not to mention up and over lung-crushing passes and onto burly singletrack trails built for full-suspension mountain bikes.

In the Groove

It never hurts the nightlife when more than 30,000 students call a place home. Whether it's big-time jazz, up-and-coming progressive rock or world-music greats, Boulder doesn't skimp on live music.

p101

Rocky Mountain National Park & Northern Colorado

National Parks
Dinosaurs
Western Culture

The Rockies

Alpine splendor, grazing elk and wildflower meadows – Rocky Mountain National Park will bewitch you. To skip the crowds, blaze your own trail in the backcountry wilderness.

Bone Yard

Dinosaur National Monument allows armchair palaeontologists to walk among nearly whole skeletons of the largest animals ever to walk on earth – eerily frozen in rock.

Cowboy Cool

From the Stetsons and chaps worn as nonchalantly as business suits in Steamboat Springs to sunset horse rides at regional dude ranches, this is the unadulterated West.

p128

Vail, Aspen & Central Colorado

Snow
Hiking
Paddling

Powder Days

From glamorous Aspen and Vail to historic Breckenridge and bare-bones Arapahoe Basin, this region boasts more tree runs, terrain parks, back bowls, cross-country trails and après-ski parties than any one aficionado can handle.

Trail Blazing

From the Colorado Trail to 54 peaks of more than 14,000ft, a trail network of over 1000 miles will take you to secluded grottos and waterfalls, fishing holes, and high-mountain passes with epic Continental Divide views.

Four Rivers

This region offers epic paddling from late May until September on Clear Creek and the Arkansas, Colorado, and Roaring Fork Rivers.

p167

Mesa Verde & Southwest Colorado

Culture
Historic Towns
Wine Tasting

Mesa Verde

Where else can you climb steep ladders to ancient cliff dwellings or drop into dark ceremonial kivas? This national park brings back the region's most mysterious inhabitants.

Wild West

Silver mining left the San Juans dotted with historic mountain villages. Quaff a microbrew in a bullet-pocked saloon in chic Telluride or ride the scenic narrow-gauge rail from Durango to Silverton.

Wine Country

Still the hub of Colorado's best peaches, locals found that Palisade's sunny, mild microclimate served another purpose: vineyards. Drive the backroads of this two-horse town to compare upstart winemakers.

p242

Southeast Colorado & the San Luis Valley

National Parks
Rafting
History

Great Sand Dunes

With massive sand dunes, snow-capped peaks and shimmering wetlands, this relatively new national park is startling and bizarre, and the best reason to visit the San Luis Valley.

Arkansas River

The Arkansas River flows from the intense Numbers section to family-friendly Brown's Canyon and culminates with the majestic Royal Gorge (the gorge is the signature trip of America's most paddled river).

Old West

America's rich gold-rushing, war-dancing, mountain-conquering history lives on along the historic Santa Fe Trail and at the state's first resort in Colorado Springs.

p301

On the Road

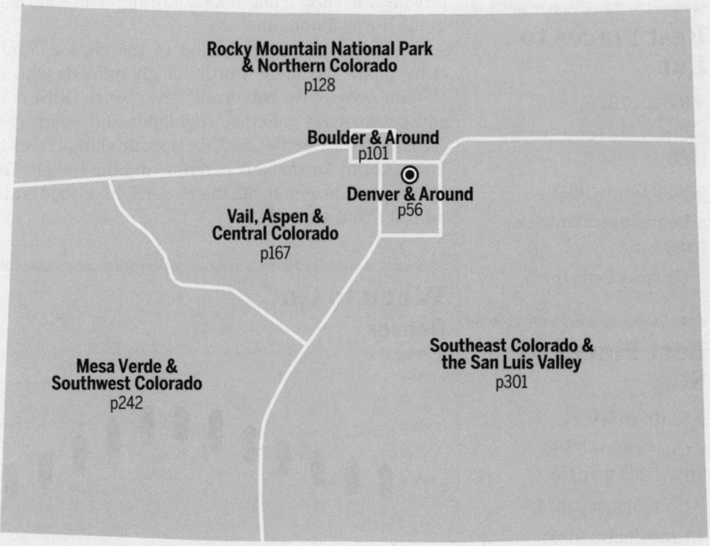

Rocky Mountain National Park & Northern Colorado
p128
Boulder & Around
p101
Denver & Around
p56
Vail, Aspen & Central Colorado
p167
Mesa Verde & Southwest Colorado
p242
Southeast Colorado & the San Luis Valley
p301

Denver & Around

Includes ➡

Best Places to Eat

- Rioja (p78)
- Steuben's Food Service (p80)
- Root Down (p81)
- Beatrice and Woodsley (p81)
- Squeaky Bean (p78)

Best Places to Stay

- Curtis (p74)
- Queen Anne Bed & Breakfast Inn (p75)
- Hotel Monaco (p74)
- Hotel Teatro (p75)
- Brown Palace Hotel (p74)

Why Go?

Denver is movement. Denver is change. Denver is a cowboy town turned cosmo crazy.

As an urban center, Denver has come a long way. Sure you'll still catch a Stetson or two walking down the 16th St Mall, but the inner-mountain West's cosmopolitan capital now delights in a growing culinary and arts scene, plus plenty of brewpubs, great parks and cycling trails, and close proximity to spectacular hiking, rafting, skiing and camping in the Rocky Mountains.

Thanks to a re-urbanization of the city's central core, Denver now has name-worthy neighborhoods with flavors all their own – Five Points and River North (RiNo) for bars and cutting-edge galleries, Highlands and South Pearl for great eateries, Cherry Creek for upscale glam, Lower Downtown (LoDo) for raucous partying and the Golden Triangle for arts and theater. In all, there's a neighborhood and a vibe for just about anybody.

When to Go

Denver

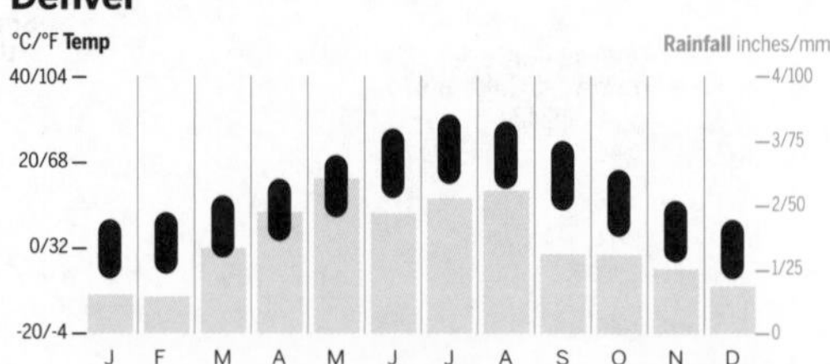

Jun–Aug Big crowds, high prices. Hot days, balmy evenings, extended daylight.

Sep–Nov Cooler temperatures see parks and mountains at their prettiest.

Dec–Mar Short days and cold weather equal skiing weather. Crowds and prices drop.

Getting Around

Getting from place to place in the Mile High City is amazingly easy, especially if you are in the downtown area. The airport is 25 miles out of town, but there are quick buses to downtown or you can shuttle it. From there, it's easy enough to get around on foot, bike (with the shared B-Cycle program), light rail or cab. If you plan to do day-hikes or head up to the mountains, rent a car.

SPRINGING INTO THE MILE HIGH CITY

Denver is smack in the middle of some of the United States' most stunning nature and, frankly, you'd be a fool to miss it. If you're flying, don't bring gear from home. The airlines' baggage fees will destroy your budget and there's tons of affordable, world-class gear to rent. The REI flagship store is a top option for camping and mountaineering supplies, kayaks, snowshoes and skis (*way* cheaper than renting at the slopes). The B Cycle program doesn't cut it for serious cyclists, so rent road or mountain bikes at Bicycle Doctor.

Most times of year, you can get a room without advance notice, but you'll always save money with the aggregators. The city has an international airport, a decent public transit system and generally permissive liberal attitudes. The altitude may affect you. Drink lots of water and watch for sun exposure.

Best Day Trips

This city has more than enough to do within its borders, but for those who have the itch to rent a car and explore a bit, here are a couple of options within an hours' drive:

- Explore Garden of the Gods and old Manitou in Colorado Springs.
- For those who love rock (or rocks): catch a show or wander through Red Rocks Park & Amphitheatre.
- Hike the front-range trails, cycle at Buffalo Creek or head to Saint Mary's Glacier for year-round sledding.
- College junket: spend the day hanging out in Boulder, and hike the Royal Arch Trail through the Flatirons.

FAST FACTS

- **Population:** 620,000 (Denver), 2.5 million (metro area)
- **Altitude:** 5280ft (1609m)
- **Marijuana dispensaries:** 300-plus (there are fewer Starbucks)

Denver's Enormous Art

- I See What You Mean (p62)
- Mesteño (p70)
- Yearling (p65)
- Big Sweep (p67)
- Dancers (p62)

For Kids

- Denver Zoo (p67)
- Denver Art Museum (p63)
- Elitch Gardens (p69)
- Lakeside Amusement Park (p70)
- Casa Bonita (p83)

Resources

- **Visit Denver** www.denver.org
- **Westword** www.westword.com
- **5280** www.5280.com
- **Denver.com** www.denver.com
- **Denver Parks and Recreation** www.denvergov.org/dpr
- **Denver Post** www.denverpost.com

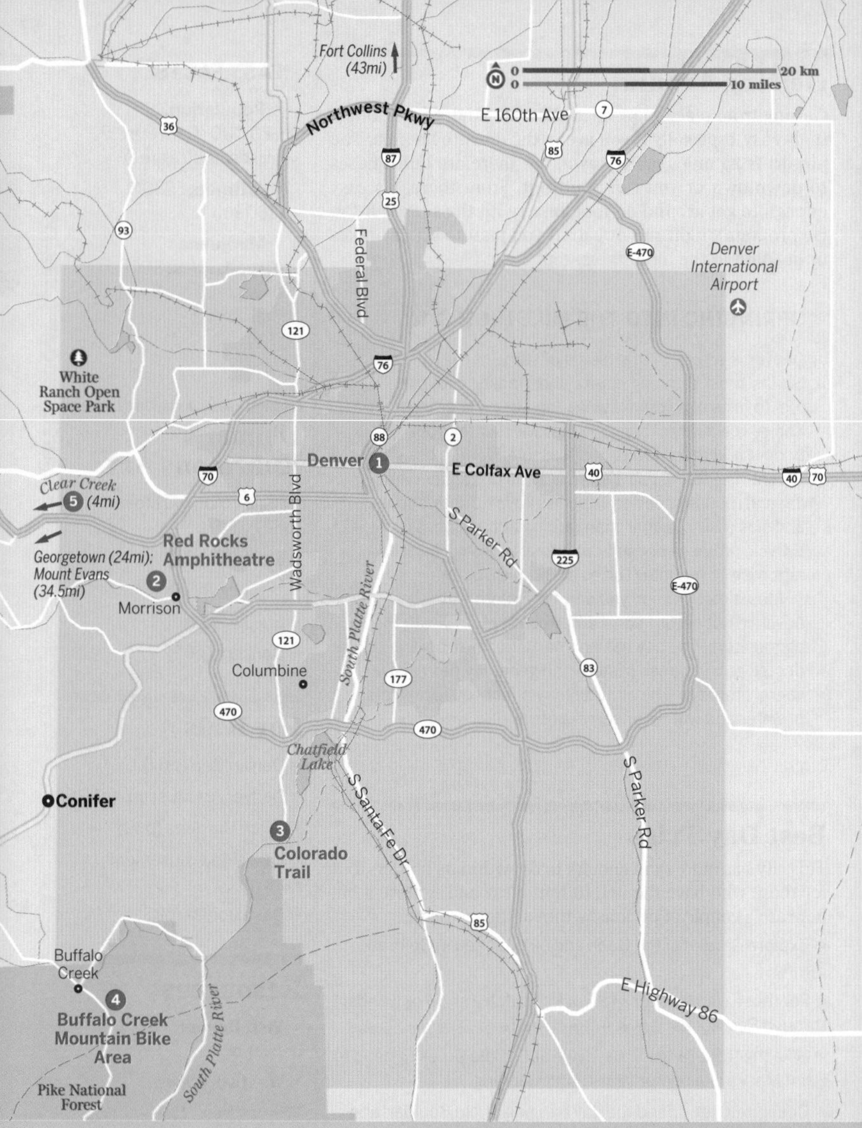

Denver & Around Highlights

1 Mix outdoor spaces with cosmopolitan modernism in the state capital, and delve into the rich art collection at **Denver Art Museum** (p63).

2 After hiking through spectacular rock formations, take in a show at **Red Rocks Amphitheatre** (p66).

3 Stretch your legs on the **Colorado Trail** (p73).

4 Bomb down a single-track trail at the **Buffalo Creek Mountain Bike Area** (p73).

5 Pay your respects to an icon of the American West at the **Buffalo Bill Museum & Grave** (p96).

6 Hike through the aspens at **Golden Gate Canyon State Park** (p73).

DENVER

POP 620,000 / ELEV 5280FT

History

Between hell-raisin' gold rushers, US Army generals, warring Native American tribes and 'unsinkable' frontier women, Denver's past is colorful and chaotic, and people here relish and romanticize the Wild West history. It was rumors of gold that brought the human tide to the Front Range in the middle of the 19th century and established Denver as a major supply point at the foot of the Rocky Mountains, but Arapaho and Cheyenne buffalo hunters already occupied hundreds of camps in the area.

General William H Larimer was the city's white founder; in late 1859 he established a township at the confluence of Cherry Creek and the South Platte River and named it after the person who appointed the area to his control, Kansas Territorial Governor James W Denver. Without water or rail transportation, however, Denver's overnight rise soon stagnated, ending the first of many boom-and-bust cycles that have defined the city's growth.

Supplying gold and silver miners fostered the city's boom until 1893, when the Silver Panic destroyed the economy and sent the state into depression. The following year discovery of gold deposits in Cripple Creek rejuvenated Denver's stature as a center of finance and commerce. When this dried up it was coupled with the Great Depression.

In 1952 Denver's 12-story height limit was repealed and the skyline sprouted high-rises, but many of these suffered during the mid-1980s when an office-construction boom went – you guessed it – bust. The cycle reversed yet again in the 1990s, and by the millennium Denver was a hub for computer, telecommunication and tech firms. Oil and gas is big in Colorado, and many firms are finding their homes somewhere on the upper floors of the Denver skyline. The city has also risen in importance on the national level, hosting the Democratic National Convention in 2008.

DENVER FOR FREE

For cheapie fun you can tour the Colorado State Capitol for free on weekdays, and almost all of the city's museums have free admission days at least once a month. The city's lovely public parks and clear skies provide tons of fresh entertainment and, if you're clever, you can use the B-Cycle program for *almost* free. After you pay the $5 daily membership, break your rides into 30-minute segments. If you check the bike in at one of the ubiquitous stations every half-hour you won't have to pay a usage fee.

Sights

Most of Denver's sights are in the downtown and Golden Triangle districts. The 16th St Mall, Larimer Sq and Cherry Creek are the focus of most retail activity, while Lower Downtown (LoDo) and Highlands are the heart of Denver's nightlife scene.

Downtown & LoDo

Museum of Contemporary Art GALLERY

(Map p60; 303-298-7554; www.mcadenver.org; 1485 Delgany St; adult/student/child/after 5pm $8/5/1/5; noon-7pm Tue-Thu, noon-8pm Fri, 10am-7pm Sat & Sun; P; 6 RTD) This space was built with interaction and engagement in mind, and Denver's home for contemporary art can be provocative, delightful or a bit disappointing, depending on the show. The focus is on contemporary mixed-media works from American and international artists.

Robischon Gallery GALLERY

(Map p64; 303-298-7788; www.robischongallery.com; 1740 Wazee St; 11am-6pm Tue-Fri, noon-5pm Sat; P; 1, 2, 12 RTD) FREE Robischon operates with a focus on emerging dialogues in art. Rotating exhibits take you to the cutting edge, and you'll be able to dig art by some of the world's foremost contemporary artists such as Robert Motherwell and Christo.

Denver Firefighters Museum MUSEUM

(Map p64; 303-892-1436; www.denverfirefightersmuseum.org; 1326 Tremont Pl; adult/child $6/4; 10am-4pm Mon-Sat; ; 7, 8, 16, 16L RTD) Fire Station No 1 was built in 1909, and in 1978 it was turned into a museum that explores the history of firefighting in Denver. See the old steam equipment, slide down a pole and get kitted out in some firefighting gear. The upstairs section is the old quarters where the firefighters slept.

The galleries include a dedicated children's section with interactive displays based on fire-safety education. Great for kids and fascinating for adults.

Denver

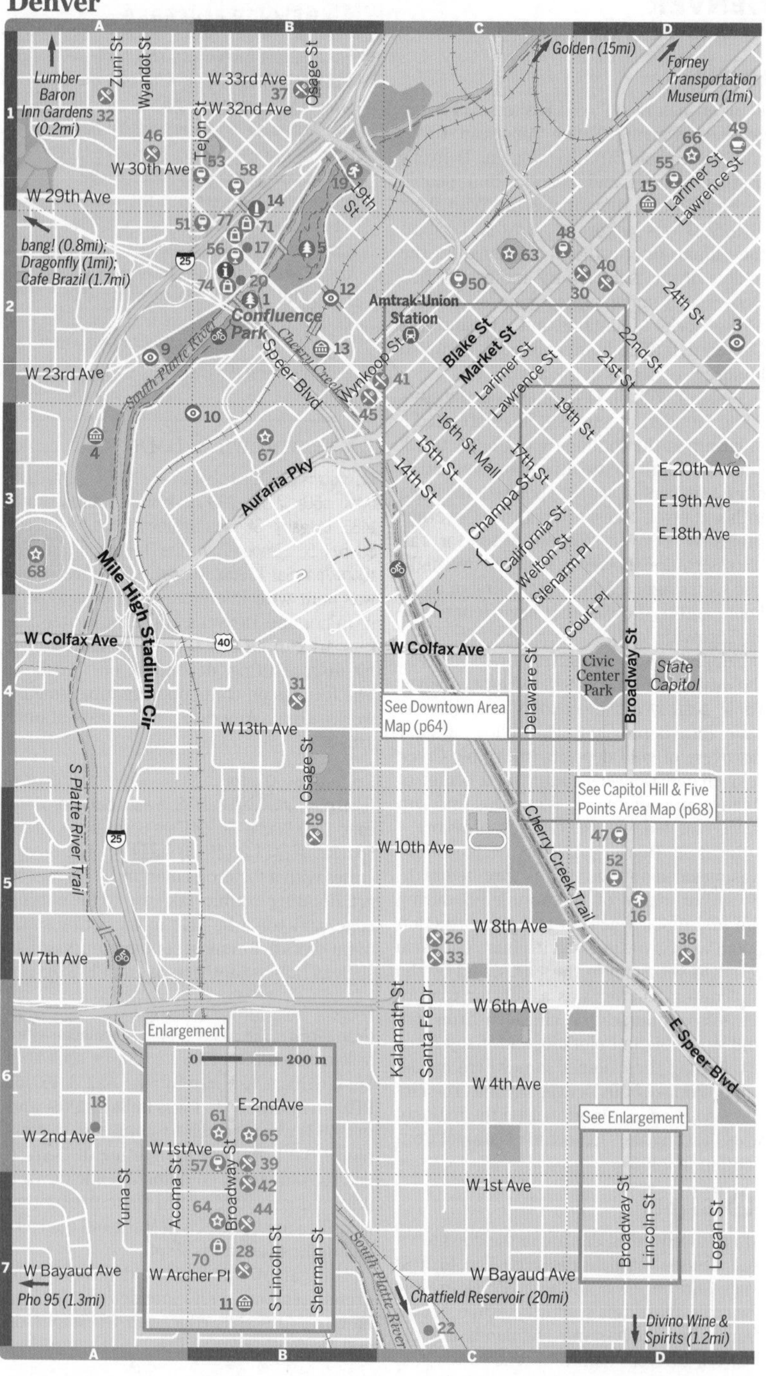
Lumber Baron Inn Gardens (0.2mi)
bang! (0.8mi); Dragonfly (1mi); Cafe Brazil (1.7mi)
Golden (15mi)
Forney Transportation Museum (1mi)
Confluence Park
Amtrak-Union Station
Civic Center Park
State Capitol
See Downtown Area Map (p64)
See Capitol Hill & Five Points Area Map (p68)
See Enlargement
Enlargement
0 200 m
Pho 95 (1.3mi)
Chatfield Reservoir (20mi)
Divino Wine & Spirits (1.2mi)
W 33rd Ave
W 32nd Ave
W 30th Ave
W 29th Ave
W 23rd Ave
W Colfax Ave
W 13th Ave
W 10th Ave
W 8th Ave
W 7th Ave
W 6th Ave
W 4th Ave
W 2nd Ave
E 2nd Ave
W 1st Ave
W Bayaud Ave
W Archer Pl
E 20th Ave
E 19th Ave
E 18th Ave
Zuni St
Wyandot St
Tejon St
Osage St
19th St
Speer Blvd
Cherry Creek
South Platte River
Auraria Pky
Mile High Stadium Cir
S Platte River Trail
Wynkoop St
Blake St
Market St
Larimer St
Lawrence St
16th St Mall
15th St
14th St
17th St
18th St
Champa St
California St
Welton St
Glenarm Pl
Court Pl
Delaware St
Broadway St
21st St
22nd St
24th St
Cherry Creek Trail
E Speer Blvd
Kalamath St
Santa Fe Dr
Yuma St
Acoma St
Broadway St
S Lincoln St
Sherman St
Lincoln St
Logan St

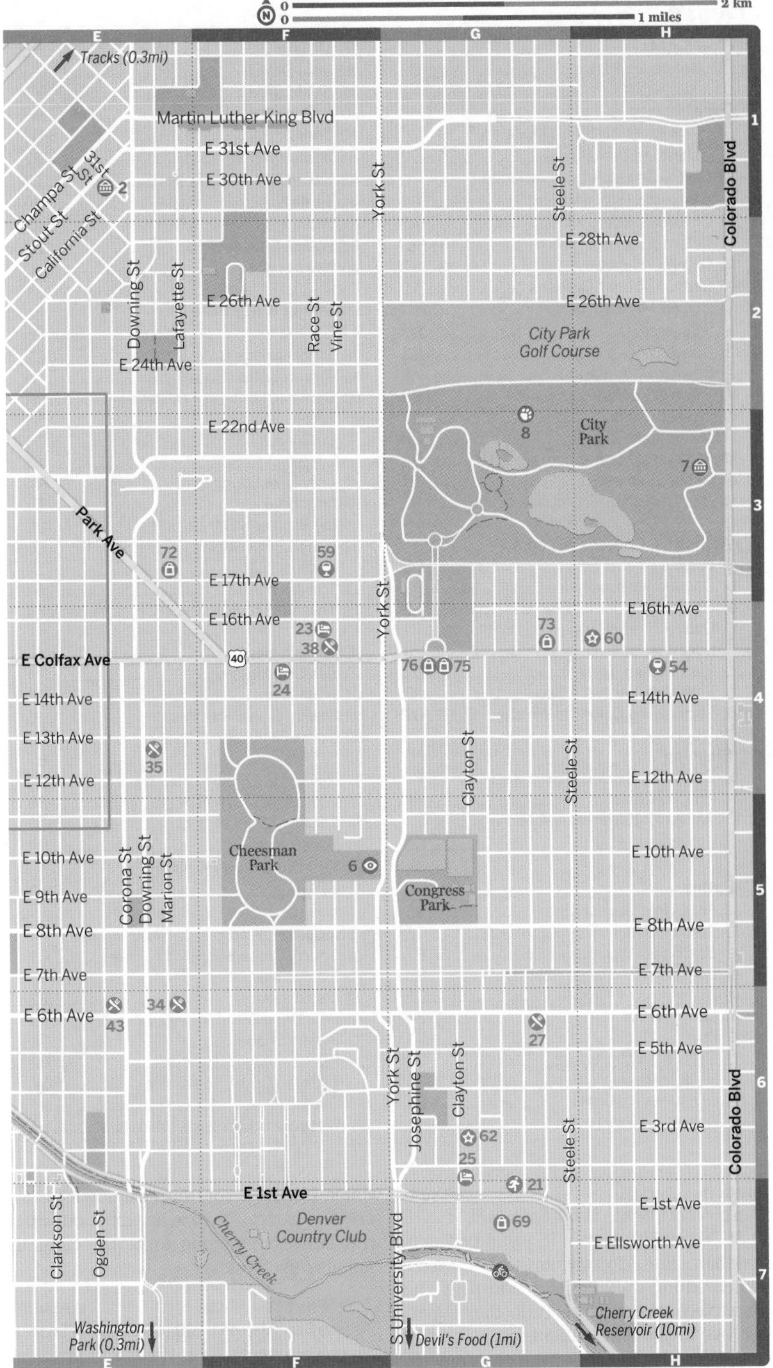

0 2 km
0 1 miles
Tracks (0.3mi)
Martin Luther King Blvd
E 31st Ave
E 30th Ave
31st St
Champa St
Stout St
California St
2
York St
Steele St
Colorado Blvd
E 28th Ave
E 26th Ave
Downing St
Lafayette St
Race St
Vine St
E 24th Ave
City Park Golf Course
E 22nd Ave
8
City Park
7
Park Ave
72
59
E 17th Ave
E 16th Ave
23
38
E Colfax Ave
40
24
76
75
73
60
54
E 14th Ave
E 13th Ave
E 12th Ave
35
Clayton St
Cheesman Park
6
Congress Park
E 10th Ave
E 9th Ave
E 8th Ave
E 7th Ave
E 6th Ave
E 5th Ave
Corona St
Marion St
34
43
27
Josephine St
E 3rd Ave
62
25
21
E 1st Ave
69
Denver Country Club
Cherry Creek
E Ellsworth Ave
Clarkson St
Ogden St
S University Blvd
Washington Park (0.3mi)
Devil's Food (1mi)
Cherry Creek Reservoir (10mi)

Denver

Top Sights

1 Confluence Park ... B2

Sights

2 Black American West Museum & Heritage Center ... E1
3 Blair-Caldwell African American Research Library ... D2
4 Children's Museum ... A3
Colorado Sports Hall of Fame ... (see 68)
5 Commons Park ... B2
6 Denver Botanic Gardens ... F5
7 Denver Museum of Nature & Science ... H3
8 Denver Zoo ... G3
9 Downtown Aquarium ... A2
10 Elitch Gardens ... B3
11 Illiterate Media ... B7
12 Millennium Bridge ... B2
13 Museum of Contemporary Art ... B2
14 National Velvet ... B1
15 Plus Gallery ... D1

Activities, Courses & Tours

16 Bicycle Doctor ... D5
17 Confluence Kayaks ... B2
18 Denver Bouldering Club ... A6
19 Denver Skate Park ... B1
Edgeworks ... (see 16)
20 Platte Valley Trolley ... B2
21 Pura Vida Fitness & Spa ... G7
22 Stranahans Colorado Whiskey ... C7

Sleeping

23 Castle Marne Bed & Breakfast ... F4
24 Holiday Chalet ... F4
25 JW Marriott Denver at Cherry Creek ... G6

Eating

26 Arada Restaurant & Bar ... C5
27 Barolo Grill ... G6
28 Beatrice & Woodsley ... B7
29 Buckhorn Exchange Restaurant ... B5
30 Buenos Aires Pizzeria ... D2
31 Domo Restaurant ... B4
32 Duo ... A1
33 El Taco De Mexico ... C5
34 Fruition Restaurant ... E6
35 Gypsy House Café ... E4
Hornet ... (see 39)
36 Mizuna ... D5
37 Root Down ... B1
38 SAME Café ... F4
39 Señor Burrito ... B6
40 Snooze ... D2
41 Squeaky Bean ... B2
42 Sweet Action Ice Cream ... B7
43 Table 6 ... E6
44 Walnut Room Pizzeria ... B7
45 Wazee Supper Club ... B2
46 Z Cuisine ... A1

Drinking & Nightlife

47 Bar Standard ... D5
48 Breckenridge Colorado Craft ... C2
49 Crema Coffee House ... D1
50 Denver Chophouse & Brewery ... C2
51 Forest Room 5 ... B2
52 La Rumba ... D5
53 Linger ... B1
54 Lost Lake Lounge ... H4
55 Matchbox ... D1
56 My Brother's Bar ... B2
57 Punch Bowl Social ... B6
Sputnik ... (see 70)
58 The Ale House ... B1
59 Thin Man Tavern ... F3

Entertainment

60 Bluebird Theater ... H4
61 BoyzTown ... B6
62 Cherry Creek Arts Festival ... G6
63 Coors Field ... C2
64 Hi-Dive ... B7
Howl at the Moon ... (see 50)
65 Landmark Mayan Theater ... B6
66 Larimer Lounge ... D1
67 Pepsi Center ... B3
68 Sports Authority Field at Mile High ... A3

Shopping

69 Cherry Creek Shopping Center ... G7
70 Fancy Tiger ... B7
71 Metroboom ... B2
72 Peppermint Boutique ... E3
73 Plastic Chapel ... G4
74 REI ... B2
75 Tattered Cover Bookstore ... G4
76 Twist & Shout ... G4
77 Wilderness Exchange Unlimited ... B2

Dancers MONUMENT

(Map p64; cnr Champa St & N Speer Blvd; ; 1, 30, 31, 36L, 48 RTD) Frozen in joyful two-step, Jonathan Borofsky's whimsical *Dancers* invite rushing traffic to stop and play. The centerpiece of Sculpture Park, they supervise live music and lounging picnickers in summer and rise eerily from the snow in winter. Initially a controversial buy for conservative citizens, they're a symbol on scale with Denver's ambition to be the cultural capital of the West.

I See What You Mean MONUMENT

(Big Blue Bear; Map p64; 700 14th St; ; D Line) Lawrence Argent's *I See What You Mean* is better known around town as the Big Blue Bear. This beloved 40ft-tall symbol of the city peers into the mammoth convention center with a friendly, playful spirit that has come to epitomize its city.

Millennium Bridge BRIDGE
(Map p60; extension of 16th St Mall) Allow us to be geeky for a second: this is the world's first cable-stayed bridge using a post-tensioned structural construction. If the technical jargon goes over your head, you'll be impressed by just looking up – the sweeping forms of the cables and white mast are a dramatic sight against Denver's consistently blue sky.

David B Smith Gallery GALLERY
(Map p64; 303-893-4234; www.davidbsmithgallery.com; 1543 Wazee St; noon-6pm Tue-Sat; 20, 28, 32, 44 RTD) David B Smith's taste for progressive American and international artists has made this space one of the most engaging small galleries in Denver.

National Velvet MONUMENT
(Map p60; 16th St Pedestrian Bridge) This much-maligned public pile of 'art' by John McEnroe appears to be a big red lingum-inspired mound of beans or boopies or sand bags. It lights up at night.

Capitol Hill & Golden Triangle

★**Denver Art Museum** MUESUM
(DAM; Map p68; ticket sales 720-865-5000; www.denverartmuseum.org; 100 W 14th Ave; adult/child/student $13/5/10, 1st Sat of each month free; 10am-5pm Tue-Thu, Sat & Sun, to 8pm Fri; P; 9, 16, 52, 83L RTD) The DAM is home to one of the largest Native American art collections in the USA, and puts on special avant-garde multimedia exhibits. The Western American Art section of the permanent collection is justifiably famous. This isn't an old, stodgy art museum, and the best part of a visit is diving into the interactive exhibits – kids love this place.

The landmark $110-million Frederic C Hamilton wing, designed by Daniel Libeskind, is quite simply awesome. Whether you see it as expanding crystals, juxtaposed mountains or just architectural indulgence, it's an angular modern masterpiece. If you think the place looks weird from the outside, look inside: shapes shift with each turn thanks to a combination of design and uncanny natural-light tricks.

Clyfford Still Museum MUSEUM
(Map p64; 720-354-4880; www.clyffordstillmuseum.org; 1250 Bannock St; adult/child $10/3; 10am-5pm, to 8pm Fri) Dedicated exclusively to the work and legacy of 20th-century American abstract expressionist Clyfford Still, this fascinating museum's collection includes over 2400 works by the powerful and narcissistic master of bold. In his will, Still insisted that his body of work only be exhibited in a singular space, so Denver built him a museum.

History Colorado Center MUSEUM
(Map p68; 303-447-8679; www.historycoloradocenter.org; 1200 Broadway; adult/student/child $10/8/8; 10am-5pm Mon-Sat, noon-5pm Sun; P) Discover Colorado's frontier roots and high-tech modern triumphs at this sharp, smart and charming museum. There are plenty of interactive exhibits, including a Jules Verne-esque 'Time Machine' that you push across a giant map of Colorado to explore seminal moments in the Centennial State's history.

Colorado State Capitol BUILDING
(Map p68; 303-866-2604; www.colorado.gov/capitoltour; 200 E Colfax Ave; 7:30am-5pm Mon-Fri, tours 10am-3pm Mon-Fri; 0, 0L, 2, 3L, 6, 7, 10, 12, 15, 16, 16L, 83L RTD) FREE Sitting commandingly atop Capitol Hill, this stately neoclassical government building looks out across the grand Civic Center Park. The ornate interior befits such a grand building, and visitors can join free tours that depart every 45 minutes.

Construction began in the 1890s from locally quarried rose onyx (Beulah red marble) and in 1908, to celebrate the Colorado gold rush, the superb dome was covered in 200 ounces of gold leaf. The 13th step sits exactly a mile above sea level.

Molly Brown House Museum HISTORIC BUILDING
(Map p68; 303-832-4092; www.mollybrown.org; 1340 Pennsylvania St; adult/child/senior $8/4/6; tours 10am-3:30pm Tue-Sat, noon-3:30pm Sun; P; 2, 10, 15, 15L RTD) This outstandingly preserved house, designed by the well-known architect William Lang, was built in 1889 and belonged to the most famous survivor of the *Titanic* disaster. You'll go through the house on a guided 45-minute tour, learning about this Colorado legend's unsinkable history.

Having survived the ill-fated voyage of 1912, Molly Brown became active in politics

Downtown Area

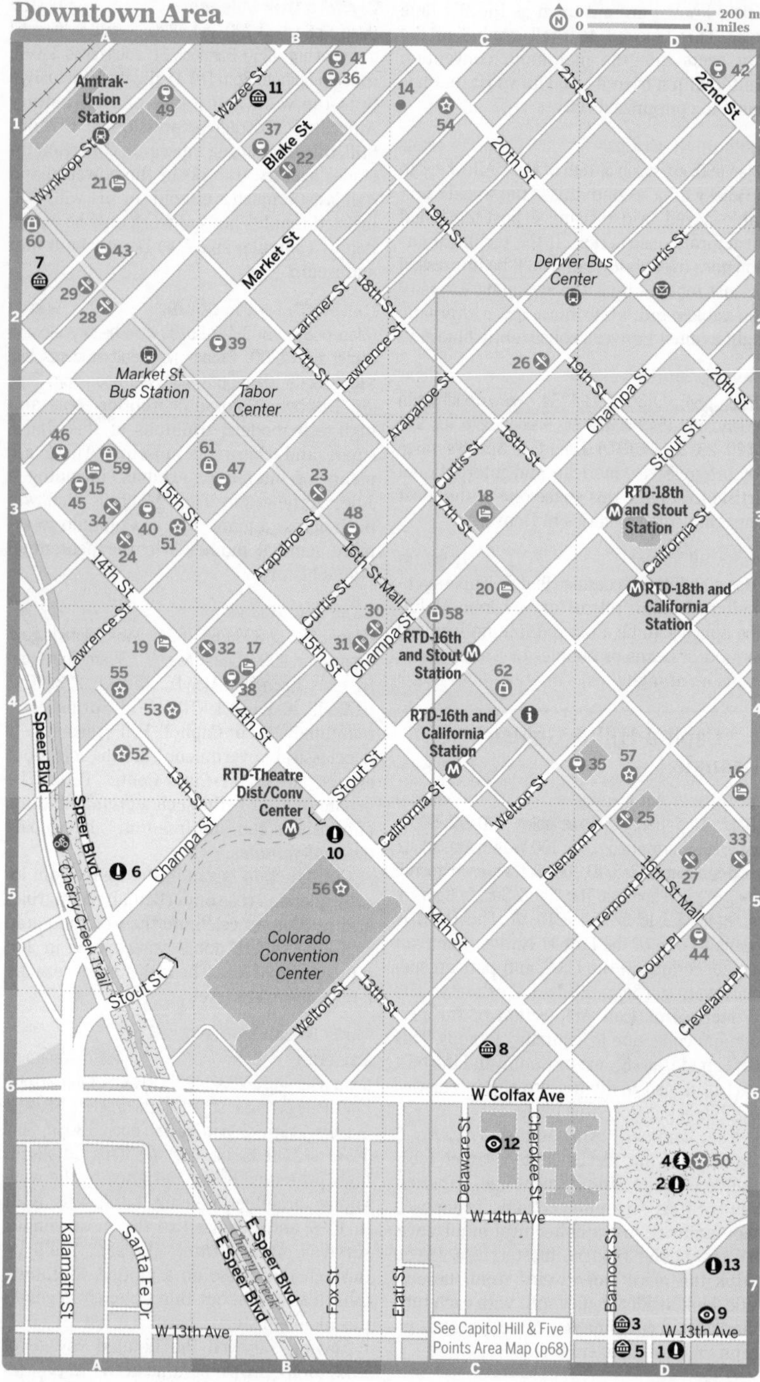

Downtown Area

Sights

- 1 Big Sweep ... D7
- 2 Bronco Buster ... D6
- 3 Byers-Evans House Museum ... D7
- 4 Civic Center Park ... D6
- 5 Clyfford Still Museum ... D7
- 6 Dancers ... A5
- 7 David B Smith Gallery ... A2
- 8 Denver Firefighters Museum ... C6
- 9 Denver Public Library ... D7
- 10 I See What You Mean ... B5
- 11 Robischon Gallery ... B1
- 12 United States Mint ... C6
- 13 Yearling ... D7

Activities, Courses & Tours

- 14 Cook Street School of Fine Cooking ... C1

Sleeping

- 15 Avenue West ... A3
- 16 Brown Palace Hotel ... D4
- 17 Curtis ... B4
- 18 Hotel Monaco ... C3
- 19 Hotel Teatro ... A4
- 20 Magnolia Hotel ... C3
- 21 Oxford Hotel ... A1

Eating

- 22 9th Door ... B1
- 23 Biker Jim's Dogs ... B3
- 24 Bistro Vendôme ... A3
- 25 Cooks Fresh Market ... D5
- 26 Elway's ... C2
- 27 Food Court at Republic Plaza ... D5
- 28 HBurger Co ... A2
- 29 Illegal Pete's ... A2
- 30 Laguna's Mexican Bar & Grill ... B4
- Little India ... (see 30)
- 31 Los Cabos II ... B4
- 32 Oceanaire Seafood Room ... B4
- 33 Pizza Colore Express ... D5
- 34 Rioja ... A3
- Vesta Dipping Grill ... (see 22)

Drinking & Nightlife

- 35 Appaloosa Bar & Grill ... D4
- 36 Beta Nightclub ... B1
- 37 Celtic Tavern ... B1
- 38 Corner Office ... B4
- 39 Croc's Mexican Bar & Grill ... B2
- 40 Crú ... A3
- 41 Falling Rock Tap House ... B1
- 42 Great Divide Brewing Company ... D1
- 43 Jet Lounge ... A2
- 44 Katie Mullen's Irish Pub & Restaurant ... D5
- 45 Mynt Lounge ... A3
- 46 Nallen's ... A3
- 47 Red Square Euro Bistro ... B3
- 48 Rock Bottom Restaurant & Brewery ... B3
- TAG ... (see 34)
- 49 Wynkoop Brewing Co ... A1

Entertainment

- Bovine Metropolis Theater ... (see 31)
- 50 Cinco de Mayo ... D6
- Colorado Ballet ... (see 53)
- Colorado Symphony Orchestra .. (see 53)
- 51 Comedy Works ... A3
- 52 Denver Center for the Performing Arts ... A4
- 53 Denver Performing Arts Complex ... A4
- 54 El Chapultepec ... C1
- 55 Ellie Caulkins Opera House ... A4
- 56 Great American Beer Festival ... B5
- Lannie's Clocktower Cabaret ... (see 23)
- Opera Colorado ... (see 53)
- 57 Paramount Theatre ... D4

Shopping

- 58 Champa Fine Wine & Liquor ... C4
- Colorado Rockies Dugout Store .. (see 35)
- Cry Baby Ranch ... (see 24)
- 59 EVOO Marketplace ... A3
- Goorin Brothers ... (see 24)
- 60 Tattered Cover Bookstore ... A2
- 61 Tewksbury & Co ... B3
- 62 Wild West Denver Store ... C4

and women's organizations, and was also a keen theater performer. She died in 1932, a woman ahead of her time.

Yearling MONUMENT

(Horse on the Chair; Map p64; 10 W 14th Ave; 16, 83L RTD) This wonderful sculpture by Donald Lipski sits outside the Denver Public Library, where it was installed in 1998 after spending a year in New York City's Central Park. The Horse on the Chair, as it's known, stands 21ft high and has a whimsy, humor and magic to it.

Bronco Buster MONUMENT

(Map p64; Civic Center Park; ; 9, 16, 52, 83L RTD) Denver sculptor A Phimister Proctor became nationally famous with this 1920 bronze of the Bronco Buster. Fun fact: Proctor's model for the cowboy was arrested for murder before the statue was done. At Proctor's insistence, the accused was allowed to continue posing until the sculpture was finished.

Denver Botanic Gardens GARDENS

(Map p60; www.botanicgardens.org; 1005 York St; adult/child $12.50/9; 9am-5pm; ; 2, 3, 6,

24 RTD) If you're hankering for greenery, this 23-acre expanse of Rocky Mountains shrubbery is the perfect place in which to hide from the hustle and bustle of the city. Local flora mixes it up with relatives from faraway continents such as Australia and Africa. Exhibitions and events are staged.

The tropical greenhouse made an appearance in Woody Allen's 1973 classic, *Sleeper*.

Denver Public Library LIBRARY

(Map p64; ☎720-865-1111; www.denverlibrary.org; 10 W 14th Ave; ⏰10am-8pm Mon & Tue, to 6pm Wed-Fri, 9am-5pm Sat, 1-5pm Sun; P; 🚌16, 83L RTD) FREE Hardly a dusty bibliotheca, the Denver Public Library is an active and hip place with whimsical post-modern architectural elements courtesy of renowned architect Michael Graves. In addition to its voluminous stacks, the library offers lectures, while shifting exhibits feature local historical and contemporary photography. On the 5th floor is the Western History & Genealogy Department.

Civic Center Park PARK

(Map p64; btwn Bannock St & Broadway; 🚌6, 7, 9, 10, 16, 16L, 52 RTD) In the shadow of the State Capitol's golden dome, this centrally located park hosts lounging drifters waiting for their bus connections, politicos yammering into Bluetooth headsets and some of the most iconic public sculptures in the city.

Byers-Evans House Museum HISTORIC BUILDING

(Map p64; ☎303-620-4933; www.coloradohistory.org; 1310 Bannock St; adult/child $6/4; ⏰10am-

DENVER IN...

Two Days

Start at rejuvenated LoDo and see its historic stables and warehouses converted into restaurants and boutiques. Check out the facade of Union Station (p94) and the Oxford Hotel (p75) before brunching at Snooze (p76) or Steuben's Food Service (p80). Check out the restaurants and boutiques of bejeweled Larimer Sq and the Big Blue Bear (p62), then head to Civic Center Park (p66) with its Greek amphitheater and stately buildings flanking three sides. Spend the afternoon touring the Mint (p67) and State Capitol (p63) before decided between Rioja (p78), Squeaky Bean (p78) and the classic Wazee Supper Club (p77) for dinner.

Day two is museum day. Head to Golden Triangle and visit either the Denver Art Museum (p63) or the Clyfford Still Museum (p63). Local history buffs can check out the History Colorado Center (p63), the Byers-Evans House Museum (p66) and the Denver Firefighters Museum (p59). The Denver Public Library (p66) is a good break spot. Hop on a B-Cycle (p88) in the afternoon to check out the **Cherry Creek Trail**, or maybe head to the foothills for a hike at the Jefferson County Open Space Parks (p73). Come nightfall, head to Linger (p87) in Highlands, or see what's happening at the Denver Performing Arts Complex (p89).

Four Days

On day three, get yourself to the Denver Zoo (p67) or the Denver Museum of Nature & Science (p67), then stroll through the huge **City Park** to stock up at the weekend farmers markets. Make you way over to Confluence Park (p67) to cool off in the river. Grab a B-Cycle and pedal down the river to Elitch Gardens (p69) amusement park to ride the Mind Eraser roller coaster. Check out Domo (p81) for a sushi dinner or head to one of the town's many arts districts for gallery browsing and bistro dining.

There's plenty more to do in Denver, but if it's summer, find some wheels and make for the mountains on day four. Head northwest through Golden Gate Canyon State Park (p73) on your way to Estes Park. It'll be almost a two-hour drive. From there, head up the stunning Old Fall River Rd to the Rocky Mountain National Park's Alpine Visitor Center (p135). The views are breathtaking. Or take a drive out to **Red Rocks Park & Amphitheater** (p99), 15 miles southwest of Denver in Morrison. The setting, between 400ft-high red sandstone rocks, is spectacular. In winter, you know what to do: head to Vail (p195), Keystone (p180), Breckenridge (p182) or Winter Park (p172), all less than two hours away, for world-class skiing.

4pm Mon-Sat; P 👪; 🚌9, 52 RTD) It's an amazing experience walking through this period house, painstakingly restored to the 1920s era; the rooms aren't roped off so you can wander into them. Guided tours run every hour from 10:30am to 2:30pm.

William Byers was the publisher of the *Rocky Mountains News* when he commissioned this grand house in 1883. He soon sold it to William Gray Evans, who was with the Denver Tramway Company.

Big Sweep — MONUMENT

(Map p64; 100 W 14th Ave) Large enough to whisk away a Volkswagen, this giant dustpan's color was chosen by Claes Oldenburg and Coosje van Bruggen to complement Denver's clear skies.

United States Mint — BUILDING

(Map p64; ☎303-405-4761; www.usmint.gov; 320 W Colfax Ave; ⊙8am-2pm Mon-Fri; 👪; 🚌7, 16, 16L RTD) FREE The Denver Mint produces about 7.5 billion coins each year and offers free guided tours each weekday. A limited number of standby tickets are available at the door, but it's best to book through the website.

CELL — MUSEUM

(Counterterrorism Education Learning Lab; Map p68; ☎303-844-4000; www.thecell.org; 99 West 12th Ave; adult/student $8/5; ⊙10am-5pm Tue-Sat, noon-5pm Sun) Indulge your fears and spy on your neighbors with the methods you learn at this rather over-the-top interactive learning center featuring plenty of footage from September 11, plus detailed exhibits on the life and work of the world's best terrorists. You may ask yourself: with centers like this, have the terrorists already won?

Five Points, Uptown & City Park

Denver Museum of Nature & Science — MUSEUM

(Map p60; ☎303-370-6000; www.dmns.org; 2001 Colorado Blvd; museum adult/child $13/8, IMAX $10/8, Planetarium $5/4; ⊙9am-5pm; P 👪; 🚌20, 32, 40 RTD) The Denver Museum of Nature & Science is located on the eastern edge of City Park. This classic natural-science museum has excellent temporary exhibits, plus those cool panoramas we all loved as kids. The IMAX theater and Gates Planetarium are especially fun.

Denver Zoo — ZOO

(Map p60; ☎720-337-1400; www.denverzoo.org; 2900 E 23rd Ave; adult/child/senior $15/10/12; ⊙9am-6pm, last admission 5pm; P 👪; 🚌24, 32 RTD) Denver's world-class zoo has more than 700 animal species housed in considerate enclosures that do their best to mirror native habitats. There are native and exotic animals, including rhinos, gorillas and giant Komodo dragons. You won't want to miss the polar bear exhibit and elephant passage. A schedule of monthly free-admission days is published on the zoo's website.

Black American West Museum & Heritage Center — MUSEUM

(Map p60; ☎720-242-7428; www.blackamericanwestmuseum.org/; 3091 California St; adult/child $10/6; ⊙10am-4pm Tue-Sat) This excellent museum is dedicated to 'telling history how it was'. It provides an intriguing look at the contributions of African Americans (from cowboys to rodeo riders) during the pioneer era – according to museum statistics, one in three Colorado cowboys were African American.

Blair-Caldwell African American Research Library — LIBRARY

(Map p60; ☎720-865-2401; www.aarl.denverlibrary.org; 2401 Welton St; ⊙noon-8pm Mon & Wed, 10am-6pm Tue, Thu & Fri, 9am-5pm Sat; 🚌38) Dedicated to the history and culture of the African American people of Denver and the Rocky Mountains region, this institution provides fabulous resources on a rich cultural heritage.

Plus Gallery — GALLERY

(Map p60; ☎303-296-0927; www.plusgallery.com; 2501 Larimer St; ⊙noon-6pm Wed-Sat; P; 🚌44, 48 RTD) When Ivar and Karen Zeile opened Plus Gallery in 2001 it was quickly established as one of the leading contemporary art galleries in the Western US.

Highlands & Platte River Valley

★Confluence Park — PARK

(Map p60; 2200 15th St; 👪; 🚌10 RTD) FREE Where Cherry Creek and South Platte River meet is the nexus and plexus of Denver's sunshine-loving culture. It's a good place for an afternoon picnic, and there's a short white-water park for kayakers and tubers.

Head south from here along the Cherry Creek Trail and you can get all the way to Cherry Creek Shopping Center and beyond

Capitol Hill & Five Points Area

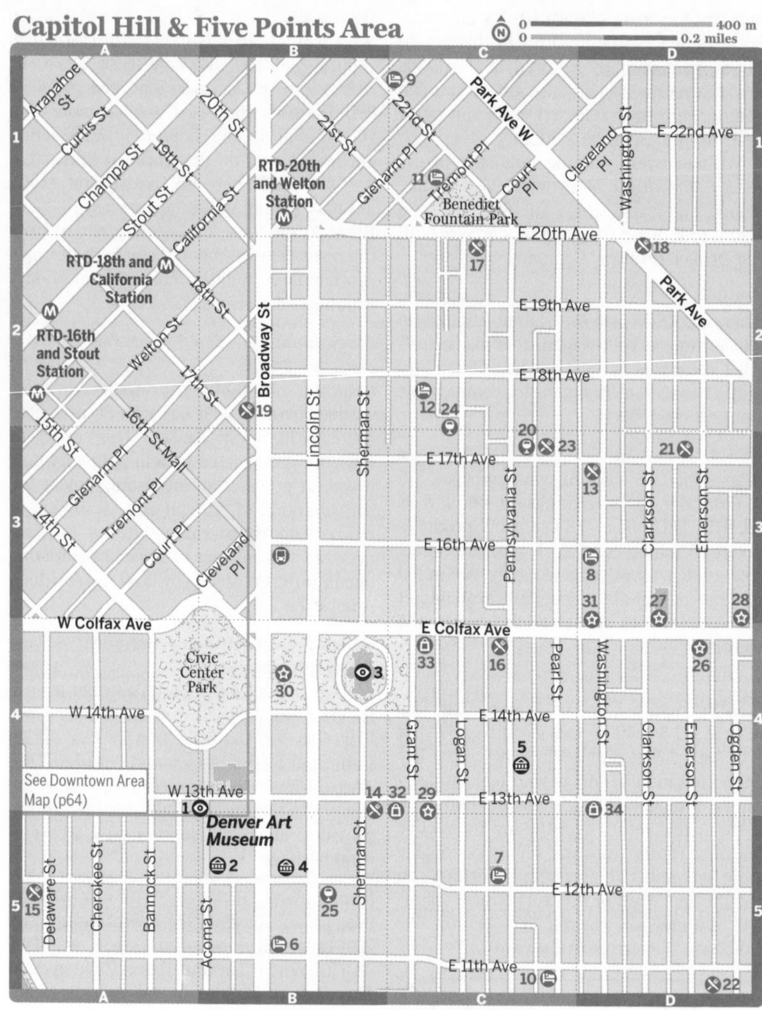

to Cherry Creek Reservoir. If you go southwest along the Platte Trail, you'll eventually ride all the way to Chatfield Reservoir. By heading north, and connecting to the Clear Creek Trail, you can get to Golden.

Commons Park PARK

(Map p60; www.denvergov.org/parksandrecreation; cnr 15th & Little Raven Sts; ; 10 RTD) FREE Affording views of the city and a bit of fresh air, this spacious, hilly patch of green has bikepaths, benches and plenty of people watching. A lyrical curving stairway to nowhere known as Common Ground, by artist Barbara Grygutis, is an undeniable centerpiece.

Children's Museum MUSEUM

(Map p60; 303-433-7444; www.mychildsmuseum.org; 2121 Children's Museum Dr; admission $9; 9am-4pm Mon, Tue & Thu, to 7:30pm Wed, to 5pm Sat & Sun;) If you've got kids, check out the Children's Museum, full of excellent interactive exhibits. A particularly well-regarded section is the kid-sized grocery store, where your little consumerists can push a shopping cart of their very own while learning about food and health.

Capitol Hill & Five Points Area

Top Sights
1 Denver Art Museum B4

Sights
2 CELL B5
3 Colorado State Capitol B4
4 History Colorado Center B5
5 Molly Brown House Museum C4

Sleeping
6 11th Avenue Hotel B5
7 Capitol Hill Mansion B&B C5
8 Denver International Youth Hostel D3
9 Melbourne International Hotel & Hostel C1
10 Patterson Historic Inn C5
11 Queen Anne Bed & Breakfast Inn C1
12 Warwick C2

Eating
13 Avenue Grill D3
14 City O' City B4
15 Cuba Cuba Café & Bar A5
16 Great Wall C4
Horseshoe Lounge .... (see 17)
17 Jonesy's EatBar C2
18 La Pasadita D2
19 Palace Arms B2
20 Steuben's Food Service C3
21 WaterCourse Foods D3
22 Wholefoods Market D5

Drinking & Nightlife
23 Ace C3
24 Denver Wrangler C2
25 The Church B5

Entertainment
26 Charlie's D4
27 Fillmore Auditorium D3
28 Ogden Theatre D3
29 Quixote's True Blue C4
30 Taste of Colorado B4
31 XBar D3

Shopping
32 Buffalo Exchange C4
33 Capitol Hill Books C4
Pandora Jewelry .... (see 32)
34 Wax Trax Records D4

Forney Transportation Museum MUSEUM
(303-297-1113; www.forneymuseum.org; 4303 Brighton Bvd; adult/child/senior $8/4/6; 10am-4pm Mon-Sat; P; 8, 38, 52 RTD) This fascinating museum exhibits antique vehicles of all types – cars, motorbikes, bicycles, tricycles, railway engines and rolling stock, fire engines, airplanes and more. Even if you're not an automotive aficionado, the shifting industrial design over the years is interesting. Among many highlights is Amelia Earhart's 1923 Kissel Speedstar in stunning canary yellow.

Elitch Gardens AMUSEMENT PARK
(Map p60; 303-595-4386; www.elitchgardens.com; 2000 Elitch Circle; adult/child $46/32; P; 1, 20 RTD) If you're finding all the museums a bit too serious, loosen up at this amusement park – your kids will love you for it. There's a water park, roller coasters and more. Go online to save on admission.

Downtown Aquarium AQUARIUM
(Map p60; 303-561-4450; www.aquariumrestaurants.com; 700 Water St; adult/child/senior $18/12/17; 10am-9pm Sun-Thu, to 9:30pm Fri & Sat; P; 10 RTD) Denver's old Ocean Journey Aquarium was sold in 2003 to a business that specializes in aquarium-themed restaurants. So it is that Downtown Aquarium is both a novelty restaurant and a public aquarium (and tiger den). It's a great place to take the kids...and a novel place to have a meal. Try the fish burger.

Colorado Sports Hall of Fame MUSEUM
(Map p60; 720-258-3888; www.coloradosports.org; 1701 Bryant St; 10am-3pm Thu-Sun Sep-May, 10am-3pm Tue-Sat Jun-Aug; P; 16, 16L, 28, 30, 30L, 31, 36L RTD) FREE This temple to Colorado's sporting prowess is in the Sports Authority Field at Mile High Stadium. It has exhibits on the Broncos and themes grouped under such purple headings as 'endurance' and 'sacrifice.' It's nothing to go out of your way for, but a good way to kill time before an event at the stadium.

South Central Denver

Washington Park PARK
(WashPark; www.washpark.com; cnr S Downing St & E Virginia Ave; P; 12 RTD) People somehow just look better in Wash Park. They are fitter, trimmer, more tanned and even taller than your average Denverite. Must be the rec center found in the middle of the park ($5 for a day pass), which includes a pool, weights and more.

Or maybe it's the bikepath and lakes, nearby restaurants, volleyball games and tennis matches that mark this park as one of the city's best.

South Broadway

Illiterate Media GALLERY

(Map p60; 303-993-4474; www.illiteratemagazine.com; 82 S Broadway; 11am-7pm Tue-Sat; ; 0 RTD) FREE This gallery grew out of *Illiterate Magazine*, a locally published art publication, and its thrust maintains a multidisciplinary edge, hosting events and hanging shows of regional artists such as Denver painter Ravi Zupa. Progressive and hip, it fits perfectly in the South Broadway neighborhood.

Beyond Central Denver

Lakeside Amusement Park AMUSEMENT PARK

(303-477-1621; www.lakesideamusementpark.com; 4601 Sheridan Blvd; gate admission/unlimited rides $2.50/$14; hr vary; ; 44, 44L, 51 RTD) This old-school fun park has rides for adrenaline junkies as well as tots and toddlers. It's in a great lakeside location with views west over the mountains – although you might not notice as you free fall from the 140ft-drop tower!

Water World AMUSEMENT PARK

(www.waterworldcolorado.com; 8801 N Pecos St, Federal Heights; adult/child $40/35; 10am-6pm, late May–Sep;) Bust out the nacho-cheese, sunscreen and water wings at this popular water park that has giant wave pools, plenty of slides and a handful of theme rides.

Mesteño MONUMENT

(Mustang; Peña Blvd) Nicknamed 'Bluecifer,' this 32ft-high blue stallion with hellish, gleaming red eyes greets visitors to and from DIA, and is the subject of much controversy in Denver. Morbid factoid: during its creation, one of the stallion's legs fell on creator Luis Jiménez, severing an artery in his leg and leading to his death.

Activities

There's a lot of talk about how the people of Denver are, on average, the slimmest in the USA, and it's easy to understand why. The city is checkered with lovely parks and green spaces, and the siren call of the rugged Front Range is ever-present. Plus, the sun is *always* shining. City elders and wags at the Chamber of Commerce are wont to brag about the 300 annual days of sunshine with which Denver is blessed, and the residents seem determined to soak up every minute of it.

The South Platte River is lined on both sides with lanes for cycling, jogging and strolling. From here, you can hook up with all of Denver's off-road cycling trails, which extend for over 100 miles across the city. Pick up a bike at one of the B-Cycle Stations that are littered around the downtown area – there are more than 80 in all. When things get hot, roll up your pants and escape into the cool currents near Confluence Park, take a kayaking lesson from Confluence Kayaks, or rent some gear at the impressive REI flagship store and head for the mountains.

Denver Parks & Recreation HEALTH & FITNESS

(720-913-1311; www.denvergov.org/dpr; day passes $6) Denver's park's department manages 27 rec centers, dozens of outdoor and indoor pools, golf courses and more. All the rec centers are open to the public, with affordable day passes.

Denver Skate Park SKATING

(Map p60; www.denverskatepark.com; 2205 19th St; 5am-11pm; 6, 10, 52 RTD) FREE Possibly the best free skate park in the US, this large outdoor area has various bowls and surfaces to suit all abilities. It's best for young skaters early on the weekends.

Pura Vida Fitness & Spa DAY SPA

(Map p60; 303-321-7872; www.puravidaclub.com; 2955 E 1st Ave; guest day pass $30; 5am-10pm Mon-Thu, to 9pm Fri, 6am-8pm Sat, 7am-8pm Sun) Sleek as the Starship Enterprise, this modern spa is Denver's best. It isn't cheap, but it's a sure bet for modern workout facilities, yoga classes, group fitness sessions and a chance to sweat alongside Denver's business class.

Bicycle Doctor BICYCLE RENTAL

(Map p60; 303-831-7228; www.bicycledr.com; 860 Broadway; 10am-7pm Mon-Fri, to 5pm Sat; 0, 6, 83L RTD) The guys behind the counter at this small shop might be the friendliest bike mechanics in the area, and their rental gear is top notch.

Edgeworks OUTDOOR EQUIPMENT

(Map p60; 303-831-7228; www.edge-works.com; 860 Broadway; 10am-7pm Mon-Fri, to 5pm Sat, varies Sun; 0, 6, 83L RTD) The superior service here meakes this one of Denver's best shops for snowboard and ski rentals.

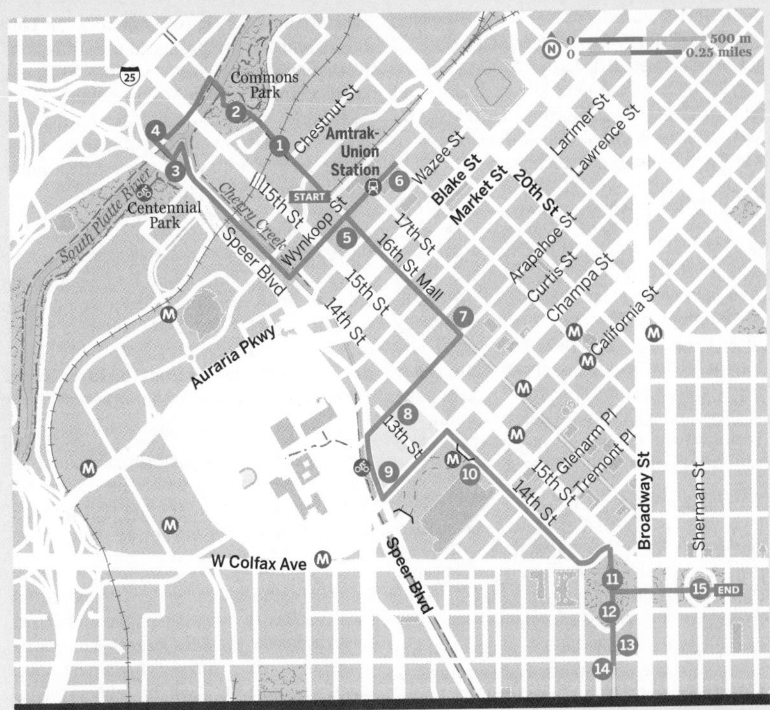

City Walk
Denver Walk

START MILLENNIUM BRIDGE
FINISH COLORADO STATE CAPITOL
LENGTH 3 MILES; 4 HOURS

This tour ventures out of the tourist turkey shoot on the 16th St Mall and into the heart of the Mile High City.

Begin by strolling across 1 **Millennium Bridge** (p63). This modernist footbridge is a bold symbol of contemporary Denver. Look ahead to the river: the city was born when gold was discovered in the currents below. Pass the rolling hills of 2 **Commons Park** (p68), where you can soak up the Denver skyline before crossing another footbridge over the South Platte River. Descend to the far bank and take the paved path upstream. Soon you'll see kids across the river splashing in 3 **Confluence Park** (p67), with its swimmable rapids where Platte River meets Cherry Creek.

If you're planning to head to the mountains, wander up to the enormous 4 **REI flagship store** (p92), where you can stock up on gadgets. Done shopping? Cross back over the water and take the footpath upstream beside Cherry Creek before taking the stairs up to Wynkoop St. At the corner you can hit 5 **Tattered Cover Bookstore** (p90), our favorite Denver bookstore. But you're getting hungry, right? Choose your own adventure: a burger and microbrew at the 6 **Wynkoop Brewing Co** (p84) or a bison sausage at 7 **Biker Jim's Dogs** (p79).

Walk your meal off by heading a few blocks over to the 8 **Denver Performing Arts Complex** (p89), where you can stand agape under 9 **Dancers** (p62) and give a hug to 10 **I See What You Mean** (p62). It's a straight shot up 14th St to 11 **Civic Center Park** (p66), where you can pose by 12 **Bronco Buster** (p65), check out the remarkable architecture of the 13 **Denver Art Museum** (p63) and 14 **Denver Public Library** (p66), and climb to the 13th step of the 15 **Colorado State Capitol** (p63) – exactly 1 mile above sea level.

Kite Surf Colorado KITE SURFING
(☎303-332-7003; www.kitesurfcolorado.com; 8547 E Arapahoe Rd, ste J111, Greenwood Village; 2hr lesson $150) Check out local kite-surfing legend Shawn Tieskotter for lessons. He'll take you out, teach you to read the winds, and keep you from drowning...which is good!

Confluence Kayaks KAYAKING
(Map p60; ☎303-433-3676; www.confluencekayaks.com; 2373 15th St, unit B; 2hr class $149-159, tube rental $20; ⏱10am-6pm Mon-Thu & Sat, to 7pm Fri, noon-5pm Sun; 🚌28, 32, 44 RTD) Situated under a health-food store, this centrally located kayak shop offers gear rental and lots of advice about the area's white water from laid-back, amiable staff. If you're a beginner, it offers lessons at nearby Confluence Park, but the classes fill fast so it's best to sign up several days in advance.

Denver Bouldering Club ROCK CLIMBING
(Map p60; ☎303-351-5588; www.denverboulderingclub.com; 2485 W 2nd Ave, No 18) The instruction for serious climbers is better at the Colorado Mountain School (p136) in Estes Park, but this climbing gym in the heart of the city is a good way to get psyched for a trip into the mountains. It's also huge: a 1500-sq-ft facility that stays open 24 hours a day.

Courses

Seasoned Chef COOKING
(☎303-377-3222; www.theseasonedchef.com; 999 Jasmine St, ste 100; classes $70-135) This well-established cooking school offers three-hour classes on everything from knife skills and cooking basics to menu building and end-to-end sessions such as 'Tapas of the Southwest.'

Cook Street School of Fine Cooking COOKING
(Map p64; ☎303-308-9300; www.cookstreet.com; 1937 Market St; classes from $89) Classes here are sharply focused, taking on ethnic flavors and cooking techniques from distant regions (such as North Africa, India or Spain), or an intense look at our favorite foods ('Scotch and Steak' class, anyone?). The instructors are well pedigreed and you'll leave stuffed.

Tours

★**Stranahans Colorado Whiskey** GUIDED TOUR
(Map p60; ☎303-296-7440; www.stranahans.com; 200 S Kalamath St; ⏱tours 11am, 1pm, 3pm & 5pm Mon, Wed, Fri & Sat) FREE Only a dozen barrels of whiskey are produced from this family distillery each week – and they're damn good. Using water from the Rockies, Colorado barley and white-oak barrels, it's a rare taste of quality over quantity. Short tours of the facility are available, though limited space means it's best to sign up online.

Denver Microbrew Tours GUIDED TOUR
(☎303-578-9548; www.denvermicrobrewtour.com; per person $29) This popular tour samples local craft beers from the boutique makers in the LoDo district. It takes a couple of hours in the afternoon on Friday, Saturday or Sunday. The tours kick off from the River North Brewery or the Rock Bottom Brewery.

Culinary Connectors GUIDED TOUR
(☎303-495-5487; www.culinaryconnectors.com; tours $39-99) Foodies will want to try the varied list of guided tours that visit Denver's best restaurants on foot or by chauffeured vehicle.

Denver Inside & Out GUIDED TOUR
(☎303-330-9871; www.denverinsideandout.com; adult/child/under 5yr $40/35/free) This outfit offers interesting historical walking tours based on the 1922 daylight robbery of the Denver Mint. They're cleverly done, with some of the robbers coming to life along the way, and mysteries and clues acted out in situ.

Platte Valley Trolley TOUR
(Map p60; ☎303-458-6255; www.denvertrolley.org; Platte St; adult/child $4/2; ⏱departures noon-3:30pm Fri-Sun; 🚌6, 10, 28, 32, 44 RTD) Ride the historic Platte Valley Trolley, which trundles along its tracks from the REI store south towards the football stadium. To be honest the sights aren't much – mostly the same stuff you see in a short walk around the area – but the stories from the history-buff staff are enlightening.

Festivals & Events

★**Denver Cruiser Ride** PARADE
(www.denvercruiserride.com) Held every Wednesday night in the summer, Denver's cruiser ride is one of the biggest in the nation. On the website, you can figure out the week's theme to get dressed in your appropriate costume. You'd hate to go as 'Bible Belt and Panties' when it's actually 'Mad Max Thunder Dome' week.

LOCAL KNOWLEDGE

BEST DAY HIKES & MOUNTAIN BIKE RIDES FROM DENVER

There are literally hundreds of day hikes within an hour of Denver. Many people choose to head up to Boulder's Mountain Parks or Colorado Springs for a day. If you're sticking to the mountains just outside of Denver, you will want to try these:

Jefferson County Open Space Parks (www.jeffco.us/openspace) Jefferson County runs along most of the western edge of Denver, and its open spaces are the best around. Top picks include Matthews Winters (right off I-70 at Morrison Rd, with trails taking you all the way to Red Rocks), Mt Falcon (near Morrison, this spot has more evergreens than most Front Range hikes), Elk Meadow (near Evergreen, with elk herds and a true mountain feel), Lair o' the Bear (between Evergreen and Morrison, also very mountainous), and White Ranch Park (south of I-70, for mountain biking).

Golden Gate Canyon State Park (303-582-3707; www.parks.state.us/parks; 92 Crawford Gulch Rd, Golden; entrance/camping $7/24; 5am-10pm) Located halfway between Denver and Nederland, this massive 12,000-acre state park can be reached in about 45 minutes from downtown Denver. Take Hwy 93 north from Golden 1 mile to Golden Gate Canyon Rd. Turn left and continue for 13 miles to the park. It has camping, a visitor center and plenty of trails. This is the best spot to see aspen trees close to Denver.

Staunton State Park (303-816-0912; www.parks.state.co.us/parks) Colorado's newest state park sits on a historic ranch site 40 miles west of Denver. It is accessed from Hwy 285 between Conifer and Bailey.

Waterton Canyon (303-634-3745; www.denverwater.org/recreation/watertoncanyon; Kassler Center) South of the city, just west of Chatfield Reservoir, this pretty canyon has an easy 6.5-mile trail to the Strontia Springs Dam. From there, the **Colorado Trail** (CTF; 303-384-3729; www.coloradotrail.org; PO Box 260876; 9am-5pm Mon-Fri) will take you all the w-ay to Durango! This trails also connects with the trails at Roxborough State Park, further south. This is probably the best area for mobility-impaired nature lovers.

Pike National Forest (303-275-5610; 19316 Goddard Ranch Ct; 8am-4:30pm Mon-Fri) Start exploring this large national forest by picking up information available at the USFS South Platte Ranger Station, about 5 miles from Morrison. One good hike is found about 45 minutes south of Denver at Devil's Head Lookout (elevation 9748ft), on the highest summit in the forested Rampart Range. Although the area offers USFS campsites ($9), they are typically full and sometimes very noisy. Picnics and day hikes, however, are highly recommended. To get there from Denver, follow US 85 south to Sedalia, then take Hwy 67 west for 10 miles to Rampart Range Rd, which leads 9 miles to the Devils Head National Recreation Trail and picnic grounds.

Buffalo Creek Mountain Bike Area (www.frmbp.org; Pine Valley Ranch Park) If you're into single-track mountain biking, this area has about 40 miles of bike trails, including the sections of the Colorado Trail that permit bikes. There are two access points: the busiest is 3.5 miles south of Buffalo Creek, where Jefferson County Rd 126 (S Deckers Rd) intersects the Colorado Trail. Another option is the Miller Gulch trailhead, reached from Bailey by taking Park County Rd 68 for 5 miles, then veering left on Park County Rd 70 for another mile before taking a left on USFS Rd 553. Miller Gulch Rd (USFS 554) will be on your right within half a mile. The South Platte Ranger Station can provide you with a free pamphlet outlining some of the rides.

First Friday CULTURE

(www.rivernorthart.com) On the first Friday of every month, Denverites come out for an art stroll, cruising galleries for free wine and fun conversations in the Santa Fe, RiNo, Cherry Creek, downtown and Tennyson Arts Districts.

Cinco de Mayo CULTURE

(Map p64; www.cincodemayodenver.com; May) Enjoy salsa music and margaritas at one of the country's biggest Cinco de Mayo celebrations, held over two days on the first weekend in May in Civic Center Park. With three stages and more than 350 exhibitors and food vendors, it's huge fun.

Cherry Creek Arts Festival ARTS
(Map p60; www.cherryarts.org; cnr Clayton St & E 3rd Ave; ⏲Jul) During this sprawling celebration of visual, culinary and performing arts, Cherry Creek's streets are closed off and over 250,000 visitors browse the giant block party. The three-day event takes place around July 4.

Taste of Colorado FOOD
(Map p68; ☎303-295-6330; www.atasteofcolorado.com; Civic Center Park; ⏲Sep) More than 50 restaurants cook up their specialties at food stalls; there's also booze, live music, and arts- and crafts vendors at this Labor Day festival.

Great American Beer Festival BEER
(Map p64; ☎303-447-0816; www.greatamericanbeerfestival.com; 700 14th St; $75; ⏲Sep or Oct; 🚇101 D-Line, 101 H-Line, 🚌1, 8, 30, 30L, 31, 48 RTD) Colorado has more microbreweries than any other US state, and this hugely popular sells out in advance. More than 500 breweries are represented, from the big players to the home-brew enthusiasts. Only the Colorado Convention Center is big enough for these big brewers and their fat brews.

Sleeping

Most Denver lodging is found in the greater downtown area. Downtown also has all the major international chains, including a top-notch Ritz (www.ritzcarlton.com/denver) and Grand Hyatt (www.granddenver.hyatt.com). There are also a number of large chain hotels located 15 miles south of downtown in the Denver Tech Center – book online to save big. Denver is downright brutal on budget-conscious backpackers; consider one of the (fairly dreary) single-story motels on E or W Colfax Ave or searching out a homestay with www.couchsurfing.org or www.craigslist.org.

Downtown & LoDo

Denver International Youth Hostel HOSTEL $
(Map p68; ☎303-832-9996; www.youthhostels.com/denver; 630 E 16th Ave; dm $19; P @ 🛜; 🚌15, 15L, 20 RTD) If cheap really matters, then the Denver International Youth Hostel might be the place for you. It's basic and vaguely chaotic, but has a ramshackle charm and a great downtown location. All dorms have attached bathroom facilities and the common area in the basement has a large-screen TV, library and computers for guests to use.

★**Curtis** BOUTIQUE HOTEL $$
(Map p64; ☎303-571-0300; www.thecurtis.com; 1405 Curtis St; d $159-279; ❄ @ 🛜; 🚌15 RTD) It's like stepping into a doobop Warhol wonderworld at this temple to postmodern pop culture. Attention to detail – be it through the service or the decor in the rooms – is paramount at the Curtis, a one-of-a-kind hotel in Denver.

There are 13 themed floors and each is devoted to a different genre of American pop culture. Rooms are spacious and very mod without being too out there to sleep. The hotel's refreshingly different take on sleeping may seem too kitschy for some – you can get a wake-up call from Elvis – but if you're tired of the same old international brands, this joint in the heart of downtown might be your tonic.

Magnolia Hotel BOUTIQUE HOTEL $$
(Map p64; ☎303-607-9000; www.magnoliahoteldenver.com; 818 17th St; r from $149; ❄ @ 🛜 👪) Housed in an old bank building, this 13-story European-style hotel offers old-world charm, modern amenities and good value in the heart of downtown. Its super-central location, good deals and bedtime milk and cookies are three major selling points.

Tasteful, stylish rooms and suites come in a variety of shapes (and prices), although some are a bit small, with a Western meets Euro flavor. Gym junkies will dig the on-site fitness center.

Hotel Monaco BOUTIQUE HOTEL $$
(Map p64; ☎800-990-1303, 303-296-1717; www.monaco-denver.com; 1717 Champa St; r from $127; P ❄ 🛜 🐾; 🚌0, 6, 30, 30L, 31, 36, 48, 52 RTD) This ultra-stylish boutique is a favorite with the celebrity set. Modern rooms blend French and art-deco styles – think bold colors and fabulous European-style feather beds. Don't miss the evening 'Altitude Adjustment Hour,' when guests enjoy free wine and five-minute massages. The place is 100% pet-friendly; staff will even deliver a named goldfish to your room upon request.

Brown Palace Hotel HISTORIC HOTEL $$$
(Map p64; ☎303-297-3111; www.brownpalace.com; 321 17th St; r from $299; P ❄ @ 🛜 👪) Standing agape under the stained-glass crowned atrium, it's clear why this palace is shortlisted among the country's elite historic hotels. There's deco artwork, a four-star spa, im-

ported marble and staff who discreetly float down the halls.

The rooms, which have been hosting presidents since Teddy Roosevelt's days, have the unique elegance of a distant era, but can be a bit small by modern standards. If it's out of budget, ask a concierge for a free self-guided tour or hang out for a while in the lobby and just pretend. The martinis are predictably perfect and served with a sterling bowl of warm pecans.

Hotel Teatro BOUTIQUE HOTEL **$$$**
(Map p64; ☎303-228-1102; www.hotelteatro.com; 1100 14th St; d from $239; ; 10, 15 RTD) Elegant surroundings and impeccable service make this luxurious boutique hotel one of Denver's best. The 112 rooms and suites are gorgeous, done up with Indonesian sandstone foyers, art-deco and cherry-wood furnishings and thick damask curtains.

Just across the street from the Denver Performing Arts Center, it's not surprising that the Hotel Teatro would incorporate the theater into its decorating scheme.

Oxford Hotel BOUTIQUE HOTEL **$$$**
(Map p64; ☎800-228-5838, 303-628-5400; www.theoxfordhotel.com; 1600 17th St; d from $230; ; 6, 20, 28, 32, 44 RTD) Marble walls, stained-glass windows, frescoes and sparkling chandeliers adorn the public spaces of this classy hotel built in 1891 in red sandstone. Denver's first hotel has large rooms decked out with imported English and French antiques.

The extensive art collection on display includes several notable works and the art-deco Cruise Room Bar is one of Denver's swankiest cocktail lounges.

Capitol Hill & Golden Triangle

11th Avenue Hotel HOTEL **$**
(Map p68; ☎303-894-0529; www.11thavenuehotel.com; 1112 Broadway; dm $19-22, r with/without bath $45/39;) This budget hotel has a good location for art lovers in the Golden Triangle district. The lobby looks vaguely like something from a Jim Jarmusch movie. The upstairs rooms, some with attached bathrooms, are bare but clean. It's safe, secure and a decent place for budget travelers.

Capitol Hill Mansion B&B B&B **$$**
(Map p68; ☎800-839-9329; www.capitolhillmansion.com; 1207 Pennsylvania St; r incl breakfast $134-219; P) Stained-glass windows, original 1890s woodwork and turrets make this delightful, gay- and family-friendly Romanesque mansion a special place to stay. Rooms are elegant, uniquely decorated and come with different special features (one has a solarium, another boasts Jacuzzi tubs).

Patterson Historic Inn HISTORIC HOTEL **$$**
(Map p68; ☎303-955-5142; www.pattersoninn.com; 420 E 11th Ave; r incl breakfast from $169; @) This 1891 grande dame was once a senator's home. It's now one of the best historic bed-and-breakfasts in town. The gardens are limited, but the Victorian charm, sumptuous breakfast and well-appointed chambers in the nine-room château will delight. Rooms come with modern touches such as silk robes, down comforters and flat-screen TVs.

Five Points, Uptown & City Park

Melbourne International Hotel & Hostel HOSTEL **$**
(Map p68; ☎303-292-6386; www.denverhostel.com; 607 22nd St; dm/s/d $20/35/45; @; 8, 48 RTD) The Melbourne is clean, comfortable and secure – though the neighborhood is still transitioning from its rough roots. It's basic but offers decent dorms, singles and doubles in a great location just minutes from the 16th St Mall. There's a common kitchen and bathrooms are shared. One family room offers sleeping for six.

★**Queen Anne Bed & Breakfast Inn** B&B **$$**
(Map p68; ☎303-296-6666; www.queenannebnb.com; 2147 Tremont Pl; r incl breakfast $135-215; P) Soft chamber music wafting through public areas, fresh flowers, manicured gardens and evening wine tastings create a romantic ambience at this eco-conscious B&B in two late-1800s Victorian homes. Featuring period antiques, private hot tubs and exquisite hand-painted murals, each room has its own personality.

Green features include mattresses made from recycled coils and green-tea insulation, organic fabrics (just like the delicious full breakfast) and products and produce purchased from local merchants when possible. It even has free bikes.

Holiday Chalet B&B $$
(Map p60; ☎303-437-8245; www.theholidaychalet.com; 1820 E Colfax Ave; d incl breakfast $94-145; P❄📶🐾; 🚌15 RTD) Big breakfasts and cozy ambience are standard at this beautifully restored Victorian mansion in Denver's historic Wyman District, just outside central downtown. Swathed in lace, floral carpets and rich woodwork, the revamped brownstone mansion features rooms with high ceilings, hardwood floors and period decor. Only downside: there's a lot of street noise.

Castle Marne Bed & Breakfast B&B $$$
(Map p60; ☎303-331-0621; www.castlemarne.com; 1572 Race St; r incl breakfast $115-300; P❄📶; 🚌15, 15L, 20 RTD) Fall under the spell of Castle Marne, one of Denver's grandest old mansions. Located in the historic Wyman District, it dates from 1889 and is on the National Register of Landmarks. The feel is pre-1900 old-world elegance with modern-day convenience and comfort. Furnishings are authentic period antiques and family heirlooms, and offer a mood of quiet charm and romance.

Each of the nine rooms is a unique experience of taste and style, and come with indoor Jacuzzi tubs or outside hot tubs.

Warwick HOTEL $$$
(Map p68; ☎303-861-2000; www.warwickhotels.com; 1776 Grant St; d $130-375; P❄📶🏊👪; 🚌20, 28, 32 RTD) Affordable luxury just east of downtown Denver is how the Warwick bills itself and, with some very cheap online specials, this can be true. Rooms here are larger than average and surprisingly modern. While the lackluster lobby leaves a bit to be desired, you are literally a jump from downtown, and the rooftop pool is a summertime perk.

Highlands & Platte River Valley

Lumber Baron Inn Gardens B&B $$
(☎303-477-8205; www.lumberbaron.com; 2555 W 37th Ave; r $149-239; P❄📶👪; 🚌38 RTD) 🌿 Murder-mystery dinners and romance-inducing suites make this elegantly quirky B&B in the cooled-out Highlands neighborhood stand out from the pack – even the locals choose to stay here for a weekend mystery getaway! The five suites are all different, although all feature Jacuzzis and giant plasma TVs.

Cherry Creek

JW Marriott Denver at Cherry Creek HOTEL $$$
(Map p60; ☎303-316-2700; www.jwmarriottdenver.com; 150 Clayton Lane; d from $245; P❄📶👪🐾; 🚌1, 2, 3, 46 RTD) Spacious digs come with high-thread-count sheets, plump beds and marble bathrooms featuring top-class soaps and shampoos. The on-site bar is also quite cool – you might even spot a Denver Bronco… or a cougar trying to land a Bronco. Local artwork and colorful blown glass grace lobbies and rooms.

Beyond Central Denver

Omni Interlocken Resort & Golf Club RESORT $$$
(☎303-438-6600; www.omniinterlocken.com; 500 Interlocken Blvd; d $300; P❄@📶🏊👪) Have a glass of champagne while checking into the impressive four-diamond Omni. Although the location isn't so hot – it's about 20 minutes from downtown Denver – rooms are spacious and well appointed, and the service is top notch, with helpful and friendly staff. A big spa, 27 golf holes and shuttle add to the list.

Eating

While the restaurants downtown offer the greatest depth and variety in Denver, insiders head to the more strollable neighborhoods such as Highlands, Cherry Creek, South Pearl St, Uptown, Five Points, Washington Park and Old Town Littleton, where little five-block commercial strips hold some of Denver's best eateries. Check out www.5280.com or www.diningout.com/denver for new eats.

Downtown & LoDo

Snooze BREAKFAST $
(Map p60; ☎303-297-0700; www.snoozeeatery.com; 2262 Larimer St; mains $6-12; ⏰6:30am-2:30pm Mon-Fri, 7am-2:30pm Sat & Sun; 👪) 🌿 This reto-styled cheery breakfast-and-brunch spot is one of the hottest post-party breakfast joints in town. It dishes up spectacularly crafted breakfast burritos and a smokin' salmon benedict. The coffee's always good, but you have the option of an early-morning Bloody Mary. The wait can be up to an hour on weekends!

Wazee Supper Club BURGERS, PIZZERIA $
(Map p60; ☎303-623-9518; www.wazeesupper-club.com; 1600 15th St; mains $9-16; ⏲11am-2am Mon-Sat, noon-midnight Sun; 👪; 🚌6, 10, 28, 32 RTD) Once you step into Wazee, there's little chance you'll turn around – it smells so delicious. Known for some of the best pizza and *stromboli* (stuffed Italian turnover) in the city, this long-time local favorite is a buzzing place day and night.

Buenos Aires Pizzeria ARGENTINE $
(Map p60; ☎303-296-6710; www.bapizza.com; 1307 22nd St; empanadas $2.50, mains $6-10; ⏲11:30am-10pm Tue-Sat, noon-8pm Sun) An authentic taste of Argentina in the heart of cow-town Colorado, this wide-angled pizzeria looks and feels like the real-deal Holyfield. You can either pig out on two or three empanadas (stuffed pastries) or dig into yummy sandwiches, above-average pizzas and pasta. Alas, no steaks.

Cooks Fresh Market SANDWICHES $
(Map p64; ☎303-893-2277; www.cooksfresh market.com; 120 16th St; sandwiches & salads $6-10; ⏲7am-8pm Mon-Fri, 9am-6pm Sat; 📶👪; 🚌Glenarm) Far and away the best deli in downtown, the attention to quality is obvious in the take-out salads and sandwiches, selection of cheeses and expert pastries. Some gourmet cooking staples and bulk selection complete the picture, making this an ideal stop for supplies if you're picnicking in the park or heading out of town.

HBurger Co BURGERS $
(Map p64; ☎720-524-4345; www.hburger.com; 1555 Blake St; mains $6-13; ⏲11am-9pm Mon-Thu, to 10pm Fri, noon-10pm Sat, noon-8pm Sun) Sure, the formidable burgers at this futuristic diner get rave reviews – especially the Angus beef, chili-infused, cheddar-crowned HBurger – but the visionary milkshake menu might be worthy of skipping the main course altogether. The Nutella marshmallow variety, topped with roasted marshmallows and infused with liquid nitrogen(!) is an icy, creamy wonder.

Laguna's Mexican Bar & Grill MEXICAN $
(Map p64; ☎303-623-5321; 1543 Champa St; mains $7-13; ⏲11am-9pm Mon-Sat; 🚌6, 10, 32 RTD) The basement space can feel a bit like a distant uncle's dim basement until you make your way out to the seating under the sunlit four-story atrium. The food leans toward cheese-laden Tex-Mex platters with sides of free chips and pleasantly *picante* (spicy) salsa.

> **SETTING YOUR DENVER BUDGET**
>
> Budget travelers can eat well in Denver: cheap restaurant meals cost $7 or $8 and there are good options for self-caterers. Inexpensive lodgings are harder to find, but the city has a handful of well-located backpacker options where a dorm bed will cost around $20 and a double costs from about $50.
>
> Mid-priced restaurant meals cost $10 to $15. Midrange travelers will be torn between cheaper $80-a-night motel rooms in the 'burbs and digs nearer downtown, where the average room costs $100 to $200 a night.
>
> Top-end travelers can choose among the many boutique hotels and B&Bs in the $180-plus bracket, often in quiet leafy streets just outside downtown. Fine-dining options are plentiful.

9th Door SPANISH $
(Map p64; ☎303-292-2229; www.theninthdoor.com; 1808 Blake St; tapas $5-9; ⏲4:30pm-2am Mon-Fri, 5:30pm-2am Sat; 🖉👪; 🚌1, 2, 12 RTD) The decor is as juicy as the Spanish tapas at this hot Denver restaurant. The ambience is intimate, with low lights, beaded glass chandeliers and booths you can disappear into – great for groups, as they easily fit six. After dinner it becomes a popular lounge with live music.

Pizza Colore Express ITALIAN $
(Map p64; ☎303-534-2111; www.pizzeriacolore.com; 1647 Court Pl; mains $7-10; ⏲8am-3pm Mon-Fri; 👪; 🚌12, 20, 16th St Shuttle) Big portions of inexpensive pasta and wood-oven pizzas are served at this casual Italian restaurant. The food is delicious (especially considering the price).

Illegal Pete's MEXICAN $
(Map p64; ☎303-623-2169; www.illegalpetes.com; 1530 16th St; mains $5-7; ⏲11am-10pm Sun-Wed, 11am-2:30am Thu-Sat; 🚌Wazee St) Around lunch, you'll queue to the door at Pete's, the best option for quick Mexican on the 16th St Mall. With rock posters plastering the window, a worn plank floor underfoot and inked-up staff behind the counter, the place has charm galore.

Food Court at Republic Plaza FAST FOOD $
(Map p64; ☎303-534-5128; 370 17th St; mains $5-12; ⏲10am-3pm Mon-Sat; 👪; 🚌Court Pl) With

chains big and small and fast-food prices, this 16th St Mall food court is easy for families and rushed office jockeys. The nosh isn't limited to the frightening thrill of Chik-fil-A patties, either; there are a few healthy options.

Little India INDIAN **$$**
(Map p64; www.littleindiadenver.com; 1533 Champa St; mains $10-15; 11am-2:30pm & 5-10pm; 15 RTD) The lunch buffet ($9) attracts a load of office workers. After dark the atmosphere gets a bit more upscale, with couples snuggling into booths for a selection of curries and generously spiced rice dishes. One of three Denver locations, this place also has a full bar in back.

Los Cabos II PERUVIAN **$$**
(Map p64; 303-595-3232; www.loscabosii.com; 1525 Champa St; mains $8-15; 11am-9pm Mon-Thu, to 10pm Fri & Sat, to 5pm Sun; ; Champa) Start things off at this popular Peruvian lunch spot with an excellent pisco sour before getting into the perfectly seasoned *lomo saltado* (grilled strips of steak with peppers, onions and veggies over fries) or a distinctly Peruvian take on chow mien. Before you leave, be sure to pet that giant stuffed llama.

★**Rioja** MODERN AMERICAN **$$$**
(Map p64; 303-820-2282; www.riojadenver.com; 1431 Larimer St; mains $18-29; 11:30am-2:30pm Wed-Fri, 10am-2:30pm Sat & Sun, 5-10pm daily; ; 2, 12, 15, 16th St Shuttle) This is one of Denver's most innovative restaurants. Smart, busy and upscale, yet relaxed and casual – just like Colorado – Rioja features modern cuisine inspired by Italian and Spanish traditions and powered by modern culinary flavors.

People in the know mix a handful of starters such as tuna sashimi and a cheese plate tapas-style, before heading into regional favorites such as Colorado lamb or pan-roasted venison.

Squeaky Bean MODERN AMERICAN **$$$**
(Map p60; 303-623-2665; www.thesqueakybean.net; 1500 Wynloop St; mains $18-24, 4-course $55; 10am-2pm & 5-10pm Sun, 5-10pm Mon-Thu, 5-11pm Fri & Sat; 32, 44 RTD) 'Shake N Bake Veal Sweetbreads' gives you a sense of the bipolar, slightly pornographic approach to high dining here – this is contemporary American cuisine with good humor, unparalleled execution and an airy vibe. Somehow, the drinks list is even better.

Palace Arms EUROPEAN **$$$**
(Map p68; 303-297-3111; www.brownpalace.com; 321 17th St; mains from $36-53; 5:30-9pm Tue-Sat; ; 16th St Shuttle) The Napoleonic decor inside the award-winning restaurant of the Brown Palace Hotel dates back to the 1700s – check out the silver centerpiece commissioned by the British royal family. The food is as impressive as the old-world ambience, and the wine list features 900 labels. Signature dishes include Wagyu rib-eye steak and rabbit in sherry jus.

Bistro Vendôme FRENCH **$$$**
(Map p64; 303-825-3232; www.bistrovendome.com; 1420 Larimer Sq; mains $18-24; 5-10pm Mon-Thu, to 11pm Fri, 10am-2pm & 5-11pm Sat, 10am-2pm Sun; 12, 15 RTD) When you discover Vendôme, tucked behind the storefronts of Larimer, it feels like your own little secret. Brunch is more casual than dinner, but both are done with scrupulous French technique: mussels in white wine and herb-roasted chicken are well-executed standards, while things get more adventurous with the avocado and scallion omelets and blackberry-glazed pork loin.

Vesta Dipping Grill BARBECUE **$$$**
(Map p64; 303-296-1970; www.vestagrill.com; 1822 Blake St; mains $18-35; 5-10pm Sun-Thu, to 11pm Fri & Sat; ; 0, 1, 2, 12 RTD) Pick your cut of meat, then choose from 30 different sauces to dip it into. It's a simple concept that works exceedingly well. The melt-in-your-mouth quality of the creative dishes – many Asian-inspired – makes Vesta one of Denver's favorite restaurants. It is especially fun for bigger groups, and the dip-tat-mosphere is relaxed and funky.

Elway's STEAKHOUSE **$$$**
(Map p64; 303-312-3107; www.elways.com; 1881 Curtis St; mains $26-50; 6:30am-10pm; 0, 1, 2, 12 RTD) Businessmen and fat cats come to wax nostalgic about Denver's all-time top-performing quarterback and carve into pricey medium-rare porterhouses at Denver's top steakhouse, located inside the Ritz Carlton. If you're at DIA or Cherry Creek, check out the sister restaurants.

Oceanaire Seafood Room SEAFOOD **$$$**
(Map p64; 303-991-2277; www.theoceanaire.com; 1400 Arapahoe St; mains $26-40; 5-10pm Mon-Thu, to 11pm Fri & Sat, to 9pm Sun; 10, 15, 20 RTD) Flying in seafood daily, this dinner spot is popular with business travelers and has some of the city's freshest seafood. The

LOCAL KNOWLEDGE

DENVER'S FOODIE UNDERGROUND

Denver's foodie scene has taken to four wheels, two wheels, trolleys and more. Check out www.roaminghunger.com and www.denverstreetfood.com for daily locations. Top finds include:

Biker Jim's Dogs (Map p64; www.bikerjimsdogs.com; cnr 16th & Araphoe Sts; hot dogs $4.25-5.75; ⏲10:30am-3pm; 👪; 🚌Arapahoe) The standard hits are an elk jalapeño cheddar brat and the Alaska reindeer sausage.

Manna from Heaven (www.mannafoodtruck.com; $7-10) Flatbreads gone worldwide crazy.

Still Smokin (☎720-300-4010; www.stillsmokinco.com; $4-10) Fusion barbecue. They hang out downtown most days at lunch.

Noble Swine Supper Club (http://nobleswine.tumblr.com; Varying locations; $10-30) Aspiring local chefs get together in new locations (almost every week) to test their recipes, inspire and share their love for everything edible.

space, styled like the dining room in a 1930s ocean liner, is large and impressive. A roost at the oyster bar offers a slightly more casual option.

Capitol Hill & Golden Triangle

City O' City VEGETARIAN $

(Map p68; ☎303-831-6443; www.cityocitydenver.com; 206 E 13th Ave; mains $8-15; ⏲7am-2am Mon-Fri, 8am-2am Sat, 8am-midnight Sun; 🍴👪; 🚌2, 9, 52 RTD) 🌿 This popular vegan/vegetarian restaurant mixes stylish decor with an innovative spin on greens, grains, faux meat and granola. The menu offers tapa boards, big salads, some good transnational noodle dishes and the best vegan pizza pie in D-Town…the bar has drinks for accompaniment. The comfy dining room also features a rotation of artworks by local artists.

WaterCourse Foods VEGETARIAN $

(Map p68; www.watercoursefoods.com; 837 E 17th Ave; mains $8-10; ⏲7am-9pm Mon-Thu, to 10pm Fri, 8am-10pm Sat, 8am-9pm Sun; 🍴; 🚌12, 20 RTD) The unrelentingly meaty menus of Denver can be a chore to navigate for vegetarians, so the smart, straightforward fare at WaterCourse is a welcome reprieve. The breakfasts are cherished by locals, and dinner options – many of them with an Asian or Mexican influence – are uniformly well done.

Vegetarians take note: the menu focuses heavily on seitan and other meat substitutes.

Gypsy House Café MEDITERRANEAN $

(Map p60; ☎303-830-1112; 1279 Marion St; mains $6-12; ⏲6:30am-11pm; @📶👪; 🚌12 RTD) This unusual, family-run operation dishes up fine Middle Eastern mains, desserts and snacks, Turkish coffee as well as espresso, and house-blended loose-leaf tea. The chaotic decor is true to theme, and there's live music, poetry, belly dancing and dub-reggae DJs performing on an erratic schedule. Internet terminals and free wi-fi make it popular with locals.

Great Wall CHINESE $

(Map p68; ☎303-832-6611; www.greatwalldenver.net; 440 E Colfax Ave; mains $5-11; ⏲11am-11pm Mon-Thu, 11am-midnight Fri & Sat, 11:30am-11pm Sun; 🍴👪; 🚌2, 7, 15 RTD) Great Wall bills itself as a New York–style Chinese restaurant. You can eat in, take out or enjoy free home delivery within a 3-mile radius (minimum order $10). The numbered menu goes to 192 – test your waiter. No MSG, and only 100% vegetable oil is used.

Wholefoods Market SELF-CATERING $

(Map p68; ☎303-832-7701; www.wholefoodsmarket.com; 900 E 11th Ave; ⏲7:30am-10pm; 🍴👪; 🚌10, 12 RTD) 🌿 Part of a national chain, Wholefoods sells organic and natural foods, products and ingredients. It has a kick-butt deli.

Cuba Cuba Café & Bar CUBAN $$

(Map p68; ☎303-605-2822; www.cubacubacafe.com; 1173 Delaware St; mains $13-24; ⏲5-11pm; 🍴👪; 🚌9, 52 RTD) Try the mango mojito at this swanky Cuban joint serving finger-lickin' BBQ spareribs, flavor-packed fried yucca, scrumptious sandwiches and a sumptuous coconut-crusted tuna. The back patio offers fantastic sunset city views; the bright blue-walled environs emit an island vibe. There's sometimes music on Thursday nights.

Five Points, Uptown & City Park

SAME Café AMERICAN $

(So All May Eat Café; Map p60; 720-530-6853; www.soallmayeat.org; 2023 E Colfax Ave; by donation; 11am-2pm Mon-Sat; ; 15 RTD) This nonprofit cafe was founded by two former food-bank workers, who wanted to provide healthy, by-donation lunches for those who were struggling to make ends meet. The standard American cafeteria fare is delicious. Walk-in volunteers are welcome, though you can reserve a spot in advance online.

Volunteering here or dropping in for lunch is one of the most unique and heartwarming experiences in Denver, and demonstrates the most progressive thinking in the city's sustainable, local, community-oriented food movement.

Horseshoe Lounge PIZZA $

(Map p68; 303-832-1180; www.thehorseshoelounge.com; 414 E 20th Ave; mains $9-14; 4pm-2am Mon-Wed, 2pm-2am Thu, noon-2am Fri-Sun; ; 28, 32 RTD) This neighborhood lounge-bar has a wonderfully laid-back atmosphere, with a pool table and sports on a large TV screen. The bar counter is composed of about 23,000 dice (they say). Pizza, subs and salad are the items *du jour,* and they're all pretty good.

La Pasadita MEXICAN $

(Map p68; 303-832-1785; 1959 Park Ave; mains $6-9; 11am-9:30pm Mon-Sat; ; 28, 32 RTD) This tiny, family-run Mexican joint is a favorite among locals. The food is authentic and cheap, and it's all handmade from whole ingredients. The restaurant sits on a small triangular allotment surrounded by streets on all sides.

★ **Steuben's Food Service** AMERICAN $$

(Map p68; 303-803-1001; www.steubens.com; 523 E 17th Ave; mains $8-21; 11am-11pm Sun-Thu, to midnight Fri & Sat;) Although styled as a midcentury drive-in, the upscale treatment of comfort food (mac and cheese, fried chicken, lobster rolls) and the solar-powered kitchen demonstrate Steuben's contemporary smarts. In summer, open garage doors lining the street create a breezy atmosphere and after 10pm it has the most unbeatable deal around: a burger, hand-cut fries and beer for $5.

Avenue Grill MODERN AMERICAN $$

(Map p68; 303-861-2820; www.avenuegrill.com; 630 E 17th Ave; mains $16-29; 11am-11pm Mon-Thu, to midnight Fri, 4pm-midnight Sat, 10am-4pm Sun; ; 2 RTD) On a quiet street corner a short walk from downtown, the Avenue Grill has been dishing up interesting fusion creations for more than 20 years. Clam chowder, baby spinach and octopus salad, and tempura prawns are some of the offerings given special treatment. The bright space is surrounded by windows with pleasant lunchtime views of passing pedestrians.

Jonesy's EatBar PUB FOOD $$

(Map p68; 303-863-7473; www.jeatbar.com; 400 E 20th Ave; mains $13-19; 5-11pm Sun-Thu, to midnight Fri, 10am-3pm & 5pm-midnight Sat, 10am-3pm Sun; ; 28, 32 RTD) This is a great place for a simple pub-style meal and a beer. This former high-end restaurant has been reborn as a gastropub with an excellent, select wine list. There's live music several nights a week, a pool table and a lovely outdoors seating area. The crowd is eclectic and the wait staff is friendly.

Highlands

Cafe Brazil BRAZILIAN $$

(303-480-1877; www.cafebrazildenver.com; 4408 Lowell Blvd; mains $16-22; 5-10pm Tue-Sat) Shake your palate to the samba beat at this beloved northwest Brazilian bistro. You woudn't think it'd be this good from the strip-mall exterior, but enter and you have warm service (what'd you expect?) and interesting plates that run from the requisite beef dishes to coconut stews and traditional country offerings. Start your meal with a caipirinha.

bang! AMERICAN $$

(303-455-1117; www.bangdenver.com; 3472 W 32nd Ave; mains $9-15; 11am-9pm Tue-Fri, 10am-9pm Sat; ; 32, 28 RTD) One of Denver's reigning kings of comfort food, bang! goes full-on for cuteness. The place has a funked-out garden in the summer, winsome and chatty wait staff, and the menu has tater tots. And you know it's clean – there's a window onto the street with the chefs on display.

★Root Down MODERN AMERICAN $$$

(Map p60; ☎303-993-4200; www.rootdowndenver.com; 1600 W 33rd Ave; small plates $7-17, mains $18-28; ⏰5-10pm Sun-Thu, 5-11pm Fri & Sat, 10am-2:30pm Sat & Sun; 🍷) In a converted gas station, chef Justin Cucci has undertaken one of the city's most ambitious culinary concepts, marrying sustainable 'field-to-fork' practices, high-concept culinary fusions and a low-impact, energy-efficient ethos. The menu changes seasonally, but consider yourself lucky if it includes the sweet-potato falafel or hoisin-duck confit sliders.

Unlike the troupe of restaurants jumping on the sustainable bandwagon, Root Down is largely wind-powered, decorated with reused and reclaimed materials, and recycles everything. It's conceptually brilliant and one of Denver's most thrilling dining experiences. It has a restaurant also at DIA Airport.

Z Cuisine FRENCH $$$

(Map p60; ☎303-477-1111; www.zcuisineonline.com; 2239 & 2245 W 30th Ave; mains $19-29; ⏰5-10pm Wed-Sat; 📶; 🚌32, 44 RTD) It'd be better if you could look at the bill before you ate at this self-styled neighborhood bistro, because when your mouth is overwhelmed by any variety of braised lamb dishes or a simple, perfect steak-and-fries combination, you'll forget it. There's no better place around for (fancy) casual French fare, a fact well noted by national critics.

Duo MODERN AMERICAN $$$

(Map p60; ☎303-477-4141; www.duodenver.com; 2413 W 32nd Ave; brunch $8-12, mains $19-24; ⏰5-10pm Mon-Fri, 10am-2pm & 5-10pm Sat, 10am-2pm & 5-9pm Sun; 🚌32 RTD) This cozy bistro-style eatery with exposed brick walls and well-worn stylings is poised, elegant, confident and, at times, simply remarkable. The seasonal menu focuses on locally sourced meats and greens. Lamb shank makes it nearly year-round. Brunch here is a three-hour affair not to be missed.

South Central Denver

El Taco De Mexico MEXICAN $

(Map p60; ☎303-623-3926; www.eltacodemexicodenver.com; 714 Santa Fe Dr; mains $5-9; ⏰7am-10pm Sun-Thu, to 11pm Fri & Sat; 🅿; 🚌1 RTD) Forget about ambience – it's a big yellow counter, fluorescent lights and a couple of slouching figures shoveling down tacos – but it's all too easy to forgive when you rip into the chili relleno burrito – a glorious disaster of peppers, cheese, refried pinto beans and salsa verde.

Devil's Food AMERICAN $

(☎303-733-7448; www.devilsfoodbakery.com; 1020 S Gaylord St; pastries $4; ⏰7am-3pm Sun-Wed, to 10pm Thu-Sat; 🚌11 RTD) It does supper and sandwiches, but the decadent pastries are reason enough to visit this lovely Washington Park cafe. The hardest to resist is the red velvet hedgehog – a moist red cake covered in cream cheese icing and shaped like a little monster. The brunch menu, crowned by an excellent salmon Benedict, is a neighborhood favorite.

★Beatrice & Woodsley TAPAS $$

(Map p60; ☎303-777-3505; www.beatriceandwoodsley.com; 38 S Broadway; small plates $9-13; ⏰5-11pm Mon-Fri, 10am-2pm & 5-10pm Sat & Sun; 🚌0 RTD) Beatrice and Woodsley is the most artfully designed dining room in Denver. Chainsaws are buried into the wall to support shelves, there's an aspen growing through the back of the dining room and the feel is that of a mountain cabin being elegantly reclaimed by nature. The menu of small plates is whimsical and European inspired. Mix up two or three with some hyper-kinetic alcoholic elixirs.

Domo Restaurant JAPANESE $$

(Map p60; ☎303-595-3666; www.domorestaurant.com; 1365 Osage St; mains $10-22) 'Japanese country food' doesn't really capture the refinement of dishes at Domo, which sports the best garden dining in all of Colorado – kind of like dining in Mr Miyagi's backyard.

The fun doesn't stop there; Danielson, the spicy maguro and hamachi donburi, is an explosively flavorful combination of fresh fish, seaweed and chili-soy dressing. Each main is served with seven traditional Japanese side dishes.

Arada Restaurant & Bar ETHIOPIAN $$

(Map p60; ☎303-329-3344; www.aradarestaurant.com; 750 Santa Fe Dr; mains $10-13; ⏰5-10pm Wed-Sat, to 8pm Tue & Sun; 👪; 🚌1 RTD) You'll use soft, slightly sour *injera* bread as the vehicle to shovel down tomato *fit-fit* (diced tomato, onion and jalapeños in vinegar-based sauce) and combination platters such as Arada Six (which includes delicious *siga wot,* a spicy beef stew). The tile floor means no frills, but for those keen to share, this place is loads of fun.

Table 6 AMERICAN $$$
(Map p60; ☎303-831-8800; www.table6denver.com; 609 Corona St; mains $19-32; ⏰5-10pm Mon-Thu, to 11pm Fri & Sat, 10:30am-2pm & 5-9pm Sun) Chef Scott Parker delivers American comfort food gone kick-ass crazy at this intimate bistro. The fryer runs overtime to deliver chicken 'n' waffles and exquisite tater tots. The seasonal menu also extends to include seafood favorites with creative touches. Brunch is much more affordable.

Mizuna MODERN AMERICAN $$$
(Map p60; ☎303-832-4778; www.mizunadenver.com; 225 E 7th Ave; mains $37-39; ⏰6-11pm Tue-Sat; 🚌6 RTD) Mizuna is exclusive, expensive and exquisite. The small dining room only adds to the rarefied atmosphere and there's a certain pride knowing you're eating at one of the country's most renowned restaurants. The menu is eclectic and ever changing, with an emphasis on fresh seafood and locally sourced seasonal produce.

Barolo Grill ITALIAN $$$
(Map p60; ☎303-393-1040; www.barologrilldenver.com; 3030 E 6th Ave; mains $20-32; ⏰6-11pm Tue-Sat; 🍷; 🚌6 RTD) This deluxe Italian restaurant is one of Denver's best. It offers a shifting à la carte menu as well as a five-course degustation menu featuring the flavors of Italy's Piedmont, Tuscany and Veneto regions. The signature dish is a braised duck with olives. There's a select wine list and an outstanding dessert menu. Bookings are essential.

Fruition Restaurant MODERN AMERICAN $$$
(Map p60; ☎303-831-1962; www.fruitionrestaurant.com; 1313 E 6th Ave; mains $28-29; ⏰5-10pm Mon-Sat, to 8pm Sun; 🚌2, 6, 12 RTD) 🌿 Alex Seidel and Blake Edmunds are heavy hitters in Denver's fine-dining scene, pulling off their contemporary American plates (potato-wrapped oysters Rockefeller, duck with red-onion marmalade) with understated panache. The food is simply conceived, carefully executed and elegantly presented. Many of the greens, the chickens and the eggs come from Seidel's farm.

Buckhorn Exchange Restaurant STEAKHOUSE $$$
(Map p60; ☎303-534-9505; www.buckhorn.com; 1000 Osage St; mains $27-56; ⏰11am-2pm & 5:30-9pm Mon-Thu, 5:30-10pm Fri & Sat, 5-9pm Sun) If you've been waiting to try Rocky Mountain oysters, you're in the right place. Founded by a scout of Buffalo Bill Cody, this out-of-the-way steakhouse has bull nuts, rattlesnake, elk and all sorts of (relatively edible) game dishes. Good luck enjoying them with a clear conscience as the hundreds of stuffed heads gaze down on your table.

South Broadway

★**Sweet Action Ice Cream** ICE CREAM $
(Map p60; ☎303-282-4645; www.sweetactionicecream.com; 52 Broadway; cones $3-6; ⏰1-10pm Sun-Thu, to 11pm Fri & Sat; 🚌0 RTD) Don't wander past this neighborhood ice-cream parlor expecting the same old chocolate chip; the seasonal, house-made flavors include baklava, salted butterscotch and five spice. In the summer there are tons of fruit-based varieties such as ginger peach and blackberry lavender. Bonus: it also does vegan varieties.

Hornet FUSION $
(Map p60; ☎303-777-7676; www.hornetrestaurant.com; 76 Broadway; mains $6-13; ⏰11am-2am Mon-Fri, 10am-2am Sat, 10am-midnight Sun; 📶; 🚌0 RTD) At first glance it might seem uninspiring – standard sandwiches, grilled meats and pasta plates dominate – but this elegant corner diner punches things up with wide-ranging Southern, Latin American and Asian influences. It's atmospheric too, with tall windows, classic black-and-white tiles and fans that spin lazily above the brunch crowd.

Señor Burrito MEXICAN $
(Map p60; ☎303-733-0747; senorburritos.blogspot.com; 12 E 1st Ave; mains $4-10; ⏰8am-9pm Mon-Sat; 🅿; 🚌0 RTD) If you need a quick fortifying bite before drinking down the South Broadway strip, Señor Burrito is adequately quick and cheap. Authentic? Not so much. Morning options include an egg-and-ham-loaded, Denver-style breakfast burrito, while the crunchy tacos – filled with ground beef, cheddar, lettuce and tomato – are just like mom used to make…back in Michigan.

Walnut Room Pizzeria PIZZERIA $$
(Map p60; ☎303-736-6750; www.thewalnutroom.com; 2 Broadway; pizzas $11-20; ⏰11am-10pm Mon & Tue, to midnight Thu, to 3am Fri, noon-3am Sat, noon-10pm Sun; 🚌0 RTD) Good, chewy thin crust and several inventive house specialties (such as the meaty, pineapple-and-jalapeño-dressed Mile High Club Pie and pesto-covered Walnut Special) make this Broadway spot impressive. Framed photos of jam bands and local rockers playing at

the associate Walnut Room venue line the tall walls of the booths.

Sushi Den SUSHI **$$$**

(☎303-777-0826; www.sushiden.net; 1487 S Pearl St; sushi $5-8, rolls $5-18; ⏲11:30am-2:30pm & 4:45pm-11:30pm Mon-Fri, 5-11pm Sat & Sun) This is the best sushi restaurant in Denver. The contemporary setting is toned and sexy, and the myriad rolls, sushi and fresh salads are creative, clever and delicious. Make reservations!

Beyond Central Denver

Pho 95 VIETNAMESE **$**

(☎303-936-3322; 1002 S Federal Blvd; mains $8; ⏲9am-9pm; ; 30 RTD) The best place for *pho* (noodle soup) in Denver is a bit out there, parked in the middle of a strip mall on a bleak stretch of Federal, but slurping your way through a big, cheap bowl of noodles is worth the hike.

Casa Bonita MEXICAN **$$**

(☎303-232-5115; www.casabonitadenver.com; 6715 W Colfax Ave, Lakewood; mains $12-18 (required for entrance); ⏲11am-9pm Sun-Thu, to 10pm Fri & Sat) The food is horrible (think chili from a button, greasy processed cheese and stone-gray guacamole), but this classic piece of American (and Mexican) kitsch is so entrenched in Denver lore, you just have to visit. There's a 30-foot waterfall and cliff divers. And the landmark restaurant even made an appearance in Colorado's other top cultural export: South Park.

Mataam Fez MOROCCAN **$$$**

(☎303-399-9282; www.mataamfez-denver.com; 4909 E Colfax; mains $30-33; ⏲5:30-9pm Tue-Sun) Colorado's first Moroccan restaurant dates back to 1976. It's friendly, festive and spirited. The menu is quite steep, but you get authentic Moroccan tastes, belly dancers and a dining experience that lasts for hours.

Drinking & Nightlife

If you consider yourself a beer snob, you might mistake Denver for a foamy, malty corner of heaven. Forget about that watery stuff made in Golden, the brewing culture around these parts is truly world class – with craft and seasonal brews by the gallon, restaurants that sideline as microbreweries and kegs that arrive from the beer regions as near as Boulder and as far as Munich. Simply put, Denver adores beer.

Top nightlife districts include Uptown for gay bars and a young professional crowd, LoDo for loud sports bars, heavy drinking and dancing, River North for hipsters, Lower Highlands for an eclectic mix and sweet decks, Cherry Creek for cougars and cougar hunters, and Broadway and Colfax for Old School wannabes.

Downtown & LoDo

Mynt Lounge BAR

(Map p64; ☎303-825-6968; www.myntmojitolounge.com; 1424 Market St; 16th St Mall Shuttle) Mynt is a minimalist lounge with a very sexy vibe. This place offers one of the best happy hours in town – from 3pm to 9pm the martinis cost around $3 and there's a massive list to choose from.

Red Square Euro Bistro VODKA BAR

(Map p64; ☎303-595-8600; www.redsquarebistro.com; 1512 Larimer St, Writer Square; vodka shots $4.50; ⏲5-9pm Sun-Thu, to 11pm Fri & Sat; 10, 15, 20 RTD) Even if the vodka list is more than 80 labels deep – including staples from Russian origin and surprise sources such as El Salvador – the most creative tipple on offer is house-infused. Horseradish vodka? Dill? Anise? Garlic? The menu of meaty bistro fare with an Eastern European influence includes fancy stroganoff, veal and wild boar chop.

Jet Lounge BAR

(Map p64; www.thejethotel.com; 1612 Wazee St; ⏲Tue-Sat 8pm-2am) This lounge is the place to see and be seen in Denver. There is a bedroom-meets-house-party vibe: candles, cozy couches, a weekend DJ and lots and lots of beautiful people. Jet Lounge was a favorite with the *Real World Denver* housemates. Order bottle service, sit back and melt into the party. The attached hotel was undergoing renovations at press time.

Corner Office LOUNGE

(Map p64; ☎303-825-6500; www.thecorneroffice denver.com; 1401 Curtis St; ⏲6:30am-11pm Sun-Thu, to midnight Fri & Sat; ; 10, 15 RTD) The cheery sensibility of this excellent retro-style lounge is demonstrated in the wall of clocks frozen at 5pm and waggish menu of cocktails ('The Secretary' comes with a rim of grape Kool-Aid powder). It's perfect for a quick, sophisticated bite before the theater, and the chicken and waffles are highlights of a killer brunch menu.

Great Divide Brewing Company BREWERY (Map p64; www.greatdivide.com; 2201 Arapahoe St; ⏲2-8pm Mon & Tue, to 10pm Wed-Sat) This excellent local brewery does well to skip the same old burger menu and the fancy digs to keep its focus on what it does best: crafting exquisite beer. Bellying up to the bar, looking onto the copper kettles and sipping Great Divide's spectrum of seasonal brews is an experience that will make a beer drinker's eyes light up.

Wynkoop Brewing Co BREWERY (Map p64; ☎303-297-2700; www.wynkoop.com; 1634 18th St; mains $9-13; ⏲11am-2am Mon-Sat, to midnight Sun; 🚌44, 48 RTD) Wynkoop's Rail Yard Ale is the city's most celebrated red ale, and beer fans file into this spacious brewpub to knock them back while tossing darts, shooting pool or taking in the breeze on the wide porch. The taps change with the season and the menu offers passable pub standards.

There's some local history here, too. Colorado Governor John Hickenlooper and a group of developers founded the brewpub in 1988, kicking off the urban renewal that took LoDo from sketchy warehouse district to the luminary upscale digs of today. The basement of the brewery hosts a long-running sketch comedy show on the weekends, and the jokes are appropriate for all ages. Call ahead for Saturday brewery tours.

Falling Rock Tap House BAR (Map p64; ☎303-293-8338; www.fallingrocktaphouse.com; 1919 Blake St; ⏲11am-2am; 🚌52, 55X, 58X, 72X RTD) High fives and hollers punctuate the scene when the Rockies triumph and beer drinkers file in to forget an afternoon of drinking Coors at the ball park. There are – count 'em – 80-plus beers on tap and the bottle list has almost 150. With all the local favorites, this is *the* place to drink beer downtown.

GAY & LESBIAN DENVER

Even though Colorado has some very socially conservative areas, Denver is as progressive and broad minded as you get in the inner-mountain west, and gay and lesbian travelers should expect no particular trouble. Overt displays of affection in public might cause some raised eyebrows, but this is probably true for heterosexual couples as well. The bohemian Capitol Hill district, especially the bars on Colfax, are the center of the gay and lesbian scene. Head to Cheeseman Park during the day. For the latest news, events and goings on, check out print and online editions of **Out Front Colorado** (www.outfrontonline.com) or www.glbtcolorado.org. Top gay bars and hang-out spots include the following:

Charlie's (Map p68; ☎303-839-8890; www.charliesdenver.com; 900 E Colfax Ave; ⏲11am-2am; 🚌15 RTD) The quintessential Denver gay cowboy bar gets Brokeback on two dance floors (there's a non-country room for you city fellows). The nightly line-dancing classes are worth it.

Boyztown (Map p60; ☎303-722-7373; www.boyztowndenver.com; 117 Broadway; ⏲3pm-1:45am Mon-Fri, noon-1:45am Sat & Sun) This gay strip club (down to their Marky Mark's) is kind of trashy, but fun for sure.

Tracks (☎303-863-7326; www.tracksdenver.com; 3500 Walnut St; ⏲9pm-2am Fri & Sat, hrs vary Sun-Thu) Denver's best gay dance club has an 18-and-up night on Thursday, Friday drag shows and lesbian nights (just once a month). There's a definite pretty-boy focus, with good music and a scene to match. Saturday is the biggest dance night.

XBar (Map p68; ☎303-832-2687; www.xbardenver.com; 629 E Colfax Ave; ⏲3pm-2am Mon-Sat, noon-2am Sun) Two stories of manly madness, with your typical gay anthems, a younger crowd and a patio, this is the 'it' spot for gay men in Denver.

Denver Wrangler (Map p68; ☎303-837-1075; www.denverwrangler.com; 1700 Logan St; ⏲11am-2am; 🚌101 RTD) Though it attracts an amiable crowd of gay male professionals after work, the central location endows Denver's premier bear bar with a flirty pick-up scene on the weekend. The sidewalk seating is a plus.

Black Crown Lounge (☎720-353-4701; www.blackcrownlounge.com; 1446 S Broadway) This piano bar caters to an older set of gay and lesbian Liberache-philes.

Crú WINE BAR
(Map p64; ☎303-893-9463; www.cruawinebar.com; 1442 Larimer St; glass of wine $9-26; ⏰4-10pm Sun-Wed, 5-10pm Thu, 3pm-2am Fri & Sat; 🚌6, 9, 10, 12, 15, 15L, 20, 28, 32, 44, 44L RTD, 16th St Mall Shuttle) This classy Larimer Sq wine bar is decked out in wine labels and posters, with dim lighting and gentle music. It looks so bespoke it's surprising to learn it's a chain (Dallas, Houston); there's another Denver branch at Park Meadows.

Breckenridge Colorado Craft BREWERY
(Map p60; ☎303-297-3644; www.breckbrew.com; 2220 Blake St; ⏰11am-11pm; 🚌8, 38 RTD) Breckenridge Brewery has a couple of locations around Denver – and across Colorado. Head through the long portfolio of beers – we bet you don't make it to the end.

Denver Chophouse & Brewery BREWERY
(Map p60; ☎303-269-0800; www.chophouse.com; 100/1735 19th St; ⏰11am-11pm Mon-Thu, to midnight Fri & Sat, to 10pm Sun) Chophouse brews are mostly European in style – pilsner, ales and lagers – and there's a good American pale ale. The Chophouse Brewery has sites in Boulder and Washington DC.

TAG COCKTAIL BAR
(Map p64; ☎303-996-9985; www.tag-restaurant.com; 1441 Larimer St; cocktails $9-12; 🚌2, 12, 15 RTD) TAG's dinner menu, with its bold and bizarre concoctions, might make more sense after a hit of acid; we still can't decide if hiramasa kingfish dressed in Pop Rocks candy is revolutionary or revolting. Apply this same mad-scientist meddling to the drinks menu, however, and it's amazing. Jalapeño kumquat mojito? Yes, please.

Nallen's IRISH PUB
(Map p64; ☎303-572-0667; www.nallensdenver.com; 1429 Market St; ⏰2pm-2am; 🚌6, 9, 10, 15L, 20, 28, 32, 44, 44L RTD) Nallen's is a venerable Irish pub, and since opening in 1992 it seems to have started a craze. Happy hour is from 2pm to 7pm.

Celtic Tavern IRISH PUB
(Map p64; ☎303-308-1576; www.celtictavern.com; 1801 Blake St; mains $6-15; ⏰11am-2am Mon-Fri, 5pm-2am Sat; 🚌1, 2, 12 RTD) The Celtic Tavern is a warm and convivial place with 50 beers on tap and a selection of top-shelf Scottish, Irish and American whiskeys to sample. The bar menu features traditional Irish stew, shepherd's pie and the like, as well as classic American favorites.

Katie Mullen's Irish Pub & Restaurant IRISH PUB
(Map p64; ☎303-573-0336; www.katiemullens.com; 1550 Court Pl; ⏰11am-2am; 📶; 🚌15 RTD) Denver's largest Irish Bar – an enormous 11,000 sq ft – maintains a surprisingly snuggled-down feel through dark wood, polished brass, book shelves and fireside seating. If the environs are a bit mannish, it seems to suit the guys who loosen their ties and talk business over a Guinness and some fine pub grub.

Croc's Mexican Bar & Grill BAR
(Map p64; ☎303-436-1144; www.crocsmexicangrill.com; 1630 Market St; ⏰11am-2am Mon-Fri, noon-2am Sat & Sun; 🚌Market St) This bar and grill is central to the Market St stumble, and is a cavernous space that turns out passable Mexican food in brawny portions and pipes in big-screen sports from every corner of the world. When the party goes off, winsome waitresses stomp along the bar pouring tequila down patrons' throats under the glassy gaze of Hal, a giant stuffed alligator.

Rock Bottom Restaurant & Brewery BREWERY
(Map p64; ☎303-534-7616; www.rockbottom.com; 1001 16th St; ⏰11am-2am; 🚌Arapahoe) Drinkers are met with the gleaming stainless sheen of brew kettles as they enter this chain brewpub, perched on the prime real estate of the 16th St Mall. It's outgrown 'micro' status and is not so hot compared to smaller craft brewers in the region, but the people-watching from the patio makes for a pleasant afternoon.

Appaloosa Bar & Grill BAR
(Map p64; ☎720-932-1700; www.appaloosagrill.com; 535 16th St; ⏰11am-2am; 🚌Welton) It's tricky to find a place on the Mall with a local feel, but plank floors, nightly local bands and kindly bartenders give the employee-owned Appaloosa a unique environment.

Beta Nightclub CLUB
(Map p64; ☎303-383-1909; www.betanightclub.com; 1909 Blake St; ⏰9am-2am Thu & Fri; 🚌52 RTD) This huge club swaps musical flavors like fashionable boutique sneakers. The best parties go off in the interior Beatport lounge, sending *au courant* bass, hip-hop and electro through a sound system that will rattle your fillings loose.

Capitol Hill & Golden Triangle

Bar Standard CLUB

(Map p60; ☎303-534-0222; www.coclubs.com; 1037 Broadway; ⏰8pm-2am Fri & Sat; 🚌0 RTD) From the sleek deco interior to the DJ roster that spins *way* outside the typically mindless thump, Bar Standard is an inimitable gem in Denver's nightclub scene. It's ice cold without the attitude, and when the right DJ is on the tables it can be some of the best dancing in town.

The attached Milk Bar takes a page from Anthony Burgess' classic *A Clockwork Orange,* with plenty of gothed-out devotcha's dancing their asses off.

The Church CLUB

(Map p68; www.coclubs.com; 1160 Lincoln St; ⏰Thu-Sun 9pm-2am) There's nothing like ordering a stiff drink inside a cathedral built in 1865. Yes, this club, which draws a large and diverse crowd, is in a former house of the Lord. Lit by hundreds of altar candles and flashing blue strobe lights, the Church has three dance floors, acrobats, a couple of lounges and even a sushi bar!

Arrive before 10pm Friday through Sunday to avoid the cover charge.

La Rumba CLUB

(Map p60; www.larumba-denver.com; 99 W 9th Ave; ⏰9pm-2am Thu-Sun) Denver's most popular salsa club gets its merengue on every weekend, with DJs Thursday and Friday and live music Saturday. Come on Thursday for some free lessons.

Five Points, Uptown & City Park

Ace BAR

(Map p68; ☎303-800-7705; www.acedenver.com; 501 E 17th Ave; ⏰11am-midnight Mon-Fri, 2pm-midnight Sat & Sun) The best ping-pong bar in Denver. Come here for fun tournaments, hipster d-bag sightings, great food and a raucous indoor-outdoor party that takes you deep into the pong underground – street rules apply.

Matchbox BAR

(Map p60; www.matchboxdenver.com; 2625 Larimer St; ⏰4pm-2am Mon-Fri, noon-2am Sat & Sun) Located in the ever-hip RiNo art district, this hole-in-the-wall appeals to the thick-glasses and blue-jeans crowd. Yep, that's a bacci court out back.

★Crema Coffee House CAFE

(Map p60; ☎720-235-2995; www.cremacoffeehouse.net; 2862 Larimer St; ⏰7am-7pm Mon-Fri, 9am-5pm Sat & Sun; 📶; 🚌44 RTD) Noah Price, a clothing-designer-turned-coffee-impresario, takes his job seriously, selecting, brewing and pouring Denver's absolute-best coffee. The espresso and French-pressed are complete perfection, but it's the oatmeal latte, delicately infused ice teas and the toast bar – with a mess of jams and toppings – that put this place over the top.

Thin Man Tavern BAR

(Map p60; www.thinmantavern.com; 2015 E 17th Ave) The Thin Man is a damn sight more stylish than most neighborhood taverns. It's decked out in all kinds of old Catholic paintings, and vintage lampshades cast the place in a warm, sentimental glow. Since a local magazine named it among the best low-key singles' spots in the city, the crowd is looking a bit more stylish, too.

In addition to a good beer selection and stiff drinks, it also hosts free art-house films in the basement-level Ubisububi Room and, during the summer, shows classic flicks outside in the parking lot.

Lost Lake Lounge BAR

(Map p60; ☎303-333-4345; www.lostlakelounge.com; 3602 E Colfax Ave; ⏰7pm-2am) According to the guys behind the bar, the photobooth in the back has 'seen more action than the Whitesnake tour bus.' This is one of the million reasons we love Denver's hipster magnet. Cheap drinks, a crackling fire and prowling 20-somethings in vintage tees are a few more.

Highlands & Platte River Valley

★Forest Room 5 BAR

(Map p60; ☎303-433-7001; www.forestroom5.com; 2532 15th St; ⏰4pm-2am) One of the best damn bars in Denver, this LoHi (that's Lower Highlands) juggernaut has an outdoor patio with fire circles (where you can smoke!), streams and a funked-out Airstream. It plays kitsch movies nightly, and has art openings in the upstairs area. It's an odd mix of Grizzly Adams meets Andy Warhol…and it works.

Linger LOUNGE

(Map p60; ☎303-993-3120; www.lingerdenver.com; 2030 W 30th Ave; mains $8-14; ⏰11:30am-2:30pm & 4pm-2am Tue-Sat, 10am-2:30pm Sun) This rambling LoHi complex sits in the former Olinger mortuary. Come nighttime, they black out the 'O' and it just becomes Linger. There's an interesting international menu, but most people come for the tony feel and light-up-the-night rooftop bar, which even has a replica of the RV made famous by the Bill Murray smash *Stripes*.

The Ale House BREWERY

(Breckenridge Brewery; Map p60; ☎303-433-9734; 2501 16th St) Head upstairs for remarkable skyline views from the Highlands' branch of this chain of microbrewery American-style pubs.

My Brother's Bar BAR

(Map p60; 2376 15th St) Classic rock and roll, lacquered booths and tables made from old wood barrels greet you inside Denver's oldest bar. Grab a seat on the leafy patio if it's nice outside. The bar is on a popular cycle path, and has been a local institution since it opened.

South Central Denver

Divino Wine & Spirits LIQUOR SHOP

(☎303-778-1800; www.divinowine.com; 1240 S Broadway; ⏰10am-10pm Mon-Thu, to 11pm Sat, to 6pm Sun; 🚌0 RTD) Bottles are stacked from floor to ceiling in this southwest shop – a little out of the way, but worth it for serious wine drinkers. It hosts events and does tastings on the weekend, and the staff know their stuff. The budget conscious will want to keep an eye on the rotating selection on the '10 under 10' rack.

South Broadway

Punch Bowl Social LOUNGE

(Map p60; ☎303-765-2695; www.punchbowlsocial.com; 65 Broadway) This adult mega-entertainment-plex has ping-pong, bowling, shuffleboard, foosball, darts and even marbles (free if you bring your own), plus plenty of good drinks and good times.

Sputnik BAR

(Map p60; ☎720-570-4503; www.sputnikdenver.com; 3 S Broadway; ⏰10:30am-2am Mon-Fri, 10am-2am Sat & Sun; 📶; 🚌0 RTD) The Sputnik does it all – it's simultaneously a plucky brunch spot, a neighborhood dive bar and an excellent place for espresso. Still, it's never more fun than when there's a show next door at the Hi-Dive and the indie rockers spill over for strong pours and a seat in the old-school photo booth.

If spending a long night of drinks, snacks and rock and roll still isn't enough for you, the long-running 'Hangover Brunch' does it right, with spicy Bloody Marys and lots of ragged morning-after style.

Beyond Central Denver

Del Norte Brewing Company BREWERY

(☎303-935-3223; www.delnortebrewing.com; 2-0/1390 W Evans Ave; ⏰3:30-6:30pm Fri) Makes a range of lightly hopped Mexican-style beers as well as the stunning 7.8% Luminaria Bock. All have won awards. You can buy direct from the sales room on Friday afternoons only.

☆ Entertainment

Live Music

★**El Chapultepec** LIVE MUSIC

(Map p64; ☎303-295-9126; www.thepeclodo.com; 1962 Market St; ⏰7am-2am, music from 9pm) This smoky, old-school jazz joint attracts a diverse mix of people. Since it opened in 1951, Frank Sinatra, Tony Bennett and Ella Fitzgerald have played here, as have Jagger and Richards. Local jazz bands take the tiny stage nightly, but you never know who might drop by.

Hi-Dive LIVE MUSIC

(Map p60; ☎303-733-0230; www.hi-dive.com; 7 S Broadway) Local rock heroes and touring indie bands light up the stage at the Hi-Dive, a venue at the heart of Denver's local music scene. During big shows it gets deafeningly loud, cheek-to-jowl with hipsters and humid as an armpit. In other words, it's perfect.

Grizzly Rose LIVE MUSIC

(☎303-295-1330; www.grizzlyrose.com; 5450 N Valley Hwy; ⏰from 6pm Tue-Sun) This is one kick-ass honky-tonk – 40,000 sq ft of hot live music – attracting real cowboys from as far as Cheyenne. The Country Music Association called it the best country bar in America. If you've never experienced line dancing, then put on the boots, grab the Stetson and let loose.

Just north of the city limits, off I-25 (you'll have to drive or cab it), the Grizzly is famous for bringing in huge industry stars – Willie

Nelson, LeAnn Rimes – and only charging $10 per ticket.

Bluebird Theater LIVE MUSIC
(Map p60; ☎303-377-1666; www.bluebirdtheater.net; 3317 E Colfax Ave; 🚌15, 15L RTD) This medium-sized theater is general-admission standing room and has terrific sound and clear sight lines from the balcony. The venue often offers the last chance to catch bands – Denver faves The Lumineers and Devotchka both headlined here – on their way up to the big time.

Ogden Theatre LIVE MUSIC
(Map p68; ☎303-832-1874; www.ogdentheatre.net; 935 E Colfax Ave; 🚌15 RTD) One of Denver's best live-music venues, the Ogden Theatre has a checkered past. Built in 1917, it was derelict for many years and might have been dozed in the early 1990s, but it's now listed on the National Register of Historic Places. Bands such as Edward Sharpe & the Magnetic Zeros and Lady Gaga have played here.

Harry Houdini performed at this theater in 1919 and it appeared in the movie *The Rocky Horror Picture Show*. Jack Nicholson drove his Winnebago past the Ogden pulling into Denver in *About Schmidt*. If the house is packed, make for the upstairs level, where the catwalk extends on the wings and you'll have a beautiful bird's-eye view and plenty of room to move.

Larimer Lounge LIVE MUSIC
(Map p60; ☎303-291-1007; www.larimerlounge.com; 2721 Larimer St; ⏰noon-2am; 🚌38, 48 RTD) This dive is a proving ground for acts from across the indie rock spectrum – last time we checked in, metal heads in clown makeup were sound checking. With shows seven nights a week, it's a reliable bet for upcoming locals and good touring indie acts. There's also a patio to escape from the noise.

Howl at the Moon LIVE MUSIC
(Map p60; ☎303-291-0880; www.howlatthemoon.com; 1735 19th St) This lively dueling piano bar is popular with bachelorette parties. It fills up quickly, so arrive around 6:30pm to score a table near the pianos. It's pretty noisy (don't expect much talking) but the atmosphere is fun. Song requests are taken (usually accompanied by $5), but many folks request the same songs.

Fillmore Auditorium LIVE MUSIC
(Map p68; ☎303-837-0360; www.fillmoreauditorium.org; 1510 Clarkson St; 🚌15 RTD) One of the major music venues in town, this big open space has hosted classic acts such as Parliament Funkadelic, big indies such as Feist, and even roller derby. The acoustics are far from perfect, but it's certainly one of Denver's essential venues.

Quixote's True Blue LIVE MUSIC
(Map p68; ☎303-861-7070; www.quixotes.com; 314 E 13th Ave; ⏰7pm-2am Mon-Wed, 4pm-2am Fri &

DENVER FOR KIDS

With loads of outdoor activities, there's plenty of space for the little ones to burn off their excess energy. Free activities in the fresh air include a drive up to Mt Evans summit, a trip to Red Rocks Amphitheatre and a swim and splash at Confluence Park. For a few bucks you can paddle a kayak from Confluence Kayaks (p72) or rent the whole family bikes from the city's **B-Cycle** (denver.bcycle.com) program. If Johnny or Jenny are keen skaters or rollerbladers, go to Denver's awesome skate park and watch them, ah, shred…dude.

Best Museums

Though the Children's Museum (p68) is perhaps a little underwhelming for moms and dads, Denver has plenty of museums that are more fun for the *whole* family.

➡ Denver Art Museum (p63) Grown-ups will love the excellent collection and kids can get creative in terrific hands-on workstations.

➡ Denver Firefighters Museum (p59) Great for a few hours of fun, this will help teach the kids how not to burn the house down.

➡ Denver Zoo (p67) Squeals of delight will greet the gross-out kids' program on animal excrement.

➡ Denver Museum of Nature & Science (p67) Egyptian mummies and dinosaur bones make this a great place to geek out.

Sat; 2, 10 RTD) Fight some windmills at this geeky-meets-freaky space kitted out with a quality PA system and a good bar. Most nights it's free, but sometimes there'll be a modest cover charge.

Comedy & Cabaret

Comedy Works — COMEDY

(Map p64; 303-595-3637; www.comedyworks.com; 1226 15th St; 6, 9, 10, 15L, 20, 28, 32, 44, 44L RTD) Denver's best comedy club occupies a basement space in Larimer Sq (enter down a set of stairs at the corner of Larimer and 15th) and routinely brings in up-and-coming yucksters from around the country. It can be a bit cramped if you're claustrophobic, but the seats are comfortable and the quality of acts is top shelf. Performances also take place at the slightly bigger **Comedy Works South** (720-274-6800; 5345 Landmark Pl, Greenwood Village) across town.

Lannie's Clocktower Cabaret — CABARET

(Map p64; 303-293-0075; www.lannies.com; 1601 Arapahoe St; tickets $25-40; 1-5pm Tue, to 11pm Wed & Thu, to 1:30am Fri & Sat; Arapahoe) Bawdy, naughty and strangely romantic, Lannie's Clocktower Cabaret is a wild-child standout among LoDo's rather straight-laced (or at least straight) night spots. A table right up near the front will get you in the sparkling heart of the action, and if you parse the schedule, you might get a glance at the sexiest drag queens in Denver.

Bovine Metropolis Theater — COMEDY

(Map p64; 303-758-4722; www.bovinemetropolis.com; 1527 Champa St; 15 RTD) This long-standing black-box theater hosts a clutch of fresh-faced improv comedy performers and shows most days of the week for under $20. It also offers afternoon workshops for tour groups.

Performing Arts

★Denver Performing Arts Complex — PERFORMING ARTS

(Map p64; 720-865-4220; www.artscomplex.com; cnr 14th & Champa Sts) This massive complex – one of the largest of its kind – occupies four city blocks and houses several major theaters, including the historic Ellie Caulkins Opera House and the Seawell Grand Ballroom. It's also home to the Colorado Ballet, Denver Center for the Performing Arts, Opera Colorado and the Colorado Symphony Orchestra. There are small spaces for experimental theater and big halls for Broadway blockbusters such as *The Book of Mormon*.

Paramount Theatre — CONCERT VENUE

(Map p64; 303-534-8336; www.paramount-denver.com; 1621 Glenarm Pl) Lots of red velvet and gold trimming deck out the Paramount, one of the premier midsized theaters in the West. Listed on the National Register of Historic Places, its recent acts include Rufus Wainwright, Margaret Cho and 'Weird Al' Yankovic.

Opera Colorado — OPERA

(Map p64; 303-468-2030; www.operacolorado.org; 950 13th St; box office 10am-5pm Mon-Thu, to noon Fri; 1, 8, 15L, 30, 31, 48 RTD) Founded in 1983, Opera Colorado is based in the Denver Performing Arts Complex.

Colorado Symphony Orchestra — CLASSICAL MUSIC

(CSO; Map p64; 303-623-7876; www.coloradosymphony.org; 1000 14th St; 1, 8, 15L, 30, 31, 48 RTD) The Boettcher Concert Hall in the Denver Performing Arts Complex is home to this renowned symphony orchestra. The orchestra performs an annual 21-week Masterworks season, as well as concerts aimed at a broader audience.

Denver Center for the Performing Arts — THEATER

(Map p64; 303-893-4100; www.denvercenter.org; 1101 13th St; 1, 8, 15L, 30, 31, 48 RTD) The Denver Center for the Performing Arts is the theater wing of the huge Denver Performing Arts Complex. Productions have included *Shrek the Musical, Billy Elliott, Les Miserables, The Lion King* and *West Side Story*.

Colorado Ballet — DANCE

(Map p64; 303-837-8888; www.coloradoballet.org; cnr 14th & Curtis Sts; box office 9am-5pm Mon-Fri; 1, 30, 30L, 31, 36L, 48 RTD) The Colorado Ballet company has 30 professional dancers who come from all over the world. Most performances are staged at the Ellie Caulkins Opera House within the Denver Performing Arts Complex.

Ellie Caulkins Opera House — THEATER

(Map p64; 303-468-2030; www.operacolorado.org; 1101 13th St; 1, 30, 30L, 31, 36L, 48 RTD) A major overhaul of this historic performance house has endowed it with luxurious acoustics, excellent sight lines and a very modern feel. It's also huge – more than 2000 seats – so if you buy cheap seats be sure to bring opera glasses.

Sports

Sports Authority Field at Mile High STADIUM
(Map p60; ☎720-258-3000; www.sportsauthorityfieldatmilehigh.com; 1701 S Bryant St;) The much-lauded Denver Broncos football team and the Denver Outlaws lacrosse team play at Mile High Stadium, 1 mile west of downtown. This stadium also has an eclectic schedule of events, including major rock concerts for superstars such as U2. Stadium tours are organized through the Colorado Sports Hall of Fame (p69).

Coors Field BASEBALL
(Map p60; ☎800-388-7625; www.mlb.com/col/ballpark; 2001 Blake St;) Denver is a city known for manic sports fans, and boasts five pro teams. The Colorado Rockies play baseball at the highly rated Coors Field. Tickets for the outfield – the Rockpile – cost $4. Not a bad deal.

Pepsi Center STADIUM
(Map p60; ☎303-405-1111; www.pepsicenter.com; 1000 Chopper Circle) The mammoth Pepsi Center hosts the Denver Nuggets basketball team, the Colorado Mammoth of the National Lacrosse League and the Colorado Avalanche hockey team. In off season it's a mega concert venue.

Dick's Sporting Goods Park STADIUM
(☎303-727-3500; www.dickssportinggoodspark.com; 6000 Victory Way, Commerce City) This smallish stadium north of the city hosts the Major League Soccer team the Colorado Rapids, plus plenty of summertime concerts.

Cinemas

Landmark Mayan Theater CINEMA
(Map p60; ☎303-744-6799; www.landmarktheatres.com; 110 Broadway; 0 RTD) Even without the fancy sound system and enormous screen, this is the best place in Denver to take in a film. The 1930s movie palace is a romantic, historic gem and – bonus! – it serves beer.

Shopping

Despite the same old American chain stores that dominate Denver's shopping scene, the city has some excellent independent boutiques scattered throughout its neighborhoods, posing a problem for serious shoppers who are in Denver without a car. If you are on foot, the best districts for browsing are LoDo, Cherry Creek, Highlands Sq and South Broadway, all of which are walkable areas with lots of appealing shops, some featuring locally designed clothes, art and housewares.

Most visitors will pass through LoDo, where the crowded and bustling, pedestrian-only 16th St Mall gets a lot of foot traffic. Unfortunately there's not much unique shopping on the mall beyond the kitschy Western souvenir shops (we're talking dream catchers, buffalo statuettes and suspect 'authentic' Native American wares). Just off the mall, the Larimer Sq area along Larimer St has a clutch of high-end boutiques suitable for more discerning shoppers. The Cherry Creek neighborhood, about 3 miles south of downtown, is another good place for shoppers to take a stroll. The massive Cherry Creek Shopping Center towers above the neighborhood – it's Denver's ritziest indoor mall – but a wander among the blocks to the north will reveal lots of galleries and spendy boutiques. The South Broadway district, where rents are cheaper, has a unique set of stores catering to alternative tastes and younger crowds. The heart of the neighborhood can be explored on foot along S Broadway between 1st and Alameda Aves.

Downtown & LoDo

★**Tattered Cover Bookstore** BOOKS
(Map p64; www.tatteredcover.com; 1628 16th St; 6:30am-9pm Mon-Fri, 9am-9pm Sat, 10am-6pm Sun) There are plenty of places to curl up with a book in Denver's beloved independent bookstore, one of two locations in the Denver area. Bursting with new and used books, it has a good stock of regional travel guides and nonfiction titles dedicated to the Western states and Western folklore and literature.

It also has an on-site cafe, and hosts free film and literature events.

Goorin Brothers ACCESSORIES
(Map p64; ☎303-534-4287; www.goorin.com; 1410 Larimer St; 1, 2, 10, 12, 44L RTD) A stylish fedora will put a little bounce in your step while strutting through the ritzy Larimer Sq district. This San Francisco–based source of hip, quality headwear has a great range for men and women.

Champa Fine Wine & Liquor DRINK
(Map p64; ☎303-571-5547; www.champaliquor.com; 1600 Champa St; 11am-midnight Mon-Sat, to 11pm Sun; Champa) This well-stocked

bottle shop opens up a heavenly find for discerning self-caterers, offering a top selection of wine (though most is imported from California) and a mix-and-match six-pack option for visitors who want to take a Colorado beer tour on the cheap.

Colorado Rockies Dugout Store CLOTHING
(Map p64; ☎303-832-8326; 535 16th St, ste 150; ⏰10am-6pm Mon-Fri, to 5pm Sat, 11am-2pm Sun) This official shop of the Rockies baseball team is tucked into a mall along 16th St, and is packed wall-to-wall with official gear, hats, pendants and team-signed baseballs. During the season you can also buy tickets and get information about games.

Wild West Denver Store SOUVENIRS
(Map p64; ☎303-446-8640; 715 16th St; ⏰9am-8:30pm Mon-Sat, to 2:30pm Sun; 🚌California) There's a mess of Western trinket stores along the upper Mall with nearly identical stock, but this is the brightest of the bunch. It's full of knickknacks, key chains, kitty sweatshirts and all manner of stuff featuring wolves, buffaloes and marginally PC depictions of Native Americans. Higher-quality items include some moccasins and gold aspen-leaf pendants.

Cry Baby Ranch WESTERN
(Map p64; ☎303-623-3979; www.crybabyranch.com; 1421 Larimer St; ⏰10am-7pm Mon-Fri, to 6pm Sat, noon-5pm Sun; 🚌12, 15 RTD) Peeking at the price tags of boots hand-tooled with skull and crossbones, it's quickly evident that this store is not for your workaday cowpoke, but the Western-themed homewares and eclectic, bizarre goods (John Wayne lunchbox, anyone?) are a blast to browse.

Tewksbury & Co WINE
(Map p64; ☎303-825-1880; www.tewksburycompany.com; 1512 Larimer St; 🚌10, 15, 20 RTD) 'Colorado's Lifestyle Store' is a real 'man cave' selling hand-rolled cigars (which you can smoke inside!), local wine and fly-fishing trips. The staff are a little surly and the bottle selection is limited, but for a glimpse into the local psyche, it's a worthy stop.

EVOO Marketplace FOOD
(Map p64; ☎303-974-5784; www.evoomarketplace.com; 1338 15th St; 375mL bottles $15-19; ⏰11am-7pm Tue-Sat, to 4pm Sun; 🚌6, 9, 10, 15L, 20, 28, 32, 44, 44L RTD) This specialty shop sells extra-virgin olive oils and balsamic vinegars from across the US and around the world.

Outdoors Geek OUTDOOR EQUIPMENT
(☎303-699-6944; www.outdoorsgeek.com; 12445 E 39th Av; ⏰8am-8pm Mon-Sat; 👪) This mom-and-pop gear outfitter puts together packages of top gear for hiking and camping and either ships it to you or arranges a time for you to pick it up at its headquarters. You can even rent llamas!

Capitol Hill, Golden Triangle & City Park

Wax Trax Records MUSIC
(Map p68; ☎303-831-7246; www.waxtraxrecords.com; 638 E 13th Ave; 🚌2, 10, 15, 15L RTD) For more than 30 years, Wax Trax Records has been trading at this Denver location, stocking a huge quantity of CDs, DVDs, vinyl and music paraphernalia. Indie, alternative, punk, goth, folk, rock, hip-hop, jazz, reggae – anything that's a bit edgy you'll either find in store or it'll order for you.

There are two adjacent shopfronts – one selling CDs and DVDs, the other exclusively vinyl.

Mod Livin' HOMEWARES
(www.modlivin.com; 5327 E Colfax Ave; ⏰10am-9pm Mon-Sat, 11am-9pm Sun; 🚌15 RTD) Fans of midcentury modern furniture will be giddy running around this enormous showroom, littered with pristine vintage gear and newly manufactured designer furnishings.

Capitol Hill Books BOOKS
(Map p68; ☎303-837-0700; www.capitolhillbooks.com; 300 E Colfax Ave; ⏰10am-6pm Mon-Sat, 11am-5pm Sun; 🚌15 RTD) It doesn't have the selection or elan of the Tattered Cover, but over its 30-year life Capitol Hill has retained the rare magic of a *real* bookshop. The rugs are threadbare. The floor creaks. Best of all, the staff of book lovers is quick with helpful suggestions.

Twist & Shout MUSIC
(Map p60; ☎303-722-1943; www.twistandshout.com; 2508 E Colfax Ave; ⏰10am-10pm Mon-Sat, 10am-8pm Sun; 👪; 🚌15, 15L RTD) The selection of used CDs at this brightly lit store is extensive, but head to the little den of used vinyl in the back for rare goodies, original pressings and surprising foreign imports. It also brings a discerning roster of in-store performances that run the gamut of musical tastes.

Peppermint Boutique CLOTHING
(Map p60; www.peppermintdenver.com; 1227 E 17th Ave; ⌚10am-7pm Mon-Sat, 11am-5pm Sun; 🚻; 🚌20 RTD) This boutique has an effortless charm, and stocks accessories, interesting jewelry and dresses that are hip and casually sophisticated. Considering the careful selection and high quality, it's also surprisingly inexpensive.

Plastic Chapel TOYS
(Map p60; ☎303-722-0715; www.plasticchapel.com; 3109 E Colfax Ave; ⌚noon-6pm Tue-Sat, 11am-4pm Sun; 🚌15 RTD) Rows of clear plastic cubes house all kinds of designer toys, collectible Japanese-made figurines and other limited-edition off-the-wall stuff to make this Denver's most wicked toy store. The toys are mostly suited for adult collectors – you're getting high-dollar stuff such as Kid Robot and StrangeCo, not Fisher Price. Also hosts design competitions and graphic-arts shows.

Tattered Cover Bookstore BOOKS
(Map p60; ☎303-322-7727; www.tatteredcover.com; 2526 E Colfax Ave; ⌚9am-9pm Mon-Sat, 10am-6pm Sun; 🚌15 RTD) Massive and bursting with new and used books, Denver's beloved independent bookstore has a particularly good selection of niche travel guides to the surrounding region and western-states nonfiction and folklore. The East Colfax location is conveniently situated just a hop from City Park.

Buffalo Exchange CLOTHING
(Map p68; ☎303-866-0165; www.buffaloexchange.com; 226 E 13th Ave; ⌚11am-8pm Mon-Sat, noon-7pm Sun; 🚻) Part of a growing nationwide chain, Buffalo Exchange in Capitol Hill is a huge space with new and used clothing: retro, futuristic, trad and garish. You want a hip 1950s shirt, or a little something for a costume party? This is the place. Garments, shoes and accessories are bought and sold.

Pandora Jewelry ACCESSORIES
(Map p68; ☎303-832-7073; www.pandorajewelrydenver.com; 220 E 13th Ave; ⌚10am-7pm Mon-Sat, 11am-5pm Sun; 🚻; 🚌2 RTD) 🍃 This is a friendly shop selling tasteful jewelry – ladies and mens – as well as cards, trinkets, gifts and novelties. The shop doesn't stock items that incorporate animal products.

Highlands & Platte River Valley

★REI OUTDOOR EQUIPMENT
(Recreational Equipment Incorporated; Map p60; ☎303-756-3100; www.rei.com; 1416 Platte St; 🚻) The flagship store of this outdoor-equipment super supplier is an essential stop if you are heading to the mountains or just cruising through Confluence. In addition to top gear for camping, cycling, climbing and skiing, it has a rental department, maps and the Pinnacle, a 47ft-high indoor structure of simulated red sandstone for climbing and rappelling.

There's also a desk of Colorado's Outdoor Recreation Information Center, where you can get information on state and national parks and an on-site Starbucks, in case you need some caffeine to accompany the adrenaline.

Dragonfly CLOTHING
(☎303-433-6331; www.dragonflydenver.com; 3615 W 32 Ave; ⌚10:30am-6:30pm Mon-Sat, 11am-5pm Sun; 🚌32 RTD) Cute, casual skirts and sweaters and a small, seasonal selection of accessories make this among the best women's clothing boutiques in Denver.

Wilderness Exchange Unlimited OUTDOOR EQUIPMENT
(Map p60; ☎303-964-0708; www.wildernessexchangeunlimited.com; 2401 15th St; ⌚10am-8pm Mon-Fri, to 7pm Sat, to 6pm Sun; 🚌10, 32 RTD) In addition to carefully selected outdoor equipment, this shop has an impressive collection of quality used gear (including good deals on hiking boots, skis and down jackets) in the basement.

Metroboom BEAUTY
(Map p60; ☎303-477-9700; www.metroboom.com; 1550 Platte St; ⌚10am-7pm Tue-Sat) This place is ideal for the man who wants a little pampering, either with custom menswear, personal grooming products, designer fashion or a shave. The packages range between the basic ('Presley') to downright luxurious ('Cary Grant'), including haircuts, hot towels and hand treatments (that's just man-talk for a manicure).

South Central Denver

Cherry Creek Shopping Center MALL
(Map p60; ☎303-388-3900; www.shopcherrycreek.com; 3000 E First Ave; ⌚10am-9pm Mon-Sat,

to 6pm Sun; ; 3, 83L RTD) A large collection of exclusive international brands (Louis Vuitton, Burberry, Ralph Lauren, Tiffany, Coach) decorate the corridors of Denver's high-end shopping facility, anchored by the large Neiman Marcus department store. Food choices range from cheap-and-quick mall standards such as Panda Express to the elegant Tuscan fare and linen-draped dining room of Brio.

5 Green Boxes HOMEWARES
(303-282-5481; www.5greenboxes.com; 1705 S Pearl St; 10am-6pm Mon-Sat, noon-5pm Sun) The sister store down the street sells simple and chic women's clothing and accessories, but this is the place to get a one-of-a-kind piece for your home. From custom remodeled furniture to home items large and small, the aesthetic is classy, vintage and whimsical.

South Broadway

Fancy Tiger CRAFT
(Map p60; 303-733-3855; www.fancytiger.com; 59 Broadway; 11am-7pm Mon-Sat, noon-6pm Sun; 0 RTD) So you dig crochet and record collecting? You knit a mean sweater and have a few too many tattoos? Welcome to Fancy Tiger, a sophisticated remodel of granny's yarn barn that's ground zero for Denver's crafty hipsters. There are classes in the basement (including ones by Jessica, 'mistress of patchwork') and a rad selection of fabric, yarn and books.

If you are a little bit more hands off with your homemade clothes, try the Fancy Tiger Boutique across the street, where local designers hock their wares.

Beyond Central Denver

Colorado Mills MALL
(303-590-1634; www.coloradomills.com; 14500 W Colfax Ave; 10am-11pm Mon-Sat, 11am-6pm Sun;) This is a shoppers' paradise: a huge shopping mall west of the downtown area with more than 200 specialty stores and 1.1 million sq ft of retail fun. All the big retailers are represented, some with discounted factory outlets, and there are restaurants and food halls. Catch a movie at the United Artists multiplex theater.

Orientation

Once you get outside the downtown area, getting around Denver's streets can be a bit of a challenge, with roads suddenly changing names, ending and running counter to the cardinal grid found in many older parts of town (save for downtown, which has a grid that sits diagonal to the cardinal points).

Keep in mind that Broadway (running north-south) and Ellsworth (running east-west) are considered '0' blocks. From these central starting points, addresses ascend by increments of 100 every block.

Information

DANGERS & ANNOYANCES

For a large city, Denver is pretty darned safe. LoDo, downtown, Highlands and Cherry Creek are safe both day and night. You may wish to excercise greater caution if you venture into the Five Points and RiNo Districts east of Park Avenue at night. Other than that, big-city smarts are the rule.

INTERNET ACCESS

If you're traveling with a laptop, you'll have no trouble finding wi-fi: it's nearly ubiquitous in Denver's restaurants, bars and cafes. There is also free wi-fi on the 16th St Mall. If you're not traveling with a computer, things get a bit more tricky, but there are free computer terminals inside almost every Denver Public Library (p66) branch.

MEDICAL SERVICES

Denver Health Medical Center (303-436-4949; www.denverhealth.org; 777 Bannock St; 52 RTD) This is where you go if you don't have health insurance.

Rose Medical Center (303-320-2121; www.rosemed.com; 4567 E 9th Ave)

St Joseph Hospital (303-837-7111; www.exempla.org; 1835 Franklin St)

University of Colorado Hospital (720-848-0000; www.uch.edu; 12605 E 16th Ave, Aurora; 24hr) Emergency services.

MONEY

ATMs are widely available and major banks will exchange foreign currency.

POST

Central Post Office (Map p64; 303-296-2071; www.usps.com; 951 20th St; 8:30am-6pm Mon-Fri, 9am-6pm Sat; 38 RTD) Main branch.

TOURIST INFORMATION

The Visit Denver (www.denver.org) website has great information about events.

DIA Information Booth (303-342-2000; Denver International Airport) Tourist and airport information is available at this booth in the terminal's central hall.

ORIC Desk (Outdoor Recreation Information Center; Map p60; ☎REI main line 303-756-3100; www.oriconline.org; 1416 Platte St; 📶) Inside REI, this information desk is a must for those looking to get out of town. It has maps and expert information on trip planning and safety information. The desk is staffed by volunteers, so hours vary wildly, but arriving on a weekend afternoon is a good bet.

Visitors & Convention Bureau Information Center (Map p64; ☎303-892-1112; www.denver.org; 1600 California St; 📶; 🚇California) When you get to town, make for the largest and most centrally located information center, on the 16th St Mall. You can load up on brochures and get information about local transport. There's also a tourist info desk in the Colorado Convention Center.

Getting There & Away

Served by the largest airport in the US, criss-crossed by major highways and intersected by one of the country's few Amtrak lines, it's easy to get to and from Denver.

AIR

Denver International Airport is a major hub for several American carriers, including Frontier Airlines and United Airlines. Private jets and charters tend to be serviced through Centennial Airport to the south and Rocky Mountain Metropolitan Airport (between Denver and Boulder).

Denver International Airport (DIA; ☎information 303-342-2000; www.flydenver.com; 8500 Peña Blvd; ⏰24hr; 📶) Twenty-four miles from downtown, DIA is connected with I-70 exit 238 by the 12-mile-long Peña Blvd. The facility has an automated subway that links the terminal to three concourses. Concourse C is almost 1 mile from the terminal, hence the need for automated transport of people and baggage, and a little extra time for finding your way around.

DIA is a major air hub and one of the country's busiest facilities. In all, DIA has 53 sq miles of land, making it the biggest airport in the country by area. The main terminal has a teflon-coated fiberglass roof that peaks out to mirror the mountains in the background, and there are always interesting public-art exhibits to help you kill time.

BUS

Greyhound (☎800-231-2222; www.greyhound.com) and affiliate TNM&O offer frequent buses on routes along the Front Range and on transcontinental routes. All buses stop at the Denver Bus Center.

The **Colorado Mountain Express** (CME; ☎800-525-6363; www.coloradomountainexpress.com; DIA; 📶) has shuttle services from DIA, downtown Denver or Morrison to Summit County, including Breckenridge and Keystone ($35 to $49, 2½ hours) and Vail ($45 to $82, three hours).

The **Colorado Springs Shuttle** (☎719-687-3456; www.coloradoshuttle.com; DIA) offers trips from DIA to Colorado Springs ($50, two hours), Castle Rock and Monument. **Powder River Coach USA** (☎800-442-3682; www.coachusa.com), offering services north to Cheyenne, WY, and on to Montana and South Dakota, also runs from the Denver Bus Center.

Regional Transportation District (RTD) buses to Boulder (route B, $5) carry bicycles in the cargo compartment and offer frequent service from the Market St Station. To reach Golden, take either the 16 or 16L bus that stops at the corner of 15th and California Sts.

Denver Bus Center (Map p64; ☎303-293-6555; 1055 19th St) Greyhound buses stop here. Services run to Boise (from $140, 18 hours), Billings (from $105, 14 hours) and Los Angeles (from $150, 20 hours).

Market St Bus Station (Map p64; cnr 16th & Market Sts) All transportation companies, including RTD, have booths near the baggage-claim area.

CAR & MOTORCYCLE

At the intersection of I-70 and I-25, Denver is pretty hard to miss. Even the poorest navigators should have no trouble finding this city.

TRAIN

Amtrak (☎800-872-7245; www.amtrak.com) Amtrak's *California Zephyr* runs daily between Chicago and San Francisco, stopping in Denver. While its usual home, Union Station, is being renovated, Amtrak has set up a temporary station at 1800 21st St. It's slated to move back to Union Station in spring 2014.

Union Station (☎Amtrak 800-872-7245; www.denverunionstation.org; cnr 17th & Wynkoop Sts; 🚇31X, 40X, 80X, 86X, 120X RTD) The red neon atop this stoic 19th-century fortress glowers down and demands you 'travel by train' – and you still can. But not until renovations are completed in spring of 2014, when the new Union Station will provide a multi-modal one-stop shop for service to Denver metro light-rail lines, commuter buses and Amtrak.

There are even plans to build a hotel on site, and you can definitely expect a number of restaurants and shops opening up here.

Getting Around

TO/FROM THE AIRPORT

A complete Ground Transportation Center is centrally located on the 5th level of DIA's terminal, near the baggage claim. All transportation companies have their booths here and passengers can catch vans, shuttles and taxis outside the doors.

Complimentary hotel shuttles represent the cheapest means of getting to or from the airport. Courtesy phones for hotel shuttles are available in the Ground Transportation Center.

RTD buses are available outside door 506 in the West Terminal and door 511 in the East Terminal. Travel time is typically less than an hour to or from the city and fares cost $9 to $13 one way – exact fare only – servicing Stapleton, downtown and other Denver suburbs. For DIA-Boulder travelers, one way fares for the 1½-hour trip cost $13.

Taxi service to downtown Denver costs around $60, excluding tip.

There are a number of airport shuttle vans and limousine services. Airport shuttles to the Front Range and mountain/ski areas are also not hard to come by.

Shuttle King Limo (☎303-363-8000; www.shuttlekinglimo.com) Private limos for about $65 from DIA to destinations in and around Denver.

SuperShuttle (☎303-370-1300; www.supershuttle.com) Van services (from $22) between the Denver area and the airport.

BICYCLE

Denver has lots of bike lanes on the city streets and an excellent network of trails to get out of town. These include routes along the Platte River Parkway, the Cherry Creek Bike Path and a network that heads all the way out to Golden (about a two-hour ride). You can get all the information you need from a pair of excellent websites, **BikeDenver** (www.bikedenver.org) and **City of Denver** (www.denvergov.org), which has downloadable bike maps for the city.

B-Cycle (☎303-825-3325; www.denver.bcycle.com; 1-day membership $8; ⏲5am-11pm) The first citywide bicycle-share program in the US was launched in April 2010. Directions are given at more than 80 stations found throughout the city. Rentals under 30 minutes are free. Helmets are not included and not required in Denver.

BUS

Regional Transportation District (RTD; Map p68; ☎303-299-6000; www.rtd-denver.com; 1500 Broadway) RTD provides public transportation throughout the Denver and Boulder area (local/express/regional fares $2.25/4/5). Free shuttle buses operate along the 16th St Mall. RTD also runs a SkyRide service to the airport from downtown Denver hourly ($11, one hour). The website has schedules, routes, fares and a trip planner.

CAR & MOTORCYCLE

Street parking can be a pain, but there is a slew of pay garages in downtown and LoDo. Nearly all the major car-rental agencies have counters at DIA, though only a few have offices in downtown Denver.

Check the ride boards at the hostels or at the north wing of Driscoll University Center at the University of Denver, which is connected to the main campus by the pedestrian walkway over E Evans Ave.

Enterprise Rent-A-Car (☎303-623-1281; www.enterprise.com; 650 15th St)

LIGHT RAIL

RTD's light-rail line currently has six lines, which service 46 stations.

The W Line runs from Union Station, past the Pepsi Center and Mile High Stadium to the Jefferson County Government Center on the outskirts of Golden.

The C Line runs along the eastern edge of downtown, continuing south to Englewood and Littleton, ending on Santa Fe and Mineral Sts. The D Line starts at 30th and Downing in Five Points, going straight through the city to hook up with the southern run of the C Line to Littleton.

The E and F lines run from either Union Station or 18th and California south along I-25 to the Denver Tech Center, ending at Lincoln Ave. The H Line from 18th and California will take you to Nine Mile, where you could potentially walk or bike to Cherry Creek Reservoir.

Fares are $2.25 for one to two stops, $4 for three fare zones, and $5 for all zones. Bikes may be taken on the train if there is space. You purchase tickets from automated kiosks before boarding. Occasional ticket checkers pass through the trains to validate your tickets.

TAXI

Two major taxi companies offer door-to-door service in Denver:

Metro Taxi (☎303-333-3333; www.metrotaxidenver.com)

Yellow Cab (☎303-777-7777; www.denveryellowcab.com)

AROUND DENVER

Golden

POP 19,000

Snuggled beneath the foothills, Table Mountain and the ugly-as-hell Coors Brewery, the town of Golden has a small historic district, a few interesting museums and the highly regarded Colorado School of Mines. Some may find Golden an interesting day trip, but it probably doesn't warrant an overnight

WORTH A TRIP

GOLD IN THEM HILLS – GAMBLING AT COLORADO'S HISTORIC MINING TOWNS

Colorado re-legalized low-stakes gambling in 1991 in historic mining towns such as Black Hawk and Central City. The stakes have gone up, with voters raising maximum bet limits to $100 in 2008. The Wild West towns still have the cool storefronts, which now lead into modern large-scale hotels and casinos such as **Ameristar** (720-946-4000; www.ameristar.com; 111 Richman St, Blackhawk; r $99-209;).

Black Hawk (www.blackhawkcolorado.com) Colorado's biggest gambling town has 18 casinos, plus hotels, spas, nearby hiking trails and all-you-can-eat buffets. Think Vegas, Wild West style. They have all the major games, and betting goes up to $100 on a single wager.

Central City (www.centralcitycolorado.com) Just a mile from Black Hawk, Central City has fewer big casinos and makes for better shopping and bopping around the historic town center. It even has an **opera company** (303-292-6700; www.centralcityopera.org; 124 Eureka St; opera tickets from $20).

stay, particularly since accommodations are fairly expensive.

History

Golden was founded in 1859 at the mouth of Clear Creek Canyon after prospectors discovered gold in the stream that flows through town. Golden served as the Colorado Territorial capital from 1862 to 1867 – apparently Denver bested Golden (then Golden City) by a single vote, one which history wags claim was rigged by then-territorial governor John Evans. You can win plenty of bar bets with visitors who assume Golden is named for the glinting yellow mineral found in them thar hills – the truth is, the seat of Jefferson County was named for Thomas L Golden, who camped near the creek in 1858.

Sights

'First Friday' events bring a pleasant street carnival with wine and local gallery openings on (you guessed it!) the first Friday of every month. The First Friday hubbub takes place along Washington St, with the epicenter at 12th St.

Coors Brewery BREWERY

(MillerCoors; 800-642-6116; www.millercoors.com; cnr 13th & Ford Sts; 10am-4pm Mon-Sat, from noon Sun; P) FREE Coors Brewery is now officially called MillerCoors, but try telling the locals that. There's been brewing on this site since 1873. Coors survived the prohibition years by producing malted milk and porcelain products, and went on to produce the world's first beer shipped in aluminum cans.

Each year 250,000 people take the brewery's free self-guided tour, which includes free samples for the over-21 crowd. A free shuttle takes people from the car park.

Colorado Railroad Museum MUSEUM

(303-279-4591; www.coloradorailroadmuseum.org; 17155 W 44th Ave; adult/child $10/5, train rides $15/5 (Sat only); 9am-5pm; P) With more than 100 railroad engines, a 500yd looping track, cabooses and rolling stock, as well as paraphernalia and regalia, this is a must-stop for train fanatics touring the region. The stars of the show are the well-restored Galloping Goose railcars (or motors, if you want to get technical).

Built in Ridgeway, Colorado, these small trains were made from converted cars (three of the original seven are now at the museum). They were used to transport small groups of people and cargo through the mountainous region and keep the Rio Grande Southern line profitable in remote Colorado. There's also a comprehensive library of all things locomotive, the Restoration Roundhouse, a working turntable and Colorado's coolest model train downstairs.

Buffalo Bill Museum & Grave MUSEUM

(303-526-0744; www.buffalobill.org; 987 1/2 Lookout Mountain Rd; adult/child/senior $5/1/4; 9am-5pm; P) This museum celebrates the life and legend of William F 'Buffalo Bill' Cody, an icon of the American West. At his request he was buried at this site overlooking both the Great Plains and the Rockies, and today it attracts a steady stream of RVs to snap pictures of his statue.

The museum and gift shop are pure kitsch and probably not recommended for those with a progressive view on Native American history. Still, Bill's biography is a fascinating one: when he began his show-business career at age 26 in Chicago in 1872, he had already spent more than a decade as a fur trapper, gold prospector, cattle herder, Pony Express rider and army scout, crossing the Great Plains many times in the West's pioneering years. His show became hugely popular and traveled to England in 1887 for Queen Victoria's Golden Jubilee celebrations.

Foothills Art Center MUSEUM
(☎303-279-3922; www.foothillsartcenter.org; 809 15th St) FREE This small, carefully managed community arts center hosts works by local artists, as well as receiving occasional traveling exhibits.

American Mountaineering Museum MUSEUM
(Bradford Washburn American Mountaineering Museum; ☎303-996-2755; www.mountaineering-museum.org; 710 10th St; adult/child $5/1; ⏲10am-5pm Tue-Fri, to 6pm Sat, 11am-4pm Sun; P 👪) If you've come to Colorado to climb, this museum will give you tingles of inspiration. There's a pile of stunning photos, historic climbing gear (some of which, like Peter Schoening's ice axe, are from legendary expeditions) and a display on the 10th Mountain Division, which trained in Colorado before the fight in WWII – you can still use its huts in the Colorado backcountry.

Activities

Cycling

Nearby parks offer plenty of opportunity for off-road rides, and road riders will find a number of loops beginning in Golden. Immediately south of I-70, along Hwy 26, Matthews Winters Park has trail access to the Mt Vernon town site, which in 1859 was the capital of the provisional Territory of Jefferson. East of Matthews Winters Park and Hwy 26, the Dakota Ridge Trail follows the spine of Hogback Park south for 2 miles before crossing Hwy 26 near Morrison to Red Rocks Trail, which returns to Matthews Winters.

If you're in good shape and don't mind a steep climb, try White Ranch Open Space Park, which has miles of challenging singletrack and fire-road rides. There are two trailheads: one just off Hwy 93 on the way to Boulder; the other 15 miles up Golden Gate Canyon Rd en route to Golden Gate Canyon State Park.

Golf

Fossil Trace Golf Club GOLF
(☎303-277-8750; www.fossiltrace.com; 3050 Illinois St; 18 holes nonresident $62) Even if you're not building your Colorado itinerary around golf, it might be worth knocking around a few holes at the Fossil Trace Golf Club. Routinely considered among America's best courses, this unique round of golf offers a glimpse of fossils, challenging play and sweeping views. The course isn't cheap, but it's certainly memorable.

This course might be the only place on Earth where you can hit the ball off the fairway and into the shadow of triceratops' tracks. The course is built in the scarred terrain of old mines, giving a fascinating landscape where rock formations jut abruptly from the grass.

Sleeping & Eating

There's no trouble finding a passable meal in Golden, though most of the sit-down eateries are serving up a fairly uninspired roster of burgers, chops, pizzas and big salads. If you're willing to look a bit harder, there are some real gems. On Saturdays between June and September, the city hosts the Golden Farmers Market at the parking lot just west of the library.

Table Mountain Inn HOTEL
(☎303-277-9898; www.tablemountaininn.com; 1310 Washington Ave; r $174-264) Not many people stay the night in Golden, but if you have an extra day, you might just want to check in for a night on the edge of the Rockies. Plus, once the sun sets, the locals take over town. The best rooms in town are found in this old adobe hotel right smack in downtown. The large Southwest-styled rooms have grand bedstands and patios looking out to Table Mesa. The cantina downstairs is worth checking out.

Empanada Express SOUTH AMERICAN $
(☎720-226-4701; www.theempanadaexpress.com; 2600 East St; dishes $4-5; ⏲10:30am-8pm; 👪) This family-operated hole-in-the-wall is worth seeking out for filling, flaky empanadas filled with savory carnitas, seasoned chicken and cheese. The chili *arepas* (fried, stuffed corn cakes) are also excellent. The tables are tiny, so it's probably best to get it on the go.

D'deli DELI $
(☎303-279-5308; www.ddelisubs.com; 1207 Washington Ave; sandwiches $6-7;) Crusty, fresh bread and stacks of ingredients make this cozy deli an excellent place for lunch. The 'Heater', a massive pile of pastrami, jalapeños, banana peppers and chipotle ranch, is the choice for spice fiends. A second location on the creek also has excellent ambience.

Woody's Woodfired Pizza & Watering Hole PIZZERIA $
(☎303-277-0443; www.woodysgolden.com; 1305 Washington Ave; all-you-can-eat pizza $10; ⏰11am-midnight) After you make it past the 'watering hole' part of the evening at Woody's, with its selection of some of the area's best brews, order up a crusty, woodfired pie. It's hard not to love the laid-back locals and sustainable-business focus.

Ali Baba Grill MEDITERRANEAN $$
(☎303-279-2228; www.alibabagrill.com; 109 N Rubey Dr; mains $10-15; ⏰11am-9pm;) Sure, it looks like another drab strip-mall joint from the parking lot, but the Lebanese and Mediterranean cuisine here is awesome and every bit as surprising as the elaborate interior, which is likely Golden's only harem-themed dining room.

Golden Farmers Market SELF-CATERING $
(www.goldencochamber.org; cnr 10th & Illinois Sts; ⏰8am-1pm Sat Jun-Sep;) On Saturdays during the summer, Golden's small farmers market hosts local food producers from throughout the region.

Shopping

Bent Gate Mountaineering OUTDOOR EQUIPMENT
(☎303-271-9382; www.bentgate.com; 1313 Washington Ave; ⏰10am-8pm Sun-Thu, to 5pm Fri) This outdoor-equipment shop focuses on skiing and mountaineering and has a good selection of high-quality gear for sale. It also hosts occasional events.

Information

You won't have trouble finding an ATM machine as the tourist areas are loaded with them.

Golden Chamber of Commerce/Visitor Center (☎303-279-3113; www.goldencochamber.org; 1010 Washington Ave; ⏰8am-5pm Mon-Fri, 10am-4pm Sat) This is the tourism nerve center for Golden, and you can stock up on brochures, maps, hotel and local info here. You can also pick up a walking-tour guide to the 12th St historic district.

Jefferson County Open Space Office (☎303-271-5925; www.co.jefferson.co.us; 700 Jefferson County Pkwy; ⏰7:30am-5:30pm Mon-Fri) This office has information and permits for camping in the county's park system. Camping permits for Reynolds Park can be obtained here or arranged through a phone call.

Post Office (☎303-216-0320; 619 12th St; ⏰9am-5pm Mon-Fri, 10am-1pm Sat) Centrally located.

Getting There & Away

BICYCLE

Riding from Denver takes about 1½ hours; the Clear Creek Bike Trail will get you most of the way along a clearly marked route.

BUS

RTD connects Golden with downtown Denver (at the corner of 15th and California Sts). Fare $5.

CAR & MOTORCYCLE

The easiest route from Denver is I-25 north to I-70, then I-70 to exit 265, from where you can catch Hwy 58 west into town. From downtown Denver, Golden is about 16 miles.

TRAIN

The Light Rail W Line ($5) runs to the Jefferson County Government Building about 5 miles south of downtown Golden. The Community Call-n-Ride ($2.25) bus passes from downtown to the light rail station every half hour.

Denver Mountain Parks & Platte River

Morrison

POP 420 / ELEV 5764FT

Billing itself as 'the nearest faraway place,' little Morrison is a National Historic District 32 miles southwest of Denver on Hwy 8, hidden from the Denver skyline by the Hogback rock formations. It echos the feel of some of Colorado's more remote mountain towns. While the spectacular upturned red rocks on the banks of Bear Creek are an attractive escape from Denver, most people visit Morrison either on the way to, or from, Red Rocks Park & Amphitheater or to fuel up before climbing the big hills in the surrounding Jefferson County Open Space Parks.

WORTH A TRIP

RED ROCKS PARK & AMPHITHEATRE

Red Rocks Amphitheatre (☎303-640-2637; www.redrocksonline.com; 18300 W Alameda Pkwy; ⏰5am-11pm; 👪) is set between 400ft-high red sandstone rocks 15 miles southwest of Denver. Acoustics are so good many artists record live albums here. The 9000-seat theater offers stunning views and draws big-name bands all summer. To see your favorite singer go to work on the stage is to witness a performance in one of the most exceptional music venues in the world. For many, it's reason enough for a trip to Colorado.

When the setting sun brings out a rich, orange glow from the rock formations and the band on stage launches into the right tune, Red Rocks Amphitheatre is a captivating experience, wholly befitting the park's 19th-century name, 'Garden of Angels.'

The natural amphitheater, once a Ute camping spot, has been used for performances for decades, but it wasn't until 1936 that members of the Civilian Conservation Corps built a formal outdoor venue with seats and a stage. Though it originally hosted classical performances and military bands, it debuted as a rock venue with style; the first rock quartet on this stage was John, Paul, George and Ringo. Since then, the gamut of artists who have recorded live albums here – such as U2, Neil Young, Dave Matthews and new-age piano tinkler John Tesh – is a testament to the pristine natural acoustics.

You scored tickets? Great. Now for the nitty gritty. Eat in Morrison beforehand as the junk food from the food vendors is predictably expensive and the restaurants are crowded. Alternatively, you can bring a small cooler into the show, as long as there's no booze and it'll fit under your seat. Climbing on the stunning formations is prohibited; however, 250-plus steps lead to the top of the theater, offering views of both the park and Denver, miles off to the east.

Amazingly, Red Rocks Park can be almost as entertaining when it's silent. The amphitheater is only a tiny part of the 600-acre space. There are miles of hiking trails, opportunities to lose the crowds and take in lovely rock formations. There's information about the entire area on the website.

Sights & Activities

You'll see plenty of cyclists in the area; the smooth pavement and undulating terrain make for excellent road biking. Excavations of what is called the Morrison Formation began in 1877 and have yielded fossils of more than 70 dinosaur species.

Dinosaur Ridge ARCHAEOLOGICAL SITE
(☎303-697-3466; www.dinoridge.org; 16831 W Alameda Pkwy; ⏰9am-5pm May-Oct, 11am-4pm Nov-Apr; P 👪) FREE Unless you are an extremely dedicated dinosaur nut, the drive out to Dinosaur National Monument is a long haul. The footprints and sandstone-encased fossils here are extremely impressive, and worth the detour, and the tours are awesome for the kids. It's about 2 miles north of Morrison along Hwy 26.

Sleeping & Eating

Cliff House Lodge B&B $$
(☎303-697-9732; www.cliffhouselodge.net; 121 Stone St; cabins from $175; @ 📶 👪) If you spend the night in Morrison, this historic brick B&B is by far the best choice. The decor might be a little overboard, but some of the cottages have hot tubs and the gardens are a peaceful place to catch up on some reading.

Mill Street Deli GRILL $
(☎303-697-1700; 401 Bear Creek Ave; mains $7-10; ⏰11am-midnight Mon-Sat; 👪) Of all the casual eats in Morrison, this place is tops. The grilled sandwiches are crispy and dripping with cheese and the Angus burger is a savory mess. You can sit next door in the bar while you wait for your order and eat late after concerts.

Willy's Wings BARBECUE $
(☎303-697-1232; www.willyswings.com; 109 Bear Creek Ave; mains $5-10; ⏰11am-8pm Mon-Sat, to 7pm Sun; 👪) Frills? Forget about it. Situated in what looks like the mobile home of a displaced Texan auntie, this place has some good wings. Stay away if you're watching your waistline – just about everything on the menu is deep fried, except the potato salad, which is thick with mayo.

Tommy's Subs DELI $
(☎303-697-5530; www.tommyssubs.com; ste J, 14011 W Quincy Ave; subs $7-11; ⊙10am-7pm Mon-Fri, to 3pm Sat; 👪) Seated in a strip mall right at the edge of the park, this locally owned sandwich shop gets a lot of lip service for the Philly cheesesteak and French dip subs. All of them come on locally baked bread rolls.

Morrison Inn MEXICAN $$
(☎303-697-6650; 301 Bear Creek Ave; mains $9-18; ⊙11am-10pm Sun-Thu, to 11pm Fri & Sat; 👪) A former drugstore and soda fountain turned Mexican restaurant-bar pours formidable margaritas and dishes out passable Mex standards and hand-cut fries. The rooftop seating is great when it's warm, and historic photos of early Morrison line the restaurant walls.

The Fort AMERICAN $$$
(☎303-697-4771; www.thefort.com; 19192 Hwy 8; mains $25-50; ⊙5:30-11pm Mon-Fri, 5-11pm Sat & Sun) This Colorado institution has been around since 1963 and is the best spot in the state to try Rocky Mountain oysters. The wild game and buffalo dishes are out of this world, as is the well-thought Western ambience in the rugged Southwestern fort perched on the foothills above Denver.

Reynolds Park

For those on a tight schedule who need a little peace and quiet, Reynolds Park (sometimes called Reynolds Ranch Park) is a perfect escape from Denver. It's the diversity of landscape that makes the place so desirable. In the park's lower elevation, visitors amble along in the gentle meadows, picnic by the stream and camp in the secluded **Idylease Campground** (www.co.jefferson.co.us; Foxton Rd; 👪). A hike in the area's rugged upper elevations offers panoramic vistas and bigger challenges to the legs. Among this varied terrain lives a large diversity of wildlife – you're likely to see mule deer, elk, wild turkey and blue grouse. You may even spot a black bear. It is a half-mile hike or horseback ride from the parking lot to the campground, where there are fire rings, grills and bear lockers. You must reserve a spot here, which you can do through the Jefferson County Open Space Office (p98) in Golden.

Boulder & Around

Includes ➡

Best Places to Eat

- Salt (p118)
- Frasca (p118)
- Tangerine (p114)
- Lucile's (p117)
- Breadworks (p115)

Best Places to Stay

- Chautauqua Lodge (p113)
- Briar Rose B&B (p113)
- Quality Inn Boulder Creek (p113)
- The Alps (p114)
- Hotel Boulderado (p114)

Why Go?

Twenty-five square miles surrounded by reality. That's the joke about Boulder that never goes away. The weather is perfect, the surroundings – stone Flatirons, gurgling creek, ponderosa trails and manicured college campus – beg idylling. And the populace – fit do-gooders with the beta on the best fair-trade coffee – seals the stereotype.

Boulder's mad love of the outdoors was officially legislated in 1967, when Boulder became the first US city to tax itself specifically to preserve open space. Thanks to such vision, people (and dogs) enjoy a number of city parks and open space while packs of cyclists whip up and down the Boulder Creek corridor.

In many ways it is Boulder, not Denver, that is the region's tourist hub. The city is about the same distance from Denver International Airport, and the hub puts you 45 minutes closer to the ski resorts west on I-70 and the extraordinary Rocky Mountain National Park.

When to Go

Boulder

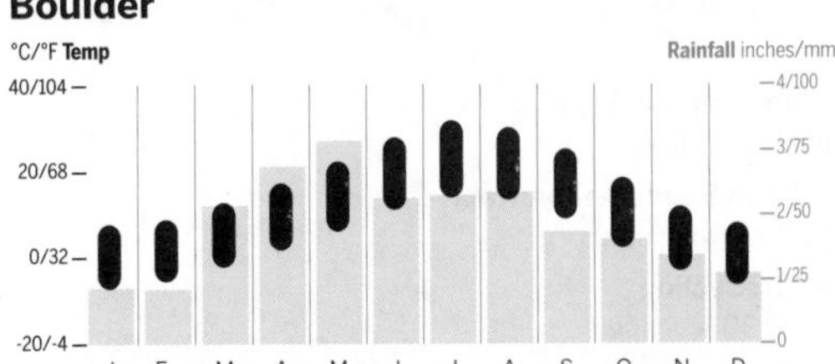

Jun–Aug Long sunny days, summer showers, farmers markets, hiking, biking and tubing.

Sep–Oct Students return, Indian Summer, fall color, warm days, cool nights.

Jan–Feb Powder at Eldora, and snowshoe or backcountry ski adventures in the Indian Peaks.

FAST FACTS

- **Population** 101,808
- **Median Resident Age** 28.7 years old
- **Altitude** 5430ft

Biking Boulder

The main vein is the Boulder Creek Bike Path, shooting directly through town to the mountains, with north-south branches. Valmont Bike Park rewards well-padded riders with jumps and a half pipe. A number of shops offer rentals and route advice. B-Cycle has stations around town with hourly rentals.

For Kids

- Chautauqua Park (p105)
- Butterfly Pavilion (p106)
- CU Wizards (p108)
- Pop Jet Fountain (p109)
- Boulder Rock Club (p110)
- Boulder Creek Bike Path (p109)

Resources

- **Boulder Downtown** www.boulderdowntown.com
- **Boulder Weekly** www.boulderweekly.com
- **Open Space & Mountain Parks** www.osmp.org
- **303Cycling** www.303cycling.com
- **Get Boulder** www.getboulder.com

Getting Around

Renting a car can be useful to get into the high country, but Boulder is perfectly manageable by bicycle or public transportation.

RTD buses travel to Denver, Denver International Airport, Nederland and within Boulder proper. Many buses have bike racks. Dedicated bike lanes and paths make the city ideal for two-wheel traffic and the downtown area is pleasantly walkable.

ADVANCE PLANNING

Each fall over 30,000 university students descend upon Boulder with few snags. You can too. The key is to start with lodging, since budget options are few. Square your reservations in advance, especially if you are coming for a festival or event.

Keep in mind that Boulder's sunny, mild climate means decent weather year-round, so consider saving money by going at off-peak times. Boulder can be a good deal quieter during the winter holiday or CU spring break, when students go home. Try not to overlap with big events like University of Colorado's May graduation week, when all restaurants and hotels are brimming.

This active town will make you want to hit the ground running, or hiking, but don't. The high altitude can take its toll, so ease into your visit with a mellow start, be mindful of sun exposure and drink lots of water, not margaritas – or at least not yet.

Best Day Trips

- Indian Peaks Wilderness Area (p127)
- Eldorado Canyon State Park (p110)
- Rocky Mountain National Park (p130)
- Eldora Ski Area (p127)

BOULDER

POP 98,900

History

The Boulder foothills were a wintering spot for nomadic Arapahoe Nation in the early 19th century. Utes, Cheyennes, Comanches and Sioux were also documented in the Boulder valley before Europeans arrived. Later in the 19th century, American explorers Zebulon Pike and John Fremont were commissioned to explore the area. One of Fremont's men, William Gilpin, became the first governor of the Colorado Territory. His speculation on gold deposits in Boulder inspired Depression-saddled easterners to set out for Colorado.

The first European settlement in Boulder County was established at Red Rocks, on October 17, 1858. One of those early settlers, AA Brookfield, organized the Boulder City Town Company. In February 1859, he divided and sold land on either side of Boulder Creek, giving birth to the present-day city.

Boulder has always had strong educational roots. Colorado's first schoolhouse was erected at the southwest corner of Walnut and 15th St in 1860. In 1872 six of Boulder's most prominent citizens donated 44.9 acres of land in an area known as 'The Hill' for the establishment of a university. Two years later the first building, Old Main, was built with a combination of public and private dollars, and it is still standing. The University of Colorado opened its doors in September of 1877, to 44 students, one professor and a president.

In 1898, Texas educators and local leaders conspired to bring a summer-long educational and cultural festival to Boulder. Part of the famed Chautauqua Movement, it drew orators, performers and educators, who traveled a national Chautauqua circuit of more than 12,000 sites bringing lectures,

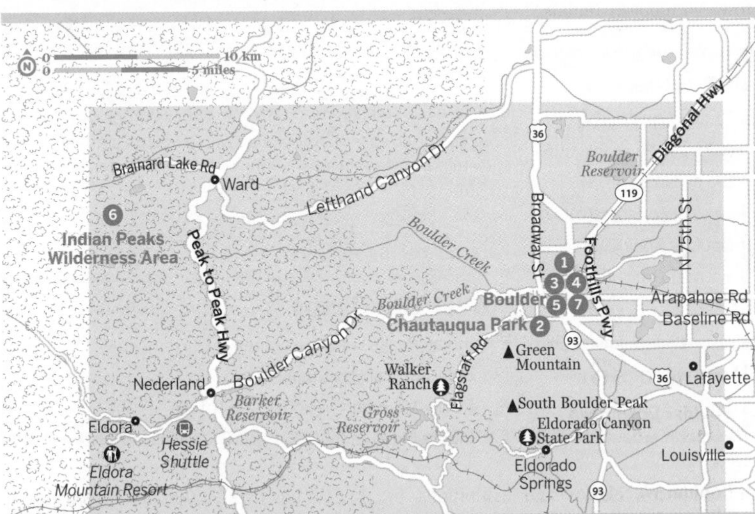

Boulder & Around Highlights

1. Coast from one end of town to the other on the scenic **Boulder Creek Bike Path** (p109).
2. Hike or pack a picnic up trails flanking the Flatirons in **Chautauqua Park** (p105).
3. Get wet paddling or tubing the **Boulder Creek** (p109) right through town.
4. Take in Shakespeare or a museum at the **University of Colorado** (p105), one of the States' finest public universities.
5. Stroll, dine, caffeinate or simply people watch on the **Pearl Street Mall** (p121).
6. Escape to the stunning backcountry of the **Indian Peaks Wilderness Area** (p127).
7. Shop for organic kale or grab exotic takeout at the **Boulder County Farmers' Market** (p116) in Central Park.

Boulder

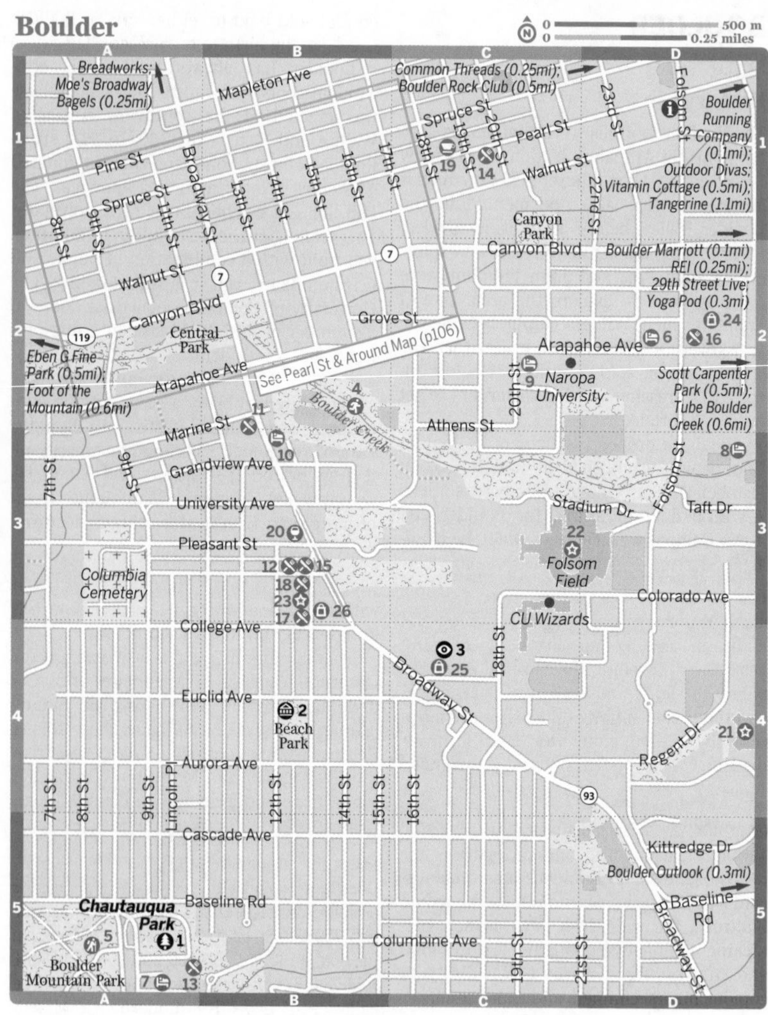

performances, classes and exhibitions to small towns and cities. Theodore Roosevelt called it, 'the most American thing in America.' Boulder's Chautauqua was completed July 4, 1898, and it had an incredible impact, not least of which was launching Boulder's parks and open-space preservation. The day after the grand opening, the city of Boulder purchased the eastern slope of Flagstaff Mountain from the United States Government.

Purchasing land for preservation became and remains one of Boulder's top priorities. It now has over 54,000 acres dedicated to parks and open space today.

In the 1950s, '60s and '70s, Boulder went through a major real-estate and business boom, with the arrival of megacompanies like IBM and Ball Aerospace and the meteoric rise of local enterprise Celestial Seasonings. Today, Boulder has around 99,000 residents and nearly 30,000 students, yet its founding themes – nature, education, culture and progress – endure.

Boulder

Top Sights
1 Chautauqua Park A5

Sights
2 Boulder History Museum B4
3 University of Colorado at Boulder C4

Activities, Courses & Tours
4 Boulder Creek Bike Path B2
5 Royal Arch Trail A5

Sleeping
6 Briar Rose B&B D2
7 Chautauqua Lodge A5
8 Millennium Harvest House D3
9 Quality Inn Boulder Creek C2
10 University Inn B3

Eating
11 Alfalfa's B2
12 Cafe Aion B3
13 Chatauqua Dining Hall A5
14 Dish C1
15 Half Fast Subs B3
16 Rincón Argentino D2
17 Salvaggio's Italian Deli B3
18 Sink B3

Drinking & Nightlife
19 Boxcar Roasters C1
20 Goose B3

Entertainment
21 CU Basketball D4
22 CU Football C3
23 Fox Theatre B3

Shopping
24 Boulder Ski Deals D2
25 CU Bookstore C4
26 Meow Meow B3

Sights

Few towns have this combination of nature and culture. Whether you're climbing the Flatirons, cycling up Flagstaff, roaming Pearl St or patrolling the campus, there are plenty of sights and activities to keep you and the family smiling. Most sites are fairly centrally located, along west Pearl St or on the Hill, where you'll also find the university.

★Chautauqua Park — PARK

(Map p104; www.chautauqua.com; 900 Baseline Rd; HOP 2) This historic landmark park is not just the gateway to Boulder's most magnificent slab of open space adjoining the iconic Flatirons: the wide, lush lawn attracts picnicking families, sunbathers, Frisbee folk, and students from nearby CU. It also gets copious hikers, climbers and trail runners.

Once an important site for the inspired rural educational organization, the Chautauqua Movement, these days the park encompasses lodgings, a good restaurant and an auditorium where world-class musicians perform each summer.

University of Colorado at Boulder — UNIVERSITY

(CU; Map p104; 303-492-6301; www.colorado.edu; Euclid Autopark; parking per hr $1.50-3; tours 9:30am & 1:30pm Mon-Fri, 10:30am Sat; P; 203, 204, 209, 225, AB, B, DASH, DD, DM, GS, J, SKIP, STAMPEDE) FREE Prospective students and curious visitors can tour one of America's finest public universities, with a beautiful campus set above downtown, on what is known as the Hill. Free tours begin with a one-hour informational session followed by a 90-minute walking tour.

Notable alumni include astronaut Scott Carpenter (one of 17 astronauts with CU diplomas), Apple's Steve Wozniak, Sidney Altman (one of six Nobel Laureates), Robert Redford (didn't graduate), *South Park* creators Trey Parker and Matt Stone (smoked a ton of dope, did graduate) and actor Jonah Hill (stopped by for one semester).

Boulder Museum of Contemporary Art — MUSEUM

(BMOCA; Map p106; 303-443-2122; www.bmoca.org; 1750 13th St; adult/child $5/free; 11am-5pm Tue-Sun; ; 203, 204, 205, 206, 208, 225, DASH, JUMP, SKIP) A historic brick house with three galleries of evocative modern art. Mixed-media exhibits can include such whimsy as neon installations and life-sized cards, while strange fashion concepts are displayed in the costume and wardrobe gallery upstairs. All exhibitions are temporary and rotate every three months. Admission is free when the farmers market blooms out the front on Wednesdays and Saturdays.

Flagstaff Mountain Trailhead — LOOKOUT

(www.osmp.org; Flagstaff Summit Rd; P) A trailhead and parking area just below the summit (elev 7283ft) and a short drive from downtown Boulder. The views over Boulder and Denver to the east are great, and the Continental Divide views to the west

Pearl St & Around

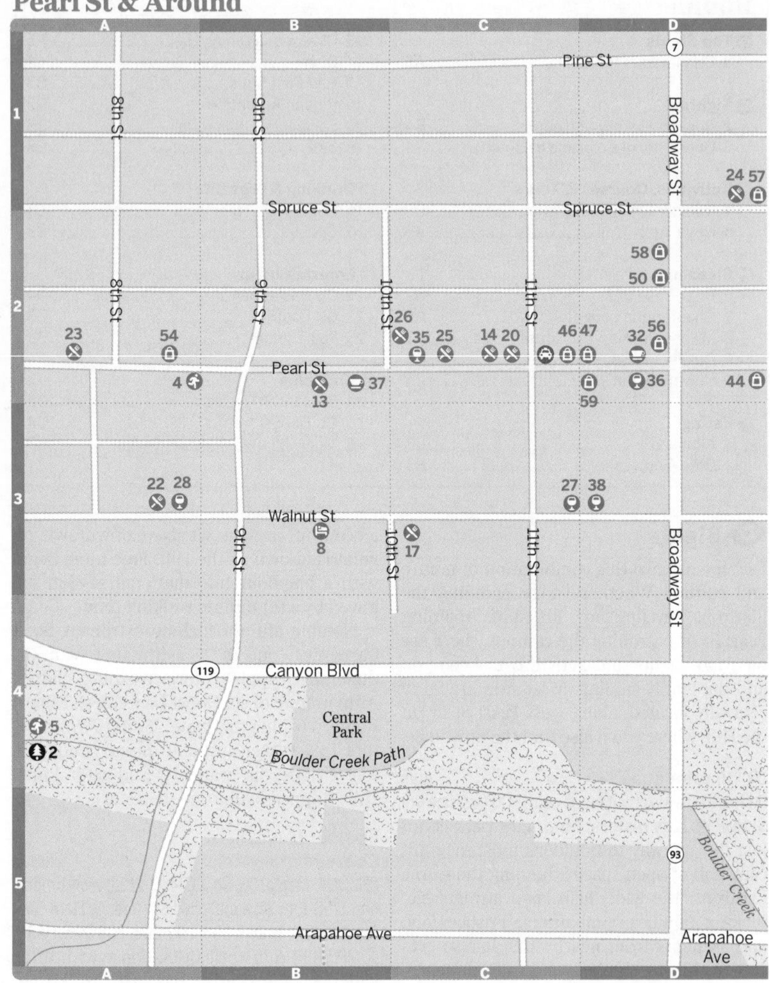

spectacular. From here, a handful of fun hikes lead to even better vistas. The super-steep climb is also popular with hardcore cyclists.

Naropa University UNIVERSITY

(Map p104; ☎303-245-4643; www.naropa.edu; 2130 Arapahoe Ave; ⏲tours 2pm Mon-Fri school year; P 👪; 🚌JUMP) FREE Founded by Tibetan Buddhist master Chögyam Trungpa Rinpoche, who escaped Tibet and climbed over the Himalayas into India as a young man. In 1970, at just 30, he began presenting teachings in the US and founded the Naropa Institute (now Naropa University) in 1974. It offers a contemplative education in psychology, environmental studies, music, performing arts and more. The university periodically hosts public talks and events.

Naropa is also home to the Jack Kerouac School of Disembodied Poetics, co-founded by his fellow Beat Allen Ginsberg, and poet Anne Waldman.

Butterfly Pavilion BOTANIC GARDEN

(www.butterflies.org; 6252 W 104th Ave, Westminster; adult/child/senior $9.50/6.50/7.50; ⏲9am-5pm; P 👪) With four indoor exhibit halls and acres of outdoor gardens fluttering with

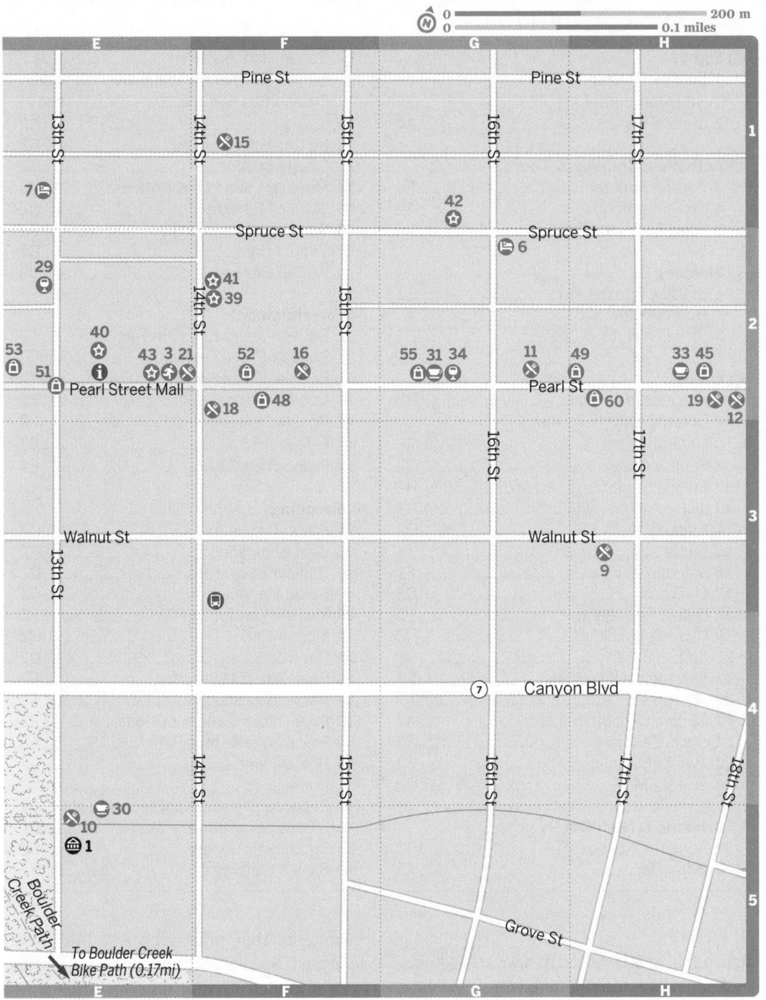

over 1200 butterflies from all the jungles and rainforests of the world – not to mention furry tarantulas, armored scorpions and fuzzy millipedes – this spot is a whirl of color, excitement and joy for the kids, and mom and dad too. It's located in Westminster, 20 miles away via Hwy 36.

Central Park PARK

(Map p106; Canyon Blvd; P 🚻; 🚌206, JUMP) A long blade of lush lawn spanning from the Contemporary Art Museum at 13th St, and encompassing the public library, a twice-weekly seasonal farmers market, the concert hatchshell and a large swatch of the Boulder Creek bike trail, it's hard to avoid this park. A ramp leads to the Boulder Creek trail and the creek itself.

Boulder Reservoir RESERVOIR

(☎303-441-3461; www.bouldercolorado.gov; 5565 N 51st St; adult/youth/senior $6.25/3.75/4.25; ⏰dawn-dusk; P 🚻) When you're this far from the ocean, this is where folks come to suntan, swim, boat and wakeboard. Dogs are not allowed into the park between May 15 and Labor Day, but are allowed in during the off-season.

Pearl St & Around

Sights

1 Boulder Museum of Contemporary Art ... E5
2 Central Park ... A4

Activities, Courses & Tours

3 Pop Jet Fountain ... E2
4 Six Persimmons ... A2
5 Yoga Rocks the Park ... A4

Sleeping

6 Bradley Boulder Inn ... G2
7 Hotel Boulderado ... E1
8 St Julien Hotel & Spa ... B3

Eating

9 Arabesque ... H3
10 Boulder County Farmers' Market ... E5
11 Foolish Craig's ... G2
12 Frasca ... H2
13 Jax ... B2
14 Kitchen ... C2
15 Lucile's ... F1
16 Mai Berry ... F2
17 Med ... C3
18 Oak at Fourteenth ... F2
19 Pizzeria Locale ... H2
20 Salt ... C2
21 Salvaggio's Italian Deli ... E2
22 Sherpa's ... A3
23 Spruce Confections ... A2
24 Sushi Zanmai ... D1
25 Two Spoons ... C2
26 Zoe Ma Ma ... C2

Drinking & Nightlife

27 Absinthe House ... C3
28 Bitter Bar ... A3
29 Bohemian Biergarten ... E2
30 Boulder Dushanbe Teahouse ... E5
Catacombs Bar ... (see 7)
31 Cup ... G2
32 Ku Cha House of Tea ... D2
33 Laughing Goat ... H2
34 Mountain Sun Pub & Brewery ... G2
35 'Round Midnight ... C2
36 Sundown Saloon ... D2
37 Trident Cafe ... B2
38 Walnut Brewery ... D3

Entertainment

39 Boulder Adventure Film Festival ... F2
Boulder Creek Festival ... (see 5)
Boulder Creek Hometown Fair ... (see 5)
40 Boulder Pride Fest ... E2
41 Boulder Theater ... F2
42 E-Town Hall ... G1
43 Proposition Gay ... E2

Shopping

44 Bayleaf on Pearl ... D2
45 Beat Book Shop ... H2
46 Boulder Bookstore ... C2
47 Goldmine Vintage ... D2
48 Into the Wind ... F2
49 Momentum ... H2
50 Oliverde ... D2
51 Pearl Street Mall ... E2
52 Pedestrian Shops ... F2
53 Peppercorn Gourmet Goods ... E2
54 Piece, Love & Chocolate ... A2
55 Posterscene ... G2
56 Prana ... D2
57 Rebecca's Herbal Apothecary ... D1
58 Savory Spice Shop ... D2
59 Smith Klein Gallery ... D2
60 Starr's Clothing Co ... H2

CU Wizards KIDS

(Map p104; ☎303-492-5011; www.colorado.edu/physics/Web/wizards/cuwizards.html; Duane Physics Bldg G1B30, Colorado Ave; ⏲program begins at 9:30am; P 👪; 🚌209, STAMPEDE) FREE Science can be cool, and kids dig the free monthly shows put on by CU's Wizards program. The science-based shows such as 'Physics of Sound' or 'Magic of Chemistry' are free, and held on one Saturday per month. Shows are geared toward fifth- to ninth-graders.

Boulder History Museum MUSEUM

(Map p104; ☎303-449-3464; www.boulderhistory.org; 1206 Euclid Ave; adult/youth/senior $6/3/4; ⏲10am-5pm Tue-Fri, noon-4pm Sat & Sun; P 👪) History buffs will want to breeze through this simple but informative museum, home to a substantial collection of old photos and documents that offer glimpses into Boulder's past. Special lectures and events range from a guided cycling tour to a history of local indigenous habitation. The first Sunday of the month is free.

Sunflower Farm FARM

(☎303-774-8001; www.sunflowerfarminfo.com; 11150 Prospect Rd; admission $7-10; ⏲closed Nov-Apr; P 👪) Set in the nearby city of Longmont, this 50-acre working farm with century-old barns welcomes families to Farmfest (its child-friendly program). Help feed baby animals, collect eggs, ride ponies and climb the giant treehouse. Opening hours and activities vary greatly by month; see the website for details.

Activities

Boulder's much-deserved reputation as an ecotopia (see: King, Stephen; *The Stand*) is rooted in the collective call for outdoors adventure. But it's also a place to go inside and tune in with your inner Om. Naropa is just one petal in the New Age/spiritual/yoga flower that's blossomed here. Aside from the various yoga studios and day spas, activities are nature oriented, with hundreds of miles of hiking and biking trails, and shady Boulder Creek running through town. Yeah, if you get bored here, it really is your own fault.

Boulder Creek Bike Path CYCLING
(Map p104; 24hr) The most utilized commuter bike path in town, this smooth and mostly straight creekside concrete path follows Boulder Creek from Foothills Parkway all the way uphill to the split of Boulder Canyon and Four Mile Canyon Rd west of downtown – a total distance of over 5 miles one-way. It also feeds urban bike lanes that lead all over town.

Six Persimmons MASSAGE
(Map p106; 303-413-9596; www.sixpersimmons.com; 840 Pearl St; 1hr massage $70-80; 10am-6pm Mon-Sat; 206) West of the Pearl Street Mall, this popular apothecary offers Chinese herbs and organic facials, and has an attached acupuncture clinic. In addition it offers a range of deep tissue, lymphatic, Swedish and sport massages by appointment. Travelers can get excellent homeopathic remedies for altitude sickness, jet lag and the common cold.

The Flatirons ROCK CLIMBING
(Chatauqua Park; HOP 2) The iconic Flatirons, three pointed rock faces that provide the backdrop to Boulder, aren't necessarily the most challenging climbs in the area, but they must be climbed. The most popular route is the Class 5.6, 10-pitch First Flatiron 'direct climb.' It's a slab crawl up 1000ft to amazing views in all directions, but it gets crowded on weekends.

The classic Third Flatiron route is the standard east face (Class 5.4, eight pitches). It's been climbed naked and in drag, but it isn't for beginners. Most push down in one 200ft 'super-rappel.' The access trail off the second-third Flatirons trail will put you at the base of this route.

Tube Boulder Creek WATER SPORTS
(720-379-6056; www.whitewatertubing.com; 3600 Arapahoe Ave; tube rental $16; 10:30am-6pm Jun-Aug) Boulder's favorite summer ritual is to pick up an inner tube at this tubing and rafting center and float down Boulder Creek from the whitewater park at **Eben G Fine Park** (Boulder Canyon Dr) to 30th St. Speak to the staff about safety.

The park's high water and sculpted ledges can get rocking in early season, and you may even get flipped. But the creek mellows below 9th St, and can get low in late summer, leaving a much more placid whitewater park as the only navigable stretch.

Valmont Bike Park PARK
(303-413-7200; www.valmontbikepark.org; Valmont Rd; 5am-11pm) FREE With dirt trails and some massive jumps, this new recreational bike park is the pride and joy of Boulder. You don't have to be an adolescent to enjoy it, but do come as padded as possible – helmet goes without saying.

Yoga Rocks the Park YOGA
(Map p106; www.yogarocksthepark.com; Central Park & Carpenter Park; per person $12; 2-4pm Aug & Sep; 206, JUMP) An ambitious melding of yoga teachings and world music. Boulder's fit, bronze yogis descend to the green grassy environs of Central Park in August or **Carpenter Park** (cnr 30th St & Arapahoe Ave) in September for this fun series that includes a sweaty asana session and some soulful live music. Discounted rate available online.

Yoga Pod YOGA
(303-444-4232; www.theyogapod.com; shop 2020 1750 29th St; adult/student & senior $17/12; 6:30am-8:45pm Mon, Tue & Thu, to 9pm Wed, to 6:45pm Fri, 9am-5:15pm Sat, to 7:15pm Sun; BOUND) One of the hippest, if most oddly located, studios in Boulder. But don't let the 29th St Mall location throw you off. There's plenty of free parking, the place isn't corporate and the instruction is first rate.

Pop Jet Fountain FOUNTAIN
(Map p106; cnr Pearl & 14th Sts; daylight hr summer; 205, 206) Bursts of water spring from the ground, sending kids squealing around in circles at this public fountain. It's a great place to bring the kiddies when the temperatures rise, but be aware that the surface underfoot isn't soft.

★Royal Arch Trail HIKING
(Map p104; Chatauqua Park) Challenging but not excruciating, this roughly two-hour, 3.6-mile, well-signed trail leads you up along the Flatirons, through a vaguely red-rock canyon, then through a keyhole and up to a wonderful natural rock arch where you'll perch on boulders, gaze at the Boulder basin and, on clear days, glimpse the Denver skyline. Grab a trail map at the park office before hiking.

Wonderland Lake Trailhead WALKING
(www.osmp.org; 4201 N Broadway St; SKIP) This easily accessed North Boulder trailhead links to 2.4 miles of trails within the City of Boulder's terrific open space mountain parks program. Fairly flat trails skirt a lovely artificial lake, surrounded by knee-high grasses and tucked up against the foothills. Dogs must be leashed.

Boulder Falls Trail HIKING
(www.bouldercolorado.gov; Boulder Canyon Dr) A quick and easy ramble along the upper reaches of Boulder Creek and into its headwaters. This trail begins approximately 10 miles west of downtown Boulder, bends into a cozy but dramatic canyon with soaring granite walls and ends at Boulder Falls, which alternates between trickling and gushing depending upon the season. A bit over 1-mile roundtrip.

Boulder Rock Club ROCK CLIMBING
(303-447-2804; http://boulderrockclub.com; 2829 Mapleton Ave; day pass adult/child $17/10; 8am-10pm Mon, 6am-11pm Tue-Thu, 8am-11pm Fri, 10am-8pm Sat & Sun) An incredible indoor climbing gym popular with local rock rats. This massive warehouse is full of artificial rock faces cragged with ledges and routes, and the auto-belay system allows solo climbers an anchor. Lessons and courses available, with a special kids' program. Staff are a great resource for local climbing routes.

Eldorado Canyon State Park OUTDOORS
(303-494-3943; visitor center 9am-5pm) Among the country's best rock-climbing areas, Eldorado has Class 5.5 to 5.12 climbs. Suitable to all visitors, a dozen miles of hiking trails also link up to Chautauqua Park. A public pool (summer only) offers chilly swims in the canyon's famous spring water.

BOULDER IN...

Two Days

No matter what time of year you land here, the first stop should always be **Chautaqua Park** (p105). If you think ahead, stop by **Arabesque** (p114) or **Dish** (p116) and bring your lunch with you. Grind on the rocks or lay out a blanket on the Chautauqua lawn. A great leg burner is the 4-mile round-trip hike to **Royal Arch** (p110). Afterwards, head down to the **Pearl Street Mall** (p121) and explore Boulder's historic downtown, then dine on fresh seafood at **Jax** (p118).

Wake up to Boulder's best brunch at **Tangerine** (p114). Grab two wheels off one of the many bike-share racks around town and explore the **Boulder Creek Bike Path** (p109). Or get a lighter roadbike and join the lycra-clad maniacs pedaling up **Flagstaff Mountain** (p105). Cap your day with happy hour drinks at the **Bitter Bar** (p119) for a Prohibition-era cocktail before an amazing locavore dinner at **Salt** (p118). Catch a show at the **Boulder Theater** (p120) or **E-Town Hall** (p120).

Four Days

In four days you can cover all of the above and overlap with one of Boulder's fabulous **farmers markets** (p116), held in Central Park on Wednesdays and Saturdays. But first, work up an appetite at one of Boulder's famed yoga studios, then head to the **Walnut** (p120) or **Mountain Sun Pub & Brewery** (p118) for an IPA. Grab a sidewalk stool and dig into a fragrant bowl of fresh Asian noodles at **Zoe Ma Ma** (p114) then get down and dirty at one of the dive bars, such as **Catacombs** (p119) or the **Sundown** (p120).

The following day, grab an early breakfast at **Moe's Broadway Bagels** (p117), then drive up to **Nederland** (p125) and go for a hike or mountain bike ride amid alpine environs. Get back in time for happy hour at the **Med** (p117), where a good cross-section of town munches cheap and tasty tapas. Stroll down the street to the **Absinthe House** (p119) for a taste of the hot, new club scene.

The park entrance is on Eldorado Springs Dr. Take Hwy 93 south from Boulder, head west on Hwy 170 to the park gates. For climbing tips, visit the Boulder Rock Club beforehand.

Tours

★Local Table Tours FOOD TOUR
(☎303-909-5747; www.localtabletours.com; tours $25-70) Go behind the scenes with one of these fun downtown walking tours presenting a smattering of great local cuisine and inside knowledge on food and wine or coffee and pastries. The tour also tries to highlight locally owned businesses with regional or sustainable food sources. The cocktail crawl is a hit.

Banjo Billy Tour BUS TOUR
(☎720-938-8885; www.banjobilly.com; adult/child $22/12) These acclaimed and entertaining 90-minute bus tours, some undertaken by the garrulous tour founder himself, mine city history for quirky tidbits and little-known incidents. Tours depart from downtown. Tickets are available online.

Festivals & Events

Boulder Creek Festival MUSIC, FOOD
(Map p106; ☎303-449-3137; www.bceproductions.com; Canyon Blvd, Central Park; ⊙May; 🚌206, JUMP) FREE Billed as the kick-off to summer and capped with the Bolder Boulder, this summer festival is massive. Over 10 event areas feature more than 30 live entertainers and 500 vendors. There will be food and drink, music and sunshine. What's not to love?

Bolder Boulder ATHLETICS
(☎303-444-7223; www.bolderboulder.com; adult from $59; ⊙May) With 54,000 runners and pros mingling with costumed racers, live bands and sideline merrymakers, this may be the most fun 10k in America, ending at the CU Stadium.

★Conference on World Affairs EVENT
(www.colorado.edu/cwa; CU Campus; ⊙early Apr) FREE This fantastic week-long event brings the campus and town together with excellent public lectures, films, music, panel discussions and debates. Presentations are given by top thinkers, artists, politicos and economists. It's really an inspiring time. In its 66th year, topics change yearly.

Colorado Shakespeare Festival THEATER
(☎303-492-8008; www.coloradoshakes.org; CU Campus; $18-54; ⊙Jun–mid-Aug) For over half a century, summer has professional actors putting on the Bard's tragedies and comedies in the lovely outdoor amphitheater at CU. The highly acclaimed series is a Boulder highlight.

29th Street Live MUSIC
(☎303-449-3137; www.bceproductions.com; 29th St Mall; ⊙various Fri & Sat Jun-Aug; 🚌205, 206, BOLT, BOUND) Boulder's corporate mall goes rock and roll on selected summer nights. Crowds can get thick and the surroundings aren't the greatest, but live bands are like pizza – good, bad…who cares? There's music in the air!

Boulder Adventure Film Festival FILM
(Map p106; www.adventurefilm.org; 2032 14th St; from $15; ⊙Oct; 🚌208) Held in early October at the Boulder Theater, this high-caliber outdoor-adventure film fest celebrates the great outdoors and the things we do in it.

Boulder Creek Hometown Fair SUMMER FESTIVAL
(Map p106; ☎303-449-3137; www.bceproductions.com; Central Park, Canyon Blvd; ⊙Labor Day Weekend; 🚌203, 204, 225, AB, B, DASH, DD, DM, GS, SKIP) This Labor Day fest caps summer with plenty of laughs, including a pie-eating contest, the Great Zucchini Race (yes, zucchinis are outfitted with wheels) and live music.

Boulder Pride Fest LGBT
(Map p106; ☎303-499-5777; www.outboulder.org; ⊙mid-Sep; 🚌208) A diverse, joyful party at Central Park. There are poetry performances and live music, speeches from community leaders, and a fair amount of wellness and health-care information.

Lights of December CHRISTMAS
(⊙1st Sat in Dec) Community floats, Scouts dressed as snowflakes, marching bands and Santa. The parade loops Pearl Street Mall.

Sleeping

With lodging that's generally overpriced, booking online can help. Special packages range from spa treatments to meal coupons or champagne.

Lodgings here are listed in order of preference within each price range.

Foot of the Mountain MOTEL $
(☎303-442-5688; www.footofthemountainmotel.com; 200 Arapahoe Ave; s/d incl breakfast

City Walk
Boulder Walk

START: CHAUTAUQUA PARK
END: BOULDER THEATER
LENGTH: 4.8 MILES; 4½ HOURS

Boulder isn't huge, but it's big enough to have pockets with different personalities. Begin at 1 **Chautauqua Park** (p105), which marked the city's initial foray into open-space preservation, a notion that now defines the city. The Chatauqua Dining Hall serves a hearty breakfast on the wraparound porch. From here, walk downhill along Baseline Rd and turn right along 9th St through one of Boulder's oldest residential neighborhoods. Turn right on Euclid Ave to the 2 **Boulder History Museum** (p108), set in one of Boulder's historic homes. Continue east on Euclid before turning left onto 13th St.

This is the Hill, a tumbledown student district with hipster-slacker appeal that is the grist of any good college town. Imbibe college life by stepping into the graffiti-clad 3 **Sink** (p116), where young Robert Redford once toiled before stardom. Continue to Broadway. Make a right onto Pleasant St, and head onto the 4 **University of Colorado** (p105) campus. Cut left after Varsity Lake and follow the walking path straight through to 17th St. Exit campus here and descend the short hill to join the 5 **Boulder Creek Bike Path** (p109).

Walk along the gurgling creek until you hit 6 **Central Park** (p107) and the 7 **Boulder Museum of Contemporary Art** (p105). On Wednesday or Saturday you can enjoy the Boulder County Farmers' Market. Stop to see the striking 8 **Dushanbe Teahouse** (p115) from Boulder's sister city.

Continue west on 13th St to Boulder's historic downtown center. If it's happy hour, stop in at 9 **Bohemian Biergarten** (p119), just past Pearl Street. Double back a block to enjoy the 10 **Pearl Street Mall** (p121) and its renowned street performers like the Yogi in a Box and Zip Code Man pleasing crowds. Browse the three-story 11 **Boulder Bookstore** (p121) before strolling Spruce St. Check out the historic 12 **Hotel Boulderado** (p114) before finishing your tour with a show at the **Boulder Theater** (p120).

$75/90; P ❄ @ 📶 👪 🐾) Nothing fancy here, but plenty of family-owned, wood-paneled charm. The motel itself looks like a cabin has been stretched out and bent around a parking lot, then tucked into a wooded glen literally at the foot of Flagstaff Mountain. Rooms are more quirky than comfy but therein lies its charm, and considering the competition, it's good value at this price.

University Inn MOTEL **$**
(Map p104; ☎303-417-1700; www.boulderuniversityinn.com; 1632 Broadway St; d $96; 🚌AB, B, JUMP, SKIP) While a Boulder motel room seems like robbery compared to its Kansan counterparts, keep in mind *it is Boulder*. Perks from this longtime business include the central location, friendly staff and decent rooms. Bicycles are available for loan and it's located just off the main bikepath.

★**Chautauqua Lodge** HISTORIC HOTEL **$$**
(Map p104; ☎303-442-3282; www.chautauqua.com; 900 Baseline Rd; r from $73, cottages $125-183; P ❄ 📶 👪 🐾; 🚌HOP 2) Adjoining beautiful hiking trails to the Flatirons, these cottages, in a leafy neighborhood inside Chautauqua Park, is our top pick. It has contemporary rooms and bedroom cottages with porches, and beds with patchwork quilts. It's perfect for families and pets. All have full kitchens, though the wraparound porch of the Chautauqua Dining Hall is a local favorite for breakfast.

★**Briar Rose B&B** B&B **$$**
(Map p104; ☎303-442-3007; 2151 Arapahoe Ave; s $139-194, d $164-219; ❄ 📶; 🚌JUMP) Gorgeous and comfy, this tranquil home is a stone's throw from Naropa University. A tall fence and landscaped garden insulate it from busy Arapahoe Ave. Inside there are cozy rooms with a Buddhist influence – no wonder since it doubles as the Boulder Zen Center. The organic vegetarian breakfast features a wide tea selection and there's one loaner bike.

Quality Inn Boulder Creek MOTEL **$$**
(Map p104; ☎303-449-7550; www.qualityinnboulder.com; 2020 Arapahoe Ave; r from $150; 🚭 ❄ 📶 🏊 👪; 🚌JUMP) A forest-green-tinted brick and shingled inn a short walk from downtown, this exceptionally well-run chain is anything but bland. Rooms are sizable and have a touch of class (read: cush linens and flatscreen TVs). Staff are top notch. This is one of the best-value stays in Boulder.

Boulder Outlook HOTEL **$**
(☎303-443-3322, 800-542-0304; www.boulderoutlook.com; 800 28th St; d incl breakfast $89-99; P ❄ 📶 🏊 👪 🐾) 🌿 Boulder's first zero-waste hotel is just off the highway at the south end of town, offering easy access from Denver. With funky colors, a sustainability focus and pet-friendly atm osphere, it feels very Boulder indeed. Strangely, motel-style rooms with outdoor access are less expensive than their counterparts in the main building with a dimly lit indoor pool and climbing wall.

The onsite restaurant and bar often hosts blues bands.

Twin Lakes Inn HOTEL **$$**
(☎303-530-2939; www.twinlakesinnboulder.com; 6485 Twin Lakes Rd; r $108-217; P ❄ 📶 👪 🐾; 🚌205W) Owned by a former Olympian, this aging midranger set in northeast Boulder is both far from fancy and from the center of town. Still, rooms are large and it accepts pets and has laundry facilities. Plus it's within walking distance of the Twin Lakes along a gravel trail. Some rooms have sofa beds and sleep up to six.

Boulder Mountain Lodge HOTEL **$$**
(☎303-444-0882; www.bouldermountainlodge.com; 91 Four Mile Canyon Rd; r from $98, cabin $194; P ❄ 📶 👪; 🚌N) Set in shady Four Mile Canyon, west of Boulder off Hwy 119, this family-owned and -operated lodge in the mountains is gorgeously placed amid pines and cottonwood trees. It offers a rather homey cabin, as well as clean, motel-style rooms with kitchenettes. The kids' fishing pond is a plus.

St Julien Hotel & Spa HOTEL **$$$**
(Map p106; ☎720-406-9696, reservations 877-303-0900; www.stjulien.com; 900 Walnut St; r from $309; P ❄ @ 📶 🏊 👪) In the heart of downtown, Boulder's finest four-star option is modern and refined, with photographs of local scenery and cork walls that warm the ambience. With fabulous Flatiron views, the back patio hosts live world music, jazz concerts and wild salsa parties. Rooms are plush, and so are the robes.

Bradley Boulder Inn INN **$$$**
(Map p106; ☎303-545-5200; www.thebradleyboulder.com; 2040 16th St; d with breakfast $264; 🚌HOP) An elegant downtown Boulder mansion with polished wood, local art and stained glass salvaged from a nearby church, this is a great upscale option. More regal than cozy, it still does the job with great

service, complimentary tea and baked goods and an afternoon wine-and-cheese hour. Rooms are unique, some with fireplaces, Jacuzzis or balconies.

Hotel Boulderado BOUTIQUE HOTEL **$$$**
(Map p106; ☎303-442-4344; www.boulderado.com; 2115 13th St; r from $264; P ❄ 📶; 🚌HOP, SKIP) With a century of service, the charming Boulderado, full of Victorian elegance and wonderful public spaces, is a National Register landmark and a romantic getaway. Each antique-filled room is uniquely decorated. The stained-glass atrium and glacial water– fountain accent the jazz-washed lobby. Guesthouse rooms across the street are slightly bigger and cheaper, but lack the historical gravitas.

The Alps B&B **$$$**
(☎303-444-5445; www.alpsinn.com; 38619 Boulder Canyon Dr; r $204-279; P ❄ @ 📶; 🚌N) Constructed in the 1870s, this inn charms with Mission furnishings, stained-glass windows and antique fireplaces. Many rooms feature private Jacuzzi for two with French doors leading to a garden, patio or private porch with views of Boulder Creek and the canyon. The generous spa amenities appeal to couples looking for a romantic stop.

Boulder Marriott HOTEL **$$$**
(☎303-440-8877; www.marriott.com; 2660 Canyon Blvd; r $230-260; P ❄ @ 📶 👪; 🚌205, 206, BOLT) One of the better options in town, this peach-tinted chain opens up to the west, which means top-floor rooms get beautiful Flatiron views. Rooms are far from fashionable but they are comfortable and spacious with a desk, sofa and queen bed. Well run, it's less a resort and more of a business hotel with free wi-fi in the lobby and hard-line internet in rooms for a fee.

If you're into amenities, it's not a bad splurge.

Millennium Harvest House HOTEL **$$$**
(Map p104; ☎303-443-3850; www.millenniumhotels.com; 1345 28th St; r $135-239; P ❄ @ 📶 🏊 👪; 🚌HX, S) Dated, formerly grand, but still a plush resort, the cylindrical flagstone and stucco Millennium has a large footprint that sprawls nearly to the edge of Boulder Creek. This place has been alive since the 1950s, and it still has the most rooms in town, along with enough zip to make you feel just a little bit like Don Draper.

Rooms are fairly large, if garishly decorated, and those in the main building have wide verandas overlooking the Flatirons; the garden includes two pools and 15 tennis courts.

Eating

Long a haven for vegetarians, Boulder's food scene is evolving. Farm to table is today's buzz phrase, and local food graces the twice-weekly farmers market and stylish restaurants. There's still a nod to health – eateries cater to everything from gluten-free to paleo diets. But beyond that, there is a marked upswing in quality, with sophistication to rival the big cities. No wonder *Bon Appetit* magazine rated Boulder the foodiest town in America.

★**Tangerine** BREAKFAST **$**
(☎303-443-2333; tangerineboulder.com; 2777 Iris Ave; mains $6-12; ⏰7am-2:30pm; 🚌BOUND) 🌿 It's worth leaving the downtown bubble for this true treat of a breakfast spot in a nondescript shopping plaza. Think polenta with poached eggs, spinach and romesco sauce, impeccable Benedicts, smoothies and ricotta lemon pancakes with blueberry sauce. The combinations are original and very well done. Sweet servers pour bottomless cups of organic coffee at tables with bright orange booths.

Arabesque MIDDLE EASTERN **$**
(Map p106; arabesqueboulder.com; 1634 Walnut St; $9-12; ⏰9am-3pm Mon-Sat; 🚌204) This authentic family-run enterprise hits the sweet spot with excellent, slightly smoky baba ganoush, fresh tabouleh and shawarma wraps made with fresh bread and plenty of greens. Cold tea comes with fresh mint and chunks of summer fruit. The food is clean-tasting and light and the chef personally greets most customers. The setting is a brick cafe with shady patio seating.

Zoe Ma Ma CHINESE **$**
(Map p106; 2010 10th St; mains $5-13; ⏰11am-10pm Sun-Thu, 11am-11pm Fri & Sat; 🚌206, SKIP, HOP) 🌿 At Boulder's hippest noodle bar you can find fresh street food at a long outdoor counter. Mama, the Taiwanese matriarch, is on hand, cooking and chatting up customers in her Crocs. Organic noodles are made from scratch, as are the garlicky melt-in-your-mouth pot stickers.

CAFFEINE EXPLOSION!

If you love lattes or kombucha tea, Boulder literally explodes with cafes, with its diverse options tailored toward lycra-clad cyclists, university students or bohemian life. These are our favorites.

Laughing Goat (Map p106; ☎303-440-4628; www.thelaughinggoat.com; 1709 Pearl St; ⏲6am-11pm Mon-Fri, from 7am Sat & Sun; 📶; 🚌203, 204, 205, 206, 208, 225, DASH, JUMP) Sure, the ambience might be diminished by the glow of two-dozen laptops, but the coffee is good enough (served in pint glasses too!) and locally roasted. The scene revolves around eyeballing college co-eds and tapping away at term papers – at least until the singer-songwriters start up. It hosts many up-and-coming musical acts.

Cup (Map p106; ☎303-449-5173; www.thecupboulder.com; 1521 Pearl St; ⏲7am-10pm; 📶; 🚌204, HOP) This groovy loftlike space opens onto Pearl St, pouring forth a tempting whiff of damn good coffee and handpicked organic loose-leaf teas. It also does fresh quiche, wonderful cakes in cups, burly sandwiches and swift wi-fi. No wonder it draws the comely and studious in numbers. Monday is open-mike night.

Boxcar Roasters (Map p104; 1825 Pearl St; ⏲8am-6pm Mon-Sat, 8am-5pm Sun; 🚌HOP) Asserting a PhD approach, this is the hot roaster of the moment, offering single-pour beaker coffee that purists swear by, set in minimalist-hipster ambience. Bags of beans are reasonably priced. There's also an interesting wine shop onsite and a great deli with craft cheeses and lovely, thick-crust bread.

Trident Cafe (Map p106; ☎303-443-3133; www.tridentcafe.com; 940 Pearl St; ⏲6:30am-11pm Mon-Sat, 7am-11pm Sun; 🚌206, SKIP) Brick walls, worn wood floors and red-vinyl booths steeped in the aromatic uplift of damn good espresso. The attached bookstore sells used and collectible titles. Add in the shady back-garden patio and fine tea selection and you'll understand why this is the longtime favorite of Boulder's literary set. A thousand secrets and plot lines have been shared and hatched here.

Boulder Dushanbe Teahouse (Map p106; ☎303-442-4993; 1770 13th St; mains $8-19; ⏲8am-10pm; 🚌203, 204, 205, 206, 208, 225, DASH, JUMP, SKIP) It's impossible to find better ambience than this incredible Tajik teahouse, a gift from Dushanbe, Boulder's sister city. The elaborate carvings and paintings were reassembled over a decade on central park's edge. It's too bad the fusion fare is surprisingly dull, but it's worth coming for a pot of tea.

Ku Cha House of Tea (Map p106; ☎303-443-3612; www.kuchatea.com; 1141 Pearl St; ⏲10am-9pm Mon-Sat, 11am-6pm Sun; 🚌208) This traditional Chinese teahouse has an enormous selection of imported loose-leaf tea, including rare finds. Upstairs, patrons snuggle over steaming cups in quiet booths. Snacks like mochi rice cake fuel the mood.

Breadworks CAFE $

(☎303-444-5667; www.breadworks.net; 2644 Broadway St; meals $8-12; ⏲7am-7pm Mon-Fri, to 6pm Sat & Sun; 🅿👪; 🚌208, SKIP) To live like a local, head to this North Boulder mecca for fresh-made soups, sumptuous pastries and breads. Salads are tossed before your eyes at the marble food bar where you'll also find pastas, gelato and hot but healthy main dishes. Cafeteria-style serving and ample seating helps you get in a quick meal that still satisfies.

Rincón Argentino ARGENTINE $

(Map p104; 2525 Arapahoe Ave; mains $3-12; ⏲11am-8pm Tue-Sun; 🚌JUMP) Hidden in a shopping plaza is a whollop of authentic Argentina. It bakes fresh empanadas – savory, small turnovers filled with spiced meat, or mozzarella and basil – which are perfect with a glass of malbec. It also offers *milanesas*-breaded beef cutlet sandwiches – and gourds of *yerba mate,* a high-octane coffee alternative.

Spruce Confections BAKERY $

(Map p106; ☎303-449-6773; 767 Pearl St; cookies from $3.25; ⏲6:30am-6pm Mon-Fri, 7am-6pm Sat & Sun; 👪; 🚌206) Boulder's go-to bakehouse, where the favorites are the Ol' B Cookie (chocolate, oats, cinnamon and coconut) and the Black Bottom Cupcake (chocolate with cheesecake filling). Pair either with the Spruce Juice, possibly the world's greatest iced vanilla latte. It has sinful scones, good homemade soups and salads too. There's a another branch at 4684 Broadway.

Dish SANDWICHES $
(Map p104; ☎720-565-5933; www.dishgourmet.com; 1918 Pearl St; mains $10; ⏰9am-6pm Mon-Fri, 11am-4pm Sat; 👪; 🚌204, HOP) Bank-length lines flank this gourmet deli at lunchtime. At $10 the sandwiches are hardly cheap but they are satisfying. Think roasted turkey carved in chunks, pate, natural beef, slow-cooked brisket and baguettes smothered with butter and top-tier cheeses. Side salads are alluring too.

Two Spoons GELATO $
(Map p106; ☎303-545-0027; www.twospoonsboulder.com; 1021 Pearl St; snacks $5; ⏰11am-8pm Mon-Wed, to 11pm Thu & Sun, to midnight Sat, seasonal variations; 👪; 🚌HOP, 203, 206, 225) Boulder's best gelato shop features homemade flavors like cappuccino brownie and fresh mint almond. It also serves excellent soups and light lunches.

Alfalfa's SELF-CATERING $
(Map p104; www.alfalfas.com; 1651 Broadway St; ⏰7:30am-10pm; 🚌AB, B, JUMP, SKIP) A small, community-oriented natural market with a wonderful selection of prepared food and an inviting indoor-outdoor dining area to enjoy it in.

Foolish Craig's AMERICAN $
(Map p106; ☎303-247-9383; www.foolishcraigs.com; 1611 Pearl St; mains $6-14; ⏰8am-10pm Mon-Sat, to 9pm Sun; 🚌204, HOP) A longtime, much loved breakfast joint famous for its build-your-own omelets and crepes. The more upscale dinner menu is worth trying, with options such as pulled pork, pan-seared trout and fried brussel sprout leaves with warm Brie.

Sink PUB FOOD $
(Map p104; www.thesink.com; 1165 13th St; mains $5-12; ⏰11am-2am, kitchen to 10pm; 🐾; 🚌203, 204, 225, DASH, SKIP) A Hill landmark since 1923, the low-slung, graffiti-scrawled Sink even employed Robert Redford during his CU years. While he dropped out, it hasn't. The dimly lit, cavernous space still churns out legendary Sink burgers and slugs of local microbrews to the latest generation of students.

Pupusa's MEXICAN, SALVADORIAN $
(☎303-444-1729; 4457 N Broadway St; mains $2.50-10; ⏰10am-9pm Mon-Fri, 9am-9pm Sat, 10am-8pm Sun; 👪; 🚌SKIP) Simple and soulful Salvadorian and Mexican food (pupusas, tacos, tortas and burritos) served in heaping portions at affordable prices in a sweet, pastel-brushed setting. A humble breath of fresh air to be sure.

Salvaggio's Italian Deli SANDWICHES $
(Map p106; ☎303-938-1981; kiosk at 14th & Pearl Sts; sandwiches $4-8; ⏰8am-6:30pm Mon-Fri, 8-11am Sat & Sun; 👪; 🚌205) Serving excellent East Coast–style subs, this busy kiosk and shop offers classic goodies such as slow-roasted prime rib subs, served on a fresh, crusty roll and dressed with horseradish and veggies. Use the nearby public benches for a simple picnic. There's also a **branch** (Map p104; 1107 13th St) on the hill.

Half Fast Subs SANDWICHES $
(Map p104; ☎303-449-0404; www.halffastsubs.com; 1215 13th St; subs $7-10; ⏰10:30am-midnight Mon, Thu & Fri, to 11pm Tue & Wed, 11am-midnight Sat, to 10pm Sun; 👪; 🚌203, 204, 225, DASH, SKIP) Deal with the line at lunch, or come for a happy hour that's 'guaranteed to kick your butt,' (the 32oz Long Island Ice Tea suggests they're serious). The extensive sandwich board has tons of stuff for vegetarians, including baked tofu. Meat eaters should go for a gooey cheesesteak.

Mai Berry FROZEN YOGURT $
(Map p106; ☎303-444-0483; www.maiberry.com; 1433 Pearl St; ⏰10am-10pm Tue-Sun, to 9pm Sat; 🚌Boulder Transport Center) With a patter of techno, this tart hipster fro-yo with mashed fruit delivers. Also serves smoothies and fresh juice.

Boulder County Farmers' Market MARKET $
(Map p106; ☎303-910-2236; www.boulderfarmers.org; 13th St btwn Canyon & Arapahoe; ⏰8am-2pm Sat Apr-Nov, 4-8pm Wed May-Oct; 🚌203, 204, 205, 206, 208, 225, DASH, JUMP, SKIP) A massive spring and summer sprawl of colorful, mostly organic local food. Here you can find flowers and herbs, as well as brain-sized mushrooms, delicate squash blossoms, crusty pretzels, vegan dips, grass-fed beef, raw granola and yogurt. The market borders the Boulder Museum of Contemporary Art, which offers free admission on market days.

Prepared food booths offer ethnic fare from Vietnamese to Mexican. Live music is as standard as the family picnics in the park along Boulder Creek.

Vitamin Cottage SELF-CATERING $
(☎303-402-1400; www.vitamincottage.com; 2355 30th St; ⏰9am-4pm Mon-Sat, 10am-6pm Sun; 👪; 🚌BOUND) Set in the same minimall complex

as the Whole Foods flagship, this less corporate and more affordable organic full-service grocer makes a nice alternative supply line for self-caterers.

Moe's Broadway Bagels CAFE $
(☎303-444-3252; www.moesbagel.com; 2650 Broadway St; bagels from $2; ⏰5:30am-5pm; P 👪; 🚌208, SKIP) Welcome to Boulder's preeminent bagel boiling and baking house – not that there's a lot of competition. You'll glimpse the trays of dough slide into the vat of briny water as you step up to the colorful menu that strays from bagels and bagel sandwiches to subs, breakfast burritos and pizza. But, listen, don't get fancy. It's the bagels. The bagels.

★**Oak at Fourteenth** MODERN AMERICAN $$
(Map p106; ☎303-444-3622; http://oakatfourteenth.com; 1400 Pearl St; ⏰11:30am-10pm Mon-Wed, Thu-Fri 11:30am-12am, 2:30pm-12am Sat, 2:30-10pm Sun; 🚌205, 206) Zesty and innovative, locally owned Oak manufactures top-notch cocktails and tasty small plates for stylish diners. Standouts include the smoky grilled eggplant in romanesco sauce and cucumber sashimi drizzled with passion fruit. Portions at this farm-to-table eatery are minimal – when it's this scrumptious you notice. Servers know all and advise well. The only downside: it tends to be noisy, so save your intimate confessions.

Cafe Aion SPANISH $$
(Map p104; ☎303-993-8131; www.cafeaion.com; 1235 Pennsylvania Ave; tapas $5-13; ⏰11am-10pm Tue-Fri, 9am-3pm Sat & Sun; 🚌203, 204, 225, DASH, SKIP) Though fancy fare on the Hill sounds odd, don't skip this one. Original and unpretentious, this side-street cafe captures the relaxed rhythms of Spain with fresh tapas and delectable house-made sangria. Papas bravas wedges have the perfect crisp, and the grilled spring onions and dolmas are light and flavorful. Happy hour goes all night on Tuesdays.

Pizzeria Locale PIZZERIA $$
(Map p106; ☎303-442-3003; localeboulder.com; 1730 Pearl Street; pizzas $9-17; ⏰Mon-Thu 11:30am-2pm, 4:30-10:30pm, Fri & Sat 11:30am-10:30pm, Sun 11:30am-9pm; 🚌204, HOP) The obvious choice for a slice with style. Beloved stepchild of upscale Frasca (they share a kitchen), this southern Italian–style pizzeria fills with locals at the bar sipping *aperol* spritzers and house wine on barrel tap. Starters like *arancini* (risotto balls with a hint of orange) show off street cred. For deals, come between 4:30pm and 5:30pm.

The double-zero crust and a fast, super-hot firing produces pies that are crispy and chewy. While Margarita is a well-done classic, combinations like egg and corn offer a happy surprise.

Lucile's CAJUN $$
(Map p106; ☎303-442-4743; www.luciles.com; 2142 14th St; mains $8-14; ⏰7am-2pm Mon-Fri, from 8am Sat & Sun; 👪; 🚌205, 206, HOP) 🍃 This New Orleans–style diner has perfected breakfast, and the Creole egg dishes (served over creamy spinach alongside cheesy grits or perfectly blackened trout) are the thing to order. Start with a steaming mug of chai or chicory coffee and an order of beignets. Powder sugar–drenched beignets are the house specialty. Go early or be prepared to wait.

Proto's Pizza PIZZERIA $$
(☎720-565-1050; www.protospizza.com; 4670 N Broadway St; pizzas $6-20; ⏰11am-9pm Sun-Thu, to 10pm Fri & Sat; 🚌SKIP) The best family pizza joint sits at the northern tip of Broadway, where parking is still plentiful (for now). Rich and savory thin-crust pies are served in an inviting interior with a full bar, or outdoors. Friday night is popular for the fresh clams and garlic pizza. Salads are fresh and well dressed, and there are gluten-free crusts available.

Med MEDITERRANEAN $$
(Map p106; ☎303-444-5335; www.themedboulder.com; 1002 Walnut St; mains $11-27; ⏰10am-10pm Sun-Thu, to 11pm Fri & Sat; 🚌HOP, 206) A Boulder classic, this friendly, festive joint brings all the many flavors of the Mediterranean under one roof (and patio). Best of all, it's consistently good. Think wood-fired pizza, gyros and terrific tapas from gambas to bacon-wrapped dates to bruschetta. It has a full bar and worthwhile desserts, and is known for its happy-hour deals. Draws a fun crowd.

Chatauqua Dining Hall AMERICAN $$
(Map p104; ☎303-440-3776; www.chautauquadininghall.com; Chautauqua Park; breakfast mains $7-13, dinner mains $8-26; ⏰8am-3pm & 5pm-close Mon-Fri, 8am-close Sat & Sun; 👪; 🚌HOP 2) With prime real estate in Chatauqua Park, this big farmhouse with a wrap-around porch is a favorite of hikers, especially for breakfast. Service isn't speedy, nor is the food a standout compared to all the local offerings – it's all ambience. The menu is

farm-to-table, supplied with produce and cured meats from a local farm.

Sushi Zanmai SUSHI $$

(Map p106; 303-440-0733; www.sushizanmai.com; 1221 Spruce St; mains $6-21; 11:30am-2pm & 5-10pm Mon-Fri, 5pm-midnight Sat, to 10pm Sun; 208, SKIP) Fresh, good and kind of goofy. The chefs shout with delight as customers fill the space, which they do early and often. Kimono-clad waitstaff serve platters of sushi, grilled and brushed eel, toro hand rolls and specialty house rolls like the Colorado, with raw filet mignon. Trout, a common sushi in the mountains of Japan, is worth trying here.

Sherpa's NEPALESE $$

(Map p106; 303-440-7151; 825 Walnut St; mains $9-15; 11am-3pm & 5:30-9:30pm Mon-Fri, 11am-3pm & 5:30-10pm Sat & Sun; 206) A friendly, fun Nepalese cafe set in a converted home at the edge of downtown. Dishes are simple, home-style choices such as Tofu Aloo and a hearty Sherpa Stew. Lunch specials are cheap, and the vine-shaded patio is a great spot for a mango lassi on a summer afternoon. The chef has summited Mt Everest 10 times!

★**Frasca** ITALIAN $$$

(Map p106; 303-442-6966; www.frascafoodandwine.com; 1738 Pearl St; mains $28; 5:30-10:30pm; HOP, 204) Deemed Boulder's finest by many (the wine service earned a James Beard award), Frasca has an impeccable kitchen and only the freshest farm-to-table ingredients. Rotating dishes range from earthy braised pork to house-made gnocchi and grilled quail served with leeks and wilted pea shoots. Reserve days or even weeks in advance. Mondays offer 'bargain' $50 set menus with wine tasting.

★**Salt** MODERN AMERICAN $$$

(Map p106; 303-444-7258; www.saltboulderbistro.com; 1047 Pearl St; mains $14-28; 11am-10pm Mon-Wed, to 11pm Thu-Sat, 10am-10pm Sun; 208, HOP, SKIP) While farm-to-table is ubiquitous in Boulder, this is one spot that delivers and surpasses expectations. The sweet pea ravioli with lemon beurre blanc and shaved radishes is a feverish delight. But Salt also knows meat: local and grass-fed, basted, braised and slow roasted to utter perfection. When in doubt, ask – the servers really know their stuff.

You may start with a cocktail: the house mixologist has repeatedly won the competition for Boulder's best.

Kitchen MODERN AMERICAN $$$

(Map p106; 303-544-5973; www.thekitchencafe.com; 1039 Pearl St; mains $18-32; 206, HOP) The pioneer of farm-to-table cuisine in Boulder, Kitchen features clean lines, stacks of crusty bread and a daily menu. Super-fresh ingredients are crafted into rustic tapas: think roasted root vegetables, shaved prosciutto and steamed mussels in cream. The pulled-pork sandwich rocks, but save room for the sticky toffee pudding. Visitors shouldn't miss the community hour, with sips and nibbles at a communal table 3pm to 5pm weekdays.

Upstairs there's a more casual atmosphere and menu.

Jax SEAFOOD $$$

(Map p106; 310-444-1811; http://jaxboulder.com; 928 Pearl St; mains $8-30; from 4pm; 206, HOP, SKIP) With two decades running, this lively seafood shack is still an exquisite treat. Belly up to the circle bar for oysters and martinis, then splurge on fresh seafood flown in daily – think wild salmon or chilled lobster. Happy hour resembles a rush-hour subway car, but it's way more fun. Produce is locally sourced and the restaurant supports sustainable fisheries.

Drinking & Nightlife

The drinking here begins before the sun goes down, with almost every restaurant and bar offering absurd happy-hour deals. Must be a student thing. You will find the student population rules the Hill (the neighborhood immediately adjacent to CU) and often spills over into downtown, making Pearl St a pedestrian party scene. Many restaurants double as bars or turn into all-out dance clubs come 10pm. Of course, the best scenes aren't usually those easily glimpsed on the surface (look for basement dives, jazz lounges, Prohibition bars…). And we haven't even mentioned the groovy cafes and coffeehouses, the microbrews or absinthe.

★**Mountain Sun Pub & Brewery** BREWERY

(Map p106; www.mountainsunpub.com; 1535 Pearl St; 11am-1am; HOP, 205, 206) Boulder's favorite brewery cheerfully serves a rainbow of fine brews and packs in all from yuppies to hippies. But best of all is its community atmosphere. The pub grub, especially the

OPEN SPACE IS NO ACCIDENT

There aren't many towns like Boulder. Even in Colorado it's an anomaly. We're not just referencing its ability to simultaneously nurture the adventurous and athletic, the intellectual and spiritual, the beer-drinking masses and the culinary-snob set. We're talking about Boulder, the place. You know, that town so close to Denver it could easily have become a mere suburb or satellite town. Just look at the Hwy 36 corridor. From the I-25 north this highway roars through one suburb after another, but as it approaches Boulder the development stops and all you spy are those gorgeous Flatirons looming to the west. Why? Because long ago the city and county of Boulder got into the land-acquisition business.

It all started back in 1898 when the city helped purchase and set aside land that was marked for gold exploration and became Chautauqua Park. In 1907 the government floated a public bond to buy Flagstaff Mountain, and in 1912 purchased and preserved 1200 more pristine mountain acres. Then, in 1967, Boulder voters legislated their love of the land by approving a sales tax specifically to buy, manage and maintain open space. This was historic. No other US city had ever voted to tax themselves specifically for open space. The sales-tax measure passed with 57% of the vote and Boulder's **Open Space & Mountain Parks** (www.osmp.org) office was launched. In 1989, 76% of voters increased the tax by nearly 100%.

Still, even with an income stream, these days the government usually can't afford to buy whole parcels, and instead purchases 'conservation easements,' a legal agreement between the city and a landowner to protect their land's conservation value. Often they're used to purchase and protect wetlands and streams, keep agricultural land from being developed, and protect forests. While a good deal of Boulder's open space has been developed with trails, mapped and opened to the public, some parcels remain closed to visitors. But residents still feel the benefits: they live in a town buffered on all sides by vast open spaces that give Boulder its serenity.

burgers and chili, is delicious and it's fully family-friendly, with board games and kids' meals. It often has live bluegrass, reggae and jam-bands on Sunday and Monday nights.

If you want to skip the hassles of downtown parking, check out its more spacious pub, called the **Southern Sun** (627 S Broadway Ave; ⌚4pm-1am Mon, 11:30am-1am Tue-Fri, 11am-1am Sat & Sun; P), at the southern end of Broadway, with free parking.

Bohemian Biergarten BEER HALL
(Map p106; ☎720-328-8328; 2017 13th St; ⌚11:30am-2am; 🚌208, HOP) A very happening spot just off Pearl St. Happy patrons drink steins of imported brews at worn communal tables filling the small brick pub and patio. The scene gets younger (and rowdier) as the hours march on, but it draws a pretty diverse crowd.

Bitter Bar COCKTAIL BAR
(Map p106; ☎303-442-3050; www.thebitterbar.com; 835 Walnut St; cocktails $9-15; ⌚5pm-midnight Mon-Thu, 5pm-2am Fri & Sat; 🚌HOP) A chic Boulder speakeasy where killer cocktails, such as the scrumptious lavender-infused Blue Velvet, make the evening slip happily out of focus. The patio is great for conversation and Thursdays at 9pm there's live music.

Absinthe House BAR
(Map p106; ☎303-443-8600; www.boulderabsinthehouse.com; 1109 Walnut St; ⌚11am-late; 🚌208, SKIP) Big and ambitious, this is Boulder's brashest club, with the rooftop bar blaring beats you might hear a block away. A top-shelf sound system rocks the dance floor, filled with college kids imbibing 16 varieties of absinthe from Europe and America, poured from table side fountains.

Catacombs Bar BAR
(Map p106; ☎303-442-4344; www.boulderado.com; 2115 13th St; ⌚4pm-1:30am Mon-Fri, from 6:30pm Sat & Sun; 🚌208, SKIP) A cavernous pool and beer joint in the Boulderado Hotel basement, this dark, dank joint really does feel like the catacombs. Expect a young and rowdy crowd with ultracheap drink specials. The dimly lit rooms are perfect for getting tangled up with a fetching stranger or two. Tuesday is trivia night and Wednesdays bring karaoke.

Walnut Brewery BREWERY

(Map p106; ☎303-447-1345; www.walnutbrewery.com; 1123 Walnut St; ⊙11am-midnight Sun-Wed, to 2am Thu-Sat; 🚌208, SKIP) A hangar-sized sports bar and brewery that crafts and serves seven varieties of microbrew, ranging from golden pilsners to midnight stouts. It also serves liquor, has all the ball games on flatscreens, and serves decent pub grub.

Augustina's Winery WINERY

(☎303-545-2047; www.winechick.biz; 4715 N Broadway; ⊙afternoons Sat mid-Mar–Jan & by appointment; 🚌204, SKIP) Augustina's is a one-woman show. She drives an old 1979 U-Haul to Palisades and Grand Junction every autumn to fetch her grapes then goes about the happy, messy business of crushing, fermenting and aging the wine all on her own. If you're looking for a bottle with a story for the campfire, grab one here.

Sundown Saloon BAR

(Map p106; ☎303-449-4987; 1136 Pearl St; ⊙3pm-2am; 🚌208, SKIP) Only come here if you can stomach outhouse chic bathrooms, throwback tunes, an impossible-to-distinguish odor upon descent into the basement, pick-up shouting (it's straight impossible to hear late night), vicious competition on the shuffle board or pool tables (free till 10pm) and waking up hungover from the cheap Pabst Blue Ribbon ($6 pitchers). Every town needs an 'end-up bar,' and you will end up here.

'Round Midnight BAR

(Map p106; ☎303-442-2176; 1005 Pearl St; ⊙5pm-2am; 🚌208, SKIP) Another divey basement bar just west of Pearl Street Mall, this spot's popularity rolls in waves, and of late it has still been prone to late-night good times thanks to the music it spins (mostly underground dub, dance-hall and hip-hop). There's free pool during happy hour.

Goose BAR

(Map p104; www.thegoosebar.com; 1301 Broadway St; ⊙3pm-late; 🚌225, SKIP) The wheel of fortune behind the bar ticks to a halt on '$3 Jager Bombs' and the howl of beefy frats is punctuated by high fives. Your choice: throw down $3 or regroup at the beer pong table. Then again, maybe you're not in any shape to be making decisions. Though utterly lacking in atmosphere, this binge drinkers' proving ground can be a riot.

Women might want to note the 'Friends with Benefits' Tuesday night, when a group of four or more women get their first shot on the house.

GAY & LESBIAN BOULDER

Boulder is tolerant and progressive, yet it is odd that such a with-it town could wind up with no gay bars. Local activists have cobbled together enough events, including Boulder Pride Fest, and organized the community so effectively that there is a gay scene here even if it lacks a sense of bar 'ownership.'

Resources

Out Boulder (☎303-499-5777; www.outboulder.org)

Proposition Gay (Map p106; kpicle@gmail.com; ⊙last Fri of the month)

☆ Entertainment

Boulder Theater CINEMA, MUSIC

(Map p106; ☎303-786-7030; www.bouldertheatre.com; 2032 14th St) This old movie-theater-turned-historic-venue brings in slightly under-the-radar acts like jazz great Charlie Hunter, the madmen rockers of Gogol Bordello and West African divas, Les Nubians. But it also screens classic films like *The Big Lebowski* and short-film festivals that can and should be enjoyed with a glass of beer.

Fox Theatre LIVE MUSIC

(Map p104; ☎box office 303-443-3399; www.foxtheatre.com; 1135 13th St; cover varies; ⊙10am-8pm Mon-Sat, 11am-8pm Sun; 🚌203, 204, 225, AB, B, DASH, SKIP) You'll be elbowing your way through students to get near the stage of this excellent mid-sized venue, so head upstairs for a perch near the sound board for better views and acoustics. Bands on stage here are national touring acts, popular jam bands and indie rock.

E-Town Hall LIVE MUSIC

(Map p106; ☎303-443-8696; www.etown.org; 1535 Spruce St) Beautiful and brand new, this is the home of etown radio show (heard on public radio), which features rising and even well-known artists combined with community awards. It's all very Boulder, and you can get in on it by attending a live taping. It's a good way to check out artists who charge a lot more for regular concerts.

CU Basketball BASKETBALL

(Map p104; ☎303-492-8337; www.cubuffs.com; 950 Regent Dr, Coors Event Center; prices vary;

games Nov-Mar; ; 209, STAMPEDE) Seldom pushovers, rarely great, CU's basketball games are always fun to watch because the competition is usually stiff. And like most great schools, it has a transcendent baller from the not-too-distant past. Chauncey 'Mr Big Shot' Billups starred here before he became an NBA champ and finals MVP.

CU Football FOOTBALL
(Map p104; 303-492-8337; www.cubuffs.com; 2400 Colorado Ave, Folsom Field; tickets $50-120; selected Sat; ; 209, STAMPEDE) Boulder sports fans may have allegiances to Denver's pro teams, but they have several teams of their own too, and they are all called the CU Buffaloes. Still, while college volleyball, gymnastics and baseball have their place, it's the football team that rules campus.

Shopping

Given the hipster student vibe, the yuppie cash flow and Boulder's status as a go-to green hot spot, it's not all that shocking to find a bit of shopping here. Along with some high-end vintage consignment houses, there are a few boutiques with happening labels, and there's plenty of eco and athletic gear on offer too. Whether you're patrolling Pearl Street Mall and its outskirts, (much) hipper East Pearl, or the more corporate 29th St Mall, you're bound to do some boutique and gallery browsing between bouts of mountain marveling.

★**Pearl Street Mall** MALL
(Map p106) The main feature of downtown Boulder is the Pearl Street Mall, a vibrant pedestrian zone filled with kids' climbing boulders and splash fountains, bars, galleries and restaurants.

★**Peppercorn Gourmet Goods** FOOD, HOMEWARES
(Map p106; 303-449-5847; www.peppercorn.com; 1235 Pearl St; 10am-6pm Mon-Thu & Sat, to 8pm Fri, 11am-5pm Sun; 208, SKIP) One of the coolest stores on Pearl, this kitchen, bed and bath supplier stocks upscale goods, locally produced foods, scores of specialized cookbooks and enough gizmos to delight all cooking geeks. It's a fun place to spend too much time and money. See the website for classes and events.

Boulder Ski Deals OUTDOOR EQUIPMENT
(Map p104; 303-938-8799; www.boulderskideals.com; 2525 Arapahoe Ave; 10am-7pm Mon-Fri, 10am-6pm Sat, 11am-5pm Sun; ; JUMP) Arguably the best deals on skis, snowboards, glasses, goggles and snow gear can be found at this laidback but professional temple to all things extreme and powdery. It sells, it rents and the staff bro out – even with the ladies. Exceptional deals on season passes to Vail, Breckenridge, Beaver Creek and Arapahoe Basin.

★**Into the Wind** TOYS
(Map p106; 303-449-5906; www.intothewind.com; 1408 Pearl St; 10am-9pm Mon-Sat, 10am-6pm Sun; 206) Your inner child will want to spend hours in this store. Not only does it sell the most beautiful kites, but there are games, puppets and toys to intrigue all ages and budgets.

Piece, Love & Chocolate FOOD
(Map p106; 805 Pearl St; 10am-6pm Mon-Thu, 10am-9pm Fri & Sat, noon-6pm Sun; 206, JUMP) This tiny shop is a chocolate emporium, with a glass case of handmade chocolates and dipped snacks whipped up on site and shelves of imports from milk to dark and every gradation in between, many fair trade and organic. A highlight is the velvety melted cup – a hot chocolate to remember.

Absolute Vinyl BOOKS, MUSIC
(303-955-1519; http://avboulder.blogspot.com; 4474 N Broadway St; 11am-6:30pm Tue-Sun; SKIP) Every town needs a temple to vinyl, a place where chilled-out clerks wipe down wax on Sunday afternoons while listening to classic Memphis blues. Bookworms comb the walls of Little Horse, the shared bookstore, for first editions, young men come here when hurting for Smiths records, and there is a paradise of jazz, blues and classical gems.

Boulder Bookstore BOOKS
(Map p106; www.boulderbookstore.indiebound.com; 1107 Pearl St;) Boulder's favorite indie bookstore has a huge travel section downstairs, along with all the hottest new fiction and nonfiction. Check the visiting-authors lineup posted at the entry.

Boulder Running Company SHOES
(303-786-8044; www.boulderrunningcompany.com; 2775 Pearl St; 10am-7pm Mon-Fri, to 6pm Sat, to 5pm Sun; ; 205, 205C, BOLT) Boulder's prime center for all the gear and specialty shoes you'll need for running track, street and trail. It even offers video analysis of your running stride on a treadmill before the fitting, which helps make sure you aren't

injury prone in your new shoes (and probably doesn't hurt the in-sole sales either). Also has info on upcoming regional races and triathalons.

Neptune Mountaineering OUTDOOR EQUIPMENT
(303-499-8866; www.neptunemountaineering.com; 633 South Broadway; 10am-7pm Mon-Fri, 10am-6pm Sat & Sun) This locally owned Boulder landmark is the best place for climbing and mountaineering gear, with a knowledgable staff who practice what they preach. There's also a good selection of camping and backcountry ski gear, guidebooks and high-end outdoor clothing.

Bayleaf on Pearl HOMEWARES
(Map p106; 720-565-2477; 1222 Pearl St; 10am-6pm Mon-Sat, to 5pm Sun; 206) A boutique selling high-end homewares with impeccable taste. Its cookbooks and kitchen goods are evidence of owner Michale Bugermeister's background as a chef. There are cool toys, oversized coffee-table books on German bookbinding and other classy curios.

Common Threads CLOTHING
(www.commonthreadsboulder.com; 2707 Spruce St; 10am-6pm Mon-Sat, noon-5pm Sun) Vintage shopping at its most haute couture, this fun place is where to go for secondhand Choos and Prada purses. Prices are higher than at your run-of-the-mill vintage shop, but clothes, shoes and bags are always in good condition, and the designer clothing is guaranteed authentic. Offers fun classes on clothes altering and innovating.

Momentum HANDICRAFTS
(Map p106; www.ourmomentum.com; 1625 Pearl St; 10am-7pm Tue-Sat, 11am-6pm Sun) Committed to socially responsible and environmentally friendly business practices, Momentum makes you feel good about shopping. It sells the kitchen sink of unique global gifts – Zulu wire baskets, fabulous scarves from India, Nepal and Ecuador – all handcrafted and purchased at fair value from disadvantaged artisans. Every item purchased provides a direct economic lifeline to the artists.

BOULDER FOR CHILDREN

It's easy to keep the kids happy and busy here: most of what makes adults so giddy about a Boulder holiday – nature and adventure – ignites kids too. There's a huge amount of outdoors options for all ages. For something a bit more academic, great free monthly shows are put on by CU's Wizards Program (p108).

Outdoors Options

Families would be happiest booking a bungalow at the Chautauqua Lodge. These rustic but pleasantly updated homes include a kitchen, a screened-in front porch and a backyard, and open onto Chautauqua Park (p105). Which means the kids can ramble through the grasses and interact with nature at ground level, while you keep one eye on them, and another on your glass of wine while you relax on the porch. The Royal Arch trail (p110) can be a long slog for a toddler, but they do fine on the Boulder Falls Trail (p110).

Kids of all ages love to go tubing (p109) on Boulder Creek, and bike shops can rent kid-sized wheels. The Boulder Creek Bike Path (p109) is a perfect family ride. The Boulder County Farmers' Market (p116) is another fun family experience, with plenty of music and color and flavors, as well as ample grass space for picnicking near the Creek. There's also the nearby Boulder Museum of Contemporary Art (p105), which offers free guided art activities on its front porch, in the thick of the market, on Saturdays (9am to 1pm).

On hot days, toddlers love the Pearl Street Mall's Pop Jet Fountain (p109). Prepare for squeals of delight, and bring a towel and a change of clothes. Among various public pools, the best is the cool spring water one in Eldorado Springs (p110).

A Drive Away

About 20 miles (20 minutes by car on the freeway) from Boulder, halfway to Denver in the suburb of Westminster, is the Butterfly Pavilion (p106). Its indoor atrium is alive with tropical gardens and 1200 butterflies from rainforests around the world – not to mention tarantulas, scorpions, giant millipedes and more. The nearby Sunflower Farm (p108) in Longmont also welcomes families on Farm Fest Sundays (May to November) to help feed baby animals, collect eggs, ride ponies and explore the giant tree house.

Savory Spice Shop FOOD

(Map p106; ☎303-444-0668; www.savoryspiceshop.com; 2041 Broadway St; ⏰10am-6pm Mon-Sat, 11am-5pm Sun; 👪; 🚌208, SKIP) Extremely popular, this growing regional chain is the place to search for a small-batch habanero hot sauce or to alchemize your own spice rub for your self-catering kit. In all there are 140 spices hand-blended from mostly organic sources. Plus, it just smells good.

REI OUTDOORS EQUIPMENT

(☎303-583-9970; www.rei.com; 1789 28th St; ⏰9am-9pm; 👪; 🚌205, 206, BOLT) The Denver flagship it is not, but the Boulder branch of America's largest and best outdoor outfitter rents sleeping bags, pads and tents, as well as anything else you might need for your stint in the Rocky Mountains.

Goldmine Vintage CLOTHING

(Map p106; ☎303-945-0845; www.goldminevintage.com; 1123 Pearl St; ⏰11am-8pm Mon-Thu, to 9pm Fri & Sat, to 7pm Sun) Hot pink fishnets and a purple wig adorn the mannequin in the window of this upscale vintage shop. There are trucker caps, *Spinal Tap* tees and turquoise cowboy boots. In back, patrons can try on Monroe-worthy gowns under the watchful gaze of a matador painted on black velvet.

Meow Meow GIFTS

(Map p104; ☎303-442-8602; 1118 13th St; ⏰10am-7pm Mon-Fri, to 8am Sun; 👪; 🚌203, 204, 225, DASH, SKIP) Pioneering the concept of 'upcycling,' this is the place for unique gifts, art, jewelry and clothes made from reused materials. It has a great local feel and lots of one-of-a-kind accessories for women. The card selection is hilarious.

Outdoor Divas SPORTS

(☎303-449-3482; www.outdoordivas.com; 2317 30th Street; ⏰10am-7pm Mon-Sat, noon-5pm Sun; 👪; 🚌208, SKIP) This specialized outdoor store for women knows its audience – the gear is top quality, the prices are competitive and the staff's knowledge on women-specific skiing, hiking and running gear is expert.

Rebecca's Herbal Apothecary HEALTH, BEAUTY

(Map p106; ☎303-443-8878; www.rebeccasherbs.com; 1227 Spruce St; classes $20-35; ⏰10am-6pm Mon-Fri, 11am-7pm Sat; 👪; 🚌208, SKIP) A groovy herbal apothecary where herbs are sold loose, in lotions and in oils. There are aromatherapy cases of tinctures and a library and expert herbalists to guide you through it all. The Western school of herbal thought dominates the thinkspace here. Classes offer the basics about herbs, infusions and salves. Not an outlet for medicinal marijuana!

Starr's Clothing Co CLOTHING

(Map p106; ☎303-442-3056; www.starrsclothingco.com; 1630 Pearl St; ⏰10am-7pm Mon-Sat, to 6pm Sun; 🚌204) Established in 1914 and still Boulder's leading denim resource, this store is damn near warehouse-sized, with all manner of stressed, smooth and relaxed denim. It also carries the odd top-end designer label such as Southern California fave Free People.

Beat Book Shop BOOKS

(Map p106; ☎303-444-7111; www.beatbookshop.com; 1717 Pearl St; ⏰varies; 🚌204) Tom Peters is the poet proprietor of this funky pile of consistently brainy, soulful books. We're talking more than 30 Kerouac titles, as well as classics from Ginsberg, Burroughs and (Beat-esque) Bukowski, among others. His hours vary but Peters claims to be here from afternoon into the night daily. Well worth a browse.

CU Bookstore BOOKS

(Map p104; ☎303-492-6411; www.cubookstore.com; 1669 Euclid Ave; ⏰8am-6pm Mon-Thu, 8am-5pm Fri, 10am-5pm Sat; 🚌203, 204, 209, 225, AB, B, DASH, SKIP, STAMPEDE) There are scads of CU merchandise outlets along the busy stretch of 13th St, but this is the school's official outfitter. In addition to textbooks and supplies, it has the largest selection of gold-and-black goods of any store in Boulder. Located in the University Memorial Center.

Oliverde FOOD

(Map p106; ☎303-442-2199; http://oliverdeoil.com; 2027 Broadway St; ⏰10am-6pm Mon-Sat, 11am-5pm Sun; 🚌208, SKIP) A unique gourmet olive-oil shop with dozens of oils sold in bulk and sampled with squares of crusty bread. There's also specialty foods and gourmet vinegars (maple is our favorite).

Pedestrian Shops SHOES

(Map p106; ☎303-449-5260; www.comfortableshoes.com; 1425 Pearl St; ⏰10am-8pm Mon-Sat, 11am-6pm Sun; 🚌203, 204, 205, 206, 208, 225, DASH, JUMP) Set smack in the midst of the Pearl Street Mall, this is where to head for the comfortable kinds of footwear that are staples in earthy Bouldertown. Think Ecco, Dansko, Keen and Born. Find the last-pair rack for the best deals, and if you buy two you'll get a third pair free.

THE THOUSAND-YEAR FLOOD

It came after a drought that followed the worst wildfire in Colorado history. On September 12, the Front Range woke up to 9in of rain and more falling. Children were kept home for an unprecedented 'rain day.' Was it the 100-year flood Boulder had long been bracing for? It turned out to be much more.

The Boulder Creek went from running at 54 cubic feet per second to 5000 cfs. First the canyons flooded, destroying homes in their path. Inundations isolated mountain communities like Jamestown and the foothills town of Lyons. Eight people died and thousands lost their homes.

The month's 17in of rainfall blasted September's usual 1.7in average. What happened is considered a thousand-year flood, as there is only 0.1% probability of a disaster of this magnitude in any given year. It's now being cited as the second-largest natural disaster in US history, after Hurricane Katrina. The affected area was roughly the size of Connecticut. Losses were estimated at $2 billion.

Changing weather patterns mean a previously rare event – tropical moisture over the usually-dry Rockies – precipitated the big flood. Researchers suspect it's part of a larger, long-term swing in weather patterns, which may mean more extreme drought-flood cycles, and decidedly more attention on climate change.

Please note that some of the businesses and mountain access roads covered here may be closed or temporarily shut down during the recovery.

Posterscene ART
(Map p106; ☎303-527-2701; www.posterscene.com; 1505 Pearl St; ⏰11am-7pm Mon-Thu, 11am-8pm Fri & Sat, 11am-5pm Sun; 🚌203, 204, 205, 206, DASH, SKIP, JUMP) Iconic images and original show posters from Janis Joplin and Dylan and the Dead make this a rock memorabilia paradise. But it isn't limited to high-end collector's items; it has a clutch of cool, inexpensive reproductions too.

Prana CLOTHING
(Map p106; ☎303-449-2199; www.prana.com; 1147 Pearl St; ⏰10am-8pm Mon-Sat, 11am-6pm Sun; 🚌208, SKIP) Monks chant to the patter of beats overhead as shoppers check out organic-dyed yoga outfits. All the clothes are organized by size – a nice touch – and the signs encourage an awareness of 'cosmic order.' Aside from all this New Age excitement, Prana is wind-powered and hosts art events.

Smith Klein Gallery ART
(Map p106; ☎303-444-7200; www.smithklein.com; 1116 Pearl St Mall; ⏰11am-6pm Mon-Thu, to 7pm Fri & Sat, noon-5pm Sun) Locally owned since 1984, this conservative-to-quirky gallery is worth a peek for some interesting paintings and the glass, bronze and wood sculptures (we like the ones crafted from vintage car doors). There's hand-blown glass and jewelry too.

Information

Boulder Convention & Visitors Bureau (Map p104; ☎303-442-2911, toll-free 800-444-0447; www.bouldercoloradousa.com; 2440 Pearl St; ⏰8:30am-5pm Mon-Thu, to 4pm Fri; 🚌204) Set in the Boulder Chamber of Commerce, this visitor center offers basic information, maps and tips on nearby hiking trails and other activities. There's a more accessible tourist info kiosk (Map p106) on the Pearl Street Mall in front of the court house.

Boulder Downtown (www.boulderdowntown.com) This alliance of downtown businesses offers comprehensive dining and event listings in the downtown area – including the Pearl Street Mall.

Get Boulder (www.getboulder.com) A local print and online magazine with helpful information on stuff to do in Boulder.

Getting There & Away

Less than an hour from downtown Denver and just over an hour from the airport, Boulder is easily accessible by public transport. However, with plenty of (paid) public parking around and the mountains beckoning, you may want to rent a car after all. Flights, tours and rail tickets can be booked online at www.lonelyplanet.com/travel_services.

BUS

Buses are run by **RTD** (☎303-299-6000; www.rtd-denver.com; per ride $2-4.50). Route B buses travel between Boulder Transit Center (p125), aka Boulder Station, and Denver Market

Street Station ($5; 55 minutes). Route AB runs between the Table Mesa Park-N-Ride on Hwy 36 in Boulder and the Denver International Airport ($13, one hour), with easy connections to downtown Boulder and the Hill.

CAR & MOTORCYCLE

Boulder sits about 30 miles northwest of Denver off Highway 36, accessible from the I-25N from downtown Denver. Hwy 36 runs through Boulder on the way to Estes Park and the Rocky Mountain National Park. Most of the major car-rental companies (Hertz, Avis, Enterprise) have shingles in Boulder, and if you rent here, you can avoid some of the hefty taxes airport branches charge.

Getting Around

TO/FROM THE AIRPORT

Green Ride (303-997-0238; http://greenrideboulder.com; 4800 Baseline Rd, D110; 1-way $25-34) Serving Boulder and its satellite suburbs, this shuttle alternative is a bit cheaper than competitors, working on an hourly schedule. The cheapest service leaves from the depot. Additional travelers in groups are discounted.

SuperShuttle (303-444-0808; www.supershuttle.com; 1-way around $27) Far pricier than the public bus, but still cheaper than a cab, the Super Shuttle is popular airport ride. But with two or more people in the mix, you'll be better served by a taxi.

BICYCLE

Owning a bicycle is almost a Boulder prerequisite. Most streets have dedicated bike lanes and the Boulder Creek Bike Path (p109) is a must-ride commuter corridor. There are plenty of places to get your hands on a rental. With rental cruisers stationed all over the city, **Boulder B-Cycle** (boulder.bcycle.com; 24hr rental $7) is a new citywide program of hourly or daily bike rentals, but riders must sign up online first.

Full Cycle (303-440-7771; www.fullcyclebikes.com; 1211 13th St; hourly rentals $18-35; 10am-7pm Mon-Fri, to 6pm Sat, 11am-5pm Sun; 203, 204, 225, AB, B, DASH, DD, GS, SKIP) This terrific bike shop rents cruisers on the cheap and higher-end road and full-suspension mountain bikes. Ask staff about the best cycling routes (from easy Boulder Creek Trail to the Tour de France level of pain that is the 4-mile ride up Flagstaff). There's another branch on East Pearl.

Pete's E Bikes (303-586-1544; www.petesebikes.com; 2710 Pearl St; half-/full-day $40/70; 10am-6pm Mon-Sat; 204) This small electric-bike showroom has engine-powered cruisers with a rechargeable battery that plugs into a wall socket. The cheapest hovers around $1800 new, but you can sample a rental.

University Bicycles (www.ubikes.com; 839 Pearl St; 10am-6pm Mon-Sat, 10am-5pm Sun; 206, JUMP) There are plenty of rental shops, but this has the widest range of rides and the most helpful staff. For $18 you can get a townie bike for the day.

CAR & MOTORCYCLE

If staying downtown you won't need a vehicle, as countless diversions are just steps away. But if you are anchored to a car, most downtown parking is paid. Weekends bring a respite: downtown parking garages are free.

And a word of warning to all drivers: Boulder's traffic cameras levy speeding fines, starting from $40 – a downer when one of these beauties lands in your mail box.

PUBLIC TRANSPORTATION

Boulder has superb public transportation, with several RTD bus routes lacing the city and connecting the Hill with downtown and North Boulder. Buses have bike racks.

Boulder Transit Center (Map p106; 303-299-6000; 1800 14th St) The city's public transportation hub is a good place to pick up maps of the transportation network. Offers free public parking on weekends; not so easy to come by elsewhere in the city.

TAXI

Boulder Yellow Cab (Map p106; 303-777-7777; www.boulderyellowcab.com; 24hr) Boulder's biggest and best cab company – actually a subsidiary of Colorado's largest taxi conglomerate. There's a taxi stand on 11th St at the Pearl Street Mall.

AROUND BOULDER

Nederland

POP 1470 / ELEV 8236FT

From Boulder, the devastatingly scenic 17-mile route through Boulder Canyon emerges in the lively, ramshackle little berg of Nederland, a mountain-town magnet for hippies looking to get off the grid. These days, Nederland has a sagging, happenstantial quality to its weather-beaten buildings, which are not without a certain rugged charm. Several worthwhile restaurants and bars feed the hungry skiers and hikers heading to or from Eldora Ski Area and the Indian Peaks Wilderness Area, as well as motorists coming down the Peak to Peak Hwy.

Sights & Activities

The nearby Indian Peaks Wilderness Area provides ample recreation in summer and winter. Road cyclists often pedal the route between Boulder and Nederland and some charge on to the scenic Peak to Peak highway, making Nederland a logical stop. Tin Shed (p127) bike shop has good information about road and mountain-bike routes.

Carousel of Happiness CAROUSEL
(20 Lakeview Dr, Nederland Mall; ride $1; 10am-8pm, late May-early Sep;) This vintage 1910 carousel with gorgeous wood-carved animals and Wurlitzer music is a real highlight for kids. Proceeds from the nonprofit organization go to children in need.

Festivals & Events

Frozen Dead Guy Days PARADE
(303-506-1048; http://frozendeadguydays.org; early Mar) This macabre, bizarre and wonderful little festival brings life to Nederland in the early spring. Basically an excuse to parade through town and drink beer, the festival celebrates Grandpa Bredo Morstoel, a Norwegian transplant who is cryogenically frozen and held locally in dry ice awaiting reanimation.

NedFest MUSIC
(www.nedfest.org; 151 E St; day ticket $55; late Aug) An annual gathering of area folkies and jam bands, perfectly suited to the ex-hippie, mountain-town vibe.

Sleeping

Most visitors do day trips to Nederland. Nearby Indian Peaks Wilderness campgrounds and backcountry campsites are managed by the Boulder Ranger District (p127).

Best Western Nederland HOTEL $$
(303-258-9463; bestwesterncolorado.com/hotels/best-western-lodge-at-nederland; 55 Lakeview Dr; d incl breakfast $126; ; N) A good value for the Boulder area, with 23 rooms featuring log furniture, mini-fridges and gas fireplaces. The hotel is within walking distance of the restaurants and reservoir, and also features a hot tub.

Rainbow Lakes Campground CAMPGROUND $
(off County Rd 116; campsite $13;) Surrounded by lodgepole pines, this campground sits at 10,000ft with access to brilliant hikes on the eastern side of Rocky Mountain National Park. Though an excellent option in the off-season, it receives lots of traffic in the summer. Bring your own water or filter from the lakes, half a mile away.

Eating

★ **Salto** CAFE $
(303-258-3509; 112 East 2nd St; mains $8-10; 7am-6pm Sun-Thu, 7am-8pm Fri & Sat; N) This lovely cafe, with roaring fires in winter and a stone patio in summer, brings some much-needed ambience to Ned. Skiers can start their day with egg sandwiches on brioche and great Ozo coffee. It offers salads and sandwiches, with gluten-free options, and beer and tap wines for the après-ski and bike crowd.

New Moon Bakery CAFE $
(303-258-3569; www.newmoonbakery.com; 1 W 1st St; mains $4-8; 6:30am-5pm Mon-Fri, 7am-5pm Sat & Sun; N) Also the town gossip hub, this hopping bakery caters to Boulder tastes. You can get your latte made with rice milk and your chocolate cookie free of gluten. Everything is superfresh and tasty.

Kathmandu NEPALESE $
(303-258-1169; 110 N Jefferson St; lunch buffet $10; 11am-9pm; ; N) Offering consistent Indian and Nepalese fare, this family-run restaurant is a longtime local staple. The lunch buffet is the best deal, there's also a kids' menu and great chai on offer.

Back Country Pizza PIZZERIA $
(303-258-0176; 20 Lakeview Dr; pizzas $12-18; 11am-10pm Sun-Thu, 11am-11pm Fri & Sat; ; N) Located in the Caribou Shopping Center, this pizzeria offers delicious, crusty pizza and hearty plates at good value. The place is an easy option for families with its casual atmosphere and video games.

Wild Mountain Smokehouse & Brewery BARBECUE $$
(303-258-9453; www.wildmountainsb.com; 70 E 1st St; mains $8-21; 11am-9pm Sun-Thu, to 10pm Fri & Sat; ; N) Harleys queue out front for a spectrum of slightly sweet, smoky or brightly spiced BBQ sauces, which complement the hoppy house brews. Happy hour is 3pm to 6pm on weekdays.

Information

Ace Hardware (303-258-3132; 74 Hwy 119 S; 8am-7pm Mon-Sat, 9am-5pm Sun; N) Across from the mall, this store sells topographic and USGS maps for the Indian Peaks area, and issues camping permits (required June to 15 September), as well as hunting and fishing licenses.

Nederland Visitors Center (☎303-258-3936; www.nederlandchamber.org; 4 W 1st St; ⏰10am-2pm Mon-Thu, 10am-4pm Fri-Sun; 🚌N) Has local information about where to eat and sleep in the area, and information on lots of local activities; located downtown, diagonally opposite the Village shopping mall.

Getting Around

Hessie Shuttle (597 County Rd, Nederland Middle-Sr High School; ⏰8am-8pm Jun–mid-Sep; 🚌N) FREE Since parking is severely limited for the Hessie hikes (including 4th of July trailhead and Arapahoe Glacier), visitors should take this convenient shuttle, which leaves roughly every half-hour in summer. Dogs on leashes are allowed. The public RTD bus from Boulder also stops at the high school.

Tin Shed (☎303-258-3509; 112 East 2nd St; ⏰9am-6pm; 🚌N) Adjacent to Salto, this bike shop offers plenty of trail maps and advice, as well as ski-tuning in winter. Mountain bike rentals are available ($35 per day). The location is between the main strip and the reservoir, with East 2nd perpendicular to 1st St.

Eldora Ski Area

Aside from the Corona Bowl, which boasts a thrilling 1400ft vertical drop, this little ski area is mostly famous for its convenience: its proximity to Boulder and the relatively inexpensive lift tickets. Four miles west of Nederland, **Eldora Mountain Resort** (☎303-440-8700; www.eldora.com; 2861 Eldora Ski Rd 140; lift ticket adult/child $79/45; 🚌N, B) primarily gets day visitors who zip around a fairly small facility with around 500 skiable acres. It's no Telluride, but there is some interesting terrain and a few expert trails. A highlight is 40km-plus of well-groomed Nordic trails.

During winter, buses leave for Eldora Mountain Resort from the corner of Boulder's 14th St and Walnut St (one-way $5).

Indian Peaks Wilderness Area

Forming the impressive backdrop to Nederland, the Indian Peaks area is the most used wilderness area in the country, thanks to hyperactive Boulderites. But what they know is that Indian Peaks has grand scenery on the scale of a national park, albeit in their own backyard. It offers many fine hiking and camping opportunities, though reservations, even for backcountry sites, are required. Dogs are allowed on almost all trails, but must be on a leash. In winter, the area is frequented by backcountry skiers and snowshoers. Equipment is easily rented in Boulder. Visitors should still go out with someone knowlegable about avalanche safety, or get recommendations for low-risk areas.

There are two main access points: one south of Nederland past the village of Eldora and the other north of Nederland along the Peak to Peak highway. South of Nederland there are the **Hessie** and **Fourth of July** trailheads. For Hessie, take the Hessie Shuttle (p127). From there you can reach Lost Lake, a good 2.7m round-trip, or head further for more lakes access. Fourth of July trail is among the most scenic, with access to Arapahoe Glacier (7.9-mile round-trip). Another recommended option from this point is the hike up to 12,000ft Arapaho Pass (6.4-mile round-trip). It's a gentle ascent but be prepared to spend the entire day – if the altitude doesn't slow you down, the scenery should. Note: the unpaved road to Fourth of July is best left to high-clearance or 4WD vehicles.

North of Nederland, the **Brainard Lake Recreation Area** has ample parking ($10) and campsites ($19), which always fill up. Brainard Lake itself is ringed by the paved entrance road. Highlights include the beautiful Lake Isabelle (4.9-mile round-trip) and the absolutely stunning (but mildly arduous) Pawnee Pass (9.1-mile round-trip), an all-day hike or a good overnight.

For more information on Indian Peaks check out the Nederland Visitors Center (p127), which has maps and guidebooks. In the mall, Ace Hardware (p126) also sells topographic and USGS maps for the Indian Peaks area and issues camping permits (required June to September 15), as well as hunting and fishing licenses. Camping permits are also available through the **Boulder Ranger District** (☎303-541-2500; 2140 Yarmouth Ave, Boulder; ⏰8am-4:30pm Mon-Fri summer).

Rocky Mountain National Park & Northern Colorado

Includes ➡

Best Places to Eat

- Backcountry Deli (p160)
- Big Horn Restaurant (p140)
- Tasty Harmony (p146)
- Bistro CV (p161)

Best Places to Stay

- YMCA of the Rockies (p137)
- Armstrong Hotel (p144)
- Longs Peak Campground (p134)
- Stanley Hotel (p139)

Why Go?

With one foot on either side of the Continental Divide and granite behemoths in every direction, Colorado's northern mountains provide a glimpse of the top of the world. Here, the northern Rockies make an irresistible call to mountain-lovers, regardless of whether the season calls for climbing them in hiking boots or shushing down them on skis. Steamboat is a world-class ski resort without the hype of other Colorado areas, and Rocky Mountain National Park and its surrounding wilderness areas and patchwork state parks is a sanctuary for wildlife and wildlife lovers alike.

In spring, summer and autumn, hiking and biking in state and national parks and forests continue to draw visitors. Many ski resorts transform into groomed mountain-biking areas, and campers make for high-altitude lakes. The region also boasts top-notch fishing, rafting and kayaking, weathered ghost towns, horseback riding, camping and mountain touring until well after autumn turns the aspens gold.

When to Go

Estes Park

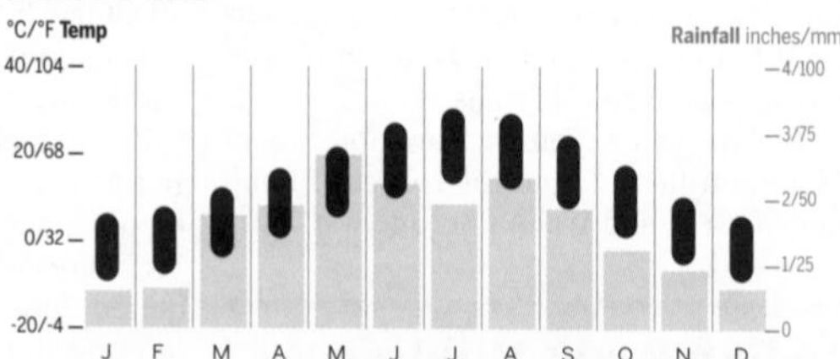

Jun–Sep Sunshine, perfect hiking and monstrous thunderheads attract visitors.

Sep–Oct Temperatures drop and the tourists vacate. The aspens turn golden.

Nov–Apr Crisp air and tons of snowfall bring skiers to low-key resort areas.

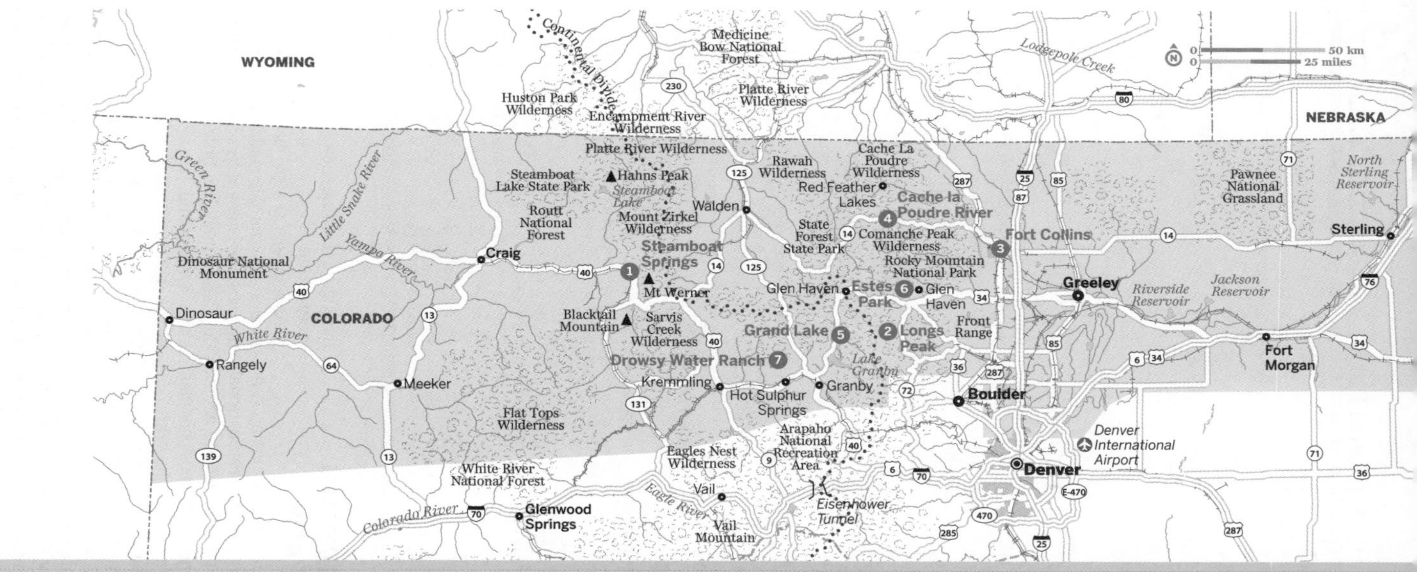

Rocky Mountain National Park & Northern Colorado Highlights

1 Watch a thunderhead roll over the lyrical peaks surrounding **Steamboat Springs** (p155).

2 Scramble to the top of **Longs Peak** (p131), one of Colorado's proud 14ers.

3 Ride a cruiser to **New Belgium Brewery** (p143) in Fort Collins for a tour and tasting of Colorado microbrew.

4 Cast a fly for wild trout in the rushing waters of the **Cache la Poudre River** (p150).

5 Hike all day before curling up by the fire at Grand Lake's **Shadowcliff Lodge & Retreat Center** (p152).

6 Visit Estes Park to climb the Rockies after some classes from **Colorado Mountain School** (p136), or creep yourself out at **Stanley Hotel** (p139), inspiration for Stephen King's thriller *The Shining*.

7 Live out the cowboy fantasy riding the range at **Drowsy Water Ranch** (p153).

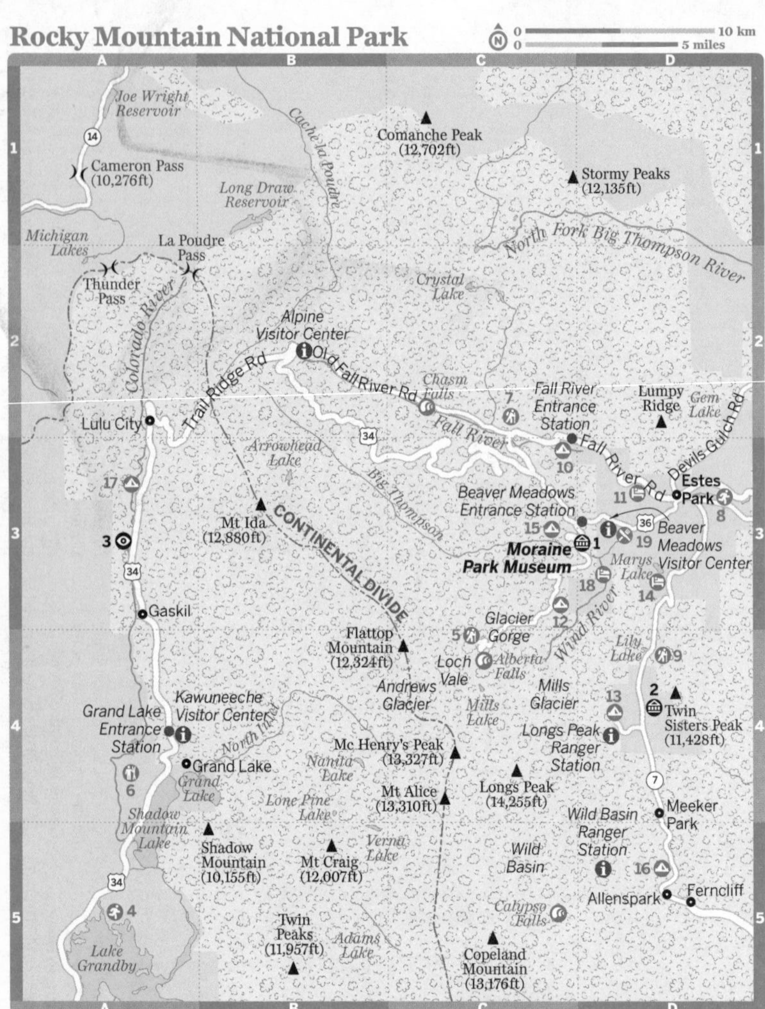

ROCKY MOUNTAIN NATIONAL PARK

Though Rocky Mountain National Park doesn't rank among the largest national parks in the USA (it's *only* 265,000 acres), it's rightly among one of the most popular, hosting four million visitors every year.

This is a place of natural spectacle on every scale: from hulking granite formations – many taller than 12,000ft, some over 130 million years old – to the delicate yellow burst of the glacier lily, one of the dozen alpine wildflowers that explode in a short, colorful life at the edge of receding snowfields for a few days every spring.

And though it tops many travelers' itineraries and can get maddeningly crowded, the park has miles of less-beaten paths, and the backcountry is a little-explored nature-lovers' wonderland. It's surrounded by some of the most pristine wild area in the west: Comanche Peak and Neota Wilderness Areas in the Roosevelt National Forest to the north and Indian Peaks Wilderness to the south. The jagged spine of the Continental Divide intersects the park through its middle. Excellent hiking trails crisscross alpine

Rocky Mountain National Park

Top Sights
1 Moraine Park Museum ... D3

Sights
2 Enos Mills Cabin Museum & Gallery ... D4
3 Holzwarth Historic Site ... A3

Activities, Courses & Tours
4 Beacon Landing Marina ... A5
5 Bear Lake Trailhead ... C4
6 Grand Lake Nordic Center & Grand Lake Golf Course ... A4
7 Lawn Lake Trailhead ... C2
Longs Peak Trailhead ... (see 13)
8 Sombrero Ranch ... D3
9 Twin Sisters Trailhead ... D4

Sleeping
10 Aspenglen Campground ... C3
11 Deer Crest Resort ... D3
12 Glacier Basin Campground ... C3
13 Longs Peak Campground ... D4
14 Mary's Lake Lodge ... D3
15 Moraine Park Campground ... C3
16 Olive Ridge Campground ... D5
17 Timber Creek Campground ... A3
18 YMCA of the Rockies – Estes Park Center ... D3

Eating
19 Rock Inn Mountain Tavern ... D3

fields, skirt the edge of isolated high-altitude lakes and bring travelers to the wild, untamed heart of the Rockies.

Sights

Wonders of the natural world are the main attractions here: huge herds of elk and scattered mountain sheep, pine-dotted granite slopes and blindingly white alpine tundra. However, there are a few museums and historic sites within the park's borders that are worthy of a glance and good for families.

★ Moraine Park Museum MUSEUM
(☎970-586-1206; Bear Lake Rd; ⊙9am-4:30pm Jun-Oct) Built by the Civilian Conservation Corps in 1923 and once the park's proud visitors' lodge, this building has been renovated in recent years to host exhibits on geology, glaciers and wildlife.

Holzwarth Historic Site HISTORIC SITE
(Never Summer Ranch; ☎park headquarters 970-586-1206; Trail Ridge Rd/US 34; ⊙10am-4pm Jun-Oct; P 🚻) When Prohibition was enacted in 1916, John Holzwarth Sr, a Denver saloonkeeper, started a new life as a subsistence rancher. This site houses several buildings kept in their original condition, and hosts historical reenactments and ranger-led programs. The **Heritage Days** celebration happens in late July.

The site lies at the end of a graded half-mile path, easily accessible with strollers.

Activities

Hiking & Backpacking

With over 300 miles of trail, traversing all aspects of its diverse terrain, the park is suited to every hiking ability. Those with the kids in tow might consider the easy hikes in the Wild Basin to Calypso Falls or to Gem Lake in the Lumpy Ridge area, while those with unlimited ambition, strong legs and enough trail mix will be lured by the challenge of summiting Longs Peak. Regardless, it's best to spend at least one night at 7000ft to 8000ft prior to setting out to allow your body to adjust to the elevation. Before July, many trails are snowbound and high water runoff makes passage difficult. In the winter, avalanches are a hazard. Dogs and other pets are not allowed on the trails. All overnight stays in the backcountry require permits.

You need not worry about getting lonesome on the 15-mile round-trip to the summit of **Longs Peak** (14,255ft). During the summer, you're likely to find a line of more than 100 parked cars snaking down the road from the Longs Peak trailhead, reached from Hwy 7, about 9 miles south of Estes Park.

After the initial 6 miles of moderate trail to the Boulder Field (12,760ft), the path steepens at the start of the Keyhole Route to the summit, which is marked with yellow-and-red bull's-eyes painted on the rock.

Even superhuman athletes who are used to the thin air will be slowed by the route's ledge system, which resembles a narrow cliffside stairway without a handrail. After this, hikers scramble the final homestretch to the summit boulders. The view from the top – snow-kissed granite stretching out to the curved horizon – is incredible. The round-trip hike takes anywhere from 10 to 15 hours.

This is a challenging climb with some scrambling on all fours. Bring more food, water and warm clothes than you think you will need.

The golden rule in Colorado mountaineering: if you haven't made the summit by noon, return (no matter how close you are). It's the best way to avoid getting hit by lightning.

Many climbers make the trail approach in early predawn hours after overnighting at Longs Peak Campground. The Keyhole Route is generally free of snow mid-July to October – otherwise you will need technical climbing skills and equipment to reach the summit. When you dial park headquarters at the Beaver Meadows Visitor Center (p135), the prerecorded message will have information about the conditions on this popular route.

Note that there are no park entrance fees for this hike, as the trailhead is outside park boundaries.

Twin Sisters Peak is an up-and-back hike that provides an excellent warm-up to climbing Longs Peak. In addition, the 11,428ft summit of Twin Sisters Peak offers unequaled views of Longs Peak. It's an arduous walk, gaining 2300ft in just 3.7 miles. Erosion-resistant quartz rock caps the oddly deformed rock at the summit and delicate alpine flowers (plenty of mountain harebell) fill the rock spaces near the stone hut. The trailhead is near Mills Cabin, 10 miles south of Estes Park on Hwy 7. No fees are required for this hike.

Accessed from the Bear Lake trailhead, **Glacier Gorge Junction** is a busy network of trails that threads through pine forest and over rushing streams, offering a spectrum of difficulty. The easy stroll to Alberta Falls is good for families. Far more strenuous 5-mile options would be to hike up Glacier Gorge, past Mills Lake and many glacial erratics to Black Lake, or via Loch Vale to Andrews Glacier on the Continental Divide. The trailhead is served by the Glacier Basin–Bear Lake shuttle.

FLOOD REPAIRS

A severe flood washed through Rocky Mountain National Park in September 2013, and several campgrounds and trails were damaged or closed as of press time. These included Twin Sisters Trail, Aspenglen Campground, Longs Peak Campground, McGraw Ranch Rd and Cow Creek Trailhead, North Fork Trail, and the Ypsilon and Lawn Lake trails. Work was underway to repair damage, and the park is open for visitors.

Rock Climbing

Many of the park's alpine climbs are long one-day climbs or require an overnight stay on the rock face. Often the only way to accomplish a long climb and avoid afternoon thundershowers is to begin climbing at dawn – this can mean an approach hike beginning at midnight! An alternative is to bivouac (temporary open-air encampment – no tents) at the base of the climb. Free bivouac permits are issued only to technical climbers and are mandatory for all overnight stays in the backcountry.

To minimize the environmental impact of backcountry use, the Rocky Mountain National Park Backcountry Office allows only a limited number of people to bivouac at four popular climbing areas. Phone reservations may be made March to May 20 for the following restricted zones: Longs Peak area, including Broadway below Diamond, Chasm View, Mills Glacier and Meeker Cirque; Black Lake area (Glacier Gorge), encompassing McHenry's Peak, Arrowhead, Spearhead and Chiefshead/Pagoda; the base of Notchtop Peak; and the Skypond/Andrews Glacier Area, including the Taylor/Powell Peaks and Sharkstooth Peak. Reservations are not needed nor accepted for other bivouacs.

Good bouldering and traditional rock climbing can be found at Lumpy Ridge, accessed less than 2 miles north of Estes Park on Devils Gulch Rd.

For climbing gear try **Estes Park Mountain Shop** (☎970-586-6548; www.estesparkmountainshop.com; 2050 Big Thompson Ave; 2-person tent $10, bear box per night $3 ; ⏲8am-9pm). A small stock of climbing gear is also available from the Colorado Mountain School (p136).

Cycling & Mountain Biking

Mountain biking and cycling have continued to gain popularity despite the park's heavy traffic. It's a splendid way to see the park and wildlife, though bicycle travel is restricted to paved roads and to one dirt road, Fall River Rd. Those looking to ride technical routes on a mountain bike should go to Roosevelt National Forest.

SAFETY

If you're in easily accessible areas during high season, the biggest annoyance in Rocky Mountain National Park will likely be the other visitors. Roads clog with RVs, garbage fills every can to the brim and screaming children seem to multiply endlessly. Brace yourself, camper: it can be annoying. But it might be more than fellow travelers giving you a headache: it could be the altitude. High elevation can play all kinds of nasty tricks here, from relatively mild problems such as a pounding head and winded breathing to fairly serious symptoms of nausea, dehydration and fatigue. Stay hydrated, protect yourself from the sun, and if symptoms get really bad, head down to a lower elevation.

If you intend to get off the heavily beaten trail, take precautions in the spring and summer to avoid bites from wood ticks, which can transmit Colorado tick fever. Also be mindful of your food, which can attract wildlife. The park is home to black bears and mountain lions. Although neither poses a serious threat to visitors, you'll need to store your food in a bear box.

Weather

Weather in the park, as in all mountainous areas, is highly variable. Summer days often reach 70°F to 80°F (21°C to 27°C), yet a sudden shift in the weather can bring snow to the peaks in July. Nevertheless, the climate follows broadly predictable patterns based on season, elevation, exposure and location east or west of the Continental Divide. Strong winds are common above the treeline. July thundershowers typically dump 2in of rain on the park, while January is the driest month. Bear Lake (9400ft) normally has a January snow base of 25in. The Continental Divide causes a pronounced rain-shadow effect: Grand Lake (west of the Divide) annually averages 20in of moisture, while Estes Park receives only about 13in.

On either a road bike or a mountain bike, climbing the paved Trail Ridge Rd has one big advantage over Fall River Rd (a 9-mile one-way climb of more than 3000ft): you can turn around should problems arise.

Less daunting climbs and climes are available on the park's lower paved roads. A popular 16-mile circuit is the Horseshoe Park/Estes Park Loop. For a bit more of a climbing challenge you can continue to Bear Lake Rd, an 8-mile long route that rises 1500ft to the high mountain basin with a decent shoulder.

If you are not up to climbing either Trail Ridge or Fall River Rds, Colorado Bicycling Adventures (p136) offers tours of Rocky Mountain National Park. It also rents bikes.

To avoid hypothermia and dehydration bring a set of dry long-sleeve clothes, plus plenty of water.

Snowshoeing & Cross-Country Skiing

From December into May, the high valleys and alpine tundra offer cross-country skiers unique opportunities to view wildlife and the winter scenery undisturbed by crowds. January and February are the best months for dry, powdery snowpack; spring snows tend to be heavy and wet. Most routes follow summer hiking trails, but valley bottoms and frozen streambeds typically have more snow cover and are less challenging. Ask about avalanche hazards before heading out – Colorado has one of the most dangerous snowpacks in the world with people dying in slides most years – and avoid steep open slopes.

Novices should consider hiring a guide or traveling with experienced leaders. Rangers lead weekend snowshoe hikes in the east side of the park from January to April, depending on snow conditions. Trailhead locations and times are available from the park headquarters.

Overnight trips require permits, and the USFS and NPS will have a list of closed trails.

You can gear up at the Estes Park Mountain Shop (p132).

Sleeping

The only overnight accommodations in the park are at campgrounds; the majority of motel or hotel accommodations are around Estes Park or Grand Lake. The closest thing the park has to the typical Civilian Conservation Corps–era lodges built by public works at parks like Yosemite and Yellowstone during the Great Depression is the YMCA of the Rockies, which is on the park's border.

FEES & PERMITS

For private vehicles, the park entrance fee is $20, valid for seven days. Individuals entering the park on foot, bicycle, motorcycle or bus pay $10 each. All visitors receive a free copy of the park's information brochure, which contains a good orientation map and is available in English, German, French, Spanish and Japanese. A good option if you plan to visit any other national parks is to buy an annual National Parks and Federal Recreational Lands Annual Pass for $80.

Backcounty permits ($20 for a group of up to 12 people for seven days) are required for overnight stays in the 260 designated backcountry camping sites in the park. They are free between November 1 and April 30. Phone reservations can be made only from March 1 to May 15. Reservations for sites and permits, by snail mail or in person, are accepted via the **Backcountry Office** (970-586-1242; www.nps.gov/romo; 1000 W Hwy 36, Estes Park, CO 80517).

A bear box to store your food in is required if you are staying overnight in the backcountry between May and October (established campsites already have them). These can be rented for around $3 to $5 per day from REI (p92) in Denver or the Estes Park Mountain Shop (p132).

Permits can be obtained in person at Beaver Meadows Visitor Center, Kawuneeche Visitor Center, and (in summer only) at the Longs Peak and Wild Basin ranger stations. Generally speaking, there are always backcountry sites available.

The park's formal campgrounds provide campfire programs, have public telephones and a seven-day limit during summer months; all except Longs Peak take RVs (no hookups). The water supply is turned off during winter.

You will need a backcountry permit to stay outside developed park campgrounds. None of the campgrounds have showers, but they do have flush toilets in summer and outhouse facilities in winter. Sites include a fire ring, picnic table and one parking spot. Most have bear boxes for food storage.

★**Longs Peak Campground** CAMPGROUND $
(970-586-1206; Longs Peak Rd, off State Hwy 7; tent sites $20; P) This is the base camp of choice for the early morning ascent of Longs Peak, one of Colorado's most easily accessible 14ers. The scenery is striking and its 26 spaces are for tents only, but don't expect much solitude in the peak of the summer.

There are no reservations, but if you're planning to bag Longs Peak after sleeping here, get here early one day before the climb – according to rangers the only way to ensure a site during peak season is to show up before noon.

Olive Ridge Campground CAMPGROUND $
(303-541-2500; State Hwy 7; tent sites $19; mid-May–Nov) This well-kept USFS campground has access to four trailheads: St Vrain Mountain, Wild Basin, Longs Peak and Twin Sisters. In the summer it can get full, though sites are mostly first-come, first-served.

Moraine Park Campground CAMPGROUND $
(877-444-6777; www.recreation.gov; off Bear Lake Rd; summer tent & RV sites $20) In the middle of a stand of ponderosa pine forest off Bear Lake Rd, this is the biggest of the park's campgrounds, approximately 2.5 miles south of the Beaver Meadows Visitor Center, and with 245 sites. The walk-in, tent-only sites in the D Loop are recommended if you want quiet. Make reservations through the website.

Reservations are accepted and recommended from the end of May through to the end of September; other times of the year the campground is first-come, first-served. At night in the summer, there are numerous ranger-led programs in the amphitheater.

The campground is served by the shuttle buses on Bear Lake Rd through the summer.

Aspenglen Campground CAMPGROUND $
(877-444-6777; www.recreation.gov; State Hwy 34; summer tent & RV sites $20) With only 54 sites, this is the smallest of the park's reservable camping. There are many tent-only sites, including some walk-ins, and a limited number of trailers are allowed. This is the quietest campground in the park while still being highly accessible (5 miles west of Estes Park on US 34). Make reservations through the website.

Timber Creek Campground CAMPGROUND $
(Trail Ridge Rd, US Hwy 34; tent & RV sites $20) This campground has 100 sites and remains open through the winter. No reservations accepted. The only established campground on the west side of the park, it's 7 miles north of Grand Lake.

Glacier Basin Campground CAMPGROUND $
(877-444-6777; www.recreation.gov; off Bear Lake Rd; campsites summer $20;) This developed campground has a large area for group camping and accommodates RVs. It is served by the shuttle buses on Bear Lake Rd throughout the summer. Make reservations through the website.

Information

MEDICAL SERVICES

There are no care facilities in the park, but most rangers are trained to give emergency treatment. Emergency telephones are at Longs Peak and Wild Basin ranger stations, as well as certain trailheads, including Bear Lake and Lawn Lake.

MONEY

The park has no banking services; for these you'll need to head to either Estes Park or Grand Lake.

TELEPHONE

Cell phone coverage? Forget it. The only place calls can be made are from public phones at visitor centers and large, established campgrounds.

TOURIST INFORMATION

The park has three full-service visitor centers – one on the east side, one on the west and one in the middle. Though they all have different displays and programs, this is where you can study maps and speak with rangers about permits and weather conditions.

Alpine Visitor Center (www.nps.gov/romo; Fall River Pass; 10:30am-4:30pm late May–mid-Jun, 9am-5pm late Jun-early Sep, 10:30am-4:30pm early Sep–mid-Oct) The views from this popular visitor center and souvenir store at 11,796ft, and right in the middle of the park, are extraordinary. You can see elk, deer and sometimes moose grazing on the hillside on the drive up Old Fall River Rd.

Much of the traffic that clogs Trail Ridge Rd all summer pulls into Alpine Visitor Center, so the place is a zoo. Rangers here give programs and advice about trails. You can also shop for knickknacks or eat in the cafeteria-style dining room.

Beaver Meadows Visitor Center (970-586-1206; www.nps.gov/romo; US Hwy 36; 8am-9pm late Jun-late Aug, to 4:30pm or 5pm rest of year) The primary visitor center and best stop for park information if you're approaching from Estes Park. You can see a film about the park, browse a small gift shop and reserve backcountry camping sites.

Kawuneeche Visitor Center (970-627-3471; 16018 US Hwy 34; 8am-6pm last week May-Labor Day, 8am-5pm Labor Day-Sep, 8am-4:30pm Oct-May) This visitor center is on the west side of the park, and offers a film about the park, ranger-led walks and discussions, backcountry permits and family activities.

Longs Peak Ranger Station (Longs Peak Rd, off State Hwy 7; 8:30am-4:30pm summer) Eleven miles south of Estes Park.

Wild Basin Ranger Station (off County Hwy 115; hours vary)

Getting There & Away

Trail Ridge Rd (US 34) is the only east–west route through the park; the US 34 eastern approach from I-25 and Loveland follows the Big Thompson River Canyon. The most direct route from Boulder follows US 36 through Lyons to the east entrances. Another approach from the south, mountainous Hwy 7, passes by Enos Mills' Cabin and provides access to campsites and trailheads on the east side of the divide. Winter closure of US 34 through the park makes access to the park's west side dependent on US 40 at Granby.

There are two entrance stations on the east side: Fall River (US 34) and Beaver Meadows (US 36). The Grand Lake Entrance Station (US 34) is the only entry on the west side. Year-round access is available through Kawuneeche Valley along the Colorado River headwaters to Timber Creek Campground. The main centers of visitor activity on the park's east side are the Alpine Visitor Center, high on Trail Ridge Rd, and Bear Lake Rd, which leads to campgrounds, trailheads and the Moraine Park Museum.

MAPS

Even though you'll get a driving map when you enter the park and some basic, non-technical photocopied maps are available at some of the most popular trailheads, it's surprising that none of the visitor centers stocks high-quality topographic maps for hikers. You'll want to pick them up beforehand in Estes Park at **MacDonald Book Shop** (970-586-3450; www.macdonaldbookshop.com; 152 E Elkhorn Ave; 8am-8pm, shorter hours in winter;).

North of Estes Park, Devils Gulch Rd leads to several hiking trails. Further out on Devils Gulch Rd, you pass through the village of Glen Haven to reach the trailhead entry to the park along the North Fork of the Big Thompson River.

Getting Around

A majority of visitors enter the park in their own cars, using the long and winding Trail Ridge Rd (US 34) to cross the Continental Divide. There are options for those without wheels, however. In summer a free shuttle bus operates from the Estes Park Visitors Center multiple times daily, bringing hikers to a park-and-ride location where you can pick up other shuttles. The year-round option leaves the Glacier Basin parking area and heads to Bear Lake, in the park's lower elevations. During the summer peak, a second shuttle operates between Moraine Park campground and the Glacier Basin parking area. The second shuttle runs on weekends only from mid-August through September.

ESTES PARK

POP 6402 / ELEV 7522FT

T-shirt shops and ice-cream parlors, sidewalks jammed with tourists and streets plugged with RVs: welcome to Estes Park, the chaotic outpost at the edge of Rocky Mountain National Park.

There's no small irony in the fact that the proximity to one of the most pristine outdoor escapes in the USA has made Estes Park the kind of place you'll need to escape from. Those expecting immediate views of the pristine beauty of Rocky Mountain National Park may be disappointed to find themselves watching brake lights on E Elkhorn Ave, the town's artery to both park entrances. But it's not all bad. Although the strip malls and low-rise motels can be unsightly, Estes Park promises every convenience to the traveler, and during the off-season the place has a certain charm, as the streets quieten down and the prices of creekside cabins drop.

The massive floods of September 2013 pummeled the town, with most of Main St flooding. Nearly every road leading to town was damaged and it took three weeks to get US 36 open again. Most businesses were able to open shortly after the flood.

Sights & Activities

On the doorstep of Rocky Mountain National Park and surrounded by national forest, Estes Park is one of the state's premier supply points for the mountains. With the exception of white-water rafting and skiing (better in other parts of the state), the area has top-notch outdoor activities of every stripe, and a stroll down Elkhorn will take you past a number of operators heading into the park via horse, jeep or hiking boots. Many of Estes Park's sights are a bit out of town and only accessible if you have a car.

Estes Park Museum MUSEUM

(970-586-6256; www.estesnet.com/museum; 200 4th St; 10am-5pm Mon-Sat, 1-5pm Sun;) FREE This ambitious community museum has a commendable rotation of exhibits on local culture. It's not only corny Ice Age mannequins either – during our last visit the main attraction was a glimpse into Estes Park's wild days in the 1960s.

Ariel Tramway CABLE CAR

(970-586-3675; www.estestram.com; 420 E Riverside Dr; adult/child/senior $10/5/9; 9am-6pm Memorial Day–Labor Day; P) In the time you wait to be herded aboard a tram to the top of Prospect Mountain, you could have climbed Lily Mountain on your own two feet, but the tram is a good option for those with modest ambitions who still want the view.

★**Colorado Mountain School** ROCK CLIMBING

(800-836-4008; www.totalclimbing.com; 341 Moraine Ave; half-day guided climbs per person from $125) Simply put, there's no better resource for climbers in Colorado – this outfit is the largest climbing operator in the region, has the most expert guides and is the only organization allowed to operate within Rocky Mountain National Park. It has a clutch of classes taught by world-class instructors.

Basic courses, such as Intro to Rock Climbing, are a great way for novices to deeply experience the Rockies. There are multiday training expeditions for those with some experience. Courses are taught in an ideal setting – whether it be a towering granite peak in the park or the 10,000-sq-ft indoor climbing facility. You can also stay on site in dorm lodging ($25).

Colorado Bicycling Adventures CYCLING

(970-586-4241; 2050 Big Thompson Ave; half-day tour $60) For years this was *the* bike shop in town, so the staff know the surrounding hills like the backs of their contoured, oversized calf muscles. Now the shop has moved to a central location, from where it leads tours.

Sombrero Ranch HORSEBACK RIDING
(☎970-586-4577; www.sombrero.com; 1895 Big Thompson Ave; horseback rides from $35) With affordable guided trips into the national park or through a huge private ranch in the foothills, this quality outfitter has a variety of options. The evening 'steak fry' is a popular ride. Sombrero Ranch operates stables throughout the region.

Kirks Flyshop FISHING
(☎877-669-1859; www.kirksflyshop.com; 230 E Elkhorn Ave; tours from $150; ⏲7am-7pm) This full-service fly-fishing shop offers a number of guided packages in Rocky Mountain National Park and the surrounding waterways of the Front Range. It also rents equipment, guides overnight hikes, and offers float fishing and group excursions.

Green Jeep Tours 4WD
(☎970-577-0034; www.epgjt.com; 157 Moraine Ave; tours from $35) Offerings start with 3½-hour guided 4WD tours to waterfalls in Rocky Mountain National Park and move up to all-day affairs. Note that green is the color of the car, and is not representative of an environmentally friendly ethos.

Sleeping

Be warned: lodgings fill up very fast during the peak July and August period, when the prices are sky high. You're likely to be out of luck if you travel west of Greeley without a reservation during summer. Off-season rates may be down to half that of summer prices, and many accommodations simply close for the winter.

Most of the cheaper midcentury motels (which still aren't that cheap) are located east of town along US 34 or Hwy 7. Most of these low-slung motels are remarkably similar: musty carpet and fairly small rooms with television and refrigerator, though some places also boast pools, hot tubs and saunas. There are plenty of cabins to rent here too, with a concentration of them along US 66.

There are some passable budget options for those trying to save money, but the best-value accommodations, hands down, are in area campgrounds, which are plentiful, easily accessible and stunning. If you didn't bring your own tent and sleeping bag, you can rent one from Estes Park Mountain Shop (p132).

Total Climbing Lodge HOSTEL $
(☎303-447-2804; www.totalclimbing.com; 341 Moraine Ave; dm $25; P@📶) A bustling hub of climbers, this lodge is the best dorm option in town. Expect simple pine bunks, a ping-pong table and a laid-back vibe. Call ahead in winter.

Estes Park Hostel HOSTEL $
(☎970-237-0152; www.estesparkhostel.com; 211 Cleave St; dm/s/d $26/38/52; 📶) This hostel, with a handful of shared rooms and simple privates, isn't going into history books as the plushest digs ever, but there's a kitchen on site, and Terri, the owner, is helpful. The price is right too.

Estes Park KOA CAMPGROUND $
(☎800-562-1887, 970-586-2888; www.estesparkkoa.com; 2051 Big Thompson Ave; tent sites $27-33, RV sites $38-48, cabins from $75; 📶👪) With so much excellent camping just up the road in Rocky Mountain National Park, it's hard to see the allure of this roadside RV-oriented camping spot. But for those in need of a staging day before a big adventure, the proximity to town is appealing.

★YMCA of the Rockies – Estes Park Center RESORT $$
(☎970-586-3341; www.ymcarockies.org; 2515 Tunnel Rd; r & d from $109, cabins from $129; P❄📶👪🐾) Estes Park Center is not your typical YMCA boarding house. Instead it's a favorite vacation spot with families, boasting upmarket motel-style accommodations and cabins set on hundreds of acres of high alpine terrain. Choose from roomy cabins that sleep up to 10 or motel-style rooms for singles or doubles. Both are simple and practical.

This very kid-friendly resort is located in a serene and ultrapristine location in the mountains just outside town. The 860-acre plot hosts lots of wide open spaces that are dotted with forests and fields of wildflowers. Just a few minutes outside Estes Park (but definitely away from the hustle of town), it offers a range of activities for adults, kids or the whole family throughout the year. This resort also runs special themed weekends and longer summer camps where environmental education is taught in a fun and engaging manner. This YMCA is unapologetically outdoorsy, and most guests come to participate in the activities.

Estes Park

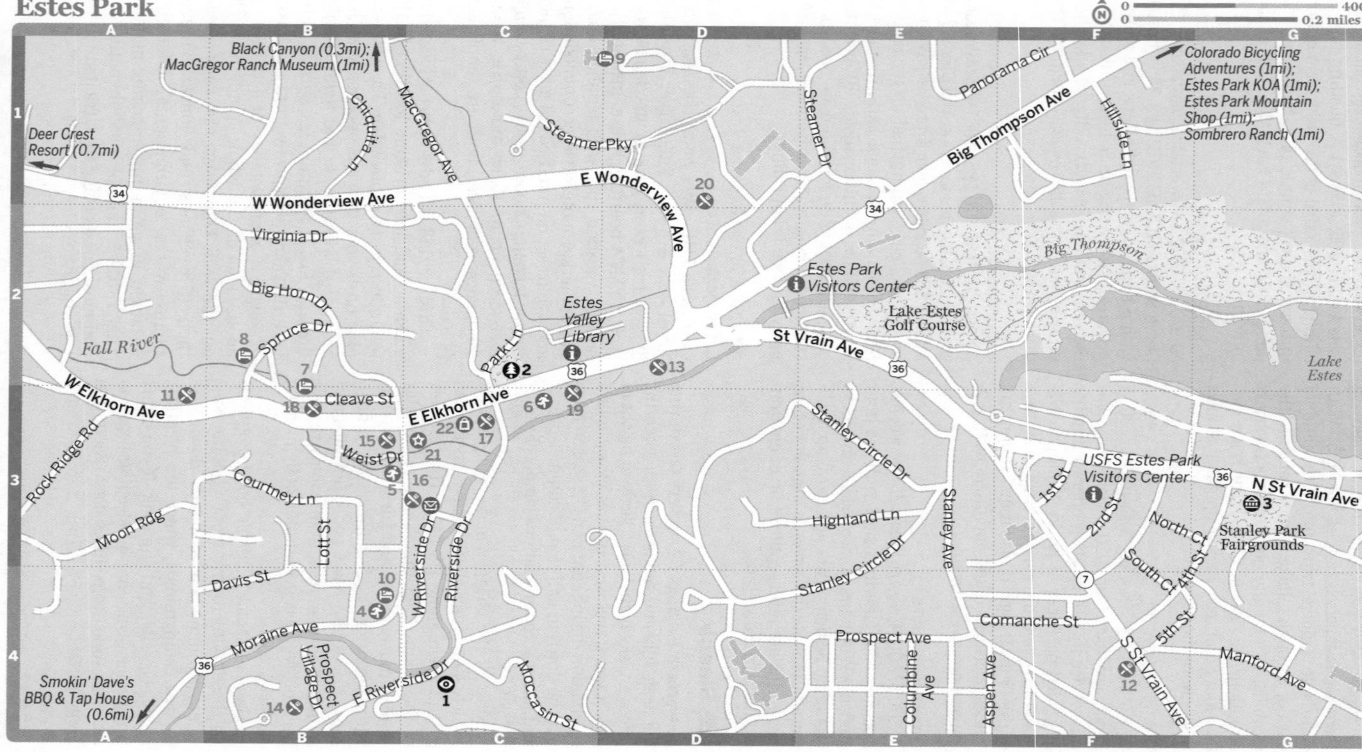
0 — 400 m
0 — 0.2 miles
Black Canyon (0.3mi); MacGregor Ranch Museum (1mi)
Deer Crest Resort (0.7mi)
Colorado Bicycling Adventures (1mi); Estes Park KOA (1mi); Estes Park Mountain Shop (1mi); Sombrero Ranch (1mi)
Smokin' Dave's BBQ & Tap House (0.6mi)
Chiquita Ln
MacGregor Ave
Steamer Pky
Steamer Dr
Panorama Cir
Big Thompson Ave
Hillside Ln
W Wonderview Ave
E Wonderview Ave
Virginia Dr
Big Horn Dr
Spruce Dr
Fall River
Cleave St
W Elkhorn Ave
E Elkhorn Ave
Park Ln
Estes Valley Library
Estes Park Visitors Center
Lake Estes Golf Course
Big Thompson
Lake Estes
St Vrain Ave
Weist Dr
Rock Ridge Rd
Courtney Ln
Moon Rdg
Lott St
Davis St
W Riverside Dr
Riverside Dr
Moraine Ave
Prospect Village Dr
E Riverside Dr
Moccasin St
Stanley Circle Dr
Highland Ln
Stanley Ave
USFS Estes Park Visitors Center
N St Vrain Ave
1st St
2nd St
North Ct
South Ct
4th St
5th St
Stanley Park Fairgrounds
Comanche St
Prospect Ave
Columbine Ave
Aspen Ave
S St Vrain Ave
Manford Ave

Estes Park

Sights
1 Ariel Tramway C4
2 Bond Park C2
3 Estes Park Museum G3

Activities, Courses & Tours
4 Colorado Mountain School B4
5 Green Jeep Tours B3
6 Kirks Flyshop C3

Sleeping
7 Estes Park Hostel B2
8 Silver Moon Inn B2
9 Stanley Hotel D1
10 Total Climbing Lodge B4

Eating
11 Big Horn Restaurant A3
12 Cables F4
13 Ed's Cantina & Grill D2
14 Estes Park Brewery B4
15 Lonigans B3
16 Molly B Restaurant C3
17 Nepal's Cafe C3
18 Penelope's Burgers & Fries B3
19 Poppy's C3
20 Safeway D1

Entertainment
21 Park Theatre C3

Shopping
22 MacDonald Book Shop C3

Deer Crest Resort HOTEL $$
(970-586-2324, 800-331-2324; www.deercrestresort.com; 1200 Fall River Rd; d $119-129, ste from $149; P ❄ ☎ ≋ 👪) There is a ton of sleeping options along the road out to Rocky Mountain National Park, but Deer Creek bests its neighbors with gas grills, lots of green space for the kids to run around in and the sound of the creek shushing guests to sleep. The on-site restaurant is also excellent.

Silver Moon Inn HOTEL $$
(970-586-6006; www.silvermooninn.com; 175 Spruce Dr; d $130-190; P ❄ @ ☎ ≋ 👪) The rooms here aren't loaded with personality, but there are plenty of thoughtful touches like fireplaces in the deluxe rooms, creekside fire pits and wheelchair access to most rooms on the 1st floor. It's tucked between a rock outcropping and a stream on the western edge of town. Go for a deluxe room for more privacy.

Mary's Lake Lodge LODGE $$
(970-577-9495; www.maryslakelodge.com; 2625 Marys Lake Rd; r & d from $99, cabins from $199; P ❄ ☎ 👪) This atmospheric old wooden lodge, perched on a ridge looking over its namesake lake, is an utterly romantic place to slumber. Built from polished pine logs, it reeks of Wild West ambience and has an amazing covered front porch with panoramic Rocky Mountain views.

The rooms and cabins are a blend of modern and historic, and many of the latter have private hot tubs. Both the saloon-style **Tavern** (mains $7-20; 11am-11pm) and fine-dining **Chalet Room** (mains $12-20; 5-10pm) serve delicious fresh lake fish (and flown-in seafood), and have seating on the heated porch. A big hot tub under the stars, fire pit and live music five nights per week round out amenities, while an on-site spa takes care of gritty hiking feet and sore muscles. Mary's is 3 miles south of Estes Park off Hwy 7.

★ **Stanley Hotel** HOTEL $$$
(970-577-4000; www.stanleyhotel.com; 333 Wonderview Ave; r from $199; P ☎ ≋ 👪) The white Georgian Colonial Revival hotel stands in brilliant contrast to the towering peaks of Rocky Mountain National Park that frame the skyline. A favorite local retreat, this best-in-class hotel served as the inspiration for Stephen King's famous cult novel *The Shining*. Rooms are decorated to retain some of the Old West feel while still ensuring all the creature comforts.

The Stanley boasts great mountain views, splendid dining and even ghost tours of the building on weekend nights! And if it's ghosts you're after, you should book room 401 to increase your chances of ghost-spotting – staff consider it the 'most haunted.' The public areas encompass vast open spaces warmed with stone fireplaces and plump leather couches.

Black Canyon LODGE $$$
(800-897-5123, 970-586-8113; www.blackcanyoninn.com; 800 MacGregor Ave; 1-/2-/3-bed r from $195/260/399; P ❄ ☎ 👪) A fine place to splurge, this lovely, secluded 14-acre property offers luxury suites and a 'rustic' log cabin (which comes with a Jacuzzi). The rooms are dressed out with stone fireplaces, dark wood and woven tapestries in rich dark colors.

Eating

Like lodgings, restaurants here often shift to shorter hours, close for several days of the week or shut down altogether in the snowy off-season. Another unfortunate similarity is poor value for your money. Most menus here are meaty American standards and humdrum pub grub, which too often come at white tablecloth prices. If you're visiting between September and May, it's wise to call ahead for reservations. Self-caterers will make out best by stocking up at the local Safeway supermarket on the way into town to picnic at **Bond Park** (E Elkhorn Ave) or in one of the national park picnic spots up the road.

Safeway SELF-CATERING $
(970-586-4447; 451 E Wonderview Ave; 9am-7pm Mon-Fri, to 6pm Sat, 10am-4pm Sun; P) This large outpost of a Western States grocery chain is the place to stock up in Estes Park. It also has a full pharmacy.

Nepal's Cafe NEPALESE $
(970-577-7035; 184 E Elkhorn Ave, Unit H; buffet $9, mains $9-13; 11am-9pm;) Lamp-heated lunch buffets are usually a no-no, but this place might make you reconsider. The curries are spiced just right and the *momo* (dumplings) are a filling option before or after a big hike. Come early for dinner, as the tiny place gets packed.

Molly B Restaurant AMERICAN $
(970-586-2766; www.estesparkmollyb.com; 200 Moraine Ave; breakfast $5-8; 7am-4pm Thu-Tue;) This classic American breakfast place in town is easy to find and has a burly omelet and other greasy-spoon delights served among wood paneling and vinyl seats. Even the healthy food is delivered jumbo size, making the 'outrageous granola' no joke.

Penelope's Burgers & Fries BURGERS $
(970-586-2277; 229 W Elkhorn Ave; mains $5-9; 11am-10pm;) This burger barn on the main drag is decorated with plenty of old-time clutter – frying pans and spoons and historic photos. The deep fryer works overtime in the back.

Poppy's PIZZERIA $
(970-586-8282; www.estesdining.com; 342 E Elkhorn Av; pizza $7-9; 11am-10pm;) Affordable and friendly, this riverfront mountain pizzeria offers a good selection of yummy wraps, burgers and sandwiches to go with its signature savory pies.

★**Big Horn Restaurant** AMERICAN $$
(970-586-2792; www.estesparkbighorn.com; 401 W Elkhorn; mains $7-18; 6am-9pm, hours vary seasonally;) This local breakfast institution offers a side of grits along with the local gossip and the best *huevos rancheros* in town. If you get here on the way into the park, order a packed lunch with your breakfast.

Cables AMERICAN $$
(970-586-1069; 451 S St Vrain Ave; mains $12-17) This new boy in town has been a northern Colorado favorite for years. It specializes in pizza and pasta with homemade noodles and plenty of Americana classics. There's a good, friendly bar packed with locals and tourists.

Ed's Cantina & Grill MEXICAN $$
(970-586-2919; www.edscantina.com; 390 E Elkhorn Ave; mains $9-13; 11am-late Mon-Fri, 8am-10pm Sat & Sun;) With an outdoor patio right on the river, Ed's is a great place to kick back with a margarita. Serving Mexican and American staples, the restaurant is in a retro woodsy space with leather booth seating and bold primary colors.

Smokin' Dave's BBQ & Tap House BARBECUE $$
(866-674-2793; www.smokindavesbbqandtaphouse.com; 820 Moraine Ave; mains $8-20; 11am-9pm Sun-Thu, to 10pm Fri & Sat;) Half-assed BBQ joints are all too common in Colorado's mountain towns, but Dave's, situated in a spare dining room, fully delivers. The buffalo ribs and pulled pork come dressed in a slightly sweet, smoky, tangy sauce and the sweet-potato fries are crisply fried. Also excellent? The long, well-selected beer list.

Lonigans PUB FOOD $$
(970-586-4346; www.lonigans.com; 110 W Elkhorn Ave; mains $9-12; 11am-2am, kitchen closes 10pm;) This pub and grill is a place to soak up Estes Park local flavor, mostly through the sidelong glances of the good ol' boys at the bar and boozy karaoke crooners. The menu – mostly burgers and American pub basics – includes Rocky Mountain Oysters, otherwise known as bull balls.

Estes Park Brewery PUB FOOD $$
(970-586-6409; www.epbrewery.com; 470 Prospect Village Dr; mains $8-12; 11am-2am; P) Ain't nothing fancy about this brewpub – it dishes out pizza, wings and house beer in a big, boxy room that's a cross between a classroom and a country kitchen. Nothing

WORTH A TRIP

PEAK TO PEAK HIGHWAY

The Peak to Peak Hwy (Hwy 72) is one of the state's most scenic drives. If you're driving between Denver and Rocky Mountain National Park, definitely consider this route.

➡ **Rainbow Lakes** Stop at the Mile 40 marker to head up to Rainbow Lakes and the Arapahoe Glacier Trails.

➡ **Brainard Lake** The lake is beautiful, and there are good trails from here into the Indian Peaks backcountry.

➡ **Saint Malo Center** On Hwy 7, just before the true start of the Peak to Peak, this wonderfully crafted church was visited by the pope.

gourmet, but pool tables and outdoor seating keep the place popping until late.

Those who are a bit indecisive can head downstairs to the tasting room before taking home a growler. Our favorites are the refreshing bright lager and the Stinger.

Rock Inn Mountain Tavern STEAKHOUSE **$$$**
(970-586-4116; www.rockinnestes.com; 1675 Hwy 66; mains $14-29; 11am-2am;) After a few days in the wilds of Rocky Mountain National Park, the rare porterhouse here seems heaven-sent (even if the country band on stage can't pass as the accompanying choir of angels). Excellent stick-to-the-ribs fare and a crackling fire make it ideal for hikers looking to indulge.

☆ Entertainment

Park Theatre CINEMA
(Moraine Av; movies $8) This 1913 historic landmark is still a great place to catch a movie.

Information

Estes Park Visitors Center (800-443-7837, 970-577-9900; www.visitestespark.com; 500 Big Thompson Ave; 9am-8pm daily Jun-Aug, 8am-5pm Mon-Fri, 9am-5pm Sat, 10am-4pm Sun Sep-May) For help with lodging come here, just east of the US 36 junction.

Estes Valley Library (970-586-8116; www.estesvalleylibrary.org; 335 E Elkhorn Ave; 9am-9pm Mon-Thu, to 5pm Fri & Sat, 1-5pm Sun;) With free wi-fi, large open spaces and tons of literature on the local area, Estes Park's central library is a good resource for travelers researching on the go.

Police Station (970-586-4000; 170 MacGregor Ave)

Post Office (970-586-0170; 215 W Riverside Dr; 8:30am-4:30pm Mon-Fri, 10am-1pm Sat) Centrally located post office with a fully staffed service desk.

USFS Estes Park Visitors Center (970-586-3440; 161 2nd St) This center sells books and maps for the Arapaho and Roosevelt National Forests and has camping and trail information for hikers and mountain bikers. Camping permits for the heavily used Indian Peaks Wilderness Area, south of Rocky Mountain National Park, are required from June to September 15 and cost $5 per person.

Getting There & Away

Estes Park is 34 miles west of Loveland via US 34, which you can access from I-25 exit 257. Many visitors also come up by way of Boulder along US 36, passing through Lyons. Both are spectacular drives through rugged foothills, red rock formations and lush forest. A slower but more scenic route is the spectacular Peak to Peak Hwy.

Getting Around

Considering the traffic, getting around Estes Park's compact downtown is easiest on foot. Estes Park has started a free shuttle service in the summer along the town's main arteries. The routes seem to change every year, but the service operates daily from about July to August, and then weekends only through September. If you're traveling into Rocky Mountain National Park, there is a free 'Hiker Shuttle,' which leaves from the Estes Park Visitors Center, making stops at Beaver Meadows Visitor Center and the park's Park & Ride lot, where you can transfer to other national park shuttles.

TO & FROM THE AIRPORT

Estes Park Shuttle (970-586-5151; www.estesparkshuttle.com) This shuttle service connects Denver's airport to Estes Park about four times a day. The trip takes two hours.

BICYCLE

Cycling is a great way to get around the area, though few visitors seem to use this mode of transport (of course the altitude does make for some huffing and puffing). In summer, bike rentals spring up in the tourist area along E Elkhorn Ave, or you can get some wheels from Colorado Bicycling Adventures (p136).

TAXI

Peak to Peak Taxi (☎970-586-6111) This mini-van taxi service makes runs throughout Rocky Mountain National Park and the Front Range.

AROUND ESTES PARK

Enos Mills Cabin Museum & Gallery

Naturalist Enos Mills (1870–1922) led the struggle to establish Rocky Mountain National Park. His infectious enthusiasm and passion for nature lived on with his daughter Enda Mills Kiley (who sadly passed away in 2009). Her father's incredible history is documented in his tiny **cabin** (☎970-586-4706; www.enosmills.com; 6760 Hwy 7; adult/child under 12yr $5/3; ⊙11am-4pm Tue & Wed summer;), built in 1885.

The Mills family maintains an interpretive nature trail leading from the parking lot to the cabin, where news clippings and photographs recount Enos Mills' advocacy for the protection of the wild. Reprints and vintage copies of many of Mills' 16 books are available for sale at the cabin, in addition to an outstanding collection of his writings edited by Enda, *Adventures of a Nature Guide* (New Past Press, 1990).

MacGregor Ranch Museum

In 1872 Alexander and Clara MacGregor arrived in Estes Park and settled beside Black Canyon Creek near Lumpy Ridge. Their granddaughter Muriel MacGregor bequeathed the **ranch** (☎970-586-3749; www.macgregorranch.org; 180 MacGregor Lane; ⊙10am-4pm Tue-Sat Jun-Aug) as an educational trust upon her death. It's a living museum featuring original living and working quarters; the ranch still raises Black Angus cattle. It's 1 mile north of Estes Park off Devils Gulch Rd.

An NPS scenic and conservation easement helps fund the operation, and provides trail access to Lumpy Ridge.

Glen Haven

Blink and you might just miss Glen Haven, a tiny outpost on the North Fork of the Big Thompson River, 7 miles east of Estes Park on Devils Gulch Rd. There isn't much here except a post office and general store, but the scenic approach makes it a worthwhile afternoon. Follow the narrow canyon road for 8 miles northwest from US 34 at Drake, site of the North Fork's confluence with the main channel in Big Thompson Canyon. Along the way there are handsome picnic spots; our favorite is right in Glen Haven on the narrow banks of the tumbling North Fork. If you forgot to pack a lunch, drop in at the **Glen Haven General Store** (☎970-586-2560; www.glenhavengeneralstore.com; 7499 Country Rd 43; ⊙9am-6pm May-Oct, shorter hours in winter; P) for gooey cinnamon rolls, cherry cobbler and deli items. In winter it's open 'from 9am to whenever we feel like it!'

The prime attraction of town is the **Inn of Glen Haven** (☎970-586-3897; www.innofglenhaven.com; 7468 Country Rd 43; d w shared bath from $95;), an effete lair of the English gentry, offering delightful B&B rooms (with names such as Lord Dunraven's Room!) and fine dining. It's almost comically stuffy, but fun in a Renaissance-fair kind of way.

FORT COLLINS

POP 138,736 / ELEV 5003FT

Sixty-five miles northwest of Denver, Fort Collins straddles Colorado's topographical divide. Look east and the plains stretch endlessly; turn around and the foothills of the Rockies begin their rise.

Though Fort Collins serves as the foil to Colorado's other Front Range college town, Boulder, the town's status as the underdog is a bit unjust. Sure, the landscape isn't as dramatic, the university isn't quite as prestigious and it doesn't have the granola-crunching socialist cultural cache, but the bicycle-packed streets of Fort Collins exude an unpretentious magnetism. This former farming community has developed into a city with lovely little pockets, especially near the Colorado State University (CSU) campus and the refurbished historical buildings of Old Town.

While the rivalry between the towns continues, there's one indisputable fact: the beer here is *way* better. People who love hoppy, handcrafted microbrews might need to pinch themselves to make sure they're not dreaming.

Sights & Activities

Like many Front Range bergs, Fort Collins' activities demand working up a sweat. Proximity to Horsetooth Mountain Park and Reservoir attracts mountain bikers, campers, hikers and cross-country skiers, while the stone's-throw distance to the Poudre River and Rocky Mountains make it a good jumping-off point for white-water and wilderness excursions. If you're staying in this college town, there are only two absolute musts: the free tour of the New Belgium Brewery (which requires advance reservations) and a cruise around town on one of the ubiquitous bicycles – free to check out from the Bike Library and many of the hotels. The city's extensive network of bicycling paths ranks among the best in the US and provides a pleasant way to see the town.

Swetsville Zoo ZOO
(970-484-9509; 4801 E Harmony Rd; entry by donation; daylight hours;) Bill Swets, a former farmer, volunteer firefighter and insomniac, created a scrap-metal menagerie during his restless nights, a whimsical roadside curiosity. Swets' creations are a coy lesson in creative recycling – from the grinning spider made from a VW bug, to the heavy metal caricature of Monica Lewinsky.

Avery House Museum HISTORIC BUILDING
(www.poudrelandmarks.com; 328 W Mountain Ave; 1-4pm Sat & Sun;) FREE This 1879 home belonged to Franklin Avery, the city surveyor of Fort Collins. Avery's foresight is evident in the tree-lined, wide boulevards that grace the city centre. The Avery House is a stop along the self-guided historic walking tour available from the Fort Collins Convention & Visitors Bureau, with free guided tours that take you through the historic building.

It's truly one of the best introductions to local history you can find.

Fort Collins Museum & Discovery Science Center MUSEUM
(970-221-6738; www.fcmdsc.org; 200 Mathews St; adult/senior over 60yr & child 3-12yr $4/3; 10am-5pm Tue-Sat, noon-5pm Sun;) The hands-on science exhibits focusing on electricity, physics and dinosaurs are designed for children, leaving adults some space to soak up the historical artifacts. The coolest thing on the grounds is an 1860s log cabin from the founding days of Fort Collins.

The Farm@Lee Martinez Park PETTING ZOO
(970-221-6665; www.fcgov.com/recreation/thefarm; 600 N Sherwood St; admission $2.50; 10am-5pm Tue-Sat, from noon Sun, to 4pm Nov-May;) Pony rides and a barnyard of cows, turkeys and chickens make this shady riverside park a draw for families. In the summer there are storytellers and special events.

Fort Collins Museum of Art MUSEUM
(MOA; 970-482-2787; www.ftcma.org; 201 S College Ave; adult/child $4/1; 10am-5pm Wed-Fri, noon-5pm Sat & Sun) In the old post office, this museum has rotating exhibits in a very cool old building. It's worth a stop, but is not a destination in and of itself.

★**New Belgium Brewery** BREWERY
(970-221-0524; www.newbelgium.com; 500 Linden St; tasting room 10am-6pm Tue-Sat, tours daily on the half-hour) FREE Touring New Belgium's brewery brings you face-to-face with the freewheeling essence of Fort Collins' character: a tripartite passion for beer, bicycles and sustainability. It's an unforgettable few hours. The tour guides are knowledgeable, smart and playful, and the special selection of beers is among the nation's best.

Tours begin with a pint of your choice before meandering through the sprawling, bicycle-cluttered brewing facility. By the time you get to the end, a colorful tasting room with long communal tables, you've probably had enough to consider getting dolled up in one of the costumes that are on hand. All told, the place is a riot. Those without the foresight to book long in advance can still enjoy a selection of brews and good-humored bartenders in the public tasting room.

Horsetooth Mountain Open Space HIKING
(970-679-5470; www.larimer.org; 4200 W County Rd 38E; parking permit $6) This large hiking, biking and boating area is located just west of Horsetooth Reservoir, 4 miles from Fort Collins. There are three backcountry camping spots here, good rock climbing and plenty of trails. Longer hikes can be had by connecting to the Blue Sky Trail or Lory State Park trails.

Fort Collins

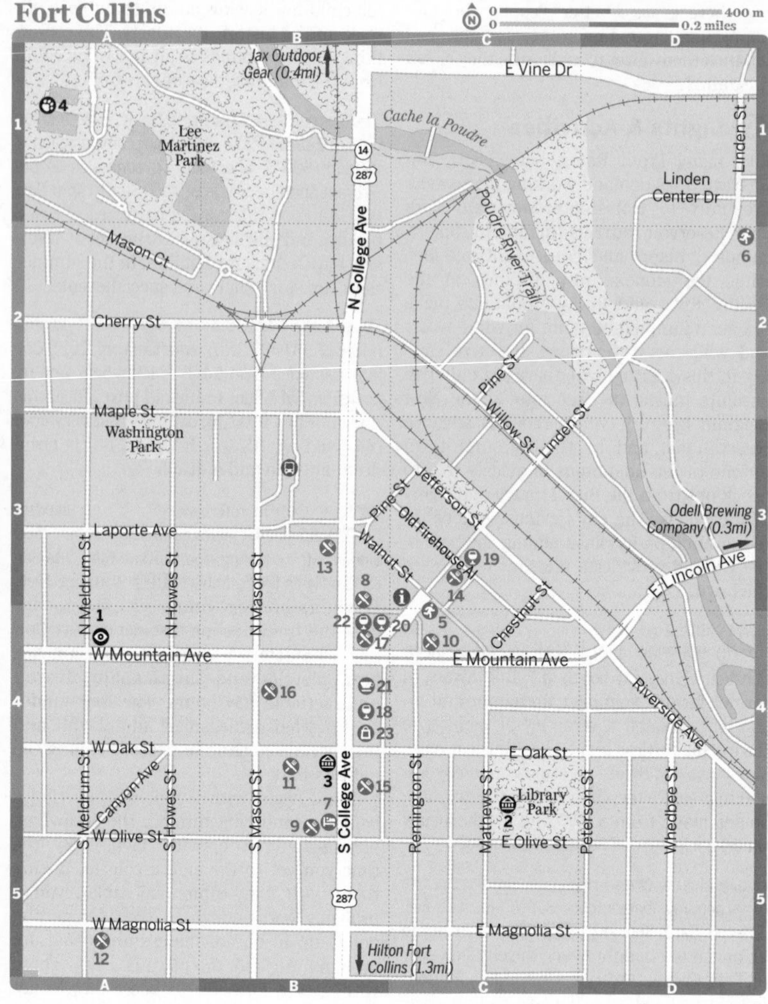

Fort Collins Bike Library BICYCLE SHARE
(☎970-419-1050; www.fcbikelibrary.org; Old Town Sq; ⏲10am-6pm Thu-Sun with seasonal variations) FREE Yes, it *really* is free. Really. You just hand over a credit-card number as a guarantee and roll out of the kiosk on Old Town Sq. Most of the well-maintained bikes are simple, sturdy cruisers for getting around town, but they also have a limited number of tandems and kids' bikes available. It costs $10 to reserve a bike for three days (that is, you don't have to return it each evening).

Sleeping

★ **Armstrong Hotel** BOUTIQUE HOTEL $$
(☎970-484-3883; www.thearmstronghotel.com; 259 S College Ave; d $129-159, studio $149-169, q $159-179, ste $169-199; P ❄ @ ☎ 👪) You'll want to extend your stay at this elegantly renovated boutique hotel in the heart of Old Town. The amenities make it: a fleet of free loaner bikes, large showers, feather duvets and gratis wi-fi. The unique rooms have a modern feel and it's one of the few spots right in the action of Old Town.

The distinct feel and stacks of charm make it one of the best places to stay in the

Fort Collins

Sights

1 Avery House Museum A4
2 Fort Collins Museum & Discovery Science Center C5
3 Fort Collins Museum of Art B4
4 The Farm@Lee Martinez Park A1

Activities, Courses & Tours

5 Fort Collins Bike Library C4
6 New Belgium Brewery D2

Sleeping

7 Armstrong Hotel B5

Eating

8 Backcountry Delicatessen B3
9 Choice City Butcher & Deli B5
10 CooperSmith's Pub & Brewing C4
11 Jay's Bistro B4
12 Lucile's Restaurant A5
13 Pueblo Viejo B3
14 Red Table Cafe C3
15 Stuft B4
16 Tasty Harmony B4
17 Yeti B4

Drinking & Nightlife

18 Crown Pub B4
19 Elliot's Martini Bar C3
20 Lucky Joe's B4
Mug's Coffee Lounge .... (see 7)
21 Starry Night B4
22 Town Pump B4

Shopping

23 Cupboard B4
White Balcony .... (see 23)

region and a perfect perch from which to explore Fort Collins in style. And it has a deal to work out at a nearby gym.

Hilton Fort Collins HOTEL **$$**
(970-482-2626; www.hiltonfortcollins.com; 425 W Prospect Rd; d $145-200; P ❄ 📶) Right at the edge of the university campus, this is a pleasant and centrally located option. The rooms are comfortably furnished, though bland.

Eating

The best eats are mostly along N College Ave, north of W Mulberry St. The walkable stretch of Old Town, just off the corner of S College and E Mountain, has a plethora of restaurants and bars as well.

★**Lucile's Restaurant** CAJUN **$**
(970-224-5464; www.luciles.com; 400 S Meldrum St; mains $7-12) Snuggled in an old house, the restaurant is a cozy dream – replete with creaking floors, winsome staff and fluffy, made-from-scratch buttermilk biscuits. The Cajun home cookin' is fantastic; try the eggs Pontchartrain, with pan-fried local trout, or the eggs New Orleans, which comes smothered in spicy sauce. Simply put, it's Fort Collins' best breakfast.

Yeti AMERICAN **$**
(Old Town Sq, Bldg 23, Suite 152; mains $9-12; 11am-2am Tue-Sun) This tony pub offers some of the best views on Old Town Sq, and serves up solid new American fare. Go for the blackened salmon burger on the patio.

Stuft BURGERS **$**
(970-484-6377; www.stuftburgerbar.com; 210 S College Ave; burgers $7-10; 11am-10pm Sun-Thu, to 2am Fri & Sat) Grab a pencil and start scribbling your dream order: the build-your-own-burger concept succeeds through a list of high-grade options like chipotle ketchup, apple-cider bacon and fire-roasted chilies. Add fresh-cut, skin-on french fries and a good list of beer specials and lunch takes on unlimited possibilities.

★**Backcountry Delicatessen** SANDWICHES **$**
(970-482-6913; www.backcountry-deli.com; 140 N College Ave; sandwiches $7-9; 7am-5pm; 👪) This brilliant little deli opens early so that outdoors-bound patrons can get out and on the trail with box lunches in their pack. The Pilgrim – a pile of turkey with cranberry sauce – was named one of the best sandwiches in America by *Esquire* magazine.

Red Table Cafe SANDWICHES **$**
(970-490-2233; 224 Linden St; sandwiches $6-9; 8am-4pm; 👪) Clean white tables and bright local art give this extraordinarily cute lunch spot a fresh ambience, even if the menu is relatively simple sandwiches. In the morning, go for an egg-and-avocado burrito; for lunch, a bowl of vegetarian chili.

Choice City Butcher & Deli SANDWICHES **$**
(970-490-2489; www.choicecitybutcher.com; 104 W Olive St; sandwiches $6-10; 7am-6pm Sun-Wed, to 9pm Thu-Sat; 👪) The butchers here are straight from central casting – all forearms and white aprons – and all of the five varieties of Reuben sandwiches win raves. They

serve dinner on the weekend, a predictably meaty selection of American mains.

★**Tasty Harmony** VEGETARIAN **$$**
(☎970-689-3234; www.tastyharmony.com; 130 S Mason St; mains $7-14; ⏲11am-9pm Tue-Thu & Sun, to 10pm Fri & Sat; ✎) Organic, vegetarian dishes at this bright lunch spot are delicious, with a menu focused on hearty sandwiches, baked tofu dishes and soups. Tacos, with tempeh and Mexican jackfruit, are the highlight of the mix-and-match daily plate. End things right with the raw key lime pie.

CooperSmith's Pub & Brewing PUB FOOD **$$**
(☎970-498-0483; www.coopersmithspub.com; 5 Old Town Sq; mains $9-20; ⏲11am-11pm Mon-Wed, to 11:30pm Thu, to midnight Fri & Sat; ♿) Of all Fort Collins' excellent brewpubs, this is the only one with a good menu. It's all about the thick-cut steak fries, chunky burgers and yards of fresh beer. The best thing on tap is also the most inventive: Sigda's Green Chili Golden Ale.

Pueblo Viejo MEXICAN **$$**
(☎970-221-1170; 185 N College Ave; mains $9-18; ⏲10am-10pm Sun-Thu, to 11pm Fri & Sat; ♿) Something of a Fort Collins institution, Pueblo Viejo serves a sizable chile relleno that's better-than-average Colorado Mexican, but the place goes one step better with rich mole dishes, big margaritas and bottomless chips and salsa. It's a bit uneven, but the place is always full. In the summer, there's a breezy patio out back.

Jay's Bistro MODERN AMERICAN **$$$**
(☎970-482-1876; www.jaysbistro.net; 135 W Oak St; mains $19-35; ⏲11:30am-8:30pm Sun-Wed, 11:30am-10:30pm Thu-Sat) Though the soft light, Frenchie paintings and jazz quartet gives off a whiff of pretension, Jay's is the most sophisticated dining room in town. The menu is straight as an arrow (calamari, lamb shank, duck breast) but well executed and paired with a big wine list.

Drinking & Nightlife

Crown Pub PUB
(☎970-484-5929; www.crownpub.net; 134 S College Ave; ⏲11am-late; 📶) All the dark-wood paneling, friendly barkeeps and a dead-center location make this no-nonsense watering hole a good place to cool your heels after walking around downtown. If you're too pressed for time to hit all the local breweries, this pub has a lot of local beer on tap.

Odell Brewing Company BREWERY
(☎970-482-2881; www.odellbrewing.com; 800 E Lincoln Ave; ⏲11am-6pm Mon, Tue & Thu, 11am-7pm Wed, Fri & Sat) New Belgium has the best tour, but Odell makes the best brew – in not only Fort Collins but all of Colorado. The bar is small and comfortable, and the brewers take pride in their work. If you taste but one Colorado beer, make it the hoppy, heady Odell IPA (India Pale Ale).

Starry Night CAFE
(☎970-493-3039; 112 S College Ave; ⏲7am-10pm Mon-Thu, to 11pm Fri & Sat, 7:30am-9pm Sun; 📶) Free wi-fi and comfortable seats make this an ideal spot near downtown to take a load off, caffeinate and catch up on email. The baked goods hit the mark as well, especially the delightfully messy whipped-cream layered chocolate-almond cake. For a bit more sustenance, order simple pasta salads or toast and jam.

Elliot's Martini Bar COCKTAIL BAR
(☎970-472-9802; www.elliotsmartinibar.com; 234 Linden St; ⏲4:30pm-2am Mon-Sat, from 8pm Sun) When you tire of all the beer, hit Elliot's for an exhaustive list of high-octane cocktails. The 'Elliot's' martini is for classicists, but

ARAPAHO NATIONAL WILDLIFE REFUGE

For birdwatchers, this is one of the best destinations in Colorado: nearly 200 species of birds frequent the summer sagebrush and wetlands of the FWS Arapaho National Wildlife Refuge, 105 (long, if lovely) miles west of Fort Collins by the Cache la Poudre–North Park Scenic Byway (Hwy 14). The star of the show is the sage grouse and its spring mating ritual, the lek, an elaborate, territorial display of spiked tail feathers, puffy chests and nearly comic braggadocio. To find the **Refuge Headquarters** (☎970-723-8202; http://arapaho.fws.gov; 953 Jackson County Rd 32; ⏲7am-3:30pm Mon-Fri), head 8 miles south of Hwy 14 via Hwy 125, then 1 mile east on Jackson County Rd 32.

If you are visiting the refuge or its surrounding backcountry, the dusty hamlet of Walden is the nearest place for a hot shower and decent shelter.

staff also entertain with way-out drinks – all served up in a martini glass, of course – including a tequila-based Smoke Monster and Death in the Afternoon, an homage to Hemingway.

Lucky Joe's IRISH PUB
(970-493-2213; www.luckyjoes.com; 25 Old Town Sq; noon-2am) Lots of wood and brick and a nightly singer-songwriter make this a warm and welcoming Irish pub in the heart of Old Town. When it snows, warm up with an Irish coffee and enjoy the tunes; in summer, hit the big patio and take in foot traffic on the square.

Mug's Coffee Lounge CAFE
(970-472-6847; www.mugscoffeelounge.com; 261 S College Ave; 6am-9pm;) Free wi-fi, strong coffee and good sandwiches keep this central, classy little place bustling throughout the day. Flat-bread sandwiches and other savory snacks are available.

Town Pump DIVE BAR
(970-493-4404; 124 N College Ave; 11am-2am) A bona fide dive bar with a century of boozing under its belt, this is a comfortable place to knock back a couple of cold ones while rubbing elbows with the locals. If you go for the Cherry Bombs, beware: they're soaked in Everclear.

Shopping

If you're on foot, Old Town Sq has lots of cute little shops for browsing, as does the nearby stretch on N College Ave.

Cupboard HOMEWARES, FOOD
(970-493-8585; www.thecupboard.net; 152 S College Ave; 9:30am-8pm Mon-Fri, to 6pm Sat, noon-5pm Sun) This is the biggest kitchen supply store in northern Colorado and as such is filled with every cooking thingamajig under the sun, plus lots of local sauces and jams. The selection of knives and cookbooks is impressive. They have demos on Saturdays and cooking classes on Wednesday evenings.

Jax Outdoor Gear SPORTS
(970-221-0544; www.jaxmercantile.com; 1200 N College Ave; 8am-9pm Mon-Fri, to 6pm Sat, 9am-6pm Sun) Half camping outfitter, half army-surplus store, Jax is Fort Collins' most well-rounded outdoor supplier – a place where you can buy a fishing rod, a Patagonia jacket and a gas mask. Its rental department has kayaks, snowshoes, sleds and skis.

White Balcony HOMEWARES
(970-493-3310; www.whitebalcony.com; 146 S College Ave; 10am-6pm Mon-Wed, to 8pm Thu-Sat, 11am-6pm Sun;) Knickknacks and off-beat collectibles are given artful attention at this unique downtown shop. It's a great place to get a one-of-a-kind gift; there are purses and homewares, kids' gifts, ladies' accessories and cards with an edgy sensibility.

Information

Colorado State Parks (970-491-1168; www.parks.state.co.us; 3745 E Prospect Rd; 8am-6pm Memorial Day–Labor Day, to 5pm winter) Sharing a building with the Colorado Welcome Center, this office can arrange permits and reservations for camping in Colorado's state parks.

Colorado Welcome Center (970-491-4775; www.colorado.com; 3745 E Prospect Rd; 8am-6pm Memorial Day–Labor Day, to 5pm winter;) Just off the highway, this office provides information about the Colorado Front Range.

Fort Collins Convention & Visitors Bureau (800-274-3678; www.visitftcollins.com; 19 Old Town Sq; 8:30am-5pm Mon-Fri, 11am-5pm Sat & Sun;) Under the green awning in Old Town Sq, this brochure-packed information center has a helpful staff who take plenty of time with their guests. History buffs will want to get a copy of the center's walking tour, which passes buildings of historical import downtown.

USFS Canyon Lakes District Office & Visitor Center (970-295-6710; 2150 Centre Ave, Bldg E; 9am-5pm Mon-Fri) The Canyon Lakes Ranger District offers year-round information, and permits for firewood gathering and grazing. It is the hub for information on four wilderness areas, three national recreation trails, two historic districts and the Cache la Poudre, Colorado's only Wild and Scenic River.

Getting There & Away

Fort Collins is 65 miles north of Denver, to the west of the I-25 corridor. Those arriving by car should take the Prospect Rd exit to reach downtown. From Boulder, take US 36 east and follow signs for the Northwest Hwy.

Fort Collins/Loveland Airport is serviced by **Allegiant Airlines** (702-505-8888; www.allegiantair.com) by connections through Denver, Las Vegas and Phoenix. This is the closest airport to Rocky Mountain National Park. You can also get here via Greyhound, which has an unmanned stop at the Downtown Transit Center.

Getting Around

TO/FROM THE AIRPORT

Green Ride Colorado (☎888-472-6656; www.greenrideco.com; 1712 Hastings Dr; DIA to Fort Collins 1-way $30) This shuttle van shares services from DIA to Fort Collins (1½ hours), the Front Range and southern Wyoming.

SuperShuttle (☎970-482-0505; www.supershuttle.com; DIA to Fort Collins 1-way $32) From DIA, it's 1½ hours to Fort Collins.

BICYCLE

This town ranks among America's most bicycle-friendly cities. There are bike lanes (and cyclists!) everywhere. To leave Fort Collins without cruising between breweries or along the Poudre River Trail would be a shame. Bikes to rent and borrow are everywhere.

PUBLIC TRANSPORTATION

Downtown Transit Center (☎970-221-6620; 250 N Mason St; ⏰7:30am-5:30pm Mon-Fri) With a customer information counter, lockers and bicycle racks, this central bus terminal also serves as Fort Collins' Greyhound stop. A train line from here to the South Transit Center is slated to open in 2014.

Transfort Bus System (☎970-221-6620; www.fcgov.com/transfort) This is the town's public transportation network.

NORTHEAST COLORADO

Pawnee National Grassland

If, like some of us, you happen to be fishtailing at high speeds along the graded dirt roads that thread through the 193,060-acre **Pawnee National Grassland** (☎camping reservations 877-444-6777, Crow Valley Recreation Area, Briggsdale 970-353-5004, Greeley Ranger District Office 970-346-5000; www.fs.usda.gov; 👪) as dusk descends on another summer day, you'll notice a few things. As the sun slants down it captures all the many shades of green and gold in this savanna that seems to roll unending in all directions. These are the Pawnee Grasslands. With more and more gas exploration in the area, you don't quite capture the atavistic adventure of yore, but there are still windmills (both old and new) and plenty of birdwatching opportunities.

The heart of the grasslands are the blond, sandstone towers that are the historic and majestic **Pawnee Buttes**. From Sterling, take Hwy 14 west to New Raymer and Weld County Rd 129, where signs will lead you to the buttes. Be sure to fill up your gas tank before you come here.

Northeast Colorado was hard hit by the 2013 floods. The Pawnee Grasslands were closed at the time of writing as a public safety precaution.

Sleeping

If you wish to camp in the grasslands, head to the **Crow Valley Recreation Area** (☎www.colorado.com/Articles.aspx?aid=42011; www.fs.usda.gov; Weld County Rd 77; sites $10-14; P 👪) off Hwy 14 near Briggsdale. It's not the most stunning campsite of your life, but it is elm and cottonwood shaded, with potable water, restrooms and fire pits. It even has a volleyball court and baseball diamond.

Fort Morgan

POP 11,315 / ELEV 4324FT

A former prairie trading post on the Overland Trail that has become an interstate city, Fort Morgan has a cute though dated center that could use an economic upturn. It's not as depressed as the prairie towns further east though, thanks to constant Interstate traffic that has brought mostly corporate franchise fast food and motels.

Sights & Activities

The best thing about Fort Morgan is its proximity to the surprisingly transporting Pawnee National Grassland and Pawnee Buttes.

Wild Animal Sanctuary ZOO
(☎303-536-0118; www.wildanimalsanctuary.org; 1946 County Rd 53, Keenesburg; adult/child $15/7.50) This large 300-acre wildlife sanctuary is about 30 minutes east of Denver by car on your way to Fort Morgan. It has over 290 large predators – including lions, tigers, bears, mountain lions, wolves and more – that have been rescued from zoos, circuses and abusive roadside attractions.

The mile-long skywalk takes you above the animals, and there are trails throughout the sanctuary.

Fort Morgan Museum & Library MUSEUM
(☎970-542-4010; www.cityoffortmorgan.com; 414 Main St; ⏰9am-6pm Mon, 10am-8pm Tue-Thu, 9am-5pm Fri & Sat; P 👪) FREE This museum tells the tale of the town of Fort Morgan

through antiques that have trickled down from the founders. There's plenty of information on American big band leader Glenn Miller, who was born here. The arrowhead collection is particularly cool.

I-76 Speedway CAR RACING
(970-867-2101; www.i-76speedway.com; 16359 County Rd S; adult/senior/child 6-12yr/child under 6yr $10/8/4/free; varies Jun-Aug, Sat evenings Apr-Oct;) Offers a summer racing season with four to six car divisions competing on Saturday evenings.

Sleeping

Day's Inn MOTEL $
(970-542-0844; www.daysinn.com; 1150 N Main St; r from $72; P) Your best bet if you plan to stay the night. You may not like the Christmas carpeting, but rooms are large, very clean and far enough from the interstate roar to get a decent night's sleep.

Sterling

POP 14,777 / ELEV 3935FT

North of the interstate, Old Sterling sits in a cozy six-block grid. Edged by an active rail yard, it still has dated brick-house charm and new natural-gas money is injecting fresh life into the once depressed burg. When the sweet old ladies at the **Visitors Information Center** (970-522-8962; www.sterlingcolo.com; 12510 County Rd 370; 9am-5pm Mon-Sat) in the rest area are asked what there is to see around here, and they reply with a shrug and 'Not much,' you get the feeling that this once major stop on the Overland Trail, a covered wagon superhighway that brought settlers west to the gold country, has seen its best and most historic days.

Sights & Activities

Sterling Overland Trail Museum MUSEUM
(970-522-3895; www.sterlingcolo.com; 21053 County Rd 370; adult/child $3/1.50; 9am-5pm Mon-Sat; P) You should definitely visit this museum, which sports a great collection handed down from the town's founding families. Out front in the gravel beds are vintage plows and tractors, and inside are rooms packed with exhibits ranging from minerals to an insane collection of authentic arrowheads, plus 19th-century firearms, bear- and buffalo-skin coats, and vintage pianos, dolls and radios.

It even has dinosaur fossils. Out back there's a 13-building replica of old Main St from the 1930s along with a covered wagon. Together it all paints a picture of Sterling's human and natural history.

Overland Trail Recreation Area HIKING
(970-522-9700; www.sterlingcolo.com; Overland Trail; 4:30am-11pm) Across the road from the visitors center this concrete path follows the Overland Trail along the river for just over half a mile. According to signs you can fish small and large mouth bass here.

Eating

J & L Cafe DINER $
(970-522-3625; 423 N 3rd St; mains $6.25-9.99; 5:15am-8pm;) A local joint steeped in country music where the men wear cowboy hats and the women talk with a hint of western twang. It serves breakfast all day, burgers, chili and chicken fried steak. And pie. Always pie. And strong coffee. Diner coffee. This is real Americana as you live and breathe.

Getting There & Away

Sterling is 125 miles northeast of Denver off I-76.

Julesburg

If you're heading into Colorado from the northeast on I-76, one of the first spots you'll see is the **Colorado Welcome Center** (970-474-2054; www.colorado.com/JulesburgWelcomeCenter.aspx; 20934 County Rd 28; 8am-6pm Memorial Day–Labor Day, to 5pm Labor Day–Memorial Day). Part rest area, part information center, it's bordered by corral fencing around waist-high grass dotted with a teepee-like shade structure and a buffalo sculpture.

There's a rather cool cast-iron monument to the Pony Express here too. On the first Pony Express expedition in 1860–61, the riders traveled 1943 miles between St Joseph and San Francisco, stopping in present-day Julesburg, then known as Overland City because it was also a major stop on the Overland Trail (over 350,000 people came through here in the mid-19th century).

Launched as a trading post in 1850 and known as the 'Wickedest City in the West' by the 1860s, the town of Julesburg moved three times before settling in its present location. First it was moved because of a raid by Native Americans, then to be closer to the railroad. In 1880 it became a rail junction for Union Pacific. These days, though, Julesburg is another dying prairie town that makes Sterling feel like a metropolis. But if you are curious about Overland Trail history, take the **South Platte River Scenic Byway** (www.byways.org; 20934 County Rd 28), a 19-mile loop that circuits Ovid, the original Julesburg site, and Fort Sedgewick, with pull-outs and interpretative panels installed throughout.

Julesburg is set just over the Colorado border from Nebraska on I-76, 180 miles northeast of Denver.

CACHE LA POUDRE RIVER

To cruise along Hwy 15 – from the mouth of the Cache la Poudre (rhymes with 'neuter') River Canyon at Laporte to Walden 92 miles west – is a stunning venture. The ribbon of pavement winds through the foothills along the aspen- and pine-edged river in some of Colorado's most scenic country. For those who want to camp without the intense backcountry commitment, the sites along the Cache la Poudre are the best highly accessible camping in the west. It offers stunning wilderness, a place where mule deer, elk and wild trout often outnumber human visitors. One of Colorado's biggest wildfires ever ran through here in 2012, and much of the area south of the river has been scorched.

The area is largely designated as a National Heritage Area and the Wild & Scenic Rivers Act protects 75 miles of the Cache la Poudre River from new dams or diversions. Thirty miles of the river meet the highest standards and are designated as 'wild' for being free of dams and diversions and having undisturbed shorelines; the remaining 45-mile protected section is designated 'recreational' – meaning it can be accessed by roads. White-water enthusiasts should check with experienced guide services or the USFS before putting into the river and finding unrunnable rapids, like the frothing Narrows, or a dam looming up ahead.

The tiny burg of Rustic, 32 miles west of the US 287–Hwy 14 junction, offers services and decent cabin lodging, but the USFS camping along Hwy 14 is the best lodging in the area by far. You can get information at the **USFS Visitor Center** (☎970-881-2152; 34500 Poudre Canyon Hwy/Hwy 14) just west of Idylwilde, which occupies the handsome Arrowhead Lodge, built in 1935 and listed on the National Register of Historic Places. Of the campgrounds under its jurisdiction, **Big Bend Campground** (☎office 970-498-2770; Poudre Canyon Hwy; tent sites $12; P 🚻) is a favorite, with shady sites within earshot of the rushing water.

Another excellent reason to head this way is the **Mishawaka Amphitheatre** (☎970-316-2001; www.mishawakaconcerts.com; 13714 Poudre Canyon Hwy/Hwy 14; ⊙summer only), a cozy 900-seat venue in the heart of the canyon. It's way out there, but the acts that are drawn to the place – everything from hip-hop acts such as Blackalicious to barefoot jam bands – are usually top notch. The food is pretty damn good too.

Stop at the self-service **Cache la Poudre Visitors Information Center**, 3 miles west of US 287 on Hwy 14, for information on wildlife viewing and fishing regulations. Watch for bighorn sheep on the steep slopes along a 35-mile section of the north bank from Mishawaka to Poudre Falls, a series of picturesque roaring cascades. The USFS recently developed a particularly good bighorn sheep-viewing site equipped with telescopes and explanatory plaques at Big Bend, 41 miles west of the US 287–Hwy 14 junction.

After Hwy 14 branches away from the river it ascends Cameron Pass (10,276ft), where the stunning 12,485ft Nohku Crags form the northernmost peaks of the Never Summer Range.

Once you're over Cameron Pass, you enter **State Forest State Park** (☎303-470-1144; www.parks.state.co.us; Hwy 12, Mile 56; day pass $7, camping $16-20). This lost piece of Colorado backcountry has mountains and alpine lakes galore, a cool backcountry huts system and even some sand dunes up north. **Never Summer Nordic** (☎970-723-4070; www.neversummernordic.com; 247 County Rd 41, Walden; yurt $60-120) maintains several yurts (canvas-walled portable structures equipped with wood-burning stoves, beds and kitchens) and one cabin in the park. It's open during the summer and winter.

RED FEATHER LAKES

Red Feather Lakes is a remote, scrappy little town in the pine-dotted hills around the Lone Pine Creek drainage, about 50 miles northwest of Fort Collins. It's far more rustic than other mountain areas and the scenery is less

TIMBER! BLACK BEETLES, BLUE FUNGI & DEAD BROWN HILLS

Sure, the family of nine camped next door with the barking Labrador is a nuisance, but nothing compared to *Dendroctonus ponderosae,* the seemingly unstoppable mountain pine beetle. About the size of a grain of rice, these little cooties have changed great swaths of the Rocky Mountain's verdant hills into a lifeless expanse of dead timber.

The females lay eggs under the bark of ponderosa, limber and lodgepole pines, which the trees resist with increased resin production. No problem, unless the beetles are dusted with blue stain fungi – a kind of pine tree Kryptonite – which halts the flow of resin and eventually suffocates the tree.

Climate change has only hastened the problem, as beetle larvae thrive during warm wintering conditions. The outlook isn't rosy: without a massive dose of chemicals or a wicked winter cold snap, some experts predict all of Colorado's mature lodgepole pine could eventually die off. In 2013, it was estimated that roughly 4.3 million acres of forest have been decimated by beetle kill. A nasty cousin, the spruce beetle, has attacked some 924,000 acres of spruce.

Interestingly, some good is being made from the dead trees. New green start-ups are making heating pellets from the trunks, and many mountain homes now sport beautifully weathered beetle-kill walls.

dramatic, but the seclusion can more than make up for it. From Fort Collins take US 287 north for 21 miles, then turn left (west) at Livermore on Larimer County Rd 74E for 24 miles to **Red Feather Lakes Ranger Station** (970-881-2937; 274 Dowdy Lake Rd; 9am-5pm Mon-Fri Memorial Day–Labor Day), operated by the Roosevelt National Forest.

Nordic ski trails for all abilities offer one-hour to full-day loops at **Beaver Meadows Resort Ranch** (970-881-2450; www.beavermeadows.com; 100 Marmot Dr 1; d $79-89, condos $139-169, cabins $109-149; P), which is open daily year-round.

Fishing and lakeside USFS campsites are available at **Dowdy Lake Campground** (reservations through Reserve America 877-444-6777; www.recreation.gov; Dowdy Lake Rd; campsites $15; May-Sep;) and **West Lake Campground** (reservations through Reserve America 877-444-6777; www.recreation.gov; off County Rd 74E; campsites $15; May-Sep;). Both campgrounds are overseen by the Canyon Lakes Ranger District. About 9 miles west along 74E/Deadman Rd, there are sites at the **North Fork Poudre Campground** (970-295-6700; 74E/Deadman Rd; sites $11; Jun-Nov).

WALDEN

POP 734 / ELEV 8099FT

Little Walden lies under the shadow of the rough Medicine Bow, Summer, Rabbit Ears and Park Ranges, at the center of an expansive valley in a region locals refer to as North Park. There isn't much to the self-proclaimed 'moose-watching capital of Colorado,' but the north–south Main St is scattered with motels, restaurants and a creaky old movie theater. The only incorporated town in Jackson County, Walden is a modest supply point for outdoor enthusiasts and hunters looking to grab a burger and get out of the elements for the night. And, by the way, we did see moose.

GRAND LAKE

POP POP 450 / ELEV 8437FT

As the western gateway to Rocky Mountain National Park, Grand Lake is a foil to the bustling hub of Estes Park. Sure, both are fairly inglorious tourist traps compared to the magnificent park in their shared backyard, but Grand Lake is more remote, suffers less traffic and exploits its history as an old mining town for the feel of an 'intimate' tourist trap. The namesake lake – with a yacht club founded in 1901 – is handsome, and offers a different suite of recreational thrills in the summer. An amble along the boardwalk lining Grand Ave is pleasant, with a hodgepodge of corny souvenir shops, decent restaurants, T-shirt stores and a few character-filled bars. Unless you're staying for a few days at the sublime Shadowcliff Lodge, Grand Lake is no destination unto itself – it's more of a lunch-and-supplies stop on the way in and out of the west side of the park.

Sights & Activities

Regardless of season, there's no problem keeping busy in Grand Lake: the town's bike and boat rentals give way to sleds and skis as the season changes. Because of its location abutting multi-use federal and state land, Grand Lake is a popular destination for snowmobiles – you can even ride in Rocky Mountain National Park. Get information about rentals and trails at the visitor center.

Several Rocky Mountain National Park trailheads are just outside the town limits, including those to the Tonahutu Creek Trail and the Cascade Falls/North Inlet Trail, both near Shadowcliff Lodge. Entering the park from these trailheads is an excellent way to dodge many of the crowds that plug up the park's eastern side.

The town is 35 miles north of **Winter Park**, a popular ski destination.

Kauffman House Museum MUSEUM
(Grand Lake Historical Society 970-627-3351; www.kauffmanhouse.org; 407 Pitkin St; entry by donation; 1-5pm Jun-Aug;) The Ezra Kauffman House is an 1892 log building that operated as a hotel until 1946. Now on the National Register of Historic Places, it contains period furniture, old skis, quilts and other dusty artifacts. Hardly hair-raising, but a nice stop for history buffs.

Grand Lake Nordic Center & Grand Lake Golf Course SKIING, GOLF
(970-627-8328; www.grandlakerecreation.com; County Rd 48; skiing per day $12, 9-hole golf $20) This facility, just west of town, hosts golf in the summer and a network of trails for skiing when the snow falls. The ski trails cover a range of difficulty, though it's not incredibly scenic – most of the trails are open, along the golf course fairways.

In winter you can also rent gear and go snowtubing. Those who travel with their dog might want to try skiing here too – there's a dedicated dog loop.

Grand Lake Metro Recreation District CYCLING, HIKING
(970-627-8328; www.grandlakerecreation.com; 928 Grand Ave, Suite 204; 8am-5pm Mon-Fri) With good maps and information about biking and hiking in the Arapaho National Forest, Nordic skiing and golf, this government office serves all-season outdoor recreation information. It can also offer dog-owners guidance about getting Fido on the trail.

Beacon Landing Marina BOATING
(970-627-3671; www.beaconlanding.us; 1026 County Rd 64; 2hr pontoon rental $75; 10am-6pm Mon-Sat, from noon Sun) This marina on Granby Lake, just south of Grand Lake, can arrange pontoons, speedboats, jet skis and other waterborne machines for rent, and hosts guided fishing expeditions on the lakes.

Sombrero Ranch HORSEBACK RIDING
(970-627-3514; 304 W Portal Rd; rides $50; rides depart on the hour 8am-4pm Jun-Aug) The best ride with this branch of Sombrero Ranch is simply named 'The Ride.' It takes two hours and traverses some lovely Rocky Mountain vistas, fields of wildflowers in the spring and rushing streams.

Sleeping

★**Shadowcliff Lodge & Retreat Center** LODGE $
(970-627-9220; www.shadowcliff.org; 405 Summerland Park Rd; dm/d/cabins $23/60/125; May 25–Sep 30;) Overlooking Grand Lake, this ecofriendly mountain resort, in a beautiful setting perched with a view of the lake and mountains, is among the best-value accommodation in Colorado. Rooms and dorms are simple and clean, and guests gather around the fire or grand piano in the book-lined common room downstairs.

Families and larger groups may also want to look into the Shadowcliff cabins, which are along the river. Shadowcliff also hosts a number of sustainability workshops, and the property abuts hiking trails into Rocky Mountain National Park. Reservations are essential. A two-night minimum stay is required for rooms.

Lemmon Lodge CABIN $$
(970-627-3314; www.lemmonlodge.com; 1224 Lake Ave; cabins $90-460;) Right on the water, these are a collection of privately owned cabins managed by one company. There's a range of prices, but quality varies widely too. This is good for a family or large group; for the best all-round stays rent either cabin 17 or 23.

Eating & Drinking

Mountain Food Market SELF-CATERING $
(970-627-3470; 400 Grand Ave; 9am-7pm Mon-Sat, to 5pm Sun;) This grocer, right at the entrance to town, is a good place to pick up supplies when heading into the park, and the best grocery store in Grand Lake. It has

a deli counter for to-go meals and a small supply of basic camping equipment.

Fat Cat Cafe BREAKFAST **$**
(☎970-627-0900; 916 Grand Ave; mains $5-10; ⏰7am-1pm; 👪) Consider yourself lucky if you find yourself rolling into Grand Junction half-starving on a Sunday morning. The Fat Cat does its breakfast buffet ($12) and brunch with hearty expertise: biscuits and gravy, bottomless drinks, scrambled 'Scotch eggs' and omelets that come drooping off the plate.

★**O-A Bistro** MODERN AMERICAN **$$**
(☎970-627-5080; www.o-abistro.com; 928 Grand Ave; prix fixe $25-30) Less than 10 tables fit inside this little jewel box, a favorite of Grand Lake's dining scene for made-from-scratch soups and a long, thoughtful wine list. A five- or six-course *prix fixe* is the best dining experience in the area; for lunch it has light snacks and crepes.

Sagebrush BBQ & Grill BARBECUE **$$**
(☎970-627-1404; www.sagebrushbbq.com; 1101 Grand Ave; mains $9-20; ⏰7am-9pm Mon-Thu, to 10pm Fri & Sat; 👪) Peanut shells litter the floor and bric-a-brac covers the walls of this BBQ joint, a place keenly balancing casual atmosphere with a slightly upscale menu of steak and local game dishes such as wild boar sausage. It's best when simplest, though, so go for the burger.

Grand Lake Brewing Co BREWERY
(☎970-627-1711; www.grandlakebrewing.com; 915 Grand Ave; mains $8-12; ⏰noon-8pm Sun-Thu, to 9pm Fri & Sat) Patrons look over the brewing tanks in this narrow pub, sipping pints of Super Chicken, an ass-kicking barley wine that's a heady 11%. The bar burgers are well built, but the Ruben is a brilliant disaster – stacked tall, loaded with sauerkraut, and served on thick slices of rye.

ℹ Information

The **Grand Lake Visitor Center** (☎970-627-3402, 800-531-1019; www.grandlakechamber.com; cnr W Portal Rd & Hwy 34; ⏰9am-5pm Mon-Sat, 10am-4pm Sun Jun-Aug) is at the junction of US 34 and W Portal Rd but it has another office downtown at 928 Grand Ave (enter from the Garfield Ave side). For information and permits for Rocky Mountain National Park, visit the Kawuneeche Visitor Center (p135), a bit north of town on US 34.

ℹ Getting There & Away

By car, Grand Lake is 102 miles northwest of Denver. Take I-70 west to the I-40 exit and continue west over the Berthound Pass, which can be a white-knuckle experience in inclement weather. If you don't have your own wheels, **Home James Transportation Services** (☎800-359-7503; www.homejamestransportation.com; DIA to Grand Lake $90) runs door-to-door shuttles to Denver International Airport (2½ hours). Reservations are required.

GRANBY

POP 1200 / ELEV 7939FT

At the junction of US 40 and US 34, Granby is a convenient and authentic homegrown stop for those heading into Rocky Mountain National Park or several other nearby recreation and ski areas. The **USFS Sulphur District Ranger Office** (☎970-887-4100; 62429 US 40; ⏰8am-5pm Mon-Fri, plus 8am-5pm Sat & Sun summer) for the Arapaho National Forest is at the east end of town and has useful hiking brochures for the Continental Divide National Scenic Trail, the Never Summer Wilderness Area and the Winter Park–Fraser–Tabernash area. It is also the place to get permits for backcountry camping in the Indian Peaks Wilderness.

Activities

Sky Granby Ranch SKIING
(www.granbyranch.com; lift ticket $58) This small family friendly ski area has night skiing, tons of beginner terrain and mountain biking in the summer.

Sleeping & Eating

Drowsy Water Ranch DUDE RANCH **$$$**
(☎970-725-3456; www.drowsywater.com; 1454 County Hwy 219; weekly rates from $1820; 🅿👪) As an all-inclusive experience, home cookin', daily guided horseback rides and evening programs are all part of the weekly price. Even though it ain't fancy, the Fosha family offer the most genuine 'dude ranch' experience in Colorado. The cabin accommodations are decked out in Western-themed coziness and it's an ideal space for families looking to escape the urban grind.

Hitting the trail on horseback is the main focus; even those with no horse sense will leave with basic riding skills.

Midtown Cafe AMERICAN $
(cnr 4th St & Agate Ave; mains $7-9; 7am-5pm;) If you're just in Granby for a bite, stop by this bookstore-slash-art-gallery-slash-cafe. The large open dining room fills with locals that enjoy the big breakfasts and excellent sandwiches.

HOT SULPHUR SPRINGS

POP 663 / ELEV 7680FT

When you roll through the sleepy little village of Hot Sulphur Springs, it's hard to imagine its glory days as a happening tourist destination. In the late 1860s William Byers, founder of the *Rocky Mountain News*, acquired most of the land in the area from itinerant Utes with a combination of legal maneuvering and the aid of the US Army, and he immediately began promoting it to tourists. At one time its rivalry with Grand Lake was so serious that a struggle over which town would be the Grand County seat led to a fatal shoot-out between elected officials. Hot Sulphur Springs prevailed politically, but never suffered the tourist invasion that has made Grand Lake so ticky-tacky – a blessing and curse, as these days it seems to be wilting in a slow economic decline.

At the foot of 12,804ft Byers Peak, Hot Sulphur Springs is midway between Granby and Kremmling on US 40. It has no formal tourist office, but Pioneer Village Museum is a good source of information.

Sights & Activities

Pioneer Village Museum MUSEUM
(970-725-3939; www.grandcountymuseum.com; 110 E Byers Ave; adult/senior/child $5/4/3; 10am-5pm Wed-Sat;) This small community museum has exhibits on early settlers (both native and white), skiing and artifacts from the nearby Windy Gap archaeology area.

Hot Sulphur Springs Resort & Spa HOT SPRING
(970-725-3306; www.hotsulphursprings.com; 5609 County Rd 20; pool adult/child $17.50/11.50, r $108-168) Unlike the hot pools in Glenwood Springs, this spa doesn't chlorinate the water, allowing the heady mix of sulfates, chloride, magnesium and other minerals to soothe bathers just as it has done for generations. The 24 pools have been enclosed by cement and tile and are separated by temperature, ranging from 95°F to a deeply satisfying, if challenging, 112°F.

Like most modern facilities of this kind, there's an added menu of spa options: body wraps, facials, massages and the like. If you want to spend the night, there is a lodge on hand with clean, comfortable motel-style facilities. You get two free days of access at the pools with your stay.

Dave Perri's Guide Service FISHING, HUNTING
(970-725-3531; www.traditionalelkhunt.com; 8hr of guided fishing for 2 adults $375) A local guide operating on the Colorado River, Perri is one of the few licensed to work the excellent waters in the area. Early spring and summer are the busiest time for wading trips. In winter, he leads week-long hunting trips in the Troublesome Basin Area for elk and mule deer, reached via a 7- to 10-mile horseback ride.

Sleeping & Eating

There's no official campground but tent campers and RVs can take advantage of the shade and good fishing at Pioneer Park on the north bank of the river, where there's not even anyone to pester you for money. Get drinking and cooking water from the standpipe across from the Riverside Hotel near the bridge; there are portable toilets, but to clean up try the pools at Hot Sulphur Springs Resort & Spa.

Canyon Motel MOTEL $
(888-489-3719; www.canyonmotelcolorado.com; 221 Byers Ave; d $64-99;) If you aren't staying at the hot springs, this roadside motel makes a clean stopover. The rooms are simple, paneled with pine and extremely clean. Some have kitchens and there's a grill for guests to use.

Glory Hole Cafe BREAKFAST $
(970-725-3237; 512 W Byers Ave; breakfast $5-10; 6am-2pm Wed-Mon;) Most of the menu is standard diner fare in lumberjack portions, but the French toast – fluffy, expertly golden slices smothered in homemade blueberry syrup – is worth a stop. It gets absolutely slammed for breakfast on the weekends, so come off-hours or be prepared to wait.

Getting There & Away

Greyhound will make a flag stop in Hot Sulphur Springs if it's arranged in advance.

KREMMLING

POP 1444 / ELEV 7313FT

It's too bad that little Kremmling doesn't get much more than a cursory glance from the rushing traffic between Steamboat Springs and the Front Range; this wide spot in the road is a great place to get out and kick the tires a bit, and the locals are friendly. There are a couple of decent lunch spots and some antique shopping in the tiny downtown area. The town has long been known as a popular base for hunters and snowmobilers and a lot of effort has recently been made to encourage mountain bikers and rafting expeditions.

Activities

Mad Adventures Whitewater Rafting RAFTING

(800-451-4844; www.madadventures.com; Hwy 40, Mile 185) Making runs on the Upper Colorado and Clear Creek, this is solid operator.

Sleeping & Eating

Hotel Eastin HOTEL, HOSTEL $

(866-546-0815; www.hoteleastincolorado.com; 105 S 2nd St; dm $18-20, d$55-60;) Built in 1906, this former sarsaparilla plant has cozy Western-themed rooms (Zane Grey stayed in Number 120), cowhide headboards and creeky floors. It has back-to-basic rooms, with a shared bathroom in the basement, that are highly passable.

Allington Inn & Suites HOTEL $$

(800-981-4091; www.allingtoninn.com; 215 W Central Ave; d $97-107;) The nicest place to stay in Kremmling happens to be one of the best-value places around. The rooms are modern and comfortable, there's an indoor swimming pool and breakfast is included. Book a room on the north side of the building for cliff views.

Quarter Circle Saloon STEAKHOUSE $$

(970-724-9765; 106 W Park Ave; mains $7-15; 11am-2am) This bar and grill serves up thick slabs of steak and pints and is about the best you'll do in Kremmling. The crowd gets rowdy, especially during pool tournaments on Tuesday night.

Information

BLM Kremmling Field Office (970-724-9004; 210 S 6th St; 8:30am-4pm Mon-Fri) This office has information about multi-use federal land, issues permits and has maps of the area.

Kremmling Chamber & Visitor Center (970-724-3472, toll free 877-573-6654; 203 Park Ave; 8:30am-5pm Mon-Fri, to 3pm Sat) The ladies at this centrally located visitor center could hardly be nicer; after chatting with them for 10 minutes you'll consider moving here. You can get information about local activities and suggestions about where to eat and sleep.

STEAMBOAT SPRINGS

POP 10,115 / ELEV 6695FT

Forget about the posturing snow bunnies in Aspen and Vail. 'Steamboat,' as it's frequently truncated, is Colorado's down-to-earth ski town, a place where hitting the slopes isn't an attitude-packed dog-and-pony show.

The town itself, situated in the shadow of Mt Werner, might be less of a rancher's hub than a resort destination, but locals still regard flashy developments and instant-rise condos with disdain – before tipping their hat, hopping into their pick-up and rumbling away. Despite the sprawling Steamboat Village, built to service skiers, the core of the town retains some of its original low-rise charm and the natural setting is lovely. Summer is almost as popular as winter, with hiking, backpacking, white-water rafting, mountain biking and a host of other outdoor activities.

Steamboat Springs consists of two major areas: the relatively regular grid of central Old Town, which straddles US 40, and the newer warren of winding streets at Steamboat Village, centered around the Mt Werner ski area southeast of town. Only the former of these is worth wandering around by foot. US 40 is known as Lincoln Ave through Old Town.

Sights

Tread of Pioneers Museum MUSEUM

(970-879-2214; 800 Oak St; adult/child/senior $5/1/4; 11am-5pm Tue-Thu;) A favorite among the area's community history museums, these restored Victorian homes host an even-handed display about the history of the Native Americans in the area and a fascinating collection on the evolution of skiing. Visitors can also take guided tours and there are regular kids' activities.

Steamboat Springs

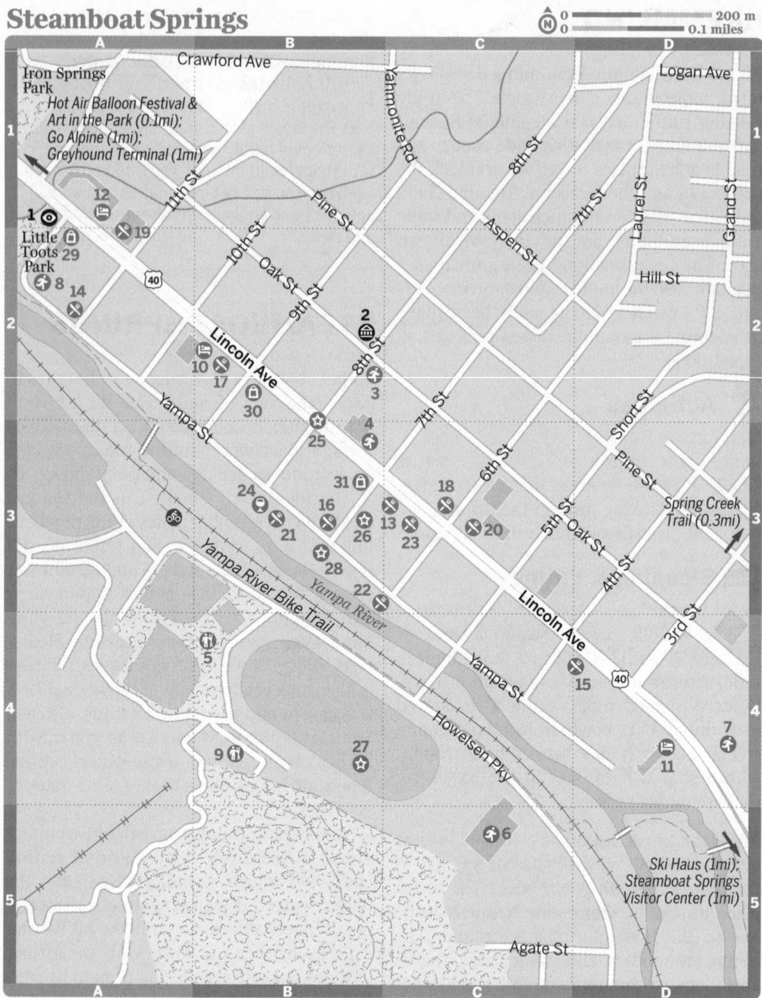

Bud Werner Memorial Library LIBRARY
(1289 Lincoln Ave; 9am-8pm Mon-Thu, 9am-6pm Fri, 9am-5pm Sat, 10am-5pm Sun;) A perfect indoor break for families, this library has awesome interactive games in the kids' area, a sweet fish tank, free wi-fi and storytime. Oh yeah, it has got books, too.

Activities

Hiking

Most of the bike ride companies also make for good hiking. Emerald Mountain has great hikes, as does Spring Creek, accessed from 3rd St, past the high school and up to two small lakes beyond. This trail eventually takes you to Buffalo Pass and Routt National Forests and can be backpacked.

Mineral Springs

Most of Steamboat's numerous springs are warm rather than hot, and some have been damaged by highway construction. The nicest spring is 3 miles from Old Town at **Strawberry Park**. It's open until midnight and you can actually bathe in it. Most of the other spas are in the area around 13th St on both sides of the river; look for the map and brochure *A Walking Tour of the Springs of Steamboat* for more information.

Steamboat Springs

Sights

1 Bud Werner Memorial Library A1
2 Tread of Pioneers Museum B2

Activities, Courses & Tours

3 BAP B2
4 Bucking Rainbow Outfitters B3
Hosted Tours Adventures & Lodging Center .... (see 13)
5 Howelsen Hill Ski Area B4
6 Howelsen Ice Arena C5
7 Old Town Hot Springs D4
8 Orange Peel Bikes A2
9 Steamboat Springs Winter Sports Club B4

Sleeping

10 Hotel Bristol B2
11 Rabbit Ears Motel D4
12 Western Lodge A1

Eating

13 Backcountry Delicatessen C3
14 Bamboo Market A2
15 Bistro CV D4
16 Carl's Tavern B3
17 Harwigs B2
18 Old Town Pub C3
19 Riggio's A2
20 Steamboat Springs Farmers Market C3
21 Sweet Pea Market B3
22 The Boathouse B3
23 Winona's C3

Drinking & Nightlife

24 Sunpies Bistro B3

Entertainment

25 First Friday Art Walk B2
26 Ghost Ranch Saloon B3
27 Steamboat Springs Pro Rodeo Series B4
28 Yampa River Festival B3

Shopping

29 Boomerang Sports Exchange A2
30 Off the Beaten Path B2
31 Urbane B3

Mountain Biking

The *Steamboat Trails Map* shows mountain-bike routes around town, in Stagecoach and Pearl Lake State Parks and in the Mt Zirkel Wilderness. It's available at the visitor information center and any bike shop in town. Steamboat Mountain Resort promotes biking on Mt Werner, allows bikes on the Silver Bullet Gondola and rents them at the Thunderhead lift.

Top rides close to town include Emerald Mountain (the big one accessed right from town), Red Dirt Trail located about 2 miles west of town off County Rd 129 and Elk River Rd, and Mad Creek Trail, located by the Strawberry Hot Springs.

Road riders can follow the Yampa River bike trail for 7 miles along the river.

Orange Peel Bikes BICYCLE RENTAL
(970-879-2957; www.orangepeelbikes.com; 1136 Yampa St; bike rental per day $20-65; 10am-6pm Mon-Fri, to 5pm Sat) In a funky old building at the end of Yampa, this is perfectly situated for renting a bike to ride the trails crisscrossing Howelsen Hill. A staff of serious riders and mechanics can offer tons of information about local trails, including maps. This is the coolest bike shop in town, hands down.

Snow Sports

Steamboat Mountain Resort SNOW SPORTS
(ticket office 970-871-5252; www.steamboat.com; lift ticket adult/child $94/59; ticket office 8am-5pm) The stats of the Steamboat Ski Area speak volumes for the town's claim as 'Ski Town, USA' – 165 trails, 3668ft vertical and nearly 3000 acres. With excellent powder and trails for all levels, this is the main draw for winter visitors and some of the best skiing in the US. In the ski area there are (overpriced) food and equipment vendors galore.

There are runs at every level, a snowshoe area in the middle and race areas near the base. The area is particularly renowned for tree skiing, and the removal of saplings and fallen trees from the glades allows high-level intermediate skiers to weave through trees without the typical hazards of tree skiing. Serious skiers will also dig a number of mogul runs on the hill, and although these runs are a virtual factory of Olympic skiers and snowboarders, you don't have to be world-class to enjoy them. Compared with its foils in the Central Mountains, the sunny north-facing slopes are generally less aggressive. Wide, well-groomed runs are ideal cruising for intermediate skiers who might be a little rusty, making this hill among Colorado's best all-rounders.

Howelsen Hill Ski Area SNOW SPORTS
(970-879-8499; Howelsen Pkwy; lift tickets adult/child $17/12; 1-8pm Tue-Fri, 10am-4pm Sat & Sun) Among the country's oldest ski areas in continuous use and on the Colorado State Register of Historic Places, this is a relatively modest hill by current standards – only 14 runs and four lifts. It's the place to go if you're minding your budget. There's an indoor ice-skating facility too, the Howelsen Ice Arena, which operates from October until April.

Steamboat Powdercats SNOW SPORTS
(970-879-5188; www.steamboatpowdercats.com; tours $375-475) Want to nail some untracked lines? This tried-and-true cat-skiing operator offers guided backcountry tours on Buffalo Pass. Your guide will provide you with beacon, shovel and probe to keep you safe... and the cats are heated!

Steamboat Ski Touring Center SNOW SPORTS
(970-879-8180; www.nordicski.net; Steamboat Blvd; day pass $18) Near the base of Mt Werner, this Nordic ski center has excellent cross-country trails, some on a golf course, others through the forest. The facility also has good food – home-cooked soups and chili served with homemade bread and baked goods.

Steamboat Central Reservations SNOW SPORTS
(877-783-2628; www.steamboat.com; Mt Werner Circle, off Gondola Sq) This central booking office is the nerve center of the Steamboat Ski and Resort Corporation and can arrange ski packages, accommodation and all sorts of rentals. It's a corporate monolith, but it occasionally has good off-season specials.

Steamboat Springs Winter Sports Club SNOW SPORTS
(970-879-0695; www.sswsc.org; 845 Howelsen Pkwy; 10am-7pm Mon-Sat, noon-6pm Sun with seasonal variations) This century-old winter sports club has scores of former and current Olympians as members. In winter it has programs and classes for all ages and ability levels.

Steamboat Ski & Snowboard School SNOW SPORTS
(877-783-2628; www.steamboat.com; Mt Werner Circle; 3-day beginner adult course $299) There are a variety of classes for learning or sharpening skills at the Steamboat Ski Area. The beginner package lasts three days and is for absolute novices, including several hours of daily instruction and lift tickets. Serious skiers can take classes from Olympic champion Billy Kidd here too.

Water Sports

The Yampa River might roll lazily past parts of downtown (great for tubing in the summer), but this dynamic stretch of water is an ideal venue for water sports. It's particularly good for kayaks, with a 4-mile Class II to III white-water run that ends in two surfable holes. Other nearby river runs include the North Platte (Class III), Eagle (Class III), Elk (Class III) and Colorado (Class II).

Bucking Rainbow Outfitters RAFTING, FISHING
(970-879-8747; www.buckingrainbow.com; 730 Lincoln Ave; inner tubes $17, rafting $43-100, fishing $150-340; daily) This excellent outfitter has fly-fishing, rafting, outdoor apparel and the area's best fly shop, but it's most renowned for its rafting trips on the Yampa and beyond. Rafting half-days start at $71. Two-hour in-town fly-fishing trips start at $155 per person. It has a tube shack that runs shuttles from Sunpies Bistro on Yampa St.

Other Activities

★ **Strawberry Park Hot Springs** HOT SPRING
(970-870-1517; www.strawberryhotsprings.com; 44200 County Rd; per day adult/child $10/5; 10am-10:30pm Sun-Thu, to midnight Fri & Sat) Steamboat's favorite hot springs are actually outside the city limits, but offer great back-to-basics relaxation. There are very rustic cabins ($60 to $70) and camping ($55) here, too – though you are probably better off back in Steamboat. It has no electricity (you get gas lanterns) and you'll need your own linens. Be sure to reserve. Weekend reservations require a two-night stay.

Note that the thermal pools are clothing optional after dark. Check website for directions.

Wild West Balloon Adventures BALLOONING
(800-748-2487; www.wildwestballooning.com; 42415 Deerfoot Lane; adult/child $200/125) Floating silently over the mountains is a breathtaking experience, and this 45-minute ride includes a snack and a champagne toast. The scenery is perhaps most stunning on clear winter mornings.

Old Town Hot Springs HOT SPRING
(970-879-1828; www.oldtownhotsprings.org; 136 Lincoln Ave; adult/child $16/9, waterslide $6; 5:30am-10pm Mon-Fri, 7am-9pm Sat, 8am-

9pm Sun) Smack dab in the center of town, the water here is warmer than most other springs in the area. Known by the Utes as the 'medicine springs,' the mineral waters here are said to have special healing powers.

The springs recently underwent a $5-million renovation and now they have a new pool, a pair of 230ft-long waterslides and, perhaps coolest of all, an aquatic climbing wall!

Hosted Tours Adventures & Lodging Center OUTDOORS
(☎970-870-7901; www.hostedtours.com; 635 Lincoln Ave; ⏰10am-7pm) This small shack sits right on the main drag and is operated by its ultra-friendly owner, Brad. His information about accommodations, activities and the local scene is excellent.

Howelsen Ice Arena SKATING
(☎970-879-8499, 970-879-0341; Howelsen Pkwy; adult/child $10/9; ⏰noon-6:15pm Mon-Wed, Fri & Sat) Call for drop-in skate hours at this covered, seasonal facility at the base of the Howelsen Ski Area.

BAP OUTDOORS
(735 Oak St; ⏰9am-5:30pm Mon-Fri, 10am-5pm Sat, 11am-4pm Sun) For camping gear rental and good advice on local trips, stop by this local outfitter.

Festivals & Events

First Friday Art Walk ARTS
(www.steamboatspringsartwalk.com; Lincoln Ave; ⏰5-9pm 1st Fri of each month) Steamboat Springs' monthly Art Walk transforms local shops into galleries and sends wine-sipping visitors along the Lincoln Ave promenade between 4th and 12th Sts.

Yampa River Festival WATER SPORTS
(www.friendsoftheyampa.com; Yampa St at 7th St; all-event ticket $30; ⏰1st weekend in Jun) This festival features a kayak rodeo – which attracts national and international world-class playboaters – an upstream slalom race, and the Crazy River Dog Contest, in which dogs retrieve sticks from the river.

Strings Music Festival MUSIC
(☎970-879-5056; www.stringsmusicfestival.com; 900 Strings Rd; ⏰Jun-Sep) This long-running summer music festival hosts some 70 performances through the summer with a range of genres, including rock, blues, bluegrass, jazz and chamber music. When the weather is nice you can snag cheap seats on the lawn.

Steamboat Springs Pro Rodeo Series RODEO
(☎970-879-1818; www.steamboatprorodeo.com; cnr 5th St & Howelsen Pkwy; adult/child $15/8; ⏰7:30-9:30pm Fri & Sat mid-Jun–Labor Day) A historic rodeo that sees some of the best riding and roping in the West. It also has a helluva BBQ stand.

Hot Air Balloon Festival & Art in the Park ARTS, BALLOONING
(☎877-754-2269; West Lincoln Park; ⏰mid-Jul) This festival sends over 40 colorful balloons into the clear skies above town, while a large arts-and-crafts show unfolds in West Lincoln Park. Call Steamboat's Chamber of Commerce for more information.

Sleeping

Western Lodge MOTEL $
(☎970-879-1050; www.western-lodge.com; 1122 Lincoln Ave; s/d $68/94; P ❄ 📶 👪) The cheapest rooms in town sport an 'Avuncular '70s Cowboyist' style, clean and comfortable beds, and basic creature comforts like microwaves and minifridges. Perfect for ski bums looking to bum.

Hotel Bristol HOTEL $$
(☎970-879-3083; www.steamboathotelbristol.com; 917 Lincoln Ave; d $129-149; 📶) The elegant Hotel Bristol has small-but-sophisticated Western digs, with dark-wood and brass furnishings and Pendleton wool blankets on the beds. It has a ski shuttle, a six-person indoor Jacuzzi and a cozy restaurant.

Rabbit Ears Motel MOTEL $$
(☎970-879-1150; www.rabbitearsmotel.com; 201 Lincoln Ave; d incl breakfast $119-169; P ❄ 👪) A diabolically chipper, pink-neon bunny welcomes guests at this simple roadside motel. The place is smart enough to exploit the kitsch appeal, which makes many other mid-century low-ride motels so drab, by keeping the rooms bright and spotless. Rooms can be a bit smoky, but with big patios upstairs, this is still good value.

★**Vista Verde Guest Ranch** DUDE RANCH $$$
(☎970-879-3858; www.vistaverde.com; 31100 Seedhouse Rd; per week per person from $2700; ❄ 📶 👪) Simply put, this is the most luxurious of Colorado's top-end guest ranches. Here, you spend the day riding with expert staff, the evening around the fire in an

elegantly appointed lodge, and the night in high-thread-count sheets. If you have the means, this is it.

The staff takes the 'all-inclusive' concept to satisfying lengths. There are cooking and photography classes, rock climbing and rafting in the summer and four-star meals that arrive with well-paired wines. If you're looking for a true-grit cowboy adventure, it's best to look elsewhere, but if luxury is a requisite, this is the best dude-ranch experience money can buy.

Sheraton Steamboat Resort HOTEL **$$$**
(☎970-879-2220; www.starwoodhotels.com; 2200 Village Inn Court; d $129-179, ste $289-310; P ❄ 📶 ≋ 👪) If skiing is paramount to your adventures here, this is the only hotel in town with direct mountain access. The remodeled amenities are standard four-star plushness: thick sheets, flatscreen TVs and, if you're willing to pay a bit extra, great views of the mountain.

Eagle Ridge Lodge RESORT **$$$**
(http://eagleridgesteamboat.com; Eagle Ridge Dr; d from $250; P ❄ 📶 ≋ 👪) The style of this 40-room four-star hotel is clean, classic and elegant – white walls, high thread-counts, fluffy robes and stone fireplaces. In summer the huge outdoor swimming pool is delightful, and when the snow flies, the location makes it simple to get on the slopes.

The lodge also has a number of high-quality two- and three-bedroom options for larger groups.

Eating

Bamboo Market MARKET **$**
(www.bamboomkt.com; 1110 Yampa St; sandwiches $6-10; ⏰8am-7pm Mon-Fri, 9am-6pm Sat & Sun) This health food market also serves the best deli sandwiches in town, piled high with natural ingredients.

Steamboat Springs Farmers Market SELF-CATERING **$**
(☎970-846-1800; www.mainstreetsteamboatsprings.com; cnr 6th St & Lincoln Ave; ⏰9am-2pm Sat Jun-Sep; 👪) 🍃 This market, held on Saturday, brings in local farmers from across northern Colorado. There are over 50 vendors selling veggies, baked goods and bread.

Backcountry Delicatessen DELI **$**
(☎970-879-3617; www.backcountry-deli.com; 635 Lincoln Ave; sandwiches $7-10; ⏰7am-5pm) This Colorado sandwich chain is magic: the bread and ingredients are fresh, it opens early to sell hikers and outdoorsy types box lunches, and it's staffed by a friendly crew of guys. The Timberline is a favorite around here: peanut butter, local honey and bananas.

The Boathouse MODERN AMERICAN **$$**
(☎970-879-4797; 609 Yampa St; mains $12-20; ⏰11am-late) You can't beat the view from the riverfront deck and the creative menu takes you on a cruise of the continents with innovative dishes like 'When Pigs Fly,' (wasabi-kissed porkchops). Great for evening stargazing, it gets moving as a favorite pub after dinner.

Sweet Pea Market MODERN AMERICAN **$$**
(☎970-879-1221; www.sweetpeamarket.com; 729 Yampa St; mains $12-20; ⏰9am-7pm Mon-Fri, 10am-5pm Sat & Sun) 🍃 With a mission dedicated to local farmers and organic food, Sweet Pea is a welcome newcomer to Steamboat's meaty scene. It stocks tons of fresh veggies and bread and to-go items for picnics. In summer, chefs also serve local, organic modern American mains in a makeshift dining room.

Carl's Tavern AMERICAN **$$**
(☎970-761-2060; www.carlstavern.com; 700 Yampa St; mains $14-31) This local's favorite has great pub grub, a happening patio, live music, hot staff and a raucous spirit that will get your heart thumping.

Winona's BREAKFAST **$$**
(☎970-879-2483; 617 Lincoln Ave; breakfast $10-15; ⏰7am-3pm Mon-Sat; 👪) Arriving here during the peak breakfast hours is a mistake: Winona's creative breakfast dishes have made it the most popular breakfast joint in town. And for good reason: gooey, monstrous cinnamon rolls and plump French toast are balanced by savory treats, such as crab eggs Benedict.

Old Town Pub PUB FOOD **$$**
(☎970-879-2101; http://oldtownpub.jimdo.com; 600 Lincoln Ave; mains $12-24; ⏰11am-late; 👪) Perhaps this Wild West pub isn't as rowdy as days of yore (check out the bullet holes in the phone booth by the bar) but locals flock here for dinner and dancing. The Old Town Pub hosts live bands most weekends, pours great margaritas and serves gourmet pub fare.

★**Bistro CV** MODERN AMERICAN $$$
(☎970-879-4197; www.bistrocv.com; 345 Lincoln Ave; mains $21-41; ⏲5-10pm) Hands down the best fine dining in Steamboat, Bistro CV excels with its carefully prepared, creative New American dishes. The regularly changing menu uses fresh, sustainable ingredients. The chicken-chorizo pot pie with a savory cornmeal crust is an excellent way to start. For mains, try the white truffle gnocchi or the $21 burger, topped with foie-gras and worth every penny.

Cafe Diva FUSION $$$
(☎970-871-0508; www.cafediva.com; 1855 Ski Time Square Dr; mains $21-40; ⏲5:30-10pm) Asian flavors with French preparation combine for the most exciting dinner in the Mountain Area. 'Colorado Never Ever Beef Tenderloin' comes sided with mushroom bread pudding – the best of the cold-weather menu – but in summer, fresh salads and a crab-and-tomato bisque is equally winning.

Harwigs FUSION $$$
(☎970-879-1919; www.lapogee.com; 911 Lincoln Ave; mains $27-41; ⏲5-10pm) This fine-dining option serves Asian-influenced French fare in elegant, candlelit environs. The mains won't blow minds – rack of lamb, duck breast with black-eyed pea hash – but on Thai Night the prices drop and the flavors get more adventuresome. Occasionally a string quartet huddles in the corner.

Riggio's ITALIAN $$$
(www.riggiosfineitalian.com; 1106 Lincoln Ave; mains $18-27; ⏲5-10pm;) An older crowd patronizes Riggio's for the classic, elegant Italian 'restaurante' atmosphere. The fresh ravioli with mixed wild mushrooms is the worthy house special.

Drinking & Entertainment

Sunpies Bistro BAR
(☎970-870-3360; 735 Yampa St; ⏲noon-2am Tue-Sun;) Overlooking the creek is a big backyard, where locals pack in to drink and swap tales. They can be rowdy, but it's a slice of the real Steamboat. The Texas Toothpicks (deep-fried jalapeños and onions) is a great snack at this bar and grill.

Ghost Ranch Saloon LIVE MUSIC
(☎970-879-9898; www.ghostranchsaloon.com; 56 7th St; ⏲11am-2am Tue-Sat) The Ghost Ranch is a sure bet. Regardless of what's on stage, the crowd here is a mix of locals and visitors, and everyone seems determined to knock a few back and cut loose. The live music ranges from middling cover bands to national touring acts.

Emerald City Opera OPERA
(☎970-879-1996; www.steamboatopera.com; adult/student $20/15; ⏲10am-8pm Mon-Sat, to 6pm Sun) This small company stages the classics: Bizet, Puccini etc. Performances are often held at the **Perry Mansfield Julie Harris Theater** (40755 County Rd 36) between fall and spring. Tickets are available through the website.

Shopping

Boomerang Sports Exchange SPORTS
(☎970-870-3050; www.brangxchange.com; 1a, 1125 Lincoln Ave; ⏲10am-6pm Mon-Sat, noon-5pm Sun) If you are minding your budget, the deals at this used-sporting-goods shop can be *amazing*. It's a very mixed bag and the quality of gear depends a lot on luck, but it's certainly worth a look if you plan on skiing, camping or getting outdoors in the area.

Off the Beaten Path BOOKS
(☎970-879-6830; www.steamboatbooks.com; 68 9th St; ⏲8am-7pm Mon-Sat, 9am-6pm Sun;) Among the crowded stacks and sharp fragrance of brewing coffee beans, patrons browse for books on local history and light vacation reads. The staff picks are good, and there is a tiny cafe on hand for cozy chats.

Urbane CLOTHING
(☎970-879-9169; www.urbanesteamboat.com; 101 7th St; ⏲10am-8pm Mon-Sat, to 6pm Sun) No doubt the hippest clothing store on the Western Slope, Urbane stocks cool urban threads for men and women. It's a great little store and the perfect place to upgrade your mountain-biking duds for a night on the town.

Ski Haus OUTDOOR EQUIPMENT
(☎970-879-0385; www.skihaussteamboat.com; 1457 Pine Grove Rd; ski & snowboard rental packages per day from $30; ⏲9am-6pm Mon-Sat, to 5pm Sun) After fitting skis for four decades, this place is the first and last stop for many snow-bound visitors. You can rent top-quality gear here, or buy used rentals or demo skis. In the summer, it also rents bikes and camping gear. It also operates a free pick-up shuttle.

Information

Steamboat Springs Visitor Center (970-879-0880; www.steamboat-chamber.com; 125 Anglers Dr; 8am-5pm Mon-Fri, 10am-3pm Sat) This visitor center, facing Sundance Plaza, has a wealth of local information, and its website is also excellent for planning.

USFS Hahns Peak Ranger Office (970-879-1870; www.fs.usda.gov; 925 Weiss Dr; 8am-5pm Mon-Sat) Rangers staff this office offering permits and information about surrounding national forests, including Mt Zirkel Wilderness, as well as information on hiking, mountain biking, fishing and other activities in the area.

Getting There & Away

Go Alpine (800-343-7433, 970-879-2800; www.goalpine.com; 1755 Lincoln Ave) This taxi and shuttle service makes several daily runs between Steamboat and Denver International Airport ($85, four hours one-way). It also makes trips to the Yampa Valley Regional Airport and operates an in-town taxi.

Greyhound Terminal (800-231-2222; www.greyhound.com; 1505 Lincoln Ave) Greyhound's US 40 service between Denver and Salt Lake City stops here, about half a mile west of town.

Storm Mountain Express (877-844-8787; www.stormmountainexpress.com) This shuttle service runs to Yampa Valley Regional Airport ($33 one-way) and beyond, though trips to DIA and Vail get very pricey.

Getting Around

Steamboat Springs Transit (970-879-3717, for pick-up in Mountain Area 970-846-1279; http://steamboatsprings.net) Steamboat Springs Transit runs a free bus service along Lincoln Ave from 12th St in the west to Walton Creek Rd in the east. It also goes up Mt Werner Rd to the gondola.

Though infrequent, it will also take you to a handful of towns to the west; the cost is $6 each way to Craig, $5 to Hayden, $3.50 each way to Milner. Check with the visitor center for seasonal schedules.

AROUND STEAMBOAT SPRINGS

Stagecoach State Park

Sixteen miles south of Steamboat Springs via US 40, Hwy 131 and Routt County Rd 14, **Stagecoach State Park** (reservation office 303-470-1144; 25500 County Rd 14; tent sites $10-20;) is the nearest inexpensive camping to Steamboat Springs. The park is on the edge of a large reservoir in a good location for trips into the Flattops Wilderness, Sarvis Creek Wilderness and Blacktail Mountain.

In summer campers entertain themselves with fishing and a modest, 8-mile network of hiking trails, while speedboats zoom along the water. In winter, camping is limited (rangers clear snow from four sites) and activities in the park include snowmobiling, Nordic skiing and ice fishing.

Mount Zirkel Wilderness

One of the five original wilderness areas in Colorado, Mt Zirkel Wilderness is an untamed, roadless expanse dotted with icy glacial lakes, granite faces and rife with opportunities for isolated backcountry hiking and camping. It's intersected by the Continental Divide and two major rivers, the Elk and the Encampment, both of which are being considered for protection under the Wild & Scenic Rivers Act.

Boldly rising from the center of the area is the 12,180ft **Mount Zirkel**, named by famed mountaineer Clarence King to honor the German petrologist with whom he reconnoitered the country in 1874. The area is *huge*, and this can provide a place to get off the grid, even during Colorado's busiest seasons.

The most popular entry points are in the vicinity of Steamboat Springs, though it's also approachable from Walden or Clark. Detailed maps and information on hiking, mountain biking, fishing and other activities in this beautiful area are available at the USFS Hahns Peak Ranger Office.

Trails Illustrated publishes Hahns Peak/Steamboat Lake and Clark/Buffalo Pass maps, while Jay and Therese Thompson describe the walks in *The Hiker's Guide to the Mt Zirkel Wilderness.*

Hahns Peak

On the windswept plain at the base of a picturesque peak lies this quasi–ghost town, 27 miles north of Steamboat Springs via Elk River Rd (Routt County Rd 129). It was once the terminus of the railroad from Wyoming, and has a rich history as a secluded harbor for outlaws. (Rumor has it that Butch Cassidy was jailed here in a bear cage.) It's an unfrequented destination that still has a handful of residents and a couple of interesting junk and crafts shops.

Nearby **Steamboat Lake State Park** (970-879-3922; www.parks.state.co.us; off County Rd 129; tent & RV sites $16-22, camper cabins $80;) and **Pearl Lake State Park** (970-879-3922; www.parks.state.co.us; off County Rd 209; tent & RV sites $16-22, yurts $60; P) are both developed state parks on the side of reservoirs with shoreline camping, some short hiking trails and opportunities for fishing and boating.

CRAIG

POP 9464 / ELEV 6198FT

Lying on the north bank of the Yampa River between the towns of Meeker and Steamboat Springs, Craig is little more than a pit stop on the way to or from Colorado's northwest corner. The downtown stands at a junction of roads leading elsewhere: US 40 goes east–west between Steamboat Springs and Dinosaur National Monument; Hwy 789/13 runs north through desolate, rolling hills near the Wyoming Border; and 394 follows the Yampa River south to Meeker.

The main drag is Yampa Ave, but its taxidermy shops, automotive suppliers and liquor stores offer a fairly grim stroll. There are big box stores and several grocers if you're stocking up for a trip out west.

Sights & Activities

Museum of Northwest Colorado MUSEUM
(970-824-6360; www.museumnwco.org; 590 Yampa Ave; 9am-5pm Mon-Fri, 10am-4pm Sat;) FREE The hats, chaps and saddles in the cowboy collection are the highlight of this community museum. But it's the handcrafted and etched spurs and hand-tooled boots that are the most cherished artifacts. It also has a small bookshop on hand with volumes on local history.

Marcia Car MUSEUM
(cnr E Victory Way & Washington St; 8am-5pm Mon-Fri Jun-Aug;) FREE This private rail car was commissioned in 1906 by David Moffat, a prominent Denver banker who owned a number of gold mines. He was also instrumental in connecting Colorado to the national rail system. You can arrange tours at the Moffat County Visitors Center.

Sleeping & Eating

There is a cluster of hotel chains in the west part of town off the intersection where Hwy 13 splits south from US 40. Just west of downtown, on US 40, there is a string of mid-century motels, but they're fairly hit-and-miss. Prices rise during hunting season, from mid-September to late November.

For eats, fast-food chains are common; the best bet for something local is downtown.

Getting There & Away

Yampa Valley Regional Airport (County Rd 51a) is midway between Craig and Steamboat Springs. Buses from the **Craig Greyhound Depot** (970-824-5161; 470 Russell St) serve Denver ($52, six hours) and Salt Lake City ($69. 6½ hours).

DINOSAUR NATIONAL MONUMENT

At the end of desolate stretches of black top in the sparsely populated northwest corner of the state, Dinosaur National Monument is Colorado's most remote destination, but for travelers fascinated by prehistoric life on earth, it is worth every lonely mile. It's one of the few places on the planet that you can reach out and touch a dinosaur skeleton, snarling in its final pose, in situ.

Although dinosaurs once inhabited much of the earth, only a few places have the proper geological and climatic conditions to preserve their skeletons as fossils. Paleontologist Earl Douglass of Pittsburgh's Carnegie Museum discovered this dinosaur fossil bed, one of the largest in North America, in 1909. Six years later, President Woodrow Wilson acknowledged the scientific importance of the area, which straddles the Utah–Colorado border, by declaring it a national monument.

Aside from the quarry, there's lots to see here. The monument's starkly eroded canyons provide the visitor with scenic drives, hiking, camping and river running.

Sights

Dinosaur Quarry PARK
(www.nps.gov/dino; per vehicle $10; 8am-7pm Memorial Day–Labor Day, 8am-4:30pm rest of year) The Jurassic strata containing the

fossils give a glimpse of how paleontologists transform solid rock into the beautiful skeletons seen in museums, and how they develop scientifically reliable interpretations of life in the remote past. Ranger-led walks, talks and tours explain the site; information can also be gleaned from brochures, audio-visual programs and exhibits.

There is also a shop selling gifts and books. The Quarry is completely enclosed to protect the fossils from weathering.

Activities

Both the Yampa River and Green River offer excellent river-running opportunities, with plenty of exciting rapids and choppy whitewater amid splendid scenery. From mid-May to early September trips range from one to five days. Adventure Bound (p295), in Grand Junction, is a popular rafting outfitter for the area. Fishing is permitted only with the appropriate state permits, available from sports stores or tackle shops in Dinosaur or Vernal, UT. Check with park rangers about limits and the best places.

Fossil Discovery Trail HIKING

This short interpretive trail is excellent for families as it's only 0.75 miles long and you can reach out and touch the bones of dinosaurs. Regardless of your knowledge or understanding of paleontology, this is a stunning walk through some 65 million years of history.

Walking along the hillside, visitors enter a small canyon, eventually arriving at the **Morrison Formation**, one of the most spectacular open-air collections of dinosaur bones in the world. The bones in these walls represent 10 species ranging in size from about 7in to 76ft.

Sleeping & Eating

There are no lodges in the monument but Vernal has a good selection of motels and restaurants, and the town of Dinosaur also has a couple of motels and eateries. There are designated backcountry campsites only on the Jones Hole Trail; otherwise wilderness camping is allowed anywhere at least one-quarter mile from an established road or trail. But lots of restrictions about backcountry camping apply, so backpackers should register at one of the visitor centers or ranger stations. Backcountry permits are free.

Green River Campground CAMPGROUND

(☎435-781-7700; Blue Mountain Rd; tent & RV sites $12; ⏰mid-Apr–early Oct) Dinosaur National Monument's main campground is Green River Campground, 5 miles east of Dinosaur Quarry along Blue Mountain Rd, with 88 sites. It has bathrooms and drinking water but no showers or hookups. A park host will sell firewood.

Split Mountain Campground CAMPGROUND

(☎435-781-7700; Blue Mountain Rd; group sites summer/winter $25/free) For camping during winter when Green River is closed, try nearby Split Mountain Campground, which is a place for group camp sites in the summer, but is open to anyone in winter, when there's no fee.

Information

Dinosaur National Monument is a 210,000-acre plot that straddles the Utah-Colorado state line. Monument headquarters and most of the land is within Colorado, but the quarry (the only place to see fossils protruding from the earth) is in Utah. There are several drives with scenic overlooks and interpretive signs, leading to a number of trailheads for short nature walks or access to the backcountry.

At the town of Dinosaur, a Colorado Welcome Center offers maps and brochures for the entire state. Information is available from **Dinosaur National Monument Headquarters Visitor Center** (☎970-374-3000; 4545 E Hwy 40; ⏰8am-4:30pm Jun-Aug, only Mon-Fri Dec-Feb), sometimes called the Canyon Visitor Center. It has an audio-visual program, exhibits and a bookstore. There's also a visitors center at Dinosaur Quarry. Entrance to the monument headquarters visitor center is free, but entrance to other parts of the monument (including Dinosaur Quarry) is $10 per private vehicle, $5 for cyclists or bus passengers.

Getting There & Away

The monument is 88 miles west of Craig via US 40 and 120 miles east of Salt Lake City, UT, by I-80 and US 40. Dinosaur Quarry is 7 miles north of Jensen, UT, on Cub Creek Rd (Utah Hwy 149). Monument headquarters is just off US 40 on Harpers Corner Dr, about 4 miles east of the town of Dinosaur.

SOUTH OF DINOSAUR NATIONAL MONUMENT

Dinosaur

POP 350

Just a few miles east of the Utah border, on the doorstep of Dinosaur National Monument, Dinosaur is easy to skip. In an effort to capitalize on its location by the monument, the town changed its name from Artesia in the mid-1960s and gave the streets dinosaur-themed monikers (Brachiosaurus Bypass, Triceratops Tce...). Junk car lots and forlorn homesteads dot the rolling hills of this windswept landscape.

Only a few things entice travelers to hit the brakes on the way through town. The well-stocked **Colorado Welcome Center** (☎970-374-2205; 101 E Stegosaurus St; ⏲8am-6pm Memorial Day–Labor Day, 9am-5pm Labor Day–Memorial Day, closed Jan & Feb; 📶) has maps for scenic drives, and information on area rafting and camping. The information is provided by a pair of doting ladies who'll help you plan your travels in Colorado's west and know every little town between here and Denver.

If you're hungry, the best bet is a greasy bite at **BedRock Depot** (☎970-374-2336; 214 W Brontosaurus Blvd; mains $3-9; ⏲11am-5:30pm Mon & Thu-Sat, 1-5pm Sun; 👪), a nostalgic ice cream and espresso shop that serves a coy menu of dino-themed sandwiches like the 'Allosaurus Delight,' a savory chicken apple sausage on a roll. The potato roll of Leona, one of the owners, is famous around here, as is the homemade ice cream. The only other place to eat is 20 miles east of town: the **Massadona Tavern & Steakhouse** (☎970-374-2324; 22927 US Hwy 40; mains $8-18; ⏲4-8pm Tue-Fri, 11am-8pm Sat & Sun; 👪). Way out on a lonely stretch of Hwy 40, it has the feel of a mid-century roadhouse and serves up passable chops, battered fish and chips, burgers and pints of beer. There are a few spare motels on Hwy 40, but none of them are recommended.

Rangely

POP 2000 / ELEV 5274FT

An isolated coal and oil town on Hwy 64, Rangely is about 56 miles west of Meeker and about 90 miles north of Fruita and Grand Junction via Hwy 139. Visitors to nearby Dinosaur National Monument may wish to detour through Rangely to access the very fine rock-art sites along Hwy 139 just south of town, but Rangely itself is not much of a destination. The **Rangely Chamber of Commerce** (☎970-675-5290; www.rangely.com; 209 E Main St; ⏲1-5pm Mon-Fri) can provide information on local businesses.

The **Rangely Museum** (☎970-675-2612; 150 Kennedy Dr; ⏲10am-4pm Jun-Aug, 10am-4pm Fri & Sat Apr-May & Sep-Oct; 👪) is a good diversion with exhibits on energy production, Native Americans and ranching. There are several notable pre-Columbian rock-art sites on nearby BLM lands; look for self-guided tour brochures along Hwy 64 East and West, the Dragon Trail south of Rangely and Cañon Pintado.

Sleeping & Eating

Rangely Camper Park CAMPGROUND $
(940 E Rangely Ave; tent & RV sites $10-15; 🅿👪) Located beneath a stand of cottonwoods, this city park has RV hookups and spacious sites. It's an excellent base for rock hounding.

Blue Mountain Inn & Suites HOTEL $$
(☎970-675-8888; www.bluemountaininnrangely.com; 37 Park St; d $140; 🅿📶🏊👪) Don't forget to wipe the oil off your boots when you enter Rangely's best hotel. It would be slightly bland if it weren't for stone fireplaces, the timber-framed entranceway and a nice little indoor pool and outdoor hot tub. The best value comes when you book directly through the website.

Cañon Pintado National Historic District

It's well worth adding a few hours to the trip between Grand Junction and Dinosaur National Monument in order to spend a few moments communing with these spectral, mysterious images – ghostly birds and life-sized flutists. The paintings, left as inscrutable messages from the region's early settlers, create Colorado's most desolate, haunting gallery.

The images are attributed to two of Douglass Canyon's first communities: the Fremont Culture, who lived here from about 0 to 1300AD, and the Ute, who lived here from around 1300 to 1881. It was the journal of Silvestre Vélez de Escalante, a Franciscan missionary who came through on the famed Dominguez-Escalante expedition of 1776, that first named this corridor Cañyon Pintado (Painted Canyon).

It's an unforgiving, arid and dusty stretch, but over the past several years the BLM has made the self-guided drive much easier to access, with educational signs and maintained turn-offs and trails. Look for green and white BLM rods that indicate the sites along Hwy 139.

MEEKER

POP 2400 / ELEV 6239FT

The picturesque seat of Rio Blanco County, Meeker takes its name from infamous government agent Nathan Meeker, whose arbitrary destruction of a Ute racetrack precipitated a fatal confrontation in 1879. Contemporary Meeker is a small oil town, surrounded by sagebrush country where Greek American sheepherders graze huge flocks for their wool and silent pumpjacks rust on the hillsides.

Sights & Activities

White River Museum MUSEUM

(970-878-9982; www.meekercolorado.com; 565 Park St; 9am-5pm summer, 10am-4pm winter;) FREE There's a rambling collection of eclectic Western memorabilia here: bear skin coats, a couple of peace pipes and Nathan Meeker's printing press.

Sable Mountain Outfitters OUTDOORS

(970-878-4765; www.sablemountainoutfitters.com; 4-day pack trips $1200) This outfitter has been conducting hunting, fishing and wilderness trips for three decades. The trips into the Flat Top Wilderness (www.flattopsbyway.com) come highly recommended by locals.

JML Outfitters FISHING, HORSEBACK RIDING

(970-878-4749; www.jmloutfitters.com; 300 County Rd 75; half-day trail rides from $55, day pack-trips from $300) It hosts multiday adventures into the Flat Top Wilderness on horseback, allowing guests to ride between a string of camps and get far into the brush. The excursions are rustic, but with horses, guides and a camp cook, it's a luxurious way to feel like you've worked for it. The riders here also have lots of programs for kids.

Sleeping & Eating

Meeker gets booked up with hunters from late September to mid-November. Note that JML Outfitters also has cabins for rent ($70), even if you don't do an expedition with them. There are several independent restaurants in the small downtown, and lots of fast-food options on the periphery.

★ **Meeker Hotel** HISTORIC HOTEL $$

(970-878-5255; www.meekerhotel.com; 560 Main St; r/ste $86/125;) Gary Cooper and Teddy Roosevelt both stayed in Meeker's best hotel, which dates back to 1896. The themed rooms have Western motifs. Some have been carefully updated, like the Billy the Kid Room, while others still have a way to go.

There's plenty of elk heads in this hunters' favorite, and the ornate tin ceiling and careful woodwork will delight turn-of-the-century architecture buffs.

Getting There & Away

On the north bank of the White River near the junction of Hwy 13 and Hwy 64, Meeker is 45 miles south of Craig and 42 miles north of Rifle. The Flat Tops Scenic Byway is a stunning 82-mile drive through the wilderness to Yampa.

Vail, Aspen & Central Colorado

Includes ➡

Best Places to Eat

- ➡ Tennessee Pass Cookhouse (p240)
- ➡ Matsuhisa (p226)
- ➡ South Ridge Seafood (p190)
- ➡ The Tenth (p203)
- ➡ Pullman (p212)

Best Places to Stay

- ➡ Devil's Thumb Ranch (p175)
- ➡ Tennessee Pass Sleep Yurts (p239)
- ➡ The Sebastian (p200)
- ➡ Avalanche Ranch (p215)
- ➡ Railroad Bridge (p235)

Why Go?

If you ask us where you can find the most trillion-dollar sights, where you can run the gnarliest rivers and charge the sickest runs, and to choose one hike that is sure to save your citified soul within a single afternoon, we would take out the map of Colorado, trim the edges and zoom into the center. Because here's where you'll find more magic per square mile than anywhere else in the state.

It's the stomping ground of war heroes and X Games athletes, and the hideaway of billionaires, ski bums and gonzo fugitives. Celebrified, intellectualized and musical, it's patrolled by bear, elk, hummingbird and eagle, laced by trail, rail and river, and linked by free transport, epic bikepaths and more friendly smiles than seems reasonable. But then again, of course these people are smiling. They freaking live here!

When to Go

Vail

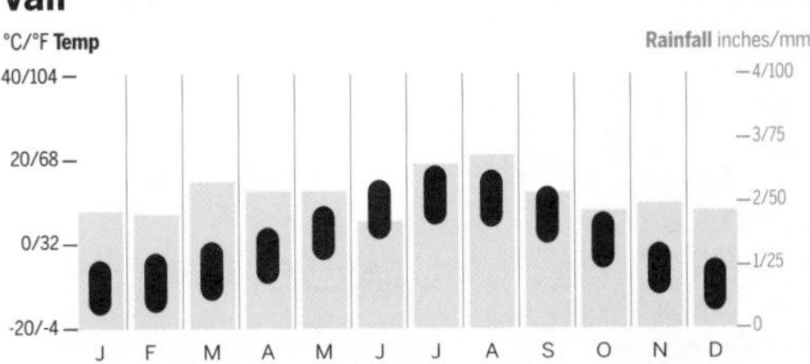

Jan–Mar Classic Colorado: fresh powder, blue skies and epic runs all day long.

Jun–Aug Long sunny days means hiking, biking, paddling and outdoor concerts.

Sep & Oct Terrific lodging deals and last gasp high-country camping amid golden aspens.

Vail, Aspen & Central Colorado Highlights

1 Experience the backcountry: climb a 14er, such as **Quandary Peak** (p186), day hike the **Colorado Trail** (p235) or ski hut-to-hut around **Shrine Pass** (p223).

2 Explore historic **Breckenridge** (p182) and ski from Peak 8 all the way down into town.

3 Hike to the Maroon Bells, soak in hot springs and fall in love with glamorous **Aspen** (p216).

4 Drive alongside the nimble mountain goats atop **Mt Evans** (p171) and **Independence Pass** (p237).

5 Toast the powder in the legendary back bowls at **Vail** (p197).

6 Cycle from **Frisco** (p177) along Summit County's bikepaths or ride epic singletrack on the **Monarch Crest Trail** (p231).

7 Ski like a local at **Winter Park** (p173), **Arapahoe Basin** (p181), **Loveland** (p175) or **Copper Mountain** (p193).

8 Paddle white water or cast for trout on the Arkansas, near **Salida** (p231).

9 Ride horseback through the high-altitude prairie of **South Park** (p191).

10 Get a glimpse of gold-rush history in ghost towns like **St Elmo** (p240) and **Crystal** (p215).

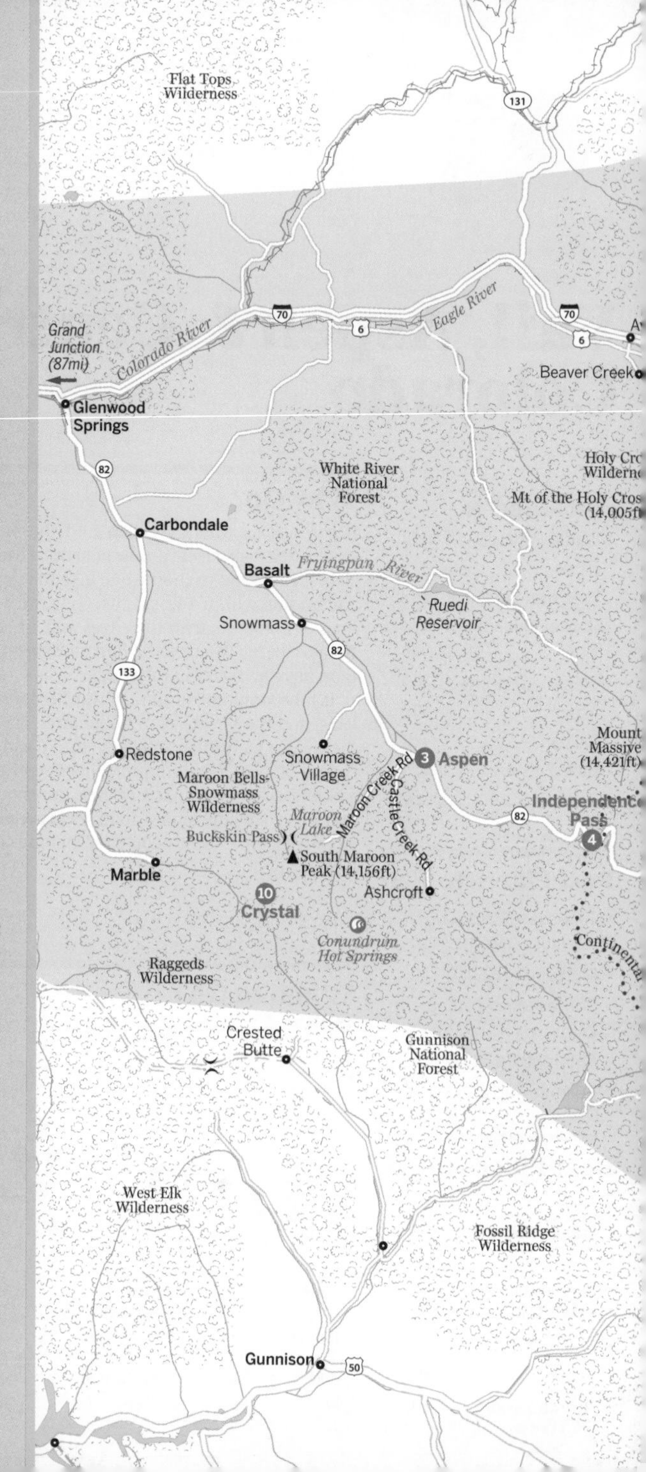

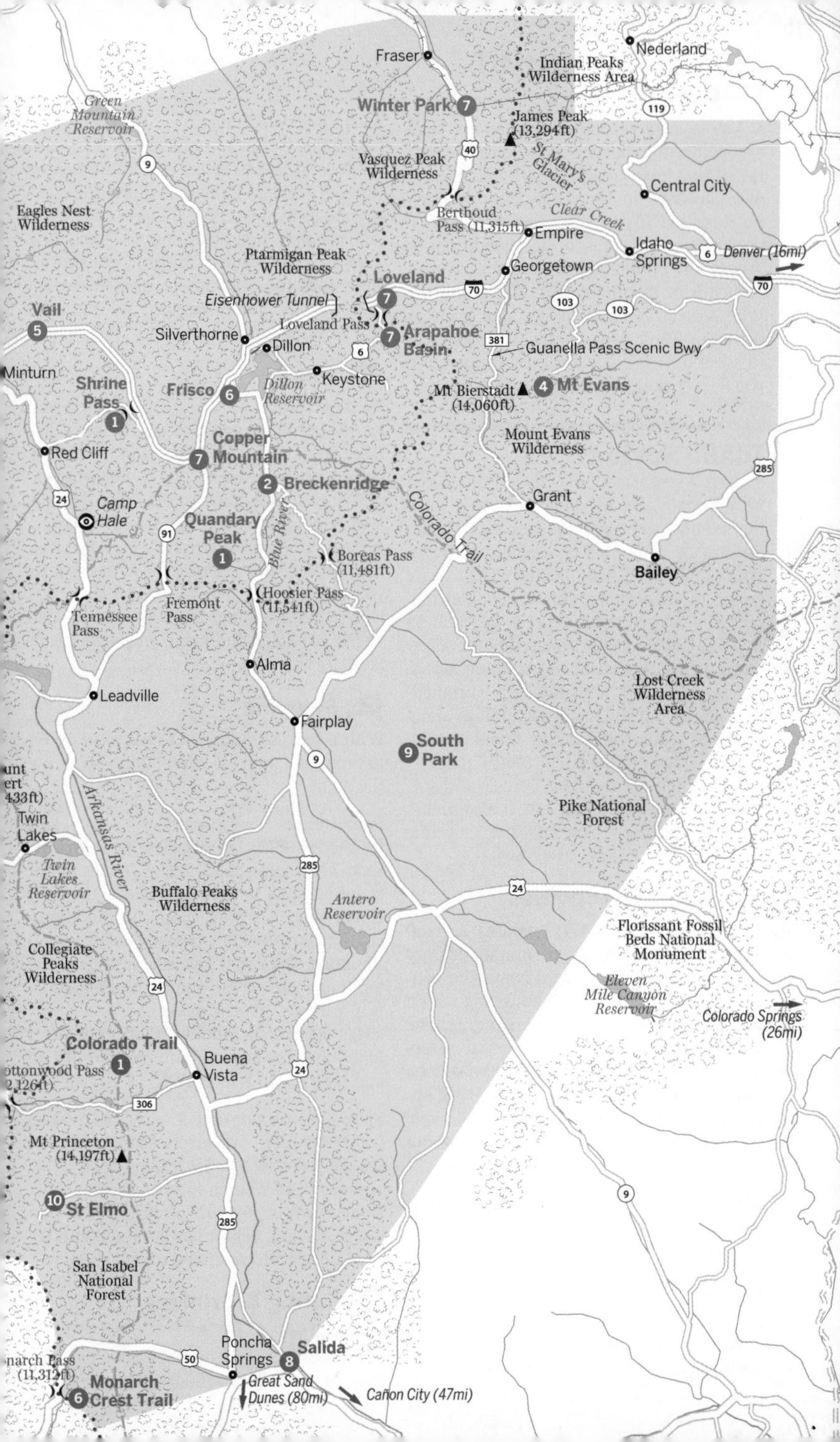

Fraser
Nederland
Indian Peaks Wilderness Area
Winter Park
James Peak (13,294ft)
Green Mountain Reservoir
St Mary's Glacier
Vasquez Peak Wilderness
Central City
Eagles Nest Wilderness
Berthoud Pass (11,315ft)
Clear Creek
Empire
Idaho Springs
Denver (16mi)
Ptarmigan Peak Wilderness
Georgetown
Loveland
Eisenhower Tunnel
Vail
Loveland Pass
Arapahoe Basin
Silverthorne
Dillon
Guanella Pass Scenic Bwy
Minturn
Keystone
Shrine Pass
Frisco
Dillon Reservoir
Mt Bierstadt (14,060ft)
Mt Evans
Red Cliff
Copper Mountain
Mount Evans Wilderness
Breckenridge
Camp Hale
Colorado Trail
Grant
Quandary Peak
Blue River
Boreas Pass (11,481ft)
Bailey
Tennessee Pass
Fremont Pass
Hoosier Pass (11,541ft)
Alma
Leadville
Lost Creek Wilderness Area
Fairplay
South Park
Twin Lakes
Arkansas River
Pike National Forest
Twin Lakes Reservoir
Buffalo Peaks Wilderness
Antero Reservoir
Florissant Fossil Beds National Monument
Collegiate Peaks Wilderness
Eleven Mile Canyon Reservoir
Colorado Springs (26mi)
Colorado Trail
Buena Vista
Mt Princeton (14,197ft)
St Elmo
San Isabel National Forest
Poncha Springs
Salida
Great Sand Dunes (80mi)
Cañon City (47mi)
Monarch Crest Trail

DENVER TO SUMMIT COUNTY

If you've had visions of powder or been eyeballing that luscious snow-dusted Front Range that looms magnificently and just out of reach above the Denver streets, then don't be surprised if you subconsciously swerve onto I-70 west and hit the gas, winding your way to the doorstep of one of the greatest stretches of mountain paradise in the US. Whether you've come to ski, hike, cycle or drive the scenic byways, this is the gateway to adventure, big sky and good times – and you'll be back in Denver in time for dinner.

Idaho Springs

POP 1893 / ELEV 7526FT

Most people who are only in Denver for a limited time can barrel up the road to Idaho Springs for a quick taste of Colorado's rough-and-tumble gold-rush history. The rowdy gaggle of prospectors, gunslingers and rapscallions who rushed here to get rich in 1859 have been mostly replaced by a notably more genteel crowd of day-tripping skiers, hikers, and bikers on blindingly chromed-up Harleys, but the historic buildings along Miner St retain the creaking floors and antique character of the city's colorful past.

About halfway between Denver and several big ski resorts along I-70, it also makes for a good pit stop – particularly when traffic on the interstate slows to a crawl.

Sights & Activities

The visitor center (p171) contains a small but interesting display of mining history and equipment, along with some Ute artifacts. Otherwise, you can't go wrong with a wander down Miner St, the main drag. The town gets its name from the thermal waters of **Indian Springs** (www.indianhotsprings.com; 302 Soda Creek Rd; day pass $19-21; 7:30am-10:30pm), but unless you're short on time, there are much better hot springs elsewhere in the state.

Clear Creek Outdoors FISHING

(303-567-1500; www.clearcreekflyfishing.com; 1524 Miner St; full-day expedition $250; 10am-6pm) Situated in a small shop selling rods, reels and outdoor gear, Rob Brozovich operates excellent fly-fishing tours to a private high-mountain lake in the area. The lake routinely gives up brown, rainbow and cutthroat trout. You can also call in for a condition report for streams in the area.

A&A Historical Trails HORSEBACK RIDING

(303-567-4808; www.aastables.com; 608 Virginia Canyon Rd; 1hr $40, additional hr $30) Traveling through Virginia Canyon is a beautiful way to soak in the history of the area. There are guided and unguided options, including a visit to the canyon's historic graveyards. Note that the stables are located several miles outside Idaho Springs – see the website for directions.

Tours

Phoenix Mine MINING

(303-567-0422; www.phoenixmine.com; Trail Creek Rd, exit 239 off I-70; tour adult/child 12yr & under $10/5, gold panning $5; 10am-6pm) One of two goldmine tours in the Idaho Springs area (the other is actually a mill), this one gets you underground with a former miner and is reasonably priced to boot. Afterwards you can pan for gold in the stream – you won't find anything, but kids love it. Call ahead in winter and bring your own headlamp if you have one.

Sleeping

With a few exceptions, it's best to move on to Summit County if you plan on spending the night.

Peck House INN $

(303-569-9870; www.thepeckhouse.com; 83 Sunny Ave, Empire; r $65-135;) As the oldest standing hotel in Colorado (1862), the Peck House manages both class and homespun charm, with creaking, crooked hallways and Victorian decor that give it loads of character. It also serves fine dinners and knows its way around a martini shaker.

It's located in Empire, 10 miles west of Idaho Springs near the intersection of I-70 and Hwy 40 (to Winter Park).

Echo Lake Campground CAMPGROUND $

(877-444-6777; www.recreation.gov; Squaw Lake Rd; tent & RV sites $17; Jun-Aug;) This popular USFS campground at the foot of Mt Evans is up at 10,600ft, so bring a hat and warm sleeping bag. It has both tent and RV sites along with water and toilets. Reserve.

Eating & Drinking

Two Brothers Deli CAFE $

(303-567-2439; www.twobrothersdeli.com; 1424 Miner St; sandwiches $7.50-9; 6am-8pm Mon-

Thu, to 9pm Fri-Sun;) The coziest cafe in town, this is an excellent option to refuel with an espresso, a smoothie or a quick meal. Breakfast wraps, fresh sandwiches and baguette pizzas are served throughout the day.

Beau Jo's PIZZERIA **$$**
(303-567-4376; www.beaujos.com; 1517 Miner St; large pizza $16-23.50; 11am-9pm;) Beau Jo's thick-crust mountain pies are far from gourmet, but if you're in need of a high-calorie meal after a hard day's play, it will certainly do you right. A Colorado institution, it's a sure-fire kid pleaser.

★ **Tommyknocker Brewery** BREWERY
(303-567-2688; www.tommyknocker.com; 1401 Miner St; mains $10-14; 11am-2am) You don't even have to like beer to know these guys are good: scores of medals from beer competitions hang over the sunlit dining space in a testament to the expert brews. Above-average pub food – from buffalo burgers to brats and sauerkraut – and an amiable staff clinch it. It also serves house-brewed root beer.

Information

Idaho Springs Visitors Center & Museum (303-567-4382; www.historicidahosprings.com; 2060 Miner St; 9am-5pm Sep-May, 8am-6pm Jun-Aug)

USFS Clear Creek Ranger Station (303-567-3000; 101 Hwy 103, exit 240 off I-70; 8am-4:30pm Mon-Fri) Information on hiking and camping in surrounding Clear Creek County.

Mt Evans

ELEV 14,264FT

The pinnacle of many trips to Clear Creek County is a drive to the summit of **Mt Evans** (www.mountevans.com; Hwy 103; per car $10; late May-early Sep), which is less than an hour west of Denver's skyscrapers. The home of shaggy, snow-white mountain goats and ancient bristlecone pine, this is the highest paved road in North America and one of three classic high-alpine drives along the Front Range (the other two being Pikes Peak Hwy and Trail Ridge Rd in Rocky Mountain National Park).

From Idaho Springs to the summit, the road ascends roughly 6600ft in altitude over 28 miles, passing through montane, subalpine and tundra ecosystems. One stop you don't want to miss is the **Mt Goliath Natural Area** (11,540ft; park at the Dos Chappell Nature Center), where you can check out some of the oldest living organisms on the planet, the gnarled, wind-sculpted bristlecone pine. The trees here range from 900 to an astounding 2000 years old.

Continuing on the road past **Summit Lake**, which freezes solid in winter, you are likely to encounter Rocky Mountain goats and bighorn sheep. From the parking lot it's then a short but lung-busting scramble to the summit's transcendent views.

Altitude change is serious business and you should come prepared, particularly if you start the day in Denver. You'll need to bring lots of water, a warm fleece (even if it's 90°F out), outer shell, sunscreen and sunglasses. There's no food up here, so a picnic is a good idea as well. Afternoon thunderstorms are always a possibility, so get an early start.

To get here, take exit 240 off I-70 at Idaho Springs and follow the signs south on Hwy 103. Near the exit, you'll pass the USFS Ranger Station, which offers information and topo maps. You can camp at Echo Lake, just before the fee station.

St Mary's Glacier & James Peak

Wildflowers and windswept trails, boulders and snowfields – these are the disproportionately big rewards for the easy hike up to St Mary's Glacier area. It's a quick day escape from Denver, and the modest elevation gains, short distance (half-mile) and summer snow and ice make it ideal even for the littlest hikers. Although the area gets fairly busy on summer weekends, the views on a clear day are remarkable, and a scramble around the lake will bring you to the glacier itself.

If you want to make a day of it, the trail to James Peak (13,294ft) continues up another 3 miles past the base of the glacier to the summit. This gentle mountain on the Continental Divide was named after the botanist Edwin James, who made the first recorded summit of Pikes Peak in 1820 (Pike, of course, never made it to the top). It's a relatively moderate but beautiful climb.

To get here, take I-70 west from Denver, past Idaho Springs to Fall River Rd (exit 238). Turn right on Fall River Rd and continue for 10 miles until you reach the parking

DRIVING I-70

Although I-70's mountain stretch can be downright scenic, the interstate – particularly on weekends and in bad weather – sometimes resembles more of a parking lot than a highway. If you're trying to trump the traffic, make use of the website or app http://goI70.com to get the latest on road conditions.

areas. There is a parking fee of $5 for these lots, and it's best not to park elsewhere; the neighbors don't tolerate strangers parking on their turf. Get here early to secure a spot.

Georgetown

POP 1088 / ELEV 8530FT

Smaller and more soulful than Idaho Springs, historic Georgetown's mix of Victorian architecture, secondhand bookshops, and cafes make it a pleasant stopover on the way up or down I-70. In summer, the town gets buzzing thanks to the daytrippers headed up the Guanella Pass byway.

Sights & Activities

Hamill House MUSEUM

(www.historicgeorgetown.org; 305 Argentine St; adult/child $4/free; noon-5pm Jul & Aug, hours vary rest of year) Originally built in 1867, this residence was renovated as a mountain estate in the late 1870s by William Hamill, who made his fortune in silver mining. Tours provide a glimpse of residential life and tastes in a 19th-century mining town.

★Guanella Pass Scenic Byway SCENIC DRIVE

(www.byways.org; late May-Sep) Built atop an old wagon road that once connected the silver-mining towns of Georgetown and Grant, this 22-mile drive (11 miles to the pass) climbs up to 11,669ft, and is an excellent staging point for fishing excursions and several alpine hikes. Sightings of bighorn sheep and mountain goats are not uncommon.

From the pass you can ascend **Mt Bierstadt** (14,060ft; 7 miles round-trip), one of the most popular 14ers along the Front Range. A shorter and less-crowded option is **Silver Dollar Lake** (3 miles round-trip); this inspiring trail is mostly above the treeline and graced with a galaxy of tiny wildflowers in summer. The trailhead is located just past Guanella Pass Campground, at 11,000ft.

Georgetown Loop Railroad RAILWAY

(888-456-6777; www.georgetownlooprr.com; 646 Loop Dr; adult/child 3-15yr $25.95/18.95; May-Oct, hours vary) Chugging along this loop is an entertaining way to leave the I-70 corridor and enjoy expansive views over Clear Creek Valley. The ride is short – only 15 minutes out and 15 minutes back, with a pause to tour a mine in between – but the scenery from one of the open passenger cars can make for a breathtaking, if chilly, afternoon.

Once part of a system that snaked through Clear Creek Canyon to connect Denver with rich mines in Silver Plume, the ride's operators have done an admirable job making it a bit more upscale, with themed events, seasonal packages and add-ons such as tours of the Lebanon Silver Mine. Plan on spending about half a day on the adventure. Book ahead.

Eating

Lucha MEXICAN $$

(www.luchacantina.com; 606 6th St; mains $9-13; 11am-midnight;) The most atmospheric spot in the old downtown area, Lucha's turn-of-the-century digs was once the legendary Red Ram, frequented by the likes of Clint Eastwood and other Hollywood gunslingers. Today it serves up fresh, homemade Mexican and American staples, from delicious fish tacos to jalapeño buffalo burgers.

Information

Georgetown Visitor Center (303-679-2312; www.georgetown-colorado.org; 1491 Argentine St; 8am-5pm summer, 9am-5pm winter)

Winter Park

POP 662 / ELEV 9000FT

Located less than two hours from Denver, unpretentious Winter Park Resort is a favorite with Front Rangers, who flock here from as far afield as Colorado Springs to ski fresh tracks each weekend. Beginners can frolic on miles of powdery groomers while experts test their skills on Mary Jane's world-class bumps. The congenial town is a wonderful base for year-round romping. Most services are found either in the ski village, which is actually south of Winter Park proper, or strung along US 40 (the main drag), which is where you'll find the visitor center. Follow Hwy 40 and you'll get to Fraser – essentially the same town – then Tabernash, and eventually the back of Rocky Mountain National Park.

Activities

Winter Park Resort SNOW SPORTS
(☎970-726-1564; www.winterparkresort.com; Hwy 40; lift ticket adult/child $104/62) Located about a mile before town, the Winter Park Resort covers five mountains and has a maximum vertical drop of more than 2600ft. Experts love it here because more than half of the runs are geared solely for highly skilled skiers. The most hair-raising rides are available off-piste at Vasquez Cirque, but there is plenty of spine-tingling action on Vasquez Ridge and Mary Jane, too.

Twenty-five lifts service more than 2500 skiable acres, which doesn't include the 1212 acres (490 hectares) of backcountry skiing. Good thing roughly one-third of the main Winter Park mountain is groomed for greenies. Winter Park also has six terrain parks geared for all levels. You can learn to ride rails and pipes at Starter and Bouncer, kick it up a notch at Ash Cat, or catch big air in the Rail Yard.

A new tubing hill ($22 per hour) is located near the Village Cabriolet lift.

Berthoud Pass HIKING, SNOW SPORTS
(www.berthoudpass.com; Hwy 40) The site of one of Colorado's first ski resorts (1937–2002), Berthoud Pass (11,307ft) remains a popular spot for backcountry skiers and snowshoers. There is significant avalanche danger here, however, so don't even think about going out unless you have the proper gear and training. **Friends of Berthoud Pass** (http://berthoudpass.org) offers free avalanche courses in winter.

The pass is also a great place to get on the Continental Divide Trail in summer. **Stanley Mountain** (12,521ft) is a 7-mile round-trip hike; from the parking lot, cross the highway to access the trail.

Rollins Pass SCENIC DRIVE
(USFS Rd 149; ⏲mid-Jun–mid-Nov) A popular though rugged 14-mile 4WD road leads almost to the top of this 11,660ft pass (now closed), which is famous for its railroad history. In the mid-1860s, JA Rollins established a toll wagon road over the pass from Nederland and Rollinsville, and early in the 20th century David H Moffat's Denver, Northwestern & Pacific Railway crossed the Continental Divide here.

First known as Boulder Pass, then Rollins Pass, it also earned the appellation 'Corona' because railroad workers considered it the crown at the 'top of the world.' Remnants of the original line (a tunnel and trestle) make it of particular interest to railroad buffs; it's also a popular ride for experienced **mountain bikers**.

There's plenty of hiking to do too. The traverse to **Rodgers Pass** (5 miles round trip) from the trestle is both mellow and beautiful. From here, you can easily summit the back of James Peak (p171).

The turnoff for Rollins Pass is located between the Winter Park resort and town; the road is extremely rocky and you definitely need 4WD-high clearance. When you reach an intersection on the way up, keep going straight. Bear in mind that the last couple of miles probably won't open until July at the earliest because of snowpack.

Colorado Adventure Park SNOW SPORTS
(http://coloradoadventurepark.com; 566 County Rd 721; per hr $18; ⏲10am-10pm mid-Dec–Mar) If you or the kids need a break from skiing, the town's two tubing hills (practically right next to each other) may be calling your name. This one has a fire pit for parents and runs divided by difficulty.

Trestle Bike Park MOUNTAIN BIKING
(www.trestlebikepark.com; day pass adult/child $39/29; ⏲mid-Jun–mid-Sep) When the snow melts, Winter Park turns into Trestle Bike Park, featuring three lifts and over 40 miles of freeride trails for all levels. You can rent bikes (from $80, including lift ticket and gear) and sign up for lessons.

Festivals & Events

Springtopia MUSIC
(www.winterparkresort.com; Hwy 40; ⏲mid-Apr) Held on the last weekend of the ski season, Springtopia is a final wave goodbye to the gods of snow. Après-ski concerts, pond-skimming races (where you combine skis and icy water) and discount lift tickets for all.

Winter Park Jazz Festival MUSIC
(☎888-409-5974; www.playwinterpark.com; Hideaway Park; ⏲mid-Jul) A two-day jazz festival held in Hideaway Park in downtown Winter Park, which has been known to attract the occasional big name.

King of the Rockies SPORTS
(www.epicsingletrack.com; Fraser River Trail; late Aug) The finale of the Epic Singletrack Race Series, this was the first and remains the best of a long summer of mountain-bike races.

Sleeping

There are two first-come first-served USFS campgrounds off Hwy 40 on the way into Winter Park: **Robber's Roost** (tent & RV sites $16), which has no water, 5 miles from town, and **Idlewild** (tent & RV sites $16), 1 mile from town.

★**Rocky Mountain Chalet** HOSTEL $
(970-726-8256; www.therockymountainchalet.com; 15 County Rd 72; dm $30, r summer/winter $89/149;) Proof that if you are affordable and reasonably cute, you will be popular among the budget traveling set. Add in the warm and welcoming staff, sparkling kitchen and international crowd and you have a winner in all categories. Both doubles and dorms are available. It's located in Fraser, just off Hwy 40.

TimberHouse Ski Lodge LODGE $
(866-726-3050; www.timberhouseskilodge.com; Winter Park Dr; dm $68-77, d $88-98; Dec-Apr;) A ski-in hostel? Yes, this groovy wooden mountain lodge is set at the base of the ski resort on the Billy Woods Trail. Sleep in a four- or six-person dorm, or grab a private room with shared or private bathroom. Rates include breakfast, dinner, tea and shuttles to the village. It's very hard to find, so get directions first.

Broome Hut HUT $
(970-925-5775; www.grandhuts.org; Hwy 40, Mile 240; per bed $35; year-round) The first project in a new hut-to-hut system that will eventually link up Berthoud Pass with Grand Lake further north, opening up new terrain for backcountry skiers. Like other backcountry huts, you'll need to reserve months in advance in winter. Broome Hut is located on the west side of Berthoud Pass.

Snow Mountain Ranch CABIN, CAMPGROUND $
(970-887-2152; www.ymcarockies.org; 1101 County Rd 53; cabins from $209, tent sites from $45, yurt $89;) This YMCA center is located 14 miles north of Winter Park off Hwy 40, and is a great spot to take the kids. A plethora of activities are available year-round, from horseback riding and challenge courses to over 60 miles of cross-country trails in the winter (rental equipment available).

Lodging is tailored to groups (six people to a yurt or dorm room, eight people to a campsite), so it's best to come with others; you can also visit as part of a day trip.

Gasthaus Eichler B&B $$
(970-726-5133; www.gasthauseichler.com; Hwy 40; r $89-149;) A notch above the various motel options in town, the rooms here are nothing fancy, but they come with a great breakfast, the requisite outdoor hot tub and two welcoming German hosts. It's located in the center of town; there's a free shuttle to the resort.

Vintage Resort & Conference Center HOTEL $$$
(800-472-7017; www.vintagehotel.com; 100 Winter Park Dr; r summer/winter from $129/259;) This somewhat dated hotel is actually in the main parking lot, but for skiers the location is better than it sounds. In the morning you can simply hop on the Village Cabriolet for direct access to the lifts. Rooms are fairly simple (think pine furnishings), but there is a pool and some rooms have kitchenettes and gas fireplaces. Minimum three-night stay in winter.

Eating & Drinking

Rise & Shine Bakery CAFE $
(970-726-5530; Park Place Plaza, 78437 Hwy 40; sandwiches $5.50-9; 7am-2pm;) Locals park their dogs out front of this funky cafe, then head in for delicious pastries, breakfast sandwiches, rich lattes and healthy bison burgers or veggie sandwiches on home-baked bread. Paintings by resident artists grace the cozy stonewashed interior. Wi-fi is temperamental.

Mirasol Cantina MEXICAN $
(78415 Hwy 40; 2 tacos $6.50-11; 4-9pm Wed-Mon;) Gourmet tacos with a Caribbean twist and Winter Park's only salsa bar ensure that you'll find something to savor here. Fillings range from buffalo and shrimp scampi to spicy tofu and beer-battered tilapia. Great happy-hour margaritas as well.

★**Tabernash Tavern** MODERN AMERICAN $$$
(970-726-4430; www.tabernashtavern.com; 72287 US Hwy 40; mains $20-34; 5-9pm Tue-Sat) Arguably the best restaurant in the Winter Park orbit. Set in Tabernash, just north of Fraser, this place is loved for its creativity and use of fresh local ingredients. The menu

WORTH A TRIP

DEVIL'S THUMB RANCH

The classiest digs in the Winter Park area, this high-altitude **ranch** (☎800-933-4339; www.devilsthumbranch.com; 3530 County Rd 83; bunkhouse $100-180, lodge $240-425, cabins from $365;) is a fantastic base for year-round adventure.

In the winter Nordic fiends descend for a scenic 65-mile network of groomed cross-country trails (adult/child $20/8), ice skating and snow-filled horseback rides. In the summer it's zip lines, hiking, biking and more horseback riding ($95 to $175) through 5000 acres of Colorado high country. Equipment rental is available on site.

Accommodations are plush, but not out of reach. The self-service bunkhouse has the cheapest rates, while the cowboy chic lodge is a must for a romantic weekend escape. Cabins are a good bet for groups. And even if you're not staying here, you won't want to miss happy hour at **Heck's** (☎970-726-7013; mains $12-26; 7:30am-9pm), where you can sink back in a leather armchair and enjoy $1 pints and half-price small plates (4pm to 6pm, Sunday to Thursday).

Note that the road in is unpaved; ensure conditions are suitable for your vehicle in the winter. Reserve well in advance.

includes inspired offerings as diverse as buffalo short rib ragu with black pepper gnocchi and Korean barbecued pork chops served with watermelon kimchi. Reservations recommended.

Fontenot's Seafood & Grill SEAFOOD $$$
(☎970-726-4021; www.fontenotswp.com; 78336 US Hwy 40; lunch $9-15, dinner $18-32; 11am-9pm;) This place has been bringing New Orleans' tasty brand of seafood love to Winter Park for over 20 years. It has everything from fried okra and steamed mussels to crawfish and crab cakes – and these are just the starters. Main courses include catfish and shrimp (fried, of course), crawfish étoufée and gumbo.

Information

Winter Park Visitor Center (☎800-903-7275; www.winterpark-info.com; 78841 Hwy 40; 9am-5pm) For maps, tips and last-minute room reservations. It's near the center of town.

Getting There & Around

Winter Park gets kudos for being one of the few ski resorts to offer free parking near the base of the mountain for day trippers. Get to the lifts via the Village Cabriolet lift or a free shuttle.

Amtrak (☎800-872-7245; www.amtrak.com; 205 Fraser Ave) Trains from Denver pass through the Moffat Tunnel and stop in Fraser ($44, two hours) at the unmanned depot on the corner of Fraser and Railroad Aves.

Greyhound (☎800-231-2222; www.greyhound.com; 78841 US Hwy 40) Buses from Denver ($24, two hours) stop at the visitor center on US 40 in Winter Park.

Home James Transportation Services (☎800-359-7536; www.ridehj.com; adult/child $65/32.50) Offers door-to-door shuttle service between Winter Park and Denver International Airport (two hours).

The Lift (7:30am-10pm) Winter Park's free shuttle carries skiers around town; it runs every 10 to 15 minutes in winter only.

Loveland Pass

ELEV 11,990FT

The alpine scenery in the Front Range is breathtaking enough, but it's not until you make it to Loveland Pass that you really begin to feel that Rocky Mountain magic. The gateway to Summit County, the pass is flanked by a ski resort on either side – Loveland and Arapahoe Basin (p181) – and offers easy access to above-treeline hiking in the summer months.

The opening of the Eisenhower Tunnel in 1973 made the pass more of a scenic detour than a necessity (except for hazmat trucks – don't tailgate!), but if you're not in a rush, the hairpin turns bring inspiring views. It remains open year-round, though it can be treacherous in winter and will close in bad weather. It's located on Hwy 6, which leaves I-70 at exit 216 on the east side and exit 205 (Silverthorne) on the west side.

Activities

★**Loveland Ski Area** SNOW SPORTS
(http://skiloveland.com; Hwy 6; adult/child $61/27; 9am-4pm Nov–mid-Apr) One of Colorado's older ski resorts (1943), Loveland may be smaller than its neighbors, but its old-school

vibe, wide-open runs, cheap lift tickets and proximity to Denver (56 miles) have guaranteed enduring popularity. With a base elevation of 10,800ft, much of the terrain is above the treeline, meaning gorgeous views when the sun shines but bitterly cold winds in bad weather. Access is via I-70 (exit 216).

Mt Sniktau & Grizzly Peak HIKING
(Hwy 6; Jun-Oct) Accessible from the Loveland Pass parking lot, the short 2-mile jaunt to Mt Sniktau (13,234ft) is a relatively easy hike and a good way to experience the thrill of hiking above treeline without having to work (too much) for it. It can get pretty windy up here, so come prepared.

If you barely broke a sweat on the way up, extend your day by following the ridge back south to Grizzly Peak (13,427ft), which ends with an exhilarating 45-degree scramble. From here the ridgeline continues to the 14ers Torreys and Grays, just beyond. All told, the Loveland-Sniktau-Grizzly traverse is 7.5 miles round-trip.

BRECKENRIDGE & SUMMIT COUNTY

Home to four big-time ski resorts, the Blue River, and historic Breckenridge, the aptly named Summit County is close enough to Denver for a day trip but far enough away to feel like you've truly escaped the Front Range sprawl. In summer, cyclists enjoy the endless miles of paved bikepaths that connect the major towns, while boaters take to the enormous Dillon Reservoir.

Dillon

POP 904 / ELEV 9111FT

The twin box-store towns of Dillon and Silverthorne are the first exit after passing through the Eisenhower Tunnel. While Dillon can't compete with the historic appeal of Frisco or Breckenridge, the marina and enormous Dillon Reservoir are certainly picturesque and a big draw for boaters in summer. One of Summit County's fabulous paved bikepaths passes the dam and wraps around the north side of the reservoir on the way to Frisco, while the Outlets at Silverthorne draw in shoppers eager to find a deal on dozens of brand names.

Activities

Dillon Marina WATER SPORTS
(970-468-5100; www.dillonmarina.com; 150 Marina Dr; 2/4hr boat rental from $105/170; 8:30am-6pm late May-Sep) Dillon's main draw in summer is the terrific marina, where you can rent motorboats and sailboats. If taking a sailboat, you should plan on shoving off after 11am when the breeze generally picks up. Pontoons and runabout powerboats are best in the morning before the cold winds blow. The marina's **Tiki Bar** has a fab deck looking out over the reservoir.

Cutthroat Anglers FISHING
(970-262-2878; http://fishcolorado.com; 400 Blue River Pkwy, Silverthorne; half-day trips from $215; 7am-7pm) River reports, gear, a variety of guided trips, fly-fishing lessons and free casting clinics.

Sleeping

Dillon offers more affordable lodging than the resort towns in winter, though don't expect anything flashy.

Prospector Campground CAMPGROUND $
(877-444-6777; www.recreation.gov; Swan Mountain Rd; tent & RV sites $18-20; late May–mid-Sep;) Dillon's main USFS campground (107 sites) is located on the south side of Dillon Reservoir, away from the traffic. It has a boat ramp and tent and RV sites, though at last check neither drinking water nor electrical hookups were available. You cannot swim in the reservoir.

Dillon Inn MOTEL $
(970-262-0801; www.dilloninn.com; 708 E Anemone Trail; r summer/winter from $70/100;) Were it not for its tremendous orientation toward those massive Buffalo and Red Mountains to the west, this stuccoed and boxy inn might not be worth considering. But it does have nice touches such as old wagons on the lawn and plenty of flowers, as well as an indoor pool and deck. Rooms are simple, clean and decent value.

Ptarmigan Lodge MOTEL $$
(800-842-5939; www.ptarmiganlodge.com; 652 Lake Dillon Dr; r summer/winter from $110/135;) The only place to stay in Dillon that looks out over the lake, rooms at the Ptarmigan Lodge all have unbroken views from their doorway. Otherwise it's a fairly plain motel disguised meekly as a lodge. Look for the Best Western sign.

Eating & Drinking

Arapahoe Cafe & Pub CAFE $$
(☎970-468-0873; www.arapahoecafe.com; 626 Lake Dillon Dr; lunch $8.95-11.95, dinner $17.50-19.75; ⏲7am-2pm & 4-11pm;) The Arapahoe Cafe began life in the 1940s as a roadside cafe and motel, and it's still the grooviest place to eat pretty much any meal in Dillon. The breakfasts are filling and original with offerings such as pork tamales and eggs, best enjoyed on the lakeview patio (weather permitting). The funky basement pub is a fun diversion after sundown.

★ **Dillon Dam Brewery** BREWERY
(www.dambrewery.com; 100 Little Dam Rd; ⏲11:30am-11:30pm;) This brewpub is one of Summit County's best and is certainly the most popular bar in town. The menu augments typical pub fare with dishes like ruby red trout finished with lemon butter sauce, and ginger glazed and seared 'sashimi grade' ahi. It does weekly live music, and, of course, there are nine kinds of suds on tap, from wheat to a black IPA.

The place is especially busy on game days, when the circle bar, in view of the vats and several flatscreens, is packed and patrolled by attentive staff.

Entertainment

Skyline Cinema CINEMA
(☎970-468-6315; http://skyline8.com; 312 Dillon Ridge Rd; adult/child $10.25/7; ⏲2-9:30pm; ; Summit Stage) The only movie theater in the area attracts moviegoers from Breck, Frisco and Keystone.

Shopping

Outlets at Silverthorne CLOTHING
(www.outletsatsilverthorne.com; ⏲10am-8pm Mon-Sat, 10am-6pm Sun) Located just off I-70 at exit 205 are three shopping villages of designer brand stores with discount prices. Brands include Calvin Klein, Nike, Levi's, Gap and dozens of others. Not only is there a shuttle that runs between the villages (free), there are also shuttles here from Vail (round-trip $20), Copper Mountain and Breckenridge (round-trip $10).

The Blue River actually runs right next to the outlets, so if your group is of a divided mind when it comes to shopping, note that fly-fishing is always a possibility.

Information

USFS Ranger Office (☎970-468-5400; www.fs.usda.gov; 680 Hwy 9, Silverthorne; ⏲8am-4:30pm Mon-Fri) Information on camping and hiking in Summit County. The office is located north of I-70 in Silverthorne.

Getting There & Around

Dillon is 70 miles west of Denver via I-70 to exit 205, then 1 mile south on US 6.

Lake Dillon Water Taxi (☎970-486-0250; www.dillontaxi.com; 150 Marina Dr; adult/child 1-way $10/8, bike surcharge $1; ⏲11am-5pm Mon-Fri, 10am-6pm Sat & Sun) The Dillon Reservoir ferry service runs between the marinas in Frisco and Dillon. Dogs and bikes welcome.

Summit Stage (☎970-668-0999; www.summitstage.com) Summit County's free bus system connects Dillon with Keystone.

Frisco

POP 2683 / ELEV 9097FT

It's almost startling to find such a cute turn-of-the-20th-century mining town, set high in the Rockies, ringed by peaks wooded and bald, and with another vast sculpted range flexing all the way to Breckenridge. It startles not because it's strange to find such a soothing, tempting setting in the central Rockies, but rather because Frisco stands alone, flaunting her 19th-century history, rather than kneeling at the foot of some recently developed ski resort. Yet it's still within 30 minutes of Vail and 10 to 20 minutes of Loveland, Arapahoe Basin, Copper Mountain, Keystone and Breckenridge, and the distance means that lodging and rental gear is cheaper here.

Historic Main St is a six-block stretch where you'll find almost everything you could need. There are cute inns and tasty dining, and it dead-ends at the scenic Dillon Reservoir where you'll find a small marina. Romantic and welcoming, with ample free parking year round, there are a lot of reasons to fall for Frisco.

Sights & Activities

Frisco Historic Park & Museum MUSEUM
(www.townoffrisco.com; cnr 2nd Ave & Main St; ⏲10am-4pm Tue-Sat, 10am-2pm Sun;) FREE Set on the site of the original town saloon in 1889, and later converted into the town's second school in 1901, this museum features a number of historical displays, including one on the Ute nation, a diorama of the original

AVALANCHE

For serious skiers and snowboarders, the lure of fresh powder and untracked backcountry terrain is a powerful temptation, a chance to experience that heady rush of feel-good dopamine that momentarily overrides the rest of the brain's circuitry. Unfortunately, the risks associated with backcountry skiing are hardly inconsequential – if you get caught in an avalanche, the odds are good that you won't survive.

While it's convenient to believe that most avalanche victims are naive and unprepared, Colorado's unstable snowpack does not discriminate: in the April 2013 avalanche at Loveland Pass, the state's deadliest in 50 years, not only were all the victims experienced, one was even a certified avalanche instructor.

Nevertheless, even if experience is no guarantee of safety, if you're going out of bounds, you need to know how to minimize risk: get trained, carry the necessary equipment and check the daily avalanche forecasts from the **Colorado Avalanche Information Center** (https://avalanche.state.co.us/index.php).

Ten Mile Canyon railroad that fed and connected the mining camps of Leadville and Frisco, and a historic map of Colorado (c 1873).

The main attractions, however, are the half-dozen old mining cabins scattered out back. Aficionados of log-construction techniques will appreciate the double-dovetail joints at the Dills Ranch House (c 1890) and the Bailey House (c 1895). Inside the Trappers Cabin, visitors will find the kind of pelts that once sustained the area's meager economy prior to mining. Other prize specimens include the Frisco Jail and the town chapel, which now screens a 15-minute documentary video.

★Summit County Bike Path CYCLING

(www.summitbiking.org) Frisco is the hub for Summit County's fabulous paved bike paths. From the Frisco Marina you can wrap most of the way around the reservoir to Dillon (7.5 miles; great family trip) and on to Keystone (13.5 miles, 1200ft elevation gain) or pedal around the other side and up to Breckenridge (9.5 miles, 500ft elevation gain); the Dillon trail has minimal elevation gain.

Alternatively, you can head off in the other direction to climb Vail Pass (12 miles, 1550ft elevation gain) and roll all the way down to Vail. Many bike shops run shuttles up to the top of the pass if you're only interested in the downhill ride. Grab a copy of the free *Summit County Bike Guide* in rental shops or the visitor center.

Note that you can take bikes on the Summit Stage (p180) if you run out of steam or only want to go one-way.

Team Managers SPORTS RENTALS

(☎970-668-3321; www.team-managers.com; 1121 Dillon Dam Rd; bicycle rental 4hr/full day $17/27, ski rental from $10; ⏲8:30am-6pm) The Frisco bike specialists, they also rent skis at very competitive rates in winter. It's near the intersection of Hwy 9 and I-70, across from Holiday Inn.

Frisco Marina WATER SPORTS

(☎970-668-4334; www.townoffrisco.com; 902 E Main St; 2hr rental canoe/motorboat/sailboat from $35/60/95; ⏲8:30am-6pm late May-Sep) The small marina at Frisco Bay, a small finger wandering off Dillon Reservoir, bobs with dozens of sailboats and motorboats available to rent in two- and four-hour intervals. Kayaks, canoes and stand-up paddleboards are also available, with numerous channel islands looming at the edge of the bay providing much needed shelter for paddlers when winds kick up 2ft swells.

It's best to paddle before noon.

Peak One HIKING

(Mount Royal Trailhead; ⏲Jun-Oct) A trail runs straight out of town, taking you right up to the beginning of the Tenmile Range. You can make this as short or long as you like, but either way get ready to sweat. It's 1.5 miles up to the ridge, where the trail forks: head right (north) to Mt Royal (10,052ft) for the easy summit.

Otherwise, opt for the tougher workout and turn left (south) to continue up the ridge to Peak One (12,805ft), which is 3.7 miles from the trailhead. Tenmile Peak (12,933ft) is another 0.6 miles from here, but be prepared for some continuous class 3 scrambling along the ridge.

Blue River Anglers FISHING
(☎970-668-2583; www.blueriveranglers.com; 281 Main St; half-day trip from $225, rods/waders rental per day $25/20; ⏰10am-6pm) Set on Main St is Frisco's best fly-fishing guide and rental outfitter, open year round, even when the rivers are ice. It takes anglers to the Blue River for three-hour lessons, five-hour half-day trips and full-day and overnight float trips. It also has evening casting clinics.

Kodi Rafting RAFTING
(☎877-747-7238; www.whitewatercolorado.com; 503 Main St; half-day trips from $60/93; ⏰late May-Sep) Summit County doesn't have Colorado's best white water, but local outfitters can take you there (the Arkansas River outside Buena Vista is the most popular destination). Alternatively, trips on the local Blue River and Clear Creek run in June and July only. Children must be seven or older.

Frisco Nordic Center & Adventure Park SNOW SPORTS
(☎970-668-0866; www.frisconordic.com; 616 Recreation Way; adult/child $20/15; ⏰9am-4pm Dec-Mar) The Frisco Nordic Center offers about 25 miles of cross-country ski trails on the Dillon Reservoir peninsula east of Frisco. Lessons and rentals are available, as are snowshoes. A **tubing hill** (10am-6pm; ⏰per hr $25) is also located here and offers a good diversion for kids. The main parking lot is off Hwy 9 about 1 mile east of Frisco.

Sleeping

Peak One Campground CAMPGROUND $
(☎877-444-6777; www.recreation.gov; Peninsula Recreation Area; tent & RV sites $19; ⏰late May–mid-Sep; 🐾) Frisco's main campground (80 sites) is located on the southwest shore of the reservoir. Both tent and RV sites are available, though there are no electric hookups. If you can't get a spot here, the nearby Pine Cove campground is first-come, first-served.

★**Frisco Lodge** B&B $$
(☎800-279-6000; www.friscolodge.com; 321 Main St; r without bath summer/winter $124/154, with bath summer/winter $164/204; P ❄ 📶 👪) Right on the main drag is Frisco's oldest hotel, which has been receiving guests since it first opened in 1885 as a stagecoach stop. The main lodge is the original log cabin (some rooms with shared bathrooms); there's also a 1960s-era annex. All rooms are lovingly detailed with antiques and Victorian-inspired flourishes, and include full breakfast and afternoon wine and cheese.

Rates drop significantly on weekdays.

Hotel Frisco INN $$
(☎970-668-5009; www.hotelfrisco.com; 308 Main St; r summer/winter $129/199; P ❄ 📶 🐾) Comfortable and modern, the up-to-date rooms here all have two-toned paint jobs, moldings and wall-mounted flatscreen TVs. King rooms are largest and brightest, and some have direct access to the hot tub on the back porch. If you reserve well in advance, you may be able to secure cheaper winter rates.

Eating & Drinking

Butterhorn Bakery & Cafe CAFE $
(☎970-668-3997; www.butterhornbakery.com; 408 Main St; mains $6.95-10; ⏰7:30am-2:30pm; 🌱 👪) This fun, bright and funky pastel-brushed diner is always packed for breakfast and lunch. In addition to house-baked breads, bagels and croissants, it does great breakfasts, salads and a variety of sandwiches, from BLTs to muffalettas to turkey Reubens, plus a couple of vegan options.

Log Cabin AMERICAN $
(☎970-668-3947; www.logcabincafe.co; 121 Main St; mains $6-10; ⏰7am-3pm; 👪) Every town has one – the unequivocal champion of all things breakfast. In Frisco, it's Log Cabin. Come for sassy, no-nonsense servers, bomb French toast, gold-medal-worthy huevos rancheros, and pan-fried Cajun trout and eggs.

★**Lost Cajun** CAJUN $$
(www.thelostcajun.com; 204 Main St; mains $10-17; ⏰11am-9pm; 📶 👪) Convivial waitstaff and a festive Louisiana soundtrack greet hungry diners here. First-timers are rewarded with five samples to help them decide (or prolong indecision) – tasty offerings from the open kitchen include jambalaya, chicken and sausage gumbo and some seriously good lobster bisque. Abita beer seals the deal.

Himalayan Cuisine INDIAN $$
(☎970-668-3330; 409 Main St; lunch buffet $7.95, dinner $12.95-15.95; ⏰11am-2:30pm & 5-9:30pm Mon-Sat, 5-9:30pm Sun) No, the name doesn't leave a lot to the imagination, but so what? Here's a little ray of Himalayan sunshine in the Rockies and a welcome change from typical mountain fare.

Bagali's ITALIAN $$
(☎970-668-0601; www.bagalisfrisco.com; 320 Main St; mains $10-20; ⏰11:30am-9pm Wed-Mon; 👪) This cute bistro is one of Frisco's most popular options, serving tasty artisan pizzas and specialties such as shrimp polenta and pasta carbonara with duck prosciutto. It also serves panini and smaller pasta dishes for lunch.

Island Grill BAR
(☎970-668-9999; www.islandgrillfrisco.com; 900 E Main St; dishes $7-9; ⏰11:30am-7pm late May–mid-Sep) Overlooking Frisco Bay, this all-outdoor marina bar has a fantastic rooftop deck and downstairs patio bar. Owners keep it simple here, offering decent grub (salads, fish tacos), but it stakes its reputation on blended island cocktails, New Belgium IPA on tap and reggae on the stereo. It has live music on Friday nights.

Shopping

★**Next Page Bookstore & Tea Bar** BOOKS
(www.nextpagebooks.com; 409 Main St; ⏰10am-6pm; 📶) A terrific bookstore that merges local naturalist literature, hiking guides, maps and children's books with modern, offbeat and classic fiction. Skinny but deep, with an excellent **tea bar** (teas $3.70) to keep you lingering.

Information

Information Center (☎800-424-1554; www.townoffrrisco.com; 300 Main St; ⏰9am-5pm; 📶) Frisco's visitor center is set in the town's original town hall, built around 1890 with volunteer labor. In addition to general info, it offers free wi-fi and internet access on in-house computers.

Getting There & Around

From Denver, take I-70 west 72 miles to exit 203. Follow Hwy 9 south for a little more than a mile, then turn right onto Main St.

Colorado Mountain Express (☎800-525-6363; www.coloradomountainexpress.com; adult/child $70/36; 📶) Shuttle service to/from Denver International Airport (two hours).

Greyhound (☎800-231-2222; www.greyhound.com; 1010 Meadow Dr) Buses traveling I-70 on the way to and from Denver ($21, 1¾ hours) stop on the outskirts of Frisco; you'll need to catch a Summit Stage into town.

Lake Dillon Water Taxi (☎970-486-0250; www.dillontaxi.com; Main St & Summit Blvd; adult/child 1-way $10/8, bike surcharge $1; ⏰11am-5pm Mon-Fri, 10am-6pm Sat & Sun) Dillon Reservoir's ferry service runs between the marinas in Frisco and Dillon. Dogs and bikes welcome.

Summit Express (☎855-686-8267; www.summitexpress.com; adult/child $64/32) Shuttle service to/from Denver International Airport (two hours).

Summit Stage (☎970-668-0999; www.summitstage.com) Summit County's free bus system connects Frisco with Breckenridge and Copper Mountain.

Keystone Resort

POP 1079 / ELEV 9280FT

In operation since 1970, Keystone is a family oriented resort on the Snake River, 5 miles east of Dillon on US Hwy 6. Keystone is definitely a resort, in that almost all accommodations, restaurants and services are owned and operated by a single company (that would be the eerily ubiquitous Vail Resorts). As a result, while the base area lacks the character and variety of nearby Breckenridge, Keystone has been well planned and it is easy to book reservations and get information. The main base area is known as River Run Village; a second base area is Mountain House, which serves true beginners and is less crowded. Although you can access some 100 miles of bike trails from Keystone, it's essentially a ghost town in summer.

Activities

The big draw is the **ski area** (www.keystoneresort.com; Hwy 6; adult/child $110/64; ⏰8:30am-4pm Nov–mid-Apr, to 8pm most days Dec-Mar), which encompasses three mountains and offers the most terrain in all of Summit County. Although it pegs itself as a family resort – and indeed, if you book two nights or more of resort lodging, kids 12 and under ski free – there's a lot of variety here. Beginners will love long cruisers like Schoolmarm (3.5 miles) and the slightly more challenging Spring Dipper, while experts can burn their quads on over 70 black diamond runs. The A51 Terrain Park is decked out with an array of jumps, jibs, rails and a Superpipe, while **snowcats** (☎970-496-4386; rides from the Outback $5; all-day tours $240) take the daring above the lifts to a string of powder-filled bowls at the summit. It's also the only big Colorado resort to offer **night skiing**, which often attracts folks from Breck. Keystone lift passes are good at Breck and A-Basin, and if you buy a pass of three days or longer, you also get access to Vail.

The resort also operates a small **Nordic Center** (☎970-496-4275; www.keystoneresort.com; 155 River Course Dr; adult/child $11/free; ⊙9am-4:40pm Dec–mid-Apr) at the western end (near Dillon), with 9 miles of groomed trails and a tubing hill for kids.

Sleeping

Keystone has six main village areas, all of which offer a variety of condo-style lodging booked through the resort. A free shuttle system serves all villages in winter. The **Keystone Lodge & Spa** (☎970-496-4242; www.keystoneresort.com; 22101 Hwy 6; r from $320, fees included; P 🛜 🏊), at Lakeside Village, offers hotel-style accommodations with comfortable rooms. The **Inn at Keystone** (☎800-328-1323; www.keystoneresort.com; 21996 Hwy 6; r from $265, fees included; P 🛜) is slightly cheaper and located at Mountain House, meaning you can walk to the lifts, though it is also less plush.

Eating & Drinking

There are more than 30 restaurants sprinkled throughout the resort, though the offerings are all fairly tame. **Kickapoo Tavern** (www.kickapootavern.com; River Run; mains $10-17; ⊙11am-10pm; 👪) is your basic, friendly Colorado eatery with veggie, buffalo and beef burgers, brisket sandwiches, rib baskets, wraps and burritos. **Inxpot** (www.inxpot.com; River Run; mains $9-11; ⊙7am-5pm; 👪), a groovy, hippie-run, rock-and-roll coffeehouse, does righteous breakfast sandwiches, jet-fueled coffee, soups and sandwiches for lunch, and it has a book nook too.

Getting There & Away

Keystone is located 75 miles west of Denver. Take exit 205 (Silverthorne) off I-70 and follow Hwy 6 east – don't go over Loveland Pass unless you plan on taking the scenic route. There are several free parking lots.

Colorado Mountain Express (☎800-525-6363; www.coloradomountainexpress.com; adult/child $70/36; 🛜) Shuttle service (two hours) to/from Denver International Airport.

Summit Express (☎855-686-8267; www.summitexpress.com; adult/child $64/32) Shuttle service to/from Denver International Airport (two hours).

Summit Stage (☎970-668-0999; www.summitstage.com) Summit County's free bus service links Keystone with Breckenridge and Arapahoe Basin in winter (Swan Mountain Flyer) and with Dillon and Silverthorne year-round.

Arapahoe Basin Ski Area

ELEV 10,780FT

Simple and rugged, this downbeat, old-school ski resort has a 'don't bother me with sissy ski fashions, just get me onto the mountain' character. Offering up some of North America's highest in-bounds ski terrain, this is the local pick to ride, especially when temps warm up enough for large tailgate cookouts and parties in the parking lot. It's the last resort standing in spring, often staying open into mid-June.

Activities

Filled with steeps, chutes and walls, **A-Basin** (☎970-468-0718; www.arapahoebasin.com; Hwy 6; lift adult/child 6-14yr $79/40; ⊙9am-4pm Mon-Fri, from 8:30am Sat & Sun) isn't beginner friendly but can't be beat for thrilling descents. The back bowl, known as Montezuma, is where you'll find two dozen or so hair-raising (but still in bounds) intermediate-to-expert runs. The **Jump** is the biggest, baddest run on Montezuma, beginning with a 10ft drop off the mountain's ledge onto a steep 35-degree slope. The **East Wall** (summit 13,050ft), which includes the hike-to Shit for Brains run, is A-Basin's other legendary backcountry-style area.

The parking lot at the foot of the mountain, aka the **Beach**, is a major tailgate spot where people come as early as 6am to stake out their space. Common sights include men in prom dresses, pole dancing, barbecues heavy with burgers, sausages and ribs, and portable hot tubs. It's a free-for-all and it's almost all first-come, first-served, except for the first five spots closest to the lift. Those are available by reservation.

There is no accommodation at A-Basin, though there are several dining options on site.

Getting There & Around

A-Basin is located 80 miles west of Denver. Take exit 205 (Silverthorne) off I-70, and follow Hwy 6 east past Keystone. Going via Loveland Pass is shorter in terms of distance, though the drive itself is longer and the pass can close in bad weather.

Summit County's free bus service links A-Basin with Breckenridge and Keystone in winter, on the Swan Mountain Flyer route.

Breckenridge

POP 4537 / ELEV 9600FT

Set at the foot of the marvelous Tenmile Range, Breck is a sweetly surviving mining town with a vibrant historic district. The down-to-earth vibe is a refreshing change from Colorado's glitzier resorts, and the family friendly ski runs and gold-nugget history make it Summit County's most atmospheric destination. Regardless of whether it's snow or shine, the BreckConnect Gondola up to the base of Peak 8 is where the fun begins.

The vast, hulking mountains here (numbered, not named) rise and fall, merging seamlessly into one another to present a perfect alpine backdrop. Smooth and sculpted, they lack the majesty of Aspen's granite knife edge – until you get to the top of Peak 8 and find enormous uplifts on all sides.

Laced with ski runs and stitched together with pine groves, they blaze gold in the morning, pink at dusk and fade into a deep shadowy blue as the sky pales then darkens, revealing endless stars best viewed from a frothing hot tub next to the roaring Blue River.

History

Like other Central Rockies towns, Breckenridge was blessed twice with sought-after natural resources. The first time, the masses came searching for gold buried in the peaks surrounding town. The second time it was for the snow-capped mountains themselves.

It all started with the discovery of gold along the South Platte River and in nearby Idaho Springs in 1859. Later that same summer, gold was discovered along the Blue River, which bisects present-day Breck. Now, where there's miners there will be whiskey, and the first bar, the Gold Pan Saloon, opened on Main St in 1859. It still stands and is the longest-tenured business in town. For the next several decades the town grew, acquired the first post office between the Continental Divide and Salt Lake City, saw the Southern Pacific Railroad arrive in town and nurtured its share of historic characters – folks like Edwin Carter and Barney Ford, an escaped slave turned pioneer, turned entrepreneur, turned politician.

In 1945, the Country Boy Mine, the last of its breed, closed down; without jobs or industry the population of Breckenridge crashed to just over 300 people in 1960. Then in July 1961 a permit was granted to build and open a ski resort in the mountains behind Breckenridge. The first lift opened on December 16, 1961, and more than 17,000 skiers visited Peak 8 that first season. Peak 9 opened in 1971 and 10 years later the world's first high-speed quad lift opened on Peak 9.

The resort innovated further in 1984 when it became the first ski resort open to snowboarders. (It even hosted the first Snowboarding World Cup on Peak 10 in 1985.) In 1997 Breckenridge and Keystone merged with Vail and Beaver Creek to form the present-day conglomerate, Vail Resorts.

Sights

Breckenridge's intriguing boomtown history, well preserved by the unsung heroes at the **Breckenridge Heritage Alliance** (http://breckheritage.com), means there's a lot to see here. Start with the displays in the visitor center (p192), partly set in a 19th-century log cabin.

★**Barney Ford Museum** MUSEUM
(http://breckheritage.com; 111 E Washington Ave; suggested donation $5; ⏲11am-3pm Tue-Sun winter, to 4pm Tue-Sun summer) FREE Barney Ford was an escaped slave who became a prominent entrepreneur and Colorado civil-rights pioneer, and made two stops in Breckenridge (where he ran a 24-hour chopstand serving delicacies such as oysters) over the course of his incredibly rich, tragic and triumphant life. He also owned a restaurant and hotel in Denver. The museum is set in his old home, where he lived between 1882 and 1890.

Edwin Carter Discovery Center MUSEUM
(http://breckheritage.com; 111 N Ridge St; suggested donation $5; ⏲11am-3pm Tue-Sat winter, to 4pm Tue-Sun summer; 👪) FREE This award-winning museum sheds light on a pioneer lured west by the Pike's Peak Gold Rush in 1858. He reached the Blue River valley in 1860. An original environmentalist, he noticed the impact of mining on wildlife early on, documenting genetic deformities (such as two-headed animals) that he suspected were linked to leaching toxins.

He eventually became a taxidermist to preserve the wildlife he encountered in the area, and his collection grew to some 3300 pieces, which were displayed in his house (now the museum). After he died, the ma-

DISCOUNT LIFT TICKETS & SKI PASSES

Sticker shock is a big part of the Colorado ski experience, and it's not just limited to Vail and Aspen. The initial slack-jawed disbelief soon changes to stubborn denial, and that's where those discount tickets come in – surely you don't have to pay $130 for a day out on the slopes, right? Well, it all depends on how much advance planning you've done.

Most resorts offer partially discounted tickets online for advance purchases through their websites. In fact, this is the only way to get discounted tickets for Vail, Aspen and Breck, where purchases must be made a minimum seven days in advance. In addition to resort websites, online vendors www.liftopia.com and www.ski.com are also worth checking out for various deals. Big resorts also offer accommodation packages that, for example, throw in a free day of skiing if you book three nights or more – but you may need to reserve before September.

If you really want to save, however, you're better off at the local hills. Winter Park, Copper Mountain, A-Basin and the like all offer coupons and special deals throughout the season, which you might find lying around at the entrance to the local brewery or, for example, a Denver Smashburger outlet. You can also get discounted tickets at grocery stores (eg King Soopers), though the savings are minimal and the choice of mountains is limited. This is more of a last-minute strategy.

The biggest savings are known as **four packs**, which are four lift tickets sold together as a block (they're non-transferable, so you can't split them with a friend or significant other). These are available throughout the year, but if you buy them before the season starts you can score some serious savings – we're talking 65% off lift tickets to both Winter Park and Copper and 33% off tickets to the five Vail resorts. You don't have to use them all at once, but watch out for blackout dates.

Of course, if you're going to be spending more than four days skiing, the obvious way to go is to get a **season pass**. The best of these cover several mountains, so you don't have to limit yourself to just one resort. The prices here are for pre-season purchases. Children, teens and seniors get reduced prices.

Epic Pass This is the Vail season pass and it covers a lot of terrain: Vail, Beaver Creek, Breck, Keystone, A-Basin and Eldora in Colorado, plus Canyons (Utah), three Lake Tahoe resorts (California) and five free days in both Switzerland and Austria. With all that skiing, who has time to work? Cost: $689

Epic Local You don't really need those 10 free days in Europe, do you? This one gives you 10 days at Vail and Beaver Creek, and unlimited access to other Epic Colorado resorts and Canyons and Lake Tahoe (blackout dates apply). Cost: $529

Summit Value Unlimited access to Breck (blackout dates apply), Keystone and A-Basin. No preferred customer shortcut through I-70 traffic jams though. Cost: $439

Mountain Collective Perfect for jetsetter types out west. You get 12 free days total: two each at Aspen, Jackson Hole, Whistler, AltaSnowbird, Squaw Valley/Alpine Meadows and Mammoth. Additional days are 50% off; lodging is 25% off. Cost: $379

Rocky Mountain Superpass+ Unlimited access to Winter Park and Copper Mountain, plus free days at Steamboat and Monarch too. Students apply here! Cost: adult/student $489/369

Rocky Mountain Superpass Unlimited access to Winter Park and Copper Mountain. Cost: $419

Keystone/A-Basin The pennypincher's pick. Only two mountains, but at this price, who's complaining? Cost: $279

jority of his collection became the original foundation of the Denver Museum of Nature and Science. A choice selection of animals remains on display along with several interactive kid-friendly exhibits.

Boreas Pass PASS

(Boreas Pass Rd; ⏲ Jun-Oct) Originally known as Breckenridge Pass (11,481ft), this road first began serving stagecoaches in 1866 when prospectors flooded into the area

Breckenridge

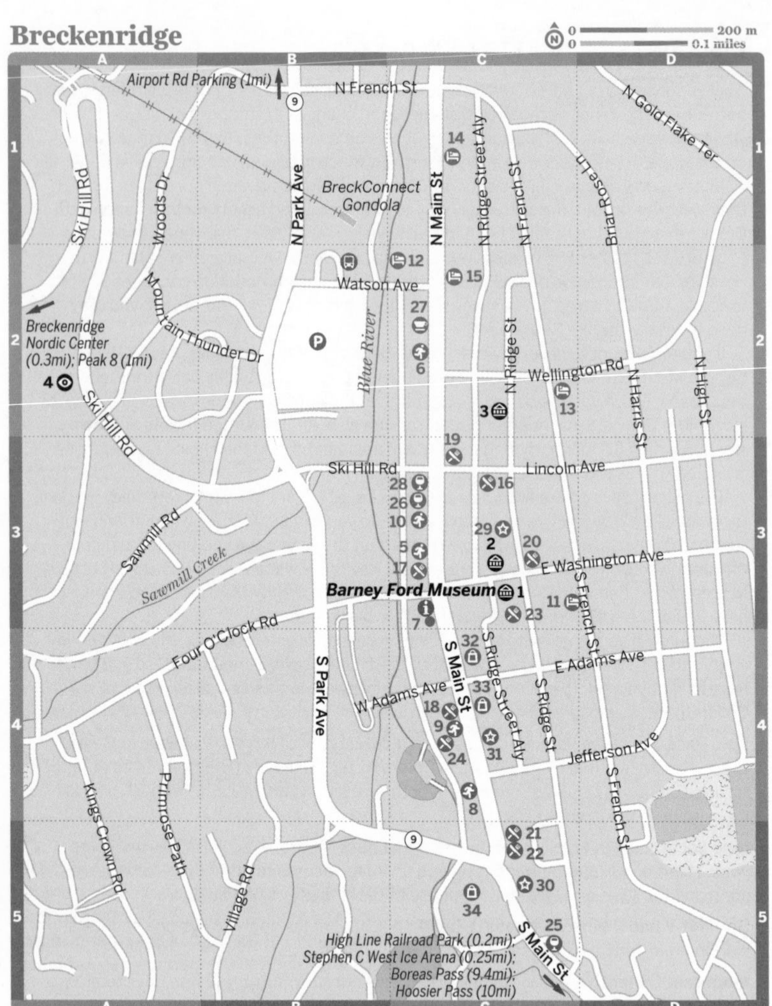

from South Park looking for gold. In 1882, a narrow-gauge railway replaced the wagon road and remained in operation until 1937. Although the upper section across the Continental Divide is unpaved, you can easily drive up in summer and in fall for spectacular views.

A parking lot halfway up the road on the Breckenridge side serves as the winter road-closure point and a trailhead for hikers in summer and snowshoers and cross-country skiers in winter. To get here, follow Main St (Hwy 9) south and turn left onto Boreas Pass Rd just outside town.

Lomax Placer Mine MINE

(970-453-9767; http://breckheritage.com; 301 Ski Hill Rd; adult/child $10/5; 11am-3pm Mon, Wed, Fri & Sat mid-Jun–Aug;) Here's a chance to pan for gold, learn how old-mining-town chemists assayed the valuable claims and check out the actual sluices and flumes used in placer (surface) mines. This site was active in the 1860s and also gives visitors the chance to sniff around a miner's cabin, complete with wood-burning stove, musical instruments, snowshoes, pack saddles and other sundry items needed for survival.

Breckenridge

Top Sights
1 Barney Ford Museum C3

Sights
2 Breckenridge Arts District C3
3 Edwin Carter Discovery Center C2
4 Lomax Placer Mine A2

Activities, Courses & Tours
5 Breck Sports C3
6 Carvers C2
7 Historic Walking Tours C3
8 Main Street Sports C4
9 Mountain Angler C4
10 Tibetan Ocean Massage C3

Sleeping
11 Abbet Placer Inn C3
12 Barn on the River C2
13 Fireside Inn C2
14 Great Western Lodging C1
15 Woodwinds Lodging C2

Eating
16 Briar Rose C3
17 Clint's Bakery & Coffee House C3
18 Crepes à la Cart C4
19 Giampetro C3
20 Hearthstone C3
21 Lucha Cantina C5
22 Park & Main C5
23 South Ridge Seafood C3
24 Wasabi C4

Drinking & Nightlife
25 Breckenridge Brewery C5
26 Downstairs at Eric's C3
27 Kava Cafe C2
28 Motherloaded Tavern C3

Entertainment
29 Backstage Theater C3
30 Cecilia's C5
31 Three20South C4

Shopping
32 Flourish C4
33 Magical Scraps C4
34 Slopeside Cowboy C5
Underground (see 33)

High Line Railroad Park HISTORIC SITE
(http://breckheritage.com; 189 Boreas Pass Rd; suggested donation $5; 11am-4pm Tue-Sun mid-Jun–Aug; P) FREE This isn't much of a park, but it is notable for its display of a vintage narrow-gauge rotary plow and the locomotives that powered it up the famed, rugged, gut-wrenching Boreas Pass railroad to keep gold-mining production open. This rail was a lifeline to miners, go-it-alone and corporate alike. Engine No 9 is on display year-round. It's also known as Rotary Snowplow Park.

Breckenridge Arts District GALLERY, STUDIO
(www.breckarts.com; S Ridge St & E Washington Ave; hours vary) This block-long stretch of historic Breckenridge is where you'll find a burgeoning arts scene. It has a live-work art space for visiting artists, a ceramics studio (Quandary Antiques Cabin) and the Tin Shop. Some permanent sculptures are on display outside the buildings. Check the website for events and workshops.

Activities

Winter Sports

When Main St is at 9600ft and the peaks are so plentiful the founders went with numbers over names, you know the skiing is going to be absurdly good. In winter, which starts early here, it's all about the snow. If you're up for some backcountry travel, Boreas Pass Rd (p183) is a good spot to strap on the snowshoes or cross-country skis. It's 6.4 miles from the parking lot (at the winter road-closure point) to the pass, and there are other trails up here.

Breckenridge Ski Area SNOW SPORTS
(800-789-7669; www.breckenridge.com; lift ticket adult/child $115/68; 8:30am-4pm Nov–mid-Apr) Breckenridge spans five mountains (Peaks 6 to 10), covering 2900 acres and featuring some of the best beginner and intermediate terrain in the state, as well as plenty of exhilarating high-alpine runs and hike-to bowls. There are also five terrain parks and two half-pipes here.

You access the mountain from the free **BreckConnect Gondola**, which runs from downtown Breckenridge Station (Watson Ave) and serves the Nordic Center, Peak 7 and Peak 8. Lift tickets are good at Keystone and A-Basin, and if you buy a three-day pass or longer, you also get access to Vail. See the website for detailed information on the ski school.

Breckenridge Nordic Center SNOW SPORTS
(970-453-6855; www.breckenridgenordic.com; 1200 Ski Hill Rd; adult/child $20/15; 9am-4pm Nov–mid-Apr) Breckenridge's Nordic Center has nine cross-country trails and five

> **REMEMBER WHEN...**
>
> A lift ticket to Breck cost $4? No, we don't either – that was back in 1961. Still, even during the prosperous '90s, it was only $39 to ski here for the day. Talk about inflation!

snowshoe trails set beneath the base of Peak 7. You can get here via a free town bus, the gondola (plus a short hike) or by car.

Stephen C West Ice Arena SKATING
(☎970-547-9974; www.townofbreckenridge.com; 189 Boreas Pass Rd; adult/child $8/6, skate rental $4; ⏰hours vary) An attractive lodge-like arena south of town houses the town ice rinks (both indoor and outdoor). It's open for public skating at least four days a week. Check the website for the latest schedule.

Mountain & Road Biking

In summer, mountain bikers can take the **chairlift** (1 haul/full-day $17/30; ⏰9:30am-5:30pm mid-Jun–mid-Sep) to the 11,000ft Vista Haus summit and cruise (or fly, depending on the run) down one of 11 designated cycle trails, two of which wander over to Peak 9.

You can rent bikes at the base of Peak 8 or in town; sports shops will also be able to suggest a few more rides (the kind where you have to work to get downhill), as there are over 200 miles of off-road trails in the area.

Summit County's fabulous network of paved bikepaths (p178) wrap around the Dillon Reservoir, stretching from Keystone to Breckenridge to Vail, and are definitely worth exploring. From Breck to Frisco is 9.5 miles along the Blue River, with only 550ft of elevation change. Breck Sports runs shuttles ($30) to the top of Vail Pass, from where you can cycle 21.5 miles back to town. If you run out of steam along the way, you can always catch a lift on the Summit Stage in Frisco (p180), which is equipped with bike racks.

The free *Summit County Bike Guide* is the best resource for both mountain bikers and road cyclists; pick it up at the visitor center or in bike-rental shops.

Equipment Rental

Carvers SPORTS RENTAL
(☎800-568-7010; www.carverskishop.com; 203 N Main St; ski rental adult $25-45, child $18-25, bikes per day $29-45; ⏰8am-9pm winter, 9am-5pm summer) A terrific indie bike and ski shop. It has a bit of everything including high-end bikes, boards, skis, boots, camelbacks and disc golf sets (not joking). It does overnight repairs, is just a short walk from the gondola, and offers a better selection than the big conglomerates.

Main Street Sports SPORTS RENTAL
(☎970-453-1777; www.mainstreetsports.com; 401 S Main St; ski rental adult $27-40, child $18-20; ⏰8am-8pm) A family owned business since it opened in 1991, this is a Spyder concept store, which means it rents rent demo skis, snowboards, and sells all the latest Spyder ski apparel too.

Breck Sports SPORTS RENTAL
(☎970-455-0215; http://breckenridgesports.com; 127 S Main St; mountain bikes half/full day $49/59, cruisers half/full day $29/39, child half/full day $19/24; ⏰10am-6pm) Offering bike rentals in summer, with two locations: one downtown and one at the base of Peak 8. It's convenient, but more expensive. It also does ski rentals in winter.

Hiking

Breckenridge offers excellent opportunities to get out and explore the Tenmile Range. In addition to the hikes listed here, the visitor center hands out descriptions of other popular options. Alternatively, check out www.summitcountyexplorer.com.

★**Quandary Peak** HIKING
(www.14ers.com; County Rd 851) Known as Colorado's easiest 14er, Quandary Peak is the state's 15th highest peak at 14,265ft. Though you will see plenty of dogs and children, 'easiest' may be misleading – the summit remains three grueling miles from the trailhead. Go between June and September.

The trail ascends to the west; after about 10 minutes of moderate climbing, follow the right fork to a trail junction. Head left, avoiding the road, and almost immediately you'll snatch views of Mt Helen and Quandary (although the real summit is still hidden).

Just below the timberline you'll meet the trail from Monte Cristo Gulch – note it so you don't take the wrong fork on your way back down. From here it's a steep haul to the top. Start early and aim to turn around by noon, as afternoon lightning is typical in summer. It's a 6-mile round-trip, taking roughly between seven and eight hours. To get here, take Hwy 9 south from Breckenridge toward Hoosier Pass. Make a right on

County Rd 850 and turn right again onto 851. Drive 1.1 miles to the unmarked trailhead. Park parallel on the fire road.

Mohawk Lakes HIKING

(Spruce Creek Rd; ⌚Jun-Oct) Deep-green Lower Mohawk is tucked onto a tundra shelf with the ruins of a miner's cabin and mining works just below. An outstanding, if slightly exposed, campsite is just south of the cabin. Upper Lake views are an even more spectacular moonscape: marbled rocks, stunted trees, inky lake views. That clear buzz is the quiet roar of the cosmos. It's 7 miles round-trip.

The trailhead is located 1.2 miles up Spruce Creek Rd; the turnoff is 2.4 miles south of Breckenridge on Hwy 9 (towards Hoosier Pass).

McCullough Gulch HIKING

(off County Rd 851; ⌚Jun-Oct) This 2.8-mile round-trip hike is short enough for families, though huffing up the 1000ft of elevation gain will require some perseverance. Luckily you'll have plenty of scenery along the way: the meandering streams that you follow from the trailhead eventually turn into thundering falls and, after that, a glacial lake.

The trail splits below the falls. One branch leads you to a lower falls and the other to a series of about eight cascades, stepping down from the lake, about 1.3 miles from the trailhead. You'll notice Quandary Peak on the south side of the lake and Pacific Peak (13,950ft) to the north.

To get here drive 7.5 miles south from Breckenridge on Hwy 9. Turn right onto County Rd 850 and right again on 851. Drive on for 2 miles and park near the water-diversion structures.

Other Activities

Peak 8 Fun Park AMUSEMENT PARK

(☎800-789-7669; www.breckenridge.com; Peak 8; day pass 3-7yr/8yr & up $34/68; ⌚9:30am-5:30pm mid-Jun–mid-Sep; 👪) This park has a laundry list of made-for-thrills activities, including a big-air trampoline, climbing wall, mountain-bike park and the celebrated SuperSlide – a luge-like course taken on a sled at exhilarating speeds. Get the day pass, do activities à la carte ($10 to $18) or simply take a scenic ride up the chairlift (without/with bike $10/17). This will eventually morph into the impressive eco-playground Epic Discovery (www.epicdiscovery.com), though not until 2016 at the earliest.

Mountain Angler FISHING

(☎800-453-4669; www.mountainangler.com; 311 S Main St; guided fishing trips per person from $210; ⌚8am-5:30pm) Fisherpeople will want to

BRECKENRIDGE SKI TIPS

Thanks to the long and relatively flat green runs on Peaks 8 and 9, the Breckenridge Ski Area has always been known as a great family mountain and a terrific place to learn. But if you're ready to step it up a notch, don't fret – there are plenty of adrenaline-addled diversions higher up on the resort's five towering peaks.

The one experience experts won't want to miss is a ride on the **highest chairlift** in North America, the Imperial Express (12,840ft). This drops you off just below the summit of **Peak 8**, from where you can traverse north along the ridge to **Whale's Tail** and **Peak 7 Bowl**, or steel yourself for the short, steep and lung-crushing hike up to the true summit (don't drop your gear!), where the views and terrain are simply spectacular. From here you can drop into the **Imperial Bowl** or the extreme **Lake Chutes**.

A favorite intermediate or 'blue' run is **Cashier** on Peak 9. Long, mellow and not too technical, it's a place to refine your skills and practice your jib tricks. It's also not a bad spot to make the switch from skis to snowboard. Another great intermediate run on Peak 7 is **Wire Patch**, featuring a series of 'rollers' – mini-hills, not moguls. In 2013, the resort opened **Peak 6** to skiers, adding access to three new bowls, two of which offer high-alpine intermediate terrain.

There's a favorite expression around Breck: 'There's no friends on powder days.' And you certainly won't catch locals waiting around for anyone when it starts dumping. They'll be skiing through the forest on the south side of **Peak 10**, where the tree runs are legendary.

In case of emergency, make sure you have the **ski patrol number** (☎970-496-7294) entered in your phone.

drop into this shop tucked inside a Main St mall. It offers a wide range of outdoor clothing, fishing gear and guided fly-fishing and float trips on the Blue, Eagle, Colorado, Arkansas and Platte Rivers.

Arkansas Valley Adventures RAFTING
(☎800-370-0581; http://coloradorafting.net; adult $54-209, child $49-189; ⊙May-Sep) Voted Summit County's best white-water outfitter three straight years, Arkansas Valley Adventures runs rafting trips down the legendary Arkansas and Colorado Rivers, as well as the mellower Clear Creek and Blue River (June and July only). The Arkansas and Colorado put-ins are over an hour's drive from Breckenridge. Children must be six and weigh at least 50lb.

Tibetan Ocean Massage SPA
(☎970-453-2085; www.tibetanoceanmassage.com; 111 S Main St, 2nd fl; 60min massage $65-80; ⊙by appointment) Not your average mountain massage joint, this healing center was started by Wangkho, a Buddhist monk, born in Amdo (northern Tibet). In 2000 he walked for 26 days over Himalayan passes out of China and into exile. He opened his first center in Dharamsala and now offers astrology readings, yoga classes and deep bodywork at his Main St studio.

Tours

Historic Walking Tours WALKING TOUR
(☎970-453-9767; www.breckheritage.com; 203 S Main St; adult/child $10/5; ⊙tours 11am & 1:30pm Tue-Sun) There are 250 historic structures in Breckenridge, making it one of the oldest surviving cities in the Central Rockies. On this tour, which meets 10 minutes ahead at the Welcome Center, you'll visit old miners' cabins, a saloon boarding house and a few museums too.

Other walking tours include the Haunted Breck Tour, Saloon Tour and the Preston Ghost Town Hike. Check the website for seasonal schedules.

Festivals & Events

Quirky parades, feats of athletic, creative and culinary agility and ingenuity, and plenty of night music: Breckenridge knows how to throw a party.

Breckenridge Music Festival MUSIC
(☎970-453-9142; www.breckenridgemusicfestival.com) Something of a kid sister to the Aspen festival, the Breckenridge Music Institute and National Repertory Orchestra offer both summer and winter seasons of stunning classical music at the Riverwalk Center, a heated amphitheater on the Blue River. There are more than 50 orchestral concerts and chamber recitals each summer, and a half-dozen dates during the shorter winter season.

Ullr Fest CULTURE
(www.gobreck.com; ⊙early to mid-Jan) The Ullr Fest celebrates the Norse god of winter, with a wild parade and four-day festival featuring a twisted version of the Dating Game, an ice-skating party and a bonfire.

International Snow Sculpture Championship ARTS
(www.gobreck.com; ⊙mid-Jan) The International Snow Sculpture Championship begins in mid-January and lasts for three weeks. It starts with 'Stomping Week,' when the snow blocks are made, proceeds with Sculpting Week, when the sculptures are created, and concludes with Viewing Week, when the sculptures decorate the River Walk and are enjoyed and judged by the public.

Mardi Gras PARADE
(www.gobreck.com; ⊙mid-Feb) Breck's take on Mardi Gras features a Fat Tuesday parade down Main St and a Bacchus Ball (New Orleans–style masquerade ball) at the Beaver Run Resort.

Spring Fever FESTIVAL
(www.breckenridge.com; ⊙mid Mar) From mid-March through closing day, Spring Fever offers a range of events, from concerts and competitions to chili cook-offs, an Easter-egg hunt and celebrity athlete shindigs.

Kingdom Days CULTURE
(www.gobreck.com; ⊙mid-Jun) The 'Kingdom of Breckenridge' was declared after it was discovered that the 1300 sq miles surrounding Breckenridge were not yet part of the US. The Kingdom Days festival celebrates this 'independence' with gold-panning, wood-carving contests, an outhouse race (someone call Steve-O) and historic walking tours.

Fourth of July CELEBRATION
(www.gobreck.com; ⊙July) Breckenridge throws one hell of a July 4 party. There are free concerts, an art festival, a parade, a reading of George Washington's Declaration of Independence, a 10km trail run and a free concert and fireworks to wrap it all up.

Breck Bike Week SPORTS
(www.gobreck.com; usually Aug) Usually coinciding with the lead-up to the US Pro Cycling Challenge, this festival on two wheels includes group rides, demo gear displays and mechanic workshops, as well as some bike-in movie nights.

Sleeping

On the whole, Breckenridge is more affordable than Vail and Aspen and a good choice for families and budgeteers. Most accommodations are condo style, so if you want one of the B&Bs listed here, reserve early. By far the easiest way to compare different rental properties is via the visitor center website (www.gobreck.com). The closest USFS campsites are near Frisco.

Fireside Inn B&B, HOSTEL $
(970-453-6456; www.firesideinn.com; 114 N French St; summer/winter dm $30/41, d $101/140; P ❄ @ 🛜 👪) The best deal for budget travelers in Summit County, this chummy hostel and B&B is a find. All guests can enjoy the chlorine-free barrel hot tub, fridge and microwave, movie nights with fellow ski bums and the resident snuggly dog. The English hosts are a delight and all but dorm dwellers get breakfast in the morning. It's a 10-minute walk to the gondola in ski boots.

Section House HUT $
(www.summithuts.org; Boreas Pass; per person $30; Nov-May) One of four Summit County huts, the Section House (sleeps 12) is located at the top of Boreas Pass Rd (p183) and is a favorite destination for backcountry skiers. It was originally built in 1882 to house railroad workers, abandoned after the line closed in the 1930s and restored in the '90s. A wood-burning stove, mattresses and solar-powered lighting are available.

Like all huts, you should reserve months in advance to secure a spot. The more intimate **Ken's Cabin** is next door.

★ **Abbet Placer Inn** B&B $$
(970-453-6489; www.abbettplacer.com; 205 S French St; r summer $99-179, winter $119-229; P ❄ @ 🛜) This violet house has five large rooms decked out with wood furnishings, iPod docks and fluffy robes. It's very low key. The warm and welcoming hosts cook big breakfasts, and guests can enjoy a lovely outdoor Jacuzzi deck and use of a common kitchenette. The top-floor room has massive views of the peaks from a private terrace. Check-in is from 4pm to 7pm.

Barn on the River B&B $$
(800-795-2975; www.breckenridge-inn.com; 303b N Main St; r $129-219; P ❄ 🛜) A centrally located barn, this B&B has five rooms with queen- or king-sized beds and antique-style furnishings. Some have soaring beamed ceilings and private balconies, and all are within earshot of the Blue River – as is the hot tub.

Great Western Lodging ACCOMMODATION SERVICES $$$
(888-453-1001; www.gwlodging.com; 322 N Main St; condos summer/winter from $125/275; P ❄ 🛜 👪) Arguably the best and most refined of the rental agencies in Breckenridge. It has a portfolio of 150 homes and condos on the west side (read: slope side) of Main St, with an emphasis on ski-in, ski-out and walk-in, walk-out properties. Two night minimum in summer; four-night minimum in winter.

WHAT'S IN A NAME?

Once gold was discovered in the Pikes Peak and Idaho Springs areas in the late 1850s, it didn't take long for prospectors to make their way to Summit County. George Spencer officially founded the town of Breckenridge in November 1859 as something of a market town and base camp to support, and profit from, the efforts of miners in the local mountains.

Spencer originally named the town 'Breckinridge' after the sitting vice president, John C Breckinridge of Kentucky. It was sheer flattery, of course. Spencer wanted a post office, and politicians being politicians, he was rewarded with the first post office between the Continental Divide and Salt Lake City, UT. But when the Civil War broke out in 1861, and the vice president became a brigadier general in the Confederate army, the decidedly pro-Union citizens of Breckinridge decided to change the town's name. An 'i' was changed to an 'e', and the place became Breckenridge forever after.

Woodwinds Lodging ACCOMMODATION SERVICES $$$
(☎800-403-6744; www.woodwindsbreck.com; 300 N Main St; condos summer/winter from $125/240; P❄📶👪) Offers one- to four-bedroom homes and condos in the flats and on the hill (including some ski-in, ski-out spots). Most require a three-night minimum stay in summer and four nights in winter. Check-in is at the office on N Main St.

Eating

Kitchens here like to flex their creative muscles, although not everyone's an Iron Chef in the upper echelons – hit après-ski specials (4pm to 6pm) for the best deals.

Clint's Bakery & Coffee House CAFE $
(131 S Main St; sandwiches $4.95-7.25; ⏰7am-8pm; 📶👪) The coolest coffeeshop in town, where brainy baristas will steam up a chalkboard full of latte and mocha flavors and dozens of loose-leaf teas. If you're hungry, the downstairs bagelry stacks burly sandwiches and tasty breakfast bagels with egg and ham, lox, sausage and cheese. Good pastries too. The bagelry closes at 3pm.

Park & Main SANDWICHES $
(http://parkandmainfood.com; 500 S Main St; sandwiches $7-12; ⏰7:30am-9pm; 🖊👪) This bright industrial space is a welcome addition to the Breck cafe scene. It runs the gauntlet of world sandwich styles, from pressed paninis on ciabatta bread and a prosciutto-laced *croque monsieur* (aka grilled ham-and-cheese) to Vietnamese *banh mi* (baguettes) and even roasted beet sliders and quinoa salad. Lots of free-range egg creations get the day started right.

Crepes à la Cart CREPERIE $
(www.crepesalacarts.com; 307 S Main St; crepes $5-11; ⏰10am-11pm Sun-Thu, 10am-2pm Fri & Sat; 👪) Breck's most popular snack stand, you can't miss this yellow gypsy cart on Main St – or the line snaking down the block in front of it. Sweet and savory crepes are made to order and folded up in the iconic Parisian wedge, but when it gets busy, oh *mon dieu*, the wait can be brutally long (like 30 minutes).

Come with time to spare and cozy up at the adjacent fire pit.

Wasabi JAPANESE $$
(☎970-453-8311; www.wasabi-breckenridge.com; 311 S Main St; lunch $8-13, dinner $17-22, sushi plates $16.50-35.50; ⏰noon-2pm Wed-Sat, 5pm-close Tue-Sun) If you're salivating for sushi, maki rolls or udon noodles, this family run hole-in-the-wall will definitely satisfy. The chef keeps it simple and affordable, especially at lunch when he offers teriyaki tofu and chicken bowls for a song ($8); the volcano bowl, piled high with wasabi tuna, salmon or albacore ($13), is the best deal in the house.

The fish served here is the same as at Matsuhisa (p226) and Osaki's (p202), and is shipped in daily from Narita. It's located in the shopping center.

Lucha Cantina MEXICAN $$
(☎970-453-1342; www.luchacantina.com; 500 S Main St; mains $10-15; ⏰11am-2am; 🖊👪) Although slightly pricey, you have to give Lucha's some credit – almost everything is housemade and healthy, with flavors that go well beyond your typical Col-Mex fare. Think wahoo fish tacos (with cilantro-dill salsa), smothered Veracruz veggie burritos and chile rellenos, along with grass-fed burgers and fresh salads. It stays open late into the night.

Giampietro ITALIAN $$
(☎970-453-3838; www.giampietropizza.com; 100 N Main St; mains $7.75-15.25, pizzas $14.50-28.50; ⏰11am-10pm; 👪) Dig into some consistently good, honest and soulful New York–style pizza. It's sold by the slice and pie, along with dishes such as baked ziti with sausage, eggplant parmigiana and lunch subs. It's all served in a bright corner room, decorated with those kitschy red-checkered tablecloths. Family-sized orders (take-out only; 24-hour notice) are also available.

★ **South Ridge Seafood** SEAFOOD $$$
(☎970-547-0063; www.southridgeseafoodgrill.com; 215 S Ridge St; mains $13-28; ⏰4pm-late; 👪) South Ridge is a gorgeous space that feels like a sophisticated saloon, with a marble bar, pressed-tin ceiling, spinning fans and stained-glass accoutrements. The kitchen whips up some delectable mains (Pacific sole with parmesan risotto cakes, grilled trout with lemon-thyme aioli), but it's the après-ski scene that garners the most acclaim, with winning small plates that go for as little as $3.

Hearthstone MODERN AMERICAN $$$
(☎970-453-1148; http://hearthstonerestaurant.biz; 130 S Ridge St; mains $26-44; ⏰4pm-late; 🖊) 🍃 One of Breck's favorites, this restored 1886 Victorian churns out creative mountain

fare such as blackberry elk and braised buffalo ribs with tomatillos, roasted chilies and polenta. Fresh and delicious, it's definitely worth a splurge, or hit happy hour (4pm to 6pm) for $5 plates paired with wine.

You can dine in the oh-so-burgundy dining room or, preferably, on the three tiered patios out front when the weather cooperates. Reserve.

Briar Rose STEAKHOUSE **$$$**
(☎970-453-9948; www.briarrosechophouse.com; 109 Lincoln Ave; mains $21-44; ⏰4-10pm; 👪) Set in a magnificent Old West frame and on the site of Breck's original saloon, this spot is named after the famed Briar Rose gold mine on Peak 10. And while it's first and foremost a chophouse, small plates (think shishito peppers, chorizo, mussels and escargot) are served in the dining room and saloon. Fine dining doesn't get any more atmospheric in Breckenridge.

Drinking & Nightlife

Downstairs at Eric's BAR
(www.downstairsaterics.com; 111 S Main St; ⏰11am-midnight) Downstairs at Eric's is a Breckenridge institution. Locals flock to this game-room-style basement joint for the brews, burgers and delicious mashed potatoes. There are over 100 beers (20 on tap) to choose from and plenty of sports bar–arcade action.

★**Kava Cafe** CAFE
(www.kavabreck.com; 209 N Main St; ⏰7:30am-5pm) This hole-in-the-wall and historic log-cabin cafe is the kind of place in which ragged miners may have procured dry goods back in the day. These days it makes

WORTH A TRIP

FAIRPLAY

Follow Hwy 9 south from Breckenridge and after 11 miles of steady climbing, you'll come to **Hoosier Pass** (11,539ft) and the Continental Divide. From here you'll be looking out over the South Park basin, a high-altitude prairie where the bison once roamed. On the other side of the pass is funky **Alma**, the highest incorporated town in the United States, standing at an elevation of 10,578ft. It's surrounded by four 14ers, thousand-year-old bristlecone pines and scores of old mining claims. If you want to explore, follow the unpaved Buckskin Rd (County Rd 8) 6 miles west toward Kite Lake – high-clearance 4WD is recommended for the last mile.

Otherwise, continue 5.5 miles down Hwy 9 until you reach **Fairplay**. South Park's main settlement was originally a mining site and supply town for Leadville (pack burros used to clop back and forth over 13,000ft Mosquito Pass to the west), and you can stop here to visit **South Park City** (www.southparkcity.org; 100 4th St; adult/child 6-12yr $10/4; ⏰9am-7pm mid-May–mid-Oct, shorter hours May & Oct; 👪), a recreated 19th-century Colorado boomtown. Get a taste of life back in the good-old, bad-old days of the gold rush through the 40 restored buildings on display, which range from the general store and saloon to a dentist's office and morgue. And yes, *South Park* fans, Fairplay does bear more than a passing resemblance to the hometown of Kyle, Cartman and the boys.

If you've been itching to slide your boots into some stirrups, South Park also offers some decent horseback-riding experiences. The **Platte Ranch** (☎719-836-1670; Hwy 9; 2hr/half-day ride $70/135) gets great reviews and offers guests a bona fide cowboy experience with rides through open country on an actual working ranch. The **American Safari Ranch** (☎719-836-2700; www.americansafariranch.com; 1484 County Rd 7; 1½/2hr rides $55/65) is another nearby option worth looking into.

There are several predictable eating options on Front St in Fairplay, but for something slightly out of the ordinary, try **Dorothy's Homemade Tamales** (123 Frontage Rd; tamales $2.25-3, enchilada plates $6.50; ⏰7am-9pm; 🌶👪), just south of town on Hwy 285 (look for Pizza Hut). The local greasy spoon dishes out all-day breakfasts and Colorado-style Mexican fare, and while the food may not be amazing, it is located in a bowling alley, which is hard to beat.

Fairplay is 21 miles south of Breckenridge and 86 miles west of Denver. If you're looking for a scenic alternative to I-70, Hwy 285 is as pretty as they come and offers a good backdoor option to Breckenridge and Buena Vista. Hoosier Pass stays open year round.

sandwiches and coffee, but is notable for its three specialties: fresh-squeezed lemonade, made-to-order mini donuts and kava ($7.50, two servings).

The latter is a Polynesian root that's been used ceremonially for centuries. Funky, earthy and served at room temperature, it's a natural relaxant and a great way to unwind at the end of the day. Take it home and pair it with your outdoor hot tub: niceness!

Breckenridge Brewery BREWERY
(www.breckbrewpub.com; 600 S Main St; ⏲11am-1am) With seven malty aromatic brews being cooked up in the kettles directly behind the bar, you know what this is all about. Sample happy-hour goodness ($3 pints) with agave wheat, vanilla porter and Lucky U IPA. Pub grub is served all day and late into the night.

Motherloaded Tavern PUB
(www.motherloadedtavern.com; 103 S Main St; ⏲11:30am-2am) The choice dive in Breckenridge isn't even all that divey. Sure, it's a bare-bones tavern, but it also attracts the local hipsters and anyone else who dreams of tasty comfort food alongside hot, steaming boozy sips. Surprisingly, there are no microbrews on tap, so it'll have to be a Pabst. There's live music every Thursday through Saturday night.

Cecilia's CLUB
(☎970-453-2243; www.cecilias.tv; 520 S Main St; ⏲2pm-2am) Ski bums love to rag on Cecilia's, but that doesn't stop them from flocking to this long-established party spot when the mood is right. It has a large dancefloor with mostly DJ-spun grooves (and occasional live acts), three bars and a bit of a frat-boy scene. It can get going on weekend nights, but other times it can be dead.

☆ Entertainment

Breck is nobody's nightclub mecca, but frequent festivals keep the Breckenridge events calendar filled with live music indoors and out, and in between you can get your fix of set-piece entertainment.

★**Three20South** LIVE MUSIC, CLUB
(☎970-368-3204; www.three20south.com; 320 S Main St; cover varies; ⏲most nights 9pm-late) Breckenridge's only 'true' nightclub brings live music to the people most nights. The taste is wide and deep, ranging from bluegrass to jazz to funk to rock. It's mostly indie acts here, but some bigger names do drift in from time to time. Check the website for upcoming showtimes and prices.

Backstage Theater THEATER
(☎970-453-0199; www.backstagetheatre.org; 121 S Ridge St; most shows $12-18; ⏲hours vary; 👪) This is a vibrant, long-running theater bringing edgy and entertaining fare to the people, staging new and classic shows. It has produced over 200 plays over the years and offers acting workshops too.

Shopping

★**Magical Scraps** CLOTHING, ACCESSORIES
(www.magicalscraps.com; 310 S Main St; ⏲10am-9pm) The girliest shop in Breck, and we mean that in the best way possible. Here are printed fabrics, stuffed toys, tot-sized tees, and dresses and hats for mom and baby. Not to mention funky handbags, scarves, skirts and luscious handmade soap.

Flourish ACCESSORIES
(226 S Main St; ⏲10am-6pm Mon-Sat, 11am-4pm Sun) This tiny boutique features original jewelry, bags and artwork from Colorado-based creators, such as Maruca in Boulder.

Slopeside Cowboy CLOTHING
(www.slopesidecowboy.com; 505 S Main St; ⏲10am-9pm, to 6pm summer) Selling snakeskin and sequin-covered cowboy boots, designer belt buckles, Stetson hats and other mother-of-pearl ranch apparel, Slopeside Cowboy is a dream come true for country-and-western fashionistas.

Underground SPORTS
(www.undergroundsnowboards.com; 320 S Main St; ⏲10am-8pm) The hippest mountain gear in Breck is found at this apparel and board shop. It sells Burton and Volcom clothing, and Analog and Anon goggles, as well as some sick boards, although it doesn't do rentals.

Information

Visitor Center (☎877-864-0868; www.gobreck.com; 203 S Main St; ⏲9am-9pm; 📶) Along with a host of maps and brochures, this center has a fantastic riverside museum that delves into Breck's gold-mining past.

Getting There & Around

Breckenridge is 80 miles west of Denver via I-70 exit 203, then Hwy 9 south. The main parking lots (Monday to Thursday $5, Friday to Sunday $12) are located across from the gondola; they are free in summer. You can also find small lots scattered throughout town; these are free for three hours, but finding a spot may be more trouble than it's worth. A free park-and-ride lot is best for skiers just up for the day; it's located on Airport Rd north of town and is connected to the gondola via shuttle.

Colorado Mountain Express (☎800-525-6363; www.coloradomountainexpress.com; adult/child $70/36; 📶) Shuttle service to/from Denver International Airport (two hours).

Free Ride (www.townofbreckenridge.com; 150 Watson Ave; ⏲8am-11:45pm) Nine free bus routes serve the town and ski area. Buses depart from Breckenridge station next to the gondola.

Fresh Tracks (☎970-453-4052; www.freshtrackstransportation.com; 1-way $20) A Breckenridge–Vail shuttle (one hour).

Summit Express (☎855-686-8267; www.summitexpress.com; adult/child $64/32) Shuttle service to/from Denver International Airport (two hours).

Summit Stage (☎970-668-0999; www.summitstage.com; 150 Watson Ave) Summit County's free bus service links Breckenridge with Keystone and A-Basin in winter (Swan Mountain Flyer) and with Frisco year-round. It leaves from Breckenridge Station.

Copper Mountain

POP 385 / ELEV 9712FT

Opened in 1973, this picturesque, self-contained resort town southwest of Frisco, just off I-70 at exit 195, was the last addition to Summit County ski country. Set high on the eastern slope of Vail Pass and tucked into a bowl, it's surrounded by mountains with long runs carved between evergreens and copious powder in the winter. In summer there's everything from golf to go-karts to cycling, and you can almost always hear that ever-present rush of Copper Creek over the roar of the nearby highway. Almost.

Activities

Copper Mountain SNOW SPORTS

(☎866-841-2481; www.coppercolorado.com; Hwy 91; adult/child $114/65; ⏲9am-4pm, from 8:30am Sat & Sun Nov–mid-Apr) The resort may be a bit too planned for some, but even the staunchest critics wouldn't thumb their noses at the mountain itself. Rising 2729ft up to the 12,441ft summit, Copper has 2450 acres of terrain, carved with over 125 trails equally divided among beginners, intermediate, advanced and expert skiers. No chichi Vail attitude here – Copper takes you back to skiing's play-hard roots.

It's an easy mountain to navigate – all levels have their own slice of paradise served by separate lifts, meaning beginners are unlikely to be run over by experts at the bottom of the mountain (and vice versa). The coup for serious skiers is the **free snowcat skiing** (10am to 1:30pm) in the back bowl on Tucker Mountain.

There are plenty of other activities here as well, including 15 miles of cross-country and snowshoe trails, a tubing hill, and a small skating rink and zip line.

Copper often has good deals going, particularly for locals, so shop around on its website in advance for discounted lift tickets and four packs.

Woodward at Copper SNOW SPORTS

(☎888-350-1544; www.woodwardatcopper.com; 505 Copper Rd; drop-in/intro sessions $29/49; ⏲hours vary) If your grommet wants to learn his or her way around a snowboard park – including those gnarly half-pipes and super pipes – send them here, a year-round ski and snowboard training camp. It serves all levels of athlete, from beginners to the young and sponsored. Choose from daylong and weeklong camps, intro classes or drop-in sessions.

During the summer it opens the indoor wing to skateboarders, BMXers and inline skaters.

Summer at Copper OUTDOORS

(☎866-841-2481; www.coppercolorado.com; activities $10-15 or day pass $44; ⏲10am-5pm, to 7pm Fri & Sat mid-Jun–Aug) All the usual activities are on offer in summer: there's a climbing wall, miniature golf and even a go-cart race track. The American Eagle lift (10am to 4pm) leaves you at Solitude Station, where you can have a BBQ lunch and take one of the two nature or hiking trails available. The chairlift is free, provided you've already spent $10 at the resort.

The Hallelujah Loop is a short nature trail, or take Andy's Encore to the alpine overlook then continue cross-country through some loose scree fields to Copper Peak (12,441ft), before hiking back down. You can haul a mountain bike up and ride down all day long for $15.

Copper Creek Golf Course GOLF

(☎866-677-1663; www.coppercolorado.com; 509 Copper Rd; peak season 9/18 holes $48/72; ⏲8am-5:50pm Jun-Oct) An affordable and scenic 18 holes are yours to play here. Check in at the Athletic Club between the two villages as you enter the resort.

Peak Sports SPORTS RENTALS
(☎970-968-2372; www.coppersports.com; 214 Ten Mile Circle; ski & snowboard packages $21-47, 4hr road-/mountain-bike rental $20/30; ⏰8am-6pm winter, 9am-5pm summer) This highly professional Copper Mountain outfitter is located just steps from the American Eagle lift. Ski and snowboard prices quoted here are walk-in rates; you'll do better if you rent online at www.rentskis.com.

Burning Stones Outdoor Theater CINEMA, LIVE MUSIC
(☎866-841-2481; www.copperchamber.com; Ten Mile Circle; ⏰concerts 6-8pm Fri) The theater would be that Stonehenge-looking building steps from the American Eagle lift, notable because it's the site of free summer concerts on Friday evenings, followed by movies projected onto a big screen. Families love it.

Festivals & Events

Copper Country Arts Festival MUSIC, ARTS
(www.villageatcopper.com/coppercountry; Ten Mile Circle; ⏰Labor Day weekend) FREE Copper Mountain's much loved country music and arts festival hosts a range of events around the Labor Day weekend, with arts and crafts exhibitions, pony rides for the kids, and lots of country music acts on the lineup, although bluesy interlopers, such as Dr John, have been known to drift in.

Sleeping

All Copper Mountain lodging comes in condo form. There are three management companies that manage the condo properties: **Copper Mountain Lodging** (☎888-219-2441; www.coppercolorado.com; condos from $233; P❄📶👪), **Copper Vacations** (☎800-525-3887; www.coppervacations.com; condos from $150; P❄📶👪🐾) and **Carbonate Lodging** (☎800-526-7737; www.carbonate-real-estate.com; condos from $150; P❄📶👪).

All properties are rated from 2-Peak to 5-Peak. The rating system corresponds to price, but also to property management. Two- and 3-Peak are the cheapest, and their owners can decorate these condos any way they want, which may be why you're waking up next to a picture of someone's Aunt Edna on the nightstand. They also tend to be more dated. A 4-Peak rating means the condos

WORTH A TRIP

SHRINE PASS

Halfway between Copper Mountain and Vail is Shrine Pass (11,178ft), accessed via an 11½-mile dirt road/ski trail that cuts south of Vail's Blue Sky Basin to link up with the town of Red Cliff along Hwy 24. In summer, this is a very popular multi-use trail: you can drive it, bike it (three to four hours), use an ATV, and of course go hiking (Shrine Mountain Trail is 4.2 miles round-trip; the trailhead is 2¼ miles up the road). From Julia's Deck (mile 3¾) you have good views of Mt of the Holy Cross. Biking is the most interesting option as once you hump the pass (2½ miles in), it's all downhill to Red Cliff. If you have two cars you can set up a shuttle, otherwise sign up for a bike tour with Bike Valet (p199) in Vail.

In winter this area is known as the **Vail Pass Recreation Area** (day/season pass $6/50) and is equally interesting. It's used by both snowmobilers and backcountry skiers and boarders (often teaming together for the uphills), but with 55,000 acres of wilderness and 52 miles of non-motorized trails, you should be able to find some seclusion. The forest service grooms 50 miles of trails back here, allowing you to get between Shrine Pass, Red Cliff and a third access point, Camp Hale (p238). Additionally, there are four huts (p223) in the area (Shrine Mt, Fowler, Jackal and Janet's Cabin) for overnight trips. It goes without saying that avalanche gear and training is a must.

To get here, take the Vail Pass exit (190) off I-70, or park in Red Cliff or Camp Hale on Hwy 24. The Minturn ranger office (p207) has maps and trail descriptions for the area. You must pick up a map before you go; it's likely you'll get lost without one. In Red Cliff, stop off at **Mango's** (www.mangosmountaingrill.com; 166 ½ Eagle St; mains $8-20; ⏰11:30am-late; 👪) for a meal or drink.

are almost always more standardized with features such as granite counters and flatscreens. The nicest are the 5-Peak properties, which have all been recently remodeled and can get downright lavish. There are no studios available.

If you book through Copper Mountain Lodging, check-in is at the Athletic Club, which you'll be able to use. It has an indoor lap pool, spa and gym.

Eating

Eating and drinking options here are pretty limited. For a night out, your best bet is to head over to Frisco.

Endo's Adrenaline Cafe CAFE $$
(209 Ten Mile Circle; mains $11-14; 8am-10pm;) A laid-back but still hard-rocking place on the main village plaza. It has kayaks dangling from the ceiling, and snowboarding stills and flatscreen TVs decorate the walls. The menu is mostly sandwiches and wraps, but it does have a few departures from the usual fare, such as beef samosas and green bean fries served with mango salsa.

Incline Bar & Grill AMERICAN $$$
(www.inclinegrill.com; Copper Mountain Village; lunch $10-16, dinner $14-31; 11am-9pm;) Set strategically at the base of Copper Mountain, steps from the American Eagle lift, this bar and grill has a roomy interior, a patio with tables overlooking the slopes, an open-minded and ambitious menu (try the goat cheese and roasted vegetable lasagna or the seared salmon dusted with Indian spices served with a smoked gouda potato cake) and more than a few earthy microbrews on tap.

Getting There & Around

Copper Mountain is 77 miles west of Denver at I-70 exit 195. Free parking is available.

Colorado Mountain Express (800-525-6363; www.coloradomountainexpress.com; adult/child $70/36;) Shuttle service to/from Denver International Airport (two hours).

Summit Express (855-686-8267; www.summitexpress.com; adult/child $64/32) Shuttle service to/from Denver International Airport (two hours).

Summit Stage (970-668-0999; www.summitstage.com) Provides free services throughout Summit County, via the Frisco Transfer Center.

VAIL & THE HOLY CROSS WILDERNESS

Tucked between the remote Eagles Nest Wilderness to the north and the Holy Cross Wilderness to the west, Vail is a universe unto itself. Famous for its massive, stylish ski resort, this is the place where many come to indulge in their deepest, darkest powder-filled fantasies. Your pockets don't have to be flush with cash to enjoy the dramatic scenery, however; the surrounding wilderness areas are truly magnificent and a great place to find inspiration, free of charge.

Vail

POP 5305 / ELEV 8120FT

Blessed with peaks, graced with blue skies and fresh powder, carved by rivers and groomed with ski slopes and bike trails, Vail is the ultimate Colorado playground. The real draw has always been Vail Mountain, a hulking domed mass of snowy joy that offers more terrain than anywhere else in the US: 1500 acres of downhill slopes on the north face and 3500 acres of back-bowl bliss. And it's those endless, naturally sculpted back bowls that have made this resort beloved and famous – though some would say current resident Lindsey Vonn (Olympic gold medalist and four-time World Cup champion for alpine skiing) has helped to boost Vail's profile in equal measure.

Factor in Vail's gourmet offerings, well-coiffed clientele and young powder-fueled staff and you have an adrenalin-addled, yuppie utopia. Indeed, stress does not cling to the bones long here…until you get the bill. And even then you'll have had such a time skiing, hiking, biking and horseback riding that the memories will last far longer than the icy splash of buyer remorse. Just remember going in that this is North America's most expensive ski resort.

If you're a Vail newbie, know that the resort has two large base areas: Vail Village and Lionshead. West Vail (north of I-70) is where you'll find grocery stores, pharmacies and the like.

Sights

Colorado Ski Museum MUSEUM
(www.skimuseum.net; 3rd fl, Vail Village parking lot exit; 10am-5pm;) FREE Humble but informative, this museum takes you from the invention of skiing to the trials of the Tenth

Vail

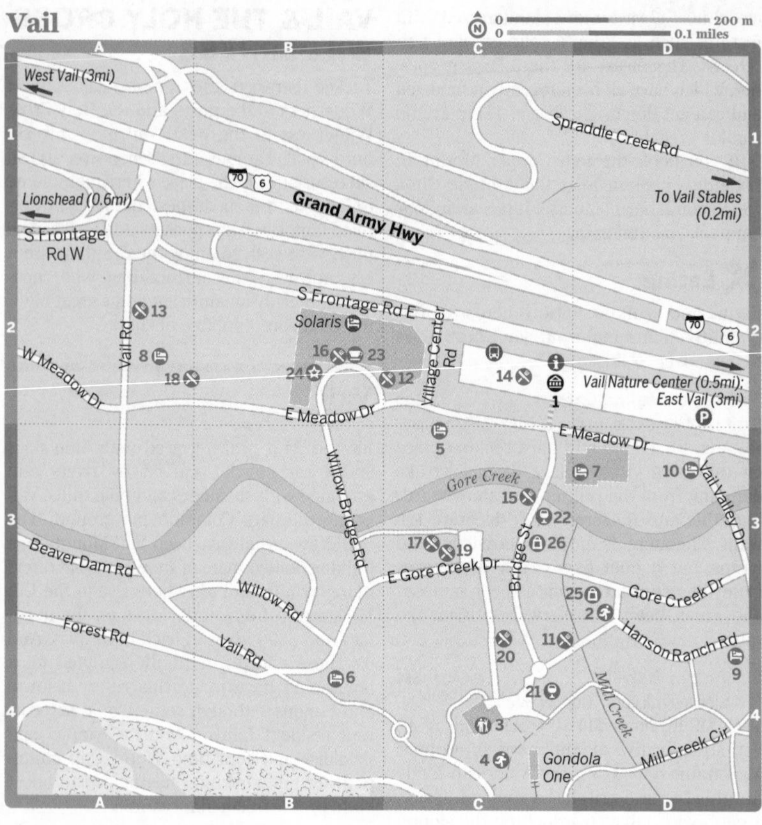

Vail

Sights

1 Colorado Ski Museum C2

Activities, Courses & Tours

Christy Sports .... (see 20)
2 Troy's Ski Shop D3
3 Vail main lift-ticket office C4
4 Vail Sports C4

Sleeping

5 Austria Haus C3
6 Lodge Tower B4
7 Mountain Haus D3
8 The Sebastian A2
9 Tivoli Lodge D4
10 Vail Mountain Lodge D3

Eating

11 Big Bear Bistro C4
12 bōl C2
13 Kelly Liken A2
14 La Cantina C2
15 Loaded Joe's C3
16 Matsuhisa B2
17 Mountain Standard C3
18 Osaki's A2
19 Sweet Basil C3
20 Vendetta's C4

Drinking & Nightlife

21 Los Amigos C4
22 Samana Lounge C3
23 Yeti's Grind B2

Entertainment

24 Cinebistro B2

Shopping

25 Buzz's Ski Shop D3
26 Kemo Sabe C3

Mountain Division, a decorated WWII alpine unit that trained in these mountains. There are also hilarious fashions from the past, as well as the fledgling Colorado Ski and Snowboard Hall of Fame.

Activities

The draw to Vail is no secret. It's the endless outdoor activities in both winter and summer that make this resort so attractive. Do remember that the mud season (mid-April to May and November) holds little attraction for visitors – you can't ski, but you can't really get up into the mountains to hike around either. If it's the backcountry you're interested in, head for the Holy Cross wilderness outside of Minturn, where you'll find several peaks to climb.

Winter Sports

★Vail Mountain SNOW SPORTS
(970-754-8245; www.vail.com; lift ticket adult/child $129/89; 9am-4pm Dec–mid-Apr) Vail Mountain is our favorite in the state, with 5289 skiable acres, 193 trails, three terrain parks and (ahem) the highest lift-ticket prices on the continent. If you're a Colorado ski virgin, it's worth paying the extra bucks to pop your cherry here – especially on a blue-sky fresh-powder day. Multiday tickets are good at four other resorts (Beaver Creek, Breck, Keystone and A-Basin).

With over 30 lifts in operation it can be tough to find your way around, so spend some time studying the trail map. The two high-speed gondolas will get you out of the base areas: **Gondola One** (heated and wifi enabled) serves Vail Village; **Eagle Bahn** serves Lionshead. The main lift-ticket office is located just northwest of Gondola One.

Dobson Ice Arena SKATING
(970-479-2271; www.vailrec.com; 321 E Lionshead Circle; adult/child $6/5, skate rental $3; hours vary) Located at the entrance to the Lionshead ski resort, this aging yet more than adequate rink offers public skate times (see schedule online). There are also much smaller outdoor rinks in Vail Village and Lionshead.

Vail Nordic Center SNOW SPORTS
(970-476-8366; www.vailnordiccenter.com; 1778 Vail Valley Dr; day pass adult/child $8/free; 9am-5pm) Vail's cross-country skiing resource offers lessons and gear rental for aspiring Nordic skiers. You can also rent snowshoes. There are 10 miles of trails; ask about backcountry access too.

VAIL SKI TIPS

True, with 5289 acres of ski terrain available it's tough to play favorites, but here are a few things to keep in mind as you explore the mountain. Beginners should stick to the groomed front side. The **Gopher Hill Lift** (#12) and **Little Eagle Lift** (#15) areas are best for first-timers. Other good green runs include Lost Boy in **Game Creek Bowl** and the Tin Pants and Sourdough in the **Sourdough Express Lift** (#14) area. Kids will dig the various adventure zones, which include banked turns and tunnels, so make sure to seek these out to break up the monotony of bunny hill–style runs.

Some good intermediate runs are Expresso, Cappuccino and Christmas in the **Mountaintop Express Lift** (#4) area. Northwoods, in the **Northwoods Express Lift** (#11) area, Avanti, Lodgepole and Columbine in the **Avanti Express Lift** (#2) area and Dealer's Choice in Game Creek Bowl are also great. Intermediate skiers also love **Blue Sky Basin** (behind the back bowls), with runs such as Big Rock Park, Grand Review and the Star. Free tours of Blue Sky Basin meet daily at Henry's Hut at 11am, across from Patrol HQ.

Advanced skiers flock to **Prima Cornice** and **Riva Ridge** at 4 miles long on the front side. The backside is where the action is, though, with its seven **legendary bowls**: Sun Down, Sun Up, China, Siberia, Teacup and Inner and Outer Mongolia. The wide-open, spruce-dotted slopes here include favorites like Over Yonder (Sun Up), Forever (Sun Down) and Bolshoi Ballroom (Siberia). Lover's Leap in Blue Sky Basin is another home run. The options are seemingly infinite and you can ski a week here without ever covering your tracks. Trickster snowboarders can find three terrain parks on the front side, plus a halfpipe at the bottom of the Riva Bahn.

In case of emergency, make sure you have the **ski patrol number** (970-754-1111) entered in your phone.

Summer Sports

Vail to Breckenridge Bike Path CYCLING

(www.fs.usda.gov) This paved car-free bike path stretches 8.7 miles from East Vail to the top of Vail Pass (elevation gain 1831ft), before descending 14 miles into Frisco (nine more if you go all the way to Breckenridge). If you're only interested in the downhill, hop on a shuttle from a Bike Valet and enjoy the ride back to Vail.

Vail Nature Center HIKING

(☎970-479-2291; www.vailrec.com; 601 Vail Valley Dr; walks adult/child $12/6, hikes from $35; ⏰Jun-Sep) The Nature Center offers guided tours all summer long, from half- and full-day backcountry hikes to more family oriented activities. Free creekside nature tours run on Sundays; other popular kids' activities include wildflower walks and evening trips to the beaver pond or stargazing with s'mores. There are also four short interpretive trails open to the public.

Booth Falls & Booth Lake Trail HIKING

(Booth Falls Rd; ⏰Jun-Oct) A 2-mile hike to the 60ft Booth Falls follows USFS Trail 1885 into the Eagles Nest Wilderness Area. The trailhead is off N Frontage Rd west of I-70 exit 180 (East Vail). Continue beyond the falls to encounter meadows filled with wildflowers and views of the Gore Range. The trail continues to Booth Lake, 4.1 miles from the trailhead, and climbs about 3000ft.

Bearcat Stables HORSEBACK RIDING

(☎970-926-1578; www.bearcatstables.com; 2701 Squaw Creek Rd, Edwards; 1/2/4hr ride $60/90/160; ⏰by reservation) One of the best horseback operations in the Vail Valley, Bearcat offers one- and two-hour rides, as well as four-hour backcountry rides, four-day rides to Aspen and horsedrawn sleigh rides in winter. Trips are always fairly intimate with an eight-person maximum. Children must be seven or older.

Vail Stables HORSEBACK RIDING

(☎970-476-6941; www.vailstables.com; Spraddle Creek Rd; rides 1/2/3hr $65/90/160; ⏰May-Sep) This family-run stable offers horse-riding classes and camps for kids, and one- to three-hour rides in the Gore Range. Kids need to be six and at least 40in tall.

Gore Creek Fly Fishermen FISHING

(☎970-476-5042; www.gorecreekflyfisherman.com; 675 Lionshead Pl; half-day/full-day trips per person $280/375; ⏰8am-6pm) This Lionshead fly-fishing shop and outfitter will set you up with new and used gear for rent or purchase. You can also get Gore Creek fishing tips and sign up for half-day and full-day fishing trips on gold-medal waters. Don't miss the free casting clinics at 10:30am daily in summer.

Lakota Guides RAFTING

(☎970-845-7238; www.lakotaguides.com; 429 Edwards Access Rd, Edwards; adult/child from $89/79; ⏰May-Sep) Lakota Guides is a reputable river outfitter serving Vail and Beaver Creek. It can get you on all the nearby rivers – the Eagle, Arkansas and Colorado – and also offers off-road trips. It's based in Edwards (west of Vail). Kids need to be seven or older, except on the Upper Colorado trip (two and older).

Zip Adventures ADVENTURE SPORTS

(☎970-926-9470; www.zipadventures.com; 4098 Hwy 131, Wolcott; per person $150; ⏰mid-Apr–Nov) Zip Adventures allows you to soar high above the Rocky Mountains, at well over 30mph, 200ft above a gushing creek. With six zip lines set up over Alkali Canyon and distances ranging from 150ft to 1000ft long, you'll get plenty of time to work on your primal scream. Easy and exhilarating, the two-hour romp is worth the splurge. It's located in Wolcott, 21 miles west of Vail on I-70.

Vail Valley Paragliding ADVENTURE SPORTS

(☎970-845-7321; www.vailvalleyparagliding.com; per person $185-250) Here's your chance to fly high above the Rocky Mountains. Join one of the tandem flights, which launch in the morning and occasionally in the afternoon. You'll lift off at 8700ft, and if the

MT OF THE HOLY CROSS

Once one of the most famous peaks in the Rockies, Mt of the Holy Cross first caught the nation's attention in 1873, when William Henry Jackson photographed the mountain while accompanying the Hayden Expedition. His photography, along with paintings of the mystical 'snow cross' (a vaguely cross-shaped snowfield on the northeast face) by fellow expedition member Thomas Moran, symbolized the Colorado wilderness to millions of 19th-century Americans. Pilgrimages to view the cross on the northeast face during the late spring and early summer led to the construction of the shelter at the summit of Notch Mountain in 1924.

ADVENTURE RIDGE & EPIC DISCOVERY

The center of family fun throughout the year is Adventure Ridge, at the top of the Eagle Bahn Gondola. Obviously it's all about snow in **winter** (☎970-754-4380; www.vail.com; ⏲10:30am-7pm Tue-Sat, to 4:30pm Sun & Mon), which can mean tubing ($32 per hour), kids' snowmobiling ($25 per hour) and snowbiking ($70 tours, ages 10 and up). Don't miss the **Nature Discovery Center** either, which offers free snowshoe tours daily at 2pm (ages 10 and up). If you don't plan on skiing, you can buy a **scenic lift ticket** (adult/child $30/19) to get up here.

In **summer** (☎970-754-8245; www.vail.com; lift ticket adult/child $26/5, activity prices vary; ⏲10am-6pm, to 9pm Thu-Sat, mid-Jun–Sep), the same area turns into a giant high-altitude playground on steroids: think ropes course, zip lines and climbing wall, as well as mellower activities like pony rides and disc and mini golf. Expect to pay $10 to $20 per activity. You can also explore the mountain trails on foot (free) or mountain bike (lift ticket including bike haul adult/child $31/10).

It's all slated to expand into the much larger eco-park **Epic Discovery** (www.epicdiscovery.com) in 2015, with everything from nature programs to a larger zip-line network and adrenaline-pumping forest coaster.

Access to Adventure Ridge is in Lionshead, but if you plan on hiking or biking in the summer, Gondola One (Vail Village) is also open and included in the lift ticket. The mountain is only open on weekends in September.

winds are cooperative, you might fly as high as 14,000ft. Duration varies, but an hour is common. Dress warmly. It gets cold in heaven.

Vail Golf Club GOLF
(☎888-709-3939; www.vailrec.com; 1778 Vail Valley Dr; 9/18 holes May-Oct $55/90) Hemmed in by Gore Creek and tucked up against the White River National Forest, this 18-hole par-71 course nestled at 8200ft elevation is a fine place to hit a small white ball. Reservations are vital in summer and can be made 60 days in advance. The pro shop can set you up with rentals, lessons and a cart.

Equipment Rental

Bike Valet BICYCLE RENTAL
(☎970-476-5385; www.bikevalet.net; 520 E Lionshead Circle; bike rental per day from $30; ⏲10am-5pm) Bike Valet is one of two independently owned bike shops in Lionshead. Rent cruisers, kids' bikes and mountain bikes and sign up for a shuttle up to Vail Pass ($39, bike included) or the offroad Shrine Pass to Red Cliff trip ($75, bike included). In winter it's **Ski Valet**, offering some of the best discount ski rentals (from $38 per day) on the mountain as well as overnight repairs.

Christy Sports SPORTS RENTALS
(☎970-476-2244; www.christysports.com; 293 Bridge St; bike/ski rental per day from $50/27; ⏲10am-6pm summer, 8am-8pm winter) This Colorado chain has stores at most resorts as well as major cities throughout the state. It rents and sells skis, boards and bikes, along with outdoor clothing and gear. Quality varies with the price.

Troy's Ski Shop SPORTS RENTALS
(☎970-476-8769; 392 Hanson Ranch Rd; ski/bike rental per day from $45/60; ⏲9am-6pm) Independently owned and with friendly staff, Troy's rents high-end, full-suspension mountain bikes in summer and the best skis and boards on the mountain in winter.

Vail Sports SPORTS RENTALS
(☎970-479-0600; www.vailsports.com; Mountain Plaza, 151 Vail Lane; bike/ski rental per day from $39/43; ⏲8am-8pm winter, 10am-7pm summer) Resort-owned and operated, you can usually get solid gear here, though it is pricey – check out www.rentskis.com for discounts. It has bikes in the summer too and a Vail Pass shuttle ($54). Locations throughout the resort, including slopeside in winter.

Alpine Quest Sports OUTDOORS
(☎970-926-3867; www.alpinequestsports.com; 34510 Hwy 6, Edwards; ⏲9am-6pm) This is Vail's top backcountry adventure kayaking resource with gear, rentals and a full kayak school with beginner, intermediate and advanced classes. It also outfits rock- and ice-climbers with gear and tips, and has telemark skis and snowshoes for rent. It's located in Edwards, west of Vail.

Tours

Apex Mountain School OUTDOORS
(☎970-949-9111; www.apexmountainschool.com) This Avon-based outfitter runs local ice climbing and backcountry skiing tours in winter and climbing trips in summer. It also hosts a variety of classes and Wilderness First Responder certification courses.

Paragon Guides OUTDOORS
(☎970-926-5299; www.paragonguides.com) Guides take guests on hut-to-hut ski tours and backcountry skiing day trips in winter, and climbing, mountain biking and mountaineering trips in summer.

Festivals & Events

Vail Film Festival FILM
(☎970-476-1092; www.vailfilmfestival.org; tickets $10; ⊙early Apr) It's not the biggest indie film fest on the block, but it brings plenty of star power. Past attendees include Kevin Smith, Paul Rudd, Olivia Wilde and Harold Ramis. Screenings take place at the Vail Plaza Hotel in Vail Village, and at the Park Hyatt and the Vilar Performing Arts Center, both in Beaver Creek.

Taste of Vail FOOD
(☎970-306-1334; www.tasteofvail.com; festival pass $495; ⊙early Apr) For more than 20 years this gourmet festival has offered some of the best mountain cuisine you can imagine. The main event is the grand tasting and auction, with every Vail restaurant included, but the lamb cook-off and après-ski wine tasting run a close second.

Spring Back to Vail FESTIVAL
(www.vail.com; ⊙mid-Apr) This weekend party officially closes the ski season with a series of free concerts and barbecues. There's always a big act for the Friday night concert – Wyclef Jean and Jimmy Cliff have been past headliners. The annual pond-skimming championships (involving a ski jump and an icy pond) might be the highlight though.

Vail Jazz Festival JAZZ
(☎888-824-5526; www.vailjazz.org; Labor Day concert $55-75; ⊙Jul-Sep) This acclaimed international jazz festival features a series of free outdoor concerts in Lionshead (Thursdays) and at the Vail Farmers Market (Sundays). The festival is anchored by the Labor Day Weekend Party, which is when the big hitters come to town.

Snow Daze MUSIC
(www.vailsnowdaze.com; ⊙early Dec) Held annually in early December, this early season party once marked the official opening of Vail Mountain. Now it's just one of the biggest early season ski-town parties on the continent. Headliners include big acts like Wilco.

Sleeping

Aside from camping, don't expect to find any budget or midrange lodging in Vail. Ski-season rates reach their peak during the Christmas and New Year holidays, but you should expect astronomical prices all winter long. Rates quoted here are for mid-February through March, when the snow is best; January prices are marginally cheaper. For the most part, you're paying for location, and location only: a lot of the lodging is condo style, and for this reason it can be very hit or miss. If you don't need to be in Vail, check out the nearby town of Minturn. Frisco, though further away, is another possible base.

Vail Village

Gore Creek Campground CAMPGROUND $
(☎877-444-6777; www.recreation.gov; Bighorn Rd; tent sites $18; ⊙mid-May–Sep;) This campground at the end of Bighorn Rd has 25 tent sites with picnic tables and fire grates nestled in the woods by Gore Creek. There is excellent fishing near here. Try the Slate Creek or Deluge Lake trails; the latter leads to a fish-packed lake. The campground is 6 miles east of Vail Village via exit 180 (East Vail) off I-70.

★ **The Sebastian** HOTEL $$$
(☎800-354-6908; www.thesebastianvail.com; 16 Vail Rd; r summer/winter from $230/500; P) Deluxe and modern, this sophisticated hotel showcases tasteful contemporary art and an impressive list of amenities, including a mountainside ski valet, luxury spa and adventure concierge. Room rates dip to reasonable in the summer, the perfect time to enjoy the tapas bar and spectacular pool area with hot tubs frothing and spilling over like champagne.

Given the prices in Vail, the Sebastian certainly offers the most bang for your buck, but you'll need to reserve months in advance for the best rates.

Vail Mountain Lodge HOTEL $$$
(☎888-794-0410; www.vailmountainlodge.com; 352 E Meadow Dr; r summer/winter from $259/419;

) With only 20 rooms and seven condos, this is about as boutique as Vail gets. Decor is rustic and simple, but rooms are nonetheless plush, featuring gas fireplaces and featherbeds, heated bathroom floors and deep soaking tubs. The amenities, too, impress: stays include breakfast, free access to the on-site Vail Athletic Club (and all drop-in classes) and indoor and outdoor hot tubs.

The cherry on the cake is the gourmet fave **Terra Bistro** restaurant, located just downstairs.

Mountain Haus CONDO **$$$**
(800-237-0922; www.mountainhaus.com; 292 E Meadow Dr; studios summer/winter from $175/350;) A laid-back spot near the village entrance. Rooms aren't huge but some have fireplaces, king-sized beds, balconies and a view from the upper reaches, and they seem to be relatively up-to-date. It has a hot tub, fitness center, pool and complimentary breakfast. One of the better deals in Vail.

Tivoli Lodge HOTEL **$$$**
(800-451-4756; www.tivolilodge.com; 386 Hanson Ranch Rd; r summer/winter from $220/483;) The only family run lodging in town, this hotel boasts incredibly personable staff and an excellent slopeside location, with hot tubs literally at the base of the mountain. While the room decor is nothing to blog about, all have kitchenettes and exude comfort. Quirky hotel fact: the owners' son, Buddy, won the Indy 500 in 1996. Kids under 12 stay free.

Austria Haus HOTEL **$$$**
(866-921-4050; www.austriahaushotel.com; 242 E Meadow Dr; r summer/winter from $250/483;) One of Vail's longest-running properties, the Austria Haus offers both hotel rooms and condos, so make sure you're clear on what you're signing up for. In the hotel, charming details such as wood-framed doorways, Berber carpet and marble baths make for a pleasant stay. Fuel up at the generous breakfast spread in the morning.

Lodge Tower CONDO **$$$**
(800-654-2517; www.lodgetower.com; 200 Vail Rd; r summer/winter from $185/395;) This tower is packed with privately owned one-, two- and three-bedroom condos, but you can rent studios too (locked-off bedrooms within a condo). Each is decorated in a different style so your furnishings will always be a surprise, though all multi-bedroom units have kitchens and fireplaces. Breakfast is included.

Lionshead

Arrabelle HOTEL **$$$**
(888-688-8055; www.arrabelle.rockresorts.com; 675 Lionshead Pl; r summer/winter from $300/800;) The grand dame of Lionshead, the Arrabelle is a massive chalet-style resort with a stone and marble lobby, top-shelf service and a variety of accommodations, from hotel rooms to four-bedroom luxury condos. All have wi-fi, flatscreen TVs, Bose sound systems, plush linens and marble baths. Call the reservations line for the best available rates or book months in advance for discounts.

Lodge at Lionshead LODGE **$$$**
(800-962-4399; www.lodgeatlionshead.com; 380 E Lionshead Circle; studios summer/winter from $175/455;) Friendly and unpretentious, this lodge offers a wide variety of private condos from studios (with Murphy bed) to four-bedroom luxury units. You'll need to book a minimum three days in summer and five days in winter. The south and east buildings were entirely renovated in 2013.

West Vail

Holiday Inn HOTEL **$$$**
(970-476-2739; www.apexvail.com; 2211 N Frontage Rd; r summer/winter from $155/280;) The Holiday Inn is as budget conscious as Vail gets. Although this is the low-rent side of the tracks, there are still a few perks, including the sauna, hot tub, and even a concrete pond of a pool. Rooms are bland but super clean, service is friendly and there's a fabulous diner next door. The West Vail location is less convenient, however.

Eating

Although Vail lacks the depth and breadth of Denver's restaurant scene, it's nonetheless one of the top spots in Colorado for a gourmet meal. During the summer, a vibrant **farmers market** is held in front of the Solaris complex (E Meadow Dr) on Sundays.

Vail Village

Big Bear Bistro SANDWICHES **$**
(970-306-7280; www.bigbearbistro.com; Hanson Ranch Rd; breakfast/lunch sandwiches from $5.95/8.50; 7am-7pm;) Unless your accommodation includes a morning buffet, this is where you come for breakfast. It serves gourmet coffee, tasty breakfast

burritos and some damn good sandwiches at lunch. We suggest 'the Masterpiece.' It comes with prosciutto, capicola, salami, maple-glazed ham, balsamic-tinged arugula, banana peppers and cracked-pepper aioli.

Loaded Joe's CAFE **$**

(www.loadedjoes.com; 227 Bridge St; breakfast/lunch from $6.50/8; 6:30am-2am;) Almost under the bridge, this low-key underground cafe serves bagels and breakfast burritos, espressos and soy lattes, and sandwiches and smoothies for lunch and dinner. You can sip and munch beneath the cedars as the creek wakes you up with its gentle hum. It does beer and wine too.

La Cantina MEXICAN **$**

(Vail Village Parking Garage, main level; burritos $4.50, dinner combos from $5.95; 11:30am-8pm) Located beneath the Transportation Center and next to the Ski Museum, it should come as no surprise that Vail's cheapest meal has a rather quirky location right at the exit of the parking garage. But no matter – where else are you going to find a salsa bar and passable $5 burritos?

★bōl MODERN AMERICAN **$$**

(970-476-5300; www.bolvail.com; 141 E Meadow Dr; mains $14-28; 5pm-1am, from 2pm in winter;) Half hip eatery, half space-age bowling alley, bōl is hands down the funkiest hangout in Vail. You can take the kids bowling in the back ($50 per hour), but it's the surprisingly eclectic menu that's the real draw: creations range from a filling chicken paillard salad with gnocchi to shrimp and grits with grapefruit. Prices are relatively affordable by Vail standards. Reserve.

Vendetta's ITALIAN **$$**

(970-476-5070; www.vendettasvail.com; 291 Bridge St; pizzas $17-26, mains $19-32; 11am-late;) In overpriced and borderline snooty Vail, this throwback pizza joint wins for aroma, ambience and, well, pizza. It does steaks and chops as well as pasta dishes, but the pies are what hit the spot.

★Matsuhisa JAPANESE **$$$**

(970-476-6628; www.matsuhisavail.com; 141 E Meadow Dr; mains $29-39, 2 pieces sushi $8-12; 6-10pm) Legendary chef Nobu Matsuhisa has upped Vail's culinary standards with this modern, airy space, set at the heart of the Solaris complex. Expect traditional sushi and tempura alongside his signature 'new-style' sashimi – Matsuhisa opened his first restaurant in Peru, and continues to incorporate South American influences into his cuisine. Star dishes include black cod with miso and scallops with jalapeño salsa. Reservations are required.Kelly Liken MODERN AMERICAN **$$$**

(970-479-0175; www.kellyliken.com; 12 Vail Rd, Suite 100; 3-course menu $74; 6-10pm) Celebrity chef Kelly Liken shows off her culinary skills in the lower lobby of the Vail Gateway building. Cooking with seasonal and mostly local ingredients, she creates exquisite dishes such as potato-crusted trout filet, pan-roasted duck served with quinoa pilaf and pickled blackberries, and starters such as elk carpaccio and braised pork cheeks with jalapeño-citrus marmalade.

The only option here is the three-course tasting menu; dessert is extra. Reserve.

Sweet Basil MODERN AMERICAN **$$$**

(970-476-0125; www.sweetbasil-vail.com; 193 Gore Creek Dr; lunch $15-24, dinner $29-45; 11:30am-2:30pm & 6pm-late) In business since 1977, Sweet Basil remains one of Vail's top restaurants. The menu changes seasonally, but the eclectic American fare, which usually includes favorites such as Colorado lamb and seared Rocky Mountain trout, is consistently innovative and excellent. The ambience is also fantastic. Reserve.

Osaki's JAPANESE **$$$**

(970-476-0977; www.osakivail.com; 100 E Meadow Dr; sushi 6/10 pieces $28/55, rolls $5.50-32; 5:30pm-late Tue-Sun) A star disciple of both his grandfather and Nobu Matsuhisa (yes, *that* Matsuhisa), Osaki worked in the Aspen restaurant before opening up this hole-in-the-wall temple, which was long Vail's go-to sushi spot. It retains its intimate (some say crowded) interior, and the sushi is definitely excellent, but there's no doubt the master's high-profile emergence – practically next door – has raised the stakes. Reserve.

Mountain Standard MODERN AMERICAN **$$$**

(970-476-0123; https://mtnstandard.com; 193 Gore Creek Dr; lunch $15-22, dinner $26-39;) A casual spin-off of Sweet Basil (which is located out front), Mountain Standard has a lovely riverside setting that spills out onto the patio in warmer weather. The open kitchen focuses on the grill (rotisserie chicken with heirloom tomatoes, grilled trout with key lime butter), with a raw bar (oyster shooters, tuna crudo) and salads to even it out.

DON'T MISS

DINNER WITH A VIEW

Two of Vail's best restaurants aren't in the village at all, but high up on the mountain, with unrivaled settings and great views.

★**The Tenth** (970-754-1010; www.the10thvail.com; Look Ma Run, Mid Vail; lunch $16-24, dinner $29-39; 9am-2:30pm daily & 3-9pm Tue-Sat Dec–mid-Apr;) And you thought ski lodge fare had to be tasteless frozen burgers and microwaved nachos. No longer: the Tenth ratchets up Vail's ski-in, ski-out dining several notches, with a smorgasbord of gourmet alpine cuisine. Think elk bolognese ziti, pheasant pot pie, and pan-seared cilantro halibut with lobster risotto. Or you could just have a brick-oven pizza.

If you're in a hurry to get back on the slopes, opt for the express menu in the bar area. Alternatively, pop in for small plates and a hot cocktail for après ski. If you're coming for a meal, you'll need to reserve.

Game Creek Restaurant (970-754-4275; www.gamecreekvail.com; Game Creek Bowl; 3/4 courses $85/95; 5:30-8:30pm Thu-Sat, 11am-2pm Sun, late-Jun–Aug, 5:30-9pm Wed-Sat Dec-Apr;) This gourmet destination is nestled high in the spectacular Game Creek Bowl. Take the Eagle Bahn Gondola to Eagle's Nest and staff will shuttle you (via snowcat in the winter) to their lodge-style restaurant, which serves an American-French fusion menu with stars like foie gras, elk steak and succulent leg of lamb. It also serves a mean brunch on Sundays in summer. Reserve.

Lionshead

Moe's Original BBQ BARBECUE $

(www.moesoriginalbbq.com; 616 W Lionshead Circle; plates $10; 11am-9pm) You'll put on some pounds at this blues-driven barbecue chain, but the unpretentious roadhouse vibe is a refreshing change from the rest of the resort. Plates get you one main (smothered in BBQ sauce) and two sides – wash it down with a can of PBR.

El Sabor MEXICAN $$

(http://elsaborvail.com; 660 West Lionshead Pl; mains $10-20; 7:30am-10pm) Located right next to the Eagle Bahn Gondola, El Sabor wins points more for its location than its cuisine. You can find some decent $7 specials (fish tacos, tamale plates) here on weekdays; otherwise, hit happy hour for the best prices.

West Vail

★**Yellowbelly** SOUTHERN $

(www.yellowbellychicken.com; 2161 N Frontage Rd, unit 14; plates $10; 11am-8:30pm;) It may be hidden in West Vail, but man is this fried chicken good. Although we could tout the healthy side of things (non GMO, free-range, veggie-fed birds), it's the dynamite gluten-free batter that earns this place its stars. Spicy, tender pieces of chicken come with two sides (brussel slaw, citrus quinoa, mac and cheese) and a drink; alternatively, order an entire rotisserie bird for the whole gang.

Westside Cafe DINER $$

(970-476-7890; www.westsidecafe.net; 2211 N Frontage Rd; mains $7-13; 7am-10pm;) Set in a West Vail strip mall, this is the most popular breakfast spot in the area among locals. It does terrific all-day breakfast skillets, like the 'My Big Fat Greek Skillet' with scrambled eggs, gyro, red onion, tomato and feta served with warm pita, along with all the usual high-cal offerings you need for a morning on the slopes.

Drinking & Nightlife

Yeti's Grind CAFE

(www.yetisgrind.com; 141 E Meadow Dr, Suite 108; 7am-7pm;) Vail's best coffee comes from this indie cafe on the ground floor of the Solaris complex. Beans are roasted by City on a Hill (p241) in Leadville; the breakfast grub and sandwiches are from bōl. It also serves beer and wine in the evening.

Vail Ale House BAR

(www.vailalehouse.com; 2161 North Frontage Rd; 11am-2am) Another notable West Vail destination, this is really the only local place to sample Colorado's diverse selection of craft beers. Enjoy 20 great picks on tap from Avery (Boulder), Great Divide (Denver), Left Hand (Longmont) and Ska (Durango), among others.

Garfinkels PUB

(www.garfsvail.com; 536 E Lionshead Circle; 10am-late) In Lionshead, this wooden lodge-style pub has a wide deck overlooking Vail Mountain. It also has a pool table, a killer circle bar with Colorado Native on tap and a dozen flatscreens showing all the sports you could want. Saturday night karaoke starts at 9pm, but before you perform, check out the wall of fame. Frank Sinatra has tossed back a couple here.

Los Amigos BAR
(400 Bridge St; ⌚11:30am-9pm) If you want views, tequila, and rock and roll with your après-ski ritual, come to Los Amigos. The Mexican food is decent at best, but the happy-hour prices and slopeside seating more than make up for any culinary shortcomings.

Samana Lounge CLUB
(www.samanalounge.com; 228 Bridge St; cover varies; ⌚9pm-late Tue & Thu-Sun) A basement nightclub in central Vail with frequent live music. It's sax-driven funk to classic-rock cover bands, as well as resident and visiting DJs. The calendar gets especially packed in summer and winter, but it brings live tunes to the Vail people in mud season too.

☆ Entertainment

Cinebistro CINEMA
(☎970-476-3344; www.cobbcinebistro.com; 141 E Meadow Dr; adult/child $15/12; ⌚noon-8pm; 👪) Located in the Solaris complex is Vail's slick contemporary cinema, with three premium theaters outfitted with cushy seats and a flash bar and restaurant serving serious cuisine in the lobby. On the big screens it plays first-rate Hollywood fare.

Ford Amphitheater CONCERT VENUE
(☎970-476-5612; www.vvf.org; 530 S Frontage Rd E) This picturesque outdoor amphitheater with lawn seating is the site of numerous summer concerts, many of which are free. It's a 10-minute walk east of Vail Village.

Shopping

Kemo Sabe CLOTHING
(www.kemosabe.com; 230 Bridge St; ⌚10am-8pm) It would be tough to find a more distinctly Western store in all of resort-land Colorado. It specializes in two things: Stetson hats and Lucchese boots. All are handmade. The boots are crafted from hide and leather, and the hats from rabbit, steer and beaver fur.

Staff will shape your hat and even distress it to make it look like you rode hard and worked hard with it. Listen for the country music and enjoy the hospitality.

Burton SPORTS
(675 Lionshead Pl; ⌚10am-7pm) Burton, arguably America's top snowboard brand, has a flagship store in Lionshead where you can get all the gear and boards you'd ever

THE VAIL DREAM

Long before two WWII vets who were hooked on powder hiked Vail Mountain to scout the possibility of a new ski resort halfway between Denver and Aspen – the only resort of its kind at the time – the Gore Range was home to Colorado's nomadic Ute Indians who used to trek from the arid rangeland into the alpine country to beat the summer heat. However, white settlers thirsty for gold arrived and the Utes didn't last.

During WWII the army founded Camp Hale, a training center off present-day Hwy 24. This is where the famous 10th Mountain Division – America's only battalion on skis – lived and trained. These troops fought hard in the Italian Alps, and when they came home, many became big players in the burgeoning ski industry.

Peter Seibert was one of them. He hooked onto the Aspen Ski Patrol then became the manager of the Loveland Basin Ski Area – one of Colorado's oldest ski resorts. Together with his friend Earl Eaton, who was a lifelong skier and ski-industry veteran, Siebert climbed Vail Mountain in the winter of 1957, and after one long look at those luscious back bowls, these men knew they'd struck gold.

At the time Vail Mountain was owned by the forest service and local ranchers. Seibert and Eaton recruited a series of investors and lawyers and eventually got a permit from the forest service and convinced nearly all of the local ranchers to sell. Much of the construction budget was raised by convincing investors to chip in $10,000 for a condo unit and a lifetime season pass.

Opening day was on December 15, 1962. Conditions were marginal, but the dream was alive. And if you'd skied there that day you would have paid $5 for a day pass and explored nine runs, accessed by two chairs and one gondola.

want. Our advice? Consider raiding the factory clearance sale in the late summer when you'll get at least 50% off last year's boards and gear.

Buzz's Ski Shop SPORTS
(☎970-476-3320; 302 Gore Creek Dr;) In tiny, corporate Vail, a laid-back place like Buzz's feels like a breath of fresh powder. Techs are knowledgeable, prices are among the cheapest on the mountain, the equipment is solid, and it's just a few minutes' walk to the Gondola in Vail Village. It's only open during the winter season; it also does rentals.

Information

Vail has free public wi-fi that, in theory, is accessible throughout the village areas, though connection speeds aren't great. Visitors get one hour of complimentary use.

Vail Visitor Center (☎970-479-1385; www.visitvailvalley.com; 241 S Frontage Rd; ⌚8:30am-5:30pm winter, to 8pm summer;) Provides maps, last-minute lodging deals and activities, and town information. It's located next to the Transportation Center. The visitor center also has a Lionshead office located at the entrance to the parking garage.

Vail Valley Medical Center (☎970-476-2451; www.vvmc.com; 181 W Meadow Dr; ⌚24hr;) Vail Valley's top hospital. It has an emergency room and is centrally located between Lionshead and Vail Village on W Meadow Dr. Provides 24-hour emergency care.

Getting There & Away

If you're driving here, note that the I-70 exits are as follows: Vail Village and Lionshead (exit 176) and West Vail (exit 173). The villages are traffic free; all drivers must park at the **Vail Village Parking Garage** ($25 per day winter, free first two hours and in summer) before entering the pedestrian mall area near the chairlifts. Lionshead is a secondary parking lot (same rates) about half a mile to the west.

To get to Breckenridge and other Summit County resorts, take the Fresh Tracks shuttle (p193).

Colorado Mountain Express (☎800-525-6363; www.coloradomountainexpress.com;) Colorado Mountain Express shuttles to/from Denver International Airport ($92, three hours) and Eagle County Airport ($51, 40 minutes).

Eagle County Airport (☎970-328-2680; www.flyvail.com; 219 Eldon Wilson Dr) This airport is 35 miles west of Vail and has services to destinations across the country (many of which fly through Denver) and rental-car counters.

High Mountain Taxi (☎970-524-5555; www.hmtaxi.com; airport $142; ⌚24hr) Vail's signature taxi service serves the entire valley from Vail to Eagle, and is equipped for pets, kids, skis and snowboards. The airport service seats six people. Book online or call.

Summit Express (☎855-686-8267; www.summitexpress.com; adult/child $84/42) Shuttles to/from Denver International Airport (three hours).

Vail Transportation Center (☎970-476-5137; 241 S Frontage Rd) Greyhound buses (☎800-231-2222; www.greyhound.com) stop at the Vail Transportation Center en route to Denver ($33, 2½ hours). This station also serves regional buses.

Getting Around

Vail has fine public transportation: it's free, it goes where you need to go and operates at short intervals. Traveling by bus is thus faster and more convenient than most car trips.

Eagle County Regional Transportation Authority (www.eaglecounty.us; per ride $4, to Leadville $7) ECO buses offers affordable transport to Beaver Creek, Minturn and even Leadville. Buses run from roughly 5am to 11pm, but check the website for the exact schedule. Buses leave from the Vail Transportation Center.

Vail Transit (www.vailgov.com; ⌚6:30am-1:50am) Serves the local golf course and loops through all the Vail resort areas – West Vail (both North and South), Vail Village, Lionshead and East Vail, as well as Ford Park and Sandstone. Most have bike and ski racks and all are free.

Minturn

POP 1023 / ELEV 7861FT

Squeezed between the burgeoning luxury condominium and resort developments of Vail and Beaver Creek, Minturn is a wonderful respite in Eagle County. This small railroad town along the Eagle River was founded in 1887 and its shops and homes retain the coziness and charm of a place that really has been around for a while. If you prefer real town ambience over faux Tyrolean architecture and fur coats, Minturn makes an excellent base.

Activities

Minturn and Red Cliff (located about 10 miles further south on US 24) are gateways to the **Holy Cross Wilderness Area**, where you'll find some of the most spectacular hiking in the region. Anyone heading up here should first check in with the Holy Cross Ranger Office. Do not head into the wilderness area without the proper information and appropriate equipment.

Given that the Eagle River runs right through town, it should come as no surprise that the fishing in and around town is pretty good. Though the fish are bigger downstream, the higher-altitude fishing is just tremendous and a terrific year-round activity. The fish are easier to find and the scenery absolutely stunning in winter.

Notch Mountain Trail HIKING

(Tigiwon Rd; ⏲Jun 21-Oct) This strenuous hike climbs over 2700ft to Notch Mountain (13,077ft), leaving many gasping for air. It's a 10.2-mile round trip that can be done in five to seven hours, but you'll be rewarded with sublime views of the Bowl of Tears and the snowy cross on Mt of the Holy Cross (through mid-July) to the west.

To get here, take the turnoff to Tigiwon Rd (USFS Rd 707, opens June 21), 3 miles south of Minturn. A high-clearance vehicle is recommended for the rough 8-mile journey to the Fall Creek Trailhead.

Half Moon Pass Trail HIKING

(Tigiwon Rd; ⏲Jun 21-Oct) The classic ascent of Mt of the Holy Cross (14,005ft), this 10.8-mile round-trip hike is best done as an overnight if you plan on making the summit, but you can also simply hike up to Half Moon Pass (1.5 miles) for a short day hike (you won't see the cross from here though). Over a dozen campsites are located 2.8 miles in.

Note that this mountain involves class 2 scrambling; it's for experienced hikers only and a compass and topo map are highly recommended – coming down can be tricky. Access is the same as for Notch Mt, but you begin at the Half Moon Trailhead.

Mountain Anglers FISHING

(☎970-827-9500; www.mountainanglers.com; 102 Main St; half-day wade trips from $285) Guides newbies along Gore Creek and the Upper Eagle River. It offers free lessons outside the Solaris in Vail Village from 9am to noon daily (May to October), rental equipment and also runs fishing camps for kids.

Sleeping & Eating

Half Moon Campground (Tigiwon Rd; tent sites $10; ⏲Jun 21-Oct) at the base of the Half Moon Pass Trail is one of several first-come, first-served campgrounds in the region. There are also five backcountry huts (p223).

★**Minturn Inn** B&B $$

(☎970-827-9647; www.minturninn.com; 442 Main St; r summer/winter from $100/150; P 📶) If you don't need to be at the heart of the action in Vail, the rustic Minturn Inn should be your pick. Set in a 1915 log-hewn building in Minturn, this cozy B&B turns on the mountain charm with handcrafted log beds, river rock fireplaces and antlered decor. Reserve one of the newer River Lodge rooms for private Jacuzzi access.

Kirby Cosmo's BARBECUE $

(www.kirbycosmos.com; 474 Main St; sandwiches $7-10.50; ⏲11:30am-9pm Mon-Fri, 3-9pm Sat & Sun; P 📶 👪) This casual Carolina BBQ spot is located at (fittingly) the south end of town, toward Leadville. It's the best choice

THE MINTURN MILE

If you're itching to head off the grid, consider the Minturn Mile. One of the most famous 'out-of-bounds' ski runs in the world, you can access it from the top of chairs 3 or 7 on Vail Mountain.

At the top of the turn on Lost Boy, stay left and hike up to Ptarmigan Ridge. Here you can take the access gate and begin a descent of 3 miles to Minturn. Advanced skills are a must as you'll encounter a wide range of terrain – starting in a bowl and veering through the trees. At about the midway point you'll find the 'beaver ponds,' a terrific place to take a break and catch your breath before hitting the Luge, an old fire road that gets narrow in spots and will lead you the rest of the way down.

Know that you'll be skiing into an area beyond the resort boundaries; it is not patrolled. If you get injured, you'll be on your own, and if you require rescue it will come at considerable expense. It's best to ski along with someone who has prior knowledge of the terrain and route, and be sure to have proper gear, equipment and an updated report on conditions (if you go too early in the season the thin coverage could be a nightmare). Of course, it is, by all accounts, a magnificent experience – one of the best in the Vail swirl – and requires a toast at the Minturn Saloon upon arrival.

for a tasty affordable meal, with stalwarts like pulled pork sandwiches, jalapeño poppers, short ribs and buffalo burgers. There are also a couple of Colorado beers on tap at the pinewood bar – need we say more?

Minturn Saloon MEXICAN **$$$**
(☎970-827-5954; www.minturnsaloon.com; 146 Main St; mains $17-37; ⏲3:30-10pm; P 👪) Sit by the crackling fireplace and knock back margaritas with everyone else who came down the Minturn Mile, then mosey through the swinging doors for dynamite Mexican in the dining room. Arguably the best après-ski in Vail. It posts regular updates of Minturn Mile conditions on its Facebook page.

Information

Holy Cross Ranger Office (☎970-827-5715; www.fs.usda.gov/whiteriver; 24747 Hwy 24; ⏲9am-4pm Mon-Fri) Info on camping and hiking in the Holy Cross wilderness. The office is 1 mile north of Minturn, shortly after you exit I-70.

Getting There & Away

Minturn is 8 miles southwest of Vail on Hwy 24 (I-70 exit 171). ECO buses (p205) connect with Vail; check the schedule online or pick up info at the Vail Transportation Center.

Beaver Creek

ELEV 8100FT

Breach the regal gates in Avon, 9 miles west of Vail just off I-70 (exit 167), and you'll emerge onto a private mountain road skirting a picturesque golf course as it climbs to the foot of a truly spectacular ski mountain. Beaver Creek feels like one of those delicious secrets shared among the rich kids, and it is indeed a privilege to ski here.

Today the perfectly maintained grounds and neo-Tyrolean buildings lend a certain looming grandeur, as do names like Park Hyatt, set in the main village, and Ritz Carlton, in nearby Bachelor Gulch. Beaver Creek is a mellower, more conservative place than Vail and typically an older scene. It's the kind of destination where grandparents bring the whole family to enjoy a slew of all-natural adventures.

Activities

Beaver Creek Mountain SNOW SPORTS
(☎800-226-0355; www.beavercreek.com; Village Rd; adult/child $129/89; ⏲9am-4:30pm) Beaver Creek isn't exactly a ghost town in the summer, but it's no secret that the winter rules. The mountain boasts a 4040ft vertical rise serviced by 16 lifts, including 10 high-speed quad chairs. There are 149 trails and a wide variety of ski terrain for all abilities.

Beginners like it in Beaver Creek because the mountain is literally turned upside down, with beginner runs at the top so they can enjoy the same spectacular mountain views. Intermediate skiers have fewer options, but the Coyote Glades and blue-cruiser Arrowhead Mountain are both good choices, as are Redtail and Harrier on the main mountain.

Experts will head to the double black diamonds at Royal Elk Glades and Bald Eagle off the Grouse Mountain Express lift – the runs are every bit as challenging as anything at Vail. Golden Eagle, the site of the Birds of Prey Men's World Cup Downhill course, gives you the chance to try out a competition-class downhill run, while the Stone Creek Chutes spike the adrenaline.

The three terrain parks – 101 (beginners), Zoom Room (intermediate) and the Rodeo (prograde with massive jumps and a half-pipe) – keep extremists happy.

Red Sky Golf Club GOLF
(☎866-873-3759; www.redskyranch.com; 376 Red Sky Rd; 18 holes $250; ⏲6:45am-7:30pm Wed-Mon, noon-7:30pm Tue Jun–mid-Sep, shorter hours May) Thirty-six holes of award-winning Tom Fazio and Greg Norman–designed fairway nirvana is available to guests of all Beaver Creek resorts and a handful of Vail lodges too. The courses are separated by a massive ridge, which, according to the Red Sky folks, serves as a wildlife corridor for deer and elk.

Golf typically being an eco-unfriendly pursuit, it's nice to know that the club transplanted or revegetated more than 25,000 native plants during the construction of the Tom Fazio golf course alone. It also applied more than the usual amount of sod to reduce, but not eliminate, fertilizers. Golf doesn't get much greener and the views are seldom finer from the tee.

Beaver Creek Summer Adventure Center OUTDOORS
(☎970-754-5373; www.beavercreek.com; Starbucks Plaza; guided hikes per person from $50; ⏲9am-4pm mid-Jun–Sep) Set on Starbucks Plaza in the village, this resort-owned concessionaire arranges 4WD tours, bike rental, and horseback rides, but it's best known for

guided hikes to some of the area's most historic mountains and 14,000ft peaks.

McCoy Park Nordic Center SNOW SPORTS
(☎970-754-5313; www.beavercreek.com; Beaver Creek Village; adult/child $30/19; ⏲8:45am-4pm mid-Dec–Mar) McCoy Park is a 20-mile playground for snowshoers and cross-country and skate skiers, where groomed and rustic trails cross pine forests, aspen groves and open glades. Nestled between Beaver Creek and Bachelor Gulch, it has terrific views of three mountain ranges.

Sleeping & Eating

Figure on an extra $50 to $100 on top of the room rate for the resort fee, valet parking and taxes. For last-minute reservations, call **Beaver Creek Reservations** (☎800-953-0844).

★Westin Riverfront Resort & Spa RESORT $$$
(☎970-790-6000; www.starwoodhotels.com; 126 Riverfront Lane; d summer/winter from $220/439; P❄📶≋👪🐾) Perched on the Eagle River, this Avon-based resort is connected by both gondola and public shuttle to nearby Beaver Creek. There's a lovely modern mountain-lodge motif in the lobby accentuated by soaring ceilings and floor-to-ceiling windows with epic mountain views, and it's arguably the most stylish choice in the area.

Rooms are likewise tastefully indulgent with wood floors in the foyer, a sitting area, a flatscreen above the fireplace, a kitchenette (in some), king beds and fabulous views. It rents multi-room condos too. The sole detractor is that it's not slopeside.

Ritz Carlton RESORT $$$
(☎970-748-6200; www.ritzcarlton.com; 130 Daybreak Ridge; d summer/winter from $350/900; P❄📶≋👪🐾) Previously listed as a top Colorado resort by *Travel & Leisure,* included on Condé Nast's gold list, lauded for family and pet friendliness and a prized wedding destination, Ritz Carlton, it's fair to say, won't disappoint. It's all about skiing in and out of luxury here and it's as grand and secluded as a 220-room hotel can be.

It's located in Bachelor Gulch, west of Beaver Creek Village.

Park Hyatt RESORT $$$
(☎970-949-1234; www.beavercreek.hyatt.com; 136 East Thomas Pl; d summer/winter $250/1200; P❄📶≋👪🐾) Definitely the star of Beaver Creek Village, this splashy hotel spills out to the foot of the mountain, practically kissing the Buckaroo Express gondola. Rooms don't quite match the location's pizzazz, but they are plush with French windows and a private terrace; everything was fully renovated in late 2013.

The outdoor pool and fire pits are tucked into a little gulch at the top of the village.

★Beano's Cabin MODERN AMERICAN $$$
(☎970-754-3463; www.beanoscabinbeavercreek.com; 5 courses per person $112; ⏲5-10pm Dec-Apr, 5-10pm Thu-Sun Jun-Sep; 🍸👪) Beaver Creek's can't-miss destination restaurant involves a 20-minute open-air sleigh ride through the snowy night to a glowing cabin on the slopes, warm from a crackling fire and with a kitchen turning out Colorado classics such as Colorado rack of lamb and almond-crusted trout. In summer, you have the option of arriving via wagon ride or a one-hour horseback trip.

Dusty Boot PUB FOOD $$$
(☎970-748-1146; www.dustyboot.com; St James Pl; lunch $11-13, dinner $18-34; ⏲11am-11pm; 🍸👪) This friendly saloon keeps it real. This food may not be for health nuts, but it's damn tasty. The burgers (including veggie burgers), handcut steaks and shaved prime-run sandwiches are all recommended. And the regulars here? All locals.

Getting There & Around

The transport options in Beaver Creek mirror those in Vail. Most folks fly to Denver International Airport and either rent a car or hop on a shuttle (p205) to Beaver Creek. Major carriers also fly into Eagle County Airport (p205).

The Beaver Creek Resort operates a useful and free private shuttle, and Avon's transit department operates a free Gondola Express shuttle for those coming up to ski for the day. Eagle County Regional Transportation Authority operates ECO buses (p205) that link Avon with Vail and Eagle. If you need a cab, High Mountain Taxi (p205) serves Beaver Creek and the Vail Valley. If you're up for the day, the daily parking fee is $33.

ASPEN & THE MAROON BELLS

Located at the south end of the Roaring Fork Valley, Aspen is Colorado at its most sublime (the scenery) and glamorous (the people). Although you can get here over Independence Pass in summer, for most of the year the town is hemmed in by the towering Sawatch Range and the rugged Elk Mountains, with the only access via Hwy 82, south from I-70. Glenwood Springs, at the north end, is commonly referred to as 'down valley,' while Aspen is considered to be 'up valley.'

Glenwood Springs

POP 9594 / ELEV 5763FT

Let's start with the fun stuff. Doc Holliday – gunfighter, gambler, Wild West legend and, uh, dentist – died here. Why he died here is the first clue to Glenwood Springs' long-standing appeal to travelers: thermal hot springs. In Holliday's day they were thought to have restorative powers; he hoped they'd ease chronic respiratory ailments.

Perched at the confluence of the Colorado and Roaring Fork Rivers at the end of gorgeous Glenwood Canyon, these hot springs have been a travel destination for centuries. Ute Indians sat in steamy thermal caves, then called *yampah* (Great Medicine). A mild climate and a range of summer and winter activities have rounded out the city's appeal, but the springs and large outdoor pools remain the town's primary draw. Glenwood Springs also represents an inexpensive down-valley winter alternative to Aspen and Vail – it's only one hour from each, which makes it a reasonable budget base for some of Colorado's best skiing.

Since 1896, Grand Ave, which extends due south from the river and now doubles as Hwy 82, has crossed the Colorado River and formed the main business street. The resort spa and pool are north of the river, reached by a highway and pedestrian/bicycle bridge.

Sights

Glenwood Caverns Adventure Park AMUSEMENT PARK, CAVE

(970-945-4228; http://glenwoodcaverns.com; 51000 Two Rivers Plaza Rd; amusement park adult/child $48/43, tram & cave tour adult/child $25/20; 9am-9pm with seasonal variations;) This family oriented destination lumps together several attractions at once: the **Fairy Caves** (once billed as the eighth wonder of the world), a full-on amusement park, and a tram ride 1300ft up to the top of **Iron Mountain**. The regular cave tour is probably the main attraction here: this is the largest cave in Colorado open to the public.

The Wild Tour ($60) of the caves is a heart-racing experience for would-be spelunkers, allowing guests to crawl through narrow passages, but our favorite ride is the canyon swing, which sends folks squealing 1300ft in the air above the Colorado River at 50mph. There are also several roller coasters, a zip line and Wild West laser tag.

Linwood Cemetery CEMETERY

(Pioneer Cemetery; cnr 12th St & Bennett Ave) Established in 1886, this is where John Henry 'Doc' Holliday was allegedly laid to rest in November 1887 (debate about this persists, since some scholars claim the ground would have been frozen). Harvey 'Kid Curry' Logan, a member of Butch Cassidy and the Sundance Kid's gang, is also here. It's a half-mile hike uphill from 12th and Bennett.

Every year in October there's a guided cemetery **ghost walk**, which can be arranged through the Frontier Historical Museum.

Frontier Historical Museum MUSEUM

(www.glenwoodhistory.com; 1001 Colorado Ave; adult/child $4/2; 10am-4pm Mon-Sat May-Sep,

DOC HOLLIDAY'S LAST LABORED BREATH

It's appropriate that the hike to the purple headstone at Linwood Cemetery might leave you breathless: the life of the legendary man underfoot was shaped by labored breathing. Seeking relief for tuberculosis (then known as consumption) Doc Holliday moved west from his native Georgia. He set up a dental practice in Texas, but the wheezing scared away patients, turning Holliday to gambling. While gambling in the saloons of the West, Holliday met Wyatt Earp, with whom he participated in the most famous shoot-out of Western lore at the OK Corral.

Biographers paint Holliday as a hot-tempered vagabond with a rapacious, caustic wit evident even in his last moments. Lying infirm in a hotel on the site of the current Hotel Colorado he gazed bemusedly at his bare feet and said, 'Well I'll be damned. This is funny.' No legendary gunfighter expects to die with his boots off. Holliday's exact place of burial is unknown; the records were lost when the cemetery was moved from an earlier location down the hill.

shorter hours rest of year) Tucked into a quiet, leafy neighborhood, this community museum has an excellent collection of historic photos and old maps. The staff are history buffs: they host the annual Linwood Cemetery Ghost Walk.

Activities

The visitor center (p213) has a town map that also details all the nearby hiking and cycling trails. For more in-depth information, stop by the USFS Ranger Office (p213).

Hot Springs

★Glenwood Hot Springs & Spa of the Rockies HOT SPRING
(☎970-947-2955; www.hotspringspool.com; 401 N River St; adult/child $19.25/11.75, lower rates off peak; ⏲7:30am-10pm late Jun-Aug, from 9am Sep-May; 📶) Glenwood Springs' main attraction, these hot springs pump out 3.5 million gallons of mineral water a day, which flow through two main pools, the 400ft-long big pool (90°F; 32°C) and the 100ft-long small pool (104°F; 40°C). It's been operating as a resort for over 125 years now, so there are plenty of other additional amenities, namely a spa, hotel, waterslides and golf.

The full-service spa is one of the nicest in the state, with a suite of offerings – massage tables, tubs to soak in (the guys' tub comes with a flatscreen ESPN overhead) and exercise equipment.

Yampah Spa HOT SPRING
(☎970-945-0667; www.yampahspa.com; 709 E 6th St; admission incl towel rental $12; ⏲9am-9pm) Entering these caves feels like descending into one of Dante's layers of hell, at least in terms of temperature. It's hot – damn hot (110°F to be exact; 43°C). First developed by the Ute hundreds of years earlier for therapeutic purposes, mineral-rich hot spring waters run along the cave floors at a temperature of 125°F (52°C), filling the interior with hot steam.

The natural caves have been a commercial facility since the 1880s, and though they've been widened and slightly remodeled in the years since, they still have a primeval feel. Additional spa treatments are available.

Rafting

Spring snowmelt reaches its peak in May and early June, when the roaring Colorado River offers tons of class 3 to 4 white water. It may not be the legendary rapids of the Grand Canyon that await much further downstream, but this section of the river still offers plenty of fun (and is easier to book a trip on).

Most trips depart from east of town, on the stretch below the Shoshone Dam. Families with young children can take shorter float trips at the Grizzly Creek turnoff from I-70, or travel the Colorado River later in the summer, during low flow. Children must weigh 50lb for class 3 and 30lb for class 2. Some companies listed here also offer trips down the Roaring Fork River during the peak run-off.

Up Tha Creek RAFTING
(☎970-947-0030; www.upthacreek.com; 309 9th St; adult/child $49/42; ⏲May-Aug) This smaller outfit has some unusual trips in its lineup, including beginner trips on less-crowded sections of the Colorado (South Canyon and Little Gore), as well as the extreme class 5 Gore Canyon. It also runs several sections of the Roaring Fork and even the Crystal River near Aspen. Definitely worth looking into if you want something different.

Rock Gardens Rafting RAFTING
(☎800-958-6737; www.rockgardens.com; 1308 County Rd 129, exit 119 off I-70; half-day adult/child from $52/42; ⏲May-Aug) Another reputable company in Glenwood Springs, this operator runs half- and full-day adventures on the Shoshone section of the Colorado River. It also rents out inflatable kayaks and offers combo raft and bike/zip line packages.

Blue Sky Adventures RAFTING
(☎877-945-6605; www.blueskyadventure.com; 319 6th St; half-day adult/child $47/35; ⏲May-Aug) One of the most established rafting companies in town, Blue Sky operates both half- and full-day trips through the Shoshone rapids on the Colorado River. Those who don't have a thirst for white water can try out one of the scenic float trips. Inflatable kayaks ($30) are available as well.

Cycling

Rolling over the smoothly paved **Glenwood Canyon Trail**, under the gorgeous canyon walls, makes an excellent afternoon for riders of all abilities. The path follows the Colorado River upstream below the cantilevered I-70, and the river often drowns out the roar of traffic. It's about 18 miles from the Yampah Vapor Caves to Dotsero at the other end of the canyon, but a good midway destination is the Hanging Lake trailhead, roughly 10 miles up the canyon. Another popular ride is along the 42-mile rail-to-trail Rio Grande (p220), which follows the Roaring Fork River all the way to Aspen.

Sunlight Ski & Bike Shop SPORTS RENTALS
(970-945-9425; www.sunlightmtn.com; 309 9th St; adult bicycles per hr/day $7/22; 9am-7pm) In summer, this downtown shop rents standard bikes, tandems, mountain bikes and a selection of children's bikes. It also runs a shuttle ($34) to Bair Ranch and Hanging Lake to let you pedal back. In winter, it has all the snow gear you need.

Canyon Bikes BICYCLE RENTAL
(800-439-3043; www.canyonbikes.com; 319 6th St; half-day rental per adult/child $19/15; 8am-8pm Jun-Aug) The paved 16-mile biking, hiking and in-line skating trail through Glenwood Canyon starts one block from this downtown bike shop. It's a great option for families too, as it operates a shuttle (adult/child $39/28, includes bike) to save you the work of pedaling uphill.

Hiking

The relatively low elevations around Glenwood Springs means that there are no alpine trails above treeline, but many are very scenic and easily accessible. Numerous trails head north from Glenwood Canyon, including the 1.2-mile **Hanging Lake Trail**, which leads to a breathtaking waterfall-fed pond perched in a rock bowl on the canyon wall. It's a strenuous 1½- to three-hour round-trip with a 1020ft elevation gain, but well worth the huffing and puffing. Keep a sharp lookout for bighorn sheep in Glenwood Canyon. If coming from Glenwood, take exit 125 off I-70 8 miles east of town. If coming from the east (Vail), you'll need to get off at exit 121 and turn around, as access is only on the eastbound side. The parking lot often fills up after 10am in summer, so arrive early or consider biking Canyon Trail up to the trailhead (10 miles) instead.

The 3.5-mile **Grizzly Creek Trail** is another popular hike that gets out of the main canyon, though it's a tougher hike than Hanging Lake. It's about 4 miles up the canyon from Glenwood Springs (exit 121).

Other Activities

Roaring Fork Anglers FISHING
(800-781-8120; www.roaringforkanglers.com; 2205 Grand Ave; half-day wade trips from $250; 8:30am-5:30pm) This full-service fly shop has been operating on the local rivers for 30 years. In addition to guided half- and full-day trips, it also offers two-hour lessons for $120 and up-to-date river reports.

Adventure Company ROCKCLIMBING
(970-945-7529; www.glenwoodadventure.com; 723 Cooper Ave; half-day climb $75) Half- and full-day climbing trips in Glenwood Canyon and beyond.

Festivals & Events

Strawberry Days FOOD
(970-945-6589; www.strawberrydaysfestival.com; Grand Ave & Hyland Park; mid-Jun) This annual carnival is one of the longest-running town festivals in Colorado.

Sleeping

Glenwood Springs Hostel HOSTEL $
(970-945-8545; www.hostelcolorado.com; 1021 Grand Ave; dm $20, r $30;) This hostel hasn't been renovated in ages and hence rooms here are cramped and run down. But if you need to save your nickels and dimes, it's the best deal you'll find in the Aspen area. The common spaces have some character, but the clientele is much more long-term residents than fellow travelers.

Private rooms are also furnished with bunk beds – don't expect a queen-sized bed. There are lockers beneath the bunks, so bring your own lock.

★**Sunlight Mountain Inn** LODGE $$
(970-945-5225; www.sunlightinn.com; 10252 County Rd 117; d $90-149;) A stone's throw from Sunlight Mountain Resort's ski area, this adorable mountain lodge has 20 Western-style rooms with quilted beds and fireplaces, and guests who congregate by the inviting fire. Somehow, the hustle of the outside world doesn't make it through the door – there are no TVs and no cell-phone reception, and when it's blanketed by snow, it achieves a languid coziness.

The comfortable dining room is open for dinner in winter, and serves breakfast all year round; there's also a bar to warm up with 'corrected' coffee after a day on the slopes. For a romantic ski getaway, this choice is excellent value and feels like a well-kept secret.

Hotel Colorado HOTEL $$
(800-544-3998; www.hotelcolorado.com; 526 Pine St; d $149;) Understandably nicknamed the 'Grand Dame,' this imposing

DOWN-VALLEY SKIING

Serious skiers head up-valley to Aspen or east on I-70 to Vail. But **Sunlight Mountain Resort** (☎800-445-7931; www.sunlightmtn.com; 10901 County Rd 117; adult/child $57/45; 9am-4pm), 12 miles south of Glenwood Springs on Garfield County Rd 117, survives by offering good deals to families and intermediate skiers. The cross-country ski area features 18 miles of groomed track and snow-skating trails, plus snowshoeing and ice-skating areas. Equipment and rentals are available at the mountain or in town at Sunlight Ski & Bike Shop (p211). In the summer, check out the horseback riding (one hour $50) and cycling activities. A shuttle (one way $5) serves Glenwood Springs; call for the latest schedule.

19th-century hotel has rooms that have seen better days, but the ghosts of its past residents (presidents and gangsters, heiresses and gunmen) make for a remarkably unique stay.

Both Howard Taft and Teddy Roosevelt were guests, but the rooms today don't match the hotel's former presidential glory. Ask to see a couple before dropping the suitcase, because they vary in size. Note there's no air-con in summer.

Glenwood Hot Springs HOTEL $$
(☎800-537-7946; www.hotspringspool.com; 415 East 6th St; r from $189;) The obvious choice if you're coming here specifically for the hot springs, the on-site hotel is as luxurious as Glenwood gets. Rooms are generic but quite comfortable. All packages include pool access and a full breakfast. Book in advance.

Eating & Drinking

If you're exploring on foot and get hungry, make for 7th St off Grand Ave – it has the highest concentration and greatest range of restaurants.

Bluebird Cafe CAFE $
(☎970-384-2024; 730 Grand Ave; sandwiches $8-9; 7am-7pm, to 6pm winter;) This organic coffee shop serves up veggie breakfast burritos and a decent lunch menu of simple sandwiches and homemade soup. Folk bands occasionally pop up outside the front window and in the summer there's breezy outdoor seating.

Taqueria El Nopal MEXICAN $
(2902 Hwy 82; tacos from $1.95, plates $9.50-15; 10am-9pm Tue-Sun;) With Salvadorian *pupusas* (thick stuffed tortillas) and a fantastic variety of tacos (from cactus to *carne asada,* skirt steak), the offerings here go well beyond the usual Col-Mex fare. There are also seafood specials and various plates (*pollo asado,* roast chicken), but it's the freshly made tortillas that seal the deal. It's located on Hwy 82 at the southern edge of town, just past 29th St.

★ **Pullman** AMERICAN $$
(☎970-230-9234; www.thepullmangws.com; 330 7th St; lunch $8-12, dinner $13-20; lunch & dinner;) This casual industrial space is easily Glenwood Springs' hippest hangout, with bare filament bulbs hanging over the tables and an open kitchen in the back. Dishes tend to have a creative twist, landing somewhere between modern American (wheat berry tabouli with cranberries and chevre) and upmarket Italian (gnocchi salad, sweet potato agnolotti).

Juicy Lucy's Steakhouse STEAK $$$
(☎970-945-4619; www.juicylucyssteakhouse.com; 308 7th St; lunch from $9.75, dinner mains from $19.75-36.50; 11am-9:30pm Mon-Thu, to 10pm Fri & Sat) Despite the cornball name, people love Lucy's because staff cook the meat perfectly and eschew the mannish brass-fitted steakhouse posture for a small-town-cafe feel. It serves game and fish dishes and has a good wine list, but the side of cheesy au gratin potatoes nearly steals the show.

Glenwood Canyon Brewing Company BREWERY
(☎970-945-1276; www.glenwoodcanyon.com; 402 7th St; 11am-11pm Mon-Thu, to midnight Fri & Sat) You'll do better to eat elsewhere, but the beers here are fresh and the night scene is lively. The lighter beers on the spectrum – particularly the Hanging Creek Honey Ale and Red Mountain ESB – are the best, though the fresh root beer is truly outstanding.

Information

USFS Ranger Office (970-319-2670; www.fs.usda.gov; 802 Grand Ave; 8am-4:30pm Mon-Fri) Information about camping and hiking in the surrounding White River National Forest.

Visitor Center (970-945-6589; www.visitglenwood.com; 802 Grand Ave; 8am-5pm Mon-Fri year-round, 9am-1pm Sat & Sun Jun-Sep) Assists with booking rooms and activities.

Getting There & Away

Glenwood Springs is 159 miles west of Denver and 90 miles east of Grand Junction along I-70.

Amtrak (970-945-9563; www.amtrak.com; 413 7th St) Amtrak's *California Zephyr* stops daily at the Glenwood Springs Amtrak Station. Trips to and from Denver ($54, 5¾ hours) happen once daily.

Greyhound (800-231-2222; www.greyhound.com; 124 W 6th St) The Ramada serves as the unmanned Greyhound station in Glenwood Springs, with service along I-70 to Denver ($44, 3½ hours).

Getting Around

Colorado Mountain Express (800-525-6363; www.coloradomountainexpress.com; adult/child $118/61;) Shuttle service to/from Denver International Airport (four hours) and Eagle and Aspen airports.

Roaring Forks Transit Authority (970-384-4984; www.rfta.com) With several lines, this network of public transportation serves the Roaring Fork Valley, from Glenwood Springs ($1 in town) to Aspen ($7). It operates several shuttles to the ski areas in the winter.

Carbondale

POP 5196 / ELEV 6181FT

Dominated by the magnificent twin-peaked Mt Sopris (12,965ft) rising up from the valley floor, Carbondale is without a doubt the most charismatic spot to cool your engine when traveling the Roaring Fork Valley. A historic settlement with an artsy, earthy community, it provides a refreshing counterpoint to the glitz and upmarket leanings of Aspen. It's hardly your typical American town, but Main St is still the place to be: take a wander to find excellent restaurants, a good selection of consignment stores and a handful of bars. Check the **town website** (www.carbondale.com) for upcoming events, and be sure to tune in to funky local radio station KDNK (88.1FM).

Festivals

5Point Film Festival FILM

(http://5pointfilm.org; late Apr) Held annually, Carbondale's film festival has gradually acquired a name for itself as the Sundance of adventure cinema. Sponsored by Patagonia, films aren't of the testosterone-driven 'look-at-me' variety, but instead explore inspiration and transformation as experienced in the great outdoors.

Sleeping

Ambiance Inn B&B $

(800-350-1515; www.ambianceinn.com; 66 N 2nd St; r $90-145;) This welcoming B&B has four personalized rooms, a nice common area (the upstairs New Orleans Library) and overall is an excellent mid-valley option. Relatively inexpensive but plenty comfortable, it's a pleasant alternative to staying in Aspen.

Eating & Drinking

Phat Thai THAI $$

(970-963-7001; www.phatthai.com; 343 Main St; mains $11-16; 5-10pm Mon-Sat;) It may not be Chiang Mai, but you're not going to find any naysayers here. Great food and cool decor – exposed brick walls, curvy counter seating – make this a very hip spot, and it gets busy every night of the week. Expect Thai classics, Vietnamese and Malaysian specialties, and a few native Colorado twists for the locavores.

Town. MODERN AMERICAN $$

(970-963-6328; www.towncarbondale.com; 348 Main St; lunch $8-14, dinner $12-20; bakery 7am-4pm Mon-Sat, restaurant 11am-10pm Mon-Sat, 10am-10pm Sun;) The most recent venture by Mark Fischer, the man behind the Pullman and Phat Thai, is this bakery/gastro cafe. Whether you're after fresh bagels and coffee, small plates (crisp pork with watermelon, lamb meatballs), pasta (burrata ravioli) or more daring dinner specials (butternut squash enchiladas), the latest gourmet fixture in the down-valley dining scene certainly merits a stop.

Sunday three-course dinners are a good deal at $28, but you'll need to reserve.

Pour House BAR

(www.skipspourhouse.com; 351 Main St; 11am-11pm;) An 1890s original, the Pour House is a local favorite and low-key choice for a drink, with six shooters and a Winchester behind the bar, Annie Oakley posters on the wall and open booths to lounge in if you're in the mood for burgers and green chili.

Entertainment

★Steve's Guitars LIVE MUSIC
(www.stevesguitars.net; 19 N 4th St) On weekend nights, this unassuming guitar shop turns into an intimate one-room venue where the focus is all about enjoying great, usually acoustic, music. Shows at this community favorite start around 8:30pm on Friday and/or Saturday nights, but it's best to turn up earlier if you want a seat. The cover charge is not always fixed, so come with a variety of bills in your pocket.

Getting There & Away

Carbondale is 13 miles south of Glenwood Springs and 29 miles northwest of Aspen on Hwy 82. RFTA (p230) runs regular buses up and down the valley.

Basalt

POP 3836 / ELEV 6611FT

Aspen's humble neighbor and down-to-earth little sister has plenty to flaunt. Set at the confluence of the Fryingpan and Roaring Fork Rivers, it's framed by gold-medal trout waters, making this cute but humble town something of a fly-fishing paradise. Most Aspen outfitters will bring you down here to cast.

The town is tiny but blessed with a historic main-street strip, plenty of tasty dining options and a couple of cute boutiques (read: not Louis Vuitton or Prada). It's only 20 minutes from the Four Mountain slopes and another 20 to artsy Carbondale down valley. It's also the gateway to little-visited Hunter-Fryingpan Wilderness area.

Activities

Taylor Creek Fly Shop FISHING
(970-927-4374; www.taylorcreek.com; 183 Basalt Center Circle; rod rental per day $15, half-/full-day trips $275/350; 8am-6pm) This fly shop, with its prime location on the banks of the Fryingpan River, has gold-medal trout waters right in its backyard. It rents rods and waders, and offers casting clinics out back and more detailed instruction on its guided trips.

Sleeping & Eating

There are numerous camping options east of Basalt along the Fryingpan River and at Ruedi Reservoir, including the Chapman Campground (p225).

Green Drake MOTEL $$
(970-927-4747; www.green-drake.com; 220 Midland Ave; r $89-129, incl kitchenettes $139;) One of the most affordable places to stay in the Aspen area, this is a simple and well-run motel. Suites can fit a family of four, but note that not all rooms have air-con. This was the original Basalt hotel when the town sprouted up c 1920. The original was set in the brick building next door.

Riverside Grill MODERN AMERICAN $$
(970-927-9301; www.riversidegrillbasalt.com; 181 Basalt Center Circle; mains $9.50-24; 11:30am-8pm;) The most atmospheric place to eat in Basalt is this old timber warehouse that opens directly onto the Fryingpan River. The more laid-back sister restaurant to Syzygy in Aspen, flatscreens strobe sports on both sides of the double-sided bar, and the menu features interesting dishes such as buffalo tacos, beer-braised Texas brisket, smoked-trout chowder, truffle fries and tasty veggie burgers.

★Cafe Bernard BISTRO $$$
(970-927-4292; www.cafebernard.net; 200 Midland Ave; lunch $7.50-13.50, dinner $16-29; 7:30am-2pm & 6pm-late Tue-Sat, 8am-1pm Sun) Owned by a French chef, this is one of the town's cutest, most beloved restaurants. Set on the main drag, it's a good spot to indulge in Gallic fare without breaking the bank: look for escargots, trout almandine and, for a bit of variety, curried shrimp. It serves breakfast and reasonably priced lunch as well.

Tempranillo MEDITERRANEAN $$$
(970-927-3342; www.tempranillorestaurant.com; 165 Midland Ave; tapas $6-14, lunch $11-22, dinner $17-35; 11am-10pm;) If you're into tapas and wine, you'll enjoy this Spanish-flavored joint set in an old, renovated Victorian. It offers a range of tapas, including Manilla clams in white-wine sauce, piquillo peppers stuffed with crab and lobster, and a sampling of Spanish sausages.

During the summer there's lovely alfresco dining on the front porch, and the interior with its high, timber-beamed ceiling and fireplaces is always inviting.

WORTH A TRIP

HIGHWAY 133

We dare you to drive down Hwy 133 and not fall in love with Colorado all over again. The scenery around Aspen may be more dramatic, but there's something about this quiet stretch of road that manages to capture that one-of-a-kind Rocky Mountain high.

Redstone

Wedged between Chair Mountain and Mt Sopris, Redstone was a true company town, quite unlike the 'every man for himself' spirit of the Gold Rush era. Founded in 1890 by John C Osgood, multimillionaire and head of the Colorado Fuel & Iron Company, Redstone was one of the early experiments in welfare capitalism, where workers were provided with higher standards of living but discouraged from forming unions. The town was created to carbonize coal from Coalbasin Mine, and the first thing you'll see as you drive up the highway are the remains of some 50 beehive coke ovens, lined up across from the town entrance. When the mine closed in 1909, the town was virtually abandoned overnight, though new residents have since moved in over the past few decades.

Several of the original buildings are still standing, including the original chalet-style workers' cottages and Osgood's personal residence, the 42-room **Redstone Castle** (www.redstonecastle.us; adult/child $15/10; ⏲ tours 1:30pm daily summer, weekends only rest of year), located 1 mile south of town on a private road (open for tours only). You can even stay at the imposing neo-Tudor **Redstone Inn** (☎970-963-2526; www.redstoneinn.com; 82 Redstone Blvd; r $99-220; ❄📶🏊👪🐾), which was built in 1902 as a dormitory to house bachelor workers.

However, the best lodging in the area is the kick-back **Avalanche Ranch** (☎877-963-9339; www.avalancheranch.com; 12863 Hwy 133; cabins $150-230; 📶👪🐾). Set on the back of Mt Sopris alongside Avalanche Creek (north of Redstone), the ranch offers 13 cabins, one gypsy wagon ($85 per night) and a ranch house. Cabins are well appointed with kitchens, sleeping lofts and front porches, but the real appeal here are the three **geothermal pools** (adult/child $15/10 Mon, Tue & Thu, adult/child $18/12 Fri-Sun, free for guests; ⏲ 9am-5pm Thu-Tue) lined with river rocks – they're one of the most scenic natural-style hot springs in the state that don't require a long hike. They are open to nonguests, but you must reserve. Cabins require a three-night minimum stay in summer.

Crystal

One of Colorado's most famous ghost towns, Crystal is also one of the most photogenic, though it is smack in the middle of nowhere – which is certainly a good thing, as long as you're up for the detour.

The first mining in the area took place in the 1860s, but access was so poor it wasn't until the 1880s that it really picked up. By 1893 there were a half-dozen mines producing silver, lead and zinc and the population spiked at several hundred. Despite having been virtually abandoned by 1915, there are several fairly intact structures still standing, including the iconic **Crystal Mill**, a turn-of-the-century power generator.

To get here, you'll need to pass through tiny **Marble**, whose quarry (still in operation) supplied stone for some of the most famous statuary in the US, including the Lincoln Memorial and Tomb of the Unknown Soldier. **Out West Guides** (☎970-963-5525; www.outwestguides.com; 7500 County Rd 3; horseback rides per hr from $50) runs a variety of horseback riding and fishing trips from town.

Marble is located 28 miles south of Carbondale, about 6 miles up County Rd 3. After Marble the dirt road to Crystal is another 6 miles, but you'll need a high-clearance 4WD vehicle to make the trip; it is only accessible from June to November. If your car isn't up to the task, contact **Crystal River Jeep Tours** (☎970-963-1991; www.smithfamilycolorado.com; 575 W Park St; tours per person $90; ⏲ Jun-Nov) or consider hiking it. The road continues on to Crested Butte, but is in very poor condition and is not recommended. Budget three or four hours for a visit to Crystal.

Getting There & Away

Basalt is 18.5 miles northwest of Aspen and 23.1 miles southeast of Glenwood Springs on Hwy 82. RFTA (p230) runs regular buses up and down the valley.

Aspen

POP 6642 / ELEV 7940FT

Here's a unique town, unlike any place else in the American West. It's a cocktail of cowboy grit, Euro panache, Hollywood glam, Ivy League brains, fresh powder, live music and lots of money. It's the kind of place where no matter the season you can bring on a head rush in countless ways. Perhaps you dropped into an extreme vertical run, or stomped to the crest of Buckskin Pass in under three hours? It could also come while relaxing at the local music festival, peering down into the bowl of a superpipe or climbing an ice wall. It's possible the horse-drawn sleigh took off too fast for you while you were peering over at yet another $10 million estate, or that cycling to the top of Independence Pass has left you exhausted but smiling. Then again it may have been that way-brainy conversation with a slurring but extraordinarily literate barfly.

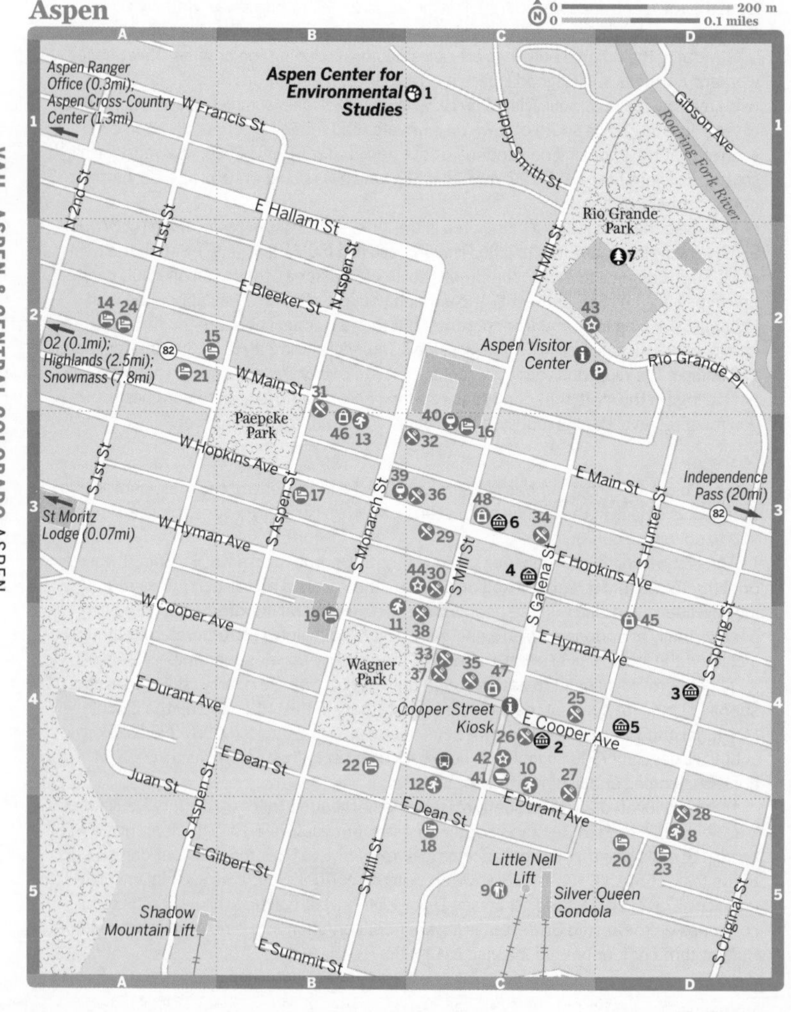

Whatever and whomever you've seen, heard or done, there is a common Aspen cure-all. One that has served every Olympic champion, gonzo journalist, world-class musician, thinker, artist or actor that has ever arrived in this athletic, cultural, intellectual, artistic, absurd ski town. Simply take your body to the frothing hot tub under the stars and leave the head behind. But do bring the bottle. After all, Aspen is nothing if not a place of excellence, extravagance and, most of all, indulgence. Just remember, whatever you do, don't stand up too fast.

Sights

Aspen, like most towns in the Rocky Mountains, is less about seeing and more about doing and experiencing. But with a handful of outstanding art venues downtown, a cutting-edge environmental center and two nearby ghost towns, this is the most culturally happening spot west of Denver.

★ Aspen Center for Environmental Studies WILDLIFE RESERVE

(ACES; ☎970-925-5756; www.aspennature.org; 100 Puppy Smith St, Hallam Lake; ⏰9am-5pm Mon-Fri; P 👪) FREE The Aspen Center for Environmental Studies is a 22-acre (10-hectare) wildlife sanctuary that hugs the Roaring Fork River. With a mission to advance 'the ethic that the earth must be respected and nurtured,' the center's naturalists provide summertime guided walks, raptor demonstrations and special programs for youngsters.

In the winter snowshoe tours are available in various locations and its weekly slide shows may give you some respite from the frigid outdoors. You can take a self-guided tour of the preserve surrounding Hallam Lake.

The sanctuary has three other centers in the region.

Aspen

Top Sights
1 Aspen Center for Environmental Studies ... C1

Sights
2 212 Gallery ... C4
3 Aspen Art Museum ... D4
4 Baldwin Gallery ... C3
5 Galerie Maximillian ... D4
6 Peter Lik ... C3
7 Rio Grande Park ... D2

Activities, Courses & Tours
8 Aspen Bike Tours & Rentals ... D5
9 Aspen Mountain ... C5
Aspen Paragliding ... (see 8)
10 Aspen Trout Guides & Outfitters ... C4
11 Hub ... B4
12 Silver Circle Ice Rink ... C4
13 Ute City Cycles ... B3

Sleeping
14 Annabelle Inn ... A2
15 Hotel Aspen ... A2
16 Hotel Jerome ... C3
17 Hotel Lenado ... B3
18 Hyatt Grand Aspen ... C5
19 Limelight Hotel ... B4
20 Little Nell ... D5
21 Molly Gibson Lodge ... A2
22 Mountain Chalet Aspen ... B4
23 Sky Hotel ... D5
24 Tyrolean Lodge ... A2

Eating
25 520 Grill ... C4
26 BB's Kitchen ... C4
27 Big Wrap ... C4
28 Butchers Block ... D5
29 Jimmy's ... C3
30 Justice Snow's ... C3
31 Main St Bakery ... B2
32 Matsuhisa ... C3
33 Meatball Shack ... C4
34 Peach's Corner Cafe ... C3
Pyramid Bistro ... (see 46)
35 Red Onion ... C4
36 Syzygy ... C3
37 Takah Sushi ... C4
38 Wild Fig ... C4

Drinking & Nightlife
39 Aspen Brewing Co ... B3
Eric's Bar ... (see 38)
40 J-Bar ... C3
41 Victoria's Espresso & Wine Bar ... C4

Entertainment
42 Belly Up ... C4
Isis Theatre ... (see 6)
43 Theatre Aspen ... C2
44 Wheeler Opera House ... C3

Shopping
45 Aspen Saturday Market ... D4
46 Explore Booksellers ... B3
47 Kemosabe ... C4
Little Bird ... (see 2)
48 Radio Boardshop ... C3

Aspen Art Museum MUSEUM
(970-925-8050; www.aspenartmuseum.org; cnr East Hyman Ave & Spring St; 10am-6pm Tue-Sat, to 7pm Thu, noon-6pm Sun) FREE No permanent collection here, just edgy, innovative contemporary exhibitions featuring paintings, mixed media, sculpture, video installations and photography by artists such as Mamma Andersson, Mark Manders and Susan Phiipszmark. Art lovers will not leave disappointed. Visit in August and you can experience its annual artCRUSH event, an art auction and wine-tasting extravaganza.

Its brand-new home was under construction at press time; it's expected to open in summer 2014, with gorgeous rooftop views.

Ice Age Discovery Center MUSEUM
(970-922-2277; www.snowmassiceage.com; Snowmass Village Mall; 10am-5pm Jun-Sep;) FREE In October 2010, a bulldozer working near Snowmass unearthed the tusk of a female mammoth. Spurred by this unusual discovery, the Denver Museum of Nature and Science moved in for the next 10 months to conduct its largest-ever fossil excavation, resulting in the discovery of some 5000 bones from 41 different Ice Age animals (including camels, horses and mastodons – distant relatives of the mammoths).

The family friendly discovery center was opened in 2011 to introduce the Snowmass site. Given the magnitude of the find, exhibits and displays will undoubtedly expand in the coming years. In the meantime, keep your eyes open for various activities: in summer you can sign up for free walks with ACES; in winter weekly ski tours are given.

Independence GHOST TOWN
(www.aspenhistorysociety.com; Hwy 82; suggested donation $3; 10am-6pm mid-Jun–Aug) FREE Just 16 miles east of Aspen at the foot of Independence Pass (p237), this gold-mining boom town turned ghost town started as a tented camp in the summer of 1879, when one lucky miner struck gold on the Fourth of July. Operated and preserved by the Aspen Historical Society, you can see the remains of the old livery, the general store and a miners cabin or three.

After its population peaked at 1500 residents, the town fell away during the harsh winter storm of 1899, when supply routes were severed due to heavy snowfall.

Ashcroft GHOST TOWN
(970-925-3721; www.aspenhistorysociety.com; Castle Creek Rd; suggested donation $3;) FREE The access point to the breathtaking Castle Creek Valley is the ghost town of Ashcroft, a silver-mining town founded in 1880. What remains are mostly miners cottages (log cabins with tin roofs), a couple of broken-down wagons stranded in the waist-high grass, and a post office and saloon.

At its height in 1893 about 2500 people worked here, but the silver veins were quickly exhausted and by 1895 the town's population plummeted to 100 residents. To get here, drive half a mile west of town on Hwy 82 to the roundabout and follow Castle Creek Rd south for 12.2 miles.

Activities

Aspen, for all it's money, taste and eccentricity, owes its current status to the surrounding slopes. Above all, this is a ski town and one of the best in America, with four mountains accessible from a single lift ticket – each offering a different flavor and an adventurous twist. But downhill is not the town's only gift.

Indeed, to come all the way to Aspen in summer or fall and not set foot in the stunning backcountry would be a veritable travesty. The most popular place to explore – and justifiably so – is the breathtaking Maroon Bells area, but there are plenty of other options. Listed here are several of Aspen's classic hikes and bike rides, but be sure to visit the ranger office (p229) for more in-depth advice and maps. The best season for hiking is from mid-June to late October; earlier is doable, but you should expect deep snow cover in places, particularly higher up.

Winter Sports

★**Aspen Mountain** SNOW SPORTS
(800-525-6200; www.aspensnowmass.com; lift ticket adult/child $117/82; 9am-4pm Dec–mid-Apr) The Aspen Skiing Company runs the area's four resorts – Snowmass (best all-around choice with the longest vertical drop in the US), Aspen (intermediate/expert), the Highlands (expert) and Buttermilk (beginner/terrain parks) – which are spread out through the valley and connected by free shuttles.

Both Aspen and Snowmass are open in summer (lift ticket adult/child $28/11; mid-June to September) for hiking, mountain biking, scenic rides and other and kids' activities.

ASPEN SKI TIPS

With four sublime mountains to choose from there's no way you can ski all the terrain on offer in a few days, but if you follow our lead, you'll find your bliss wherever you ski.

➡ **Snowmass** With something for everyone and the most terrain in Aspen, Snowmass is the best all-round choice. The best beginner run is **Assay Hill**. It's short, typically free of crowds and sloped perfectly for newbies. Access it via the Assay Hill lift or the Elk Camp Gondola. The top intermediate choice is **Sneaky's**. Offering sweeping views of the Roaring Fork Valley, this wide-open cruiser is the perfect blue groomer, and those looking for a challenge can ski into powder and trees on either side of the run at anytime. Access it with the Sheer Bliss or Big Burn lifts. Any run in the **Hanging Valley Headwall** will suit the adrenaline set. Make the 10-minute hike to the top of Headwall and head down Roberto's to Strawberry Patch where you can often find fresh powder. It's accessed via the High Alpine lift. There are also three terrain parks here.

➡ **Aspen Mountain** Accessed from town, this is the only mountain with no beginner terrain. It can get crowded, so expect bumps. Intermediate skiers and riders will dig **Ruthie's**, a wide-open groomed run with sweeping views. This is the same terrain skied by Women's World Cup racers late November/early December each year when the FIS Women's World Cup comes to Aspen. Local tip: stay skier's right at the top of Ruthie's and you'll head into the Jerry Garcia Shrine, accessed from the FIS and Ruthie's lifts. **Walsh's**, on the other hand, is for experts. It is steep, deep and breathtaking (visually and physically), with jaw-dropping views of Independence Pass.

➡ **Aspen Highlands** You know all those amazing promo shots of beautiful people joyfully hiking atop an exposed snow-covered ridge with skis hoisted on one shoulder and incredible alpine scenery in the background? That's here. Although there are some beginner and intermediate runs here (**Apple Strudel**, accessed by the Exhibition lift, and the groomed **Golden Horn** run to Thunderbowl), the Highlands is all about extreme skiing in the stunning hike-to Highland Bowl: expect chutes, vertiginous drop-offs and glades. Try **G-4** for a steep, deep, tree run and **Hyde Park** for one of the longest bump and tree runs you've ever taken. It's accessed by Loge Peak and Deep Temerity lifts, then hop a free snowcat ride part-way or just hike it.

➡ **Buttermilk** Buttermilk beginners head to **Westward Ho** via the Summit Express and West Buttermilk Express. The Summit Express and Upper Tiehack lifts take intermediate skiers to the blue runs at **Buckskin**, and the best advanced terrain is **Buttermilk Park**, starting on Jacob's Ladder. This is where you can ski/ride the same hits and 22ft superpipe as Shaun White, Peter Olenick and all your favorite X Games athletes. You read that right: this is one of the venues for the Winter X Games.

Aspen-Snowmass Nordic Trail System SNOW SPORTS
(☎970-429-2039; www.aspennordic.com) FREE This European-style village-to-village trail system incorporates over 60 miles of free trails that link up the towns of Aspen, Snowmass, Woody Gulch and Basalt. The hub is the local golf course, where you'll find the **Aspen Cross-Country Center** (☎970-925-2145; www.utemountaineer.com; 39551 Hwy 82; ski rentals adult/child $23/10; ⊙9am-5pm Dec-Mar), which rents out equipment and gives lessons.

Ashcroft Ski Touring SNOW SPORTS
(☎970-925-1971; www.pinecreekcookhouse.com/tours; 11399 Castle Creek Rd; adult/child $15/10) This local Nordic outfitter serves 20 miles of groomed trails through 600 acres of back-country – it's a bit more wild than your typical Nordic center. The mountain backdrop is spectacular, the Ashcroft ghost town eerie. Rent classic cross-country ski equipment, ski gear or snowshoes. Individual and group lessons, as well as snowshoe and ski tours, run daily.

Shuttles ($35) to and from Aspen are also available.

Silver Circle Ice Rink SKATING
(☎970-925-1710; 433 E Durant Ave; adult/child $7/5.50, skate rental $3; ⊙noon-9pm Nov-Mar) Set at the front of the Hyatt Grand Aspen,

this small but centrally located ice rink is ideal for a family skate.

Hiking

Conundrum Hot Springs HOT SPRING

(Conundrum Creek Rd) The steaming, healing Conundrum Hot Springs, west of Castle Peak (14,265ft), are the reward for 8.5 miles of tough climbing on the Conundrum Creek Trail (USFS Trail 1981). There are several pools hewn from craters, some larger than others, varying in temperature from 102°F (39°C) to 105°F (41°C).

No matter which you sink into, you'll have outrageous alpine views, including glimpses of steep avalanche chutes and waterfalls. Most people spend the night at the nearby campsite, unofficially called 'The Bluffs.' From here you can either retrace your steps or continue over the little-visited Triangle Pass (12,907ft) and return on East Maroon Creek Trail (13 miles) to catch a bus from Maroon Lake back to Aspen.

To get here, drive half a mile west of town on Hwy 82 to the roundabout, follow Castle Creek Rd south for 5 miles, then turn right on Conundrum Creek Rd.

Cathedral Lake Trail HIKING

Particularly stunning in autumn when the aspens shimmer gold, the Cathedral Lake Trail is one of the most popular in Aspen, though with 2000ft of elevation gain over 3 miles, it's definitely no walk in the park.

To get here, drive half a mile west of town on Hwy 82 to the roundabout and follow Castle Creek Rd south for 12.2 miles. The trailhead is located not far beyond the Ashcroft ghost town.

Hunter-Fryingpan Wilderness Area HIKING

Accessible from town, the easy Hunter Creek Trail (USFS Trail 1992) follows Hunter Creek northeast about 3 miles through wildflower meadows to the Sunnyside and Hunter Creek Trails, which lead into the 82,026-acre Hunter-Fryingpan Wilderness Area. Less visited than other slices of Central Rockies wilderness, you can find some nice campsites and rugged peaks here, as well as the headwaters of two rivers.

To get to the trailhead from downtown, follow N Mill St across the river, then turn left on Red Mountain Rd and then right onto Lone Pine Rd.

> **CYCLING TO MAROON BELLS**
>
> According to the Aspen cycling gurus, the most iconic road-bike ride in Aspen is the ride to Maroon Bells, mainly because it climbs a lung-wrenching 11 miles to the foot of one of the most picturesque wilderness areas in the Rockies. Most folks drive it or take the shuttle, but if you crave sweet, beautiful pain, let your quads sing.

Cycling & Mountain Biking

Bike Snowmass MOUNTAIN BIKING

(☎800-525-6200; www.aspensnowmass.com; bike haul adult/child $38/21; ⊙10am-4pm mid-Jun–Sep) Yeehaw! A good 3000ft of downhill and 50 miles of mountain-bike trails at Snowmass guarantee good times in the summer. Most trails are accessible from either the Elk Camp Gondola or Elk Camp Lift. Some of the classic cross-country trails, such as Government and Tom Blake, don't require a lift ticket.

Check out www.laysometread.com or ask around at rental shops for other good singletrack rides in and around the valley.

Rio Grande Trail CYCLING

(www.riograndetrail.com; Rio Grande Trail) FREE This bike trail rambles for 42 mostly paved miles along a former railroad corridor from Aspen to Glenwood Springs, passing through Basalt and Carbondale.

Hub BICYCLE RENTAL

(☎970-925-7970; www.hubofaspen.com; 315 E Hyman Ave; bicycle rental per day from $69; ⊙9am-6pm) Arguably the best of the Aspen bike shops. This place offers a cycling school, sponsors a weekly road race and bike club, and acts as a booster for local talent, pointing out that Aspen is home to some of the best cyclists in the US, including two top-five time trialists, Tour de France competitors and Olympic medalists.

It rents cruisers, full-suspension mountain bikes and carbon-fiber road bikes, and will offer advice on the best road routes and single tracks plying Aspen and Smuggler Mountains, the Montezuma Basin, and Pearl and Independence Pass, but staff aren't always sweet about it. Their motto? 'It's not rude. It's the Hub.'

Ute City Cycles BICYCLE RENTAL

(☎970-920-3325; www.utecitycycles.com; 231 E Main St; bike rental per 24hr $75; ⊙9am-6pm) A high-end road and mountain-bike retailer, this place also offers limited rentals from

LOCAL KNOWLEDGE

ASPEN ART GALLERIES

Among the inevitable 'Western' galleries selling hackneyed cowboy paintings and the like are a few jewels for serious art lovers.

Baldwin Gallery (www.baldwingallery.com; 209 S Galena St; ⌚10am-6pm Mon-Sat, noon-5pm Sun) A two-floor gallery begun in 1994 and specializing in contemporary American art. It's among the best in the Rocky Mountains.

212 Gallery (☎970-925-7117; www.212gallery.com; 525 E Cooper Ave; ⌚10am-9pm) This forward-thinking art gallery hosts events such as Andy Warhol pop-up exhibits and Daniel Beltra's aerial photos of the BP oil spill.

Galerie Maximillian (www.galeriemax.com; 602 E Cooper Ave; ⌚10am-8pm Mon-Sat, 11am-7pm Sun) Come here for famous 20th-century names from Chagall to Lichtenstein, mixed in with works from contemporary American and British artists.

Peter Lik (www.lik.com; 406 E Hopkins Ave; ⌚10am-10pm) Displays the work of the self-taught Aussie photographer. Lik focuses on vibrant panoramic landscapes, with a fine selection of local Aspen shots that sometimes appear to be in 3D.

Anderson Ranch Art Center (☎970-923-3181; www.andersonranch.org; 5263 Owl Creek Rd, Snowmass; ⌚hours vary) Exhibits from resident artists, lectures, auctions and an excellent selection of workshops for adults and children. Check the website to see what's on.

its demo fleet: there's nowhere else in town where you can rent $6500 Orbea road bikes or $2700 Yeti mountain bikes. Rentals are $75 per day with a two-day maximum; no reservations. Staff can also point you in the direction of Aspen's best cycling.

Aspen Bike Tours & Rentals BICYCLE RENTAL
(☎970-925-9169; www.aspenbikerentals.com; 430 S Spring St; half-/full-day adult from $33/40, child $22/29; ⌚9am-6pm) Easily the most laid-back bike shop in town – shaved legs and Lycra bravado are nowhere to be found here. Along with premium road and mountain bikes for rent, it also has a network of private guides who can set you up on terrific mountain-biking tours onto trails seldom glimpsed by tourists. Allow 24-hours' notice for staff to set it up.

Other Activities

Maroon Bells Outfitters HORSEBACK RIDING
(☎970-920-4677; www.maroonbellsaspen.com; 3125 Maroon Creek Rd; 1hr rides from $65) Saddle up at this working ranch down the slope from the Maroon Bells Wilderness Area. Shorter rides (one hour to full day) head into the spectacular Maroon Bells Wilderness, while overnight rides ($535) take you all the way to Crested Butte. It does sleigh rides in the winter too.

Aspen Trout Guides & Outfitters FISHING
(☎970-379-7963; www.aspentroutguides.com; 520 E Durant Ave; half-day trips from $245; ⌚9am-5pm) Based out of Hamilton Sports Pro Shop, this has been Aspen's top fly-fishing outfitter since 1981. Trips to the Fryingpan and Roaring Fork Rivers, Maroon, Castle and Hunter Creeks or nearby lakes, including Thomas, Blue and Little Gem, are customized to clients' wishes and include casting instruction. Family trips also available.

O2 MASSAGE, YOGA
(☎970-925-4002; www.O2aspen.com; 500 W Main St; yoga class $18, massage $130-180) Get your yoga, Pilates and massage at this cute, Victorian-style house-turned-studio just off of the main downtown swirl. Highly recommended by locals. Check the website for seasonal schedules.

Aspen Paragliding ADVENTURE SPORTS
(☎970-925-6975; www.aspenparagliding.com; 426 S Spring St; tandem flights $250; ⌚flights 6:45am, 8:30am & 10:30am) Feel like flying? This paragliding outfitter runs tandem flights year round. During the summer, flights take off from the Silver Queen Gondola on Aspen Mountain. In winter, lift off is either from Sam's Knob on the top of Snowmass or on Aspen Mountain. Private instruction and group courses are also available.

Tours

Aspen Historical Society TOUR
(970-920-5770; www.aspenhistorysociety.com; tours from $15; Jun-Sep) Sign up for local walking and biking tours of historic Aspen and around. It also runs visits to several smaller museums.

Blazing Adventures OUTDOORS
(800-282-7238; www.blazingadventures.com; 48 Upper Village Mall, Snowmass) A popular Snowmass-based outfitter that will get you in a raft, kayak or jeep, or on a bike or high-altitude ridge at sunset. It's based in the upper mall (main mall) and consistently gets rave reviews, most notably for the white-water-rafting trips on the nearby Colorado River.

Aspen Expeditions OUTDOORS
(970-925-7625; www.aspenexpeditions.com; 115 Boomerang Rd) Based in the Aspen Highlands ski area, this guiding company is notable for its adventurous itineraries, including some stellar hiking, mountaineering and rock-climbing trips to some of Aspen's most spectacular destinations, as well as ice climbing and cross-country and downhill ski trips in winter. It also runs level one and two avalanche courses.

Festivals & Events

Jazz Aspen Snowmass JAZZ
(970-920-4996; www.jazzaspen.org; Jun & Labor Day) Aspen's June festival is true to its jazz roots, with horn players such as Christian McBride and Nicholas Payton, crooners such as Harry Connick Jr and Natalie Cole and fusionists such as Pink Martini gracing the Benedict Music Tent or the downstairs venue at the Little Nell in the week leading up to the Fourth of July. A second concert series is held over the Labor Day weekend.

Aspen Music Festival MUSIC
(970-925-9042; www.aspenmusicfestival.com; Jul & Aug) Every summer for the past 60 or so years, some of the best classical musicians from around the world have come to play, perform and learn from the masters of their craft. Students form orchestras led by world-famous conductors and perform at the Wheeler Opera House or the Benedict Music Tent, or in smaller duos, trios, quartets and quintets on Aspen street corners.

The event schedule is also peppered with classical music stars, many of whom are themselves alumni. All told there are more than 350 classical music events taking place over eight weeks. You can't escape, nor would you want to. And if you're hungry to hear the best music in the sweetest venue, the Benedict is a must. And you don't even have to pay – just unfurl a blanket on the grass outside the tent and let the music wash over you.

Sleeping

Aspen is a cute town to nest in and there are more than a few charming inns to consider – and although pricey, it's still more affordable than Vail. If the winter prices make you balk or you simply can't find a room, consider a down-valley option in Basalt, Carbondale or Glenwood Springs. Once the snow melts (early June), Aspen's breathtaking wilderness areas draw campers from around the world – ask at the ranger office for up-to-date info on backcountry sites. Wherever you stay, even if you're car camping, make sure to reserve well in advance.

Aspen

St Moritz Lodge HOSTEL $
(970-925-3220; www.stmoritzlodge.com; 334 W Hyman Ave; dm summer/winter $60/66, d summer $130-269, winter $155-299; P) St Moritz is the best no-frills deal in town. Perks include a heated outdoor pool and grill overlooking Aspen Mountain, and a lobby with games, books and a piano. The European-style lodge offers a wide variety of options, from quiet dorms to two-bedroom condos; the cheapest options share bathrooms. There's a kitchen downstairs.

Annabelle Inn HOTEL $$
(877-266-2466; www.annabelleinn.com; 232 W Main St; r incl breakfast summer/winter from $169/199; P) Personable and unpretentious, the cute and quirky Annabelle Inn resembles an old-school European-style ski lodge in a central location. Rooms are cozy without being too cute, and come with flatscreen TVs and warm duvets. We enjoyed the after-dark ski video screenings from the upper-deck hot tub (one of two on the property).

Tyrolean Lodge LODGE $$
(970-925-4595; www.tyroleanlodge.com; 200 W Main St; r summer/winter from $135/155; P) One of the few midrange lodges in Aspen, the Tyrolean is a popular, family owned option, located within walking distance of downtown. The white condo-style

LOCAL KNOWLEDGE

10TH MOUNTAIN DIVISION HUT-TO-HUT TRIPS

Exploring the Colorado wilderness is already quite an adventure in summer, but imagine the thrill of gliding through the backcountry on skis: just you, your friends and quiet snowfall blanketing the mountainside. Well, thanks to the **10th Mountain Division Hut Association** (☎970-925-5775; www.huts.org; per person from $33), which manages a system of 34 huts (some with wood-burning saunas), it can be done – without having to spend the night in a snow cave.

The huts are connected by a 350-mile trail network ideal for cross-country skiing and snowshoeing in the winter, and mountain biking and hiking in the summer. The majority are located between Vail Pass and Aspen (10th Mt Huts and Braun Huts), but there are growing networks in Summit and Grand counties. You'll be out in the wilderness, so you should be a decent backcountry skier and be familiar with avalanche safety before reserving a bunk. It's best to go as a group (some huts only accept group reservations), with at least one experienced leader who knows how to find a trail in a storm.

So how do you sign up for all this winter fun? The catch, of course, is securing reservations: these huts are incredibly popular and space is limited. Winter reservations for the following year begin with a member-only lottery on March 1 (annual membership $25). Call-in reservations for non-members open up on June 1. In other words, you have to plan your trip six to 12 months in advance and be somewhat flexible with your dates (avoiding weekends is key).

Summer is generally easier to arrange, though not all huts are open; call-in reservations for the following year open October 1.

building is adorned with a giant bronze eagle and crossed skis mounted on the outside walls. It's built to resemble a Native American version of an Austrian ski lodge, and is hard to miss.

The rooms here are spacious, and even though they resemble your garden-variety American motel chain, with pine furniture and colored, fire-retardant bedspreads, the Tyrolean goes above and beyond with some nifty decorating features. Each room is slightly different, featuring accents such as fire-engine-red kitchenettes, stone fireplaces and dark-wood paneling behind the two queen beds.

★Hotel Aspen HOTEL **$$$**
(☎970-925-3441; www.hotelaspen.com; 110 W Main St; r summer/winter from $135/300; P❄📶🏊👪🐾) The hip Hotel Aspen is one of the best deals in town, with a casual vibe and affordable luxury. The modern decor features rust-hued walls, a wet bar and stylish furnishings – if you go for the fireplace suite, you'll also have access to your own private solarium. Whichever room you choose, the heated pool and four frothing hot tubs are another plus.

Book well in advance for the best rates; Colorado residents get 20% off.

★Limelight Hotel HOTEL **$$$**
(☎800-433-0832; www.limelighthotel.com; 355 S Monarch St; r summer/winter from $245/395; P❄📶🏊👪🐾) Sleek and trendy, the Limelight's brick-and-glass modernism reflects Aspen's vibe. Rooms are spacious and have their perks: granite washbasins, leather headboards and mountain views from the balconies and rooftop terraces. In addition to the ski valet and transportation services, you can also catch live music most winter nights in the lobby's Italian restaurant. Breakfast is included.

Molly Gibson Lodge HOTEL **$$$**
(☎970-925-3434; www.mollygibson.com; 101 W Main St; r summer/winter from $159/339; P❄@📶🏊👪🐾) One of two tasteful good-value properties across from each other on the edge of downtown. The owners re-do the rooms every spring, which means parquet floors, fresh paint and lush linens. It's all very mod and Ikea-ish but with an upscale slant. Some rooms are huge with fireplaces and massive hot tubs. Online deals lower the rates. Breakfast included.

Mountain Chalet Aspen HOTEL **$$$**
(☎970-925-7797; www.mountainchaletaspen.com; 333 E Durant Ave; r summer/winter from $139/300; P❄📶🏊👪) Just two short blocks from the gondola, the Mountain Chalet has a great

location. Rooms at this family run hotel are a bit outdated and bland, but clean and comfortable nevertheless. The hot tub and sauna are perfect after a long day on the slopes. The best deals here are the recently redone apartment suites ($600), which sleep six.

Hotel Lenado BOUTIQUE HOTEL **$$$**
(☎970-926-6246; www.hotellenado.com; 200 S Aspen St; r summer/winter from $245/395; P❄🛜👪🐾) There's a certain B&B-style intimacy at this very cute boutique hotel set in what feels like a modern farmhouse. Rooms have old-school woodburning stoves, flatscreen TVs, high ceilings and large stylish wardrobes decked out with vanities. There's also a wood-barrel hot tub on the roof deck, and a chef shows up every morning to prepare a gourmet breakfast.

Sky Hotel BOUTIQUE HOTEL **$$$**
(☎800-882-2582; www.theskyhotel.com; 709 E Durant Ave; r summer/winter from $191/439; P❄🛜🏊👪🐾) At the base of the Aspen ski area, this oh-so-hip hotel is an elegant affair with a funky twist. Rooms are minimalist, but playful – yellow walls meet Southwestern wooden beams, while animal-print bathrobes and faux-fur throws offset the white Frette linens.

Be sure to check out the huge lobby with its oversized leather chairs, rock wall, lit Aspen trees and table strewn with board games for guests to borrow. Outside, the hot tub and splash pool beckon after a day on the slopes.

Hyatt Grand Aspen HOTEL **$$$**
(☎970-429-9100; www.hyatt.com; 415 E Dean St; studio summer/winter from $289/510; P❄🛜🏊👪) Soak in your private hot tub on your private deck and take in the gorgeous mountain views at sunset. It's the perfect way to end a perfect Aspen day. Specializing in pampering, everything here is pure luxury, and the service and location are spot on. Right next to the Silver Queen Gondola, you couldn't ask for a better slopeside location.

All the rooms here are actually multi-bedroom apartments – featuring oak floors, granite-counter kitchens, gas fireplaces – but you can rent studios too.

Hotel Jerome HOTEL **$$$**
(☎800-331-7213; www.hoteljerome.com; 330 E Main St; r summer/winter $459/725; P❄🛜🏊👪🐾) Superb service and relaxed elegance are the trademarks at the historic Hotel Jerome. A long-time favorite with Aspen's old-money crowd, the Jerome occupies an 1889 landmark brick building constructed during Colorado's silver heyday. Rooms are individually decorated with period antiques, double-marble vanities and baths with oversized tubs.

Beds feature lots of pillows and fluffy, feather-down comforters for cold winter nights. If you just want to enjoy the view, sink into one of the armchairs facing Aspen Mountain. The hotel also has a great restaurant and lobby, where a hand-carved fireplace is the centerpiece and guests dine on fish and game served by friendly waiters.

Those interested in the building's storied history can sign up for a tour with the Aspen Historical Society (p222).

Little Nell HOTEL **$$$**
(☎970-920-4600; www.thelittlenell.com; 675 E Durant Ave; r summer/winter from $595/940; P❄🛜🏊👪🐾) A legendary ski-in, ski-out Aspen landmark offering understated, updated elegance and class at the foot of Aspen Mountain. Gas-burning fireplaces, high-thread-count linens and rich color schemes make up the recently remodeled modernist decor. There are fabulous Balinese pieces in the lobby and hallways decorated with wonderful ski photography. The Greenhouse Bar is perfect for après-ski unwinding, while Element 47 serves gastronomic cuisine.

Snowmass

Wildwood Snowmass LODGE **$$**
(☎970-923-8400; www.wildwoodsnowmass.com; 40 Elbert Lane; r summer/winter from $79/159; P🛜🏊👪🐾) This aging lodge was given a slick, colorful makeover in 2012. The 145 rooms are still motel-like in their layout and comfort level – renovations were mostly skin-deep – but if you're OK with that, it's definitely an affordable choice located close to the slopes. Wi-fi is free in the lobby, but costs an additional $20 per day for room access. No air-con in summer.

Westin Snowmass HOTEL **$$$**
(☎970-923-8200; www.westinsnowmass.com; 100 Elbert Lane; r summer/winter from $109/369; P❄🛜🏊👪🐾) Opened in 2012, the ski-in, ski-out Westin delivers the most comfort for your money in Snowmass. Rooms are spacious and feature modern alpine decor: think varnished wooden headboards, contemporary art on the walls and a beige and tan color scheme. Wi-fi is an extra $10 per day; parking is valet only.

Viceroy HOTEL $$$

(☎970-923-8000; www.viceroysnowmass.com; 130 Wood Rd; studios summer/winter from $175/625; P ❄ 📶 🏊 👪 🐾) This is a great choice in Snowmass, with ski-in, ski-out convenience in winter and cut-rate prices in summer to make for seriously affordable luxury. Here you'll find stylish studios and condos steeped in glamor, with high ceilings, full kitchens, deep soaker tubs, mosaic showers, seagrass wallpaper, fireplaces and flatscreen TVs.

Camping

Difficult CAMPGROUND $

(☎877-444-6777; www.recreation.gov; Hwy 82; tent & RV sites $21; ⏱mid-May–Sep; 🐾) The largest campground in the Aspen area, Difficult is one of four sites at the foot of Independence Pass and the only one that takes reservations. Located 5 miles west of town, it also has the lowest altitude (8000ft). Higher up are three smaller campgrounds: Weller, Lincoln Gulch and Lost Man. Water is available, but no electrical hookups for RVs.

Silver Bell CAMPGROUND $

(☎877-444-6777; www.recreation.gov; Maroon Creek Rd; tent & RV sites $15; ⏱late May-Sep) If you want to pitch a tent near the Maroon Bells but don't have time to get into the backcountry, this is your spot. There are three small campgrounds along the access road, all of which take reservations. The other two are Silver Bar and Silver Queen. Water is available, but there are no electrical hookups for RVs.

Chapman CAMPGROUND $

(☎877-444-6777; www.recreation.gov; Fryingpan Rd; tent & RV sites $20-22; ⏱mid-May–Oct; 👪 🐾) Located upstream from Ruedi Reservoir (good for boaters), this is one of six campgrounds along the Fryingpan River. It's fairly developed as far as USFS campgrounds go, with volleyball courts, a horseshoe pit and some seriously good fishing holes nearby. Water is available, but no electrical hookups. It's 29 miles east of Basalt.

Eating

For a mountain town, Aspen has a refreshingly diverse culinary scene. From hole-in-the-wall sandwich joints to top-shelf sushi, raw bars and grass-fed, locally sourced beef, you should have no problem replenishing your calorie count in style after an action-packed day. It goes without saying that you'll need to reserve a table for dinner.

Aspen

Big Wrap SANDWICHES $

(520 E Durant Ave, Suite 101; wraps $6.95; ⏱10am-6pm Mon-Sat; 🥕 👪) One of Aspen's most beloved spots for a quick, cheap meal, the Big Wrap's creative and vaguely healthy concoctions have won over legions of fans. In addition to Thai-, Mexican- and Greek-inspired wraps, there are tacos, salads and smoothies. It's located downstairs from the main sidewalk on Hunter St, despite the Durant St address. Cash only and no seating.

Butchers Block DELI $

(☎970-925-7554; 424 S Spring St; sandwiches from $9; ⏱8am-6pm) The depth and breadth of the gourmet spirit of this ski-town deli is striking. Here you'll find gouda, stilton and goat cheese, wild salmon and sashimi-grade ahi, caviar and gourmet olive oil, maple-glazed walnuts, dried mango, good deli sandwiches, and terrific roast chicken and salads. It's open until 6pm, but stops making sandwiches at 5pm.

520 Grill SANDWICHES $

(☎970-925-9788; 520 E Cooper Ave; sandwiches & salads $8-11; ⏱11am-9pm Tue-Sun; 📶 🥕) A (mostly) healthy (kinda) fast-food grill, if there is such a thing. Sandwiches are creative, spicy concoctions. The achiote chicken is grilled and piled on the pita with roasted red peppers, avocado and cheese. The Veg Head is an alchemy of roasted portobello mushrooms and garlic, with a pepper medley dressed in balsamic.

It also serves a good-looking, much-loved kale and quinoa salad, along with sweet potato fries and New Belgium beers.

★ Justice Snow's MODERN AMERICAN $$

(☎970-429-8192; www.justicesnows.com; 328 E Hyman Ave; mains $10-22; ⏱11am-2am; 📶 🥕) Located in the historic Wheeler Opera House, Justice Snow's is a retro-fitted old saloon that marries antique wooden furnishings with a deft modern touch. Although nominally a bar – the speakeasy cocktails are the soul of the place – the affordable and locally sourced menu ($10 gourmet burger! in Aspen!) is what keeps the locals coming back.

Don't miss the peepholes outside the bathrooms.

Pyramid Bistro CAFE $$

(☎970-925-5338; http://pyramidbistro.com; 221 E Main St; mains $11-18; ⏲11:30am-9pm;) Set on the top floor of Explore Booksellers (p229), this gourmet veggie cafe serves up some delightful creations, including sweet potato gnocchi with goat cheese, truffled mushroom burgers and quinoa salad with mango, avocado and goji berries. Definitely Aspen's top choice for health-conscious fare.

Main St Bakery CAFE $$

(☎970-925-6446; 201 E Main St; breakfast $8-15, lunch from $11; ⏲7am-4pm;) Step into this time-worn cafe for fresh-baked giant cinnamon rolls, raspberry-cream cupcakes and cherry pie. It also does full-on breakfasts if you've got an inclination to sit down, as well as simple lunch options. Even though French chef Jacques Pépin has been spotted here on occasion, it remains a refreshingly down-home destination.

Peach's Corner Cafe CAFE $$

(http://peachscornercafe.com; 121 S Galena St; mains $8-13; ⏲7am-6pm Mon-Sat;) This busy organic cafe is good for affordable coffee and a quality meal at any time of the day. When the sun shines – which is often – everyone decamps to the patio seating out front. Look for monster slices of quiche, yummy pizzas, sandwiches and smoothies.

HIKING TO THE GROTTOS

One of the most popular summer playgrounds in Aspen and a great family hike, the Grottos area is accessed via a complex web of short trails (most about half a mile in length) that sprout from old Weller Station on the original Independence Pass wagon road, leading to waterfalls and sculpted gorges. The shortest, wheelchair-accessible trail visits a series of thundering falls and swimming holes on the Roaring Fork River.

On the opposite bank, the Old Stage Rd leads upstream to Lincoln Creek, and an offshoot heads to unique water-carved slots known locally as the **Ice Caves**. These are worth hunting for. Head up Independence Pass east of town for 9 miles on Hwy 82 and look for a 'Trailhead' sign on the right-hand side of the road, nearly a mile after passing Weller Campground. Leave your car or bike in the small parking area and start exploring. Be warned: the rocks are slippery and the water icy. Deaths are not frequent, but have been known to happen.

★ **Pine Creek Cookhouse** AMERICAN $$$

(☎970-925-1044; www.pinecreekcookhouse.com; 12700 Castle Creek Rd; lunch & summer dinner mains $13-41, winter dinner prix-fixe with ski tour/sleigh $90/110; ⏲11:30am-2:30pm daily, 2:30-8:30pm Wed-Sun Jun-Sep, seatings at noon & 1:30pm daily, plus 7pm Wed-Sun Dec-Mar;) This log-cabin restaurant, located 1.5 miles past the Ashcroft ghost town at the end of Castle Creek Rd (about 30 minutes from Aspen), boasts the best setting around. In summer you can hike here; in winter it's cross-country skis or horse-drawn sleigh in the shadow of glorious white-capped peaks. Sample alpine delicacies like house-smoked trout, buffalo tenderloin and grilled elk brats.

Matsuhisa JAPANESE $$$

(☎970-544-6628; www.matsuhisaaspen.com; 303 E Main St; mains $29-39, 2 pieces sushi $8-12; ⏲from 6pm) The original Colorado link in Matsuhisa Nobu's iconic global chain that now wraps around the world. This converted house is more intimate than the Vail sibling and still turns out spectacular dishes such as miso black cod, Chilean sea bass with truffle, and flavorful uni (sea urchin) shooters.

Meatball Shack ITALIAN $$$

(☎970-925-1349; www.themeatballshack.com; 312 S Mill St; lunch $13, dinner $21-28; ⏲11:30am-11:30pm;) Helmed by Florentine chef Eddie Baida and NYC transplant Michael Gurtman, the shack specializes in – you guessed it – fettuccine and meatballs (nonna's, chicken or veal). It's quite the happening place come evening, but forget about the scene for a minute and concentrate on what's on your plate: those locally sourced ingredients definitely make a difference.

For lunch you'll have to settle for one of the meatball parmigianas, but come dinner you can order up the good stuff, along with tempting starters like truffle bruschetta or the *buratta du jour*.

Jimmy's AMERICAN $$$

(☎970-925-6020; www.jimmysaspen.com; 205 S Mill St; mains $24-48; ⏲4:30pm-late daily, 10:30am-2pm Sun brunch) Jimmy's is a soulful tequila bar and steakhouse with attitude that attracts a very A-list crowd. Settle into a booth and check out the guest graffiti on the wall in the main dining room, or skip the high-priced grill and try to wrangle a spot at the perpetually packed bar, which serves a cheaper menu and 105 types of tequila and mescal.

BB's Kitchen MODERN AMERICAN **$$$**
(☎970-429-8284; www.bbskitchen.com; 525 E Cooper Ave, 2nd fl; brunch $14-20, dinner $24-39; ⏰10am-9pm) A local darling and winner of several awards, this 2nd-floor patio is the best spot for a leisurely gourmet brunch (think lobster Benedict or wild morel omelet). This isn't show food – the chef-owners are committed to quality, down to curing their own meats.

For dinner, slip into a red booth for delicious black truffle flatbread or poached halibut served over a gorgeous mint-pea puree.

Syzygy EUROPEAN **$$$**
(☎970-925-3700; www.syzygyrestaurant.com; 308 E Hopkins Ave; mains $26-55; ⏰from 6pm) Tucked into a basement on Aspen's restaurant row, this elegant dining room showcases the considerable talents of a local chef who's been feeding Aspen Jazz Festival VIPs for years (through his catering company). Think herb-crusted Colorado lamb, elk tenderloin and pan-seared scallops with gnocchi.

Wild Fig MODERN AMERICAN **$$$**
(☎970-925-5160; www.thewildfig.com; 315 E Hyman Ave; mains $22-38; ⏰11:30am-3pm summer, 5:30pm-close year round) This bright, tiled dining room and patio edged with flower boxes packs plenty of gourmet cheer. It does a nightly risotto, a tender grilled-octopus salad and an enticing fig-glazed pork chop. Its small plates are also worth considering – we loved the marinated figs with pancetta, the pan-seared scallops and the fire-roasted clams with chorizo.

Takah Sushi JAPANESE **$$$**
(☎970-925-8588; www.takahsushi.com; 320 Mill St; mains $26-31, rolls $9-16; ⏰5:30pm-late) It's not as celebrated as Matsuhisa, but Takah Sushi is not quite as expensive either and this fun basement and patio sushi bar has tasty cooked small plates too. Think sirloin-wrapped asparagus, Kobe beef sliders, atomic lobster (yeah, it's spicy), the usual sushi and some creative rolls, such as the ninja (tempura avocado and crab salad wrapped in tuna).

Red Onion PUB FOOD **$$$**
(☎970-925-9955; www.redonionaspen.com; 420 E Cooper Ave; lunch $10-14, dinner $18-21; ⏰11am-2am; 👪) Open since 1892, this saloon has been recently renovated with a certain mountain-bistro flair. The fusion menu has a brainy side, starring mango and brie quesadillas, and grilled lamb chops in a habanero preserve, plus you've gotta love a joint that serves chicken and waffles for (late) breakfast. The kitchen stays open well into the night.

Snowmass

Fuel CAFE **$**
(☎970-923-0091; 45 Village Sq, Snowmass; mains $5.20-8.90; ⏰7am-5:30pm) This hard-rocking Snowmass cafe does two things exceptionally well: jet-fueled espresso and world-class breakfast burritos. It also has protein bars and energy food to keep you going on the slopes and ridgelines, no matter the season, as well as bagels, paninis, wraps and smoothies.

Staff will pack lunches for the slopes if you ask nicely. It's located just off lot 6 in the lower (main) mall.

★ **Ranger Station** PUB FOOD **$$**
(www.rangerstation.org; 100 Elbert Lane; mains $8-18; ⏰noon-9pm Wed-Sun summer, 11am-9pm winter) OK, so this place is much more a bar than a restaurant, but given the dearth of dining choices in Snowmass, you may as well eat here too. The stars of the show are the 10 New Belgium beers on tap, but where else are you going to get Bavarian pretzels with yummy dipping sauces, bison chili or ciabatta-style grilled cheese? Ski-in, ski-out. Yes!

Drinking & Nightlife

★ **Aspen Brewing Co** BREWERY
(www.aspenbrewingcompany.com; 304 E Hopkins Ave; ⏰noon-late; 📶) With six signature flavors and a sun-soaked balcony facing the mountain, this is definitely the place to unwind after a hard day's play. Brews range from the flavorful This Year's Blonde and high-altitude Independence Pass Ale (its IPA) to the mellower Conundrum Red Ale and the chocolatey Pyramid Peak Porter.

Woody Creek Tavern PUB
(☎970-923-4585; www.woodycreektavern.com; 2 Woody Creek Plaza, 2858 Upper River Rd; ⏰11am-10pm) Enjoying a 100% agave tequila and fresh-lime margarita at the late, great gonzo

journalist Hunter S Thompson's favorite watering hole is well worth the 8-mile trek from Aspen. Here since 1980, the walls at this rustic funky tavern, a local haunt for decades now, are plastered with newspaper clippings and paraphernalia (mostly dedicated to Thompson).

The lunch menu features organic salads, low-fat but still juicy burgers and popular Mexican food including some quality guacamole. The dinner menu is less imaginative, but there's plenty of alcohol. Eleven gallons of margaritas a day can't be wrong.

Victoria's Espresso & Wine Bar CAFE
(970-920-3001; www.aspenespressobar.com; 510 E Durant St; 7am-7pm;) Victoria's serves up delish pastries, wine by the glass, full breakfasts and tempting curries for afternoon grazing, but the must-try here is the vanilla latte. Made with housemade syrup crafted from real vanilla bark, it isn't too sweet – just immediately and completely addictive.

J-Bar BAR
(www.hoteljerome.com; 330 E Main St; 11:30am-2am;) Once Aspen's premier saloon, back when the word 'saloon' had its own unique meaning, this bar was built into the Hotel Jerome in 1889 and remains full of historic charm. It's packed with everyone from local shopkeepers to Hollywood stars. The signature cocktail, the Aspen Crud, is a delicious blend of bourbon and ice cream.

Eric's Bar BAR
(www.sucasaaspen.com; 315 E Hyman Ave; 7pm-2am) One of three bars in the Su Casa complex, all of which are owned by one savvy fellow. This one is by far the coolest. It's a brick-walled lounge with DJs on Thursday nights when the midnight freaks dance like mad. If the crowd gets too tight, head over to the billiard hall or upstairs to the cigar lounge.

☆ Entertainment

★ Belly Up LIVE MUSIC
(970-544-9800; www.bellyupaspen.com; 450 S Galena St; cover varies; hour vary) Long the top nightspot in Aspen, Belly Up has built and maintained its street cred by bringing the best live acts to the Aspen people. That means everything from local bluegrass bands to hip-hop globalist K'naan and intimate, up-close throwdowns with all-timers such as BB King.

No matter who you see, the room will be intimate and alive with great sound. Easily the best venue this side of Denver.

Theatre Aspen THEATER
(970-925-9313; www.theatreaspen.org; 470 Rio Grande Pl; prices vary; hours vary;) A nonprofit theater and drama school that hosts classes, workshops and periodic productions (mostly in the summer and early autumn) from its gorgeous, tented complex in the heart of Rio Grande Park. Matinees include bonus views of the nearby mountains, evening productions play beneath a starry sky. Check the website for details of upcoming shows and see one if you can.

Wheeler Opera House PERFORMING ARTS
(970-920-5770; www.aspenshowtix.com; 320 E Hyman Ave; prices vary; box office 11am-7pm winter, 9am-5pm summer;) Built in 1887, one of Aspen's oldest and finest examples of Victorian architecture has been a working theater since it first opened – with the exception of the 30 or so years during which things were interrupted by fire, depression and reconstruction. Part of Aspen's postwar revival, it still presents opera, films, concerts and musicals. During summer the Aspen Music Festival holds concerts here.

Isis Theatre CINEMA
(970-925-7584; www.metrotheatres.com; 406 E Hopkins Ave; adult/child $10.50/7.50; 1:15-9:45pm;) The only movie house in Aspen proper plays first-run Hollywood fare, but thankfully spices up the blockbusters with an occasional pinch of art-house and foreign cinema. This is Aspen, after all.

Shopping

Aspen is for the professional shopper. Part Malibu, part Rodeo Dr, part Champs-Élysées, this is Colorado's only luxury brand haute-couture strip. Everything from high-end hoodies to pro-grade outdoor gear to designer bling is available. That said, you won't find many local boutiques here. If Louis Vuitton's not your thing, head down valley to Basalt or Carbondale.

Little Bird CLOTHING
(970-920-3830; http://thelittlebirdinc.com; 525 E Cooper Ave; 10am-6pm Mon-Sat, noon-5pm Sun) This gem of a consignment store has new and vintage luxury designer scarves, dresses, handbags, shoes and more. Gucci, Jimmy Choo, Blahnik – all the handsome boys are here. You can bargain too, and if

staff have had the gear for more than 30 days, you may strike a deal. But it still won't be cheap. You are in Aspen, after all.

Kemosabe CLOTHING
(www.kemosabe.com; 434 E Cooper Ave; ⏲10am-5pm) The sister to Vail's cowboy apparel depot, Kemosabe vends the same handmade boots and Stetson hats – steam shaped to please. Expect friendly faces, a stuffed buffalo head, gleaming belt buckles and a bluegrass soundtrack.

Explore Booksellers BOOKS
(☎970-925-5336; www.explorebooksellers.com; 221 E Main St; ⏲10am-7pm; 📶👪) A sweet and intimate local bookshop, the kind that must survive if humanity is to preserve its literate soul. Little alcoves are stacked with biographies, history, adventure and nature tomes, new and classic literature, and the staff tips are rock solid. By far the best excuse in Aspen to put down the iPad/Kindle and turn a page.

Aspen Saturday Market MARKET
(S Hunter St, E Hopkins Ave & E Hyman Ave; ⏲8:30am-3pm Sat mid-Jun–mid-Oct; 👪) 🍃 This market blooms on Saturday mornings. It's more than just a farmers market, though self-caterers can grab their organic fruits and veggies, artisan cheese, and naturally and locally grown beef, bison and elk here. It also has tons of crafts, including handmade soap, silver jewelry and fixed-gear bikes built with vintage frames.

The market runs in a U-shape from Hyman to Hopkins on Hunter before turning down both Hyman and Hopkins to Galena.

Radio Boardshop SPORTS
(☎970-925-9373; www.radioboardshop.com; 400 E Hopkins Ave; skateboards incl helmets & pads per day $10-15; ⏲10am-6pm; 👪) On the shortlist for the coolest shop in Aspen, this place does stylish top-shelf skateboards and snowboards, and sells the gear, shoes and boots to match. It's a mom-and-pop store with style to spare. Unfortunately, it doesn't rent snowboards, but does rent skateboards at great prices in the summer.

Information

MEDIA

Aspen Magazine (www.aspenmagazine.com)

Aspen Times (www.aspentimes.com) The local paper has a decent website packed with relevant local and regional news and events.

MEDICAL SERVICES

Aspen Valley Hospital (☎970-925-1120; www.aspenvalleyhospital.org; 401 Castle Creek Rd; ⏲24hr) A small but up-to-the-minute community hospital with 24-hour emergency services.

TOURIST INFORMATION

Aspen Ranger Office (☎970-925-3445; www.fs.usda.gov/whiteriver; 806 W Hallam St; ⏲8am-4:30pm Mon-Fri) The USFS Aspen Ranger District operates twenty-some campgrounds and covers Roaring Fork Valley and from Independence Pass to Glenwood Springs, including the Maroon Bells Wilderness. Come here for maps and hiking tips.

Aspen Visitor Center (☎970-925-1940; www.aspenchamber.org; 425 Rio Grande Pl; ⏲8:30am-5pm Mon-Fri) Located across from Rio Grande Park.

Cooper Street Kiosk (cnr E Cooper Ave & S Galena St; ⏲10am-6pm)

Getting There & Away

Aspen is 41 miles south of Glenwood Springs on Hwy 82. From Denver, Aspen is 200 miles via I-70 and Hwy 82. The road to Aspen via Independence Pass is only open from late May to early November.

Aspen-Pitkin County Airport (☎970-920-5380; www.aspenairport.com; 233 E Airport Rd; 📶) Four miles northwest of Aspen on Hwy 82, this surprisingly spry airport has direct flights from Denver, Los Angeles, Dallas and Chicago. Several car-rental agencies operate here. Roaring Forks Transportation Authority also runs a twice hourly free bus to and from the airport.

Colorado Mountain Express (☎800-525-6363; www.coloradomountainexpress.com; adult/child to DIA $118/61; 📶) Colorado Mountain Express runs frequent shuttles to/from the Denver International Airport (four hours). It also offers local shuttle services.

Getting Around

It should come as no surprise that street parking in Aspen is both expensive and a headache. If you're just up for the day, or if your hotel doesn't have parking spots (it happens), save yourself the trouble and head straight for the town parking garage (per hour/day $1.50/15) next to the visitor center on Rio Grande Pl. Skiers not staying in Aspen generally go to the free Park-and-Ride lot on Brush Creek Rd, which is opposite the turnoff for Snowmass off Hwy 82. The free shuttles here serve all mountains.

High Mountain Taxi (☎970-925-8294; www.hmtaxi.com; airport to/from Aspen $19-30; ⏲24hr) Serves the airport and offers Aspen-area metered fare services 24 hours a day.

Taxis seat up to six people and are equipped with child seats.

Roaring Fork Transportation Authority (RFTA; ☎970-925-8484; www.rfta.com; 430 E Durant Ave; ⏰6:15am-2:15am) RFTA buses connect Aspen with the Highlands, Snowmass and Buttermilk via free shuttles, as well as the down-valley towns of Basalt ($4, 30 minutes), Carbondale ($6, one hour) and Glenwood Springs ($7, 80 minutes). Drivers don't handle money, so passengers must have exact change. Most buses are equipped with ski/bike racks; bikes are an additional $2.

The Aspen depot is located at Durant Ave and Mill St at the Rubey Park Transit Center.

SALIDA & THE COLLEGIATE PEAKS

The Arkansas River Valley, running from Leadville in the north to Salida in the south, is a picturesque slice of high-desert landscape whose natural diversity is such that you never tire of looking at it. The mighty Sawatch Range, and the Collegiate Peaks in particular, are the dominant geological feature, forming the backdrop to one of the most popular stretches of white water in the entire country.

DON'T MISS

MAROON BELLS

If you have but one day to enjoy a slice of pristine wilderness, you'd be wise to spend it in the shadow of Colorado's most iconic mountains: the pyramid-shaped twins of North Maroon Peak (14,014ft) and South Maroon Peak (14,156ft). The parking area spills onto the shores of Maroon Lake, an absolutely stunning picnic spot backed by the towering, striated summits. The surrounding wilderness area contains nine passes over 12,000ft and six 14ers. Some jut into jagged granite towers, others are a more generous slope and curve, nurturing a series of meadows that seem to gleam from the slopes.

The most important thing to know when visiting the Maroon Bells is that you can't just drive in and park your car whenever you want – this area sees some 20,000 visitors each summer, hence access is strictly controlled. The road in is only open to outside traffic from 5pm to 9am ($10 access fee) from mid-June to September; the majority of visitors will need to park at or take an RFTA bus to the Aspen Highlands (half-mile west of Aspen on Hwy 82) and then take a **shuttle** (Aspen Highlands; adult/child $6/4; ⏰9am-4:30pm daily Jun 15-Aug, Fri-Sun Sep-Oct 6). Exceptions to the road closure include visitors with disabilities and campers at any of the three USFS campgrounds off Maroon Creek Rd. The access road is not plowed in winter, when you can cross-country ski in to Maroon Bells Lake.

Hikes

You can spend an hour up here or several days: the choice is yours. Free guided naturalist hikes are led by ACES (p217) guides daily at 10:15am and 1:15pm, leaving from the visitors center. The one-hour walk along the shore of Maroon Lake is the best choice for novice hikers. Assemble 10 minutes before each departure.

ACES also runs a more strenuous trip to **Crater Lake**, leaving at the same times. If you're in reasonable shape, though, you might as well do this one yourself. Although steep in spots, it's only 1.8 miles one-way, making for a nice, short day hike. Surrounded by gorgeous sculpted peaks and fed by a creek flowing down from the high country, the setting is stunning, though the lake itself is shallow in late summer. If you're hungry for a little bit more altitude, we suggest pressing on to **Buckskin Pass** (12,462ft; 4.8 miles one-way). From the narrow granite ledge you can see mountains erupt in all directions. If you continue over the pass for three additional miles you'll wind up at Snowmass Lake, a terrific campsite.

Alternatively, you can diverge from the Buckskin Trail and head over Willow Pass (12,600ft) and camp at **Willow Lake** (11,795ft; 6.5 miles one-way). Views are marvelous the entire way, especially at the top where you can see the Continental Divide.

As is the usual protocol in the Rockies, it's best to get below treeline before noon, as afternoon lightning is a real danger.

Salida

POP 5274 / ELEV 7083FT

When a town of about 5200 people has three microbreweries, you know something's up. A former railroad hub turned ranching community turned outdoor mecca, this is quintessential Colorado: where mud-spattered pickup trucks cruise the streets alongside battered Subarus adorned with rooftop kayaks, and mighty peaks form distant postcard panoramas everywhere you look.

Blessed with one of the state's largest historic districts, Salida is not only an inviting spot to explore, it also has an unbeatable location, with the Arkansas River on one side and the intersection of two mighty mountain ranges on the other. The plan of attack here is to hike, bike or raft during the day, then come back to town to refuel with grilled buffalo ribs and a cold IPA at night.

And did we mention that the sun always shines?

Sights & Activities

Salida doesn't have any major sights, but the historic downtown contains around 100 buildings that date to the turn of the century. Look for the free booklet *Historic Chaffee County* (pick it up at the tourist office or try your hotel), which contains an in-depth and informative walking tour of the city. History buffs can check out the small museum next to the tourist office, though opening hours are very sporadic.

Both bikers and hikers should note that some big-time trails – the Continental Divide (www.continentaldividetrail.org), the Colorado Trail (www.coloradotrail.org) and the Rainbow Trail (p335) – are all within spitting distance of town. If you don't want to sweat it, a **gondola** (http://monachcrestscenictramway.webs.com; adult/child $10/5; ⌚8:30am-5:30pm mid-May–mid-Sep) can haul you from Monarch Pass nearly 1000ft up to the Continental Divide.

Mountain Biking

Salida has no shortage of epic singletrack. Grab a copy of the *Upper Arkansas Valley Cycling Guide* (free) or stop by a bike shop for tips and maps.

★ **Monarch Crest Trail** MOUNTAIN BIKING

One of the most famous rides in all of Colorado, the Monarch Crest is an extreme 28-mile adventure. It starts off at Monarch Pass (11,312ft), follows the exposed ridge 12 miles to Marshall Pass and then either cuts down to Poncha Springs on an old railroad grade or hooks onto the Rainbow Trail. A classic ride, but not for the inexperienced.

Salida Mountain Trails MOUNTAIN BIKING

(http://salidamountaintrails.org) If you don't want to bother with a shuttle, the best place to start riding in Salida is the Arkansas Hills Trail System just across the river (look for the giant S). Open year round – yes, you can ride here in winter – it offers a nice variety of short rides for all levels.

South of town, Methodist Mountain is another spot to check out for fun cross-country traverses through the high desert. The Little Rainbow Trail (4.7 miles) is a great one for families.

Absolute Bikes BICYCLE RENTAL

(☎719-539-9295; www.absolutebikes.com; 330 W Sackett Rd; bike rental $40-80, tours from $90; ⌚9am-7pm) The place to go for bike enthusiasts, offering maps, gear, advice and rentals. Check out the selection of guided rides, ranging from St Elmo ghost town to the Monarch Crest.

Hiking

With a dozen 14ers poking up from the mighty Sawatch Range, there is some serious mountain adventure to be had here. Head up Hwy 50 west to Monarch Pass to access the Colorado Trail, the Waterdog Lakes day hike or the Continental Divide Trail. Hwy 285 south to Poncha Pass passes the Rainbow Trail. The Collegiate Peaks are best accessed from Buena Vista. The Sangre de Cristo Range is a 1½-hour drive and can be accessed via Westcliffe (p334) or Crestone (p337). Stop by the ranger office (p233) for maps, route descriptions and camping info.

Other Activities

Rocky Mountain Outdoor Center OUTDOORS

(RMOC; ☎800-255-5784; http://rmoc.com; 14825 Hwy 285; climbing trips from $125) The local Swiss Army knife of outdoor adventure, RMOC offers all sorts of guided activities, but is particularly good for rafting, kayaking and rock-climbing trips. If you want to learn some basic techniques, it also offers instruction in kayaking and stand-up paddling. Rent river gear here.

Captain Zipline EXTREME SPORTS

(☎877-947-5463; www.captainzipline.com; 331 H St; zip-line tour $89) This popular zip-line tour takes in seven cables through the high desert, some of which send you flying above some pretty deep canyons. Expect to spend two to three hours on the tour. Plans are in the works to add via ferrata (assisted climbing) and a large aerial park. Children must be seven or older.

Ark Anglers FISHING
(☎719-539-4223; www.arkanglers.com; 7500 Hwy 50; half-day wade trip $225; ⏰8am-6pm) The Arkansas is a great place to cast for trout and the Ark is the best spot to meet the local fisherfolk and get up-to-date reports on current river conditions. It also has a shop in Buena Vista.

Monarch Mountain SNOW SPORTS
(☎888-996-7669; www.skimonarch.com; 23715 Hwy 50; adult/child $65/25; ⏰Dec–mid-Apr) Cut along the same lines as Eldora and Ski Cooper ski resorts, Monarch is a great local mountain. Although the resort's 800 acres is on the small side, you'll still find lots of varied terrain, great powder and some very affordable tickets – the season pass gets you days at 12 different Colorado resorts, including Crested Butte. It's located just below Monarch Pass, on Hwy 50.

Sleeping

The Arkansas Headwaters Recreation Area operates six campgrounds (bring your own water) along the river. The nicest is **Hecla Junction** (☎800-678-2267; http://coloradostateparks.reserveamerica.com; Hwy 285, Mile 135; tent/RV $16/24 ;), located 14 miles north of town off Hwy 285. It's fairly secluded and boasts fabulous riverside scenery. Rincon is another nearby site if Hecla is full. Reservations are essential in summer.

RAFTING THE ARKANSAS

The headwaters of the Arkansas is Colorado's best-known stretch of white water, with everything from extreme rapids to mellow ripples. Although most rafting companies cover the river from Leadville to the Royal Gorge, the most popular trips descend Brown's Canyon, a 22-mile stretch that includes class 3 to 4 rapids. If you're with young kids or just looking for something more low key, Bighorn Sheep Canyon is a good bet. Those after more of an adrenaline rush can head upstream to the Numbers or downstream to the Royal Gorge, both of which are class 4 to 5. If you'd like to go solo, most outfitters also rent duckies (inflatable kayaks).

Water flow varies by season, so time your visit for late May or early June for a wilder ride – by the time August rolls around, the water level is usually pretty low. If you're rafting with kids, note that they need to be at least six (sometimes older depending on the trip/outfitter) and weigh a minimum of 50lb.

Most companies are based just south of Buena Vista, close to where Hwys 24 and 285 diverge. The larger ones have Cañon City (p314) locations as well. We recommend the following:

Buffalo Joe's (☎866-283-3563; www.buffalojoe.com; 113 N Railroad St; half-/full-day adult $64/98, child $54/78; ⏰May-Sep) One of the top river outfitters in the Buena Vista–Salida swirl, offering a range of trips that run every bit of the Arkansas.

Wilderness Aware Rafting (☎800-462-7238; www.inaraft.com; 12600 Hwys 24/285; half-/full-day adult $60/94, child $51/80; ⏰May-Sep) This adventure company offers rafting, horseback riding, mountain biking and more.

River Runners (☎800-723-8987; www.riverrunnersltd.com; 24070 County Rd 301; half-/full-day adult $60/98, child $50/88; ⏰May-Sep) One of the largest rafting companies, though being big has its drawbacks.

American Adventure Expeditions (☎719-395-2409; www.americanadventure.com; 12844 Hwy 24; half-/full-day adult $60/98, child $55/88) Another company offering both rafting and land-based tours, it comes recommended by locals in the know.

Arkansas River Tours (☎800-321-4352; www.arkansasrivertours.com; 19487 Hwy 50; half-/full-day adult $57/95, child $47/85; ⏰May-Sep) This outfitter runs from Brown's Canyon downstream, specializing in Royal Gorge trips. It has an office in Cotopaxi, 23 miles east of Salida.

★ **Simple Lodge & Hostel** HOSTEL $
(☎719-650-7381; www.simplelodge.com; 224 E 1st St; dm/d/q $24/55/76; P 📶 👪 🐾) If only Colorado had more spots like this. Run by a super-friendly husband-wife team (Jon and Julia), this hostel is simple but stylish, with a fully stocked kitchen and a comfy communal area that feels just like home. It's a popular stopover for touring cyclists following the coast-to-coast Rte 50 – you're likely to meet some interesting folks here.

Palace Hotel BOUTIQUE HOTEL $$
(☎719-207-4175; www.salidapalacehotel.com; 204 N F St; ste $130-210; P ❄ 📶 🐾) 🍃 The most atmospheric digs in Salida, the three-story Palace is an old railway hotel (1909) that was entirely renovated in 2012 by Vicki and Fred Klein. It's now a smart, solar-powered boutique option, with 14 personalized suites and a vintage claw-foot-bathtub-style decor. Some suites sleep up to four people; all include kitchenettes and continental breakfast.

Eating

Thai Mini Cafe THAI $
(11150 Hwy 50; mains $9-13; ⏰10am-8pm Thu-Tue; 📶 🌱) The Thai Mini Cafe is known as far away as Glenwood Springs, proving that if you want something besides burgers in central Colorado, you may have to travel for it. Located out on Hwy 50, past Poncha Springs and on the way to Monarch Pass, this no-frills diner offers home-cooked Thai classics – pad thai, curries and papaya salad.

★ **Amícas** PIZZERIA $$
(www.amicassalida.com; 136 E 2nd St; pizzas & paninis $8-12; ⏰11:30am-9pm; 🌱 👪) Thin-crust wood-fired pizzas and six microbrews on tap? Amícas can do no wrong. This laid-back, high-ceilinged hangout (formerly a funeral parlor) is the perfect spot to replenish all those calories you burned off during the day. Savor a Michelangelo (pesto, sausage and goat cheese) or Vesuvio (artichoke hearts, sun-dried tomatoes, roasted peppers) alongside a cool glass of Headwaters IPA.

Fritz TAPAS $$
(☎719-539-0364; http://thefritzdowntown.com; 113 East Sackett St; tapas $4-8, mains $9-14; ⏰11am-2am; 📶) This fun and funky riverside watering hole serves up clever American-style tapas. Think three-cheese mac with bacon, fries and truffle aioli, shrimp curry, and even bone marrow with red-onion jam. It also does a mean grass-fed beef burger and other sandwiches at lunch. Good selection of local beers on tap.

Laughing Ladies MODERN AMERICAN $$$
(☎719-539-6209; http://laughingladiesrestaurant.com; 128 W 1st St; lunch $9-16, dinner $13-23; ⏰Thu-Mon) 🍃 For the most sophisticated cuisine in town, head to this intimate brick-walled bistro. The bluesy soundtrack and changing art exhibits provide a dash of urban chic, though the tantalizing local specialties (cornmeal-crusted snapper, goat cheese chile relleno, rosemary grilled buffalo) keep you rooted in the valley. Both chefs previously worked in Napa; unsurprisingly, the wine list is excellent.

Drinking

★ **Cafe Dawn** CAFE
(www.cafe-dawn.com; 203 W 1st St; ⏰6am-6pm; 📶) 🍃 The place to go for your morning cappuccino and raspberry scone. This great community cafe is run by Phillip and Dawn out of a former Volkswagen repair shop, and features organic beans, local ingredients in the lunch menu and damn good lattes. Phillip has also written two local guidebooks (climbing and mountain biking), which you can find here. Cash only.

Boathouse Cantina BAR
(228 N F St; ⏰11am-10pm; 📶) If you can snag a table by the river, this is a pretty sweet spot. It's got 20 craft beers on tap, including local brew Elevation. The buffalo chili and fish tacos ain't bad either.

Information

Salida Chamber of Commerce (☎877-772-5432; www.nowthisiscolorado.com; 406 Hwy 50; ⏰9am-5pm Mon-Fri) General tourist info.

USFS Ranger Office (☎719-539-3591; www.fs.usda.gov; 5575 Cleora Rd; ⏰8am-4:30pm Mon-Fri) Located east of town off Hwy 50, with camping and trail info for the Sawatch and northern Sangre de Cristo Ranges.

Getting There & Away

Located at the 'exit' of the Arkansas River Valley, Salida occupies a prime location at the crossroads of Hwys 285 and 50. Indeed, this used to be a major railroad hub, and you'll likely spot an abandoned line or two while exploring the area. Gunnison, Colorado Springs, the Great Sand Dunes and even Vail are all within one to two hours' drive, provided you have your own car.

It's also a good stopover for those traveling between Denver and Santa Fe.

LOCAL FARMERS MARKETS

The **Central Colorado Foodshed Alliance** (CCFA; http://ccfa.coop) runs farmers markets from June through mid-October in Salida (8am to 12.30pm Saturday), Buena Vista (9am to 1pm Sunday) and Cañon City (9am to 1:30pm Saturday). They're a great resource for finding out more about where to find locally grown food in Central Colorado. See the website for details.

Buena Vista

POP 2638 / ELEV 7954FT

With Mt Princeton (14,197ft) and the rest of the Collegiate Peaks providing a dramatic backdrop to the west, and the icy Arkansas River rushing by the boulder-filled hills east of town, Buena Vista certainly lives up to its name. Whether you're after hiking, biking, paddling, hot-spring soaking or simply stupendous landscapes, this is a town that has adventure playground written all over it.

Historic E Main St, the town's main drag, runs perpendicularly (away from the mountains) off Hwy 24. Follow Main St to the end and you'll come to the Arkansas River. Heading west (towards the mountains) off Hwy 24 is W Main St, which turns into Rte 306 and heads up to Cottonwood Pass.

Activities

Among the many diversions available to the thrill-seeking wanderer in Buena Vista, the top attraction has always been and will always be the Arkansas River (p232): 99 miles of white water accessible from Main St. If you have your own boat and know what you're doing, check out the Buena Vista Whitewater Park at the end of E Main St.

Hiking & Mountain Biking

★Collegiate Peaks Wilderness HIKING

Who said the Ivies had to be stuck-up and boring? Encompassing 166,938 acres laced with 105 miles of trails, the Collegiate Peaks has the highest average elevation of any wilderness area in the US: eight peaks exceed 14,000ft, including the state's third and fifth highest summits, Mt Harvard and La Plata Peak. (Princeton, Yale, Oxford and Columbia are the 20th, 21st, 26th and 35th highest respectively.)

But the best hikes here don't necessarily involve peak bagging. Popular day trips include Ptarmigan Lake (6.6 miles; 14 miles from town on County Rd 306), Kroenke Lake (8 miles; access County Rd 365) and as much of the Colorado Trail as you want to do (access Avalanche Trailhead, 9 miles from town on County Rd 306). For detailed descriptions and maps, stop by the ranger office in Salida (p233) .

Barbara Whipple Trail MOUNTAIN BIKING, HIKING

(Whipple Trail; www.garna.org; Buena Vista River Park) Good for hikers, bikers and picnickers, this trail system is about as idyllic as town parks get. Accessed from the end of E Main St (turn north), it follows an old stage road through the arid hills and funky rock formations east of the Arkansas River, with stupendous views back towards the Collegiates.

The main trail is about a mile long, but you can combine it with numerous other trails (eg Broken Boyfriend).

Hot Springs

Mt Princeton Hot Springs Resort HOT SPRINGS

(☎888-395-7799; www.mtprinceton.com; 15870 County Rd 162; day pass adult/child from $18/12; ⏰8am-10pm; 📶) A sprawling four-star hot-springs resort, this is a terrific destination for families. There are 30 natural pools on the property that differ in size and atmosphere, including soaking pools, an expansive swimming pool and a 400ft water slide. Many guests stay the night, but it is also possible to purchase a day pass.

Room rates (from $124) include hot-spring access. Private cabins (from $164) are fully equipped and a full-service spa is onsite, offering body wraps, exfoliations and five types of massage.

Cottonwood Hot Springs HOT SPRING

(☎719-395-6434; www.cottonwood-hot-springs.com; 18999 County Rd 306; adult/child from $15/12; ⏰8:30am-9pm) Take Main St across Hwy 24 and keep going up the mountain toward Cottonwood Pass, and you'll soon come to the hippiest of the Collegiate hot springs. These renovated pools are set on leafy grounds and are somewhat kitsch, with gushing fountains of hot water, dangling vines and wind chimes (but no water slide).

Other Activities

Mt Princeton Hot Springs Stables HORSEBACK RIDING
(☎866-877-3630; www.coloradotrailrides.com; 14582 County Rd 162; 1hr ride $35) Located down the hill from the hot-springs resort, this stable offers a variety of trips, from one-hour nose-to-tail rides to overnight pack trips. Children must be five or older.

Trailhead SPORTS RENTALS
(☎719-395-8001; www.thetrailheadco.com; 707 Hwy 24; mountain bikes half-/full-day adult $30/35, child $15/18; ⏰10am-6pm Thu-Tue, noon-5pm Sun) Located north of town on Hwy 24, this outdoor shop rents out bikes, Nordic skis, snowshoes and climbing shoes. Also sells useful topo maps and plenty of gear.

Cottonwood Pass SCENIC DRIVE
(County Rd 306; ⏰Jun-Oct) Ever wonder what it's like to drive to the moon? Wind your way past the Collegiate Peaks Campground to Cottonwood Pass (12,126ft). This is the Continental Divide and the border between the San Isabel National Forest on the eastern slope and the Gunnison National Forest to the west.

On the eastern side of the road as you head uphill is a turnoff to the Avalanche Trailhead, which is a spur of the Colorado Trail with access to the Collegiate Peaks Wilderness. Further uphill you'll come to Denny Creek Trail, then Ptamargian Lake trailhead. The drive to the pass goes from moderately sinuous to downright jagged as you approach the edge of the timberline, and to the east the Collegiate Peaks spread out against the big blue sky. Just a 30-minute drive up County Rd 306 (head west on Main St and keep going), it's spectacular country and a great place for a picnic or hike.

Sleeping

Apart from faceless motels, the sleeping options in Buena Vista are very limited, with the most distinctive choices being the Liars' Lodge and Mt Princeton Hot Springs Resort. There are a number of campgrounds, however, including Railroad Bridge and the **Collegiate Peaks Campground** (www.reserveamerica.com; Hwy 306; tent & RV sites $17; ⏰May-early Sep; 🐾). The road up to St Elmo has three additional campgrounds (p240), though these can get very busy.

★Railroad Bridge CAMPGROUND $
(☎800-678-2267; www.coloradostateparks.reserveamerica.com; County Rd 371; tent & RV sites $16; ⏰year-round; 🐾) Just after passing through the series of blasted tunnels that give this stretch of graded earth its name – Tunnels Rd – you'll find Elephant Rock looming over the Arkansas River with a wide, flat, sheltered patch that makes an exquisite campsite. There are no bathroom facilities and you need to bring your own water, but dig those massive mountain views.

It's a popular spot (there are bolted climbs across the road and you're on the banks of the Arkansas), so you'll need to reserve

CLIMBING MT PRINCETON

Although experienced hikers will probably want to tackle Yale's east ridge, those looking for a more accessible 14er can opt for Mt Princeton, a terrific (if long) day trip from Buena Vista.

The road itself is often harder to find than the trail. From the center of town, drive west on County Rd 306 for 0.7 miles. Turn left on County Rd 321 and continue south for 7.2 miles. Turn right onto County Rd 322 at a large sign. On County Rd 322, drive 0.8 miles to a fork in the road. Bear right and you'll be on Mt Princeton Rd.

If you have a two-wheel-drive vehicle, you'll be leaving it here at the large parking area (8900ft) and starting your walk up the road. If you begin here the total distance will be 13 miles. If you have a high-clearance 4WD, you can continue up the narrow road. Bear right at the fork, and drive 3 miles to the radio towers (10,800ft). There is parking here for a couple of vehicles, or turn left and continue on 322A Rd for just over 3 miles to park near small camping spots at about 11,000ft. If you start from here (and at this point everyone is on foot) the total distance will be about 6.25 miles.

After hiking about a half-mile, the road curves up to the left and heads south to the Lucky Mine. The Mt Princeton Trail will be on the right; follow it all the way to the summit. Remember that storms in the Collegiates can blow in fast, so don't hesitate to turn back if the weather gets dicey.

online during the summer. To get here, turn north on Colorado Ave off E Main St.

★**Liars' Lodge B&B** B&B $$
(☎719-395-3444; www.liarslodge.com; 30000 Co Rd 371; r $138-168, cabin $265;) This airy, spectacularly set log cabin is perched on a finger of the Arkansas River, so close that the river will sing you to sleep. It has five rooms and a cabin, which sleeps up to five people. Breakfast is served on an outstanding riverside terrace, weather permitting. This place represents outstanding value and is easily the best in Buena Vista, so reserve ahead.

Rates drop by as much as $60 in winter. It's set just off Co Rd 371; to get here, turn north onto Colorado Ave from E Main St and keep going.

Eating & Drinking

Evergreen Cafe DINER $
(☎719-395-8984; www.evergreencafebv.com; 418 US Hwy 24; mains $5-8.95; ⏲6:30am-2pm daily;) Fun and funky, this canary-yellow traincar of a diner on Hwy 24 north of Main St is where you'll find some seriously tasty offerings, such as zucchini fries, milkshakes and sinful bread pudding, not to mention killer omelets, melts, burgers and salads.

Asian Palate ASIAN $$
(☎719-395-6679; www.theasianpalate.com; 328 E Main St; mains $12-22; ⏲11:30am-10pm Mon-Fri, 5-10pm Sat & Sun;) Eclectic Asian fare is what passes for haute cuisine in Buena Vista. Dishes such as massaman curry, pork larb and beef with udon noodles are typical kitchen fare, while raw morsels appear from the sushi bar. All are served in minimalist environs – think high-beamed ceilings and burgundy walls strategically cracked to reveal swatches of original brick.

Eddyline Restaurant & Brewery PUB FOOD $$
(☎719-966-6000; www.eddylinepub.com; 926 S Main St; pizzas $9-12; ⏲11am-9pm;) With sunny patio seating just steps from the Arkansas River, it's no surprise this South Main brewpub is the local hangout. The food – woodfired pizzas and grass-fed local beef – is solid if unspectacular. You can't go wrong with the seven beers on tap, however.

To get here, take E Main St to the end of town, then follow the signs south.

★**Buena Vista Roastery** CAFE
(www.bvroastery.com; 409 E Main St; ⏲7am-6pm;) Known among locals as the Roastery, this wonderful, aromatic cafe roasts and sells fair-trade and organic beans, supporting local nonprofit organizations through its Coffees for a Cause program. It's a nice space with patio seating and delectable pastries available throughout the day.

Getting There & Away

Buena Vista is 93 miles west of Colorado Springs and 35 miles south of Leadville on Hwy 24, and 25 miles north of Salida on Hwy 285.

Twin Lakes

POP 171 / ELEV 9200FT

An alternative to staying in Leadville, Twin Lakes is a gorgeous historic mining camp set on the shores of the largest glacial lakes in Colorado, at the base of the sinuous climb to Independence Pass. Fed by steady stagecoach lines, this was log-cabin mining country in the late 19th century, and a convenient rest stop between Aspen and Leadville. First called Dayton during the 1860s gold rush, it was renamed Twin Lakes in 1879 when the silver rush revived the village.

Sights & Activities

Several historic structures still stand on the lake shore, including the Red Rooster Tavern (aka the town brothel), now the visitor center. On the south shore of the main lake is **Interlaken**, the vestiges of what was once Colorado's largest resort, built in 1889. The ruins have good signage and you can even walk inside and explore the abandoned buildings. You can get here along the Colorado and Continental Divide trails; it's about 5 miles round-trip with little elevation gain. The turnoff for the Interlaken trailhead is 0.6 miles after you turn onto Hwy 82, after Lost Canyon Rd.

The cross-country skiing and snowshoeing in the area is magnificent too (though you'll have to source your own gear), and, of course, you can fish and boat on the lakes in summer. Canoe rentals are available in the village.

If you're up for some higher-altitude views, La Plata Peak and Independence Pass lie just west of town. You'll find several campsites in the area.

Sleeping & Eating

Twin Lakes Lodge HOTEL $$
(☎719-486-7965; www.thetwinlakesinn.com; 6435 Hwy 82; r $100-160, cabin from $250, all incl break-

DON'T MISS

INDEPENDENCE PASS

Looming at 12,095ft, **Independence Pass** (Hwy 82; ⏲ late May-Oct) is one of the more high-profile mountain passes along the Continental Divide. Perhaps it's the proximity to Aspen (just 20 miles away on Hwy 82), or maybe it's the celeb quotient (Kevin Costner lives on its western slope). But we think it's the drive itself.

A narrow ribbon of road swerves above the timberline with gentle then hairpin turns. Views range from pretty to stunning to downright cinematic, and by the time you glimpse swaths of snow along the ridges just below the knife edge of peaks you'll be living in your own IMAX film. Late season you'll see everyone from bow hunters dressed in camo gear and last-gasp family vacationers (or a cocktail of the two) to two kinds of bikers: unshaven Harley riders with frayed bedrolls on the tailgate, and leg-shaven millionaire road bikers with iPhones in their saddle bags.

A paved nature trail wanders off the parking area at the top of the pass. It's tundra country up here, so dress warmly and stay on trails lest you cause decades of unknowable damage in a single step.

If you've got some mountaineering experience, consider climbing 14,336ft **La Plata Peak** (www.14ers.com; ⏲ Jun-Sep), the state's 5th highest. The trail leaves from South Fork Lake Trailhead on the eastern slope of Independence Pass. From the parking area, walk over the bridge and continue on the fire road for about a quarter of a mile to find a trailhead sign on the left. There's a trail fork about 100m after crossing the bridge over La Plata Gulch. Stay right on the main trail and follow it up to the top. It starts out mellow, but soon intensifies – once you reach Ellingwood Ridge, it's almost all class 3 the rest of the way up, with moderate exposure in places. It's a 9.5-mile round-trip, but you'll need extra time to traverse the ridge. Note that this is definitely not a climb for beginners.

There are some fantastic eastern slope campgrounds to stay at if you're here to climb the peak. Both **Parry Peak Campground** (Hwy 82; tent sites $15; ⏲ Jun-Aug), 2.5 miles west of Twin Lakes, and the stunning **Twin Peaks Campground** (Hwy 82; tent sites $15; ⏲ Jun-Aug; 🐾), nestled at the base of two peaks, have great locations and are first-come, first-served.

fast; 📶👪) Over 130 years old, this green-shuttered inn was reopened in 2013 after three years of restoration. Some rooms are on the small side and not all have private bathrooms, but you can't argue with the lakeside location. The downstairs restaurant (lunch $7 to $12, dinner $15 to $27) and saloon is the main hangout in Twin Lakes.

ℹ Getting There & Away

Twin Lakes is 37 miles from Aspen, just over Independence Pass (open late May through October) on Hwy 82. Hwy 24 is just east of the lakes, providing access to Leadville (22 miles north) and Buena Vista (26 miles south).

Leadville

POP 2602 / ELEV 10,152FT

Originally known as Cloud City, Leadville was once Colorado's second-largest city (population 40,000) and a quintessential Wild West town, where fortunes were made and lost overnight, swindlers ruled the roost, and Doc Holliday got into a shootout with the law and won.

It was silver, not gold, that brought riches to the lucky few, but after the bottom dropped out of the silver market in 1893, Leadville took a serious nosedive. Other minerals kept the town alive, however, particularly after the discovery of molybdenum (atomic number 42), which was extremely popular in wartime as it helped to reinforce steel: Germany, Japan and the Soviet Union were the three biggest customers of Climax Mine during the 1930s. Unsurprisingly, the US government subsequently designated Climax (atop Hwy 91 and still in operation) the nation's most important mine in the following decade.

Today, Leadville may feel slightly abandoned, but there's adventure to be had in them there hills. You can climb the two tallest peaks in Colorado, run a 100-mile race, mountain bike for 24 hours straight, cross-country ski to a gourmet meal or simply hop on a historic train to glimpse wildflowers. Well, what are you waiting for?

Sights

Healy House Museum & Dexter Cabin MUSEUM

(www.historycolorado.org; 912 Harrison Ave; adult/child 6-12yr $6/4.50; 10am-4:30pm mid-May–Sep) Two of Leadville's oldest surviving homes are decked out with the owners' original gear and period pieces resembling what they may have enjoyed. The Dexter Cabin was the original mining digs of wealthy gold-mining investor, James V Dexter. The much grander 1878 Greek Revival home, now known as Healy House, was built by August R Meyer.

Healy House features lavish Victorian furnishings collected in Leadville, including objects belonging to silver tycoon Horace Tabor and his wife Augusta (Baby Doe), among other Leadville pioneers.

National Mining Hall of Fame MUSEUM

(www.mininghalloffame.org; 120 W 9th St; adult/child 6-12yr $7/3; 9am-5pm Jun-Oct, 11am-6pm Nov-May;) Although it sounds both cheesy and dreary, this is a surprisingly informative museum, with mineral displays, gold-mining dioramas, a mock-up coal mine, and an introduction to the local mining industry. Kids will find enough here to stay entertained for an hour or two. You can get a combo ticket (adult/child $10/5) that includes a visit to the Matchless Mine.

Matchless Mine HISTORIC SITE

(E 7th Rd; adult/child 6-12yr $7/3, combo ticket with National Mining Hall of Fame $10/5; 9am-5pm, Jun-Sep) This is where silver magnate and Colorado senator Horace Tabor made and then lost millions in the 1880s, and where his glamorous and sensational wife, Baby Doe, eventually froze to death after spending the last three decades of her life in poverty.

The 45-minute tours visit Baby Doe's cabin and the mine's hoist tower, but don't actually descend into the mine itself. In summer, tours leave every half hour; get tickets at the National Mining Hall of Fame.

Camp Hale MEMORIAL

(Hwy 24) About 16 miles north of Leadville on Hwy 24, just over Tennessee Pass, lies the former US Army facility, Camp Hale. Established in 1942, it was created specifically for the purpose of training the 10th Mountain Division, the Army's only battalion on skis. At its height during WWII, there were over 1000 buildings and some 14,000 soldiers housed in the meadow here.

After the war Camp Hale was decommissioned, only to be brought back to life again in 1958, this time by the CIA. Over the next six years, CIA agents trained Tibetan freedom fighters in guerrilla warfare, with the goal of driving the communist Chinese out of Tibet. In 1965 Camp Hale was officially dismantled, and the land returned to the US Forest Service.

Nova Guides (719-486-2656; www.novaguides.com; bike tours $100) is based here, offering mountain-bike tours and various other outdoor activities.

Tabor Opera House HISTORIC BUILDING

(www.taboroperahouse.net; 308 Harrison Ave; adult/child $5/2.50; 10am-5pm Mon-Sat Jun-Aug) Built in 1879 by multimillionaire Horace Tabor, this was once one of the premier entertainment venues in all Colorado, if not the West, and hosted the likes of Houdini, Oscar Wilde and Anna Held. You can visit the interior on a tour; there are also occasional performances.

Activities

Mt Elbert HIKING

(www.14ers.com; Jun-Sep) Colorado's tallest peak and the 2nd highest in the continental US, Mt Elbert (14,433ft) is a relatively gentle giant. There are three established routes to the top, none of which are technical. The most common approach is via the northeast ridge; it's a 9-mile round-trip hike with 4700ft of elevation gain, so expect to spend most of the day.

The turnoff for the trailhead is just south of Leadville on Rte 300. If you have 4WD, the South Mt Elbert Trailhead is accessed via Hwy 82, just east of Twin Lakes. It's a slightly shorter hike with only 4100ft of elevation gain.

★Mt Massive HIKING

(Jun-Oct) The state's second-tallest peak, Mt Massive (14,421ft) lives up to its name: it has four summits and a 3-mile-long ridge, giving it more total area above 14,000ft than any other peak in the state. From Hwy 24, it dominates the western horizon.

The classic route up the east slope is a real bruiser; you'll put in a grueling 13.6 miles of hiking round-trip. The southwest slope is much shorter at 8 miles, but you'll need

4WD and high clearance to reach the trailhead. Both trailheads are accessed via Rte 300, south of Leadville. The Tour de Massive is for those who enjoy punishment – it takes in all four summits, with nearly 15 miles (11 hours) of hiking. Start before dawn.

Tennessee Pass Nordic Center SNOW SPORTS
(☎719-486-1750; www.tennesseepass.com; Hwy 24; trail pass adult/child $14/10; ⏲8:30am-5pm Dec–mid-Apr) Snowshoers and cross-country skiers come here to get their Leadville fix. Some 15 miles of groomed trails extend from the base of Ski Cooper, but the highlight is the 1-mile haul to your favorite gourmet yurt: the Tennessee Pass Cookhouse (p240).

Ski Cooper SNOW SPORTS
(☎800-707-6114; www.skicooper.com; Hwy 24; lift ticket adult/child $47/27; ⏲9am-4pm Dec–mid-Apr) Ski Cooper offers about 500 acres of skiable terrain, a dedicated snowboard terrain park, and backcountry thrills through the snowcat tours on Chicago Ridge ($299). It's small but affordable, and a great place for beginning and intermediate skiers and boarders. It's just north of Leadville on Hwy 24, at Tennessee Pass.

Leadville, Colorado & Southern Railroad RAILWAY
(☎866-386-3936; www.leadville-train.com; 326 E 7th St; adult/child $35/20; ⏲late May-early Oct) Originating in Leadville, the LC&S follows the old Denver, South Park and Pacific, and Colorado and Southern lines to the Continental Divide. Time it right and you'll see fields of wildflowers give way to panoramas across the Arkansas River Valley. Your tour guide will fill you in on Leadville's bawdy past along the way. All trips are 2½ hours; engine and caboose seating is extra.

Festivals & Events

Leadville Trail 100 CYCLING
(www.leadvilleraceseries.com; ⏲Jun-Jul) The Leadville 100 is one of the most famous and longest mountain-bike races in the world. Imagine 100 miles of lung-crushing, adrenaline-fueled riding on the old silver-mining roads that go from 9200ft to 12,424ft and back again. But the Leadville Trail races are not just about the mountain bikers.

The whole thing started as a 100-mile foot race (45 racers started, only 10 finished), and they still offer that run every year, along with a half-marathon, a 50-mile bike race and a 24-hour mountain-bike race. If you're interested in the run, you should also think about attending the annual training camp.

Sleeping

★ **Tennessee Pass Sleep Yurts** YURT $
(☎719-486-1750; www.tennesseepass.com; Tennessee Pass; per yurt $225; 👪) Sleeping in the backcountry has never been so luxurious. With a woodburning stove, kitchenette and even luggage delivery and room service, this is a great way to enjoy all the magic of a quiet winter night without having to wake up with frostbitten toes. Yurts sleep up to six people and are located 1.3 miles from the Tennessee Pass Nordic Center.

Part of the appeal is that you have to ski, snowshoe or hike in: gear can be rented at the Nordic Center, and the yurts are a great base for exploring the Tennessee Pass trail system. You can cook your own meals, but

LEADVILLE MOUNTAIN BIKING

There's a reason that one of the largest mountain-bike races in the world – the Leadville Trail 100 – happens here. There are simply so many trails that you could bike for weeks and never retrace your path. **Mosquito Pass** presents a unique opportunity to ride above 13,000ft in treeless alpine scenery. This extremely challenging 7-mile ascent follows E 7th St from Leadville.

Another good destination where you can enjoy panoramic vistas is **Hagerman Pass** (11,925ft), west of Leadville. Riders follow a relatively easy railroad grade on USFS Rd 105 for 7 miles to Hagerman Pass from the junction on the south bank of Turquoise Lake Reservoir. On the way you pass **Skinner Hut** (☎970-925-5775; www.huts.org; per person $25), maintained by the 10th Mountain Division Hut Association.

An easy ride follows the shoreline trail on the north side of Turquoise Lake Reservoir for 6 miles between Sugar Loaf Dam and May Queen Campground. Another follows the Colorado Trail north from Tennessee Pass for 2½ miles to Mitchell Creek. For other suggestions, pick up a map from the USFS Leadville Ranger Station.

WORTH A TRIP

ST ELMO

An old gold-mining ghost town tucked into the base of the Collegiate Peaks, St Elmo makes for a fun excursion. The drive is the best part: the road wends its way past stands of redolent ponderosa pine, a wildlife-viewing meadow and jagged peaks before petering out at what is Colorado's best-preserved ghost town.

Of course, it wasn't about the scenery back in the good ol' days. There was gold in this here creek! Most buildings were built in or around 1881: the schoolhouse, an old mercantile, and a miners exchange are among the best kept of the bunch.

The only catch to this spectacular setting is that St Elmo is also a staging point for ATV and snowmobile enthusiasts, who follow the forest service road up to Tincup Pass. The revving of not-too-distant engines can take away some of the charm, so try to avoid weekends.

If you've got the time and energy, you can continue on 5 miles to Hancock; the turnoff is just before St Elmo. From here it's a 3-mile hike up to the **Alpine Tunnel** – a failed attempt to get a railroad through the mountain – and amazing views from the Continental Divide. Ready to tackle it on bike? Sign up for a tour with Absolute Bikes (p231) in Salida.

If you want to have the place to yourself, stay the night: the **Ghost Town Guest House** (☎719-395-2120; www.ghosttownguesthouse.com; r incl 2 meals $165-185; @) is a local B&B (really!), and there are three very popular USFS campgrounds on the way up. They're all nice, but **Chalk Lake** (☎877-444-6777; www.recreation.gov; tent & RV sites $17 ; 🐾) has a choice location with views of Mt Princeton. Reservations are essential. Just before the turnoff to the campground is a parking lot for the **Agnes Vaille Trail** (on your right), a short half-mile hike up to a waterfall. It's the perfect spot to stretch your legs.

St Elmo is on County Rd 162, 11.5 miles past Mt Princeton Hot Springs. The road turns to dirt about halfway up. In summer it's not a problem, but in winter or muddy weather you'll probably want 4WD.

ordering dinner from the cookhouse (mains $14 to $20) is highly recommended.

Leadville Hostel HOSTEL $
(☎719-486-9334; www.leadvillehostel.com; 500 East 7th St; dm/d $25/60; 📶👪) A true travelers' hostel, this place is run by Wild Bill and is one of the coziest budget choices in the state. Guests get the run of the place, which includes two common areas, a downstairs games room and movie niche, and a large kitchen (hot breakfasts $7). It's within reach of several ski resorts: Cooper (15 minutes), Copper Mountain (30 minutes) and Vail (one hour).

Delaware Hotel HOTEL $
(☎800-748-2004; www.delawarehotel.com; 700 Harrison Ave; tw/d from $60/80, in Aug from $80/109; ⏰mid-May–Oct; P❄📶👪🐾) If you're here in summer, consider this Victorian mining-era hotel, which dates back to 1886. The innkeeper enjoys her burlesque hat and gloves, and the antique-strewn rooms feature high ceilings and lace curtains. It's nothing fancy but certainly solid value.

Eating & Drinking

High Mountain Pies PIZZERIA $$
(☎719-486-5555; 115 W 4th St; medium pizza $14-17; ⏰11am-10pm; 🌱👪) An ultra-popular pizza joint with great toppings, but unfortunately there are only about 10 seats, so make sure you either arrive early or order to go.

Tennessee Pass Cafe CAFE $$
(222 Harrison Ave; sandwiches $9-13, mains $9-16; ⏰7am-9pm; 🌱👪) This artsy cafe (no relation to Tennessee Pass Cookhouse) has the most inventive menu in town, with specials ranging from veggie enchiladas and buffalo burgers to Thai-style stir-fries. It serves crepes (breakfast) and pizza too.

★**Tennessee Pass Cookhouse** MODERN AMERICAN $$$
(☎719-486-8114; www.tennesseepass.com; Tennessee Pass; lunch from $14, 4-course dinner $80; ⏰lunch Sat & Sun, dinner daily Dec–mid-Apr, dinner only Thu-Sun late Jun-Sep; 🌱) If you've never had a gourmet dinner in a yurt before, this is your chance. Diners get to hike, snowshoe or cross-country ski one mile to the yurt, where an elegant four-course meal featuring elk tenderloin, local rack of lamb and wild sock-

eye salmon awaits. Departures are from the Tennessee Pass Nordic Center (p239), at the base of Ski Cooper. Reservations only.

City on a Hill CAFE
(508 Harrison Ave; ⏲6am-6pm, to 9pm Fri;) Freshly roasted beans and delectable espresso drinks are available in this attractive coffeehouse with high ceilings, exposed brick walls and comfy couches. It serves sandwiches, soups, pastries and freshly baked quiches, and is one of the few spots in town with free wi-fi.

Shopping

★**Melanzana** CLOTHING
(www.melanzana.com; 716 Harrison Ave; ⏲10am-6pm;) A unique outdoor clothing shop where stylish adventure wear is made right behind the counter. The factory doubles as a store; browse for hoodies, skirts, bombproof pants, ultrawarm hats and thermal wear. Definitely worth checking out.

Information

Leadville Ranger District (☎719-486-0749; 2015 N Poplar St; ⏲8am-4pm Mon-Fri) Has information, books and topo maps on the Mt Massive Wilderness Area and other forest sites like the Turquoise Lake Reservoir.

Leadville Visitor Center (☎719-486-3900; www.leadvilleusa.com; 809 Harrison Ave; ⏲10am-4pm summer, closed Sun & Mon winter) Connected to the Lake County Area Chamber of Commerce; you can grab maps and brochures here.

Getting There & Away

Leadville is 23 miles southwest of Copper Mountain (Hwy 91), 38 miles south of Vail (Hwy 24) and 34 miles north of Buena Vista (Hwy 24). Bus service runs to Summit County and Vail in the morning, and returns in the evening.

Dee Hive Tours & Transportation (☎719-486-2339; www.leadville.com/deetours; tours $10-20; ⏲by appointment) Welcomes hikers, skiers and cyclists in need of local shuttle transportation. Rides to trailheads or ski areas cost $10 to $20 per person for groups of four to six. Dee Hive also offers 4WD tours on the backroads to old mines and mountain passes.

ECO (☎970-328-3520; www.eaglecounty.us; per ride $7) The ECO bus links Leadville with Vail, leaving twice in the morning and returning twice in the evening.

Summit Stage (☎970-668-0999; www.summitstage.com; per ride $5) Summit Stage's Lake County Link connects Leadville with Copper Mountain and Frisco, leaving twice in the morning and returning twice in the evening.

Mesa Verde & Southwest Colorado

Includes ➡

Best Places to Eat

- James Ranch (p273)
- 626 on Rood (p295)
- New Sheridan Chop House (p259)
- Secret Stash (p288)

Best Places to Stay

- Willowtail Springs (p249)
- Jersey Jim Lookout Tower (p249)
- Kelly Place (p251)
- Wiesbaden (p264)

Why Go?

The West at its most rugged, this is a landscape of twisting canyons and ancient ruins, with burly peaks and gusty high desert plateaus. Centuries of boom and bust, from silver to real estate, tell part of the story. There's also the lingering mystery of its earliest inhabitants, whose relics have been found at the abandoned cliff dwellings in Mesa Verde National Park.

Southwestern Colorado can be a heady place to play. Some of the finest powder skiing in the world melts to reveal winding singletrack and hiking trails in summer. Vineyards are sprouting up on the western slope. A sense of remove keeps the Old West alive in wooden plank saloons and aboard the chugging Durango railroad.

With all that fresh mountain air, local attitudes – from the ranch hand to the real-estate agent – are undoubtedly relaxed. Dally a bit under these ultra-blue skies and you will know why.

When to Go

Durango

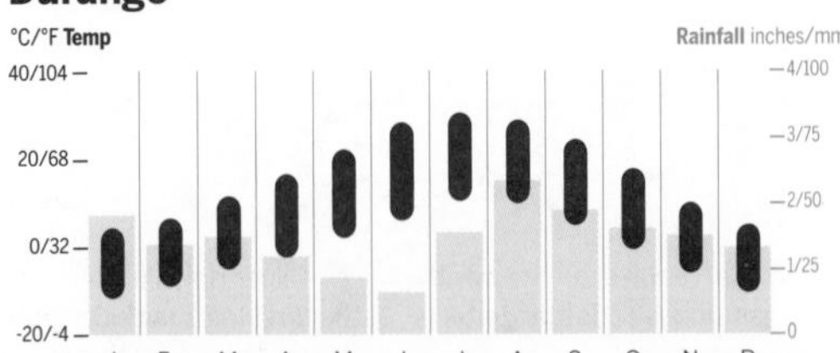

Jun–Aug Prime time for hiking and camping in the legendary San Juans.

Sep–Nov Cool days in the desert and fewer crowds in Mesa Verde.

Dec–Apr Powder hounds hit the famed slopes of Telluride.

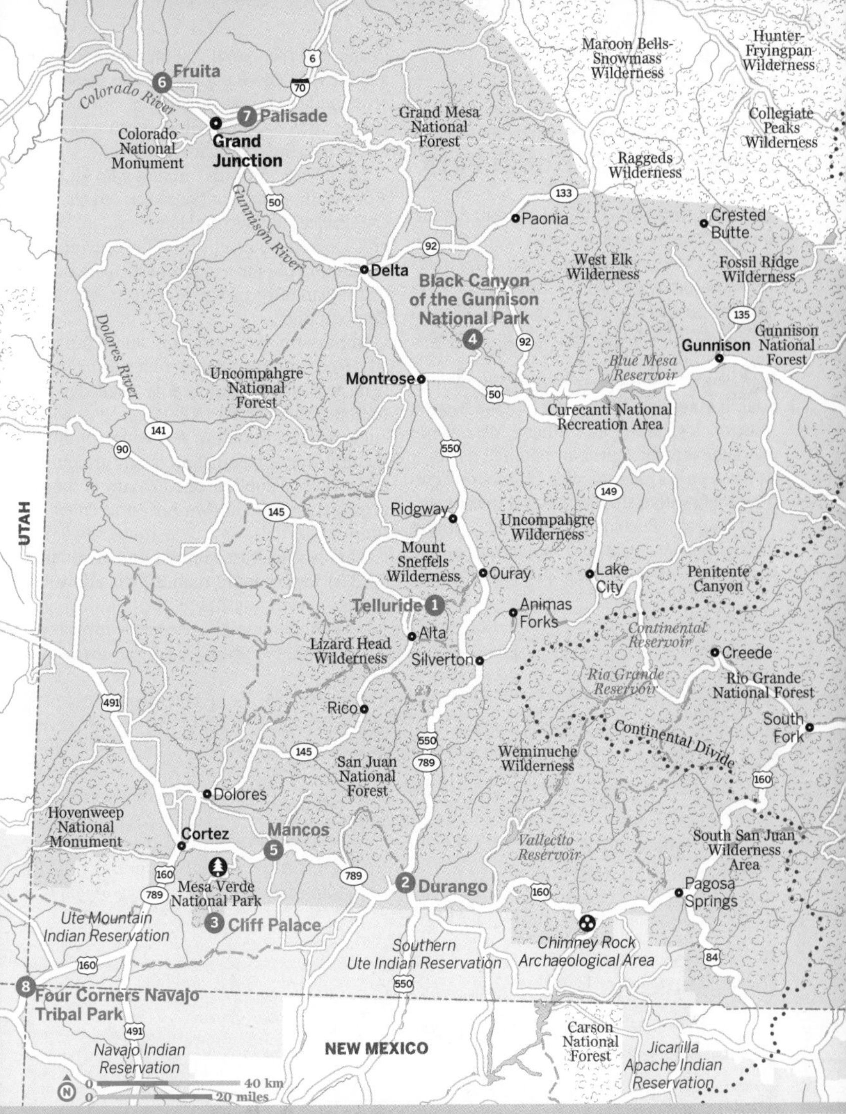

Mesa Verde & Southwest Colorado Highlights

1. Carve turns on the world-class slopes of **Telluride Ski Resort** (p255).
2. Climb aboard the **Durango & Silverton Narrow Gauge Railroad** (p269) for jaw-dropping scenery.
3. Retrace the steps of Ancestral Puebloans at **Cliff Palace** (p246).
4. Climb down to the floor of the dizzying **Black Canyon of the Gunnison National Park** (p283).
5. Poke around the friendly, offbeat town of **Mancos** (p249).
6. Ride the dizzy desert singletrack of **Fruita** (p297).
7. Savor the bold reds while exploring the Colorado wine country of **Palisade** (p298).
8. Drive to the point where four states (almost) meet: **Four Corners Navajo Tribal Park** (p253).

MESA VERDE & THE FOUR CORNERS

Mesa Verde National Park

ELEV 7000-8000FT

More than 700 years after its inhabitants disappeared, the mystery of **Mesa Verde** (☎970-529-4465; www.nps.gov/meve; 7-day pass cars/motorcycles Jun-Aug $15/8, low season $10/5; P ♿) remains unsolved. It is here that a civilization of Ancestral Puebloans appears to have vanished into thin air in the 1300s. Today their last known home is preserved as Mesa Verde, a fascinating, if slightly eerie, national park. Anthropologists will love it here: Mesa Verde is unique among American national parks in its focus on maintaining this civilization's cultural relics rather than its natural treasures.

Ancestral Puebloan sites are found throughout the canyons and mesas of the park, perched on a high plateau south of Cortez and Mancos. If you only have time for a short visit, check out the Chapin Mesa Museum and try a walk through the Spruce Tree House, where you can climb down a wooden ladder into the cool chamber of a kiva.

Mesa Verde rewards travelers who set aside a day or more to take the ranger-led tours of Cliff Palace and Balcony House, explore Wetherill Mesa (the quieter side of the canyon), linger around the museum or participate in one of the campfire programs run at Morefield Campground.

Preserving the Ancestral Puebloan sites while accommodating ever-increasing numbers of visitors continues to challenge the National Park Service (NPS). The NPS strictly enforces the Antiquities Act, which prohibits the removal or destruction of any antiquities and prohibits public access to many of the approximately 4000 known Ancestral Puebloan sites.

The North Rim summit at Park Point (8571ft) towers more than 2000ft above the

Mesa Verde National Park & Around

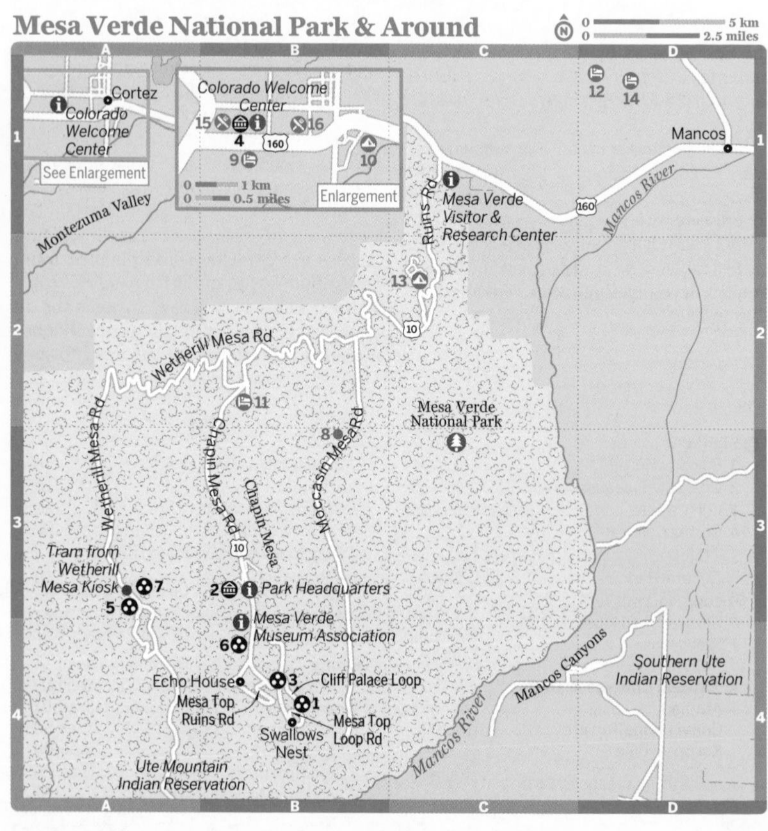

Montezuma Valley. From Park Point the mesa gently slopes southward to a 6000ft elevation above the Mancos River in the Ute Mountain Tribal Park. Parallel canyons, typically 500ft below the rim, bisect the mesa-top and carry the drainage southward. Mesa Verde National Park occupies 81 sq miles of the northernmost portion of the mesa and contains the largest and most frequented cliff dwellings and surface sites.

History

A US army lieutenant recorded the spectacular cliff dwellings in the canyons of Mesa Verde in 1849–50. The large number of sites on Ute tribal land, and their relative inaccessibility, protected the majority of these antiquities from pothunters.

The first scientific investigation of the sites in 1874 failed to identify Cliff Palace, the largest cliff dwelling in North America. Discovery of the 'magnificent city' occurred only when local cowboys Richard Wetherill and Charlie Mason were searching for stray cattle in 1888. The cowboys exploited their 'discovery' for the next 18 years by guiding both amateur and trained archaeologists to the site, particularly to collect the distinctive black-on-white pottery.

When artifacts started being shipped overseas, Virginia McClurg of Colorado Springs was motivated to embark on a long campaign to preserve the site and its contents. McClurg's efforts led Congress to protect artifacts on federal land, with the passage of the Antiquities Act establishing Mesa Verde National Park in 1906.

Sights

Park Point

The fire lookout at Park Point is the highest elevation (8571ft) in the park and offers panoramic views. To the north are the 14,000ft peaks of the San Juan Mountains; in the northeast are the 12,000ft crests of the La Plata Mountains; to the southwest, beyond the southward-sloping Mesa Verde plateau, is the distant volcanic plug of Shiprock; and to the west is Sleeping Ute Mountain, whose profile resembles a supine human.

Chapin Mesa

There is no other place in Mesa Verde where so many remnants of Ancestral Puebloan settlements are clustered so closely together, providing an opportunity to see and compare examples of all phases of construction – from pothouses to Pueblo villages to the elaborate multiroom cities tucked into cliff recesses. Pamphlets describing the most excavated sites are available at either the visitor center (p248) or Chapin Mesa Museum.

On the upper portion of Chapin Mesa are the Far View Sites, which make up what was perhaps the most densely settled area in Mesa Verde after 1100AD. The large-walled Pueblo sites at Far View House enclose a central kiva and planned room layout that was originally two stories high. To the north is a small row of rooms and an attached circular tower that probably once extended just above the adjacent 'pygmy

Mesa Verde National Park & Around

Sights

1	Balcony House	B4
2	Chapin Mesa Museum	B3
3	Cliff Palace	B4
4	Cortez Cultural Center	B1
	Cultural Park	(see 4)
5	Long House	A3
6	Spruce Tree House	B4
7	Step House	A3

Activities, Courses & Tours

8	Aramark	B3
	Come Dance Tonight	(see 15)
	Kokopelli Bike & Board	(see 4)

Sleeping

9	Best Western Turquoise Inn & Suites	B1
10	Cortez-Mesa Verde KOA	B1
11	Far View Lodge	B2
12	Flagstone Meadows Ranch Bed & Breakfast	D1
13	Morefield Campground	C2
14	Willowtail Springs	D1

Eating

	Far View Terrace Café	(see 11)
15	Farm Bistro	B1
	Metate Room	(see 11)
	Pepperhead	(see 15)
	Stonefish Sushi & More	(see 15)
16	Tequila's Mexican Restaurant	B1

forest' of piñon pine and juniper trees. This tower is one of 57 in Mesa Verde that may once have served as watchtowers, religious structures or astronomical observatories for agricultural schedules.

South from park headquarters, the 6-mile Mesa Top Rd circuit connects 10 excavated mesa-top sites, three accessible cliff dwellings and many vantages of inaccessible cliff dwellings from the mesa rim. It's open 8am to sunset.

Chapin Mesa Museum MUSEUM
(970-529-4475; www.nps.gov/meve; Chapin Mesa Rd; admission incl with park entry; 8am-6:30pm Apr–mid-Oct, 8am-5pm mid-Oct–Apr; P) The Chapin Mesa Museum has exhibits pertaining to the park. It's a good first stop. Staff at the museum provide information on weekends when the park headquarters is closed.

Spruce Tree House ARCHAEOLOGICAL SITE
(Chapin Mesa Rd; admission incl with park entry; P) This Ancestral Puebloan ruin is the most accessible of the archaeological sites, although the half-mile round-trip access track is still a moderately steep climb. Spruce Tree House was once home to 60 or 80 people and its construction began around AD 1210. Like other sites, the old walls and houses have been stabilized.

During winter, there are free ranger-led guided tours at 10am, 1pm and 3:30pm.

Cliff Palace & Mesa Top Loops

This is the most visited part of the park. Access to the major Ancestral Puebloan sites is only by ranger-led tour, and tickets must be pre-purchased at the Far View Visitor Center.

Cliff Palace ARCHAEOLOGICAL SITE
(Cliff Palace Loop; 1hr guided tour $3;) The only way to see the superb Cliff Palace is to take the hour-long ranger-led tour. The tour retraces the steps taken by the Ancestral Puebloans – visitors must climb down a stone stairway and four 10ft ladders. This grand engineering achievement, with 217 rooms and 23 kivas, provided shelter for 250 to 300 people.

Its inhabitants were without running water. However, springs across the canyon, below Sun Temple, were most likely their primary water sources. The use of small 'chinking' stones between the large blocks is strikingly similar to Ancestral Puebloan construction at distant Chaco Canyon.

Balcony House ARCHAEOLOGICAL SITE
(Cliff Palace Loop; 1hr guided tour $3; P) Tickets are required for the one-hour guided tours of Balcony House, on the east side of the Cliff Palace Loop. A visit is quite an adventure and will challenge anyone's fear of heights or small places. You'll be rewarded with outstanding views of Soda Canyon, 600ft below the sandstone overhang that once served as the ceiling for 35 to 40 rooms.

The Balcony House tour requires you to descend a 100ft staircase into the canyon, then climb a 32ft ladder, crawl through a 12ft tunnel and climb an additional 60ft of ladders and stone steps to get out. It's the most challenging tour in the park but might just be the most rewarding, not to mention fun!

Wetherill Mesa

The less-frequented western portion of Mesa Verde offers a comprehensive display of Ancestral Pueblo relics. The Badger House Community consists of a short trail connecting four excavated surface sites depicting various phases of Ancestral Puebloan development.

Long House ARCHAEOLOGICAL SITE
(Wetherill Mesa Rd; 1hr guided tour $3;) On the Wetherill Mesa side of the canyon is Long House. It's a strenuous place to visit and can only be done as part of a ranger-led guided tour (organized from the visitor center). Access involves climbing three ladders – two at 15ft and one at 4ft – and a 0.75-mile round-trip hike, and there's an aggregate 130ft elevation to descend and ascend.

Step House ARCHAEOLOGICAL SITE
(Wetherill Mesa Rd; admission incl with park entry) Step House was initially occupied by Modified Basketmaker peoples residing in pithouses, and later became the site of a Classic Pueblo–period masonry complex with rooms and kivas. The 0.75-mile trail to Step House involves a 100ft descent and ascent.

Activities

Hiking

Hiking is a great way to explore the park, but remember to follow the rules. Backcountry access is specifically forbidden and fines are imposed on anyone caught wandering off designated trails or entering cliff dwellings without a ranger. Please respect these necessary regulations so that the fragile and irreplaceable archaeological sights and artifacts remain protected for centuries to come.

When hiking in Mesa Verde always carry water and avoid cliff edges. Trails can be muddy and slippery after summer rains and winter snows, so wear appropriate footwear. Most park trails, except the Soda Canyon Trail, are strenuous and involve steep elevation changes. Hikers must register at the respective trailheads before venturing out.

The 2.8-mile **Petroglyph Loop Trail** is accessed from Spruce Tree House. It follows a path beneath the edge of a plateau before making a short climb to the top of the mesa, where you'll have good views of the Spruce and Navajo Canyons. This is the only trail in the park where you can view petroglyphs.

The 2.1-mile **Spruce Canyon Loop Trail** also begins at Spruce Tree House and descends to the bottom of Spruce Tree Canyon. It's a great way to see the canyon bottoms of Mesa Verde.

Mountain Biking

Finding convenient parking at the many stops along Mesa Top Loop Rd is no problem for those with bikes. Only the hardy will want to enter the park by bike and immediately face the grueling 4-mile ascent to Morefield Campground, quickly followed by a narrow tunnel ride to reach the North Rim. An easier option is to unlimber your muscles and mount up at Morefield, Far View Visitor Center or park headquarters.

Skiing & Snowshoeing

Winter is a special time in Mesa Verde. The crowds disperse and the cliff dwellings sparkle in the snow. The skies are often blue and sunny, and you may be the only person around. In recent years there has been enough snow to ski or snowshoe on most winter days after a snowstorm (although Colorado's dry climate and sunshine cause the snow to melt quickly). Before setting out, check the current snow conditions by calling the park headquarters.

Two park roads have been designated for cross-country skiing and snowshoeing when weather permits. The Cliff Palace Loop Rd is a relatively flat 6-mile loop located off the Mesa Top Loop Rd. The road is closed to vehicles after the first snowfall, so you won't have to worry about vehicular traffic. Park at the closed gate and glide 1 mile to the Cliff Palace overlook, continuing on past numerous other scenic stopping points. The Morefield Campground Loop roads offer multiple miles of relatively flat terrain. The campground is closed in winter, but skiers and snowshoers can park at the gate and explore to their heart's content.

Tours

The NPS and the park concessionaire **Aramark** (www.visitmesaverde.com; adult/child $35/17.50) run various organized tours for walkers as well as small-group bus tours.

Wetherill Mesa Experience HIKING
(per person $18; departs 9:45am late May-early Sep;) Limited to 14 people, this five-hour ranger-led walking tour departs from the Wetherill Mesa Kiosk – catch the free **tram** (operates 9:20am to 3:30pm, every half hour) from the kiosk. Binoculars are recommended for walkers as the trail has superb views across the canyon to multiple cliff dwellings.

Spring House Hiking Tour HIKING
(per person $40; departs 8am May 26-Jun 5, Sep 1-Oct 6) If you're really fit and equipped with hiking boots, sun protection and adequate water, you'll enjoy this premium experience. Rangers lead these 6-mile interpretive hiking tours that take eight hours and involve strenuous climbs and descents, and rough trails. Remote sites such as Buzzard House and Teakettle House are part of the itinerary.

Festivals & Events

12 Hours of Mesa Verde SPORTS
(www.12hoursofmesaverde.com; per rider $80; May) This annual 12-hour relay-endurance mountain-bike event is popular. Teams race against each other over an incredible network of trails across the national park. There's also a kids' ride. All proceeds raised go to the Montezuma County Partners – a mentoring program for youth at risk.

Sleeping

There are plenty of accommodation options in nearby Cortez and Mancos, and Mesa Verde can be easily visited as a day trip from Durango (36 miles to the east). Within the national park, visitors can stay in luxury at the lodge, or rough it camping. An overnight stay in the park allows convenient access to the many sites during the best viewing hours, participation in evening programs and the sheer pleasure of watching the sun set over Sleeping Ute Mountain from the tranquillity of the mesa top.

Morefield Campground CAMPGROUND $
(970-529-4465; www.visitmesaverde.com; North Rim Rd; tent/RV site $29/37; May-early Oct;) The park's camping option, located 4 miles from the entrance gate, also has 445 regular tent sites on grassy grounds conveniently located near Morefield Village. The village has a general store, gas station, restaurant, showers and laundry. It's managed by Aramark. Dry RV campsites (without hookup) cost the same as tent sites.

Far View Lodge LODGE $$
(970-529-4421, 800-449-2288; www.visitmesaverde.com; North Rim Rd; r $115-184; mid-Apr–Oct;) Perched on a mesa top 15 miles inside the park entrance, this tasteful Pueblo-style lodge has 150 Southwestern-style rooms, some with kiva fireplaces. Don't miss sunset over the mesa from your private balcony. Standard rooms don't have air-con (or TV) and summer daytimes can be hot. You can even bring your dog for an extra $10 per night.

Eating

Far View Terrace Café CAFE $
(970-529-4421, 800-449-2288; www.visitmesaverde.com; North Rim Rd; dishes from $5; 7-10am, 11am-3pm & 5-8pm May–mid-Oct;) Housed in Far View Lodge immediately south of the visitor center, this self-service place offers reasonably priced meals and a convenient espresso bar. Don't miss the house special: the Navajo Taco.

Metate Room MODERN AMERICAN $$$
(800-449-2288; www.visitmesaverde.com; North Rim Rd; mains $15-28; 5-7:30pm year-round & 7-10am Apr–mid-Oct;) With an award in culinary excellence, this upscale restaurant in the Far View Lodge offers an innovative menu inspired by Native American food and flavors. Interesting dishes include stuffed poblano chilies, cinnamon chili pork tenderloin and grilled quail with prickly pear jam.

Orientation

The park entrance is off US 160, midway between Cortez and Mancos. From the entrance, it's about 21 miles to park headquarters, Chapin Mesa Museum and Spruce Tree House. Along the way are Morefield Campground (4 miles), the panoramic viewpoint at Park Point (8 miles) and the Far View Visitor Center opposite the Far View Lodge – about 11 miles. Towed vehicles are not allowed beyond Morefield Campground.

South from park headquarters, Mesa Top Rd consists of two one-way circuits. Turn left about a quarter-mile from the start of Mesa Top Rd to visit Cliff Palace and Balcony House on the east loop. From the junction with the main road at Far View Visitor Center, the 12-mile mountainous Wetherill Mesa Rd snakes along the North Rim, acting as a natural barrier to tour buses and indifferent travelers. The road is open only from Memorial Day in late May to Labor Day in early September.

Information

Good maps are issued to visitors at the national park gate on entry. Quality topographical maps can be bought at the visitor center and the museum as well as in stores in Durango and Cortez.

Mesa Verde Museum Association (970-529-4445, 800-305-6053; www.mesaverde.org; Chapin Mesa Rd; 8am-6:30pm Apr–mid-Oct, 8am-5pm mid-Oct–Apr;) Attached to the Chapin Mesa Museum, this nonprofit organization sponsors research activities and exhibits. It has an excellent selection of materials on the Ancestral Puebloans and modern tribes in the American Southwest, and has books, posters and glossy calendars for sale.

Mesa Verde Visitor & Research Center (800-305-6053, 970-529-5034; www.nps.gov/meve; North Rim Rd; 8am-7pm Jun-early Sep, 8am-5pm early Sep–mid-Oct, closed mid-Oct–May;) Visitor information and tickets for tours of Cliff Palace, Balcony House or Long House.

Park Headquarters (970-529-4465; www.nps.gov/meve; Chapin Mesa Rd; 7-day park entry per vehicle $15, cyclists, hikers & motorcyclists $8; 8am-5pm Mon-Fri;) The Mesa Verde National Park entrance is off US 160, midway between Cortez and Mancos. From the entrance it is 21 miles to the park headquarters. You can get road information and the word on park closures (many areas are closed in winter).

Getting There & Around

Although there are some operators running tours to and around Mesa Verde National Park from Durango – contact the Durango Welcome Center (p274) – most people visit with a private car or motorcycle. Vehicular transportation is necessary to get to the sites from the front park gate as well as to get between them.

Mancos

POP 1330 / ELEV 7028FT

A quick sprint through tiny Mancos and you'll think you've stumbled upon yet another Colorado ghost town. But slow down for a minute and wander amid the boutiques, artists co-op and landmark buildings and you'll be in for a great surprise. Sleeping and eating options are limited, but the ones that do exist are charming and eclectic. Mesa Verde National Park is just 7 miles to the west, so if visiting the park is on your itinerary, staying in Mancos makes an appealing alternative to the rather nondescript motels in Cortez. From June through September, the town puts on Grand Summer Nights, a series of gallery walks that local restaurants and shops also participate in. It's held the last Friday of the month.

Sleeping

★Jersey Jim Lookout Tower LOOKOUT TOWER $

(☎970-533-7060; r $40; ⊙mid-May–mid-Oct) How about spending the night in a former fire-lookout tower? Standing 55ft above a meadow 14 miles north of Mancos at an elevation of 9800ft, this place is on the National Historic Lookout Register and comes with an Osborne Fire Finder and topographic map. But no water.

The tower accommodates up to four adults (bring your own bedding) and must be reserved long in advance; there's also a two-night minimum stay. The reservation office opens on the first workday of March (1pm to 5pm) and the entire season is typically booked within days.

Enchanted Mesa Motel MOTEL $

(☎970-533-7729; www.enchantedmesamotel.com; 862 W Grand Ave; s/d $71/82;) Hipper than most independent motels, this place has shiny lamps and solid wooden furniture, along with king- and queen-size beds. There's a big playground out front for the kids. Best of all, you can play a game of pool while waiting for your whites to dry – there's a billiards table in the laundry room!

Flagstone Meadows Ranch Bed & Breakfast B&B $$

(☎970-533-9838; www.flagstonemeadows.com; 38080 Rd K-4; d incl breakfast $115-125;) This elegant ranch is a decidedly more romantic option than any of the motels in town. Guests sit on the deck to enjoy the stars at night, or warm themselves by the field stone fireplace. During the day it's dead quiet; you can take in big views across the plain to Mesa Verde or walk on nearby trails.

Echo Basin Ranch DUDE RANCH $$

(☎970-533-7000; www.echobasin.com; County Rd M; cabins per night/week from $139/722;) Traveling with horse? Stop for the night at Echo Basin Ranch, an affordable unstructured dude ranch. The A-frame cabin accommodations are very cool (as long as you don't mind rustic, and by that we mean basic). We love the pitched roof and big windows – very Rocky Mountain high.

The deluxe cabins are not posh, but plenty comfortable, with multiple rooms and more-artistic decor. There is a two-night minimum to stay here, and it is much cheaper (and in scale with what you pay for, amenities-wise) if you stay at least four nights. Dogs are welcome, and horses stay for $10 per night. The ranch offers a host of activities, from guided horseback riding to a putting green. The on-site restaurant and saloon mean you don't have to drive to eat. Echo Basin is about 7 miles from Mancos.

★Willowtail Springs LODGE, CABINS $$$

(☎800-698-0603; www.willowtailsprings.com; 10451 County Rd 39; cabins $229-279;) Peggy and Lee, artist and tai chi master, have crafted a setting that inspires and helps you to slow down to the pace of their pond's largemouth bass. These exquisite camps sit within 60 acres of gardens and ponderosa forest. Two immaculate cabins and a spacious lake house (sleeping six) feature warm and exotic decor including a real remnant beehive.

There are also clawfoot tubs, Peggy's fabulous original art, a hot tub and a canoe hitched to the dock. Kitchens are stocked with organic goodies and extras include candlelight chef dinners, reasonable catered meals and massages. It's also a wildlife sanctuary (raptors are released here) and, for roamers, a little slice of heaven. It's well outside town; get directions from the website.

Eating & Drinking

★Absolute Baking & Cafe BREAKFAST, SANDWICHES $

(☎970-533-1200; 110 S Main St; mains $6-10; ⊙7am-2pm;) The screen door is always swinging open at this town hot spot with giant breakfasts. Try the green chili on eggs – it's made from scratch, as are the organic breads and pastries. Lunch includes salads, big sandwiches and local, grass-fed beef burgers. Grab a bag for the trail, but don't forgo a square of gooey, fresh carrot cake.

If you're in the market for a new read, the cafe has a decent collection of used books for sale, so grab a cup of coffee, chat with friendly waitstaff and just chill out.

Olio CAFE **$$$**

(114 W Main St; mains $18-28; 4-9pm Tue-Sat) This friendly, upscale cafe is the spot to hit for a glass of wine and cheese boards with fig jam. Highlights include deviled eggs, and light items like watermelon salad, and local lettuce served with shaved fennel, cherries and aged balsamic. In addition to being pretty original, it also caters well to vegan and gluten-free diets.

Fahrenheit Coffee Roasters CAFE

(201 W Grand Ave; 6:30am-5pm Mon-Fri, 7am-5pm Sat;) Imbued with the aroma of fresh-roasted beans, this quality espresso house also serves slices of homemade pie and cheap breakfast burritos to go. It also provides interesting atmosphere, with small-talking locals, outdoor sofas and Oz-like art installations.

Mancos Valley Distillery DISTILLERY

(www.mancosvalleydistillery.com; 116 N Main St; 5pm-late Fri & Sat) If you're interested in tasting something *really* local, make your way to this alley-side rum distillery, where artisan distiller Ian James crafts delicate rum. He opens up his distillery to live blues and bluegrass, but generally only for special occasions. Check the website for more information.

Columbine Bar BAR

(970-533-7397; 123 W Grand Ave; 10am-2am) Established in 1903, one of Colorado's oldest continuously operating bars is still going strong. Think divey old saloon. The mounted animal heads keep watch as you shoot pool.

Information

Mancos Valley Visitors Center (702-533-7434; www.mancosvalley.com; 101 E Bauer St; 9am-5pm Mon-Fri) Historic displays and a walking-tour map are available at the visitor center. It also has information on outdoor activities and local ranches that offer horseback rides and Western-style overnight trips.

Cortez

POP 8450 / ELEV 6201FT

Cortez fails to beguile, but its location 10 miles west of Mesa Verde National Park makes it a logical base, and the surrounding area holds quiet appeal. Mountain bikers will covet the hundreds of great singletrack rides nearby.

Typical of small-town Colorado, Cortez is lined with strip malls containing fast food, trinket and rifle shops with far-off mountain vistas to complete the picture. But the downtown seems to be revitalizing: three great restaurants on just one city block proves it. The surrounding desert is also a pleasure, with surprises like archaeological sites and the occasional desert winery.

Sights

Cortez Cultural Center MUSEUM

(702-565-1151; www.cortezculturalcenter.org; 25 N Market St; 10am-9pm Mon-Sat May-Oct, to 5pm Nov-Apr;) FREE Exhibits on the Ancestral Puebloans, as well as visiting art displays, make this museum worthy of a visit if you have a few hours to spare. Summer evening programs feature Native American dances on Tuesdays, Fridays and Saturdays at 6pm, followed at 8pm by cultural programs that often feature Native American storytellers.

Guy Drew Vineyard WINERY

(www.guydrewvineyards.com; 19891 Road G; 10am-6pm Tue-Sat) A fun stop if you are headed to or from Kelly Place, this well-regarded small family-run vineyard has informal tastings in the straw-bale farm kitchen. Owned by happy corporate drop-outs, it may have only 13 years of production under its belt but it has lots of good stories to tell.

Cultural Park MUSEUM

(10am-9pm Mon-Sat summer, to 5pm winter) FREE The Cultural Park is an outdoor space at the Cortez Cultural Center where Ute, Navajo and Hopi tribe members share their cultures with visitors through dance and crafts demonstrations. Weaving demonstrations and Ute mountain art are also displayed and visitors can check out a Navajo hogan.

Crow Canyon Archaeology Center ARCHAEOLOGICAL SITE

(970-565-8975, 800-422-8975; www.crowcanyon.org; 23390 Rd K; adult/child $60/35; 9am-

5pm Wed & Thu Jun–mid-Sep;) This cultural center, about 3 miles north of Cortez, offers a day-long educational program that visits an excavation site west of town. Programs teach the significance of regional artifacts and are an excellent way to learn about Ancestral Puebloan culture first-hand.

Travelers who want to stay longer can partake in week-long sessions, where guests share traditional Pueblo hogans and also study excavation field and lab techniques.

Activities

Kokopelli Bike & Board BICYCLE RENTAL
(970-565-4408; www.kokopellibike.com; 130 W Main St; front-suspension bike per day $35; 9am-6pm Mon-Fri, to 5pm Sat) The friendly staff at this local bike shop are happy to talk trail with riders, and also rent and repair mountain bikes. The rental price includes helmet, air pump, water bottle and tools. For some pre-trip planning the shop's website has great trail descriptions.

Come Dance Tonight BALLROOM DANCING
(www.comedancetonight.com; 30 W Main St; drop-in dance lessons $10; evenings, hr vary) Behind the trophy-cluttered windows, this nondescript storefront opens onto a surreal world, where Friday nights find couples cha-cha-cha-ing across the wide wooden floor along to the buoyant clapping of Denise. A ballroom studio and social club that seems from another era, this is a truly weird and awesome scene.

Sleeping

Cortez has heaps of budget motels along its main drag, and rates and rooms are much the same at most. In winter, prices drop by almost half.

Cortez-Mesa Verde KOA CAMPGROUND $
(%970-565-9301; http://koa.com/campgrounds/cortez; 27432 E Hwy 160; campsites $32-100, cabins $58; hApr-Oct; Ws) The only campground in town not right next to a highway or dedicated to RVs, this is the at the east end of town.

Tomahawk Lodge LODGE $
(970-565-8521, 800-643-7705; www.angelfire.com/co2/tomahawk; 728 S Broadway; r from $59;) Friendly hosts welcome you at this clean, good-value place. It feels more personable than the average motel, and offers coffee and pastries in the morning. A few rooms allow pets, but they might be a little intimidated by the sweet pony-sized Great Danes kept by the host.

★ **Kelly Place** B&B $$
(970-565-3125; www.kellyplace.com; 14663 Montezuma County Rd G; r & cabins $105-150, 2-person campsite/RV site $35/45;) A rare gem B&B with archaeological ruins and desert trails with nary another soul in sight. Founded by late botanist George Kelly, this lovely adobe-style lodge sits on 40 acres of orchards, red-rock canyon and Native American ruins abutting Canyon of the Ancients, 15 miles west of Cortez. Rooms are tasteful and rates (even camping) include an enormous buffet breakfast.

It has a range of cabins, the best sporting a private flagstone patio and whirlpool tub. A pamphlet helps you locate and understand the ruins (including a kiva), in addition to identifying local plants. It also has horseback riding, cultural tours and archaeological programs. At night watch DVDs or chill with a glass of wine or a tasty microbrew; the lodge serves both.

Best Western Turquoise Inn & Suites HOTEL $$
(970-565-3778; www.bestwestern.com; 535 E Main St; r from $132;) With two swimming pools to keep the young ones entertained, this is a good choice for families (kids stay free, and the restaurant has a kiddy menu). Rooms here are spacious, and bigger families can grab a two-room suite. If you're exploring Mesa Verde all day and just want an affordable and clean, if slightly bland, hotel to crash at for the night, this comfortably laid-out Best Western will do the trick.

Eating

★ **Farm Bistro** CAFE $
(970-565-3834; www.thefarmbistrocortez.com; 34 W Main St; mains $7-10; 7am-9pm Thu-Sat, 11am-3pm Mon-Wed;) With a mantra of 'mostly local, mostly organic,' this brick cafe with mismatched seat-yourself tables is a hub for healthy appetites. On the menu are grass-fed beef burgers with tomato jam, zucchini fritter salad and homemade green chili with a worthy zing. Ingredients come from an organic farm down the road in Mancos and some fare is vegan or gluten free.

Pepperhead SOUTHWESTERN $$
(970-565-3303; www.pepperheadcortez.com; 44 W Main St; mains $7-12; 11am-9pm Tue-Sat;) A haven of smoky Southwestern spice, this newish favorite sits in a colorful room adorned by a beautiful mural. Start with a

black-cherry margarita – it's tart perfection. Also worthwhile are the *posole* (hominy stew), thin steaks *tampequeña* and delicious *chiles rellenos* (stuffed peppers) made with the famous Rocky Ford variety.

Stonefish Sushi & More JAPANESE $$
(☎970-565-9244; 16 W Main St; mains $10-16; ⏰11am-2pm Tue-Fri, 4:30-10pm Thu-Sat) With blues on the box and a high tin ceiling, this is sushi for the Southwest. Specialties like potstickers with prickly-pear chili and Colorado rancher seared beef and wasabi liven things up. Cool light fixtures, black tiles and globe-shaped fish tanks behind the bar complete the scene.

Tequila's Mexican Restaurant MEXICAN $$
(☎970-565-6868; 1740 E Main St; mains $8-12; ⏰11am-10pm; 👪) Good-tasting food at bargain prices draws the crowds on any given night. Though a chain, it does a great job. The chicken mole, seafood tacos and carne asada all win raves, as do margaritas with fresh lime juice. Expect a wait on weekends.

ℹ Information

Colorado Welcome Center (☎970-565-4048; 928 E Main St; ⏰9am-5pm Sep-May, to 6pm Jun-Aug) Maps, brochures and some excellent pamphlets on local activities like fishing and mountain biking.

Southwest Memorial Hospital (☎970-565-6666; 1311 N Mildred Rd) Emergency services.

ℹ Getting There & Away

In the extreme southwest corner of the state, Cortez is easier to reach from either Phoenix, AZ, or Albuquerque, NM, than from Denver, 379 miles away by the shortest route. East of Cortez, US 160 passes Mesa Verde National Park on the way to Durango, the largest city in the region, 45 miles away. To the northwest, Hwy 145 follows the beautiful Dolores River through the San Juan Mountains on an old Rio Grande Southern narrow-gauge route over Lizard Head Pass to Telluride, 77 miles distant.

Cortez Municipal Airport (☎970-565-7458; 22874 County Rd F) is served by United Express, which offers daily turboprop flights to Denver. The airport is 2 miles south of town off US 160/666.

MOUNTAIN BIKING FOUR CORNERS

The Four Corners area around Cortez offers some epic mountain-bike trails through woodlands and over the otherworldly 'slickrock' mesa.

With 32 miles of singletrack rolling through piñon-juniper trees, **Phil's World** is the mecca for mountain bikers, located five miles out of Cortez. It's also apt for all levels. Another local favorite is **Boggy Draw**, located north of Dolores, with dispersed camping in the ponderosa pines.

If you are still hungry for more, **Sand Canyon** can be fun, though it gets overly hot in summer. The 18-mile trail starts at the same-named archaeological site west of Cortez. It follows a downhill trail west to Cannonball Mesa, where there is also dispersed BLM camping, near the state line. If you're looking for a shorter ride, at the 8-mile mark the Burro Point overlook of Yellow Jacket and Burro Canyons is a good place to turn back.

You can also test your skills riding the 27-mile **Stoner Mesa Loop**, a challenging intermediate to expert ride beginning with 8 miles of paved road along the west fork of the Dolores River. The tough part comes during the 7-mile dirt-road climb (you'll gain nearly 2000ft in elevation) to the top of Stoner Mesa. When (or maybe if) you reach the top, the views are splendid, and you'll be rewarded with a long, mellow downhill through amazing forests of aspens and open meadows. The last 2 miles are the most technical, consisting of an endless number of tight switchbacks and rock and root steps that take you down to the trailhead in a steep descent. Stoner Mesa is best in fall when temperatures cool and aspens glow.

Pick up a copy of *Mountain and Road Bike Routes for the Cortez-Dolores-Mancos Area*, available at the Colorado Welcome Center (p252) and at local chambers of commerce. It provides maps and profiles for several road and mountain-bike routes.

Try Kokopelli Bike & Board (p251) for mountain bike rental and repairs and see their website for good trail descriptions.

Four Corners Navajo Tribal Park

Don't be shy: do a spread eagle for the folks on top of the **Four Corners Navajo Tribal Park** (☎928-871-6647; www.navajonationparks.org; off US 160; admission $3; ⏰7am-5pm Oct-May, 7am-8pm Jun-Sep) corners marker that signifies you're in four states at once. Great photo op, even if it's not 100% accurate – government surveyors have admitted that the marker is almost 2000ft east of where it should be, but it is a legally recognized border point marking the intersection of Arizona, New Mexico, Utah and Colorado.

The monument is really in the middle of nowhere. Services include a small visitors center, picnic tables and portable toilets. The nearest gas station is 6 miles south in Teec Nos Pos. Vendors set up nearby sell food, Native American crafts and jewelry and knickknacks. The best snack to nosh on is a flat piece of fried dough from a **Navajo Fry Bread Cart** (Four Corners Navajo Tribal Park; fry bread $3; ⏰11am-5pm), to your right as you exit the parking area.

Ute Mountain Indian Reservation

Ute people once inhabited this entire region – from the San Luis Valley west into Utah – and, after a series of forced relocations and treaties from the 1860s to 1930s, control only this small strip of land in the dry high plains of the Colorado Plateau. The relationship between Utes and the federal government is one of conflict and ongoing tension; the Ute tribe won their first rights for potable water on this arid reservation in 1988. The tribal land includes a number of archaeological sites, including petroglyphs and cliff dwellings, but can only be accessed through guided tour. The **Ute Mountain Tribal Park** (☎970-749-1452; www.utemountaintribalpark.info; Morning Star Lane; half/full-day tours per person $29/48; ⏰by appointment) can set up tours, which include lots of rough and dusty driving over back roads.

The tribe operates the **Ute Mountain Casino, Hotel & Resort** (☎hotel reservations 800-258-8007; 3 Weeminuche Dr; d $75-95, campsites $30), near Sleeping Ute Mountain.

Hovenweep National Monument

Hovenweep, meaning 'deserted valley' in the Ute language, is a remote area of former Ancestral Puebloan settlements straddling the Colorado–Utah border, 42 miles west of Cortez via McElmo Canyon Rd from US 160. This was once home to a large population before drought forced people out in the late 1200s. Six sets of unique tower ruins are found here, but only the impressive ruins in the Square Tower area are readily accessible. For people who love ticking off a checklist of America's national parks and monuments, this is only a half-day diversion from the sites at Mesa Verde National Park.

Activities

Three easy-to-moderate loop hiking trails (none longer than 2 miles) leave from near the ranger station and pass a number of buildings in the Square Tower area. The trails give both distant and close-up views of the ancient sites whose fragile unstable walls are easily damaged – please stay on the trail and don't climb on the sites. Visitors are reminded that all wildlife is protected – including rattlesnakes – but you are more likely to see the iridescent collared lizard scampering near the trail. Brochures are available for self-guided tours and also describe plant life along the trails.

Sleeping

Hovenweep NPS Campground CAMPGROUND **$**
(tent sites $10) This campground is about a mile from the ranger station and is open year-round on a first-come, first-served basis. The 31 sites rarely fill, but are busiest in summer. There are toilets and picnic facilities. Spring water is available when weather permits, usually from April to October only.

Information

Hovenweep National Monument Ranger Station (☎970-562-4282; www.nps.gov/hove; McElmo Rte; vehicles/individuals $6/3; ⏰8am-6pm Apr-Sep, to 5pm Oct-Mar; ♿)

Getting There & Away

From US 160/US 666 south of Cortez, turn at the sign for the Cortez Airport onto Montezuma County Rd G, which follows McElmo Canyon east through red-rock country north of Sleeping Ute Mountain and Ute tribal lands. At the Utah border you cross onto the Navajo Reservation and can expect sheep, goats or even cattle on the road. A signed road to the monument turns right (north) from McElmo Creek.

Dolores

POP 933 / ELEV 6936FT

Scenic Dolores, sandwiched between the walls of a narrow canyon of the same name, has a treasure trove of Native American artifacts and sits near the sublime river of the same name – only rafted in spring. But on a more permanent basis, the McPhee Lake boasts the best angling in the Southwest. Food and lodging options here are slim. The **Dolores Visitor Center** (☎800-807-4712, 702-882-4018; 421 Railroad Ave; ⏰9am-5pm Mon-Fri) is housed in a replica of the town's old railroad depot; it has regional information on lodging and outdoor activities.

Sights & Activities

Anasazi Heritage Center MUSEUM

(☎970-882-5600; www.blm.gov/co/st/en/fo/ahc.html; 27501 Hwy 184; admission $3, free Dec-Feb; ⏰9am-5pm Mar-Nov, 10am-4pm Dec-Feb; P) The BLM manages the Anasazi Heritage Center, a good stop for anyone touring the area's archaeological sites. It's 3 miles west of town, with hands-on exhibits such as weaving, corn grinding, tree-ring analysis and an introduction to the way in which archaeologists examine potsherds.

You can walk through the Dominguez Pueblo, a roofless site from the 1100s that sits in front of the museum and compare its relative simplicity to the Escalante Pueblo, a Chacoan structure on a nearby hillside.

McPhee Lake RESERVOIR

The second-largest body of water in Colorado, McPhee Lake is one of the top fishing spots in the San Juan basin. With the best catch ratio in southern Colorado, it's great for new anglers. The artificial reservoir is 8 miles long and 2 miles wide, stretching north and west of town. Fishers should have a valid Colorado fishing license.

Many of its angling spots are accessible only by boat. Wakeless boating zones in skinny, tree-lined side canyons allow for great still-water fishing without the buzz and disturbance of motor craft.

Art Girls' Studio ARTS CENTER

(200 S 4th St; ⏰10am-5pm Tue-Sat) This fully decked-out quilt and crafts shop is a do-it-yourselfer's dream. Classes are offered and finished products such as art quilts are on sale; some of the stock, such as Japanese quilting patches, is truly original.

Sleeping

If you want to camp, you can find out about nearby sites in the San Juan National Forest from the **USFS Dolores Ranger Station** (☎970-882-7296; www.fs.usda.gov/sanjuan; 29211 Hwy 184; ⏰8am-5pm Mon-Fri), which has the best camping options.

Dolores River RV Park CAMPGROUND $

(☎970-882-7761; www.doloresriverrvparkandcabins.com; 18680 Hwy 145; tent/RV sites $25/35, cabins $45) This place is fine enough if you're just looking for a place for the night, and is especially easy for RVs. It is located about 1.5 miles east of town and has pleasant enough (if overpriced) sites. The small cabins are the best deal going.

Outpost Motel MOTEL $

(☎970-882-7271, 800-382-4892; www.doloreslodgings.com; 1800 Central Ave; d with/without kitchen $75/70, cabins $125-150, RV sites $31) At the east end of town, this friendly motel has small but clean rooms with pine beds and quilts, as well as cabins. Some rooms have kitchenettes and the courtyard features a pleasant little wooden deck overlooking the Dolores River. The motel also takes RVs.

Rio Grande Southern Hotel HOTEL $$

(☎866-882-3026; www.rgshotel.com; 101 S 5th St; r incl breakfast $69-79;) Norman Rockwell prints and an old-world front desk welcome guests at this National Historic Landmark where Zane Gray wrote *Riders of the Purple Sage* (in room 4). Today it's a bit misshapen; in fact, you might be turned away if the host is napping. Features include a cozy library and small, antique-filled guest rooms.

Circle K Guest Ranch MOTEL $

(☎970-562-3826; www.ckranch.com; 27758 Hwy 145; tent/RV site $25/35, d $55-70, cabins from $132; P) South of Rico, this largely utilitarian riverside ranch is popular for family reunions. There's a homestyle restaurant serving family-style and horses to ride (from $43 per hour). Lodgings are sprawled out but include simple private cabins, worthwhile renovated motel rooms, dated and basic lodge rooms (very cheap), and a place to park the RV.

Eating & Drinking

Rio Grande Southern Restaurant GERMAN $$
(☎866-882-3026; www.rgshotel.com; 101 S 5th St; mains $9-15; ⏰7am-8pm Wed-Sat; 👪) Downstairs from the historic hotel, this welcoming dining room functions as a German restaurant with generous portions of bratwurst and Wiener schnitzel. Repeat customers swear it's the best German food in the region. You can also let off some steam on Karaoke Sundays (2pm to 8pm).

★**Dolores River Brewery** BREWERY
(☎970-882-4677; www.doloresriverbrewery.com; 100 S 4th St; pizzas $9-13; ⏰4pm-late Tue-Sun) Welcome to Dolores nightlife, with live bluegrass bands and cask-conditioned ale. Hickory wood-fired pizzas are the specialty here, with toppings like goat's cheese, chipotle peppers and grilled eggplants spicing it up. Drawing patrons from Cortez, it's easily the best pizza in the Four Corners region, and worth the torturous wait (entertain yourself with a pint or two).

Getting There & Away

Dolores is 11 miles north of Cortez on Hwy 145, also known as Railroad Ave.

Rico

POP 264 / ELEV 8825FT

At the base of a steep climb to Telluride, it's probably no surprise that Rico (meaning 'rich') was founded when prospectors sought silver in the hills, and local wags will claim that it is Colorado's last boom town. Stiff Ute resistance thwarted the first efforts at mining here, but the Utes signed the Brunot Agreement to effectively surrender the entirety of the San Juan Mountains in 1878, meaning the miners came rushing back. A boom from the Enterprise Lode brought some 5000 residents at the town's peak in 1892, but the timing was too late. Things went bust with the Silver Panic of 1893, and the town all but folded up. There's little history left, aside from a few historic buildings and the Van Winkle Headframe and Hoist Structure, a towering piece of mining equipment alongside the road, which makes a quick photo op. Today the town feels a little depressed.

Sights & Activities

Summer brings fabulous fishing along the Dolores River (which runs through town). Anglers score big with cutthroat, rainbow and brown trout. You can also hike the 9-mile loop from the top of Lizard Head Pass to the base of Lizard Head Peak, a crumbling 13,113ft tower of rock. Aside from that, it's mostly a place to gas up and move on.

Sleeping & Eating

Rico Hotel & Mountain Lodge LODGE $
(☎970-967-3000; www.ricohotel.com; 124 S Hwy 145; r incl breakfast $79-108; 📶) This rambling old roadside lodge offers mostly bare-bones rooms in a refurbished miners' boarding house. Room size varies widely. The on-site Argentine Grille isn't always open – check ahead – but it usually offers dinner and Sunday lunch. On the menu are delicious beef tenderloin tacos with mango, chili and cilantro.

SAN JUAN MOUNTAINS

Telluride

POP 2368 / ELEV 8750FT

Surrounded on three sides by mastodon peaks, exclusive Telluride is quite literally cut off from the hubbub of the outside world. Once a rough mining town, today it's dirtbag-meets-diva – mixing the few who can afford the real estate with those scratching out a slope-side living for the sport of it. The town center still has palpable old-time charm, though locals often villainize the recently developed Mountain Village, whose ready-made attractions have a touch of Vegas. Yet idealism remains the Telluride mantra. Shreds of paradise persist with the town's free box – where you can swap unwanted items (across from the post office) – the freedom of luxuriant powder days and the bonhomie of its infamous festivals.

Activities

Telluride Ski Resort SNOW SPORTS
(☎888-288-7360, 970-728-7533; www.tellurideskiresort.com; 565 Mountain Village Blvd; lift tickets $98) Covering three distinct areas, Telluride Ski Resort is served by 16 lifts. Much of the terrain is for advanced and intermediate skiers, but there's still ample choice for beginners.

Telluride

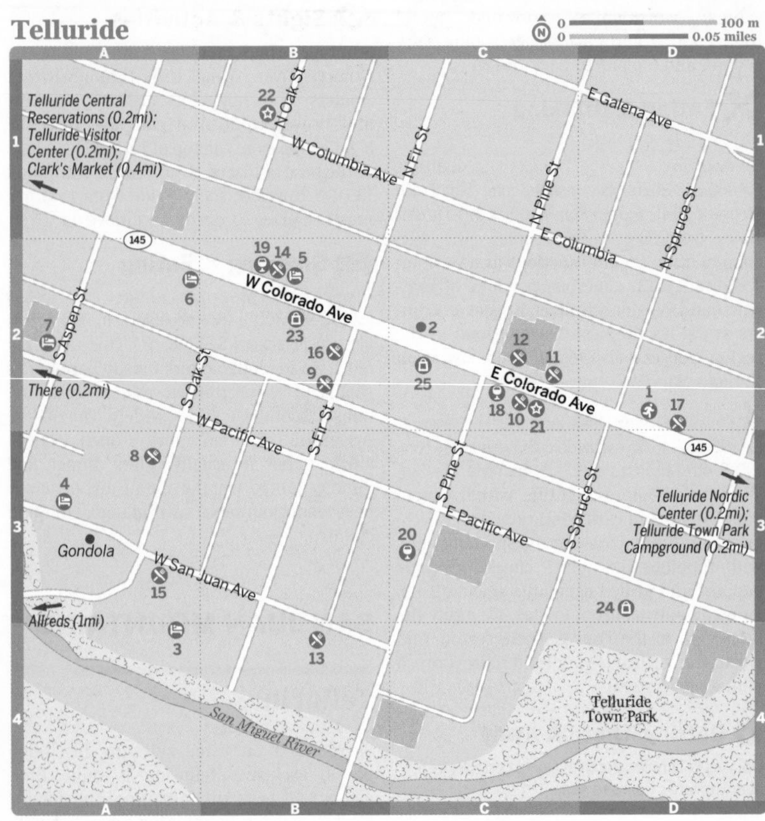

Telluride Ski & Snowboarding School

SNOW SPORTS

(☎970-728-7507; www.tellurideskiresort.com; 565 Mountain Village Blvd; adult group lesson full day $170, 2hr $75; 👪) If you'd like to sharpen your skills, the Telluride Ski Resort offers private and group lessons with good teachers through this school, which offers classes for children and sessions specific to women, with women instructors.

San Juan Hut System

SNOW SPORTS, MOUNTAIN BIKING

(☎970-626-3033; www.sanjuanhuts.com; per person $30) Experienced cross-country skiers will appreciate the strong series of basic huts along a 206-mile route stretching from Telluride west to Moab, Utah. In summer these huts, equipped with bunks and cooking facilities, are popular with mountain bikers. Book well in advance, as huts fill quickly.

Telluride Flyfishers

FISHING

(☎800-294-9269; www.tellurideflyfishers.com; half-day fly-fishing $225) Housed in Telluride Sports, this outfit offers fishing guides and instruction.

Ride with Roudy

HORSEBACK RIDING

(☎970-728-9611; www.ridewithroudy.com; County Rd 43ZS; 2hr trips adult/child $85/45; ⏲closed Sun; 👪) Offers all-season trail rides through the surrounding hills. Roudy moved here as 'one of the old hippies' in the 1970s and has been leading trips for 30 years. Just don't show up wearing shorts! His rugged hospitality recalls Telluride's yesteryear. Call for an appointment and pricing details.

Telluride Nordic Center

SNOW SPORTS

(☎970-728-1144; www.telluridetrails.org; 500 E Colorado Ave) There are public cross-country trails in Town Park, as well as along the San Miguel River and the Telluride Valley

Telluride

Activities, Courses & Tours
1 Gravity Works D2
2 Telluride Outside C2

Sleeping
3 Camel's Garden A4
4 Hotel Columbia A3
5 New Sheridan Hotel B2
6 Telluride Alpine Lodging A2
7 Victorian Inn A2

Eating
8 221 South Oak A3
9 Baked in Telluride B2
10 Brown Dog Pizza C2
Cosmopolitan .... (see 4)
11 Honga's Lotus Petal C2
12 La Cocina de Luz C2
13 La Marmotte B4
14 New Sheridan Chop House B2
15 Oak A3
16 Over the Moon B2
17 The Butcher & The Baker D2

Drinking & Nightlife
18 Last Dollar Saloon C2
19 New Sheridan Bar B2
20 Smugglers Brewpub & Grille C3

Entertainment
21 Fly Me to the Moon Saloon C2
22 Sheridan Opera House B1

Shopping
23 Between the Covers B2
24 Scarpe D3
25 Telluride Sports C2

floor west of town. Instruction and rentals are available from the Telluride Nordic Center.

Gravity Works SPORTS RENTAL
(☎970-728-4143; www.telluridegravityworks.com; 205 E Colorado Ave; full-day bicycle hire $40-85; ⏱9am-8pm) This locally owned full-service bike and ski shop sells gear and offers demos and rentals. Kids rentals are also available. As a mountain-sports center, it also boasts an indoor climbing wall and fitness center.

Tours

Telluride Food Tours TOUR
(☎301-758-3555; www.telluridefoodtours.net; tours $65; ⏱4:30pm Wed-Sat; 🐾) Run by a young couple, this walking food tour gives visitors a taste of both Telluride and its varied eats. The course takes two to three hours. After seven to eight tastings with drinks, you may still need to take a walk. Bookings can be made online.

Telluride Outside ADVENTURE TOUR
(☎970-728-3895; www.tellurideoutside.com; 121 W Colorado Ave) In business for over 30 years, this longtime local operation is the go-to guide service for fly-fishing, mountain-bike tours, 4WD tours, rafting and more. In winter it does snowmobile tours. Check the website for fishing reports and blog.

Festivals & Events

★**Mountainfilm** FILM
(www.mountainfilm.org; ⏱Memorial Day weekend, May) A four-day screening of outdoor adventure and environmental films.

Telluride Bluegrass Festival MUSIC
(☎800-624-2422; www.planetbluegrass.com; 4-day pass $195; ⏱late Jun) This festival attracts thousands for a weekend of top-notch rollicking alfresco bluegrass. Stalls sell all sorts of food and local microbrews to keep you happy, and acts continue well into the night. Camping out for the four-day festival is very popular. Check out the website for info on sites, shuttle services and combo ticket-and-camping packages – it's all very organized!

Telluride Mushroom Festival FOOD
(www.tellurideinstitute.org; ⏱late Aug) Fungiphiles sprout up at this festival.

Telluride Film Festival FILM
(☎603-433-9202; www.telluridefilmfestival.com; ⏱early Sep) National and international films are premiered throughout town, and the event attracts big-name stars. For more information on the relatively complicated pricing scheme, visit the film-festival website.

Brews & Blues Festival BEER, MUSIC
(www.tellurideblues.com; 3-day pass $170; ⏱mid-Sep) Telluride's festival season comes to a raucous end at this event, where blues musicians take to the stage and microbrews fill the bellies of fans.

Sleeping

Aside from camping, there's no cheap lodging in Telluride. If you arrive during the summer or winter peak seasons, or during one of the city's festivals, you'll pay dearly. Rates drop quite a bit during the off season, sometimes up to 30%. If you are coming during festival time, contact the festival organizers directly about camping.

Some of the huge properties in Mountain Village offer decent online rates, but none have the character of the smaller hotels downtown. Most skiers opt to stay in vacation rentals – there are scores of them. If you're interested in booking a room in one, the most reputable agency is **Telluride Alpine Lodging** (☎888-893-0158; www.telluride-lodging.com; 324 W Colorado Ave).

★**New Sheridan Hotel** HOTEL $$
(☎970-728-4351, 800-200-1891; www.new-sheridan.com; 231 W Colorado Ave; d from $188;) Elegant and understated, this historic brick hotel (erected in 1895) provides a lovely base camp for exploring Telluride. High-ceilinged rooms feature crisp linens and snug flannel throws. Check out the hot-tub deck with mountain views. In the bull's-eye of downtown, the location is perfect, but some rooms are small for the price.

CAMPING

Right in Telluride Town Park, the excellent **Telluride Town Park Campground** (☎970-728-2173; 500 E Colorado Ave; campsite with/without vehicle space $23/15; mid-May–mid-Oct;) offers 42 campsites, showers, and swimming and tennis. There's even a bit of beach at a couple of riverside spots. Campsites are all on a first-come, first-served basis, unless it is festival time (consult ahead with festival organizers).

Two campgrounds in the Uncompahgre National Forest are within 15 miles of Telluride on Hwy 145 and cost $20 per site. **Sunshine Campground** (☎970-327-4261; off County Rd 145; sites $20; late May–late Sep) is the nearest and the best, with 15 first-come, first-served campsites; facilities at **Matterhorn Campground** (☎970-327-4261; Hwy 145; sites $20; May-Sep), a bit further up the hill, include showers and electrical hookups for some of the 27 campsites.

Inn at Lost Creek BOUTIQUE HOTEL $$
(☎970-728-5678; www.innatlostcreek.com; 119 Lost Creek Lane; r $146-281;) This lush boutique-style hotel in Mountain Village knows cozy. At the bottom of Telluride's main lift, it's also very convenient. Service is personalized, and impeccable rooms have alpine hardwoods, Southwestern designs and molded tin. There are also two rooftop spas. Check the website for packages.

Victorian Inn LODGE $$
(☎970-728-6601; www.victorianinntelluride.com; 401 W Pacific Ave; r incl breakfast from $124;) The smell of fresh cinnamon rolls greets visitors at one of Telluride's better deals, offering comfortable rooms (some with kitchenettes) and a hot tub and dry sauna. Best off all, there are fantastic lift-ticket deals for guests. Kids aged 12 years and under stay free, and you can't beat the downtown location.

Hotel Columbia HOTEL $$$
(☎970-728-0660, 800-201-9505; www.columbiatelluride.com; 300 W San Juan Ave; d/ste from $175/305;) Since pricey digs are a given, skiers might as well stay right across the street from the gondola. Locally owned and operated, this stylish and swank hotel pampers. Store your gear in the ski and boot storage and head directly to a room with espresso maker, fireplace and heated tile floors. With shampoo dispensers and recycling, it's also pretty ecofriendly.

Other highlights include a rooftop hot tub and fitness room. Breakfast is included, but food at the connected Cosmopolitan is also excellent.

Lumière HOTEL $$$
(☎866-530-9466, 907-369-0400; www.lumiere-hotels.com; 118 Lost Creek Lane; d incl breakfast from $250;) In Mountain Village, this ski-in, ski-out luxury lodge commands breathtaking views of the San Juans. Plush and fluff, it boasts seven-layer bedding, Asian-inspired contemporary design and suites with top-of-the-line appliances that few probably even use. But even with the hip sushi bar and luxuriant spa menu, its greatest appeal is zipping from the slopes to a bubble bath in minutes.

Camel's Garden HOTEL **$$$**
(970-728-9300; www.camelsgarden.com; 250 W San Juan Ave; r from $158;) This modern and luxurious choice is located at the base of the gondola. The lobby is filled with local artwork and the large rooms feature custom-crafted furniture and Italian marble baths with oversized tubs. Don't miss the giant 25ft hot tub on the top level.

The complex also features restaurants, bars and spa treatments. The Chair 8 Bar is a favorite with the après-ski crowd.

Eating

Meals and even groceries can be pricey in Telluride, so check out the food carts and the taco truck on Colorado Ave with picnic table seating for quick fixes. Gaga for sustainability, many local restaurants offer grass-fed beef or natural meat; we indicate those with the greatest commitment to sustainability.

Clark's Market SELF-CATERING
(www.clarksmarket.com; 700 W Colorado Ave; 7am-9pm) Put the condo kitchenette to good use after picking up supplies at Clark's, the nicest market in town. It stocks specialty goods and scores of treats, with fresh fruit and deli meats.

Baked in Telluride BAKERY **$**
(970-728-4775; www.bakedintelluride.com; 127 S Fir St; mains $6-12; 5:30am-10pm) Don't expect ambience. This cafeteria-style Telluride institution serves up XL doughnuts, mom's meatloaf, sourdough wheat-crust pizza and some hearty soups and salads. The front deck is a fishbowl of local activity and the vibe is happy casual.

★ **La Cocina de Luz** MEXICAN, ORGANIC **$$**
(www.lacocinatelluride.com; 123 E Colorado Ave; mains $9-19; 9am-9pm;) As they lovingly serve two Colorado favorites (organic and Mexican), it's no wonder that the lunch line runs deep at this healthy taqueria. Order the *achiote* pulled pork and you might be full until tomorrow. Delicious details include a salsa and chip bar, handmade tortillas, and margaritas with organic lime and agave nectar. With vegan and gluten-free options, too.

The Butcher & The Baker CAFE **$$**
(970-728-3334; 217 E Colorado Ave; mains $10-14; 7am-7pm Mon-Sat, 8am-2pm Sun;) Two veterans of upscale local catering started this heartbreakingly cute cafe, and no one beats it for breakfast. Hearty sandwiches with local meats are the perfect takeout for the trail and there are heaps of baked goods and fresh sides.

Brown Dog Pizza PIZZA **$$**
(970-728-8046; www.browndogpizza.net; 10 E Colorado Ave; pizzas $10-22; 11am-10pm) The pizza? It's thin crust and fair enough, but the crowd makes the place interesting. Ten minutes after you belly up to the bar for a slice and a cheap pint of Pabst, you'll be privy to all the local dirt. It's one of the most affordable meals on the strip.

Over the Moon TAPAS **$$**
(www.overthemoonfinefoods.com; 200 W Colorado Ave; cheese plates $12-15; 11am-6pm Mon-Tue, 10am-7pm Wed-Sat, noon-5pm Sun) Over the alleyway, this gourmet wine and cheese shop would be a boon to Wallace and Gromit. Cheeses are organized by country of origin, plus it offers fig confit, truffled honey and charcuterie. Sure, it's not without pretension, but its few tables offer travelers the pleasure of fine wines by the glass alongside some exotic cheeses.

Oak BARBECUE **$$**
(970-728-3985; www.oakstelluride.com; 250 San Juan Ave; mains $10-15; 11am-10pm;) You can pick something off the chalkboard or just take what the other guy has his face in – a cheap and messy delight. Go for the pulled-pork sandwich with coleslaw on top. Do it right by siding it with a bowl of crispy sweet-potato fries. The can beer specials are outrageous.

★ **New Sheridan Chop House** MODERN AMERICAN **$$$**
(970-728-4531; www.newsheridan.com; 231 W Colorado Ave; mains from $19; 5pm-2am) With superb service and a chic decor of embroidered velvet benches, this is an easy pick for an intimate dinner. Start with a cheese plate, but from there the menu gets Western with exquisite elk shortloin and ravioli with tomato relish and local sheep ricotta. Top it off with a flourless dark chocolate cake in fresh caramel sauce.

Breakfasts are gourmet and noteworthy, too.

221 South Oak MODERN AMERICAN **$$$**
(970-728-9505; www.221southoak.com; 221 S Oak St; mains $19-25; 5-10pm;) A great pick, this is an intimate restaurant in a historic home, with a small but innovative

menu spinning world flavors with fresh ingredients. Dishes are flavorful and usually based on meat, fish and seafood, with ample vegetable accents. There's also a vegetarian menu with depth and diversity. Tuesdays have two-for-one mains.

La Marmotte FRENCH **$$$**
(☎970-728-6232; www.lamarmotte.com; 150 W San Juan Ave; mains from $20; ⊙5pm-late Tue-Sat) Seasonal plates of French cuisine, white linen and candlelit warmth contrast with this rustic 19th-century icehouse. Dishes like the *coq au vin* with bacon mashed potatoes are both smart and satisfying. There are some organic options and an extensive wine list. Parents should check out the Friday-night winter babysitting options.

Cosmopolitan MODERN AMERICAN **$$$**
(☎970-728-0660; www.columbiatelluride.com; 300 W San Juan Ave; mains from $20; ⊙dinner) The on-site restaurant at the Hotel Columbia is one of Telluride's most respected for fine modern dining with a twist – can you resist Himalayan yak rib eye or lobster corn dogs? The food is certainly inventive, and cheap if you come at happy hour (5pm to 6pm), when sushi and cosmos are half-price.

Allreds MODERN AMERICAN **$$$**
(☎970-728-7474; www.allredsrestaurant.com; gondola station St Sophia; mains $29-49; ⊙5:30-9:30pm, bar 5-11:30pm) Midway up the gondola, Allreds stuns with San Juan mountain panoramas – though the bar boasts the best views. Upscale and very exclusive, it emphasizes Colorado and organic ingredients, and has five-course dinners with wine pairings. Smaller budgets can cheat the system: hit the bar for sunset drinks with glorious handcut truffle fries and burgers. Summer alpenglow peaks just before 8pm.

Honga's Lotus Petal ASIAN **$$$**
(☎970-728-5134; www.hongaslotuspetal.com; 135 E Colorado Ave; mains $16-25; ⊙6pm-late) For pan-Asian cuisine, make your way to this two-story dining space. Prices are dear but the presentation – ranging from sushi to curries – is lovely and the outstanding mojitos have plenty of rock and roll. Korean short ribs just about fall off the bone. So lively and fresh, we can even forgive the pan flutes.

Drinking & Nightlife

New Sheridan Bar BAR
(☎970-728-3911; www.newsheridan.com; 231 W Colorado Ave; ⊙5pm-2am) Well worth a visit in low season for some real local flavor and opinions. At other times, it's a rush hour of beautiful people. But old bullet holes in the wall testify to the plucky survival of the bar itself, even as the adjoining hotel sold off chandeliers and antiques to pay the heating bills when mining fortunes waned.

There COCKTAIL BAR
(☎970-728-1213; http://therebars.com; 627 W Pacific Ave; appetizers from $4; ⊙5pm-midnight Mon-Fri, 10am-3pm Sat & Sun) A hip social alcove for cocktails and nibbling, plus weekend brunch. Bigger appetites can dine on shareable mains such as whole Colorado trout. On a comic-book-style menu, East-meets-West in yummy lettuce wraps, duck ramen and sashimi tostadas, paired with original hand-shaken drinks. We liked the jalapeño kiss.

Smugglers Brewpub & Grille PUB
(☎970-728-5620; www.smugglersbrewpub.com; 225 S Pine St; ⊙11am-10pm; 👪) Beer-lovers will feel right at home at casual Smugglers, a great place to hang out, sample local brew and eat fried stuff. With at least seven beers on tap, it's a smorgasbord, but go for the chocolatey Two Plank Porter or the Smugglers' Scottish Strong Ale.

Last Dollar Saloon BAR
(☎970-728-4800; www.lastdollarsaloon.com; 100 E Colorado Ave; ⊙3pm-2am) All local color – forget about cocktails and grab a cold can of beer at this longtime late-night favorite, popular when everything else closes. With pool tables and darts.

Entertainment

Fly Me to the Moon Saloon LIVE MUSIC
(☎970-728-6666; 132 E Colorado Ave; ⊙3pm-2am) Let your hair down and kick up your heels to the tunes of live bands at this saloon, the best place in Telluride to party hard.

Sheridan Opera House THEATER
(☎970-728-4539; www.sheridanoperahouse.com; 110 N Oak St; 👪) This historic venue has a burlesque charm and is always the center of Telluride's cultural life. It hosts the Telluride Repertory Theater, and frequently has special performances for children.

Shopping

Telluride Sports SPORTS
(970-728-4477; www.telluridesports.com; 150 W Colorado Ave; 8am-8pm) There are branches and associated shops in Mountain Village, making this the biggest network of outdoor suppliers in town. It covers everything outdoors, has topographical and USFS maps, sporting supplies and loads of local information.

Between the Covers BOOKS
(970-728-4504; www.between-the-covers.com; 224 W Colorado Ave; 9am-7pm Mon-Sat, 9am-6pm Sun) Bookworms flock to this homey shop with a big selection of local interest, creaking floors and a doting staff. Check online for readings and events. Local secret: the coffee counter in back turns out a mean espresso milkshake.

Scarpe CLOTHING
(970-728-1513; www.shopscarpe.com; 250 E Pacific Ave; 10am-7pm) The hand-picked selection of women's shoes, skirts and accessories makes Scarpe the best clothing boutique in town. Things here feel timeless, designed by a fleet of names that includes a good number of locals.

Orientation

Colorado Ave, also known as Main St, has most of the restaurants, bars and shops. You can walk everywhere, so leave your car at the intercept parking lot at the south end of Mahoney Dr (near the visitor center) or at your lodgings.

From town you can reach the ski mountain via two lifts and the gondola. Located on S Oak St, the gondola also links Telluride with Mountain Village, the base for the Telluride Ski Resort. Located 7 miles from town along Hwy 145, Mountain Village is a 20-minute drive east, but only 12 minutes away by gondola (free for foot passengers).

Ajax Peak, a glacial headwall, rises up behind the town to form the end of the U-shaped valley. To the right (or south) on Ajax Peak, Colorado's highest waterfall, Bridal Veil Falls, cascades 365ft down; a switchback trail leads to a restored Victorian powerhouse atop the falls. To the south, Mt Wilson reaches 14,246ft among a group of rugged peaks that form the Lizard Head Wilderness Area.

Information

Telluride Central Reservations (888-355-8743; 630 W Colorado Ave; 9am-5pm Mon-Sat, 10am-1pm Sun) Handles accommodations and festival tickets. Located in the same building as the visitor center.

Telluride Medical Center (970-728-3848; 500 W Pacific Ave) Handles skiing accidents, medical problems and emergencies.

Telluride Visitor Center (970-728-3041, 888-353-5473; www.telluride.com; 630 W Colorado Ave; 9am-5pm winter, to 7pm summer) This well-stocked visitor center has local info in all seasons. Restrooms and an ATM make it an all-round useful spot.

Getting There & Around

In ski season Montrose Regional Airport (p291), 65 miles north, has direct flights to and from Denver (on United), Houston, Phoenix and limited cities on the east coast.

Gondola (S Oak St; 7am-midnight) The world's most beautiful commute, this free gondola takes a 15-minute ride up to the Mountain Village through aspen trees.

Telluride Express (970-728-6000; www.tellurideexpress.com) Shuttles from the Telluride Airport to town or Mountain Village cost $15. There are also shuttles to Montrose airport (adult/child $50/30); call to arrange pickup.

Telluride Regional Airport (970-778-5051; www.tellurideairport.com; Last Dollar Rd) Commuter aircraft serve the mesa-top Telluride Airport, 5 miles east of town on Hwy 145. If weather is poor, flights may be diverted to Montrose, 65 miles north. For car rental, National and Budget both have airport locations.

Ridgway

POP 900 / ELEV 6985FT

Ridgway, with its local quirk, zesty history and scandalous views of Mt Sneffels, is hard to just blow through. On top of that, the town also served as the backdrop for John Wayne's 1969 cowboy classic, *True Grit*.

It sits at the crossroads of US 550, which goes south to Durango, and Hwy 62, which leads to Telluride. The downtown area is tucked away on the west side of the Uncompahgre River. Through town Hwy 62 is called Sherman and all the perpendicular streets are named for his daughters. Ridgway Area Chamber of Commerce has a lot of information about local activities.

Sights & Activities

Ridgway Railroad Museum MUSEUM
(970-626-5181; www.ridgwayrailroadmuseum.org; 150 Racecourse Rd; 10am-6pm May-Sep, reduced hr Oct-Apr) FREE Ridgway was the birthplace of the Rio Grande Southern Railroad, a narrow-gauge rail line that

connected to Durango with the 'Galloping Goose,' a kind of hybrid train and truck that saved the struggling Rio Grande Southern for a number of years. This museum is dedicated to the plucky rail line.

The volunteers who staff the museum are true railroad zealots – one even reconstructed a Galloping Goose engine outside from photos and sketches. The permanent collection has maps, historical photos and a really cool diorama of the Pleasant Valley Trestle and Motor No 2. It's also the de facto historical museum for the town, and it has good brochures for a short self-guided tour.

Orvis Hot Springs HOT SPRING
(☎970-626-5324; www.orvishotsprings.com; 1585 County Rd 3; per hour/day $10/14) The attractive rock pools make this outdoor, clothing optional, hot spring hard to resist. Yes, it does get its fair share of exhibitionists, but the variety of soaking areas, ranging from 100°F to 114°F (38°C to 45°C) mean you can probably scout out the perfect spot. Less appealing are the private indoor pools that feel a little airless. It's 9 miles north of Ouray, outside Ridgway.

Rigs Fly Shop & Guide Service FLY-FISHING
(☎970-626-4460, 888-626-4460; www.fishrigs.com; Suite 2, 565 Sherman St; half-day fishing tours per person from $225; ⏰7am-7pm; 👪) Rigs Fly Shop offers guided fly-fishing tours out of Ridgway from half-day beginners' trips to multiday campouts for more-experienced anglers. Riggs also does white-water rafting and other soft-adventure itineraries in and around southwest Colorado. Costs drop significantly with the number of guests.

★**Chicks with Picks** CLIMBING INSTRUCTION
(☎970-316-1403, office 970-626-4424; www.chickswithpicks.net; 163 County Rd 12) This group is dedicated to getting women onto the rocks and ice, giving instruction for all-comers (beginners included) about typical male pursuits such as rock climbing, bouldering and ice climbing. The programs change frequently and often involve multiday excursions or town-based courses. Men are included on some activities, but most are women-only.

Ridgway State Park & Recreation Area FISHING
(☎970-626-5822; www.parks.state.co.us/parks/ridgway; 28555 US Hwy 550; admission $7; ⏰dawn-dusk) Fishing aficionados should head to Ridgway State Park and Recreation Area, 12 miles north of town. The reservoir here is stocked with loads of rainbow trout, as well as German brown, kokanee, yellow perch and the occasional largemouth bass. There are also hiking trails and campsites.

Sleeping

Ridgway State Park & Recreation Area CAMPGROUND $
(☎800-678-2267; www.parks.state.co.us/parks/ridgway; 28555 US Hwy 550; tent/RV/yurt sites $18/22/70) With almost 300 sites, the three campgrounds here offer good availability with gorgeous water views, hiking and fishing. Tent campers have 25 walk-in sites, but the path is short and there are wheelbarrows to transport your stuff. Or check out the cool canvas yurts. Restrooms have coin-op showers and there's a playground for kids. Book online or over the phone.

★**Chipeta Solar Springs Resort** LODGE $$$
(☎970-626-3737; www.chipeta.com; 304 S Lena St; r $175-275; 🚭) This Southwestern adobe-style lodge is a swank, upscale sleeping option. Rooms feature hand-painted Mexican tiles, rough-hewn log beds and decks with a view. It's very classy and upmarket, and there are wonderful public areas on the property.

Have a read in the Great Room or a chat in the solarium, or head out to the hot tubs on the property for a quiet soak. The on-site spa features treatments developed by the Utes and daily yoga classes. Check Chipeta's website for ski, soak and stay deals, where you can ride the slopes at Telluride, soak in the hot springs pools in Ouray and spend the night in Ridgway.

Eating & Drinking

★**Kate's Place** BREAKFAST $$
(☎970-626-9800; 615 W Clinton St; mains $9-13; ⏰7am-2pm; 👪) Consider yourself lucky if the morning starts with a chorizo-stuffed breakfast burrito and white cheddar grits from Kate's: it's the best breakfast joint for miles. The restaurant's dedication to local farmers, cute and colorful interior and bubbly waitstaff seal the deal.

Thai Paradise THAI $$
(☎970-626-2742; 146 N Cora St; mains $12-16; ⏰11am-2pm Mon-Fri, 5-9pm Mon-Sun) Serving up all the standard curries in light, spicy and fragrant preparations, this tiny house of flavor is a hit. Pad Thai, crispy duck and tempura round out the menu, with brown rice and Asian beers also on offer. If it's warm

out, you can enjoy the few tables set on the outdoor patio.

True Grit Cafe AMERICAN $$
(☎970-626-5739; 123 N Lena Ave; mains $8-15; ⏲lunch & dinner; 📶👪) Scenes from the original *True Grit* were filmed at this appropriately named cafe and watering hole. It's a kind of shrine to John Wayne, with pictures and memorabilia hung on the walls. Quarter-pound burgers, tasty chicken and fried steaks are served, and a crackling fire warms patrons in the winter.

★**Colorado Boy** BREWERY, PIZZERIA
(602 Clinton St; pizzas $10; ⏲4-9pm Tue-Sun) Baking goat's-cheese pizzas with fennel sausage and serving craft beer by the barrel, congenial Colorado Boy is a boon to locals, who rush to claim the outdoor picnic tables early. Wash the artisan pizza down with the house-brewed Irish Red, with caramel and toffee notes, or a Mexican Coke.

Cimmaron Coffee House CAFE
(☎970-626-5858; 380 Sherman St; mains $3; ⏲7am-6pm) Coffee addicts collect at this unassuming cafe and bookstore to get a fix and a smothered breakfast burrito. There are also smoothies. With patio seating.

Information

Ridgway Area Chamber of Commerce
(☎800-220-4959, 970-626-5181; www.ridgwaycolorado.com; 150 Racecourse Rd; ⏲9am-5pm Mon-Fri) Lots of information about local activities.

Ouray & the Million Dollar Highway

POP 982 / ELEV 7760FT

With gorgeous icefalls draping the box canyon and soothing hot springs dotting the valley floor, Ouray (you-ray) is one privileged place, even for Colorado. For ice climbers, it's a world-class destination, but hikers and 4WD fans can also appreciate its rugged and sometimes stunning charms. The town is a well-preserved quarter-mile mining village sandwiched between imposing peaks.

Between Silverton and Ouray, US 550 is known as the Million Dollar Hwy. Some credit the name to roadbed rich in valuable gold ore. Others say it cost $1 million per mile to build. The whole of US 550 has been called the Million Dollar Hwy, but more properly it's the amazing stretch of road south of Ouray through the Uncompahgre Gorge up to Red Mountain Pass at 11,018ft, passing abandoned mine headframes and slag piles from the former Idarado Mine.

The alpine scenery is truly awesome and driving south towards Silverton positions drivers on the outside edge of the skinny, winding road, a heartbeat away from freefall. Vehicles traveling north sit more snugly on the inside edge. Much of the road is cut into the mountainsides and gains elevation in tight hairpin turns and S-bends. The brooding mountains loom large and close, their bulk and flanks intimidating, with snow clinging to their lofty misty peaks even in high summer. In good weather the road is formidable. In drizzle or rain, fog or snow, the Million Dollar Hwy south of Ouray is downright scary, so take care.

Ouray is named after the legendary Ute chief who maintained peace between the white settlers and the crush of miners who descended on the San Juan Mountains in the early 1870s. Ouray relinquished the Ute tribal lands, preventing the slaughter of his people.

Sights

Little Ouray, 'the Switzerland of America,' is very picturesque and littered with old houses and buildings. The visitor center and **museum** (☎970-325-4576; www.ouraycountyhistoricalsociety.org; 420 6th Ave; adult/child $6/1; ⏲hours vary, closed Dec-mid-Apr; 👪) issue a free leaflet with details of an excellent walking tour that takes in two dozen buildings and houses constructed between 1880 and 1904.

Birdwatchers come to Ouray to spot rare birds. The Box Canyon Falls have the USA's most accessible colony of protected black swifts. There are surprising numbers of unusual birds in town, including warblers, sparrows and grosbeaks. The visitor center has resources for bird-watchers, and the excellent **Buckskin Booksellers** (☎970-325-4071; www.buckskinbooksellers.com; 505 Main St; ⏲9am-5pm Mon-Sat; 👪) has books and guides.

Activities

There are stacks of things to do in and around Ouray. Remember that Ouray falls within the purview of tour and activities providers in nearby Ridgway, Montrose and Silverton, and even Durango and Gunnison so check the Activities sections in those towns too.

Ouray Ice Park ICE CLIMBING
(☎970-325-4061; www.ourayicepark.com; Hwy 361; ⏱7am-5pm mid-Dec–Mar; 👪) FREE Enthusiasts from around the globe come to ice climb at the world's first public ice park, spanning a 2-mile stretch of the Uncompahgre Gorge. The sublime (if chilly) experience offers something for all skill levels. Get instruction through a local guide service.

Ouray Hot Springs HOT SPRING
(☎970-325-7073; www.ourayhotsprings.com; 1200 Main St; adult/child $12/8; ⏱10am-10pm Jun-Aug, noon-9pm Mon-Fri & 11am-9pm Sat & Sun Sep-May; 👪) For a healing soak, try the historic Ouray Hot Springs. The natural springwater is crystal-clear and free of the sulfur smells plaguing other hot springs around here, and the giant pool features a variety of soaking areas at temperatures from 96°F to 106°F (36°C to 41°C). The complex also offers a gym and massage service.

Tours

Ouray Mule Carriage Co CARRIAGE TOURS
(☎970-708-4946; www.ouraymule.com; 834 Main St; adult/child $15/5; ⏱hourly departures 1-6pm Jun-Aug; 👪) The mule-drawn coach you see clip-clopping along Ouray's main streets is the nine-person dray that takes visitors (and locals) around on interpretive tours of the old town. Charters are available for larger groups.

Ouray Livery HORSEBACK RIDING
(☎970-708-7051, 970-325-4340; www.ouraylivery.com; 834 Main St; 1hr ride $40; 👪) The old Ouray Livery has been in the same family since 1944. It offers short and day-long guided horseback riding in the mountains surrounding the town. This group has special permits to tour the Grand Mesa, Uncompahgre and Gunnison National Forests.

San Juan Mountain Guides CLIMBING, SKIING
(☎800-642-5389, 970-325-4925; www.ouray-climbing.com; 725 Main St; 👪) Ouray's own professional guiding and climbing group is certified with the International Federation of Mountain Guides Association (IFMGA). It specializes in ice and rock climbing and wilderness backcountry skiing.

San Juan Scenic Jeep Tours 4WD, FISHING
(☎970-325-0089; http://sanjuanjeeptours.com; 206 7th Ave; adult/child half-day tours $59/30; 👪) The friendly folks at the Historic Western Hotel operate a customized Jeep-touring service. Abandoned ghost towns of the old mining days are always popular, as are off-road tours of the nearby peaks and valleys. Hiking, hunting and fishing drop-offs and pick-ups can be arranged.

Festivals & Events

Ouray Ice Festival ICE CLIMBING
(☎970-325-4288; www.ourayicefestival.com; donation for evening events; ⏱Jan; 👪) The Ouray Ice Festival features four days of climbing competitions, dinners, slide shows and clinics. There's even a climbing wall set up for kids. You can watch the competitions for free, but various evening events require a donation to the ice park. Once inside, you'll get free brews from popular Colorado microbrewer New Belgium.

Sleeping

Amphitheater Forest Service Campground CAMPGROUND $
(☎877-444-6777; www.recreation.gov; US Hwy 550; tent sites $16; ⏱Jun-Aug) With great tent sites under the trees, this high-altitude campground is a score. On holiday weekends a three-night minimum applies. South of town on Hwy 550, take a signposted left-hand turn.

Historic Western Hotel, Restaurant & Saloon HOTEL $
(☎970-325-4645; www.historicwesternhotel.com; 210 7th Ave; r without/with bath $49/98; P📶) Open by reservation in shoulder season, this somewhat threadbare Wild West boardinghouse serves all budgets. Huge, floral widow's-walk rooms are straight out of a Sergio Leone flick, with saggy beds and a clawfoot tub in room. It's probably wise to skip the cramped shared-bath rooms. The saloon serves affordable meals and grog under a wall of mounted game.

★**Wiesbaden** HOTEL $$
(☎970-325-4347; www.wiesbadenhotsprings.com; 625 5th St; r $132-347; 🚭📶🏊) Quirky, quaint and new age, Wiesbaden even boasts a natural indoor vapor cave, which, in another era, was frequented by Chief Ouray. Rooms with quilted bedcovers are cozy and romantic, but the sunlit suite with a natural rock wall tops all. In the morning, guests roam in thick robes, drinking the free organic coffee or tea, post-soak, or awaiting massages.

The on-site Aveda salon also provides soothing facials to make your mountain detox complete. Outside, there's a spacious hot-spring pool (included) and a private,

WORTH A TRIP

SCENIC DRIVES: SAN JUAN ROUTES

If you have a high-clearance 4WD and four-wheeling skills, these rugged routes are a blast. Jeep tours may also be available.

Alpine Loop Demanding but fantastic fun, this 63-mile drive into the remote and rugged heart of the San Juans begins in Ouray and travels east to Lake City before looping back. Along the way you'll cross two 12,000ft mountain passes, with spectacular scenery and abandoned mining haunts. Allow six hours.

Imogene Pass Every year, runners tackle this rough 16-mile mining road, but you might feel that driving it is enough. Ultra-scenic, it connects Ouray with Telluride. Built in 1880, it's one of the San Juans' highest passes, linking two important mining sites.

In Ouray, head south on Main St and turn right on Bird Camp Rd (City Rd 361). Pass Bird Camp Mine, once one of the San Juans' most prolific, climbing high into the mountains. There are stream crossings and sheer cliff drops – a total adrenaline rush! Eventually the route opens onto high alpine meadows before the summit of Imogene Pass (13,114ft). Descending toward Telluride, you will pass the abandoned Tomboy Mine, which once had a population as large as present-day Ouray. The pass is open in summer, allow three hours one-way.

clothing-optional soaking tub with a waterfall, reservable for $35 per hour.

Box Canyon Lodge & Hot Springs LODGE **$$**
(☎970-325-4981, 800-327-5080; www.boxcanyonouray.com; 45 3rd Ave; r $110-165, apt $278-319; wi-fi) 🍃 It's not every hotel that offers geothermal heated rooms, and pineboard rooms prove spacious and fresh. Spring-fed barrel hot tubs are perfect for a romantic stargazing soak. With good hospitality that includes free apples and bottled water, it's popular, so book ahead.

Ouray Victoria Inn HOTEL **$$**
(☎970-325-7222, 800-846-8729; www.victorianinnouray.com; 50 3rd Ave; d incl breakfast from $99; P non-smoking wi-fi) Refurbished in 2009, 'The Vic' has a terrific setting next to Box Canyon Park on the Uncompahgre River near Ouray Ice Park. Rooms have cable TV, fridges and coffeemakers; some have balconies and splendid views. Kids will appreciate the deluxe swing set with climbing holds. Rates vary widely by season, but low-season rates are a steal.

St Elmo Hotel HOTEL **$$**
(☎970-325-4951, 866-243-1502; www.stelmohotel.com; 426 Main St; d incl breakfast $125-190; non-smoking air-con) 🍃 Effusively feminine, this 1897 hotel is a showpiece of the Ouray museum's historic walking tour. Nine unique renovated rooms have floral wallpaper and period furnishings. Guests have access to a hot tub and sauna and there's even some of Ouray's best dining, Bon Ton Restaurant, on-site downstairs.

Beaumont Hotel HOTEL **$$$**
(☎970-325-7000; www.beaumonthotel.com; 505 Main St; r from $179; P non-smoking) With magnificent four-post beds, clawfoot tubs and hand-carved mirrors, this 1886 hotel underwent extensive renovations to revive the glamour it possessed a century ago. Word has it that Oprah stayed here, and you'll probably like it too. It also has a spa and boutiques, but due to the fragile decor, pets and kids under 16 years old are not allowed.

✕ Eating & Drinking

Beaumont Grill MODERN AMERICAN **$$**
(☎970-325-7050; http://beaumonthotel.com/dine.html; 507 Main St; mains $16-35; ⏲11am-10pm; family-friendly) In Colorado, gourmet can also mean a really nice burger, which isn't a bad bet here. With a beautiful courtyard, this contemporary bistro offers everything from rib eye burgers to homemade mac n' cheese, though it is on the pricey side. Choose from the wine cellar's 300 vintages from all over the world.

Buen Tiempo Mexican Restaurant & Cantina MEXICAN **$$**
(☎970-325-4544; 515 Main St; mains $7-20; ⏲6-10pm; vegetarian) This good-time spot bursts with bar-stool squatters and booths of families. From the chili-rubbed sirloin to the *posole* with warm tortillas, Buen Tiempo delivers. Start with a signature margarita with chips and spicy homemade salsa. End with a satisfying scoop of deep-fried ice cream. But

to find out how the dollars got on the ceiling, it will cost you.

O'Briens Pub & Grill PUB FOOD $$
(☎970-325-4386; 726 Main St; mains $8-14; ⊙11am-midnight) Somewhere between the thick soups and greasy plates, this classic pub fare gets motors started. Perhaps for the lack of pretension, or the very friendly service, it's among the most popular haunts in town, packing in locals and visitors alike. Happy hour is daily from 4pm to 6pm.

Bon Ton Restaurant FRENCH, ITALIAN $$$
(☎970-325-4951; www.stelmohotel.com; 426 Main St; mains $15-38; ⊙5:30-11pm Thu-Mon; ☑) Bon Ton has been serving supper for a century in a beautiful room under the historic St Elmo Hotel. The French-Italian menu includes specialties like roast duck in cherry peppercorn sauce and tortellini with bacon and shallots. The wine list is extensive and the champagne brunch comes recommended.

Silver Eagle Saloon SALOON
(617 Main St; ⊙2pm-2am) With an 1886 barback and Wild West attitude to spare, this smoky saloon is a favorite of locals. Unless you're smoking (it's grandfathered in to tobacco sale sites), the only thing to do is drink. No food is served but bartenders display an expert pour. It boasts the only pool table in town, though it will take gumption to play.

Ouray Brewery BREWERY
(☎970-325-7388; www.ouraybrewery.com; 607 Main St; ⊙11am-9pm) With a rooftop deck to spy on Main Street or chairlift bar stools, this pub is something of a flytrap for visitors; in fact, there is a notable lack of locals around. The brewery offers a brew sample tray and growlers to go.

Information

Ouray Visitors Center (☎800-228-1876, 970-325-4746; www.ouraycolorado.com; 1230 Main St; ⊙10am-5pm Mon-Sat, 10am-3pm Sun; 📶👪) Staffed by volunteers, this useful visitor center has brochures and the usual information. It's near the Ouray hot-springs pool.

Post Office (☎970-325-4302; 620 Main St; ⊙9am-4:30pm Mon-Sat)

Getting There & Away

Ouray is on Hwy 550, 70 miles north of Durango, 24 miles north of Silverton and 37 miles south of Montrose. There are no bus services in the area and private motorcar is the only way to get to and around the town.

Silverton

POP 630 / ELEV 9318FT

Ringed by snowy peaks and steeped in the sooty tales of a tawdry mining town, Silverton would seem more at home in Alaska than the Lower 48. But here it is. Whether you're into snowmobiling, biking, fly-fishing, beer on tap or just basking in some very high altitude sunshine, Silverton delivers.

It's a two-street town, but only one is paved. Greene St is where you'll find most businesses (think homemade jerky, fudge and feather art). Still unpaved, notorious Blair St runs parallel to Greene and is a blast from the past. During the silver rush, Blair St was home to thriving brothels and boozing establishments.

A tourist town by day in summer, Silverton reverts to local turf once the final Durango-bound steam train departs. Visit in winter for a real treat. Snowmobiles become the main means of transportation, and town becomes a playground for intrepid travelers, most of them serious powder hounds.

One of Silverton's highlights is just getting here from Ouray on the Million Dollar Hwy – an awe-inspiring stretch of road that's one of Colorado's best road trips.

Sights & Activities

★**Silverton Railroad Depot** RAILWAY
(☎970-387-5416, toll-free 877-872-4607; www.durangotrain.com; 12th St; deluxe/adult/child return from $189/85/51; ⊙departures 1:45pm, 2:30pm & 3pm; 👪) You can buy one-way and return tickets for the brilliant Durango & Silverton Narrow Gauge Railroad at the Silverton terminus. The Silverton Freight Yard Museum is located at the Silverton depot. The train ticket provides admission two days prior to, and two days following, your ride on the train.

The train service offers combination train-bus return trips (the bus route is much quicker). Tickets are also available on the website. Hikers use the train to access the Durango and Weminuche Wilderness trailheads.

Mining Heritage Center MUSEUM
(☎970-387-5838; www.silvertonhistoricalsociety.org; 1559 Greene St; adult/child $7/3; ⊙9am-5pm Jun-Oct; P👪) This specialist museum is

dedicated to Silverton's mining history. Old mining equipment is displayed and there's a re-created machine shop and blacksmith shop.

Silverton Museum MUSEUM
(970-387-5838; www.silvertonhistoricsociety.org; 1557 Greene St; adult/child $5/free; 10am-4pm Jun-Oct;) Installed in the original 1902 San Juan County Jail, the Silverton Museum has an interesting collection of local artifacts and ephemera.

Mayflower Gold Mill HISTORIC BUILDING
(970-387-0294; www.silvertonhistoricsociety.org; County Rd 2; adult/child $8/free; 10am-4pm May 25-Sep 30;) This mill was once a major employer in Silverton. The Aerial Tram House is a highlight of the self-guided tour.

★ **Silverton Mountain Ski Area** SKIING
(970-387-5706; www.silvertonmountain.com; State Hwy 110; daily lift ticket $49, all-day guide & lift ticket $99) Not for newbies, this is one of the most innovative ski mountains in the US – a single lift takes advanced and expert backcountry skiers up to the summit of an area of ungroomed ski runs. Numbers are limited and the mountain designates unguided and the more exclusive guided days.

The lift rises from the 10,400ft base to 12,300ft. Imagine heli-skiing sans helicopter. You really need to know your stuff – the easiest terrain here is comparable to skiing double blacks at other resorts.

Kendall Mountain Recreation Area SKIING
(970-387-5522; www.skikendall.com; Kendall Pl; daily lift tickets adult/child $20/15; 11am-4pm Fri & Sat Dec-Feb;) Managed by the town, with just one double 1050ft chairlift and four runs, all of them suitable for beginners. People goof around on sleds and tubes. It's cheap and family-friendly. Skis, tubes, sleds and snowboards can be rented from the Kendall Mountain Community Center.

Tours

Old Hunded Gold Mine Tour TOURS
(970-387-5444, 800-872-3009; www.minetour.com; County Rd 4A; adult/child $18/9; hourly 10am-4pm May 15-Oct 15;) Fifteen minutes east of town, the hour-long Old Hundred Mine Gold Tour is hugely popular. A tram travels a third of a mile into a tunnel where passengers alight and are guided around the old gold-mine workings. There are demonstrations of drilling equipment and 1930s-era mining machinery.

Panning for gold is included in the tour price – an area is regularly 'salted' with gold dust. Significantly, the tour is totally wheelchair accessible.

San Juan Backcountry TOURS
(970-387-5565, 800-494-8687; www.sanjuanbackcountry.com; 1119 Greene St; 2hr tour adult/child $60/40; May-Oct;) Offering both 4WD tours and rentals, the folks at San Juan Backcountry can get you out and into the brilliant San Juan Mountain wilderness areas around Silverton. The tours take visitors around in modified open-top Chevy Suburbans.

Sleeping

Silverton Hostel HOSTEL $
(970-387-0115; www.silvertoninnandhostel.com; 1025 Blair St; dm $20) In the summer this creaky home gets overrun with college groups on geology field trips, but if you are on a shoestring it's probably your best bet. It has a fire pit, a grill and communal showers that definitely merit wearing flip-flops.

Silver Summit RV Park CAMPGROUND $
(970-387-0240, 800-352-1637; www.silversummitrvpark.com; 640 Mineral St; RV sites $36 plus electricity $4; May 15-Oct 15;) Like so much else in Silverton, Silver Summit is a mixed business running rental Jeeps out of the RV park headquarters (two-/four-door Jeep Wranglers $155/185). The park has good facilities, including a laundry, hot tub, fire pit and free wi-fi.

Inn of the Rockies at the Historic Alma House B&B $$
(970-387-5336, 800-267-5336; www.innoftherockies.com; 220 E 10th St; r incl breakfast $109-173;) Opened by a local named Alma in 1898, this inn has nine unique rooms furnished with Victorian antiques. The hospitality is first-rate and its New Orleans–inspired breakfasts, served in a chandelier-lit dining room, merit special mention. Cheaper rates are available without breakfast. There's also a garden hot tub for soaking after a long day.

Bent Elbow HOTEL $$
(970-387-5775, toll-free 877-387-5775; www.thebent.com; 1114 Blair St; d $112-122;) Located on notorious Blair St, these creaky rooms once served as a bordello. For what you get these days, prices are a little steep, but the decoration is pleasingly quaint and Western. The restaurant (mains $10 to $22)

is a cheerful dining room with a gorgeous old wood shotgun bar that serves Western American fare.

Red Mountain Motel & RV Park MOTEL, CAMPGROUND $$
(☎970-382-5512, toll-free 800-970-5512; www.redmtmotelrvpk.com; 664 Greene St; motel r from $110, cabins from $120, tent/RV sites $22/38; P) The tiny log cabins stay warm and make good use of their limited space with a double bed, a bunk, a tiny TV and a fully outfitted kitchenette. The managers are friendly and keen to make sure guests and customers have a good time. It's a pet-friendly place that stays open year-round.

This operation covers everything from tent camping and RV facilities, cabins and motel rooms to Jeep and ATV hire and guided tours, snowmobiling, fishing and hunting. The river, with good fishing, is just a few minutes' walk away.

Wyman Hotel & Inn B&B $$$
(☎970-387-5372; www.thewyman.com; 1371 Greene St; d incl breakfast $140-240; closed Nov;) A handsome sandstone on the National Register of Historic Places, this 1902 building brims with personality. Local memorabilia lines long halls with room after room of canopy beds, Victorian-era wallpaper and chandelier lamps. Every room is distinct, none more so than the caboose that you can rent out back. Includes a full breakfast plus afternoon wine and cheese tasting.

Eating & Drinking

Stellar ITALIAN $$
(☎970-387-9940; 1260 Blair St; mains $8-20; 4-9:30pm;) This friendly place is a good choice for lunch or dinner. Locals come here for the stellar pizzas, friendly service and easy atmosphere. There's a full bar with beers on tap, and the lasagna and freshly made salads are always good.

Handlebars AMERICAN $$
(☎970-387-5395; www.handlebarssilverton.com; 117 13th St; mains $10-22; lunch & dinner May-Oct;) Steeped in Wild West kitsch, this place serves worthy baby-back ribs basted in a secret BBQ sauce, and other Western fare. The decor, a mishmash of old mining artifacts, mounted animal heads and cowboy memorabilia, gives this place a ramshackle museum-meets-garage-sale feel. After dinner, kick it up on the dance floor to the sounds of live rock and country music.

★Montanya Distillers BAR
(www.montanyadistillers.com; 1309 Greene St; mains $6-13; noon-10pm) Under new management, this regional favorite still delivers, now in a spacious minimalist bar on Greene St. On a summer day, score a seat on the rooftop deck. Bartenders here can talk you into anything, crafting exotic cocktails with homemade syrups and their very own award-winning rum. It's worth it just for the fun atmosphere. Note: low season hours change.

Information

Silverton Chamber of Commerce & Visitor Center (☎970-387-5654, toll-free 800-752-4494; www.silvertoncolorado.com; 414 Greene St; 9am-5pm;) Staffed by friendly volunteers, this center provides information about the town and surrounds. You can buy tickets for the Durango & Silverton Narrow Gauge Railroad here. Radio KSJC 92.5 FM, a nonprofit community radio station, broadcasts out of an adjoining room in the same building – think about that when you're stomping down the hallway to the public restrooms.

Getting There & Away

Silverton is on Hwy 550 midway between Montrose, about 60 miles to the north, and Durango, some 48 miles to the south. Other than private car, the only way to get to and from Silverton is by using the Durango & Silverton Narrow Gauge Railroad, or the private buses that run its return journeys.

Durango

POP 17,100 / ELEV 6580FT

An archetypal old Colorado mining town, Durango is a regional darling that's nothing short of delightful. Its graceful hotels, Victorian-era saloons and tree-lined streets of sleepy bungalows invite you to pedal around soaking up all the good vibes. There is plenty to do outdoors. Style-wise, Durango is torn between its ragtime past and a cool, cutting-edge future where townie bikes, caffeine and farmers markets rule.

The town's historic central precinct is home to boutiques, bars, restaurants and theater halls. Foodies will revel in the innovative organic and locavore fare that is making it one of the best places to eat in the state.

But there's also interesting galleries and live music that, combined with a relaxed and congenial local populace, make it a great place to visit. Durango is also an ideal base for exploring the enigmatic ruins at Mesa Verde National Park, 35 miles to the west.

Sights & Activities

All sorts of outdoor activities can be arranged in this hub for travel and soft adventure. Listen for the train drivers riding the steam whistles of the locomotives traveling the famous 1882 Durango & Silverton Narrow Gauge Railroad, issuing plumes of steam as they pull into the town's historic railyards.

★Durango & Silverton Narrow Gauge Railroad RAILWAY

(☎970-247-2733, 877-872-4607; www.durangotrain.com; 479 Main Ave; adult/child return from $85/51; ⏰departures at 8am, 8:45am & 9:30am; 👪) Riding the Durango & Silverton Narrow Gauge Railroad is a Durango must. These vintage steam locomotives have been making the scenic 45-mile trip north to Silverton (3½ hours each way) for more than 125 years. The dazzling journey allows two hours for exploring Silverton. This trip operates only from May through October. Check online for different winter options.

Durango Mountain Resort SNOW SPORTS

(☎970-247-9000; www.durangomountainresort.com; 1 Skier Pl; lift tickets adult/child from $75/45; ⏰mid-Nov–Mar; 👪) Durango Mountain Resort, 25 miles north on US 550, is Durango's winter highlight. The resort, also known as Purgatory, offers 1200 skiable acres of varying difficulty and boasts 260in of snow per year. Two terrain parks offer plenty of opportunities for snowboarders to catch big air.

Check local grocery stores and newspapers for promotions and two-for-one lift tickets and other promotional ski season specials before purchasing directly from the ticket window.

Trimble Spa & Natural Hot Springs SPRING, MASSAGE

(☎970-247-0111, toll-free 877-811-7111; www.trimblehotsprings.com; 6475 County Rd 203; day pass adult/child $18/912; ⏰9am-9pm Sun-Thu, 9am-10pm Fri & Sat; 👪) If you need a pampering massage or just a soak in some natural hot springs after hitting the ski runs or mountain bike trails, this is the place. Qualified massage therapists can work out those knotted muscles and tired limbs with treatment ranging from acupressure to trigger-point myotherapy. Five miles north of Durango.

Phone or check the website for last-minute specials, which sometimes include two-for-one deals and other discounts.

Mild to Wild Rafting RAFTING

(☎970-247-4789, 800-567-6745; www.mild2wildrafting.com; 50 Animas View Dr; trips from $38; 👪) In spring and summer white-water rafting is one of the most popular sports in Durango. Mild to Wild Rafting is one of numerous companies around town offering rafting trips on the Animas River. Beginners should check out the one-hour introduction to rafting, while the more adventurous (and experienced) can run the upper Animas, which boasts class III to V rapids.

Durango Rivertrippers RAFTING

(☎970-259-0289, 800-292-2885; www.durangorivertrippers.com; 720 Main Ave; adult/child 2hr trip $25/17, half-day $29/20; 👪) This family-operated outfit is the oldest accredited rafting operator in Durango and highly reputed. It offers various river-rafting trips on the Delores and Animas Rivers, from two-hour family runs to six-day wilderness adventures.

Duranglers FISHING

(☎970-385-4081, 800-347-4346; www.duranglers.com; 923 Main Ave; day trip 1/2-person $325/350) It won't put the trout on your hook, but Duranglers will do everything to bring you to that gilded moment; serving beginners to experts.

Big Corral Riding Stable HORSEBACK RIDING

(☎970-884-9235; www.vallecitolakeoutfitter.com; 17716 County Rd 501, Bayfield) Highly recommended by locals, this outfitter does day rides and overnight horseback camping for the whole family in the gorgeous Weminuche Wilderness. If you're short on time, try the two-hour breakfast ride (including sausage, pancakes and cowboy coffee) with views of Vallecito Lake. Located 25 miles northeast of Durango.

Festivals & Events

San Juan Brewfest BEER

(www.cookmanfood.com/brewfest; Main Ave, btwn 12th & 13th Sts; admission $25; ⏰early Sep; 👪) Showcasing 30-odd specialist brewers from Durango, around Colorado and interstate, this annual festival is a highlight. Official judging takes place late in the afternoon but

Durango

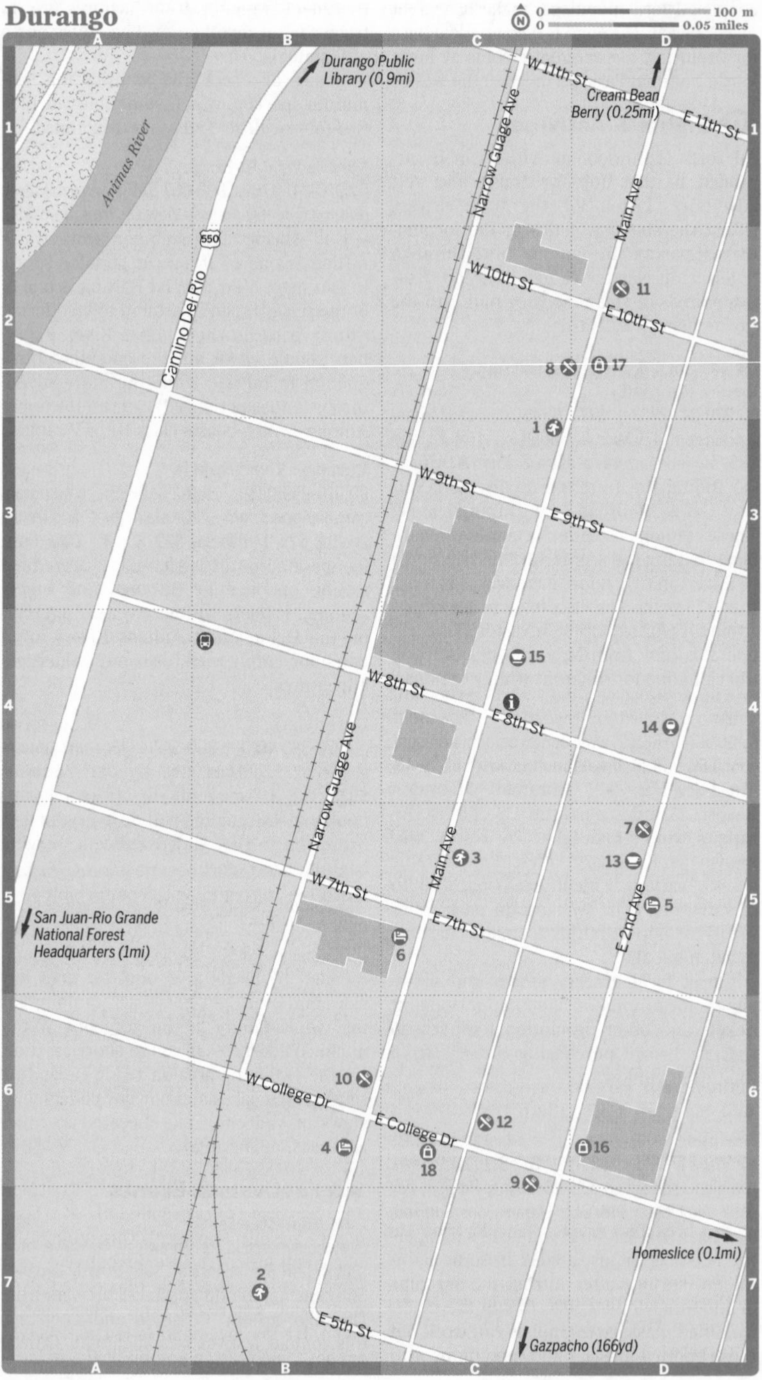

0 100 m
0 0.05 miles

A B C D
1 2 3 4 5 6 7

Durango Public Library (0.9mi)
Cream Bean Berry (0.25mi)
W 11th St
E 11th St
Animas River
550
Camino Del Rio
Narrow Guage Ave
Main Ave
W 10th St
E 10th St
11
8
17
1
W 9th St
E 9th St
15
W 8th St
E 8th St
14
Narrow Guage Ave
Main Ave
7
13
3
5
E 2nd Ave
W 7th St
E 7th St
6
San Juan-Rio Grande National Forest Headquarters (1mi)
10
W College Dr
E College Dr
12
4
18
16
9
Homeslice (0.1mi)
2
E 5th St
Gazpacho (166yd)

Durango

Activities, Courses & Tours
1 Duranglers ... C3
2 Durango & Silverton Narrow Gauge Railroad ... B7
3 Durango Rivertrippers ... C5

Sleeping
4 General Palmer Hotel ... B6
5 Rochester House ... D5
6 Strater Hotel ... C5

Eating
7 Cyprus Cafe ... D5
8 Durango Diner ... C2
9 East by Southwest ... C6
10 Jean Pierre Bakery ... B6
11 Olde Tymers Café ... D2
12 Ore House ... C6

Drinking & Nightlife
Diamond Belle Saloon ... (see 6)
13 Eno ... D5
14 Steamworks Brewing ... D4
15 White Dragon Tea Room ... C4

Entertainment
Henry Strater Theatre ... (see 6)

Shopping
16 2nd Avenue Sports ... D6
17 Maria's Bookshop ... D2
18 Pedal the Peaks ... C6

all attendees (must be aged 21 and over to taste) get to vote for the San Juan Brewfest's People's Choice award. There are bands and food and a carnival atmosphere.

Sleeping

Adobe Inn MOTEL $

(970-247-2743; www.durangohotels.com; 2178 Main Ave; d $84;) Locally voted the best lodging value, this friendly motel gets the job done with clean, decent rooms and friendly service. You might even be able to talk staff into giving their best rate if you arrive late at night. Check out the Durango tip sheet.

Siesta Motel MOTEL $

(970-247-0741; www.durangosiestamotel.com; 3475 N Main Ave; d $72; P) This family-owned motel is one of the town's cheaper options, sparkling clean and spacious but admittedly dated. If you're self-catering, there's a little courtyard with a BBQ grill.

★ **Rochester House** HOTEL $$

(970-385-1920, 800-664-1920; www.rochesterhotel.com; 721 E 2nd Ave; d $169-229;) Influenced by old Westerns (movie posters and marquee lights adorn the hallways), the Rochester is a little bit of old Hollywood in the new West. Rooms are spacious, with high ceilings. Two formal sitting rooms, where you're served cookies, and a breakfast room in an old train car are other perks at this pet-friendly establishment.

Check out the free summer concert series on Wednesdays at 4:30pm, in the courtyard.

General Palmer Hotel HOTEL $$

(970-247-4747, 800-523-3358; www.generalpalmer.com; 567 Main Ave; d incl breakfast $155-200;) With turn-of-the century elegance, this 1898 Victorian has a damsel's taste, with pewter four-post beds, floral prints, and teddies on every bed. Rooms are small but elegant, and if you tire of TV, there's a collection of board games at the front desk. Check out the cozy library and the relaxing solarium.

Strater Hotel HOTEL $$$

(970-247-4431; www.strater.com; 699 Main Ave; d $197-257;) The past lives large in this historical Durango hotel with walnut antiques, hand-stenciled wallpapers and relics ranging from a Stradivarius violin to a gold-plated Winchester. Rooms lean toward the romantic, with comfortable beds amid antiques, crystal and lace. The boastworthy staff goes out of its way to assist with inquiries. The hot tub is a romantic plus (reserved by the hour), as is the summertime melodrama (theater) the hotel runs. In winter, rates drop by more than 50%, making it a virtual steal. Look online.

Eating

★ **Cream Bean Berry** ICE CREAM $

(http://creambeanberry.com; 1309 E 3rd Ave, Smiley Bldg; ice cream $4; 9am-5.30pm Mon-Thu, 9am-8pm Fri; from 1pm Sat) Handmade, organic and local, this stuff tastes like happiness. It's also inventive – with flavors, some seasonal, like salted caramel, beet poppyseed and peach cardamom. It's the love child of journalists who grabbed inspiration sampling the *helados* of Mexico. If you are on the Animas River path, look for the bicycle freezer cart, from noon to 5.30pm.

Homeslice PIZZERIA $
(☎970-259-5551; http://homeslicedelivers.com; 441 E College Ave; slice $4; ⏲11am-10pm) Locals pile into this no-frills pizza place for thick pies with bubbly crust and sriracha sauce on the side. It has patio seating, gluten-free crust options and salads too.

Doughworks BREAKFAST $
(☎970-247-1610; 2653 Main Ave; mains $5-10; ⏲6am-3pm) For mammoth breakfasts or diner-style lunch, this busy hub by the high school has your back. A brisk takeout business offers bagels and doughnuts, with about a dozen self-serve coffee stations to keep you caffeinated. Or grab a booth and peruse the large menu. For some kick, add the homemade green chili to a burrito or egg sandwich.

Durango Diner DINER $$
(☎970-247-9889; www.durangodiner.com; 957 Main Ave; mains $7-18; ⏲6am-2pm Mon-Sat, 6am-1pm Sun;) To watch Gary work the grill in this lovable greasy spoon is to be in the presence of greatness. Backed by a staff of button-cute waitresses, Gary's fluid, graceful wielding of a Samurai spatula turns out downright monstrous plates of eggs, smothered potatoes and plate-sized French toast. The best diner in the state? No doubt.

Jean Pierre Bakery FRENCH, BAKERY $$
(☎970-247-7700; www.jeanpierrebakery.com; 601 Main Ave; mains $9-22; ⏲8am-9pm;) A charming patisserie serving mouthwatering delicacies made from scratch. Breakfasts are all-out while dinner is a much more formal affair. Prices are dear, but the soup-and-sandwich lunch special with a sumptuous French pastry (we recommend the sticky pecan roll) is a deal.

Gazpacho MEXICAN $$
(☎970-259-9494; 431 E 2nd Ave; mains $10-28; ⏲11:30am-10pm;) A crowd pleaser, this tiled quasi–New Mexican restaurant dishes up local beans, savory *carne adovada* (red chili pork) and green chili cheeseburgers. Families love it and the friendly bar is a good spot to grab a margarita and fresh, hot *sopaipillas* (fried pastries). Also has good gluten-free and vegetarian options, like the vegan burger piled high with smoked chilies.

Olde Tymers Café BURGERS $
(☎970-259-2990; www.otcdgo.com; 1000 Main Ave; mains $5-10; ⏲11am-10pm;) Voted Durango's best burger by the local paper, the Olde Tymers is popular with the college crowd, especially on Monday's $5.50-burger nights. Well-priced American classics are served at cozy booths under pressed-tin ceilings in a big open dining room or on the patio outside. Ask about the cheap daily specials.

East by Southwest FUSION, SUSHI $$$
(☎970-247-5533; http://eastbysouthwest.com; 160 E College Dr; sushi $4-13, mains $12-24; ⏲11:30am-3pm & 5-10pm Mon-Sat, 5-10pm Sun;) Low-lit but vibrant, it's packed with locals on date night. Skip the standards for goose-bump-good sashimi with jalapeño or rolls with mango and wasabi honey. Fish is fresh and endangered species are off the menu. Fusion plates include Thai, Vietnamese and Indonesian, well matched with creative martinis or sake cocktails. The best deals are the happy-hour food specials (5pm to 6:30pm).

Ore House STEAKHOUSE $$$
(☎970-247-5707; www.orehouserestaurant.com; 147 E College Dr; mains $18-68; ⏲5-10pm;) The

PEDALING DURANGO

That post-bike beer is a Colorado tradition, so it's little surprise that a town supporting such a lively microbrew community is also paradise to mountain bikers.

Durango is home to some of the world's best cyclists, who regularly ride the hundreds of local trails ranging from steep singletrack to scenic road rides.

Start easy with the **Old Railroad Grade Trail**, a 12.2-mile loop that uses both US Hwy 160 and a dirt road following the old rail tracks. From Durango, take Hwy 160 west through the town of Hesperus. Turn right into the Cherry Creek Picnic Area, where the trail starts.

For something a bit more technical, try **Dry Fork Loop**, accessible from Lightner Creek just west of town. It has some great drops, blind corners and copious vegetation.

Sports shops on Main Ave rent mountain bikes.

WORTH A TRIP

JAMES RANCH

A must for those road-tripping the San Juan Skyway, the family-run **James Ranch** (970-385-9143; http://jamesranch.net; 33800 US 550; 11am-7pm Mon-Sat), 10 miles north of Durango, features a market and outstanding farmstand grill featuring the farm's own organic grass-fed beef and fresh produce. Steak sandwiches and fresh cheese melts with caramelized onions rock. Kids dig the goats.

Burger and band nights are held every Thursday from July to October (adult/child $20/10). There's also yoga hosted on the terraces in summer. A two-hour farm tour ($18) is held on Mondays and Fridays at 9:30am and Tuesdays at 4pm.

best steakhouse in town, with food served in casual and rustic environs. Order a hand-cut aged steak, or try the steak, crab leg and lobster combo known as the Ore House Grubsteak, easily serving two people. The meat is natural and antibiotic free and organic vegetables are the norm. There's also a large wine cellar.

Cyprus Cafe MEDITERRANEAN $$$
(970-385-6884; www.cypruscafe.com; 725 E 2nd Ave; mains $13-29; 11:30am-2:30pm & 5-9pm, closed Sun;) Nothing says summer like live jazz on the patio at this little Mediterranean cafe, a favorite of the foodie press. With a farm-to-table philosophy, it offers locally raised vegetables, wild seafood and natural meats. Favorites include warm duck salad with almonds and oranges and Colorado trout with quinoa pilaf.

Drinking & Nightlife

★Ska Brewing Company BREWERY
(970-247-5792; www.skabrewing.com; 225 Girard St; mains $7-13; 11am-3am Mon-Wed, 11am-3pm & 5-8pm Thu, 11am-8pm Fri) Big on flavor and variety, these are the best beers in town. Although the small, friendly tasting-room bar was once mainly a production facility, over the years it's steadily climbed in the popularity charts. Today it is usually jam-packed with friends meeting for an after-work beer.

Despite the hype, the place remains surprisingly laid-back and relaxed. Ska does weekly BBQs with live music and free food; call for dates – they are never fixed.

Eno CAFE, WINE BAR
(970-385-0105; 723 E 2nd Ave; tapas $3-5; 8am-10pm Sun-Thu, 8am-11pm Fri & Sat) Serving excellent pour-over coffee by day and dangerous cocktails at night, this tiny house is an intimate spot to socialize. The award-winning 'alpenglow' pairs local rum with muddled cucumber, mint and hibiscus. Highlights include deviled eggs and the Colorado cheese plate, though big appetites should go elsewhere. The later happy hour (8pm to 10pm) makes it a good after-dinner spot.

White Dragon Tea Room TEAHOUSE
(970-385-7300; http://teadurango.com; 820 Main Ave; 10am-6pm Mon-Sat, noon-5pm Sun) A wonderful find, this modern teahouse run by an ex-monk serves organic Chinese and Japanese teas bought direct from farmers. Chocolate-lovers shouldn't miss the $5 sipping cups: on offer is Thomas Jefferson's recipe for hot chocolate and a delicious ancho chili cocoa aptly nicknamed 'high as a kite.'

Steamworks Brewing BREWERY
(970-259-9200; www.steamworksbrewing.com; 801 E 2nd Ave; mains $10-15; 11am-midnight Mon-Thu, 11am-2am Fri-Sun) Industrial meets ski lodge at this popular microbrewery, with high sloping rafters and metal pipes. It has a large bar area, as well as a separate dining room with a Cajun-influenced menu. At night there are DJs and live music.

Durango Brewing Co BREWERY
(970-247-3396; www.durangobrewing.com; 3000 Main Ave; tap room 9am-5pm) While the ambience is nothing special, serious beer fans can appreciate that this place concentrates on the brews. There are taproom tastings and it's open seven days a week.

Diamond Belle Saloon BAR
(970-376-7150; www.strater.com; 699 Main Ave; 11am-late) In a rowdy corner of the historic Strater Hotel, this elegant old-time bar has waitresses flashing Victorian-era fishnets and live ragtime that packs in out-of-town visitors with standing room only at happy hour (4pm to 6pm). The food isn't an attraction. Also in the Strater, The Office Spiritorium serves cocktails in an upscale and much more low-key atmosphere.

Henry Strater Theatre LIVE MUSIC
(970-375-7160; www.henrystratertheatre.com; 699 Main Ave;) Internationally renowned, producing old-world music-hall shows, live bands, comedy, community theater and more for nearly 50 years.

Shopping

Pedal the Peaks SPORTS
(970-259-6880; www.pedalthepeaks.biz; 598b Main Ave; full-suspension rentals $45; 9am-5pm Mon-Sat, 10am-5pm Sun;) This specialist bike store offers the works from mountain- and road-bike sales and rentals to custom-worked cycles, trail maps and accessories. The staff are all hardcore riders, and their friendly advice and local knowledge are second to none.

2nd Avenue Sports SPORTING GOODS
(970-247-4511; www.2ndavesports.com; 600 E 2nd Ave; 9am-6pm Mon-Sat, 9am-5pm Sun) Skiing and extensive cycling and mountain-biking gear for sale and rental.

Maria's Bookshop BOOKS
(970-247-1438; www.mariasbookshop.com; 960 Main Ave; 9am-9pm) Maria's is a good general bookstore – independently owned and well stocked. It does e-reader orders too.

Information

Durango Public Library (970-375-3380; www.durangopubliclibrary.org; 1900 E 3rd Ave; 9am-8pm Mon-Wed, 10am-5:30pm Thu, 9am-5:30pm Fri & Sat) Free internet access and great resource for regional maps and outdoor information.

Durango Welcome Center (970-247-3500, 800-525-8855; www.durango.org; 802 Main Ave; 9am-7pm Sun-Thu, 9am-9pm Fri & Sat;) A great resource, with live help plus iPad guides, in addition to free sunscreen dispensed in big bottles. There is a second visitor center south of town, at the Santa Rita exit from US 550.

Mercy Regional Medical Center (970-247-4311; www.mercydurango.org; 1010 Three Springs Ave) Outpatient and 24-hour emergency care.

San Juan-Rio Grande National Forest Headquarters (970-247-4874; www.fs.fed.us/r2/sanjuan; 15 Burnett Ct; 9am-5pm Mon-Sat) Offers camping and hiking information and maps. It's about a half-mile west on US Hwy 160.

Getting There & Away

Durango lies at the junction of US Hwys 160 and 550, 42 miles east of Cortez, 49 miles west of Pagosa Springs and 190 miles north of Albuquerque in New Mexico.

Durango-La Plata County Airport (970-247-8143; www.flydurango.com; 1000 Airport Rd) This airport is 18 miles southwest of Durango via US Hwy 160 and Hwy 172. Both United and Frontier Airlines have direct flights to Denver; US Airways flies to Phoenix.

Durango Transit (970-259-5438; www.getarounddurango.com; 250 W 8th St) Greyhound buses run daily from here north to Grand Junction and south to Albuquerque, NM.

Getting Around

Check the website www.getarounddurango.com for local travel information. All Durango buses are fitted with bicycle racks. A free bright-red T shuttle bus travels Main St.

Chimney Rock Archaeological Area

Like the architects of the elaborate structures in Chaco Canyon – with which this community was connected – the people of the **Chimney Rock Archaeological Area** (off-season 970-264-2287, visitor cabin 970-883-5359; www.chimneyrockco.org; Hwy 151; guided tours adult/child $12/5; 9am-4:30pm mid-May–late Sep, additional evening hr for special events;) were dedicated astronomers and this was a place of spiritual significance. Remains of 100 permanent structures are at the base of two large red-rock buttes. Walking tours are at 9:30am, 10:30am, 1pm and 2:30pm.

Today, the rock monuments remain, though the thriving religious and commercial center has been reduced to sketches in stone – hearths and shafts for ventilation, holes for roof beams and storage areas. The largest pair of buildings here, the Great Kiva and Great House, are both impressive examples of Chacoan architecture. Designated an Archaeological Area and National Historic Site in 1970, the entire area covers more than 4000 acres of the **San Juan National Forest** land. If the local politicos get their way, Chimney Rock Archaeological Area will soon be designated a National Monument.

Pagosa Springs

POP 1717 / ELEV 7126FT

Pagosa Springs may seem to be a large slice of humble pie, but it has the bragging rights to the biggest snowfall in Colorado – at Wolf Creek Ski Area – nearby. Pagosa, a Ute term for 'boiling water,' refers to the other local draw: hot springs. Natural thermals provide heat for some of the town's 1900 residents.

The town sits east of Durango, on US 160 at the junction with US 84 south to New Mexico. The historic downtown, with most of the visitor services, is near the intersection of Hot Springs Blvd and US 160. Condos and vacation rentals flank a winding series of roads 2 miles to the west, over a small rise.

Sights & Activities

★Fred Harman Art Museum & the Red Ryder Roundup MUSEUM
(☎970-731-5785; www.harmanartmuseum.com; 85 Harman Park Dr; adult/child $3/50¢; ⏲10:30am-5pm Mon-Sat; P ♿) The Red Ryder's image might be lost on today's whippersnappers, but Fred Harman's comic book hero was born in Pagosa Springs, and today Harman's home is a small museum. It's a kitschy and off-beat roadside attraction, but Harman himself is often on hand to show you around his studio.

Pagosa Springs' biggest annual event is the Red Ryder Roundup, a carnival with a rodeo and art show that ends in fireworks. It's held near 4th of July.

Springs Resort & Spa SPA
(☎970-264-4168; www.pagosahotsprings.com; 165 Hot Springs Blvd; adult/child from $25/14; ⏲7am-11pm; ♿ 🐾) These glorious pools along the San Juan River have healing, mineral-rich waters from the Great Pagosa Aquifer, the largest and deepest hot mineral spring in the world. Man-made pools look fairly natural, and the views are lovely. Temperatures vary from 83°F to 111°F (28°C to 44°C).

The terraced pink adobe hotel (rooms from $189) features a spa, offers ski packages and welcomes pets. The cheapest rooms are nothing special, while sprawling deluxe rooms feature thicker mattresses, higher thread-count sheets and kitchenette.

Pagosa Outside RAFTING
(☎970-264-4202; www.pagosaoutside.com; 350 Pagosa St; full-day Upper Piedra trips $150; ⏲10am-6pm, reduced hr winter; ♿) Check out this outfitter's springtime white-water trips (class III) on the San Juan and Piedra Rivers. The most exciting travels Mesa Canyon, ideal to sight eagles and other wildlife. Rivers mellow in summer and the focus turns to river tubing ($15 for two hours) and mountain-biking trips, including a thrilling singletrack route at Turkey Creek, and rentals ($35 per day).

Sleeping

Since the hot springs are a year-round draw, hotels in the area hold their rates fairly steady. A number of motels and new hotels sprawl out from the town center on US 160. Usually, the equation is fairly straightforward: the further away from the hot springs, the better the deal.

Pagosa Huts CABINS $
(☎970-264-1543, 970-264-2268; www.pagosahuts.com; San Juan National Forest; cabins $60) These remote, basic huts are perfect for people trying to get out into the national forest, and they are available to both hikers and recreational motorists. Getting here is a little rough – the roads can be a mess in the spring – but they offer excellent solitude. Inquire about availability and exact location through the Forest Service.

Alpine Inn Motel MOTEL $
(☎970-731-4005; www.alpineinnofpagosasprings.com; 8 Solomon Dr; d incl breakfast $69; P ❄ @ 📶) A converted chain motel, this roadside option is excellent value. The rooms, each with dark carpet and balconies, are a standard size, but the owners are great guides to the local area and there's a deluxe continental breakfast.

★Fireside Inn Cabins CABINS $$
(☎888-264-9204; www.firesidecabins.com; 1600 E Hwy 160; cabins from $105, 2-bedroom cabins from $198; P ⊖ ❄ 📶) Hands down our favorite place in town – each log cabin comes with a Weber grill and planters of wildflowers. Pine interiors have immaculate kitchenettes, quilts and flatscreen TVs. The San Juan River flows through the property. Equestrians can use the corral, and the games available at the central office are great for families.

Eating & Drinking

Pagosa Brewing Company PUB FOOD $
(☎970-731-2739; www.pagosabrewing.com; 118 N Pagosa Blvd; mains $5-12; ⏲11am-10pm Mon-Sat; ♿) Brewmaster Tony Simmons is a professional beer judge, and the Poor Richard's Ale

OFF THE BEATEN TRACK

THE SECRET POWDER STASH

Boasting Colorado's highest annual snowfall, little old **Wolf Creek Ski Area** (☎970-264-5639; www.wolfcreekski.com; lift ticket adult/child $56/30; ⊙Nov–mid-Apr; 👪) offers a white-carpet ride without comparison. Steep and deep, it's awesome for advanced skiers and boarders, with waist-high powder after a big storm blows through.

Located 25 miles north of Pagosa Springs on US 160, this family-owned ski area gets over 465in of light and dry powder per year – that's 150in more than Vail. Eight lifts service 70 trails, from wide-open bowls to steep tree glades. The on-site ski school has lessons for beginners and children.

For cross-country skiing, many backcountry and groomed trails that lead into quiet, pristine forest are available. It's some of the most remote Nordic skiing in the state. Contact the USFS Pagosa Ranger Station for details.

Long considered a Colorado secret, its distance from major airports and big urban areas has reinforced its happy isolation. There are no lodgings onsite, so it's not a destination ski area. Your best bet is to stay in Pagosa Springs, on the west side of the pass, or South Fork, on the east.

is brewed according to historical standards – the corn and molasses mix is inspired by the tipple of Ben Franklin. After a few, move on to a menu of made-from-scratch pub food, at this, Pagosa's fun dinner spot.

JJ's Riverwalk Restaurant Pub MODERN AMERICAN **$$$**
(☎970-264-9100; 356 E Hwy 160; mains $15-40) Overlooking the San Juan River, JJ's has a great vibe, tasty food, a decent wine list and pleasant service. It can be very spendy, but the menu includes early-bird cheap meals and a nightly happy hour. In summer sit outside on the patio overlooking the river and watch the kayakers float by.

Information

Pagosa Springs Area Chamber of Commerce (☎970-264-2360; www.visitpagosasprings.com; 402 San Juan St; ⊙9am-5pm Mon-Fri) A large visitor center across the bridge from US Hwy 160.

USFS Pagosa Ranger Station (☎970-264-2268; 180 Pagosa St; ⊙8am-4:30pm Mon-Fri)

South Fork

POP 377 / ELEV 8300FT

The appeal of visiting South Fork is hardly evident in the low-slung stretch of buildings along US 160, 31 miles west of Monte Vista. But its position at the confluence of the South Fork and Rio Grande Rivers makes it an excellent base from which to fish the Gold Medal waters of the Rio Grande.

In ski season, South Fork is a more affordable lodging alternative than Pagosa Springs for skiers at Wolf Creek. Exceptional backcountry hiking in the Weminuche Wilderness of the Rio Grande National Forest, Colorado's largest pristine area, is readily accessible from trailheads near South Fork. An abundance of nearby campgrounds also attracts vacationers who want to enjoy a forested mountain setting.

At South Fork, US 160 turns south from the Rio Grande toward Wolf Creek Pass 18 miles away, and Hwy 149 continues upstream 21 miles to Creede before crossing the Continental Divide to Lake City.

Sleeping

★**Ute Bluff Lodge** MOTEL **$**
(☎800-473-0595, 719-873-5595; www.utebluff-lodge.com; 27680 US Hwy 160; d from $55, cabins $75-185; P ⊖ ❄) This impeccably clean hotel is the best option in town. Run by a South Carolina transplant named Debbie, the rooms have new carpet, wood paneling and a great location on the border of USFS land where there are hiking trails. There are also a couple of moderately priced cabins which are a good option for families.

Blue Creek Lodge LODGE, CABINS **$**
(☎719-658-2479; http://bluecreeklodge.net; 11682 Hwy 149; d $54, cabins $80-125, RV sites $27) This lodge, 7 miles up the road, is a faux-rustic B&B, restaurant and beauty salon. It's housed in a former saloon with lots of deer heads on the wall and a juicy chicken fried-steak breakfast.

Spruce Lodge B&B $
(☎719-873-5605, 800-228-5605; www.sprucelodges.com; 29431 US Hwy 160; d/ste/cabin $89/129/109;) Bed and breakfast with shared bath are on offer at this woodsy lodge, which is about 1 mile east of the visitor center, and has a relatively plush Jacuzzi room.

Chinook Lodge & Smokehouse MOTEL $$
(☎719-873-9993, 888-890-9110; www.chinooklodge.net; 29666 US Hwy 160; cabins $70-110; P) Carnivorous folk will appreciate this lodge and smokehouse, where copious meats are smoked on the premises (sample its amazing beef jerky). Guests stay in rustic, century-old cabins, most with handsome rock fireplaces and kitchens.

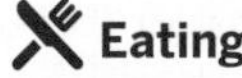

Eating

Rockaway Cafe CAFE $
(☎719-873-5581; 30333 US Hwy 160; mains $5-12; 7am-6pm;) This humble, friendly diner sends out a good breakfast of big pancakes and enormous cups of coffee. For dinner, the fresh grilled trout doesn't disappoint. If you are headed into the wilderness and need to do a little planning, it also has complimentary wi-fi and a little book exchange.

Information

South Fork Chamber of Commerce (☎719-873-5512, 800-571-0881; www.southfork.org; 29803 W Hwy 160; 9am-5pm Mon-Fri, 10am-4pm Sat & Sun Jun-Aug) The center has information on outdoor activities and lodging and sells biking and hiking trail maps. Consult the website for information on recreation and activities following the 2013 fire.

Around South Fork

Coller State Wildlife Area

The grassy riverbanks in the Coller State Wildlife Area attract elks, deer and moose in winter. From South Fork, follow Hwy 149 toward Creede for about 7 miles, where there's a sign on the left; turn there and you enter the area after a couple hundred yards. You can see bighorn sheep throughout the year on the south-facing Palisade cliffs extending from the Coller State Wildlife Area to Wagon Wheel Gap. At the gap, golden eagles soar above the cliff faces and fish the Rio Grande.

Weminuche Wilderness Area

Named for a band of the Ute tribe, the Weminuche Wilderness Area is the most extensive wilderness in Colorado, with an area of more than 700 sq miles. The Weminuche extends west along the Continental Divide from Wolf Creek Pass to the Animas River near Silverton.

From June to July 2013, the West Fork Complex fire burned over 100,000 acres, mostly affecting the Weminuche Wilderness area. The cause of the fire was lightning strikes combined with strong winds that spread the fire. Today, public access is affected mainly in the areas west of Creede.

Along the Continental Divide National Scenic Trail (USFS Trail 813) you will find many secluded hiking opportunities as the trail passes through 80 miles of the Weminuche Wilderness between Wolf Creek Pass and Stony Pass. One trail of particular interest leads to an undeveloped natural hot spring west of the Divide. To reach **Wolf Creek Pass Hot Spring** take USFS Trail 560 west from the Divide, descending more than 6 miles through the Beaver Creek drainage to the West Fork headwaters of the San Juan River. The spring, with water hotter than 100°F (38°C), is to the right on USFS Trail 561, about half a mile above the trail junction.

Visitors should have maps of both the Rio Grande and San Juan National Forests. Ranger stations for the Rio Grande National Forest are in either Del Norte or Creede; the nearest San Juan National Forest ranger station is in Pagosa Springs.

Creede & Around

Welcome to the middle of the mountains and the middle of nowhere. Creede is the only incorporated city in Mineral County, which joins neighboring Hinsdale County as one of Colorado's least-populated counties: each has less than 900 people.

If you couldn't tell by the name, Mineral County dug its wealth from the ground: underfoot are huge reserves of silver, lead and zinc. Since 1988 all the silver mines of Mineral County have ceased operation and become tourist attractions. Today you can tour the rugged mining landscape north of town, where tremendous mills cling to spectacular cliffs. Below the vertical-walled mouth of Willow Creek Canyon, narrow

Creede Ave is a mix of galleries and shops in historic buildings.

For scenic beauty, the country surrounding Creede is difficult to beat. Relatively untrampled trails lead into the immense surrounding wilderness areas and provide appreciative hikers and backpackers with beauty and solitude, as well as access to unique sights like the bizarre volcanic spires and pinnacles of the Wheeler Geologic Area.

Sights

Creede Historic Museum MUSEUM
(☎719-658-2303; http://museumtrail.org/creedehistoricmuseum.asp; 17 Main St; adult $2; ⊙10am-4pm late May-early Sep) Mineral treasures attracted miners by the trainload, but this museum chronicles the more intriguing opportunists and scoundrels who took advantage of Creede's short-lived prosperity. It's in the former railroad depot, behind City Park.

Creede Underground Mining Museum MUSEUM
(☎719-658-0811; www.undergroundminingmuseum.com; 407 N Loma Ave; adult/child $5/3; ⊙10am-4pm Jun-Aug, 10am-3pm Sep-May, closed weekends Dec-Feb; 👪) Opened in 1992, this fascinating museum was hewn from the ground by mine workers, and the tours, which really bring home the grim reality of life in the mines, are also led by miners. It's a chilling exhibit in more ways than one: with the temperature a steady 51°F (11°C) year-round, visitors are advised to bring jackets.

North Clear Creek Falls WATERFALL
Twenty-five miles west of Creede and only half a mile from signs on Hwy 149, the impressive falls are visible from an overlook on the fenced edge of a deep gorge. From the parking area, a short walk over the ridge away from the falls takes you to another viewpoint above the sheer-walled canyon with Bristol Head in the distance.

Far below your feet a metal aqueduct carries Clear Creek away from its natural course to the Santa Maria Reservoir as part of a massive effort to regulate the flow of the Rio Grande headwaters.

Activities

Hiking & Backpacking

The hike through the upland meadow called Phoenix Park is especially appealing, as it begins at the King Solomon Mill at the top of East Willow Creek Canyon and proceeds past waterfalls and beaver ponds. You can pick up maps at the **Amethyst Emporium** (☎719-658-2430; 129 N Main St; ⊙9am-6pm Mon-Sat Jun-Aug).

Hiking options are nearly limitless within the extensive Weminuche and La Garita Wilderness Areas on either side of the Rio Grande Valley. A good source of information if you wish to explore the Continental Divide east of Stony Pass is Dennis Gebhardt's *A Backpacking Guide to the Weminuche Wilderness*. You can rent hiking packs and tents at **San Juan Sports** (☎888-658-0851, 719-658-2359; www.sanjuansports.com; 102 Main St; bike rental per day $19; ⊙10am-5pm).

Visiting the dramatic stone forms of the **Wheeler Geologic Area** – resembling rows of sharp animal teeth, and bearing names like City of Gnomes, White-Shrouded Ghosts, Dante's Lost Souls – makes a specular and fairly strenuous full-day hike. Carved by wind and rain into volcanic tuff framed by evergreen forest, the bizarre area was declared a national monument in 1908. But the remote 11,000ft setting near the Continental Divide kept all but the hardiest visitors away and by 1950 its monument status was removed. In 1993, the Wheeler Geologic Area was again granted wilderness protection when federal lawmakers approved the area's addition to La Garita Wilderness.

The USFS East Bellows Trail (Trail 790) is a 17-mile round-trip hike that climbs nearly 2000ft from the Hanson's Mill campground to the base of the geologic formations. To get to the trailhead, drive southeast along Hwy 149 for slightly more than 7 miles and turn left on USFS Rd 600 (Pool Table Rd). Continue for 9½ miles to Hanson's Mill campground. The trail affords some great views and there are lots of places to camp along the way. From Hanson's Mill there is also a 14-mile 4WD road that leads to the area.

Rafting

On the Rio Grande below Wagon Wheel Gap, scenic float trips with a few rapids and quality fishing are the primary attractions of the 20-mile run to South Fork. A good place to put in along Hwy 149 is the Goose Creek Road Bridge immediately west of the gap. During high water, rafters should beware the closely spaced railroad bridge abutments at Wagon Wheel Gap. Rafting tours and equipment rental are available from **Mountain Man Rafting & Tours** (☎719-658-2663; www.mountainmantours.com; 702 S Main St; Rio Grande half-day adult/child $59/49).

Fishing

Above the Wagon Wheel Gap on the Rio Grande, anglers have two choice sections of the river with special regulations for catch-and-release of rainbow trout using either artificial fly or lure. There's a two-bag limit on brown trout more than 12in long. One section between Creede's Willow Creek and Wagon Wheel Gap is mostly private and boat access is necessary. Further upstream, however, you can fish from public lands on both sides of the Rio Grande at USFS Marshall Park and Rio Grande campgrounds.

The fishing is good at Ruby Lakes (11,000ft), accessible by USFS Trail 815, a 4-mile hike or horseback ride along Fern Creek. The trailhead is about 1¼ miles along USFS Rd 522, 16 miles southwest of Craig off Hwy 149. The Brown Lakes State Wildlife Area (9840ft) is stocked by the Division of Wildlife (DOW) with rainbow and brook trout, but the large browns and native cutthroat are the real attraction. The lakes are surrounded by spruce and fir forests and are located 2 miles west of Hwy 149 and the USFS Silver Thread Campground, 25 miles west of Creede.

Fishing supplies, information and guide services are available at the **Rio Grande Angler** (☎719-658-2955; www.southforkanglers.com; 13 S Main St; half-day wading $275; ⏰10am-6pm Mon-Sat Jun-Aug). Guided river fishing is offered by Mountain Man Rafting & Tours.

Driving Tour

While in Creede, bouncing along **Bachelor Loop**, the 17-mile loop tour of the abandoned mines and town sites immediately north of town, is a fun, DIY adventure and a good way to punish the rental car. The loop is well signposted and easy to follow with a 25-page booklet ($1) from the Chamber of Commerce. It offers outstanding views of La Garita Mountains (San Luis Peak is 14,014ft) and Rio Grande Valley. Sections of the road are very narrow and steep, but not difficult, so long as the road is dry and you drive slowly enough to avoid destroying your car.

Sleeping

Bruce's Snowshoe Lodge MOTEL $
(☎719-658-2315; www.snowshoelodge.net; cnr 202 E 8th & Hwy 149; d $75-139; P) Rates at this clean, friendly place, on the southeast edge of town, include a continental breakfast and, unlike a lot of places around, it's open all year.

Creede Hotel B&B HOTEL $$
(☎719-658-2608; www.creedehotel.com; 120 N Main St; d $105-115) This hotel has four rooms with private baths. Both the hotel and its excellent restaurant are closed October to May.

FAT TIRE CREEDE

Creede's awesome mountain biking is free from the frustrating bikejams you might find elsewhere. The main area is about 9 miles north of town, starting from the **West Willow Creek** trailhead. Although it's a rough road, you won't need a 4WD most of the year. Even so, it's a tough start on the bike: the 2000ft rise in elevation during the initial 2 miles along West Willow Creek was called the 'Black Pitch' by miners. Below the Black Pitch, failed brakes on loaded teamster wagons often pulled unfortunate animals to their end at Dead Horse Flats.

Continue up this treacherous section to arrive at the Amethyst, one of Colorado's richest silver mines. You can still see part of the high-rotary tram system that sent ore down the steep canyon. There's remnants of the tall towers up the steep slope to the east of the Black Pitch.

Some cyclists may prefer to tour mines along the gentler grades of **East Willow Creek**, which are accessed via the same trailhead, with dilapidated mining equipment that is slowly being overtaken by nature.

An excellent illustrated tour booklet ($1) prepared by local historians is available from the Creede/Mineral County Chamber of Commerce, the USFS, the Creede Museum or from a dispenser at the first interpretive stop: the West Willow–East Willow Creek junction, immediately north of the rock spires that mark the gateway to Willow Creek Canyon.

You can rent a mountain bike or camping gear at San Juan Sports. The shop also carries a thorough collection of USGS topographic maps. Guided mountain-bike tours and bike rentals are offered by Mountain Man Rafting & Tours.

Antlers Rio Grande Lodge RANCH $$
(☎719-658-2423; www.antlerslodge.com; 26222 Hwy 149; d from $149, cabins per week from $975, RV sites $39; 📶) Families are welcome at Antlers Ranch, which is 5 miles southwest of Creede and offers motel-style rooms and cabins on both banks of the Rio Grande. Cabins are rented at a weekly rate and amenities include a riverside hot tub.

Soward Ranch RANCH $$
(☎719-658-2295; 4698 Middle Creek Rd; cabins $95-250; ⊙May-Oct) About 8 miles southwest of Creede is this beautiful centennial ranch – this means it has been operated by the same family for more than 100 years. Guests can enjoy fishing from four lakes as well as 4 miles of trout creek on the 1500-acre property. Twelve cabins range in price depending on size and amenities on offer.

To get there, take Hwy 149 southwest for 7 miles, turn left on Middle Creek Rd, continue for a mile and when you get to the fork in the road, bear right, following the signs to the ranch.

Wason Ranch RANCH $$$
(☎719-658-2413; www.wasonranch.com; 19082 Hwy 149; d $350, cabins $325, 3-night minimum) Two miles southeast of Creede, this ranch has two-bedroom cabins equipped with kitchenettes (available May through October). Riverside cottages with three bedrooms and two baths are available year-round with a minimum stay of three days. The ranch also offers fly-fishing lessons, fishing guides and a dory for use by guests.

Information

Creede/Mineral County Chamber of Commerce (☎800-327-2102, 719-658-2374; www.creede.com; 904 S Main St; ⊙8.30am-4.30pm Mon-Sat) Pick up a copy of an excellent illustrated tour booklet ($1) prepared by local historians.

USFS Divide District Ranger Station (☎719-658-2556; cnr 3rd St & Creede Ave; ⊙8:30am-4pm Mon-Fri)

Getting There & Away

Creede is 23 miles northwest of South Fork on the Silver Thread National Scenic Byway, which follows Hwy 149 for 75 miles between South Fork and Lake City.

Lake City & Around

POP 400 / ELEV 8671FT

It's hard to believe that this tiny town, lovingly referred to by residents as the 'flyspeck' seat of Hinsdale County, was once known as the Metropolis of the Mines. But back in the 1870s, while so many other mining towns would swell and dwindle with the prosperity of the lodes, Lake City boasted a population of 5000 people who seemed here to stay. Settlers built Greek and Gothic Revival buildings and tree-lined streets that reflected a nostalgia for their homes back east. Today, less than a fifth of that population remains, making this remote town a quiet base for exploring the mountains.

Lake City is on Hwy 149 (Gunnison Ave in town), 47 miles south of the intersection with US 50, which in turn leads east to Gunnison and west to Montrose. It lies west of the Continental Divide at Spring Creek Pass and the giant Slumgullion landslide, which dammed the Lake Fork of the Gunnison River and formed Lake San Cristobal south of town. To the west rises Uncompahgre Peak and four others peaks over 14,000ft, creating a barrier between Lake City and Ouray. This wall of mountains is crossed only by the USFS Alpine Loop Byway, which requires 4WD vehicles or a mountain bike and a strong pair of legs. From Lake City it's 50 miles south on Hwy 149 to Creede.

Activities

A full-service outfitter and a godsend in Lake City, **Sportsman Outdoors & Fly Shop** (☎970-944-2526; www.lakecitysportsman.com; 238 S Gunnison Ave; daily rental bike/tent/car camping kit $25/15/125; ⊙7am-7pm Jun-Aug, 9am-6pm Tue-Sat Sep-Dec, 10am-4pm Jan-Apr) rents camping and fishing gear and bikes, with cheaper rates after the first night. It offers tons of local information and leads trips into the area.

Mountain Biking & Driving

After 16 miles up Hensen Creek, the unpaved **Alpine Loop Byway** (www.alpineloop.com) becomes a rugged route over Engineer Pass suited only for 4WDs and mountain bikes headed to Ouray. Another part of the 4WD loop heads south along the Lake Fork of the Gunnison River and crosses Cinnamon Pass to Silverton. Fat-tire bikes can be rented at the Sportsman Outdoors & Fly Shop. You can rent from a fleet of cute red

ANIMAS FORKS

When the wind whips through the graying wood frames at Animas Forks, and clear, cold air whistles through the former bedrooms and parlors of long-dead 19th-century prospectors, there's something truly ghostly about this abandoned mining town.

It's one of the most photogenic stops on the Alpine Loop. If you're coming up the road from Lake City in the middle of the summer, inquire with locals before you attempt the trip here in a 2WD vehicle, but you'll probably make it. In spring or fall, you'll probably need a 4WD. In winter? Your best bet is a dogsled.

This high mountain mining outpost suffered an unfortunately timed founding in 1883, the year the bottom fell out of the silver market. The community of 300 residents limped along for a few years; many survived by spending the brutal winters further down the mountain and returning in the warmer months. But the last mill closed in 1910 and the last resident moved away in 1920.

Today, the 10 remaining buildings are a playground for yellow-tailed marmots and the alpine plain is punctuated with the shells of a couple of cars, wildflowers and rusting mining equipment. The biggest home is the grand Gothic Duncan residence, which you can enter safely thanks to the efforts of the Bureau of Land Management, which has stabilized many of the dilapidated structures.

Jeeps at the **Pleasant View Resort** (☎970-944-2262; www.pleasantviewresort.net; 549 S Gunnison Ave; cabins $125-175, Jeep rentals from $165; P). The resort is at the south end of Lake City, on Hwy 149 near Mile 72. There's a lot of great information about driving, biking and hiking on the byway's website.

Hiking & Backpacking

Alpine wildflowers are a prime attraction on the many summer trails in the area. West of Lake City and north of Hensen Creek is the Big Blue Wilderness Area, featuring many stunning peaks that are more than 13,000ft, including two 14ers: Uncompahgre Peak and Wetterhorne Peak.

Northeast of Lake City, the Powderhorn Wilderness Area features the 4-mile Bureau of Land Management (BLM) Trail 3030 to Powderhorn Lakes, crossing a huge alpine meadow loaded with wildflowers.

South of Lake San Cristobal, day hikes in the BLM's Alpine Loop Byway offer high altitude scenery and peak ascents, but the lower parts of most trails are shared with 4WD vehicles that disperse wildlife and disrupt the solitude.

You can rent tents and other gear in Lake City, at Sportsman Outdoors & Fly Shop, which packages together a 'car camping' kit. The shop also has complete information and leads trips into the area.

Rafting

Local white-water enthusiasts enjoy the uncrowded Lake Fork of the Gunnison River stretching from High Bridge Creek, 8 miles north of Lake City, for 30 miles to the BLM Redbridge Campground, where the river is stilled as it enters Blue Mesa Reservoir. On the way, the river passes through the spectacular volcanic columns breached by the river to form the Gate, a giant notch visible for miles. There are two companies that raft in the area, **Scenic River Tours** (☎970-641-3131; www.scenicrivertours.com; 703 W Tomichi Ave; half-day adult/child $49/39; 👪), out of Gunnison, and **Three Rivers Resort** (☎970-641-1303, toll-free 888-761-3474; www.3riversresort.com; 130 County Rd 742, Almont; rafting from $40; 👪), from Almont.

Nordic Skiing

For cross-country skiing there's an excellent opportunity in the area thanks to the **Hinsdale Haute Route** (☎970-944-2269; www.hinsdalehauteroute.org; yurts 1st night $110, subsequent nights $80), a nonprofit organization that maintains four yurts on the Divide between Lake City and Creede. Among the niche of hut-to-hut backcountry skiers, this system has a flawless reputation for the scenery and the quality of the huts. Even novice skiers can enjoy the 2 miles of backcountry travel from Hwy 149 to an overnight stay at the first yurt. The yurts sleep up to eight people, and have cooking facilities.

Sleeping

★**Matterhorn Motel** MOTEL **$$**
(☎970-944-2210; www.matterhornmotel.com; 409 Bluff St; d/cabin from $99/125; 📶🐾) Our favorite motel in the downtown area is the

Matterhorn, a smartly remodeled 1940s motel with red trim and scalloped siding, where some rooms have kitchenettes.

Inn at the Lake MOTEL **$$**
(☎936-499-1323; www.innatthelake.org; 600 Country Rd 33; d incl breakfast $125; P⊖❄📶) On the shores of Lake San Cristobal, this is a log-fitted motel where potted flowers sway in the breeze. It has 10 rooms, all with water views.

Camping & Cabins

There are a couple of private campgrounds in town, but the state and federal land nearby is a better option. For RVs, try the **Elkhorn RV Resort & Cabins** (☎970-944-2920; www.elkhornrvresort.com; 713 N Bluff St; cabins $49, tent/RV sites $21/37; P📶), where there are RV hookups, some utilitarian tent camping and simple 'camping cabins,' which come without linens. Dispersed camping is available on USFS lands along Hensen Creek immediately east of town. Free BLM riverside campsites are available at the Gate, 20 miles north next to Hwy 149, and at Gateview and Redbridge along Lake County Rd 25, which continues beside the river where Hwy 149 turns east from the river course.

Nine miles southwest of town, immediately below Slumgullion Pass (11,361ft), the USFS Slumgullion Campground offers 21 campsites for $10 per site. The **Wupperman Campground** (☎970-944-2225; County Rd 33; campsites $15) on Lake San Cristobal is a good option if you want to be near the water.

Additional primitive sites are available by continuing east on Cebolla Creek Rd, where rarely used trails enter La Garita Wilderness Area in the Gunnison National Forest's Cebolla Ranger District.

Eating

Lake City Bakery BAKERY **$**
(☎970-944-2613; 922 Hwy 149; snacks $4-6) The best snacks in town come from this family-run bakery just north of town. It is only open in the summer, but the pies and doughnuts are delicious and always very fresh.

Information

Lake City/Hinsdale County Chamber of Commerce (☎800-569-1874, 970-944-2527; www.lakecity.com; 800 Gunnison Ave; ⏲1-4pm Mon, Tue, Thu & Fri) The chamber also acts as the USFS and BLM visitor center, selling topo maps and offering free trail information. Booklets with maps of local fishing spots are available for $1.

CRESTED BUTTE & GUNNISON

This region of Colorado's southwest is a playground for outdoorsy types, with skiing dominating in the winter and hiking, rafting and mountain biking popular in summer. Fly-fishing is another activity that draws both locals and domestic tourists in waders to the icy waters of the great Gunnison River. Others come to hunt, and antlers and trophy mounts are a popular decorative feature in homes and ranch houses.

The Gunnison River, whose headwaters gather near Crested Butte, 8867ft above sea level, has carved its way through this incredible terrain that shifts from alpine forests to desert-scape tablelands. The physical drama of the Black Canyon of Gunnison National Park is breathtaking – one of the world's longest, narrowest and deepest gorges. The park brings hikers, campers and a steady stream of day-trippers all trying to squeeze the magnificent panorama into a photo frame.

Hwy 50 and the roads around the Gunnison region carry lots of RVs, many bigger than school buses, with Jeeps, boats or trailers of all-terrain quad bikes in tow behind. There are also monster SUVs towing enormous caravans, and the region is a popular touring route for thundering gangs of Harley-Davidson riders. This, after all, is recreation country – some of the greatest of the great outdoors.

Getting There & Around

Avis (☎970-641-0263; www.avis.com; 711 W Rio Grande Ave, Gunnison; ⏲9am-5pm)

Gunnison County Airport (☎970-641-2304) Gunnison airport is serviced by American Airlines, Delta and United. Avis, Budget and Hertz rental cars are represented at the airport.

Hertz (☎970-641-2881; www.hertz.com; 711 W Rio Grande Ave, Gunnison; ⏲9am-5pm)

Dolly's Mountain Shuttle (☎970-349-2620, cell 970-209-9757; www.crestedbutteshuttle.com; to Crested Butte from $115; 🐾) Dolly's runs private groups of up to 10 around the Gunnison Valley, to the ski fields and mountain-bike trailheads.

Mountain Express (Gunnison Valley RTA; ☎970-349-5616; www.gunnisonvalleyrta.org; ⏲6:30am-8pm) The Gunnison Valley RTA runs the free Mountain Express between Gunnison and the Crested Butte mountain top.

Black Canyon of the Gunnison National Park

The Colorado Rockies are, of course, famous for their mountains, but the **Black Canyon of the Gunnison National Park** (800-873-0244, 970-249-1915; www.nps.gov/blca; 7-day admission per vehicle $15; 8am-6pm summer, 8:30am-4pm fall, winter & spring;) is the inverse of this geographic feature – a massive yawning chasm etched out over millions of years by the Gunnison River and volcanic uplift.

Here a dark, narrow gash above the Gunnison River leads down a 2000ft chasm that's as eerie as it is spectacular. No other canyon in America combines the narrow openings, sheer walls and dizzying depths of the Black Canyon, and a peek over the edge evokes a sense of awe (and vertigo) for most.

The 32,950-acre park takes its name from the fact that it's so sheer, deep and narrow, sunlight only touches the canyon floor when the sun is directly overhead. In just 48 miles of traveling through the canyon, the Gunnison River loses more elevation than the entire 1500-mile Mississippi. This fast-moving water, carrying rock and debris, is powerfully erosive. In fact, if it weren't for the upstream dams, the river would carry five times its current volume of water.

Head to the 6-mile-long South Rim Rd, which takes you to 11 overlooks at the edge of the canyon, some reached via short trails up to 1.5 miles long (round-trip). At the narrowest part of Black Canyon, Chasm View is 1100ft across yet 1800ft deep. Rock climbers are frequently seen on the opposing North Wall. Colorado's highest cliff face is the 2300ft Painted Wall. To challenge your senses, cycle along the smooth pavement running parallel to the rim's 2000ft drop-off. You definitely get a better feel for the place than you do trapped in a car.

In summer the East Portal Rd is open. This steep, winding hairpin route takes you into the canyon and down to the river level where there are picnic shelters and superb views up the gorge and the craggy cliff faces. This area is popular with fly-fishers.

For a surreal experience, visit Black Canyon's South Rim in winter. The stillness of the snow-drenched plateau is broken only by the icy roar of the river at the bottom of the canyon, far, far below.

The park is 12 miles east of the US Hwy 550 junction with US Hwy 50. Exit at Hwy 347 – well marked with a big brown sign for the national park – and head north for 7 miles.

History

This massive canyon has presented an impassable barrier to human beings since they first trod these lands. Utes had settlements along Black Canyon's rim, but there's no evidence of human habitation within the chasm itself. Early Spanish records of sojourns through this part of the country make no mention of the gorge. John W Gunnison, who was commissioned to survey the Rockies for a future Pacific railroad, sought a crossing over the river that would later bear his name. He bypassed the canyon in 1853 and continued west until he and his party were massacred near Lake Sevier, Utah, by Utes (though there are some who believe they were killed in a Mormon conspiracy).

The 1871 Hayden geological survey – again seeking a route for a Pacific railroad – was the first to document the canyon. By 1900 settlers seeking water for irrigating crops in the nearby Uncompahgre Valley

SLUMGULLION SLIDE

In AD 1270 a catastrophic earth flow moved almost 5 miles down the mountainside and dammed the Gunnison River to form Lake San Cristobal, creating Colorado's second-largest lake. The land is still moving, but it has slowed down; today the persistent flow that began about 350 years ago continues to advance between 2ft and 20ft per year. This active section of the slide, whose name comes from the yellowish mud's resemblance to the watery miner's stew, is mostly barren, and spotted in patches with forests of crooked trees. It's best viewed in the morning from Windy Point Overlook, south of Lake City off Hwy 149, at 10,600ft. Another good view is from the top of Cannibal Plateau Trail (USFS Trail 464), the site where prospector Alfred Packer is said to have had his companions for dinner. The trailhead is below Slumgullion Campground, off Cebolla Creek Rd.

looked to the river as a source. In 1901, Abraham Fellows and William Torrence floated through the canyon on rubber mattresses, traveling 33 miles in nine days. By 1905 construction of the 5.8-mile Gunnison Diversion Tunnel had begun and it still provides water to farms today.

Though moves were afoot to protect the canyon as a national park as early as the 1930s, it took until 1999 for its park status to be declared, protecting 14 of the canyon's 48 miles.

Activities

Hiking

The South Rim Visitor Center has maps and information on the park's hiking trails.

The Rim Rock Trail connects Tomichi Point with the visitors center only a quarter of a mile away. From the visitor center, the easy 1.5-mile Oak Flat Trail passes through Gambel oak, Douglas fir and aspen, and offers good views of Black Canyon. Take the Warner Point Nature Trail, a 1.5-mile round-trip beginning at the end of South Rim Rd, before watching the sunset from either High Point or Sunset View overlooks. From the remote North Rim, the SOB Draw Trail heads to the river.

Rangers at the visitor center can issue a backcountry permit, if you want to descend one of the South Rim's three unmarked routes to the infrequently visited riverside campsites.

Fishing

The Gunnison River, designated as Gold Medal Water and Wild Trout Water, offers some of the best fishing in Colorado. (Of the 9000 miles of trout rivers in Colorado, less than 2% qualify as Gold Medal Water.) However, strict regulations are enforced to maintain this status. A Colorado fishing license is required and bait fishing is not allowed – only lures and flies. If caught, all rainbow trout must be released, and a limit of four brown trout per person per day (with a bag limit of eight) applies. Fishing within 200 yards of the Crystal Dam is prohibited.

The best access to the river is down the summer-only East Portal Rd. Anglers can also access the river from one of the many tracks leading into the canyon; however, they are extremely steep and difficult, and anyone attempting this should be very fit. A free backcountry permit must be obtained from the South Rim Visitor Center or the **North Rim Ranger Station** (8.30am-4pm, closed mid-Nov–mid-Apr).

Rock Climbing

Mountain climbers who know what they are doing and have their own equipment can get their kicks in Black Canyon – this is not a place for beginners. Routes are not well charted and even the easier climbs are multi-pitch traditional routes in remote areas of the canyon.

If you are an experienced climber, this is a wonderful site. Most of the climbing in the park occurs on the North and South Chasms, which measure 1820ft. Black Canyon is also home to Colorado's tallest vertical cliff, Painted Wall, measuring 2300ft from the bottom of the canyon and named for its fabulous marble stripes. There are a number of different climbing routes to the top of Painted Wall. Check the park website for updates – when we visited, some routes were closed due to nesting raptors (it's a national park after all).

For information on specific routes and difficulty levels, visit the park's excellent website. Also check out *Black Canyon Rock Climbs* by Robbie Williams.

Sleeping

The park has three campgrounds although only one is open all year round. Water is trucked into the park and only the **East Portal Campground** (970-249-1915; www.nps.gov/blca; campsites $12; spring–fall) has river-water access. Firewood is not provided and may not be collected in the national park – campers must bring their own firewood into the campgrounds.

Information

South Rim Visitor Center (800-873-0244, 970-249-1915; www.nps.gov/blca; 8am-6pm summer, 8:30am-4pm fall, winter & spring) Two miles past the park entrance on South Rim Dr, the visitor center is well stocked with books and maps, and enthusiastic National Parks Service staff offer a wealth of information on hiking, fishing and rock climbing. There's also a mini-theater, which shows interesting orientation and historical films.

Curecanti National Recreation Area

The Gunnison River, which once flowed freely through the canyons, is now plugged by three dams creating the Curecanti National Recreation Area. Its official title, the Wayne N Aspinall Storage Unit, is more apt – named for a US representative, in office between 1948 and 1973, who never met a water project he did not like. Many RVs are strangely attracted to the bleak and windy shores of chilly Blue Mesa Reservoir, which Curecanti surrounds. The calm waters of the Blue Mesa are popular with windsurfers, as well as boating and fishing families. Stunning landforms that survived immersion are the unsinkable Curecanti Needle and Dillon Pinnacles, a volcanic breccia capped by welded tuff.

There are no entrance fees for Curecanti, unless entering through the main entrance of the Black Canyon of the Gunnison National Park.

Tours

Morrow Point Boat Tour BOAT TOUR
(970-641-2337, ext 205; adult/child $16/8; 10am & 12:30pm Wed-Mon;) The popular Morrow Point boat tour is run by the National Park Ranger Service, and takes visitors on a gentle 1½-hour tour through the upper Black Canyon on a 42-seat pontoon. Access to the Pine Creek boat dock is via a 1½-mile round-trip trail that includes 232 steps. The trailhead is just off Hwy 50, between Montrose and Gunnison, at the 130-mile marker. Bookings are essential.

The views from the boat are superb and the ranger delivers a commentary on the stunning scenery and wildlife. Allow an hour to walk from the trailhead to the boat dock.

Sleeping

Curecanti has 10 campgrounds, and some, such as **Elk Creek** (970-641-2337; www.nps.gov/cure; US Hwy 50; per night Loops B & C $12, Loop A $12 plus $3 booking fee, Loop D $18 plus $3 booking fee; year round; P) and **Lake Fork** (970-641-2337; www.nps.gov/cure; US Hwy 50; per night $12 plus $3 booking fee; year round), are developed, with showers and flush toilets, while others are more basic. For hikers there are also small campgrounds at the end of the Curecanti Creek Trail (2 miles) and Hermit's Rest Trail (3 miles). The latter descends 1800ft, so be prepared for a steep climb back out.

Information

There are information centers at Cimarron and Lake Fork, which only operate from late May to late September.

Elk Creek Visitor Center (970-641-2337, ext 205; www.nps.gov/cure; 102 Elk Creek; 8am-6pm summer, 8am-4:30pm rest of yr) Part of the Black Canyon of Gunnison National Park, the Elk Creek visitor center is the main office serving the Curecanti National Recreation Area and offers topographic maps and exhibits describing the area's cultural and natural history. It's on US 50, 6 miles west of the junction with Hwy 149 to Lake City.

Gunnison

POP 5886 / ELEV 7703FT

Long ago Ute tribes hunted on the plains surrounding the present-day town of Gunnison in summer. Now this western town – nondescript and functional for the most part – is home to the handsome campus of Western State College of Colorado, which opened in 1911. The giant W on the hill southeast of town is a reference to the college. However, a walk through the older residential neighborhoods will reveal numerous Victorians and masonry homes.

Few people stop in Gunnison, other than to restock and refuel, but it can be a good base for the outdoor activities that abound. In winter, a free shuttle bus plies between Gunnison and Crested Butte continuously each day, and staying off the mountain can make skiing vacations a little less expensive.

Sleeping

★ **Wanderlust Hostel** HOSTEL $
(970-901-1599; www.thewanderlusthostel.com; 221 N Boulevard St; dm $23, d $40-50; P) A find! Think bright and clean rooms, a garden with pickable berries and grill, and a large and well-equipped communal kitchen. Amy, the owner, is an adventure guide with an encyclopedic knowledge of the area and a cute hostel dog. At festival times, guests can raid the incredible costume closet. Emphasis on sustainability, and loaner bikes for guests.

Vintage Inn B&B $
(970-596-1848; www.vintageinngunnison.com; 123 N Boulevard St; r $99;) An adorable cottage home in a leafy residential district, this spot oozes ease and charm. Both the interior and landscaped exterior are loaded with personality. Breakfast options include

smoothies, greek yogurt and bagel sandwiches with fruit. Amenities include hair dryers, free airport pickup and bikes for loan.

Alpine Inn HOTEL $
(☎970-641-2804, toll-free 866-299-66; www.gunnisonalpineinn.com; 1011 W Rio Grande; d incl breakfast from $80; P) A good budget choice, this super-clean remodel has a range of rooms with nice bedding, cable TV and hearty breakfasts that include biscuits, gravy and eggs. There's an indoor pool and pets are welcome.

Tall Texan Campground CAMPGROUND $
(☎970-641-2927; www.talltexancampgroundofgunnison.com; 194 County Rd 11; tent/RV sites $21/36, cabin $75-100; P) In 10 acres off the Crested Butte road north of Gunnison, this places has RV hookups, cabins and site for campers with tents.

Eating & Drinking

★**Firebrand Deli** SANDWICHES $
(☎970-641-6266; 108 N Main St; sandwiches $8-9; 7am-3pm Wed-Sun;) If you're after a healthy breakfast and lunchtime eating in Gunnison, it's hard to go past the Firebrand Deli. The freshly made sandwiches are always terrific with a great selection of breads and fillings. Vegetarians (who have it hard in Gunnison) get more than lip service.

Gunnisack BURGERS, STEAK $$
(☎970-641-5445; 142 N Main St; mains $8-17; 11am-9pm Tue-Sat, to 4pm Sun;) This upbeat 'cowboy bar and bistro' makes 16 kinds of burgers (maple pecan, anyone?) from scratch plus fried chicken and steaks. It's a family-friendly place, with a kids' menu and some wicked deserts.

Gunnison Brewery BREWERY
(☎970-641-2739; www.gunnisonbrewery.com; 138 N Main St; 11am-midnight Mon-Thu, 11am-2am Fri & Sat, 4pm-midnight Sun;) With cool ambience, Gunnison's only brewery serves Hopalicious IPA alongside its other craft beers on tap, plus pub meals and bar snacks.

Information

Gunnison Chamber of Commerce (☎970-641-1501, toll-free 800-323-2453; www.gunnisonchamber.com; 500 E Tomichi Ave; 9am-5pm Mon-Sat;) Pick up a self-guided historic walking tour booklet, maps of area mountain-bike trails and lists of accommodations and activities.

Gunnison Valley Hospital (☎970-641-1456; www.gvh-colorado.org; 711 N Taylor St)

Getting There & Away

Denver is about 3½ hours' drive away, while Colorado Springs is about three hours. Gunnison lies on US Hwy 50, 65 miles east of Montrose and 34 miles west of Monarch Pass. The highway to the Divide is a scenic trip following Tomichi Creek.

Crested Butte

POP 1500 / ELEV 8885FT

Powder-bound Crested Butte has retained its rural character better than most Colorado ski resorts. Ringed by three wilderness areas, this remote former mining village is counted among Colorado's best ski resorts (some say the best). The old town center features beautifully preserved Victorian-era buildings refitted with hip shops and businesses. Two-wheel traffic matches the laidback, happy attitude.

In winter, the scene centers around Mt Crested Butte, the conical ski mountain emerging from the valley floor. But come summer, these rolling hills become the state wildflower capital (according to the Colorado State Senate), and many mountain bikers' fave for sweet alpine singletrack.

Sights

★**Crested Butte Mountain Heritage Museum** MUSEUM
(☎970-349-1880; www.crestedbuttemuseum.com; 331 Elk Ave; adult/child $4/free; 10am-8pm summer, noon-6pm winter; P) In one of the oldest buildings in Crested Butte. It's a worthwhile visit for the Mountain Bike Hall of Fame or to see a terrific model railway. Exhibits range from geology to mining and early home life.

Crested Butte Center for the Arts ARTS CENTER
(☎970-349-7487; www.crestedbuttearts.org; 606 6th St; prices vary; 10am-6pm; P) With shifting exhibitions of local artists and a stellar schedule of live music and performance pieces, there's always something lively and interesting happening here.

Crested Butte Cemetery CEMETERY
(Gothic Rd) Many of the town's pioneers are buried in the cemetery, about 0.25 miles north of town towards Mt Crested Butte. Also interred here are 59 miners who died in

the Jokerville Mine explosion of 1884, many of them boys and adolescents.

Mountain Bike Hall of Fame MUSEUM
(970-349-1880; www.mtnbikehalloffame.com; 331 Elk Ave; adult/child $3/free; 10am-8pm summer, noon-6pm winter;) Inside the Crested Butte Mountain Heritage Museum is the Mountain Bike Hall of Fame. There's a great collection of historic photos and some very cool old bikes to see.

Activities

★**Crested Butte Mountain Resort** SKIING
(970-349-2222; www.skicb.com; 12 Snowmass Rd; lift ticket adult/child $98/54;) Catering mostly to intermediates and experts, Crested Butte Mountain Resort sits 2 miles north of the town at the base of Mt Crested Butte. Surrounded by forests, rugged mountain peaks, and the West Elk, Raggeds and Maroon Bells-Snowmass Wilderness Areas, the scenery is breathtaking. It comprises several hotels and apartment buildings, with variable accommodations rates.

Crested Butte Nordic Center CROSS-COUNTRY SKIING
(970-349-1707; www.cbnordic.org; 620 2nd St; day passes adult/child $15/10; 8:30am-5pm;) With 50km of groomed cross-country ski trails around Crested Butte, this center issues day and season passes, manages hut rental and organizes events and races. Ski rentals and lessons are available, in addition to ice skating, snowshoeing and guided tours of the alpine region.

Adaptive Sports Center OUTDOORS
(970-349-2296; www.adaptivesports.org; 10 Crested Butte Way;) This nonprofit group is dedicated to providing opportunities for people with disabilities to participate in outdoors activities and adventure sports.

Fantasy Ranch HORSEBACK RIDING
(970-349-5425, toll-free 888-688-3488; www.fantasyranchoutfitters.com; 935 Gothic Rd; 1½hr rides $60;) Offers short trail rides (for guests over seven years and under 240lbs), wilderness day rides and multiday pack trips. One highlight is a stunning ride from Crested Butte to Aspen round-trip.

Alpineer MOUNTAIN BIKING
(970-349-5210; www.alpineer.com; 419 6th St; bike rental per day $20-55;) Serves the mountain-biking mecca with maps, information and rentals. It also rents out skis and hiking and camping equipment.

Crested Butte Guides OUTDOORS
(970-349-5430; www.crestedbutteguides.com; off Elk Ave) Guide service for hardcore backcountry skiing, ice climbing or mountaineering. With over a decade of experience, these guys can get you into (and out of) some seriously remote wilderness. They can also provide equipment.

Black Tie Ski Rentals SNOW SPORTS
(970-349-0722, toll-free 888-349-0722; www.blacktieskis.com; Unit A, 719 4th St; 7:30am-10pm winter;) Black Tie hires out skis, skiing equipment and snowboards.

Christy Sports SNOW SPORTS
(970-349-6601, toll-free 877-754-76278; www.christysports.com; 10 Crested Butte Way;) Ski-equipment hire. Rental snowboards, snowshoes and sales too, and clothing.

Festivals & Events

★**Crested Butte Arts Festival** ARTS
(970-349-1184; www.crestedbutteartsfestival.com; Elk Ave;) FREE For 38 years the Crested Butte Arts Festival, in late July or early August, has drawn huge crowds and hundreds of artists, musicians and food and wine vendors to Elk Ave for a wonderful free street party. Artists from all over the US come to display and sell their weird and wonderful works.

Sleeping

Visitors to Crested Butte can stay either in the main town, which is better for restaurants and nightlife, or in one of the many options at the mountain resort. Some of the Mt Crested Butte hotels and apartment buildings close over the shoulder seasons in spring and fall, but others offer great discounts and longer-stay incentives – check the websites, compare prices and bargain. If you've come for the hiking and mountain biking or to enjoy the wildflowers, you can do very well at these times.

Crested Butte Mountain Resort Properties ACCOMMODATION SERVICES
(CBMR Properties; 888-223-2631; www.skicb.com) This property-management group, part of the Crested Butte Mountain Resort, handles reservations for dozens of the lodges, hotels and apartment buildings at Mt Crested Butte.

Crested Butte International Hostel HOSTEL $

(☎970-349-0588, toll-free 888-389-0588; www.crestedbuttehostel.com; 615 Teocalli Ave; dm $35, d with shared bath $89, r $99-109; 📶) For the privacy of a hotel with the lively ambience of a hostel, grab a room here at one of Colorado's nicest hostels. The best private rooms have their own baths. Dorm bunks come with reading lamps and lockable drawers, and the communal area has a stone fireplace and comfortable couches. Rates vary with the season, with winter being high season. Extended stays attract discounts.

★ **Ruby of Crested Butte** B&B $$$

(☎800-390-1338; www.therubyofcrestedbutte.com; 624 Gothic Ave; d $129-249, ste $199-349; P⊖❄📶🐾) Thoughtfully outfitted, down to the bowls of jellybeans and nuts in the stylish communal lounge. Rooms are brilliant, with heated floors, high-definition flatscreen TVs with DVD players (and a library), iPod docks and deluxe linens. It also has a Jacuzzi, a library, a ski-gear drying room, free wi-fi and use of retro townie bikes. Hosts help with dinner reservations and other services.

Pets get a first-class treatment that includes their own bed, bowls and treats.

Inn at Crested Butte BOUTIQUE HOTEL $$$

(☎970-349-2111, toll-free 877-343-211; www.innatcrestedbutte.net; 510 Whiterock Ave; d $199-249; P❄📶) This refurbished boutique hotel offers intimate lodgings in stylish and luxurious surrounds. With just a handful of rooms, some opening onto a balcony with views over Mt Crested Butte, and all decked out with antiques, flatscreen TVs, coffee makers and minibars, this is one of Crested Butte's nicest vacation addresses.

Elevation Hotel & Spa HOTEL $$$

(☎970-349-2222; www.skicb.com; 500 Gothic Rd; r from $139; P) At the base of Crested Butte Mountain Resort and just steps from a major chairlift, this swank address offers oversized luxury rooms ready for first call on powder days. Check online for specials, particularly at the start or end of the season.

On-site, 9380 Prime is a trendy place for dining, while the hotel's slope-side deck is the spot for a beer by the fire pit while you watch snowboarders whizz by.

✖ Eating & Drinking

Izzy's CAFE $

(218 Maroon Ave; mains $7-9; ⏲7am-1pm Wed-Mon) Start your day right with breakfast from this buzzing cafe. Latkes, egg dishes and homemade bagels are all done up right. Don't skip the sourdough made with a 50-year-old starter. It's by the creek between Maroon and Elk Aves.

★ **Secret Stash** PIZZA $$

(☎970-349-6245; www.thesecretstash.com; 303 Elk Ave; mains $8-20; ⏲8am-late; 🍸👪) With phenomenal food, the funky-casual Secret Stash is adored by locals, who also dig the original cocktails. The sprawling space was once a general store, but is now outfitted with teahouse seating and tapestries. The house specialty is pizza; its Notorious Fig (with prosciutto, fresh figs and truffle oil) won the World Pizza Championship. Start with the salt and pepper fries.

Avalanche Bar & Grill PUB FOOD $$

(www.avalanchebarandgrill.com; off Gothic Rd; mains $8-30; ⏲7:30am-9pm winter, from 11:30am summer; 🍸👪) One of the favorite après-ski venues, Avalanche is right on the slopes and has a big menu of American comfort foods (tuna melts, burgers, club sandwiches, pizzas) as well as an impressive lineup of desserts, beverages and a kids' menu.

Bacchanale ITALIAN $$$

(☎970-349-5257; www.bacchanale.net; 209 Elk Ave; mains $13-28; ⏲5-10pm; 👪) Serving natural Colorado beef, polenta fries and fresh pastas, this is the original fine-dining restaurant in Crested Butte, revamped in lovely minimalist style. In addition to Italian staples, there's a good selection of veggie sides and cured meats and cheeses to start. Save room for chocolate *budino* and strawberries in balsamic caramel. The kids' menu is good too.

Soupçon FRENCH $$$

(☎970-349-5448; www.soupconcrestedbutte.com; 127 Elk Ave; mains $17-32; ⏲6-10:30pm; 👪) 🌿 Specializing in seduction, this petite French bistro occupies a characterful old mining cabin with just a few tables. Chef Jason has worked with big NYC names and keeps it fresh with local meat and organic produce. Reserve ahead.

★ **Montanya** BAR

(130 Elk Ave; snacks $3-12; ⏲11am-9pm) The original Montanya distillery has moved

here, with wide acclaim. Its basiltini, made with basil-infused rum, fresh grapefruit and lime, will have you levitating. It also offers tours, free tastings and worthy mocktails.

Camp 4 Coffee CAFE
(www.camp4coffee.com; 402 1/2 Elk Ave; ⌚5am-midnight) Grab your caffeine fix at this serious local roaster, the cutest cabin in town, shingled with license plates (just as local miners once did when they couldn't afford to patch their roofs).

Princess Wine Bar WINE BAR
(☎970-349-0210; 218 Elk St; ⌚8am-midnight; 👪) Intimate and perfect for conversation while sampling the select regional wine list. There's regular live acoustic music featuring local singer-songwriters. A popular après-ski spot.

Lobar CLUB
(☎970-349-0480; www.thelobar.com; 303 Elk Ave; mains $9-18; ⌚5pm-late; 👪) Nightclub-cum-sushi-bar, it's warmly lit with Japanese lanterns and candles. Then the disco lights and the mirror balls transform the place into an upbeat dance room with DJs or live music.

☆ Entertainment

Eldo Brewery LIVE MUSIC
(☎970-349-6125; www.eldobrewpub.com; 215 Elk Ave; cover charge varies; ⌚3pm-late, music from 10:30pm; 👪) With a great outdoor deck, this lively microbrewery doubles as the club where most out-of-town bands play. The pub grub is just OK, but the riffs are sweet and the beats deadly.

Crested Butte Mountain Theatre THEATER
(☎970-349-0366; www.cbmountaintheatre.org; 403 2nd St; 👪) The best local and community theatre. For deals, check out dress-rehearsal shows.

ℹ Information

Crested Butte Visitor Center (☎970-349-6438; www.cbchamber.com; 601 Elk Ave; ⌚9am-3pm) Crested Butte's visitor center is packed with information and staffed by helpful people.

Post Office (☎970-349-5568; www.usps.com; 217 Elk Ave; ⌚7:30am-4:30pm Mon-Fri, 10am-1pm Sat)

ℹ Getting There & Away

Crested Butte is about four hours' drive from Denver, and about 3½ hours from Colorado Springs. Head for Gunnison on US Hwy 50 and from there head north for about 30 minutes to Crested Butte on Hwy 135.

Montrose

POP 19,000 / ELEV 5974FT

Montrose is an agricultural center and a wholesale supply point for Telluride, 65 miles to the south. With the lofty San Juan Mountains to the south, the Black Canyon of the Gunnison National Park to the east, the Grand Mesa to the north and the Uncompahgre Plateau to the west, it's a handy starting point for adventure. Historic buildings grace the old center with atmosphere, one that is distinctly missing on the north–south US 550 route with huge chain stores, motels and fast-food restaurants.

Though rather perfunctory, there are some good museums, antique stores and a clutch of decent restaurants. But perhaps the best reason to stay in Montrose is to day-trip to the awesome Black Canyon of the Gunnison National Park and to try your hand at mountain biking on the Uncompahgre Plateau.

◉ Sights

The vestiges of the old town can be found along Main St and near the old Denver & Rio Grande Railroad Depot on N Rio Grande Ave. Some of the buildings date from the early 1880s, although the grander edifices were constructed around the turn of the 20th century as Montrose moved from frontier railroad town to significant financial center. A set of 12 interpretive signs is installed in the historic five-block central area around Main St.

Montrose is also a good base from which to explore the **Cimarron Railroad Exhibit** (www.nps.gov/cure/; P👪), a restored steam locomotive, boxcar and caboose sitting on a narrow-gauge bridge crossing the Cimarron River, about 20 miles east of town.

★**Ute Indian Museum** MUSEUM
(☎970-249-3098; www.historycolorado.org/museums/ute-indian-museum-0; 17253 Chipeta Dr; adult/child $4.50/2; ⌚9am-4pm Tue-Sat; P👪) 🌿 One of the few American museums dedicated to one tribe. The Ute are the traditional people of western Colorado. The museum is situated on a homestead that belonged to legendary Uncompahgre Ute chief Ouray and his wife Chipeta. A visitor center is attached to the museum.

Museum of the Mountain West MUSEUM
(☎970-249-4162; www.mountainwestmuseum.com; 68169 E Miami Rd; adult/child $10/5; ⊙8:30am-4:30pm Mon-Sat; P) On display are a staggering number of pieces from the 1880s to the 1930s. There's a re-created Old West town replete with storefonts, a saloon, drugstore and doctor's surgery. The original Diehl Carriage Works building is where 1919–26 world heavyweight boxing champion Jack Dempsey trained.

Activities

BMX

BMX Complex CYCLING
(☎970-417-1824; www.facebook.com/montrosebmx; 1001 N 2nd St;) FREE This excellent BMX complex is located at the Montrose County Fairgrounds. The local BMX community is very welcoming to new and visiting riders.

Fishing

This area offers some of the best trout fishing in the US. The Gunnison River has been designated Gold Medal Waters and the Uncompahgre River, which flows through Montrose, offers outstanding year-round angling. Anglers must have a license and comply with local regulations and bag limits. (Rainbow trout are strictly catch-and-release.) There are several companies that can get you kitted out and onto the water.

Toads Guide Shop FISHING
(☎970-249-0408; www.toadsguideshop.com; 309 E Main St; tours from $225;) This angler's shop provides customized guided fly-fishing tours to the Gunnison and Uncompahgre Rivers and beyond.

Hiking

The great variety here ranges from simple strolls to more challenging overnight hikes and mountaineering expeditions. Contact the Montrose Chamber of Commerce & Tourism for maps and more information.

Mountain Biking

Surrounded by wonderful and varied landscapes, and with a network of cycling trails in and around town, mountain bikers are spoilt for choice. For more challenging mountain biking head out on Hwys 50 and 347 for the Black Canyon and ride along the paved edge of the Southern Rim. *Bicycling the Uncompahgre Plateau,* by Bill Harris, is a comprehensive guide to cycling the plateau, including the famous Tabeguache Trail. For bike rentals, gear and advice, go to Jeans Westerner or Cascade Bicycles.

Rafting

Like much of southwest Colorado, Montrose makes a great base for river rafting. The Gunnison Gorge, downstream from the Black Canyon, is a popular spot, with rapids ranging from Class II to IV. Several regional companies can get you out on the water, as well as Montrose outfitter Toads Guide Shop.

Skateboarding

★**Montrose Skate Park** SKATING
(540 S Rio Grand Ave;) FREE If you've got your deck or rollerbades, head for Montrose Skate Park, 15,000 sq ft of concrete action judged one of the best in the USA by *Thrasher Magazine*.

Sleeping

For the most part Montrose's sleeping options are dominated by the big motel chains, but there are a couple of terrific B&Bs and a few places to pitch a tent or hook up an RV. There are several camping areas around Montrose run by the Bureau of Land Management and the National Park Service; ask at the Montrose Chamber of Commerce & Tourism for more information.

Black Canyon Motel MOTEL $
(☎970-249-3495, toll-free 800-348-3495; www.blackcanyonmotel.com; 1605 E Main St; d incl breakfast $70-100; P) East Main St heading into Montrose is lined with chain motels. This is one of the few independents, offering good lodgings at a reasonable price and very welcoming service. It's spotless, with some family rooms and complimentary breakfast. Some pets OK.

Cedar Creek RV Park CAMPGROUND $
(☎877-425-3884, toll-free 970-249-3884; www.cedarcreekrv.com; 126 Rose Ln; tent/RV sites $23/37, cabins from $48; P) One of several RV parks in Montrose, this facility is well equipped. Includes a coin-laundry.

Canyon Creek Bed & Breakfast B&B $$
(☎970-249-2886, toll-free 877-262-8202; www.canyoncreekbedandbreakfast.com; 820 E Main St; d incl breakfast $135; P) This beautiful 1909 house on the town's busy main street has been carefully refurbished into an immaculate B&B – the only one of it's type in Montrose. Each of the three suites is uniquely decorated. Flatscreen TVs and a

wine hour welcome wagon are some of the perks on offer.

Eating & Drinking

★Colorado Boy PIZZERIA $
(☎970-240-2790; 320 E Main St; mains $6-9; ⊙11:30am-9pm; 🚸) Worth stopping at if you're just passing through, this wonderful spot dishes up spinach salads and amazing, mouthwatering pizzas with names like molto carne or rustica, with artichokes and capicola. The setting, a bare but refurbished spot with worn brick and carved tin ceilings, offers a cool ambience to match.

Horsefly Brewing Co BARBECUE $
(846 E Main St; mains $8-10; ⊙11am-9pm Sun-Thu, 11am-11pm Fri & Sat) This very popular brewhouse and BBQ hut serves baskets of nachos, hot wings and burgers alongside pitchers of its signature Tabano Red. It has pleasant outdoor patio seating and bluegrass on the speakers.

Camp Robber SOUTHWESTERN $$
(☎970-240-1590; www.camprobber.com; 1515 Ogden Rd; mains $12-22; ⊙11am-9pm Mon-Sat, 9am-2pm Sun; 🚸) Fine dining without being too stuffy or pretentious, Camp Robber's eclectic menu offers Americana tricked-up with contemporary Mexican and Italian accents. The signature dish is the green-chili pistachio-crusted pork medallions served in a rich cream sauce. 'Camp Robber' refers to the gray jaybird that pilfers campers' provisions.

Stone House SEAFOOD, STEAK $$$
(☎970-240-8899; www.stonehousemontrose.com; 1415 Hawk Pkwy; mains $12-26; ⊙11am-10pm; 🚸) With prompt, affable service and a menu as long as your arm, the Stone House offers a catalog of Modern American, Italian and Caribbean-style dishes. Fresh fish and seafood are specialties, and prime beef comes in 8oz, 12oz or 14oz cuts.

Coffee Trader CAFE
(☎970-249-6295; 845 E Main St; ⊙6am-7pm Mon-Fri, 7am-5pm Sat, 6am-5pm Sun) In a big old house with a lovely shaded patio, this caffeine stop offers frozen and hot coffee drinks and Italian sodas as well as some pastries and breakfast burritos.

Shopping

Montrose is renowned for its antique stores; pick up the detailed *Montrose Antique Trail* brochure from the Montrose Chamber of Commerce & Tourism.

Cascade Bicycles SPORTS
(☎970-249-7375; www.cascadebicyclesllc.com; 21 N Cascade Ave; ⊙10am-6pm Mon-Fri, 10am-4pm Sat; 🚸) This local bike shop has been outfitting cyclists and supporting local cycling events for years. For great local advice on mountain biking, touring and BMX, talk to the friendly owners.

Information

Montrose Chamber of Commerce & Tourism (☎970-249-5000; www.visitmontrose.com; 1519 E Main St; ⊙9am-5pm) Right near the outskirts of town as you approach from the east, this tourist office is well stocked with brochures, maps and travel information on Montrose and its environs. The friendly folks can help you out with itineraries, and information on mountain biking, skiing and rafting, as well as cultural information on Montrose's museums and historic buildings.

Getting There & Away

Montrose Regional Airport (☎970-249-3203; www.montroseairport.com; 2100 Airport Rd) is serviced several times each day from Denver airport by United Express (round-trip from $433), the regional flier of **United Airlines** (☎800-864-8331; www.united.com). United also has direct flights from Houston. American Airlines flies to Montrose on weekends from Dallas and Chicago during winter.

Getting Around

Montrose airport has rental car agencies represented on-site, including **Avis** (☎970-240-4802; www.avis.com; ⊙9am-7:15pm & 10:15pm-10:45pm Wed-Mon, 9am-5pm & 10:15pm-10:45pm Tue), **Budget** (☎970-249-6083; www.budget.com; ⊙8am-11pm Sun-Fri, 8am-9pm Sat) and **Hertz** (☎970-240-8464; www.hertz.com; ⊙9am-5pm & 10-11pm). **Enterprise** (☎970-240-3835; www.enterprise.com; 437 N Townsend Ave; ⊙8am-5pm Mon-Fri, 8am-noon Sat) has a rental yard in town.

Delta

POP 8780 / ELEV 4890FT

Once known as Uncompahgre, Delta is the gateway to the north rim of Black Canyon of the Gunnison National Park. It's a small crossroads town that travelers to southwest Colorado can hardly miss, though in recent times its population has doubled. It's also home to a large state prison, which along with a number of empty storefronts, may lend to the town's general lack of cheer. It's worth checking out the lovely postwar-style murals along Main St, which depict the region's agricultural tradition.

Sights & Activities

★Dry Mesa Dinosaur Quarry DINOSAUR SITE
(970-874-6638; Uncompahgre National Forest; P) FREE Within the borders of the Uncompahgre National Forest, this bone-rich area yielded one of the most diverse Jurassic vertebrate collections in the world. Over a dozen different dinosaurs have been unearthed here since the first dig in 1971, including the terrifying *Torvosaurus* and various birds, crocodiles and mammals.

Currently, the quarry is southeast of town, along Escalante Creek. The location of the quarry will vary because the dig remains ongoing. For more information about the visit, inquire at the USFS forest station. A short hike will also bring you to a Ute rock-art site.

Fort Uncompahgre HISTORIC BUILDING
(970-874-7566; 205 Gunnison River Dr; admission $3; 9am-3pm Apr-Sep;) Delta's history as a fur-trading center and frontier outpost comes alive with a self-guided tour behind the rough timber walls of this 1828 fort. Allow about an hour for a visit.

Gunnison River Expeditions FISHING, RAFTING
(970-874-8184; www.gunnisonriverexpeditions.com; 14494 F Rd; half-day rafting $75;) This adventure-tour company offers fly-fishing, river-rafting and hunting trips. It has a hunting lodge bedecked in trophy mounts near Hotchkiss.

Sleeping

Frankly, Delta isn't so pretty, but its location makes it a likely stopover. You won't have trouble spotting any number of mid-century roadside motels along the central corridor. It's not an easy choice, since none of them are too nice.

Eating

El Tapatio MEXICAN $
(970-874-4100; 353 Main St; mains $8; 10am-10pm Sun-Thu, 10am-11pm Fri & Sat;) The bright booths are ornately carved, and the plates of Mexican food are moderately priced and delicious. Lunch deals, like the green chili and cheese smothered *enchiladas Suizas* are both filling and satisfying. Pair them with *aguas frescas* (fresh fruit drinks).

Entertainment

Tru Vu Drive-In CINEMA
(970-874-9556; 1001 Hwy 92; tickets $7.50; summer only;) When the evening air is warm and dusk falls on Delta, this historic drive-in has a magical atmosphere. It is one of the few remaining such facilities in Colorado, and there are only a handful in the entire USA. Check out Tru Vu's Facebook page to find out what's showing.

Information

Delta Chamber of Commerce (970-874-8616; www.deltacolorado.org; 301 Main St; 9am-5pm Mon-Fri;) The volunteer staff doesn't have encyclopedic information about the area, but this place is wall-to-wall with brochures and maps; also has free coffee and wi-fi.

USFS Grand Mesa, Uncompahgre & Gunnison National Forest Headquarters (970-874-6600; 2250 US Hwy 50; 9am-4:30pm Mon-Fri)

Getting There & Away

The **Delta TNM&O/Greyhound Station** (970-874-9455; 270 E Hwy 92) sends buses to Montrose, Durango, Salida and Pueblo, and to Albuquerque, NM. There are also daily buses to Grand Junction, where you can connect with buses and trains to Denver, Salt Lake City, UT, and points beyond.

Delta lies 40 miles southeast of Grand Junction and 21 miles northwest of Montrose via US 50.

Paonia

POP 1427 / ELEV 5674FT

A worthy stop between Carbondale and Montrose, rural Paonia has the right mix of quirk, calm and Wild West tradition. The city's founder wanted to name the town 'Paeonia,' the Latin name for the peony flower, but according to local legend an austere postmaster wouldn't allow the city moniker to have so many vowels.

For its size, Paonia offers a surprising combination of natural beauty, working-class society and liberal culture. It's the home of *High Country News*, one of the country's most outspoken environmental publications. Surrounded by farms and wildlands, it also has some late-19th-century buildings in superb condition. Coal mining is still a significant local industry. Today, most of its residents are a mix of coal miners, farmers (also cultivating the state's newest cash crop - pot) and boomers gone off the grid.

The historic downtown - all 10 or so blocks of it - is just south of the highway. As you descend into the valley of the North Fork River, the Grand Mesa flanking one side and Mt Lamborn towering on the other, Hwy 133 runs right through town.

Sleeping & Eating

★Fresh & Wyld Farmhouse Inn B&B $$
(☎970-527-4374; www.freshandwyld.com; 1978 Harding Rd; d incl breakfast $110-140) Guests at this 1908 farmhouse, with seven bright bedrooms, are fed organic breakfasts grown out back. Owner Dava Parr also hosts cooking classes ('Cooking in a Crockpot' and the like), so even if you don't get a bed, there's a chance to soak in the homespun warmth of the place. Dogs OK in some rooms - beware there's chickens too!

Backcountry Bistro CAFE $
(☎970-527-5080; 210 3rd St; mains $3-8;) The town meeting spot is this shoebox cafe serving strong coffee alongside fresh and organic baked goods and sweet-potato breakfast burritos. If it's hot, go for the ginger or mint house lemonade, with herbs plucked from the garden the moment you order. Breakfast is served all day.

Information

Paonia Chamber of Commerce (☎970-527-3886; www.paoniachamber.com; 130 Grand Ave; ⏲10am-noon, 1-3pm Thu-Sat) A good source of local information.

USFS Paonia Ranger Station (☎970-527-4131; 403 N Rio Grande; ⏲8am-4pm)

WESTERN SLOPE & GRAND JUNCTION

With bluebird skies, dusty byways and red-rock formations on a grand scale, it's easy to sense the great American West in Grand Junction. Minus the pavement, it's just like the backdrop of an old cowboy movie. The Western Slope is all of Colorado west of the Continental Divide, but Grand Junction is the population hub of the whole region, merging interstate traffic from Utah and the Front Range.

Beyond the hub, this is small-town Colorado or just plain wilderness, so travel long distances well supplied. Visitors to the region will find truly enchanting drives, like Hwy 141 south along the twisting Dolores River canyon.

But there's also adventure: Fruita boasts some of the best singletrack around and then there's the underrated Colorado National Monument, a huge red-rock mesa standing sentinel over the Grand Junction metropolis. If you are not a jock, or if it's your day off, don't despair. There's always the rolled-up shirtsleeve charm of Palisade's wine country.

Colorado National Monument

The crown jewel of the Western Slope, here the setting sun seems to kindle otherworldly red-rock formations. Hike its starkly beautiful landscape or watch from camp as lightning storms roll across the distant plains.

These canyons rise from the Uncompahgre Uplift of the Colorado Plateau, 2000ft above the Grand Valley of the Colorado River to reveal a stunning view. The twinkling lights of Grand Junction, the green strip of the Colorado River, the black ribbon of I-70, the tree-lined farm fields of the Grand Valley - these are all far below, together a memorable juxtaposition of Colorado's ancient geological past and modern present.

Once dinosaur country, this 32-sq-mile scenic wonder is one of the most rewarding side trips possible from an interstate highway, well worth a detour by car but even better for backcountry exploration. Open all year, the Colorado National Monument is an exceptional area for hiking, camping and road biking.

Activities

A variety of hiking trails start on Rim Rock Dr, most of them relatively short, such as the half-mile hike starting from the **Coke Ovens Trailhead** or a quarter-mile stroll starting at the **Devils Kitchen Trailhead**. The numerous canyons are more interesting, but the rugged terrain makes loop hikes difficult or impossible; a steep descent from the canyon rim means an equally steep ascent on the return. One alternative is to use either a car or bicycle shuttle, since some trailheads outside the park are reached most easily from Hwy 340, the Broadway/Redlands Rd between Fruita and Grand Junction.

Perhaps the most rewarding trail is the 6-mile **Monument Canyon Trail**, leading from Rim Rock Dr down to Hwy 340, past many of the park's most interesting natural features, including the Coke Ovens, the Kissing Couple and Independence Monument. Another possibility is the less precipitous Liberty Cap Trail, which links up with the much steeper Ute Canyon Trail to form a lengthy 14-mile loop.

If you have half a day and lots of ambition, it's interesting to make for **Rattlesnake Arches**, the largest collection of natural arches anywhere outside Arches National Park. Getting there is a bit tricky, since the arches can be accessed by trailheads in the BLM Black Ridge Wilderness Area or within the national monument. Inquire about directions at the BLM office in Grand Junction or the Saddlehorn Visitor Center.

Sleeping

Saddlehorn Campground CAMPGROUND $
(970-858-3617; www.nps.gov/colm; Rim Rock Dr; campsites $20) The only organized camp in the monument has good car camping with expansive views. It's easy for RVs and near the visitor center.

Information

Saddlehorn Visitor Center (970-858-3617; www.nps.gov/colm; Rim Rock Dr; 9am-6pm Mon-Sun Jun-Oct, low season hr vary) Rangers are happy to suggest hikes, climbs and outings and they issue backcountry camping permits. There's also a small on-site bookstore.

Grand Junction

POP 58,700 / ELEV 4586FT

In truth, Grand Junction is as utilitarian as its name suggests. Near two major rivers, its intersecting highways are built over centuries-old trading routes. It's admittedly not much to look at. Amid one of Colorado's most fertile agricultural zones, Grand Junction is a cow town at heart – despite being western Colorado's main urban hub. It's worth browsing downtown Main St, revamped into a pleasant pedestrian mall with fountains, benches and sculptures that capture some small-town atmosphere away from the sprawl.

Sights

Most of the banner sights of the area are actually outside city limits. The sightseeing action in the town itself is concentrated in the pleasant downtown. The self-explanatory Art on the Corner program makes for a enjoyable stroll along Main St.

Museum of Western Colorado MUSEUM
(970-242-0971; www.museumofwesternco.com; 462 Ute Ave; adult/child/senior $6.50/3.75/5.50; 9am-5pm Tue-Sat) The most impressive of Grand Junction's sites, this well-arranged museum is the largest in the region, featuring impressive multidisciplinary displays on regional history (such as the awesome Thrailkill Collection of firearms) and special exhibits. Look for the modern bell tower downtown, the most central of the museum's three facilities.

Western Colorado Botanic Gardens GARDENS
(970-248-3288; www.wcbotanic.org; 655 Struthers Ave; adult/child/student & senior $5/3/4; 10am-5pm Tue-Sun; P) The Orchid Display is the jewel in the crown of this small community botanic gardens, which takes an hour to leisurely stroll through.

Activities

Mountain Biking

Some of Colorado's finest mountain biking is to be had around Grand Junction, and travelers with even a cursory interest in it would be remiss not to spend a couple of hours exploring.

Major trails include the 142-mile Grand Junction to Montrose Tabegauche Trail (pronounced 'tab-a-watch'), and the 128-mile Kokopelli Trail, which stretches from nearby Fruita to Moab in Utah. The latter is an epic, requiring multiday planning, and traversing miles of ruggedly beautiful terrain. While doing the full length of any of these trails requires extensive preparation, both offer plenty of loops and other shorter ride possibilities.

If time is short, go up the road to Fruita, where numerous sights are an easy pedal north of the village.

Other Activities

Fine climbing is found in Unaweep Canyon and Monument Canyon in the Colorado National Monument. Visit Summit Canyon Mountaineering (p296) for climbing equipment, books, topographic maps and tips on where to go.

Adventure Bound WATER SPORTS

(☎970-245-5428, 800-423-4668; www.adventure-boundusa.com; 2392 H Rd; 1-day trip from $90; 👪) This excellent operator is fully licenced on all BLM and NPS land and runs extended excursions on isolated, pristine sections of western Colorado's rivers. Day trips raft the Ruby and Horsethief Canyons. The Yampa River multiday offers great rapids and excellent scenery, running through Dinosaur National Monument following the route of mid-19th-century explorer John Wesley Powell.

Sleeping

Grand Junction has abundant accommodations. If you're blowing through town on the highway, the I-70 exit for Horizon Dr is downright silly with hotels from just about every major chain. The walkable downtown is more pleasant, with higher-end chains flourishing.

Skip Grand Junction's RV-loaded private camping for some of the excellent state and national land in the area.

James M Robb Colorado River State Park CAMPGROUND $

(☎970-434-3388; www.parks.state.co.us; tent/RV site $16/24; P) Conceived as a 'string of pearls' along the Colorado, it's five small parks in one. The Fruita Section is within walking distance of Dinosaur Journey (p297) and has over 60 sites, including a nice loop for tents along a small lake.

Castle Creek B&B B&B $$

(☎970-241-9105; www.castlecreekbandb.com; 638 Horizon Dr; d incl breakfast $125; P ⊖ ❄ 📶) From the driveway, Castle Creek looks like little more than an enormous suburban mansion, but the details are spot on – independent entrances, chocolates on the pillow, a big selection of movies, popcorn by the microwave, and a hot tub from which to take in the fresh night air. Adults-only; the spacious grounds allow for a quiet stay.

Grand Junction Bookcliffs Bed & Breakfast B&B $$

(☎970-261-3938; www.grandjunctionbnb.com; 3153 F Rd; d incl breakfast $115-150; P ⊖ ❄ 📶) North of town, this family-operated B&B has immaculate country-style rooms. Though on a busy road, it's an excellent alternative to Grand Junction's mostly bleak hotels. Rooms are bright and cozy, and there's a backyard and nearby park for the kids to run around.

Eating

★Pablo's Pizza PIZZA $

(☎970-255-8879; www.pablospizza.com; 319 Main St; mains $6-10; ⏰11am-8:30pm Sun-Thu, to 9pm Fri & Sat; 👪) These creative pies are easily the best pizza in town and we love the bike-to-dinner incentives. With sidewalk seating and a small-town vibe, this place serves steaming thin-crust pizzas with names like Dracula's Nemesis, The Cowboy, and Naked Truth. Pair with a microbrew. Lunches feature an $8 buffet.

Dream Café BREAKFAST $

(☎970-424-5353; 314 Main St; breakfast $6.50-12; ⏰6:45am-2:30pm Mon-Sun; 👪) Hit this bright, sleek cafe for Grand Junction's best breakfast. Our favorite of the five eggs Benedict dishes is the California Dreamin' Bene, topped with red peppers, avocado, asparagus and hollandaise. Those who prefer something sweet could opt for the pineapple upside-down pancakes.

Nepal Restaurant INDIAN, NEPALESE $

(☎970-242-2233; 356 Main St; mains $6-12; ⏰11am-2:30pm & 5-9pm Mon-Sat; 🌶) In a town without much ethnic food, the Nepalese lunch buffet fills a niche. The meat curries are better-than-average Indian and vegetarian dumplings, dipped in a spicy oil, make for a tasty, easy snack. There are plenty of vegan dishes as well.

Blue Moon Bar & Grille AMERICAN $$

(☎970-242-4506; www.bluemoongj.com; 120 N 7th St; $7-26; ⏰11am-2am Mon-Sat) With a cute retro setting, this hopping grill serves up classic fare like burgers, salads and prime rib with salad and a baked potato. Huge sandwiches come with curly fries and there's a laundry list of bottle beers and microbrews on offer.

★626 on Rood MODERN AMERICAN $$$

(☎970-257-7663; www.626onrood.com; 626 Rood Ave; mains $19-34; ⏰11am-11pm Mon-Sat, 4-10pm Sun) 🍃 Elegant and inventive, this is contemporary American at its best, like whole plates of stunning heirloom tomatoes in season, house-made mozzarella and lobster mac and cheese. Artful mains change with the seasons and are paired with an excellent wine list. Servers know their stuff and can highlight regional wines, many of which are sustainable and biodynamic. Tuesday is farm-to-patio night.

At lunch, uptown versions of classic sandwiches dominate the menu for around $10.

Drinking & Entertainment

★Kannah Creek Brewing Company BREWERY
(☎970-263-0111; www.kannahcreekbrewingco.com; 1960 N 12th St; mains $8-16; ⏰11am-10pm Sun-Thu, to 11pm Fri & Sat) Kannah's Broken Oar is probably the best IPA on the Western Slope, and the Black Bridge Stout – an Irish-style dry stout with lots of depth – isn't fooling around either. Students from Mesa State, beer-lovers and mountain bikers pack this place to drink and eat off the menu of calzone and brick-oven pizza in creative combos.

Rockslide Brewery BREWERY
(☎970-245-2111; www.rockslidebrewpub.com; 401 Main St; ⏰11am-midnight Mon-Sat, 8am-11pm Sun) Though locals like it more for the beer than the food, Rockslide has a huge patio and is an amiable gathering place on summer weekends.

Avalon Theatre CINEMA, LIVE MUSIC
(☎970-263-5700; www.tworiversconvention.com/avalon; 645 Main St; 👪) This enormous historic theater hosts art-house films, live comedy shows and live music. It might be the only stage in the world that can boast hosting both composer John Philip Sousa and pop songstress Pat Benatar. During movies, it serves beer and wine.

Mesa Theater & Club CLUB
(☎970-241-1717; www.mesatheater.com; 538 Main St) With occasional live music, this small theater serves more as a nightclub, popular with students from the local university who come to dance to hip-hop and drink away the weekend. The website details upcoming events and evenings.

Shopping

Grand Valley Books BOOKS
(☎970-242-3911; 350 Main St; ⏰10am-7pm Mon-Sat, to 4pm Sun) By exchanging store credit for used books, this downtown shop is a godsend for avid readers. It has a big selection of titles about regional history, Native American culture and the West.

Summit Canyon Mountaineering SPORTS
(☎800-360-6994, 970-243-2847; www.summitcanyon.com; 461 Main St; ⏰9am-7pm Mon-Sat, 10am-5pm Sun) You're in good hands here: the bearded dude behind the desk greets you as 'bro,' breaks down the region's climbs with back-of-hand familiarity and, a moment later, reminds his female counterpart (an avid mountain biker herself) that it's Jerry Garcia's birthday.

REI SPORTS
(☎970-254-8970; www.rei.com/stores/70; 644 North Ave; ⏰10am-8pm Mon-Fri, 10am-6pm Sat, 11am-5pm Sun) It's not as mammoth as some of the other sporting-good outlets in town, but for camping and climbing, REI sells the best gear and the enthusiastic staff gives the best advice.

Information

BLM Grand Junction Field Office (☎970-244-3000; www.blm.gov; 2815 H Rd; ⏰7:30am-4:30pm Mon-Fri) The Grand Junction branch of the Bureau of Land Management, located opposite the airport, has helpful staff and a good selection of books.

USFS Grand Junction Ranger District Office (☎970-242-8211; 764 Horizon Dr; ⏰8am-5pm Mon-Fri) This office has permits, maps and information about the Grand Mesa, Uncompahgre and Gunnison National Forests and camping.

Visitors Center (☎970-256-4060, toll-free 800-962-2547; www.visitgrandjunction.com; 740 Horizon Dr; ⏰8:30am-6pm Mon-Sat, from 9am Sun; 📶) This volunteer-staffed information center is a quick minute from the highway, and offers information about accommodations, attractions and local events.

Getting There & Away

Hertz, Avis, National and Budget have locations at the airport. Grand Junction is on I-70, 248 miles west of Denver via and 30 miles east of the Utah state line.

Grand Junction Amtrak (www.amtrak.com; 339 S 1st St; ⏰ticket office 9am-6pm) Amtrak's daily *California Zephyr* between Chicago, IL, and Oakland, CA, stops at the passenger depot; there's a small information booth here. There is one train to and from Denver via the *California Zephyr* (eight hours, $64 one-way).

Grand Junction Regional Airport (Walker Field Airport; ☎970-244-9100; www.gjairport.com; 2828 Walker Field Dr) Grand Junction's commercial airport is 6 miles northeast of downtown. It connects to six cities in the western US, including Las Vegas, Phoenix and Los Angeles, but most flights go to and from

Denver. It is served by Delta, America, United, US Airways and Allegiant.

Greyhound Station (☎970-242-6012; www.greyhound.com; 230 S 5th St) Bus services to Denver ($65, five hours); Las Vegas, NV; and Salt Lake City, UT.

Getting Around

Grand Valley Transit (GVT; ☎970-256-7433; http://gvt.mesacounty.us; 525 S 6th St; $1.50; ⏲5:45am-6:15pm Mon-Sat) There are 11 Fixed Routes serving Grand Junction, Palisade, Clifton, Orchard Mesa and Fruita. All buses allow bikes.

Fruita

POP 12,646 / ELEV 4514FT

Home to some of the best singletrack mountain biking in the US, modest Fruita has thus far escaped a dire fate as an extended suburb of Grand Junction. It's cute two-block 'downtown' has traveler services that wisely cater to cyclists, beyond the odd antique shop and Saturday farmers market. The town is also the gateway to the 550-mile Dinosaur Diamond Prehistoric Highway, a recent addition to the Scenic & Historic Byways network, which leads north to Dinosaur National Monument and into Utah.

Sights & Activities

Mountain Biking

Aside from those in Moab, Utah, the singletrack rides around Fruita are the best in the West – drawing serious enthusiasts from afar. The dry, mild high-desert climate allows for a long riding season that stretches from late April to mid-November.

You can ride 142 miles of dirt to Moab on the Kokopelli Trail, but there's tons of options in two areas near town: the 18 Road area, more suited to beginners, and the Kokopelli area trails, best for high-intermediates and experts. Maps are available at Fruita's bike shops.

Over the Edge Sports BICYCLE RENTAL
(www.otefruita.com; 202 E Aspen Ave; bicycle rental $50-80; ⏲9am-6pm) This is the shop that put Fruita on the map. A full-service bike shop offering guided rides like the Kokopelli Trail, it continues to advocate for responsible trail use.

Single Tracks BICYCLE RENTAL
(☎970-858-3917, 800-878-3917; www.singletracks.com; 150 South Park Sq; ⏲9am-6pm Mon-Sat, to 3pm Sun, shorter hr winter) Sells, services and rents bikes.

Dinosaur Sites

Dinosaur Journey MUSEUM
(☎970-858-7282; www.museumofwesternco.com; 550 Jurassic Ct; adult/child $8.50/6.50; ⏲9am-5pm May-Sep, 10am-4pm Mon-Sat & from noon Sun Oct-Apr; 👪) Situated between Grand Junction and Fruita, this small museum is a fantastic collection of grizzly animatronic dinos that snort steam and jerk around, bestial skeletons and interesting multimedia demonstrations. It's a little bit corny at times, but thrilling for the younger members of the party.

Fruita Paleontological Area HIKING
(www.blm.gov; Horsethief Rd, off Kings View Rd; ⏲dawn-dusk) FREE Maybe it's the desolation of the dry, rumbling country; maybe it's the lack of anything man-made in your view. Whatever the reason, it seems entirely possible to imagine dinosaurs roaming Fruita Paleontological Area. A half-mile loop trail leads past good interpretive signs explaining the six types of dinosaurs found here during 100 years of off and on excavation.

Trail Through Time HIKING
(www.blm.gov; I-70, exit 2, McInnis Canyons National Conservation Area; ⏲dawn-dusk) FREE The best of four interpretive dinosaur trails around Fruita. On this 1.5-mile loop you can learn loads about the prehistoric landscape from interpretive signs, touch in-situ bones and, in summer, check out the active Mygatt-Moore Quarry.

Sleeping

If you're looking for an overnight in town, there are some national chain hotels on the south side of I-70, off the Fruita exit.

Balanced Rock Motel MOTEL $
(☎970-858-7333, ext 4; http://balancedrockmotel.com; 126 S Coulson St; r $50-80; ❄📶) Tidy and well maintained, Balanced Rock is excellent value for the price. The two-story, exterior-access motel is popular with mountain bikers.

Eating

Aspen Street Coffee CAFE $
(☎970-858-8888; 136 E Aspen Ave; dishes $2-8; ⏲6:30am-5pm Mon-Sat, 7am-1pm Sun; 📶) With simple wraps, strong coffee and homemade granola, this is a great spot to stock up before the ride.

★Hot Tomato Cafe PIZZA $$
(☎970-858-1117; www.hottomatocafe.com; 124 N Mulberry St; small pizzas $12-16; ⏲11am-9pm Tue-Sat) This pizza joint and cyclist hangout is run by Jen and Anne, a pair of bike enthusiasts who espouse a sustainable business ethos. The pizza here comes in thick slices and there is a row of Colorado beer on tap. When it gets late, there's a fun scene on the small outdoor patio.

Information

Fruita Chamber of Commerce (☎970-858-3894; www.fruita.org) Call for more info on local attractions, lodgings and events.

GoFruita.com (www.gofruita.com) The local tourism website.

Palisade

Famous for growing Colorado's best peaches, this small town owes its luck to a warm, dry microclimate that later turned out to also be ideal for vineyards. Bordeaux-style grapes do well here, though you will find a bit of everything on offer. Relatively new on the scene, Palisade vineyards cannot compare to those in Napa Valley, but they do offer a fun outing into this blue-sky farmland. Palisade also offers good mountain biking that's not yet widely known with the newly developed Palisade Rim Trail.

Utes were the first inhabitants of the Grand Valley, followed by white settlers around 1881. It didn't become a popular area for agriculture until the Bureau of Reclamation built irrigation canals to divert water from the Colorado River in the early 1900s Today it's a pleasant small town with a farm feel and entrepeneurs focused on developing the accoutrements of a wine-country culture.

Sights & Activities

★Suncrest Orchard, Alpacas and Fiber Mill FARM
(☎970-464-4862; www.suncrestorchardalpacas.net; 3608 E 1/4 Rd; ⏲9am-5pm Tue, Thu, Sat; P) If cute were currency, Mike and Cindy McDermott would be sitting on a gold mine with their combination alpaca and lavender farm. While Mike patiently explains the fiber processing, kids stand agape before the inquisitive beasts. The on-site store, with its selection of natural yarns, hats and stuffed bears, has one-of-a-kind gifts.

Sage Creations Organic Farm FARM
(☎970-464-9019; www.sagecreationsorganicfarm.com; 3555 E Rd; ⏲9am-4pm Wed-Sat) Tour this organic farm with pick-your-own lavender from its gorgeous fields. The lavender eye pillows make great gifts. It also sells bags of juicy cherries and heirloom tomatoes. The farm is generous about sharing growing tips with do-it-yourselfers.

Little Book Cliffs Wild Horse Range WILDLIFE RESERVE
(☎970-244-3000; P) FREE One of three federally designated areas for wild horses in the US, where over 100 wild horses get the run of some 30,000 acres of craggy canyons and plateaus. To catch a glimpse of them, get ready for the grueling 10¼-mile Tellerico Loop, which rises 2300ft from the canyon floor to the top of the Bookcliffs.

High Country Orchards FARM
(☎970-464-1150; www.highcountryorchards.com; 3548 E 1/2 Rd; ⏲10am-5pm; P) While campaigning for the 2008 presidential election, the Obamas picked up a box of peaches at this family-operated outfit. They grow fruit so succulent the juice dribbles down your chin. The tractor tours are a fun way for families to get out into the fields and the on-site store stocks yummy peach salsa.

★Colterris WINERY
(☎970-464-1150; www.colterris.com; 3548 E 1/2 Rd; tours $4; ⏲10am-5pm) Sold in Colorado's finest restaurants, Colterris sits in a league of its own – a sip of its earthy, balanced Cabernet Sauvignon confirms. The inviting tasting patio has cheese with wine pairings and a general store sells crates of peaches and apricots. Servers are very knowledgable. The three-hour tour takes you from the vines to the packing shed, with beautiful river views. Reserve ahead.

Masion La Belle Vie Winery WINERY
(☎970-464-4959; www.amyscourtyard.com; 3575 G Rd; ⏲11am-5pm Mon-Sat; P) Owner John Barbier is a gregarious oenophile of the most lovable sort and his 'House of Beautiful Life' produces some of the area's finest Cab, Syrah and Rosé. On site there's also Amy's Courtyard, an elegant little space that doubles as a piano bar. Things get lively after a few bottles go dry.

Canyon Wind Cellars WINERY
(www.canyonwindcellars.com; 3907 North River Rd; ⏲10am-5pm Mon-Sun) In the shadows of

red canyon walls, this is an unpretentious, well-established tasting room. The eco-friendly estate is a postcard representation of the area, and its respectable Cab flaunts surprising sophistication. Tours are available on summer weekends at 11am, 1pm and 3pm.

Carlson Vineyards WINERY
(☎970-464-5554; www.carlsonvineyards.com; 461 35 Rd; ⏰10am-6pm Mon-Sun; 👪) When the hunt for the state's fine wine leads to this pole building, your expectations might take quite a dip. But if Carlson's reds are nothing special, this family winery rewards the search with fine whites and interesting fruit-based wines, including one from Palisade peaches. It's Colorado's third-oldest winery, with expansive views.

Sleeping

★Wine Valley Inn B&B $$
(☎970-464-1498; www.winevalleyinnpalisade.com; 588 West 1st St; d incl breakfast $129-149; ❄📶) From the wraparound porch to the comfortable quilted beds and clawfoot tubs, this welcoming Victorian inn is pure romance. In a quiet neighborhood setting, this is the ideal basecamp for wandering the vineyards. With welcoming hosts and a pleasant 24-hour hot tub in a private, landscaped garden.

Colorado Wine Country Inn HOTEL $$
(☎970-464-5777; www.coloradowinecountryinn.com; 777 Grande River Dr; d/ste $139/249; P 🚭 ❄ @ 📶 🏊) More chain hotel than B&B, this newish 80-room lodging sits right next to I-70. Hopefully, the pool and white rocking chairs looking out on surrounding vineyards might help you forget. Staff are helpful and there's a social atmosphere with Friday night BBQs and wine receptions for guests. Includes a hot buffet breakfast. The adjoining winery has self-guided tours.

Eating & Drinking

★Inari's A Palisade Bistro BISTRO $$
(☎970-464-4911; www.inarisbistro.com; 336 Main St; mains $11-25; ⏰5-9pm Tue-Sat, 10am-2pm Sun) Just taking a whiff of the cheese menu makes it evident that there's no contest for Palisade's finest dining room. The seasonal menu features a dash of Mediterranean and Asian influences. The honey-soy-glazed grilled salmon is terrific.

Palisade Brewing Company BREWERY
(☎970-464-1462; www.palisadebrewingcompany.com; 200 Peach Ave; sandwiches $9-11; ⏰noon-10pm) The unadorned warehouse demonstrates a single-minded focus on beer making. On nice days the patio fills up with families eating brats and paninis while listening to live music (Wednesday and Friday). The popcorn machine is a nice touch; a few salty handfuls pique your thirst for some Dirty Hippie, a dark American wheat. Kids get homemade rootbeer.

TOURING WINE COUNTRY

Colorado's tiny wine region boasts the surreal backdrop of the wide Colorado River, red-rock canyons and big blue skies. Here hot summers and volcanic soil produce wines that are as bold as the surroundings. It's nothing like France, or Northern California. Grand Valley's plucky producers are mostly small-scale family farms along dirt roads, but that's part of the attraction.

According to locals, Palisade is the smallest town in the USA with an all-of-the-above approach to producing booze: a winery, meadery, distillery and brewery all within the city borders. Exploring area wineries and orchards makes for a fun weekend trip, though you can enjoy more peace if you go midweek. All offer free tastings, some have extensive tours available with reservations for a small fee.

Across from the town plaza, **Rapid Creek Cycles** (☎970-464-9266; http://www.rapidcreekcycles.com; 237 S Main St; per day from $36; ⏰9am-6pm Mon-Sat, 10am-4pm Sun) offers bikes apt for touring the vineyards. It also has John Hodge's handy area map. To vineyard hop in air-conditioned comfort, contact **American Spirit Shuttle** (☎970-523-7662; www.americanspiritshuttle.net; ⏰noon-4pm Sat), with scheduled four-stop tours of the Grande Valley AVA wineries.

The Palisade Tourism Board and Chamber of Commerce have useful maps you can download from their websites. You can also find useful information at www.coloradowine.com.

Peach Street Distillers DISTILLERY
(☎970-464-1128; www.peachstreetdistillers.com; 144 Kluge Ave; ⏰noon-10pm) From the moment you size up this room – more work-a-day warehouse than an uppity tasting room – it's clear that Peach Street is dead serious about its booze. Sure, the sign behind the bar reminds you that this is a tasting room and *not* a bar, but locals pack in. Bring in dinner from the food truck parked alongside.

If you're taking a bottle home, go for the boutique and seasonal stuff, such as limited edition pear-vodka (with a whole pear inside the bottle), or Peach Goat Vodka, infused with the famous local peaches. If you're just here for a drink, the Bloody Mary is to die for.

Information

Palisade Chamber of Commerce (☎970-464-7458; www.palisadecoc.com; 319 Main St; ⏰9am-5pm Mon-Fri) Offers a website with more information about Palisade. Useful downloads include regional maps and driving tours.

Palisade Tourism Board (www.palisadetourism.com) This website has a useful index of lodgings, wineries, orchards and other attractions. It also lists upcoming events.

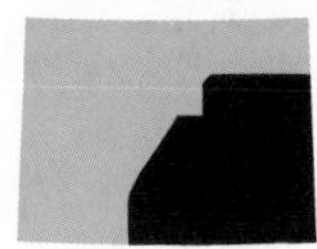

Southeast Colorado & the San Luis Valley

Includes ➡

Best Places to Eat

- Marigold (p309)
- Adam's Mountain Cafe (p309)
- San Luis Valley Brewing Co (p329)
- Calvillo's (p329)
- Jim & Michelle's Farm Table (p338)

Best Places to Stay

- Broadmoor (p309)
- Cliff House at Pikes Peak (p308)
- Zapata Falls Campground (p326)
- Elk Creek Campground (p331)
- Tarabino Inn (p321)

Why Go?

Colorado's arid southeast is a place of high desert landscapes backed by craggy peaks and flat-topped mesas, where silvery sage and scraggly juniper trees begin to replace the aspen and pine forests of the central mountains. Dotted with signature landmarks – Pikes Peak, the Great Sand Dunes, the Royal Gorge – southern Colorado interweaves dramatic vistas with hardscrabble history to great effect.

In this stripped-down setting, the bones of the earth are particularly evident: fossilized dinosaur footprints, massive petrified sequoias and the volcanic vestiges of the Spanish Peaks serve as a stark reminder of a geological timescale in which human life is no more than the blink of an eye. But a fascinating human element lingers here, too: come discover a time when the Southwest belonged to Mexico and played host to the Santa Fe Trail, which brought together the intersecting lives of Native Americans, Mexican pioneers, French trappers, Pikes Peak-or-bust miners and the covered wagon trains of hope-filled American homesteaders.

When to Go

Colorado Springs

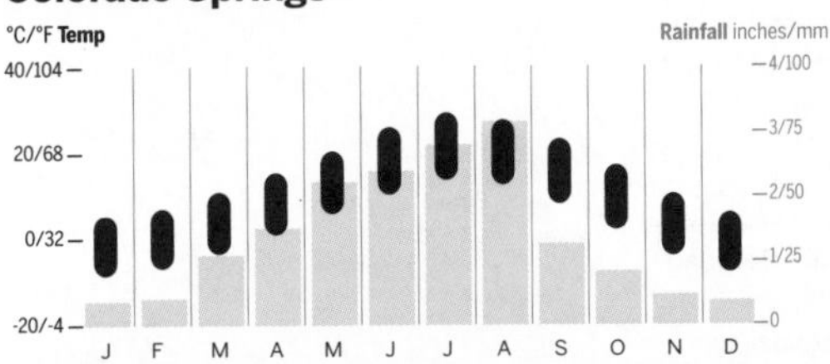

May–Jun Explore the Sand Dunes before the heat of summer.

Jun–Aug Climb 14ers, bike the back roads and enjoy summer music festivals.

Sep–Oct Golden aspens light up Pikes Peak and the Sangres.

Southeast Colorado & the San Luis Valley Highlights

1 Marvel at the sight of North America's highest dunes at **Great Sand Dunes National Park** (p324).

2 Ascend **Pikes Peak** (p304) or gaze at its lofty heights from the magical **Garden of the Gods** (p306).

3 Drive the twists and turns of **Phantom Canyon** (p313) on the way to Cripple Creek.

4 Follow a herd of bighorn sheep through the Sangre de Cristo mountains on the **Comanche-Venable Loop Trail** (p335).

5 Hike past the ancient volcanic walls erupting from the earth on the **Spanish Peaks Wilderness** (p318).

6 Ride the wild Arkansas River through the precipitous **Royal Gorge** (p314).

7 Find solitude in the desert landscapes of **Penitente Canyon** (p332).

8 Chug up a high mountain pass on the **Cumbres & Toltec Scenic Railroad** (p334).

9 Relax in the natural hot springs at **Valley View** (p336).

10 Explore old trading posts and dinosaur footprints along the **Santa Fe Trail** (p317).

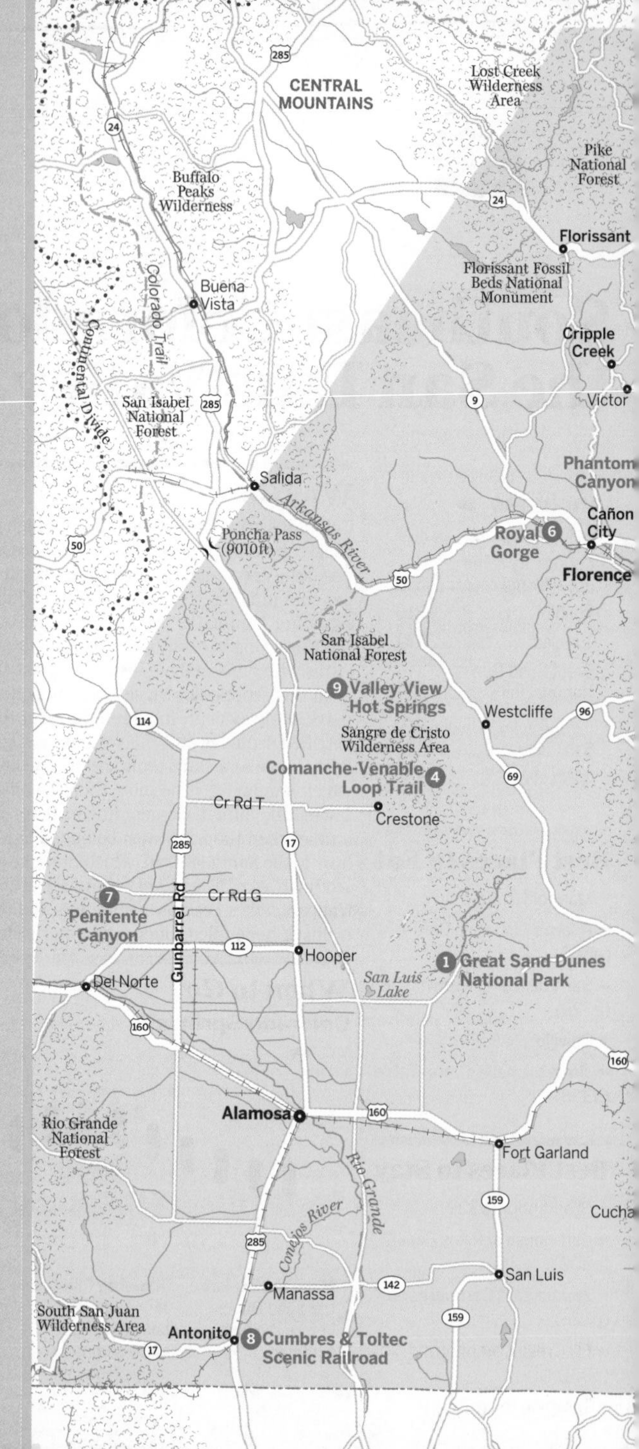

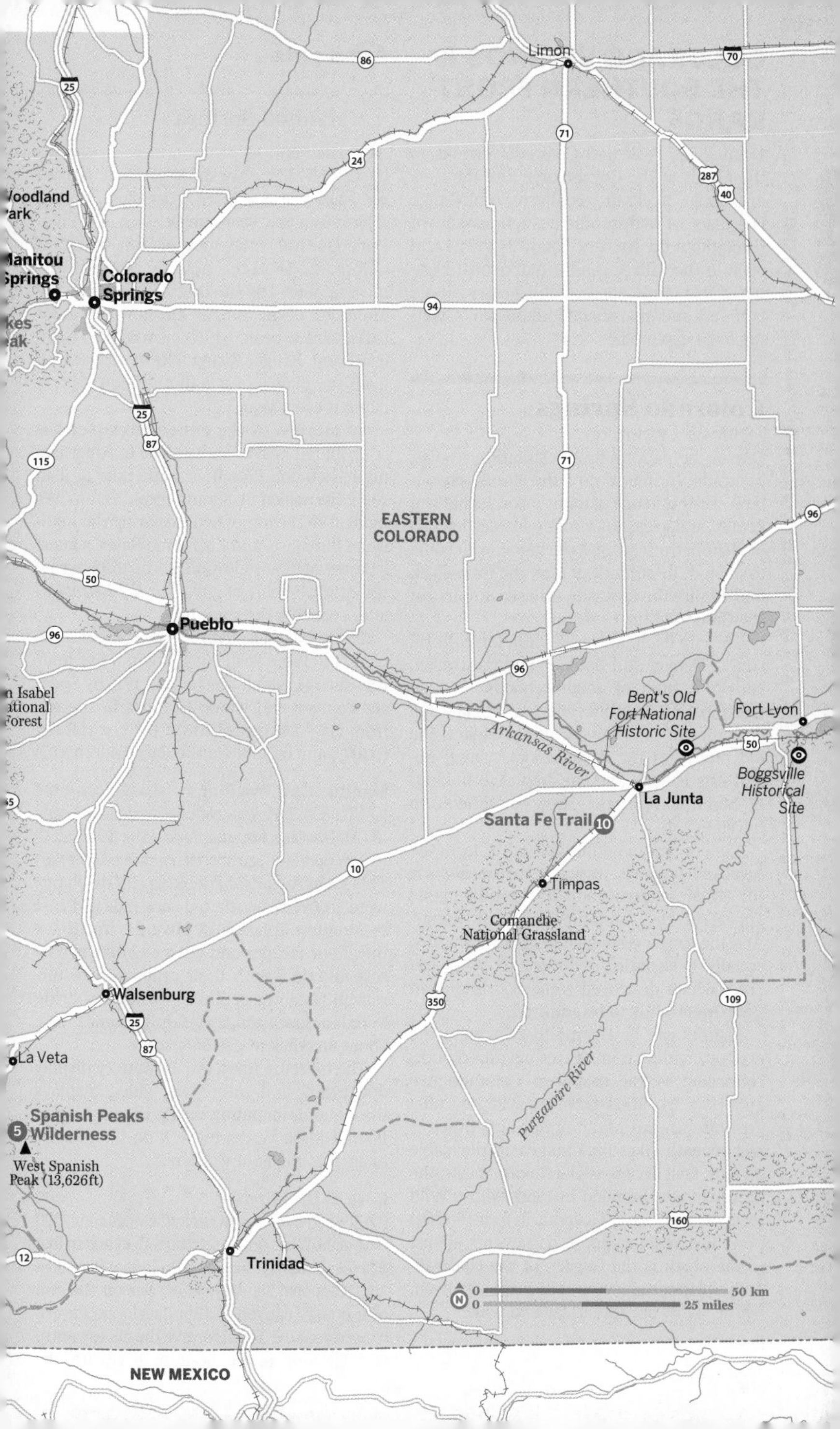

Limon
70
86
25
71
24
287
40
Woodland
Park
Manitou
Springs
Colorado
Springs
94
25
87
115
71
EASTERN
COLORADO
96
50
Pueblo
96
96
Isabel
National
Forest
Bent's Old
Fort National
Historic Site
Fort Lyon
Arkansas River
50
Boggsville
Historical
Site
La Junta
Santa Fe Trail
10
10
Timpas
Comanche
National Grassland
Walsenburg
350
109
25
87
La Veta
Purgatoire River
5
Spanish Peaks
Wilderness
West Spanish
Peak (13,626ft)
160
12
Trinidad
0
50 km
0
25 miles
NEW MEXICO

COLORADO SPRINGS & THE SOUTHERN FRONT RANGE

From Pikes Peak and Colorado Springs to the rapids of the Royal Gorge and the slots of Cripple Creek, the southern Front Range is a place of high-profile attractions known throughout the country. Follow Hwys 24 and 50 into the hills to find a marvelous country of arid landscapes, jumbled rose-colored boulders and pine-shaded hiking trails waiting to be explored.

Colorado Springs

POP 416,427 / ELEV 6010FT

One of the nation's first destination resorts, Colorado Springs is now the state's second-largest city and one of many faces. Its natural beauty and pleasant climate attract legions of visitors from around the globe, who come to ascend the summit of majestic Pikes Peak and admire the exquisite sandstone spires of the Garden of the Gods.

The city itself, however, lacks the cultural soul of Denver and Boulder, and its strange, sprawling quilt of neighborhoods - which encompass four military bases, the national epicenter of the evangelical movement, the old money of the Broadmoor, a small liberal arts college and the New Age holdout of Manitou Springs - can be difficult to navigate.

Nonetheless, a handful of sights, from the excellent fine-arts museum to the historic Air Force Academy, add to the undeniable appeal of the monumental Front Range. And the town's resilience in overcoming two equally devastating wildfires in 2012 and 2013, which destroyed some 850 homes in total, is certainly to be admired.

Visitors can best come to grips with the area by dividing it into three neighborhoods, connected by the east–west Colorado Ave and Hwy 24. Most travelers will naturally gravitate toward Manitou Springs, which is just beneath Pikes Peak and easily navigable on foot. East of here is Old Colorado City, the original town founded in 1860, whose Wild West dens of vice (21 saloons in four blocks!) now host restaurants and souvenir shops; to the north is the Garden of the Gods. Finally, further east across I-25 is the city itself, whose sights are spread far and wide.

Sights

Manitou Springs

★Pikes Peak MOUNTAIN

(719-385-7325; www.springsgov.com; highway per adult/child $12/5; 7:30am-8pm Jun-Aug, 7:30am-5pm Sep, 9am-3pm Oct-May;) Pikes Peak (14,110ft) may not be the tallest of Colorado's 54 14ers, but it's certainly the most famous. The Ute originally called it the Mountain of the Sun, an apt description for this majestic peak, which crowns the southern Front Range. Rising 7400ft straight up from the plains, over half a million visitors climb it every year.

Its location as the easternmost 14er has contributed heavily to its place in American myth. Zebulon Pike first made note of it in 1806 (he called it 'Grand Peak' but never made it to the top) when exploring the Louisiana Purchase, and Katherine Bates, a guest lecturer at Colorado College in 1893, wrote the original draft of *America the Beautiful* after reaching the summit.

Today there are three ways to ascend the peak: the Pikes Peak Hwy (about a five hour round-trip), which was built in 1915 by Spencer Penrose and winds 19 miles to the top from Hwy 24 west of town; the cog railway (p307); and on foot via the Barr Trail (p307).

Manitou Cliff Dwellings ARCHAEOLOGICAL SITE

(800-354-9971; www.cliffdwellingsmuseum.com; 10 Cliff Dwellings Rd; adult/child 7-11yr $9.50/7.50; 9am-6pm May-Sep, shorter hours Oct-Apr; P) This set of Ancestral Puebloan cliff dwellings were grooved into the red-rock hills just east of Manitou Springs off Hwy 24. You'll see the adobe facades and get a feel for the cool cave interiors with their grain-storage turrets and beamed ceilings in what is a string of half-a-dozen multiple family homes. Talk about an efficient use of space!

The museum has a terrific pottery display downstairs and interesting video displays throughout, including inside the bathroom. It's not Mesa Verde, but it'll do if you can't make it to the Four Corners.

Cave of the Winds CAVE

(719-685-5444; www.caveofthewinds.com; 100 Cave of the Winds Rd; adult/child 6-11yr Lantern Tour $24/14, Discovery Tour $18/9; 9am-9pm Jun-Aug, 10am-5pm Sep-May; P) Set on the rim of a craggy canyon is this developed cavern concessionaire. You'll forgive the cheesy entry and elevator music because here are the

Colorado Springs

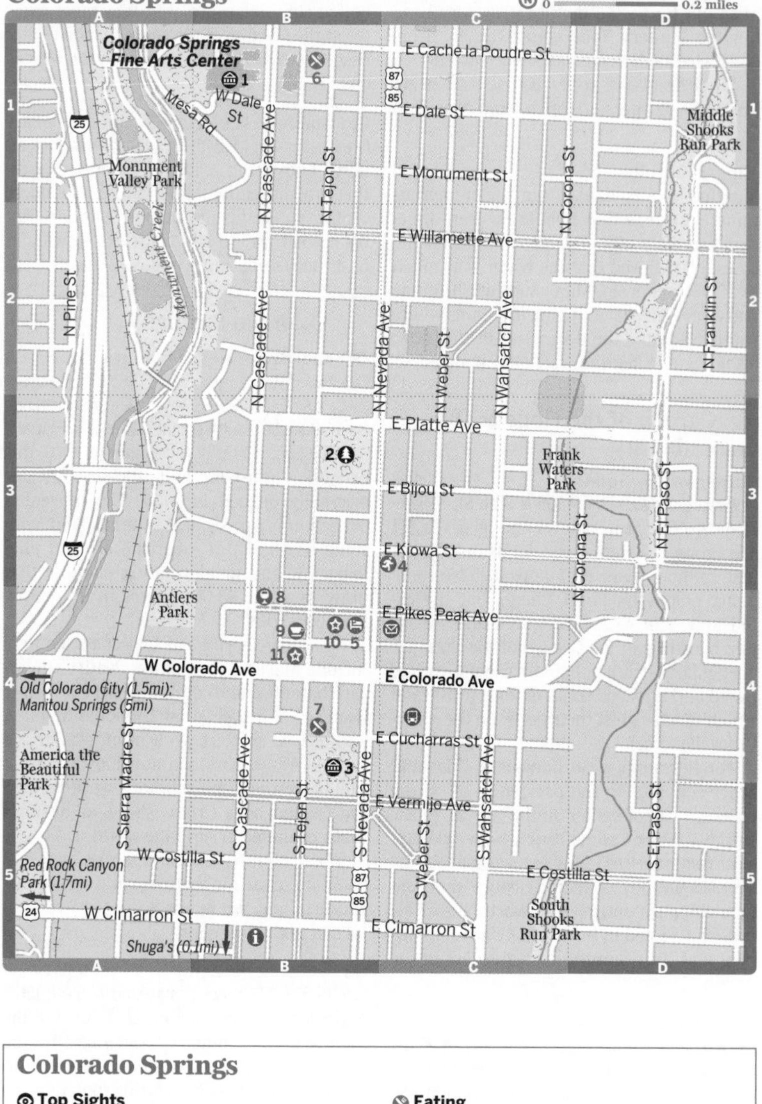

stalactites and stalagmites of your dreams. Most opt for the 45-minute Discovery Tour, but the Lantern Tour goes twice as deep, gets twice as dark and lasts twice as long.

There is also a ropes course and a zip line ($20 per person), open from March to October.

Mineral Springs SPRING

Manitou got its name from the numerous mineral springs that bubble up from limestone aquifers along Manitou Ave. In some cases, it's believed that the water is as much as 20,000 years old. Many, such as Shoshone and Cheyenne, have sipping fountains where you can sample the distinctive-tasting (OK, it's not San Pellegrino) carbonated water.

Garden of the Gods & Old Colorado City

Garden of the Gods PARK

(www.gardenofgods.com; 1805 N 30th St; 5am-11pm May-Oct, 5am-9pm Nov-Apr; P) FREE This gorgeous vein of red sandstone (about 290 million years old) appears elsewhere along Colorado's Front Range, but the exquisitely thin cathedral spires and mountain backdrop of the Garden of the Gods are particularly striking. Explore the network of paved and unpaved trails, enjoy a picnic and watch climbers test their nerve on the sometimes flaky rock.

For information on horseback rides and other activities in the park, stop off at the excellent visitor center on the way in. In the summer, **Rock Ledge Ranch** (www.rockledgeranch.com; adult/child $8/4; 10am-5pm Wed-Sat Jun–mid-Aug;), a living history museum near the park entrance, is worth a visit for those interested in the lives of Native Americans and 19th-century homesteaders in the region.

Red Rock Canyon Park PARK

(www.redrockcanyonopenspace.org; Hwy 24 at 31st St;) FREE A former quarry and part of the sandstone vein that runs through the Garden of the Gods, this 787-acre park was nearly developed into a golf course and townhouses. But thanks to committed residents who fought the good fight, it's now a fabulous local park, where you can hike, mountain bike and rock climb, without all the tourist hoopla.

If you want to link up with a longer hike, the Section 16 trail leads out of the southwestern corner of the park on a nice 6-mile loop. Rock climbers have access to over 80 bolted climbing routes, but they must register at the Garden of the Gods Visitor Center first. The main access is off Hwy 24 west of Old Colorado City at 31st St.

Old Colorado Historical Society MUSEUM

(www.occhs.org; 1 S 24th St; 11am-4pm Tue-Sat) FREE Located in a former Baptist church, this tiny museum and bookstore introduces visitors to the history of Old Colorado City. It's a good way to add context to a wander past today's boutiques and restaurants.

Colorado Springs

★**Colorado Springs Fine Arts Center** MUSEUM

(FAC; 719-634-5583; www.csfineartscenter.org; 30 W Dale St; adult/student $10/8.50; 10am-5pm Tue-Sun; P) Fully renovated in 2007, this expansive museum and 400-seat theater originally opened in 1936. The museum's collection is surprisingly sophisticated, with some terrific Latin American art and photography, and great rotating exhibits that draw from the 23,000 pieces in its permanent collection.

Other pieces you can expect to see here include Mexican clay figures, Native American basketry and quilts, wood-cut prints from social justice artist Leopoldo Mendez, and terrific abstract work from local artists such as Vance Kirkland and Floyd Tunson. The biggest and most famous work is Richard Diebenkorn's *Urbana No 4*, an abstract that's exhibited around the world.

The sculpture garden and vast lawn out back are great for lounging and occasional concerts, and the Bemis School of Art is attached to the museum.

US Air Force Academy MILITARY ACADEMY

(719-333-2025; www.usafa.af.mil; I-25 exit 156B; visitor center 9am-5pm; P) FREE One of the highest-profile military academies in the country, a visit to this campus offers a limited but nonetheless fascinating look into the lives of an elite group of cadets. The visitor center provides general background on the academy; from here you can walk over to the dramatic chapel (1963) or embark on a driving tour of the expansive grounds.

The entrance is via the North Gate, 14 miles north of Colorado Springs on I-25.

US Olympic Training Center OLYMPIC SITE

(888-659-8687; www.teamusa.org; 1750 E Boulder St; 9am-4:30pm Mon-Sat; P) FREE

Fans of Olympic sports will enjoy a guided spin through one of three official United States Olympic and Paralympic training centers (the other two are in Lake Placid and Chula Vista). This is the chief training facility for various sports such as gymnastics, judo, swimming and volleyball. It begins with an inspirational up-to-date highlight reel.

Afterward you'll stroll through the 37-acre campus, glimpse weight rooms and gyms, and hear legends of athletes past. The tour ends at the US Olympic Hall of Fame in the lobby. Recent inductees include the spectacular sprinter Michael Johnson, volleyballer Karch Kiraly and the great marksman Lones Wigger.

Cheyenne Mountain Zoo ZOO

(☎719-633-9925; www.cmzoo.org; 4250 Cheyenne Mountain Zoo Rd; adult/child May-Aug $17.25/12.25, Sep-Apr $14.25/10.25; ⏰9am-6pm, last admission 4pm; P 👪) High up on Cheyenne Mountain, the largest private zoo in the country was launched with holdovers from Penrose's private animal collection. These days it takes conservation more seriously and is proud of its giraffe breeding program. The habitats are decent with instructional elements built in, and there are some nice play areas for kids.

The Mountaineer Sky Ride (adult/child $5/4), a brief chairlift experience, will give you a bird's-eye view of the entire zoo.

Pioneers Museum MUSEUM

(www.cspm.org; 215 S Tejon St; ⏰10am-5pm Tue-Sat; 👪) FREE Colorado Springs' municipal museum is set in the old El Paso County Courthouse, built in 1903. The collection and exhibition of some 60,000 pieces sums up the region's history. Particularly good is the Native American collection, which features hundreds of items from the Ute, Cheyenne and Arapaho Nations.

Activities

Pikes Peak Cog Railway RAILWAY

(☎719-685-5401; www.cograilway.com; 515 Ruxton Ave; round-trip adult/child $35/19; ⏰8am-5:20pm May-Oct, reduced hours Nov-Apr) Travelers have been making the trip to the summit of Pikes Peak (14,110ft) on the Pikes Peak Cog Railway since Zalmon Simmons had it constructed in 1891. Today's diesel-powered, Swiss-built trains make the round-trip in three hours and 10 minutes, which includes 40 minutes at the top. Make sure you bring enough clothing, no matter how hot it may be at the base.

The train usually stays open in winter, though departures are entirely dependent on weather conditions – it's definitely a roll of the dice. Trains depart from the Manitou Springs Depot, 6 miles west of Colorado Springs on US Hwy 24. Engineers will drop hikers at Mountain View (1.5 miles from Barr Camp) on the first and last trips of the day only. This is the best way to day hike Pikes Peak; a one-way ticket is $22.

Barr Trail HIKING

(www.barrcamp.com; Hydro St) The tough 12.5-mile Barr Trail ascends Pikes Peak with a substantial 7400ft of elevation gain. Most hikers split the trip into two days, stopping to overnight at Barr Camp (p308), the halfway point at 10,200ft. The trailhead is near the Manitou Springs cog railway depot; parking costs $5.

If you're interested in doing it as a day hike, you can buy a one-way ticket ($22; first or last departure only) from the Cog Railway. You'll be let out onto a spur trail 1.5 miles from Barr Camp where you can join the main trail to the summit (7.5 miles total).

CityRock ROCK CLIMBING

(☎719-634-9099; www.climbcityrock.com; 21 N Nevada Ave; half/full day $139/169, gym day pass $15; ⏰11am-10pm Mon-Fri, 10am-8pm Sat, noon-8pm Sun) Learn to climb with this local association, which runs an indoor gym and leads trips to Garden of the Gods, Red Rock Canyon and Shelf Road. Rental equipment available.

Challenge Unlimited CYCLING

(☎800-798-5954; www.bikithikit.com; 204 S 24th St; per person $95-120; ⏰May-Oct) An Old Colorado City–based outfitter who for 20 years has led cyclists on the lovely, fully supported downhill ride from the Pikes Peak summit into Manitou Springs. There are rides twice a day, in the morning and afternoon. Advance reservations are a must. It has a handful of other Colorado cycling itineraries, too.

CS West Bikes CYCLING

(☎719-633-5565; www.cswestcyclinghub.com; 2403 W Colorado Ave; mountain bike rental per 4/24hr $20/30; ⏰10am-6pm Mon-Fri, 9am-5pm Sat, 10am-4pm Sun; 🚌3) Based in Old Colorado City, CS West rents high-quality road and mountain bikes, does repairs and will suggest the best mountain-bike trails in the area. A terrific resource.

Festivals & Events

MeadowGrass MUSIC

(☎719-495-2743; www.meadowgrass.org; 6145 Shoup Rd; tickets $50; ⏰Memorial Day weekend, May) Three days of bluegrass at the La Foret retreat center, just north of Colorado Springs. For the complete experience, buy a full festival/camping pass.

Pikes Peak International Hill Climb RACE

(☎719-685-4400; www.ppihc.com; tickets $40-50; ⏰last weekend in Jun) A legendary car race first launched by Spencer Penrose after he built the road to Pikes Peak. These days the cars are faster and the drivers more skilled. The course along Pikes Peak Toll Road is 12.42 miles in total, beginning at 9390ft just uphill from the tollgate. There are 156 turns and the finish line is at the 14,110ft summit.

It's an interesting race as the thin air usually saps up to 30% off an engine's horsepower and, of course, there are occasionally some spectacular crashes. The race has around 10 classes, including super stock car, pro truck and motorcycle classes in a combined field approaching 200 competitors.

Colorado Balloon Classic BALLOONING

(www.balloonclassic.com; 1605 E Pikes Peak Ave; ⏰Labor Day weekend, Sep) For the past 40 years running, hot-air ballooners, both amateur and pro, have been launching Technicolor balloons into the sky just after sunrise for three straight days over Labor Day weekend. You'll have to wake with the roosters to see it all, but it's definitely worth your while.

Emma Crawford Coffin Races RACE

(www.manitousprings.org; Manitou Ave; ⏰Oct) In 1929 the coffin of Emma Crawford was unearthed by erosion and slid down Red Mountain. Today, coffins are decked out with wheels and run down Manitou Ave for three hours on the Saturday before Halloween.

Great Fruitcake Toss CATAPULT

(☎719-685-5089; www.manitousprings.org; ⏰1st Sat in Jan) Don't miss this famous post-Christmas fruitcake toss, when locals make homemade slingshots to catapult the suckers. One rule: you must hate fruitcake. The cake that flies furthest wins. Held on the Manitou Springs High School Track.

Sleeping

Manitou Springs

Barr Camp CAMPGROUND $

(www.barrcamp.com; tent sites $12, lean-tos $17, cabin dm $28;) At the halfway point on the Barr Trail, about 6.5 miles from the Pikes Peak summit, you can pitch a tent, shelter in a lean-to or reserve a bare-bones cabin. It has drinking water and showers; dinner ($8) is available Wednesday to Sunday. Reservations are essential and must be made online in advance. It's open year-round.

Two Sisters Inn B&B $$

(☎719-685-9684; www.twosisinn.com; 10 Otoe Pl; r incl breakfast without bath $79-94, with bath $135-155; P) A longtime favorite among B&B aficionados, this place has five rooms (including the honeymoon cottage out back) set in a rose-colored Victorian home, built in 1919 by two sisters. It was originally a boarding house for school teachers, and has been an inn since 1990. It has a magnificent stained-glass front door and an 1896 piano in the parlor. The inn has won awards for its breakfast recipes.

Avenue Hotel B&B $$

(☎719-685-1277; www.avenuehotelbandb.com; 711 Manitou Ave; r incl breakfast $120-145; P) This Victorian mansion, on a hill in downtown Manitou Springs, began as a boarding house in 1886. One hundred years later, it reopened as the city's first B&B. Decorated in warm colors, the seven rooms, reached via a fantastic three-floor, open turned staircase, have claw-foot tubs, lush fabrics and canopied wrought-iron beds.

Families should ask about the bigger Carriage House, which has a private kitchen.

★**Cliff House at Pikes Peak** HOTEL $$

(☎719-785-1000; www.thecliffhouse.com; 306 Canon Ave; r from $149; P) Nestled at the foot of Pikes Peak, the Cliff House offers the discriminating traveler a Victorian boutique experience in charming Manitou Springs. It started as a 20-room boarding house and stagecoach stop in 1844. Today it's a luxurious country inn with an old-fashioned vibe and fabulous mountain views.

Complete with turrets and amazing views of Pikes Peak and the surrounding mountains, rooms are styled in late-1800s decor. Warm yellow wallpaper, soothing white duvets and thick gilded drapes set an old-fashioned tone, while 21st-century conveniences such as towel warmers, steam showers, gas fireplaces and spa tubs built for two bring this four-diamond-rated hotel up to modern standards.

Out of season, room rates can drop to as low as $100; a hefty service fee and parking fee are extra.

Colorado Springs

Mining Exchange HOTEL $$
(719-323-2000; www.wyndham.com; 8 S Nevada Ave; r $135-200;) Opened in 2012 and set in the former turn-of-the-century bank where Cripple Creek prospectors traded in their gold for cash (check out the vault door in the lobby), the Mining Exchange takes the prize for Colorado Springs' most stylish hotel. Twelve-foot-high ceilings, exposed brick walls and leather furnishings make for an inviting, contemporary feel, though its downtown location is better suited to businesspeople than tourists. Excellent-value rates.

Broadmoor RESORT $$$
(855-634-7711; www.broadmoor.com; 1 Lake Ave; r from $280-500;) One of the top five-star resorts in the US, the 744-room Broadmoor sits in a picture-perfect location against the blue-green slopes of Cheyenne Mountain. Everything here is exquisite: acres of lush grounds and a lake, a glimmering pool, world-class golf, myriad bars and restaurants, an incredible spa and ubercomfortable guest rooms (which, it must be said, are of the 'grandmother' school of design).

There's a reason that hundreds of Hollywood stars, A-list pro athletes and nearly every president since FDR have made it a point to visit.

Eating

Manitou Springs

Heart of Jerusalem Cafe MIDDLE EASTERN $
(719-685-1325;www.heartofjerusalemcafe.com; 718 Manitou Ave; mains $7-14; 11am-9pm Mon-Sat, to 8pm Sun;) A fabulous Middle Eastern greasy-spoon haunt, and exactly the kind of place you wouldn't expect to find in Manitou Springs. It does savory shawarma and falafel sandwiches as well as tasty kebab plates. There's also a delectable veggie plate, with hummus, tabouleh, falafel, dolmas dripping in olive oil and lemon juice and served warm, and warm pita seasoned with za'atar spice mix.

Pikes Peak Chocolate & Ice Cream ICE CREAM $
(www.pikespeakchocolate.com; 805 Manitou Ave; 10:30am-7pm;) The place to refuel in Manitou Springs, with local Josh and John's ice cream, espresso and smoothies.

Adam's Mountain Cafe MODERN AMERICAN $$
(719-685-1430; www.adamsmountain.com; 934 Manitou Ave; mains $9-19; 8am-3pm daily, 5-9pm Tue-Sat;) In Manitou Springs, this slow-food cafe makes a lovely stop. Breakfast includes orange-almond French toast and huevos rancheros (eggs and beans on a tortilla). Lunch and dinner are more eclectic with offerings such as Moroccan chicken, pasta gremolata and grilled watermelon salad. The interior is airy and attractive with marble floors and exposed rafters, and there is patio dining and occasional live music too.

Garden of the Gods & Old Colorado City

Pizzeria Rustica PIZZA $
(719-632-8121; http://pizzeriarustica.com; 2527 W Colorado Ave; pizzas $11-14; noon-9pm Tue-Sun summer, shorter hours rest of year;) Wood-fired pizzas, local ingredients and a historic Old Colorado City locale makes this pizzeria a happening place. Reserve for dinner.

★**Marigold** FRENCH $$
(719-599-4776; www.marigoldcafeandbakery.com; 4605 Centennial Blvd; lunch $8.25-11, dinner $9-19; 11am-2:30pm & 5-9pm Mon-Sat, bakery 8am-9pm) Way out by the Garden of the Gods is this buzzy French bistro and bakery that's easy on both the palate and the wallet. Feast on delicacies such as snapper Marseillaise, garlic and rosemary rotisserie chicken, and gourmet salads and pizzas, and be sure to leave room for the double (and triple!) chocolate mousse cake and lemon tarts.

Jake & Telly's GREEK $$
(719-633-0406; www.greekdining.com; 2616 W Colorado Ave; lunch $9-12, dinner $16-25; 11:30am-9pm;) One of the best choices in Old Colorado City, this Greek eatery looks and sounds slightly touristy – lots of Greek monument murals on the walls and themed music on the stereo – but the food is absolutely delicious. It does a nice Greek-dip sandwich as well as traditional dishes such as souvlaki, dolmades and spanakopita. It's

WORTH A TRIP

CRIPPLE CREEK

Just an hour from Colorado Springs yet worlds away, Cripple Creek hurls you back into the Wild West of lore. This once lucky lady produced a staggering $413 million in gold by 1952.

The booze still flows and gambling still thrives, but yesteryear's saloons and brothels are now modern casinos. If you're more interested in the regional history or simply need a break from the slots, check out the **Heritage Center** (www.visitcripplecreek.com; 9283 Hwy 67; ⌚8am-7pm; 👪), the popular **gold mine tour** (www.goldminetours.com; 9388 Hwy 67; adult/child $18/10; ⌚8:45am-6pm mid-May–Oct; 👪) or the **narrow gauge railway** (http://cripplecreekrailroad.com; Bennet Ave; adult/child $13/8; ⌚10am-5pm mid-May–mid-Oct) to historic Victor.

Cripple Creek is 50 miles southwest of Colorado Springs on scenic Hwy 67, but there are three other beautiful unpaved roads leading here. If you're headed back to Colorado Springs, check out the old Gold Camp Rd out of Victor on the way home. It's narrow but provides spectacular views. It takes about 1½ to two hours down to the Springs; you'll be let out near Cheyenne Mountain. Even more spectacular are Phantom Canyon (p313) and Shelf Road (p314), both of which lead to Cañon City.

Alternatively, if you don't want to drive, catch the **Ramblin' Express** (☎719-590-8687; www.ramblinexpress.com; round-trip tickets $25; ⌚departures 7am-midnight Wed-Sun) from Colorado Springs' 8th Street Depot.

set on a 2nd-story terrace above a magic wand shop.

Colorado Springs

Shuga's CAFE $

(www.shugas.com; 702 S Cascade St; dishes $8-9; ⌚11am-midnight; 📶👪) If you thought Colorado Springs couldn't be hip, stroll to Shuga's, a Southern-style cafe with a knack for knockout espresso drinks and hot cocktails. Cuter than buttons, this little white house is decked out in paper cranes and red vinyl chairs. There's also patio seating. The food – brie BLT on rosemary toast, Brazilian coconut shrimp soup – comforts and delights. Don't miss vintage-movie Saturdays.

La'au's MEXICAN $

(www.laaustacoshop.com; 830 N Tejon St; dishes $6.25-8.25; ⌚11am-9pm; 🖉👪) Tucked into Spencer Center, near Colorado College, this creative Hawaiian taco shack offers tasty, fast and healthy fare in the form of taco, bowl, (massive) burrito or salad. Choose your protein (shrimp, steak, mahi, chicken or pork), and your salsa and toppings style (Baja, Kona, Hilo or Maui) and grab some coconut flan for dessert.

Nosh MODERN AMERICAN $$

(☎719-635-6674; www.nosh121.com; 121 S Tejon St; small plates $9-16; ⌚11am-9pm; 📶🖉) Everyone's favorite downtown dining room. Color and art are everywhere you look, from the giant koi swimming by on the walls to the wide patio with dangling lights and fire pits, and especially in the kitchen where delicious small plates are created. Think chili-glazed burgers, crispy Korean wings and all manner of roasted veggies.

Blue Star MODERN AMERICAN $$$

(☎719-632-1086; www.thebluestar.net; 1645 S Tejon St; mains $21-35; ⌚from 3pm; 🅿🖉) One of Colorado Springs' most popular gourmet eateries, the Blue Star is in the gentrifying Ivywild neighborhood just south of downtown. The menu at this landmark spot changes regularly, but always involves fresh fish, top-cut steak and inventive chicken dishes, flavored with Mediterranean and Pacific Rim rubs and spices.

The colorful bar area, with metal and sleek wood decor and booth or high-top tables, is more social than the open-kitchen dining room in the back. There's occasional live jazz here, and the menu is slightly less expensive. Blue Star also has an impressive 8500-bottle wine cellar that includes organic varietals.

Drinking & Nightlife

Manitou Springs

★**Swirl** WINE BAR

(www.swirlwineemporium.com; 717 Manitou Ave; ⌚noon-10pm Sun-Thu, to midnight Fri & Sat)

Behind a stylish bottle shop in Manitou Springs, this nook bar is intimate and cool. The garden patio has dangling lights and vines while inside are antique armchairs and a fireplace. If you're feeling peckish, sample the tapas and homemade pasta.

Garden of the Gods & Old Colorado City

Trinity Brewing Co BREWERY
(www.trinitybrew.com; 1466 Garden of the Gods Rd; 11am-midnight Thu-Sat, 11am-10pm Sun-Wed;) Inspired by Belgium's beer cafes, the ecofriendly Trinity Brewing Co is a cool addition to the Colorado Springs pub scene. Owned by two self-admitted beer geeks, it serves 'artisanal beers' (made from rare ingredients and potent amounts of alcohol) and has a veggie-friendly menu – though don't expect miracles from the kitchen. Look for the brewery in a strip mall one block west of Centennial Blvd.

Jives Coffee Lounge CAFE
(16 Colbrunn Ct; 7am-11pm Sun-Thu, to midnight Fri & Sat;) Easily the hippest hand on the Old Colorado City stretch, this large brick-wall coffee lounge has ample sofas, wi-fi and a bandstand featuring regular live music (weekends) and a Wednesday open-mike night. It does coffee and a selection of all-fruit, no-sugar smoothies. Food is limited. It's located between 24th and 25th Sts.

Colorado Springs

Bristol Brewing Co BREWERY
(www.bristolbrewing.com; 1604 S Cascade Ave; 11am-10pm;) Although a bit out of the way in south Colorado Springs, this brewery – which in 2013 spearheaded a community market center in the shuttered Ivywild Elementary School – is worth seeking out for its Laughing Lab ale and pub grub from the owner of the gourmet Blue Star. Other back-to-school tenants include a bakery, deli, cafe, art gallery and movie theater in the old gym.

Pikes Perk Coffeehouse CAFE
(14 S Tejon St; 6am-10pm Mon-Sat, to 9pm Sun;) With a fantastic rooftop boasting unobstructed views of Colorado Springs' signature mountain, Pikes Perk is a favorite regional coffee shop. Read a magazine, write a novel or just chat with friends in the cozy 2nd-floor lounge or on the rooftop deck when the weather's nice. It also serves sandwiches.

Phantom Canyon Brewing BREWERY
(719-635-2800; www.phantomcanyon.com; 2 E Pikes Peak Ave; 11am-late;) In an old exposed warehouse building saved from the wrecking ball in 1993, this local brewery serves a variety of pints in a casual atmosphere with wood floors and furnishings. It's not the best brewery in town, but it's definitely the most central. Locals flock to the upstairs billiards room at night.

Entertainment

Kimball's Twin Peak Theater CINEMA
(www.kimballstwinpeak.com; 113 E Pikes Peak Ave; adult/child $9/6.50; screenings 2:30-8:30pm) A beer-drinking, wine-swilling downtown indie cinema. It's staffed by artsy movie geeks who present first-run foreign and indie films.

Thirsty Parrot BAR
(www.thirstyparrot.net; 32 S Tejon St; from 4pm Tue-Sat) However cheeseball this place looks – and it certainly does – it provides a blast of much-needed nightlife on Tejon St when DJs spin dance music on Fridays.

Loft LIVE MUSIC
(www.loftmusicvenue.com; 2506 W Colorado Ave; hr vary) This Old Colorado City spot features diverse artists in an underground performance space sans liquor license. There's usually one show per week and swing dancing once a month.

Shopping

All the best shopping can be found along the main drags in Old Colorado City and Manitou Springs. It's mostly souvenir shops and New Age vendors plying crystals and magic wands, but it makes for a fun browse.

Information

Colorado Springs Convention and Visitors Bureau (719-635-7506; www.visitcos.com; 515 S Cascade Ave; 8:30am-5pm;) All the usual tourist pamphlets.

Manitou Springs Visitor Center (800-642-2567; http://manitousprings.org; 354 Hwy 24; 8:30am-5pm) The most helpful tourist office in the area.

Getting There & Away

Colorado Springs Airport (719-550-1900; www.springsgov.com; 7770 Milton E Proby Pkwy;) A smart alternative to Denver. The local airport is served principally by United and

Delta and flies to 11 major cities around the country. There is no public transportation into town, however, so you'll have to rent a car or take a cab.

Greyhound (☎719-635-1505; 120 S Weber St) Greyhound buses heading north and south on I-25 roll through town daily.

Getting Around

All street parking is meter only; if you have your own wheels, bring lots of quarters. Manitou Springs is served by a free shuttle from mid-May to mid-September, so you can park at the entrance to town on Colorado Ave, where there are designated lots.

Mountain Metropolitan Transit (www.springsgov.com; per trip $1.75, day pass $4) A reliable bus line that serves the entire Pikes Peak area. Bus 3 is the most useful, running from downtown through Old Colorado City and on to Manitou Springs. Maps and schedule information is available online. Exact change only.

Yellow Cab (☎719-777-7777) The Yellow Cab fare from the airport to the city center is about $30. It's about $48 to Manitou Springs.

Florissant Fossil Beds National Monument

In 1873, Dr AC Peale, as part of the United States Geological Survey (USGS) Hayden expedition, was on his way to survey and map the South Park area, when he reputedly discovered these ancient lake deposits, which were buried by the dust and ash from a series of volcanic eruptions. This has since been recognized as one of the world's greatest collections of Eocene fossils (34 million years old), though unfortunately most of it lies beneath your feet. The excellent **visitor center** (☎719-748-3253; www.nps.gov/flfo; County Rd 1; adult/child $3/free; 8am-6pm summer, 9am-5pm rest of yr) does contain a small sampling of some of the 50,000 fossils that have been excavated (which includes the only fossilized tsetse flies in existence), but the only thing you can really see in the open are a series of spectacular petrified sequoia stumps.

Sights & Activities

Although the sights apart from the petrified stumps are pretty underwhelming, the location itself is quite beautiful and a great place for a hike. The gorgeous swatch of high country features dozens of wildflower-freckled meadows, boulder-crusted hills and views of the back of Pikes Peak. The park has 15 miles of trails through open meadows and rolling hills. The most accessible trails include the half-mile **Ponderosa Loop** and the 1-mile **Petrified Forest Loop**. The latter leads to several petrified stumps, including the remains of a truly giant sequoia measuring 38ft in circumference.

Signs of mule deer and elk are often seen along the southeastern segment of the **Hornbeck Wildlife Loop** (4 miles), which crosses the highway in front of the visitor center. After a mile it intersects the **Shootin' Star Trail** (1.2 miles), which leads to the Barksdale Picnic area, near Lower Twin Rock Rd. Between late June and mid-August, visitors make special trips to Florissant (French for 'blooming') for ranger-guided walks held at 10:30am on Friday. Admire, but don't pick.

Another sight on the Hornbeck Wildlife Loop is the **Hornbeck House**, a 160-acre homestead settled by Adeline Hornbeck in 1878 with her four children. The outbuildings include a bunkhouse, carriage shed, barn and root cellar. All have been restored or rebuilt by the NPS.

Getting There & Away

Florissant is located about 35 miles west of Colorado Springs on Hwy 24. The visitor center is in the middle of the monument on Teller County Rd 1, some 2 miles south of Hwy 24.

Around Florissant

Sights

Rocky Mountain Dinosaur Center MUSEUM
(www.rmdrc.com; Hwy 24 at S Fairview St; adult/child $11.50/7.50; 9am-6pm Mon-Sat, 10am-5pm Sun;) This fun dinosaur center is located in Woodland Park, 19 miles west of Colorado Springs. The kids won't want to miss this private museum owned by working paleontologists, where you can watch lab techs assemble casts and clean fossils from digs across the Western states, from Montana to Texas.

Most of the 35 pieces on display are casts based on the fossils they've found. There's a massive *Toxochelys* and *Protostega gigas,* giant marine turtles, but, as always, the T-Rex is the star of the show.

As you drive up Hwy 24 into Woodland Park, look for the cheesy fake palms in the rock garden. But don't snicker too much. When the dinosaurs roamed Colorado, these were the native trees.

Colorado Wolf & Wildlife Center WILDLIFE SANCTUARY

(☎719-687-9742; www.wolfeducation.org; County Rd 42; adult/child $10/7; ⏰Tue-Sun; P 👪) Located between the town of Divide and Florissant off Hwy 24, this private, nonprofit wildlife sanctuary shelters three subspecies of wolf (timber, arctic and Mexican gray), two species of fox (red and swift) and coyotes. It offers three to four one-hour walking tours per day to educate the public about the importance of these creatures to the ecosystem of the Rocky Mountains. You must reserve in advance.

Cañon City & the Royal Gorge

POP 16,499 / ELEV 5332FT

There's no getting around it. This here's a prison town. In fact, if you drive into town from Royal Gorge on Hwy 50 the first thing you'll see is the prison. Gleaming, rambling and tucked up against the Rocky Mountains, it's almost beautiful.

But before you start judging, consider the fact that there's something honest about a small town with a prison on Main St. And because it's an honest place, locals will soon inform you that there are actually 13 prisons in the immediate area. A factoid which, we concur, takes a second to digest.

Sights

Royal Gorge Bridge & Park BRIDGE

(☎719-275-7507; www.royalgorgebridge.com; 4218 County Rd 3A; adult/child $26/20; ⏰10am-7pm mid-Jun–mid-Aug, hr vary rest of yr; 👪) The most hyped-up attraction in all of south Colorado is this impressive 950ft-deep canyon, which stretches for 10 miles west of Cañon City. A 1260ft-long suspension bridge was built across the gorge in 1929, further promoting the already popular area as a tourist destination. Tragically, the 2013 Cañon City wildfire ravaged the surrounding landscape and destroyed the vast majority of the park attractions, including the visitor center and aerial tram, but miraculously spared the bridge.

The park estimates that the bridge will remain open to traffic, but the rest of the park may stay closed through 2015 while renovations are undertaken. Both raft trips and the Royal Gorge Route Railroad (p314) will continue to run through the gorge.

Check the website for the latest updates and ticket prices.

Garden Park Fossil Area PALEONTOLOGICAL SITE

(Red Canyon Rd) The second-largest Jurassic graveyards in Colorado, but still one of the largest in North America, these are one of the quarries that spawned the Bone Wars and produced such dinosaur stars as *Stegosaurus*, *Diplodocus* and *Allosaurus* back in the late 1800s. They're still standing in the Smithsonian today. The world's most complete *Stegosaurus* skeleton was excavated here in 1992.

It's pretty unlikely that you'll spot a giant femur sticking up out of the ground, but it's still an easy quarter-mile hike out to the Marsh-Felch Quarry from the turnoff, and you can combine a visit with a drive along Shelf Rd (p314). To get here, turn north onto Field Ave from Hwy 50 at the east end of town.

Cañon City Municipal Museum MUSEUM

(612 Royal Gorge Blvd; ⏰10am-4pm Wed-Sat; 👪) FREE Good for that rare rainy day is this municipal museum, which introduces the region's early history. In 2013 it incorporated the local dinosaur museum collection (it's here indefinitely), consisting of a *Stegosaurus* cast and a few skull replicas. Visits are by tour only.

Prospect Heights HISTORIC SITE

(4th St) When United Artists were making John Wayne Westerns in Cañon City, this is where they lived and worked. A turn-of-the-20th-century Colorado Fuel & Iron company town before Hollywood came and went, Cañon City was legally dry, so the drinkers, like Wayne and cowboy actor Tom Mix, came down to this area to drink and fight. You'll see remnants of the old stone jail and brick storefronts. To get here follow 4th street from Main over the river and across the tracks.

Activities

★**Phantom Canyon** SCENIC DRIVE

(www.goldbeltbyway.com) Even if you weren't planning on heading to Cripple Creek, this incredible 35-mile drive might make you change your mind – anyone with a sense of adventure and history will enjoy this trip. It follows a sinuous old railroad grade (the Florence & Cripple Creek; 1894–1912) through gorgeous red sandstone cliffs and blasted-out tunnels to historic Victor.

To get here from Cañon City, follow Hwy 50 six miles east, then turn north onto County Rd 67. The dirt road climbs 4500ft in elevation; expect to spend 1½ to two hours going one way. You can drive this in a car, as long as the weather permits. Taking Shelf Road back down to Cañon City makes for a great day trip.

★Shelf Road SCENIC DRIVE

(www.goldbeltbyway.com) An old stagecoach road that once connected Cañon City with Cripple Creek, much of this drive – with its red earth, low-growing piñon pines and juniper, and sheer limestone cliffs – feels like you've entered the set for an old Western. The final 8 miles of this 26-mile road are unpaved and definitely not for those with vertigo.

Coming from Cañon City, the first site you'll pass is the Garden Park Fossil Area (p313), the site of major dinosaur discoveries.

Further along is the Shelf Road Recreation Area, home to one of the top **sport climbing** destinations in the state. The 1000 or so bolted climbs are generally short (60ft to 140ft), but are accessible year- round – although the sun can be scorching in summer. You can camp at Sand Gulch Campground.

Past the climbing area is the 'shelf', where the drive narrows and really starts to get interesting. Originally a toll road ($1.75 stagecoach, 30¢ horse and rider), the next few miles were carved out of the canyon wall. Take it slow in this section as fallen rocks on the road and oncoming cars can pose a major hazard – you wouldn't want to suddenly swerve. Give yourself two hours to reach Cripple Creek.

Royal Gorge Route Railroad RAILROAD TRIP

(☎888-724-5748; www.royalgorgeroute.com; 330 Royal Gorge Blvd; adult/child from $39/28; ⏰9am, 12:30pm, 3:30pm & 6:30pm summer, reduced hr rest of yr) In 1999, following a 32-year hiatus, passenger service on the Royal Gorge Route, a 12-mile segment of the old Denver & Rio Grande train line, was restored. Visitors can make the two-hour ride in carriages or open-air observation cars from Cañon City to Parkdale and back through the majestic gorge. Riding these rails along the Arkansas River is unforgettable.

Trips range from the basic to more eventful journeys with lunch, dinner, wine, and even a murder. Make that a staged murder, which you can help solve. Then there's the Santa Express, a popular family trip during the Christmas season. Trips begin and end at the old Santa Fe Depot in Cañon City.

Fort Royal Stables HORSEBACK RIDING

(☎866-678-8880; www.fortroyalstables.com; 44899 Hwy 50; per person per hr $30; ⏰9am-5pm) Cañon City's top horseback outfitter, just east of the Royal Gorge turnoff, offers some tremendous rides through high plains country with massive mountain and Royal Gorge views. It accepts walk-ins, but the three-hour rides require a reservation and a four-person minimum.

RAFTING THE ROYAL GORGE

The best way to see the Royal Gorge is on a raft, but the 7 miles of class IV and V Arkansas River white water are not for the timid. Half-day trips start a few miles upriver from the gorge and are 10 to 12 miles in length. Full-day trips are approximately 20 to 22 miles. Tour operators typically require rafters to be over 18 years of age in the early season (May to June) or over 12 years when the flow diminishes by midsummer (July to September). Thrills are at their highest in the early season.

There's a large gathering of rafting guides near the Royal Gorge turnoff, 8 miles west of Cañon City, and a few others who operate out of Salida and Buena Vista also run the trip. The following operators are recommended:

Buffalo Joe's (☎866-283-3563; www.buffalojoe.com; 45000 Hwy 50, Buena Vista; half/full day $76/125)

Raft Masters (☎719-275-6645; www.raftmasters.com; 2315 E Main St, Cañon City; half/full day $75/120)

Echo Canyon River Expeditions (☎800-755-3246; www.raftecho.com; 45000 Hwy 50, Cañon City; half/full day $76/125)

River Runners (☎800-723-8987; www.whitewater.net; 44641 Hwy 50, Cañon City; half/full day $75/125)

Arkansas River Tours (☎800-321-4352; www.arkansasrivertours.com; Hwy 50, Cañon City; half/full day $70/115)

Sleeping & Eating

Cañon City is no pageant winner, and as almost all sleeping options are right on the highway, you'd be better off spending the night in Salida or Florence if possible.

Sand Gulch Campground CAMPGROUND $
(www.blm.gov; Red Canyon Rd; tent sites $7) This first-come, first-served BLM-managed campground is north of Cañon City on Red Canyon/Shelf Rd and is mostly used by climbers; the desert location is ideal. There is no water here. A similar site, the Banks, is further north.

Best Value Inn MOTEL $
(719-275-3377; www.americasbestvalueinn.com; 1925 Fremont Dr; d $89; P) Rooms are decent value and three-star quality with fresh paint, a rather nice showerhead and crown moldings. Family units are huge with two queen beds and a sofa, but you do get Hwy 50 traffic noise here. The sign outside says 'Royal Gorge Lobby.'

American Inn MOTEL $
(719-269-1158; 1231 Royal Gorge Blvd; r $45; P) No frills, and as clean and cheap as rooms get in Cañon City. Sure, you get a touch of the prison-visitor traffic, but that's all part of the adventure.

Hampton Inn HOTEL $$
(719-269-1112; www.canoncity.hamptoninn.com; 102 McCormick Pkwy; r incl breakfast from $175; P) Stark and standing alone at the eastern end of town, past Walmart, this is the most comfortable choice in the area. It's a chain, but rooms are large (all have two queen beds) with wood furnishings and flat-screen TVs.

El Caporal MEXICAN $
(719-276-2001; 1028 Main St; lunch $5.75-7, dinner $6.75-12; 11am-9pm;) This funky, family-owned diner serves up decent Mexican fare. Tuck into *carne asada,* grilled chicken dinners with refried beans, rice and guacamole, tasty chicken *tacos al carbon,* enchiladas, burritos, chimichangas and a fine *arroz con pollo* (chicken with rice). The tortilla and green chili soups get rave reviews, too.

Merlino's Belvedere Restaurant ITALIAN $$$
(719-275-5558; www.belvedererestaurant.com; 1330 Elm Ave; lunch $7-12, dinner $15.50-28.50; noon-2pm & 5-8pm Mon-Fri, noon-9pm Sat, noon-7:30pm Sun;) Back when Cañon City was less enlightened the Italian immigrants – who came here to work the land and grow food – were confined to these plains south of the river. A generation later in 1945, Merlino's opened up and it's still running, with hearty American-Italian meals served in a basement dining room that resembles something from the *Love Boat.*

There are lavender booths, kitschy fountains and silk plants, but you aren't here for the decor. If you don't get a steak, order the handmade *cavatelli* (potato pasta), spaghetti, manicotti or fettuccine and top it with chicken, meatball or house-made sausage. Lunch is not served on weekdays in the off-season.

Information

Ranger Office (719-269-8500; www.fs.usda.gov; 3028 E Main St; 8am-4pm Mon-Fri) Sharing an office with the Bureau of Land Management (BLM), this office has topo maps and camping and hiking tips for the Spanish Peaks Wilderness, the Gold Belt Byway and the southern Sangre de Cristos.

Getting There & Away

Cañon City is on US 50, 40 miles west of Pueblo and 59 miles east of Salida.

Florence

Lying in the southeastern Colorado lowlands, amid the old pasturelands and, relatively speaking, devoid of the sort of mountain views that define much of the state, is the flowering of something funky and beautiful. Here's a town in transition from depressed farming community to regional magnet for the antique-collector set. People come from across Colorado to sift through bins and hunt for gems almost every weekend, while the area's shop owners work together to promote their goods. It's a nice cooperative movement, with more than a dozen galleries lined up on historic Main St.

The award-winning **Florence Rose** (719-784-4734; www.florencerose.net; 1305 W 3rd St; r $139-239;) is a cute B&B that provides a nicer alternative to staying in Cañon City.

Florence is about 8 miles southeast of Cañon City. To get here take 9th St south across the river and you'll be on Colorado Hwy 115, which takes a rather sinuous route on its way to Florence. You'll need to look out for the signs to make sure you stay on the right road.

PUEBLO & THE SANTA FE TRAIL

For those who like to walk along the old wagon ruts of history, back to a more rugged day when 'cowboys and Indians' wasn't a game, but a way of life, driving the Santa Fe Trail will offer a fun day of diversion. For others, well, it's just a series of informational plaques along the highway – but no one will be able to miss the real beauty of the journey.

From the wild sunny prairie around Bent's Fort to the high mesas and billowing clouds outside Trinidad on the New Mexico border, without forgetting a stopover to admire the ancient volcanic walls of the twin Spanish Peaks near La Veta, this long-traveled route provides just the right balance of history and superb landscapes.

Pueblo

POP 107,577 / ELEV 4695FT

When America first expanded west, one pioneer at a time, the Arkansas River – which bisects Pueblo – was the border between the United States and Old Mexico. Following the Mexican-American War (1846–48), developers began turning this eastern Colorado market town into a railroad hub and steel manufacturing center. It went on to become Colorado's second-largest city and eventually earned the moniker 'Pittsburgh of the West', thanks to the success of Colorado Fuel & Iron.

However, business flagged after WWII and with the steel market crash in 1982, Pueblo's steady decline turned into a free fall, which has only recently abated. But all that history makes for an interesting downtown wander. Seventy buildings and places are listed on the National Historic Register, and plaques have been installed detailing local history along Grand and Union Aves, between 1st and B Sts.

While you wouldn't go out of your way to visit, Pueblo continues to occupy an important crossroads – today it's the intersection of I-25 and Hwy 50 – and for the many road-trippers that are passing through, it's certainly worth a stopover.

Sights & Activities

★El Pueblo History Museum MUSEUM

(www.historycolorado.org; 301 N Union Ave; adult/child $5/4; 10am-4pm Tue-Sat; P) Set on central plaza, the original site of Fort Pueblo (an American fort established in 1842 and held until 1854, when a Ute and Apache raid on Christmas Day caused the fort to be abandoned), this airy, modern museum with a stunning interior houses treasures from the Pueblo past.

Exhibits include an old cannon, a family teepee and a cut from a massive old tree that once stood over present-day Union Ave and was ominously called the hanging tree. Saturday is family day, when kids under 12 are granted free admission.

Rosemount Museum MUSEUM

(www.rosemount.org; 419 West 14th St; adult/child 6-18yr $6/4; 10am-3.30pm Tue-Sat, closed Jan;) Pueblo's premier historic attraction is this three-story, 37-room Victorian mansion, constructed in 1893 of pink rhyolite stone. It contains elaborate stained glass and elegant, original furnishings. The top floor features an Egyptian mummy and other assorted booty from philanthropist Andrew McClelland's global travels during the early 20th century.

Nature & Raptor Center of Pueblo WILDLIFE SANCTUARY

(719-549-2414; www.natureandraptor.org; 5200 Nature Center Rd; per car $3; grounds 6am-10pm daily, Raptor Center 11am-4pm Tue-Sun; P) Riverside trails, reptile displays, picnic and playground areas and a raptor center bring people beneath the cottonwoods on the Arkansas River. The raptor program began in 1981 to assist the Department of Wildlife in rehabilitating injured birds of prey. The turnoff for Nature Center Rd is 3 miles west of downtown, north of the Pueblo Ave Bridge.

Sangre de Cristo Art Center MUSEUM

(719-295-7200; www.sdc-arts.org; 210 N Santa Fe Ave; adult/child 3-16yr $4/3; 11am-4pm Tue-Sat) Set in three brick buildings, housing seven galleries that feature both fine and regional historical arts and crafts, this is more than just Pueblo's art museum. It's also an arts center with more than 100 music, dance and fine-arts classes each quarter. Admission also includes entrance to the Buell Children's Museum.

THE SANTA FE TRAIL

One of the great overland trade routes of the 19th century, the Santa Fe Trail stretched from Missouri to New Mexico (a Mexican province from 1821 to 1848), bringing manufactured European and American goods west, and Mexican silver and Native American jewelry, blankets and furs east. The 800-mile route took seven to eight weeks to cross with a covered wagon, and was defined by monotony and hardship. Near Dodge City in Kansas, the route divided in two: the southern road (Cimarron Route) cut down into New Mexico, and was shorter but more dangerous, due to a lack of water and hostile Native Americans. The northern road (Mountain Route) continued through Bent's Fort and Trinidad in Colorado and was longer but safer. With the expansion of the railroad west, trade along the route eventually diminished, coming to a close in 1880. You can drive the route today, following Hwys 56, 50 and 350.

Buell Children's Museum MUSEUM
(☎719-295-7200; www.sdc-arts.org/buellchildrensmuseum.html; 210 N Santa Fe Ave; adult/child 3-16yr $4/3; ⏱11am-4pm Tue-Sat; 👪) This is the place to climb into classic cars, jam to old rock-and-roll, build bridges, swim with jellyfish, create magical fairy lands and discover the power of numbers while exploring exhibits that help kids learn with a smile on their faces. It should appeal to kids up to the age of 14.

Riverwalk WATERFRONT
(www.puebloriverwalk.org; 101 S Union Ave; pedal boats per 30min $10, gondola tours $5; ⏱boat rental & tours weekends May-Aug; 👪) FREE A pedestrian-friendly and peacefully lazy channeled slice of the Arkansas – the rest of it is running more fiercely underground – this is the center of historic Pueblo. There are sidewalks on both sides of the river and plenty of shady seating too. It runs for about four blocks and during the summer months you can book pedal boats or take a gondola tour. The city also hosts occasional concerts and events here.

Sleeping

With one exception, Pueblo's sleeping options are all chains. Eagleridge Blvd (I-25, exit 102) in north Pueblo has more than a half-dozen familiar names; **Hampton Inn** (☎719-543-6500; http://hamptoninn.hilton.com; 4790 Eagleridge Cir; r $109-169; ❄📶🏊👪) is the best of the bunch.

Edgar Olin House B&B
(☎719-544-5727; www.olin-house.com; 727 W 13th St; r $79-159; P❄📶) This three-story brick home is set in Pueblo's architecturally interesting, though somewhat dilapidated, historic residential district. With period furnishings in the Victorian interior and welcoming hosts, this is the finest place to stay in town.

Eating

Franco's Bistro BISTRO $
(210 N Santa Fe Ave; kids' menu $2.50, mains $5.50-6.75; ⏱9am-7pm) Parents with kids in tow should definitely consider this family restaurant in the Buell Children's Museum.

Hopscotch Bakery BAKERY, ICE CREAM $
(333 S Union Ave; sandwiches $8; ⏱7am-4pm Tue-Sat; 👪) If you are just passing through long enough to see a few sights and grab a bite to eat, make that bite happen here. There are fresh pastries and quiche of the day, cookies, tarts and home-made ice cream, and some terrific gourmet sandwiches with capicola ham, chicken breast and balsamic-vinegar-soaked portobello mushrooms. No seating.

Bingo Burger BURGERS $
(www.bingoburger.com; 101 Central Plaza; burgers $5.75-9.75; ⏱11am-8pm Mon-Sat; 👪) A locally owned downtown burger joint – it's conveniently right across from the History Museum – Bingo uses only locally produced grass-fed lamb and beef, and it does chicken and portobello burgers too. Cheese options include blue and goat's cheese and it has both sweet potato and regular fries. Shakes and malts are made with Hopscotch ice cream

dc's on B Street BISTRO $$
(☎719-584-3410; 115 West B St; lunch $8-12, dinner $12-20; ⏱lunch Mon-Sat, dinner Wed-Sat) This cute B St bistro (located in the old Coors Building) offers some of the best eats in town. It does a terrific Reuben on marbled rye and a Poulet Pueblo with tomato chutney for lunch, and fancier fare for dinner. Think steak au poivre, Colorado lamb and

lemon-pepper fettuccine. It's several blocks south of the Riverwalk.

Information

Pueblo Chamber of Commerce (800-233-3446; www.pueblochamber.org; 302 N Santa Fe Ave; 8am-5pm Mon-Fri)

Ranger Office (719-553-1400; www.fs.usda.gov/psicc; 2840 Kachina Dr, off Hwy 50; 8:30am-4pm Mon-Fri) This ranger office supervises all offices in the San Isabel and Pike National Forests, and the Comanche Grasslands to the east.

Getting There & Away

Pueblo is 112 miles south of Denver and 45 miles south of Colorado Springs at the crossroads of I-25 and US 50.

Greyhound (800-231-2222; www.greyhound.com; 123 Court St) Pueblo's Greyhound bus depot offers service north to Colorado Springs and Denver, and south into New Mexico.

La Veta & the Spanish Peaks

POP 857 / ELEV 7013FT

Beautifully set in high country rangeland and at the base of the stunning Spanish Peaks, La Veta, a small historic town, is undiscovered Colorado at its finest.

It comes with all the magnificent beauty of the best of the Rockies with none of the crowds, and a touch of small-town charm too. Here's a place where paved streets are outnumbered by churches. It would take a serious effort to get lost in La Veta – its compass-oriented grid is divided by north-south Main St (Hwy 12). Most businesses are at the north end near the old narrow-gauge railroad. Following Hwy 12 south from town will take you on the Hwy of Legends byway, which wraps around the Spanish Peaks before reaching Trinidad.

Sights & Activities

Francisco Fort Museum MUSEUM

(719-742-5501; www.franciscofort.org; 306 S Main St; adult/child $5/free; 10am-4pm Tue-Sat, 11am-3pm Sun Jun-Aug;) This museum is set on the site of the original 1862 fort, with a couple of the real deal buildings still left. It was built by 12 men as a base of operations for settlement, trade and Indian protection – meaning protection from Native Americans, which involved attacking the Ute and surrounding tribes.

SPACe Gallery GALLERY

(Gallery in the Park; www.spanishpeaksarts.org; 132 W Ryus St; hr vary) More than two-dozen artists display paintings, pottery, glasswork and weavings at this cooperative gallery built in 1983 by the origins of what has become the Spanish Peaks Arts Council. It's a two-minute walk east of Railroad Park.

★ **Spanish Peaks Wilderness** HIKING

(www.spanishpeakscountry.com; Jun-Oct) Long before you make it into town the twin Spanish Peaks, named for their past life as part of Old Mexico, loom majestically over this valley. The East Spanish Peak is 12,708ft, while West Spanish Peak is nearly 1000ft higher at 13,625ft.

With incredible vertical stone dikes erupting from the earth and down their shoulders like some kind of primordial fence line, these are mountains begging to be explored.

If you drive up Hwy 12, you'll arrive at Cuchara Pass (9994ft), from where you can follow a forest service road 6.5 miles east to the **Cordova Pass Trailhead** ($5 parking

WORTH A TRIP

WALSENBURG MINING MUSEUM

This **museum** (www.spanishpeakscountry.com; 112 W 5th St; adult/child 12-18yr $2/1; 10am-4pm Mon-Fri, 10am-1pm Sat) is the only reason to stop in Walsenburg on the way to or from the Spanish Peaks. Set in the old jailhouse (built in 1896), it's a monument to the struggle for labor laws in the Colorado mining industry, in the days leading up to the 1913 Ludlow Massacre.

That's when Mary Harris 'Mother' Jones was held for civil disobedience in the basement of the county courthouse next door. She was held there for 20 days when she was 82 years old! There's a great picture of her leading a march through Trinidad. There is also an interesting display on the 1927 strike by the Industrial Workers of the World (IWW; also known as Wobblies), and it has old mining equipment like bellows and trip hammers and old lanterns. The docent will lead you through the museum.

GREAT DIKES OF THE SPANISH PEAKS

Some of the Kapota band of the Ute tribe aptly referred to the volcanic Spanish Peaks as *wahatoya* – 'breasts of the earth.' Spanish and American travelers relied on these twin sentinels to guide their approach to the Front Range across the eastern Great Plains.

On closer inspection, you'll find hundreds of magnificent rock walls radiating like fins from the peaks. Called 'dikes,' they were formed from fissures, surrounding the volcanic core, being filled up with magma, later turning into solid rock as it cooled. Subsequent erosion has exposed the dikes, leaving a peculiar landscape of abrupt perpendicular rock walls protruding from the earth. This is the largest collection of such dikes in the world.

For an opportunity to see wildlife and wildflowers, you can explore the great dikes on foot by following the **Wahatoya Trail** along the saddle between the East and West Spanish Peaks, or from the road along scenic Hwy 12, which intersects the dikes at several different points.

fee; there are also three campsites here). From the trailhead it's a steep 2.5-mile climb to the summit of the West Peak over scree and stones; this is the most popular route up. Figure on 2½ hours up and make sure you're off the summit by noon.

The Wahatoya Trail (12 miles one-way) traverses the saddle between the peaks. As you approach the peaks, you may see the remnants of the 2013 wildfire that burned the north side of the East Peak.

All told there are 65 miles of trails in the area: all three campgrounds offer hiking in the Sangre de Cristos to the west. Stop by the ranger offices in Cañon City (p315), Pueblo (p318) or (if you're lucky) La Veta for maps and trail info.

Sleeping & Eating

La Veta Inn HOTEL $$

(☎719-742-3700; http://lavetainn.com; 103 W Ryus Ave; r $109-149; ❄ 📶) This inviting hotel has 18 comfortable rooms, equipped with feather mattresses and each personalized by a different artist. Just south of the railroad tracks, it's the main place to sleep, eat and drink in town. The restaurant serves up tempting Southwestern fare.

Information

Ranger Office (103 S Main St; ⏰hr vary) This is actually a work station, not a true ranger office, so you'll be very lucky if you actually catch someone inside. That said, you should be able to find some brochures and basic maps outside the door. It's at the south end of town.

Highway of Legends

Following Hwy 12 south from town will take you on the Hwy of Legends byway, which wraps around the west side of the Spanish Peaks before reaching Trinidad to the south. This road offers the best access to the hiking and camping opportunities in the area.

Cuchara

A stunning stretch of Hwy 12 connects La Veta with Cuchara, a small ranch town in the Spanish Peaks Wilderness. Here are lush green hills crowned with the Spanish Peaks' Great Dikes: stark vertical granite walls jutting like an archaic boundary up from somewhere deep. They rise and recede through meadows and on mesas, and always looming behind them are those Spanish Peaks, which happen to be two million years older than the Continental Divide.

The town of Cuchara is even smaller than La Veta, with just one dirt road (Cuchara Ave). That's where you'll find its only restaurant and a couple of inns. All around here are unbelievable snowshoeing and cross-country skiing trails in winter, and hiking and climbing routes in summer. If you attempt to bag the peaks, know that because they stand alone lightning is a real hazard. Get off the high ground before noon and you'll be fine.

Sleeping & Eating

Yellow Pine Guest Ranch DUDE RANCH $$

(☎719-742-3528; www.yellowpine.us; 15890 Hwy 12; cabins $105-180; horseback rides per hr $30; ⏰May-Oct; P 🚭 👪 🐾) The Yellow Pine is located up in Cuchara, where you can rent cute red cabins (two to eight people) oriented perfectly with marvelous valley, meadow and West Peak views. There are horse professionals to take you riding, old wagon wheels lining the driveway and a stream meandering through the property.

★Dog Bar & Grill PUB FOOD $
(☎719-742-6366; www.dogbarcuchara.com; 34 Cuchara Ave; sandwiches from $8, large pizza from $19; ⏱from 11am in summer, reduced hr winter;) The Dog Bar is a Cuchara institution with its wood bar, wide inviting patio, pool table, live music on weekends and damn good pizzas.

Monument Park

Evergreen forests surround Monument Park, 29 miles south of La Veta and 38 miles west of Trinidad on Hwy 12. The park is named for a rock formation rising from the waters of an attractive mountain reservoir. Numerous summer activities are offered, including fishing on the trout-stocked lake, horseback riding and mountain biking.

Monument Park Lake Resort CAMPGROUND $
(☎719-868-2226; www.monumentlakeresort.com; 4789 Hwy 12; tent sites $20, RV sites $20-29, cabins & lodges $99-119; hmid-May–mid-Sep;) This popular resort has camping and RV sites, as well as showers and coin-operated laundry. There are also lodge rooms and cabins decorated in Southwestern style. The resort's restaurant serves decent home-style American food. The resort is only open in the summer, though you can fish here year round ($7 day pass per vehicle).

Purgatoire Campground CAMPGROUND $
(☎877-444-6777; www.recreation.gov; Hwy 12; tent sites $16; ⏱May–mid-Oct;) One of three campgrounds in the Spanish Peaks Wilderness Area, Purgatoire is the only one that you can reserve. It's located 4 miles west of Monument Lake, off Hwy 12, at the base of the Sangre de Cristos. Closer to La Veta, just before Cuchara Pass, are the first-come, first-served Blue Lake and Bear Lake campgrounds, also 4 miles west of the highway.

TRINIDAD

POP 9125 / ELEV 6025FT

Tucked into a chimney-top mesa, quiet Trinidad sits on the Purgatoire River, which flows down from the heights of the Sangre de Cristo Mountains and the Spanish Peaks in the west. The town's past – from its origins as a Spanish outpost and Santa Fe Trail stopover to its coal-mining period when it played a central role in a groundbreaking labor dispute – is documented in its museums and on the brick-paved streets.

While the history buffs may want to take their time here, road-trippers will smell adventure on the pine-tinged winds streaming down Rte 12 from Cucharas Pass on the Highway of Legends, the scenic drive that passes through the Spanish Peaks Wilderness (p318).

Sights & Activities

★Trinidad History Museum MUSEUM
(www.coloradohistory.org; 312 E Main St; adult/child $8/3; ⏱9am-4pm Mon-Sat May-Sep) This is a lot of museum, a full city block in fact, set smack dab on Main St. There are three sights here: the adobe Baca House (1870), the French-style Bloom Mansion (1882) and the Santa Fe Trail museum. Early settlers Felipe and Dolores Baca, who came to Trinidad in the 1860s, bought the unusual two-story Baca House for 22,000 pounds of wool in 1873. Entry is by tour only (open 10am to 3pm).

Next door is the Bloom Mansion, a symmetrical brick building with French eaves and moldings on the exterior and wrought iron on the roof and terraces.

But the real prize here is the Santa Fe Trail museum, set in the Baca's workers cottage. Displays trace the course of early Trinidad – an interesting mix of Mexicans and settlers from as far off as Nova Scotia – through its heyday during the Santa Fe Trail peak and on to its transformation as a railroad and mining town.

Arthur Roy Mitchell Memorial Museum of Western Art MUSEUM
(☎719-846-4224; www.armitchell.us; 150 E Main St; adult/child $3/free, Sun free; ⏱10am-5pm Tue-Sat, noon-4pm Sun May-Sep;) Also known as 'The Mitch,' this pleasant gallery was built in honor of local cowboy artist, and the original, if unofficial, town historian, AR Mitchell. Set in a late-19th-century department store (those tiled ceilings are original), the ground floor is the permanent collection of Mitchell's work: cowboys, horses, Western landscapes, more horses and more cowboys.

Upstairs, there's a rotating exhibition space, and the basement has a terrific collection of historic Trinidad photos. There are Mitchell pieces for sale along with turquoise jewelry and quirky cowboy gifts in the adjacent gift shop.

Louden-Henritze Archaeology Museum MUSEUM
(600 Prospect St; 10am-3pm Mon-Thu) FREE This small museum is located on the campus of Trinidad State Junior College, north of I-25. It's only one room and the exhibits could do with some more context, but it's nonetheless a quick intro to the area's geology and prehistory. In addition to fossils and artifacts, there's even a mammoth tusk.

Ludlow Massacre Memorial MONUMENT
(Colorado County Rd 44) FREE In 1914 striking migrant workers were living in a large tent city in Ludlow. After a series of conflicts, the Colorado National Guard were called in. An ensuing clash saw the tent city razed, resulting in the deaths of 21 people – including two women and 11 children. This well-executed stone monument, just north of Trinidad, was dedicated by the United Mine Workers to tell the story.

Displays include testimonials of those involved with the strike and tent camp, and a timeline of the mine workers' struggle. There's also a display about company towns, a practice used by management to create a climate of indentured servitude.

Trinidad Lake State Park OUTDOORS
(719-846-6951; www.parks.state.co.us; Hwy 12; vehicle pass per day $7) Three miles west of the city, off Hwy 12, this park sits on a bluff above the Purgatoire River, downstream from the reservoir dam. Hiking, wildlife viewing, an interpretive nature trail, fishing and boating on the reservoir are available.

Southside Park SKATEBOARDING, DISC GOLF
(1309 Beshore Dr; 8am-10pm) FREE This viable community center at the south end of Trinidad has acres of athletic fields, a public pool and, according to the legendary Tony Hawk, one of the top skate parks in the US. The sport's longest grind is possible on the 120ft flat wall. Next to the skate park is Trinidad's disc golf course.

Sleeping

Trail's End Motel MOTEL $
(719-846-4425; 616 E Main St; s/d $44/49; P ❄ wi-fi) Blessed with a vintage neon sign and a nice flowery sundeck, this hole-in-the-wall motel isn't fancy, but it is great value and very friendly. Family-owned and operated, it has small rooms with recently remodeled bathrooms, satellite TV and wi-fi, and will do for a one-night pit stop.

Carpios Ridge Campground CAMPGROUND $
(http://coloradostateparks.reserveamerica.com; tent sites $10-16, RV sites $20-24) About a mile west of the dam at Trinidad Lake State Park, this campground has flush toilets, showers and coin laundry, along with 62 sites for RVs and tents. There's a $10 booking fee if you reserve.

★ **Tarabino Inn** B&B $$
(719-846-2115; www.tarabinoinn.com; 310 E 2nd St; r $84-129; wi-fi, family, pets) There are four guest rooms in this beautifully restored Italianate villa, by far the classiest sleep in Trinidad, with antique-style furnishings. The cheaper rooms on the 3rd floor share a bath (though they do have prime access to the top-floor widow's walk), while the two suites have private baths with huge claw-foot tubs. This place is listed among ghost hunters as a possessor of benevolent spirits. Guests have felt a presence. Even the skeptical host admits to the possibility.

Holiday Inn & Suites HOTEL $$
(719-845-8400; www.holidayinn.com; 3130 Santa Fe Trail; r $109-135; P ❄ wi-fi pool family pets) This is the best of the chains that are scattered a couple of miles south of downtown. Rooms are large with a king or two queen beds, huge Samsung flatscreens, free wi-fi throughout and excellent service.

Eating

Although there are a handful of restaurants in this sleepy town, it's worth noting that most are closed Sundays, Mondays and/or Tuesdays.

CH...CH...CH...CHANGES

Before arriving here you'll probably hear that Trinidad is unofficially credited with being the sex-change capital of the USA. However, you won't find much evidence among the local population. Dr Stanley Biber, who passed away in 2006, was chiefly responsible for this reputation via his supposedly cash-only practice, which changed the genders of 4500 people.

★**The Cafe** CAFE $

(135 E Main St; dishes $3.50-10; 8am-4pm Mon-Fri, 9am-2pm Sat;) This cafe, set in the Danielson Dry Goods building, is a terrific find. In the morning it does gourmet egg wraps, such as the Santa Fe (eggs, bacon, spicy corn salsa, Anaheim chili, cheese and crème fraiche) or the Farmers Market (eggs, artichoke hearts, oven-roasted tomatoes, Parmesan and creamy basil spread). Tantalizing sandwiches and salads for lunch.

Nana & Nano's ITALIAN $

(719-846-2696; 418 E Main St; mains $6.75-12.25; 10:30am-7:30pm Wed-Sat) Given the historical connection of Italian miners to the area, it shouldn't be a surprise that there are several Italian restaurants in town. This deli is a Trinidad institution with fine meats, specialty cheeses and homemade sandwiches. It does tasty meatball and sausage heroes as well as a 'heavenly combo' with a roasted green chili.

The pasta dinners are less impressive, however – stick to the sandwiches.

Bella Luna PIZZA $$

(719-846-2750; 121 W Main St; pizzas $11-18.50; 11am-3pm & 5-9pm Mon & Wed-Sat, noon-6pm Sun;) Wood-fired pizza in an antiquated dark-wood Main St dining room with exposed brick walls, high ceilings and good beer on tap. Locals rave.

Rino's ITALIAN $$$

(719-845-0949; www.rinostrinidad.com; 400 E Main St; mains $12-25; 5-9pm Wed-Sun) Situated in an antiquated stone church, Rino's is where Las Vegas meets Little Italy, and your chicken parmigiana is served by a singing waiter. No joke. Hey Frankie, keep the wine coming.

Information

Colorado Welcome Center (719-846-9512; www.colorado.com; 309 Nevada Ave; 8am-6pm Jun-Aug, to 5pm Sep-May) One of 10 state-run welcome centers in the state, this one serves travelers coming north from New Mexico and offers an array of maps and brochures detailing tourism options in southeast Colorado.

Getting There & Away

Greyhound buses stop at **JR's Travel Shoppe** (719-846-7271; www.greyhound.com; 639 W Main St), a Conoco gas station near I-25 exit 13B. **Amtrak's** (800-872-7245; www.amtrak.com; 110 W Pine St) *Southwest Chief* passes through Trinidad on its daily Chicago–Los Angeles route.

Bent's Old Fort National Historic Site

Seven miles east of La Junta is **Bent's Old Fort National Historic Site** (www.nps.gov/beol; 35110 Hwy 194; adult/child $3/2; 8am-5:30pm Jun-Aug, 9am-4pm Sep-May;), easily the best site in the Colorado plains. Set just north of the Arkansas River, the natural and official border between the US and Old Mexico, the fort (1833–49) was once a cultural crossroads and the busiest settlement west of Missouri. Built by the Bent brothers (Charles and William), it was a place where information and goods were exchanged, and it provided shelter for every culture and type of person traveling in the West at that time: traders, trappers, explorers, soldiers, naturalists and pioneers.

Although the Bents are credited with having established the fort, the local Cheyenne chief, Yellow Wolf, was instrumental in determining the fort's location. Yellow Wolf offered the Bents access to the surrounding land and intertribal trade networks, hoping to forge an important alliance with the new wave of settlers. The Bents, too, saw the wisdom of creating local alliances; soon after building the fort, William married Owl Woman, the daughter of another important chief, White Thunder. Tragically, after the closure of Bent's Fort, Yellow Wolf was betrayed by the new settlers and murdered during the Sand Creek Massacre (p323).

Today, the old fort has been restored beautifully and is staffed by knowledgeable guides in period clothing. It has a blacksmith's shop and a wood shop, and the general store is stocked with rifles, sacks of grain, barrels of sugar, cases of wine, whiskey, ammo and buffalo pelts, and furnished with 19th-century antiques.

A paved trail leading from the parking lot to the fort skirts a natural wetland, and a very flat, easy hiking trail (about 1 mile) runs around the fort to the edge of the Arkansas River and back to the parking lot. Staff offer two tours per day most of the year (10:30am and 1pm) and four during summer.

Boggsville Historic Site

You can continue in Kit Carson's footsteps to the **Boggsville Historic Site** (719-456-0453; Hwy 101; 10am-4pm Fri-Sun May, 10am-5pm daily Jun-Oct;) FREE, about 16 miles east of Bent's Fort and 2 miles south on Colorado Hwy 101. Nestled on the Purgatoire River, this was Carson's homestead and trading center, which he built in the 1860s after the demise of the fort. Eventually it became the first county seat for Bent County when the railroad arrived in 1873.

Fort Lyon

The Bents did build another fort east of their old fort in 1853 and it was a profitable trading post until 1857, when a Colorado gold strike and the resulting land grab coupled with the mass slaughter of bison by Americans and Europeans spurred unrest among the Native Americans of the plains. As a result, the US cavalry built Fort Fauntleroy to protect settlers.

Later renamed Fort Lyon, it was from here that on November 29, 1864, John Chivington led the Colorado Volunteers in a dawn attack on Chief Black Kettle and his band, who had been told they would be safe if they moved to this desolate reservation. Over 100 Cheyenne and Arapahoe men, women and children were slaughtered and their corpses grotesquely mutilated, bringing a new wave of conflict to the Santa Fe Trail. The event is commemorated at the **Sand Creek Massacre National Historic Site** (www.nps.gov/sand; cnr County Rd 54 & County Rd W; 9am-4pm; P) FREE. Fort Lyon is located 19 miles east of Bent's Old Fort along Hwy 50.

Timpas & the Comanche National Grassland

Heading west from La Junta along Hwy 350 toward Trinidad, you'll pass another of the Santa Fe Trail's signature sites in Timpas: the gateway to the **Comanche National Grassland**, an unforgiving wilderness of hip-high grasses and wild grains, rising into small hills and diving into shallow canyons. After several thousand wagon crossings, the clay soil here was worn into ruts, which you can actually see at **Iron Spring** (cnr County Rd 9 & Hwy 350), just a mile down a well-graded dirt road off Hwy 350. Walking along the ruts, with the dry wind in your hair, it's easy to imagine the challenges that traders and settlers faced.

Iron Spring is a 1-mile drive down County Rd 9. It intersects Hwy 350 about 11 miles west of Timpas.

Picketwire Dinosaur Tracksite

Also in the Comanche National Grassland, but only accessible by organized tour, or on foot, is a whole different kind of tracksite. This one is all about the migration of dinosaurs.

The quarter-mile **Picketwire Dinosaur Tracksite** (719-384-2181; www.recreation.gov; 1420 E 3rd St; adult/child $15/10.50; by reservation, May-Jun & Sep–mid-Oct) is the largest documented site of its kind in North America, with as many as 1300 visible dinosaur tracks. Some 150 million years ago, two types of dinosaurs, *Allosaurus* and *Apatosaurus* (*Brontosaurus*), migrated along the muddy shoreline of a large prehistoric lake.

You must reserve a guided auto tour through La Junta Ranger District if you intend to drive. You can also hike from the Withers Canyon trailhead, which is an 11.3-mile round-trip hike along Picketwire Canyon Trail to the dinosaur prints.

GREAT SAND DUNES & THE SAN LUIS VALLEY

The strange and mysterious San Luis Valley is the driest part of Colorado, hemmed in by the San Juan Mountains to the west and the Sangre de Cristos to the east. Despite the seemingly barren landscape, however, the valley holds many surprises – the most famous of which is the rippling sea of sand at the Great Sand Dunes.

The valley was also the first part of Colorado to be permanently settled, when Hispanic pioneers set out from Taos in the mid-19th century to find new homesteads, and their influence still defines valley culture today.

But the most important thing of all to know is that this is one of the top areas in the world for alien sightings and abductions. Don't say we didn't warn you!

Fort Garland

POP 433 / ELEV 7936FT

Fort Garland (1858–83) was established to protect Hispanic and white settlers in the San Luis Valley from Ute raids, and Union troops stationed here marched in a campaign against Confederates in Texas during the Civil War. For a short time the outpost was under the direction of famed frontier scout Kit Carson. Though Carson successfully negotiated a period of peace with Utes, all hell broke loose following the Meeker Massacre in 1879. After that, the fort became a major base of operations in the forcible removal of Utes from the area.

Today Fort Garland – all five square blocks of it – is the first town encountered by westbound travelers in the San Luis Valley. The **fort** (www.historycolorado.org; Hwy 159, off Hwy 160; adult/child $5/3.50; 9am-5pm daily Apr-Oct, 10am-4pm Thu-Mon Nov-Mar;) contains five of the original 22 buildings and is a good spot to cool the engine.

Sleeping & Eating

Fort Garland Motor Inn MOTEL $
(719-379-2993; www.garlandmotorinn.com; 411 Hwy 160; d $79-105;) Although there's not really any reason to stay in Fort Garland – unless you're looking for an alternative base from which to explore the Sand Dunes – this clean and well-run motel is a good spot in a pinch. Rates vary depending upon occupancy.

All Gon Pizza AMERICAN $
(719-379-2222; http://allgonrestaurant.com; 319 Beaubien Ave, off Hwy 160; mains $7-9, pizzas $14; 11am-9pm, closed Sun in winter;) This popular restaurant serves up pizza, pasta, Mexican fare and peach and mango milkshakes, and is generally regarded as the best place to eat for miles around (and we mean miles).

Getting There & Away

From Fort Garland it's 8.5 miles east to the Hwy 150 turnoff to the Great Sand Dunes National Monument, 26 miles east to Alamosa or 17 miles south to San Luis via Hwy 159.

Great Sand Dunes National Park

ELEV 8200FT

For all of Colorado's striking natural sights, this sea of sand – the country's youngest, quietest and most diverse national park – is a place where nature's magic is on full display.

At the center of the **park** (719-378-6399; www.nps.gov/grsa; 11999 Hwy 150; adult/child $3/free; visitor center 8:30am-6:30pm summer, shorter hr rest of yr) is a 55-sq-mile dunefield, surrounded by steep mountain peaks on one side and glassy wetlands on the other. After long drives on the straight highways of the San Luis Valley or twisting mountain byways, it's a bit unnerving to find yourself so suddenly standing amid the landscape of the Sahara.

This is a place of stirring optical illusions. From the approach up Hwy 150, watch as the angles of sunlight make shifting shadows on the dunes; the most dramatic time is the day's end, when the hills come into high contrast as the sun drops low on the horizon. Hike past the edge of the dune field to see the shifting sand up close; the ceaseless wind works like a disconsolate sculptor, constantly creating and revising elegant ripples underfoot. Lose all perspective in the shadow of the dunes – the largest of which rise over 700ft. In this monochromatic, uninterrupted landscape, the only tool by which to judge distance is the sight of other hikers, trudging along like ants on the faraway dunes in this surreal, misplaced desert.

Activities

Most visitors limit their activities to the area where Medano Creek (pronounced *med*-ano) divides the main dune mass from the towering Sangre de Cristo Mountains. The remaining 85% of the park's area is designated wilderness – almost all major ecosystems are represented here, with the exception of volcanoes and coastline.

From the visitor center, a short trail leads to the Mosca Picnic Area next to ankle-deep Medano Creek, which you must ford (when the creek is running) to reach the dunes. Across the road from the visitor center, the Mosca Pass Trail climbs up into the Sangre de Cristo Wilderness.

The area beyond the Point of No Return parking lot is a good spot to get further out into the backcountry on backpacking trips; a road theoretically leads up to Medano Pass (9982ft) at the top of the Sangres, but because of the sand it's not recommended unless you have a suitable off-road vehicle.

Regardless of where you go, take a hat, closed shoes, sunscreen, water and bandanna to protect your face if the wind picks up.

Medano Creek

One of the most curious spectacles in the entire park, the snowmelt Medano Creek flows down from the Sangre de Cristos and along the eastern edge of the dunes. Peak flow is usually in late May or early June, and the rippling water over the sand creates a temporary beach of sorts, which is extremely popular with families. In years when the

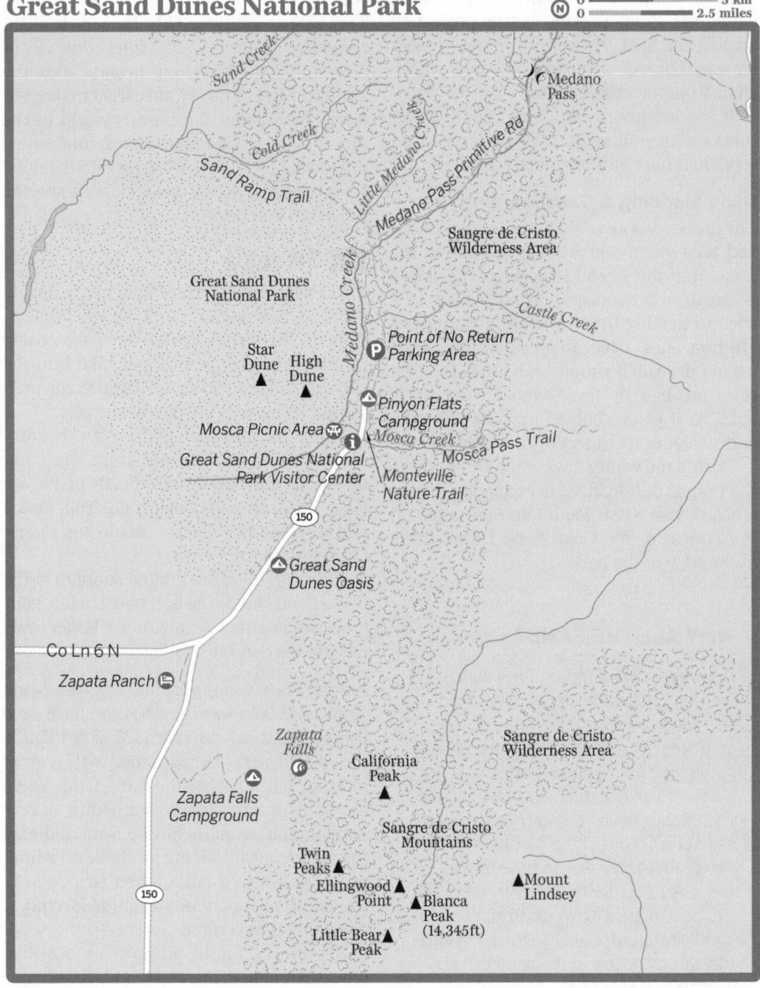

water is high enough (check the park website for daily water-level reports; the level of late has been very low), children can even float down the creek on an inner tube, right along the dunes. The combination of the creek's appeal and the end of the school year means that this is the park's peak season.

Hiking

There are no trails through this expansive field of sand, but it's the star attraction for hikers. Two informal hikes afford excellent panoramic views of the dunes. The first is a hike to High Dune (strangely, not the highest dune in the park), which departs from a parking area just beyond the visitor center. It's about 2.5 miles out to the peak and back, but be warned: it's not easy. As you trudge along up the hills of sand, it feels like you're taking a half-step back for every one forward. If you're up for it, try pushing on to the second worthy goal. Just west of High Dune is Star Dune (750ft), the tallest in the park.

In the middle of the summer, hikers should hit the hills during the morning, as the sand can reach 140°F (60°C) during the heat of the day. Although you might think sandals would be the footwear of choice, closed-toe shoes provide better protection against the heat. Those with limited mobility can borrow a dunes-accessible wheelchair from the visitor center.

If you are hiking with children, don't let them out of your sight. It is very easy to get separated once you've entered the dunes.

Dune Sledding & Sandboarding

The heavy wooden sled may seem like a bad idea when you're trudging out to the dunes, but the gleeful rush down the slopes is worth every footstep. There's a bit of a trick to making this work. Sand conditions are best after a recent precipitation; when it's too dry you'll simply sink. Also, the best rides are had by those who are relatively light, so if you've bulked up on microbrew and steaks, don't expect to zip down the hill.

During the winter days when snow covers the dunes, the sledding is excellent. To rent a board, visit Kristi Mountain Sports (p329) in Alamosa or the Great Sand Dunes Oasis at the edge of the park.

WHY ALL THE SAND?

Upon your first glimpse of the dunes, you can't help but wonder: where did all this sand come from, and why does it stay here? The answer lies in the unique geography and weather patterns of the San Luis Valley. Streams, snowmelt and flash floods have been carrying eroded sand and silt out of the San Juan Mountains (about 60 miles to the west) to the valley floor for millions of years.

There, prevailing winds from the southwest gradually blow the sand into the natural hollow at the southern end of the Sangre de Cristo range. At the same time, streams and stronger prevailing winds from the eastern mountains push back in the other direction, causing the sand to pile up into what are now the highest dunes in North America.

If you look closely at the sand (the visitor center has a magnifying glass) you'll see a spectrum of shapes and colors: 29 different rock and mineral types – from obsidian and sulfur to amethyst and turquoise – are represented in the sand's makeup.

Tours

Throughout summer NPS rangers lead interpretive nature walks from the visitor center and hold evening programs at the amphitheater. This is an excellent way to learn more about the unseen world of the dunes – surprising thickets of sunflowers, burrowing owls and even tiger salamanders! Inquire at the visitor center about specific programs and times.

Sleeping

Plan a visit to this extraordinary park during a full or new moon. Stock up on supplies, stop by the visitor center for a free backcountry camping permit and hike into the surreal landscape to set up camp in the middle of nowhere (bring plenty of water).

There are also half-a-dozen backcountry sites that can be accessed from the Point of No Return parking lot, north of Pinyon Flats. These sites vary in terrain, from alpine and woodland to desert – ask at the ranger office for details.

Although there are limited supplies at the Great Sand Dunes Oasis, it's best to buy your groceries in either Alamosa or a larger town outside the San Luis Valley.

Pinyon Flats Campground CAMPGROUND $
(888-448-1474; www.recreation.gov; Great Sand Dunes National Park; campsites $20;) This is the official park campground, with a great location not far from the dune field. There are 88 sites here, but be warned: it is very popular and regularly fills up from mid-May through August. Half are available on a first-come, first-served basis (open year-round); the other 44 (open May to mid-November) can be reserved online.

Reserve as far in advance as possible; otherwise, show up early and cross your fingers. Water and toilets are available here.

Zapata Falls Campground CAMPGROUND $
(www.fs.usda.gov; BLM Rd 5415; campsites $11; year-round;) Seven miles south of the national park, this campground offers glorious panoramas of the San Luis Valley from its 9000ft perch in the Sangre de Cristos. There are 23 first-come, first-served sites, but note that there is no water and that the 3.6-mile access road is steep and fairly washed out, making for slow going.

The payoff, however, is worth it, especially if you prefer a secluded location.

RECOMMENDED HIKES

Montville Nature Trail

The Montville Store once stood at the foot of Mosca Pass Trail. It was built in the 1830s by fur trader Antoine Robidoux, who used the pass to transport supplies to his posts in western Colorado and eastern Utah. Many miners passed here on their way west to the San Juan Mountains. Today, a half-mile trail next to Mosca Creek provides a self-guided tour through a variety of ecosystems, leading to a grand view of the San Luis Valley and the dunes. The Montville Nature Trail starts north of the visitor center, and is a good option for those visiting the area with children or who just want a quick walk.

Mosca Pass Trail

This is a moderate hike (7 miles round-trip) that climbs through meadows and stands of aspen along Mosca Creek. Near the start of the trail is a bronze plaque etched with the impression of Zebulon Pike, who described the dunes as 'appearing exactly as a sea in storm except as to color.' It begins at the Montville Nature Trail trailhead.

Zapata Falls

This short half-mile hike higher up in the Sangre de Cristos provides a refreshing change from slogging through the dunes. The falls, though small, are hidden at the end of a slot canyon and the last 150 yards are loads of fun (though not without risk), as you'll need to scramble through ankle-deep ice-cold water and over slippery rocks to get there. This is a good family hike.

Grippy water shoes are a good idea. If you want to make a day of it, you can continue on to South Zapata Lake (8 miles round-trip). The turnoff for the falls is 7 miles south of the park entrance along Hwy 150. It's a further 3.5 miles up a dirt road from here, from where you'll have an excellent view of the dunes.

Great Sand Dunes Oasis CAMPGROUND, HOTEL **$**
(719-378-2222; www.greatdunes.com; 5400 Hwy 150; tent/RV sites $25/38, cabins $55, r $100; Apr-Oct) At the park entrance, the Oasis serves as a general store, restaurant, and campground and motel. It has a convenient location and there are facilities to shower and do laundry, but overall the sites are fairly bleak. This is very much a Plan B choice. The cabins are also very spartan.

Zapata Ranch DUDE RANCH **$$$**
(719-378-2356; www.zranch.org; 5303 Hwy 150; d with full board $300;) Ideal for horseriding enthusiasts, this exclusive preserve is a working cattle and bison ranch set amid groves of cottonwood trees. Owned and operated by the Nature Conservancy, the main inn is a refurbished 19th-century log structure, with distant views of the sand dunes.

Information

Great Sand Dunes National Park Visitor Center (719-378-6399; www.nps.gov/grsa; 11999 Hwy 150; 8:30am-6:30pm summer, shorter hr rest of yr) Stop by this informative center before venturing out to learn about the geology and history of the dunes or to chat with a ranger about hiking or backcountry camping options. Be sure to ask about scheduled nature walks and nightly programs held at the amphitheater near Pinyon Flats.

Getting There & Away

Great Sand Dunes National Park is 33 miles northeast of Alamosa. To get here, travel east on US 160 for 14 miles toward prominent Blanca Peak, turn left (north) on Hwy 150 and follow the road for 19 miles to the visitor center, 3 miles north of the park entrance. You can also get here from the north, turning west off Hwy 17 onto County Ln 6 N (look for signs).

San Luis State Park

This state park is a patch of bleak terrain on the edge of the Great Sand Dunes National Park, where dunes covered with saltbush and rabbitbrush stand in contrast to the grassy wetlands – the secondary beneficiary of this governmental largesse. Waterfowl, shorebirds and birdwatchers enjoy the recently restored wetlands.

The **Mosca Campground** (719-378-2020; www.parks.state.co.us; Lane 6 N; campsites $20, daily vehicle fee $7; May-Sep;) has a bathhouse, laundry and drinking fountains and is a convenient alternative to camping in the Great Sand Dunes National Park, though the park is only open for camping between May and the end of September. The park is 8 miles west of Hwy 150 on Alamosa County Ln 6N. To get from Alamosa to the park, drive 13 miles north on Hwy 17, then turn right (east) on County Ln 6N for 8 miles.

Alamosa

POP 8937 / ELEV 7543FT

In the heart of the San Luis Valley, Alamosa (Spanish for cottonwood) is the largest town in the valley, thanks mostly to a small university, Adams State College. From the highway, its car garages and Mexican joints aren't so different to other towns in the valley, but the students bring some life to its restaurants and bars. Its greatest appeal for travelers is its convenience as an overnight stop for visiting nearby Great Sand Dunes National Park or riding the excellent Cumbres & Toltec Scenic Railroad steam train from Antonito to the south.

Main St, with its small walking district, runs parallel to US 160, one block north of the highway. It's far more enjoyable to approach downtown on foot by walking along the river. The river walk starts at the information depot in Cole Park and offers views of Blanca Peak and a stroll through tree-lined neighborhood streets to the downtown area. Paths follow the Rio Grande on both banks from the information depot, but most walkers and joggers will prefer the wide, well-drained levee on the east side.

Sights & Activities

★Alamosa National Wildlife Refuge WILDLIFE SANCTUARY

(719-589-4021; www.fws.gov/alamosa; 9383 El Rancho Lane; sunrise-sunset) FREE This wildlife refuge on the banks of the Rio Grande is a special spot, and will give you some idea of what the valley must have looked like before it was developed for agriculture. It's best to visit at dawn or dusk, when wildlife is the most active and when you'll hear the amazing soundscape of bird calls and whistles.

If you're lucky, some of the animals you might see here include bald eagles, elk, coyotes and porcupines; in the spring and fall look for migrating sandhill cranes and numerous other seasonal travelers.

The refuge is located 3 miles southeast of Alamosa on Hwy 160. A 2.5-mile trail along the Rio Grande and a panoramic overlook on the east side of the refuge give visitors views of the wetland marshes, ponds and river.

San Luis Valley Museum MUSEUM

(www.sanluisvalleymuseum.org; 401 Hunt Ave; adult/child $2/free; 10am-4pm Tue-Sat) Located behind the Chamber Depot, this museum has a small but well-arranged collection of 'then and now' photographs and artifacts from early farm life in the valley. Knowledgeable volunteers answer questions and can help plan excursions to historical sites.

For a regional museum, there's some offbeat stuff here, including an interesting exhibit about the nearby La Jara Buddhist Church, the story of the Japanese in the valley and a Nazi uniform worn by a prisoner of war stationed near here during WWII.

Blanca Wetlands WILDLIFE RESERVE

(719-274-8971; www.blm.gov; County Rd 2S; mid-Jul–mid-Feb) FREE The Bureau of Land Management (BLM) has restored the wildlife habitat at Blanca Wetlands, northeast of Alamosa. Activities include fishing for bass or trout in newly created ponds and viewing waterfowl, shorebirds and other species. Hiking trails lead throughout the many marshes and ponds, but are closed in the nesting season from February 15 to July 15.

To get here from Alamosa, travel 6 miles east on Hwy 160, then 5 miles north on Alamosa County Rd 116S.

UFO WATCHTOWER

Don't panic! The visiting aliens are harmless. Or mostly harmless anyway. And if you're eager for a glimpse (or perhaps want to leave an offering for a weary interstellar hitchhiker), then a stop at the **UFO Watchtower** (www.ufowatchtower.com; 2502 County Rd 61; $5 donation per car;) is a must. About 15ft high, the tower is unlikely to improve your chances of actually spotting a flying saucer, however the garden and its assorted treasures is definitely something to behold. The watchtower is located off Hwy 17 near Hooper (about 30 miles west of the Great Sand Dunes National Park), and is easiest to access if you're driving south toward the dunes from Salida.

Kristi Mountain Sports OUTDOORS
(☎719-589-9759; www.slvoutdoor.com; 3323 Main St; bike/sandboard per day $20/18; ⊙9am-6pm Mon-Sat) These extremely friendly folks rent bikes and sandboards and have a good selection of camping gear; they're located west of town on Main St/Hwy 160.

Sleeping

For chain accommodations, you have your pick – just head out along Hwy 160 to the western edge of town.

Valley Motel MOTEL $
(☎719-589-9095; http://valleymotelalamosa.com; 2051 Main St; r incl breakfast $55-75; ❄📶👪🐾) Completely renovated in 2012, this family-run motel is the best-value option in Alamosa. It's located west of town on Hwy 160.

Comfort Inn Alamosa MOTEL $$
(☎719-587-9000; www.comfortinn.com; 6301 Hwy 160; d incl breakfast $100-165; P❄📶🏊👪🐾) One of the nicer chain hotels, with a good breakfast, plasma TVs, and a pool and hot tub. There's also a coin laundry.

Eating & Drinking

Calvillo's MEXICAN $$
(☎719-587-5500; 400 Main St; buffet lunch/dinner $10/12; ⊙8am-9pm; 📶👪) The first place you'll see as you turn onto Main St, Calvillo's is *the* place to eat in town – mostly thanks to its legendary buffet. Chiles rellenos, enchiladas, tacos, fajitas, *chicharonnes*, and on and on…the buffet also includes *agua fresca* (fruit-flavored water) and dessert, and there are enough customers to ensure that fresh servings are constantly being dished out.

★**San Luis Valley Brewing Co** PUB FOOD $$
(☎719-587-2337; www.slvbrewco.com; 631 Main St; mains $8-18; ⊙11am-2am; 📶👪) Housed in an old bank, the local brewery has some winning drinks on tap – notably the green-chili-infused Valle Caliente – as well as $3 margaritas during happy hour and home-made black-cherry cream soda. The food, which ranges from pub fare to pasta to Rocky Mountain trout, is better than expected.

Milagro's Coffee House CAFE
(529 Main St; ⊙7am-8pm Mon-Sat, 8am-4pm Sun; 📶) This is a great little stop-off for travelers; it has wi-fi, comfy couches and a shelf of used books for sale. There are also pastries and breakfast burritos on offer, but it's best for drinks.

Information

Alamosa County Chamber of Commerce (☎800-258-7597; www.alamosa.org; 610 State Ave; ⊙8am-5pm) This visitor center offers tourist information for both the area and the entire state at the Narrow-Gauge Engine, Car & Depot History Center.

Getting There & Away

Alamosa is 73 miles west of Walsenburg and I-25 on Hwy 160, 35 miles southwest of the Great Sand Dunes and 82 miles south of Salida on Hwy 17.

Alamosa San Luis Valley Regional Airport (☎719-589-4848; 2500 State Ave), South of the central district there are daily flights to Denver on Great Lakes Airline, an independent partner of United.

Greyhound (☎719-589-2567; www.greyhound.com; 2005 Main St) Buses stop at the Best Western in Alamosa just west of downtown on the daily Denver–Albuquerque service.

San Luis

POP 800 / ELEV 7965FT

Tucked into the far southeast margin of the San Luis Valley is the town of San Luis, which happens to be Colorado's oldest settlement (1851). It largely escaped the 'progress' that revoked Hispanic tenure in other parts of the valley following the arrival of the railroad; today the town remains almost 90% Hispanic, a harbor of cultural diversity among Colorado's largely white population. It's an appealing, friendly place, worth a detour for those who want to experience the scenic, slow pace of the deep San Luis Valley.

The character of San Luis – today and throughout history – is largely the result of its isolation. For Spain, the upper Rio Grande was a lost province best left to the nomadic Native American tribes that Spain was unable to dominate. Mexico encouraged civilian settlement and agriculture with the Sangre de Cristo Land Grant in 1843, yet did not establish a plaza at San Luis until 1851. Under the threat of Ute raids, and far from the mercantile and spiritual centers at Taos and Santa Fe, San Luis developed as a self-sufficient outpost.

Sights

★Stations of the Cross RELIGIOUS

(cnr Hwys 142 & 159) Following a path up a small hill, local sculptor Huberto Maestas' 15 dramatic life-sized statues of Christ's crucifixion are a powerful testament to the Catholic heritage of communities near the 'Blood of Christ' Mountains. They are stationed along a 1-mile pathway, an excellent chance to stretch the legs.

Beginning with Jesus being condemned to death, the bronze statues continue through the Resurrection. From the crucifixion on the mesa summit during late afternoon sunsets you can observe the reddish light cast on the Sangre de Cristo mountain range, including Culebra Peak (14,069ft), giving the mountains their 'Blood of Christ' name. You can also look out over San Luis and its surrounding fields and pasture. For many years, San Luis residents re-enacted the capture, trial and crucifixion of Christ during Holy Week (Easter) and also made pilgrimages to the Stations of the Cross every Friday during Lent. During the Centennial Jubilee of the Sangre de Cristo Parish in 1986, parish members conceived the Stations of the Cross Shrine to formalize this re-enactment.

San Luis Museum & Cultural Center MUSEUM

(☎719-672-3611; 401 Church Pl; adult $2; ⏲10am-4pm summer, 9am-4pm Mon-Fri winter; 👪) This handsome museum and gallery chronicles Hispanic culture in southern Colorado, in a modern building that blends sustainable concepts with traditional regional architecture. Exhibits on the Penitente Brotherhood are especially intriguing for their insight into this formerly secretive local sect of Catholicism. It was undergoing renovations at the time of writing, but should be open in 2014.

Viejo San Acacio CHURCH

(Costilla County Rd 15) The beautiful Viejo (Old) San Acacio is a historic Catholic church where mass is still occasionally held. To get here, go 4 miles east of San Luis on Hwy 142, then turn left (south) on Costilla County Rd 15. The church is near Culebra Creek.

Sleeping & Eating

Although there are two or three restaurants here, your best bet is All Gon Pizza (p324), just up the road in Fort Garland.

San Luis Inn Motel MOTEL $

(☎877-672-3331; 138 Main St; d $75; ❄) A simple choice, this is the only option in town.

Information

San Luis Visitors Center (☎719-672-3002; 408 Main St; ⏲9am-1pm Thu-Sun)

Getting There & Away

San Luis is 41 miles southeast of Alamosa and 17 miles south of Fort Garland. West on Hwy 142 is Los Caminos Antiguos Byway, a scenic stretch of road along the New Mexico border dotted with mesas and chamisa shrubs. It runs through Manassa and on to Antonito.

JACK DEMPSEY MUSEUM

Manassa is home to a tiny one-room **cabin** (412 Main St; ⏲9am-5pm Tue-Sat Jun-Aug) FREE where Jack Dempsey was born as the ninth child of a poor mining family. It was a destitute childhood, but Dempsey channeled his hardship into boxing, and from 1919 to 1926 reigned as the heavyweight world champion. Boxing fans will enjoy the collection of memorabilia. Manassa is located in between the towns of San Luis and Antonito.

Antonito

POP 785 / ELEV 7890FT

Pickup trucks with fishing tackle in the back rumble through the dusty, run-down little burg of Antonito. It's sadly fitting that the only two real attractions here are means of getting somewhere else: there's the northern terminus of the Cumbres & Toltec Scenic Railroad (C&TS), a narrow-gauge railway that goes over the mountains to Chama, New Mexico; and scenic Hwy 17, which follows the Conejos River into the Rio Grande National Forest.

The Cumbres & Toltec Scenic Railroad Depot is a mile south of Antonito at the junction of Hwy 285 (Main St) and Hwy 17. The **Antonito Visitors Center** (☎800-835-1098; www.conejosvacation.com; 200 Main St; ⏲9am-5pm Mon-Fri Jun-Aug) is opposite the railroad depot and only open in summer.

Visitors can take a short detour to the north along the river, passing the scrawny county seat at Conejos and Colorado's oldest church, the **Nuestra Señora de Guadalupe**, before rejoining Hwy 17. Another example of early Spanish architecture is the adobe **San Pedro y San Rafael Church** at Paisaje. This handsome building, topped by an octagonal wooden bell tower, can also be reached by Hwy 17; turn right on Conejos County Rd 1075, 3 miles west of Antonito.

With lodging and campsites available along the beautiful Conejos River to the west on Hwy 17 and no shortage of motels in Alamosa to the north, there's little reason to stay here. Likewise, eating options are scarce: you're best off stocking up on supplies in Alamosa.

Conejos River & the South San Juans

If you truly want to get away from it all, the South San Juans are certainly a good option. Hwy 17 follows the Conejos River west out of Antonito and into the San Juan wilderness, providing a scenic detour over the Cumbres Pass (10,022ft) on the road to Chama and Santa Fe in New Mexico. Superb fishing, camping and hiking are the main attractions here. The volcanic character of the San Juan Range from this angle is vivid, with ragged rock outcrops that rise before drivers who make it over Cumbres Pass.

Activities

Hiking

There is a lot of good hiking and camping in the remote South San Juan Wilderness Area, a part of the Rio Grande National Forest. Don't expect a crowded trail; this area is probably the least used wilderness in southern Colorado.

The **Elk Creek Trailhead** makes for a good base; from here you can hike in to Duck Lake (3 miles) or First Meadows (2 miles); for a longer backpacking trip, continue past First Meadows to the Dipping Lakes (13 miles) and the Continental Divide Trail. Elk Creek is 24 miles west of Antonito, just off Hwy 17.

You can also access the Continental Divide Trail from the top of Cumbres Pass, near the depot.

For maps and information about these hikes and surrounding campgrounds, contact the **USFS Conejos Peak Ranger District** (719-274-8971; 15571 County Rd T5; 8am-4:30pm Mon-Fri), 11 miles north of Antonito (3 miles south of La Jara) on Hwy 285.

Fishing

Specially managed Wild Trout Waters are designated by the Colorado Division of Wildlife on the uppermost Lake Fork, plus sections of the Conejos River next to the South San Juan Wilderness and below the Menkhaven Lodge for 4 miles. These streams support self-sustaining native cutthroat trout populations. The Division of Wildlife manager in Antonito prepares a map and handout on fishing the Conejos River for each season; it's available at the Antonito Visitors Center (p330) and tackle shops. Alternatively, stop in at **Conejos River Anglers** (719-376-5660; www.conejosriveranglers.com; 34591 Hwy 17; half-day per person from $185), 5 miles west of Antonito, for information on fishing conditions and specific regulations for the season. The shop offers fishing guides for trips on the Conejos River and its tributaries from May to November; it also rents cabins for $89 a night.

Sleeping

There are five USFS campgrounds along Hwy 17, between Antonito and Cumbres Pass. The first three (Aspen Grove, Mogote, and Spectacle Lake) are nice enough, but the scenery definitely improves the higher up into the mountains you go. **Elk Creek** (Hwy 17; tent sites $18; late May–mid-Sep) is a choice location; free dispersed camping is also available just down the road at Elk Creek Trailhead. Another good spot is Trujillo Meadows near the top of the pass. A reservoir stocked with trout is nearby, as is the Continental Divide.

Comfortable cabins and B&B accommodations, all with private bath, are available at **Conejos River Ranch** (719-376-2464; www.conejosranch.com; 25390 Hwy 17; cabins $140-235, lodges d $98-125), 14 miles west of Antonito. Six fully equipped riverside cabins are on hand – our favorite is the bright and airy La Casita – and there are eight comfortably furnished lodge rooms. All of them include breakfast. There are even facilities for horses.

Getting There & Away

To reach the Conejos River from Antonito, travel directly west on Hwy 17.

Penitente Canyon

ELEV 8000FT

The best desert experience in the San Luis Valley, Penitente Canyon offers visitors the chance to climb, hike and bike among a never-ending tumble of strangely shaped giant boulders, spread out through four separate canyons. The main canyon takes its name from Los Hermanos Penitentes and is symbolized by the fading, blue-cloaked mural of the Virgin of Guadalupe painted on a canyon wall. Local legend has it that the mural was painted by three men, one of whom descended sitting on a suspended tire; the inscription reads 'Consuelo y Espiritu' (Comfort and Courage).

However, history here stretches back much earlier. Some 27 million years ago, an enormous volcanic explosion (one of the largest in the earth's history) spewed an incredible 1000 cubic miles of ash that was over 100ft deep,: the origin of the rock formations you see today. After the eruption the underground chamber collapsed, forming the caldera (a geologic depression – this one is 22 miles wide by 47 miles long!) west of Penitente, where these ancient ash formations and volcanic plugs rise like spires in a haunting landscape.

Also of note are the scattered pictographs on the canyon walls, painted by either ancestral Puebloans, Apache or Ute, who possibly used the area for game drives. Most will be hard to find, although you can easily spot one at the entrance to the main canyon, near the parking lot.

Activities

Rock Climbing

Sport climbers are attracted to Penitente's bolted face climbs on the canyon's pocketed rhyolite rock walls. The walls are short – usually ranging from 40ft to 100ft in height – but there are over 300 climbs here, some of which are extremely challenging (ranging from 5.2 to 5.13c) and lots of fun. Further climbs are located in the Rock Garden and Witches Canyon.

Hiking & Mountain Biking

The surrounding desert landscape makes for some excellent hiking, but be aware that this is rattlesnake country – watch your step. A great trail is the Penitente Canyon Loop

LONESOME SONG OF THE PENITENTE

Of the characters who populate the pre-American history of Colorado's deep south – native Utes, Franciscan missionaries, Spanish prospectors – none are more mysterious than Los Hermanos Penitente, a secretive religious sect of men that thrived in the early 19th century. Some say the Penitente's membership drew from the furthest outcasts of 19th-century Southwestern society, a servant class of Native Americans who worked as housekeepers and shepherds, called *genízaros*. Because of their remote location and cast-off social status, Los Hermanos had limited access to the sacred traditions of Spanish Catholicism, which had taken root in the region – some communities were visited by a priest as little as once a year. So they took matters into their own hands. Meeting in humble meeting houses called *moradas*, their ceremonies evolved into a fairly grisly brand of mystical Catholicism that sought spiritual awakening through the suffering of the Passion of Christ. *Penitente* rituals involved lashing each other with amole weed or binding themselves to a heavy wooden cross. Some sects ended their Good Friday ceremonies with an actual crucifixion, the last fatal instance of which was recorded in the 1890s. If you visit San Luis near Easter, the echoes of this tradition are evident in the town's elaborate Holy Week celebrations.

The mournful songs of Los Hermanos Penitente are called *alabados*, haunting, unaccompanied hymns that blend Hispanic *folclórica* with elements of droning Native American song. Often sung at death rituals, funeral processions and burials, *alabados* have themes that are, like the group itself, fixated on the suffering and torture of Christ. New World Records has compiled an excellent compilation of salvaged historical recordings of Penitente chapters singing *alabados – Dark & Light in Spanish New Mexico: Alabados y Bailes*, the only released recording of the music and the perfect soundtrack to the long, dry scenery of a drive through the region. For more information about Los Hermanos Penitente, look to Dr Marta Weigle's definitive study, *Brothers of Light, Brothers of Blood*, published by the University of New Mexico Press.

(2 miles), which follows the lush canyon, shaded by groves of aspen and thickets of chokecherry, before climbing back up into the desert where you'll be rewarded with glorious views across the valley to the Sangre de Cristo Mountains. Along the way you can take a detour to view some old wagon (*carreta*) tracks grooved into the stone. Numerous other trails connect with other canyons; pick up a brochure at the local ranger office (p334) in Del Norte.

Seventeen miles of the same trails (but not the Penitente Canyon Loop) are also open to mountain bikers.

Sleeping & Eating

Penitente Canyon Campground CAMPGROUND $
(campsites $11; 🐾) There are 13 first-come, first-served tent sites at the main campground and a further eight sites at Witches Canyon. In theory there is a water pump here near the turnoff for the canyon, but play it safe and bring plenty with you. The campground is open year-round.

La Garita Cash Store AMERICAN
(⏲7am-6pm Tue-Sat, 7am-11pm Sun) The cash store is the closest place to stock up on supplies (gas, firewood, groceries) and get a bite to eat for breakfast or lunch. It's located in La Garita (which barely qualifies as a town), 2 miles west of Penitente.

Getting There & Away

Penitente Canyon is located 7.5 miles west of Hwy 285, off County Rd 38A. From Hwy 285, take County Rd G to La Garita, then continue on County Rd 38A to Penitente. You can also get here from Del Norte, 13 miles south. Take Oak St (County Rd 112) north out of town, then turn onto County Rd 33 which will turn into County Rd 38A.

You'll pass a turnoff for a natural arch 3 miles south of Penitente. Although the arch is not particularly impressive (in addition to being quite hard to find), the drive through the caldera is quite beautiful.

Del Norte

POP 1683 / ELEV 7879FT

Sun-bleached and lazy, Del Norte (rhymes with 'port') is a place most travelers blast through on the way to or from sites in Colorado's southwest. The town is seated next to the Rio Grande del Norte, for which it was named, in the San Juan foothills on Hwy 160. One of Colorado's oldest towns, it was founded in 1860 and by 1873 it was a thriving supply point for mining in the San Juan Mountains. Now Del Norte marks the beginning of Gold Medal fishing on the Rio Grande and is the closest big town for rock climbers and hikers on their way to Penitente Canyon.

Sights

Rio Grande County Museum & Cultural Center MUSEUM
(☎719-657-2847; 580 Oak St; admission $1; ⏲10am-4pm Tue-Fri, 10am-2pm Sat Apr-Oct; 👪) This museum and cultural center features Pueblo and Ute rock art, Hispanic history and early photographs of Monte Vista's 'potato row' wagons loaded high with valley spuds at the turn of the 20th century. Special programs include talks and outdoor excursions led by local historians and naturalists. The museum has information for people who want to visit local rock-art sites.

Activities

Mountain Biking

Fat-tire bikes are permitted on all public trails with the exception of designated wilderness areas. One ride recommended by the USFS follows an old stock driveway along an alpine ridge on USFS Trail 700 from Grayback Mountain (12,616ft) east 7 miles to Blowout Pass (12,000ft). To reach the Grayback Mountain trailhead, you have to travel about 20 miles south of Del Norte on USFS Rd 14, then continue another 5 miles on USFS Rd 330. Otherwise, the dirt roads heading into the caldera area near Penitente Canyon are easy riding and offer some remarkable scenery. It is hot and dry out there, though, so come prepared.

Fishing

Gold-medal fishing on the Rio Grande begins a mile upstream at the Farmer's Union Canal. From here to the Hwy 149 bridge at South Fork is one of Colorado's most productive fisheries, producing 16in to 20in trout. You access the river and signed public property via the bridges on Rio Grande County Rds 17, 18 and 19, plus the Hwy 149 bridge above South Fork. See www.fishtheupperrio.com for more info.

WORTH A TRIP

CUMBRES & TOLTEC SCENIC RAILROAD

One of several historic narrow-gauge trains in the state, this impressive ride is a chance to mount the Cumbres Pass (10,022ft) by power of steam.

In 1880 the Denver & Rio Grande Western Railroad (D&RG) completed a track over Cumbres Pass, linking Chama, New Mexico, with Denver by way of Alamosa. The twisting, mountainous terrain was suited to narrow-gauge track, which is only 3ft wide instead of the standard gauge of 4ft 8in. Within a few years the line was extended to Durango, Farmington and the Silverton mining camp, 152 miles away. Railroad buffs encouraged Colorado and New Mexico to buy the scenic Cumbres Pass segment when the Antonito–Farmington line came up for abandonment in 1967. Their efforts led to a compact between Colorado and New Mexico to save the railway as a National Register site, and churning along its track, past hills of pine and aspen and expansive views of the high plains and mountains, makes an excellent way to spend a day.

Trains run daily, roughly from Memorial Day to mid-October, from the **Cumbres & Toltec Scenic Railroad Depot** (☎888-286-2737; www.cumbrestoltec.com; 5234 Hwy 285, Antonito; adult/child from $89/49). Dress warmly as the unheated cars, both enclosed and semi-enclosed, can get extremely cold. There are currently six day-trip options to choose from, but whichever you select, expect to be out the entire day. Call ahead or check the website for current schedules and reservations.

Sleeping & Eating

Windsor Hotel HOTEL $$
(☎719-657-9031; http://windsorhoteldelnorte.com; 605 Grand Ave; r from $165; ❄️📶) This landmark 1874 hotel has been lovingly restored, from the original color schemes all the way down to the hardwood floors. The 22 rooms are simple but cozy, and the ground-floor restaurant (mains $8 to $22) is the nicest dining option west of Alamosa, with specialties such as pan-seared rainbow trout and goat's cheese polenta.

Boogie's Restaurant AMERICAN, MEXICAN $
(www.boogiesdelnorte.com; 410 Grand Ave; mains $8-12; ⏲6am-7pm Thu-Tue, 6am-2pm Wed; 👪) Del Norte's greasy spoon has a menu that's all over the place (Tex Mex, burgers, salads) but it's the local fave and the portions are big.

Drinking & Nightlife

Three Barrel Brewery BREWERY
(www.threebarrelbrew.com; 586 Columbia Ave; ⏲10:30am-9pm Tue-Sat, 3-9pm Sun & Mon) Welcome to one of Colorado's smallest breweries. It produces only 350 barrels of beer from the nondescript brick building just a block off the main drag. But it's damn good beer. The 'just one more' inclination inspired by brews such Pemba Sherpa or Black Yak might be the best reason to spend the night in town.

Information

Del Norte Chamber of Commerce (www.delnortechamber.org; 505 Grande Ave; ⏲8:30am-5pm Mon-Fri)

USFS Divide District Ranger Station (☎719-657-3321; 13308 W Hwy 160; ⏲8am-4:30pm Mon-Fri)

SANGRE DE CRISTO MOUNTAINS

In a state full of dazzling mountains, the shark-toothed Sangre de Cristo (Blood of Christ) range certainly holds its own. These mountains are steep and jagged, rising as much as 6000ft in about 4 miles, and three – Kit Carson, Crestone Peak and Crestone Needle – were the last of Colorado's 14ers to be summitted (Colorado College professors Albert Ellingwood and Eleanor Davis managed the feat in July 1916, after walking over 100 miles from Colorado Springs). It's a rugged range with limited acccess points: the main ones include Westcliffe (eastern side), Crestone (western side) and the Great Sand Dunes (southwest).

Westcliffe

POP 563 / ELEV 7867FT

The full panorama of the rugged north-south Sangres is best viewed coming into

Westcliffe on Hwy 96, where you'll see peak after jagged peak rise up dramatically from the valley floor. The town itself is a down-to-earth ranching community; outside of the bluegrass festival and rodeo in July, it's mainly of interest for travelers as the staging ground for excursions into the eastern Sangre de Cristo wilderness.

Sights

Westcliffe has a historic Main St, with a few 19th-century buildings scattered around town. The old state bank on 2nd St is where scenes from *Comes a Horseman,* the 1978 flick starring James Caan and Jane Fonda, were shot.

Silver Cliff Museum MUSEUM
(610 Main St; 1-4pm Sat & Sat summer) FREE This small museum is housed in a former town hall and fire station, built in 1879. You can view relics and photographs of the regional history. It's located in Silver Cliff, just east of Westcliffe.

Activities

Hiking

There are three 14ers here (and countless 13ers!), which include Crestone Peak (14,294ft) and Crestone Needle (14,197ft), among the toughest ascents in Colorado. Luckily, there are plenty of hikes that don't require technical expertise. However, many do require a high-clearance 4WD vehicle to get to the main trailhead. Talk to the ranger offices in either Salida (p233) or Cañon City (p315) for detailed information on trails and campgrounds. For maps, try Valley Ace Hardware, south of Westcliffe on Hwy 69.

★ **Comanche-Venable Loop Trail** HIKING
(Jun-Sep) For outstanding views on the crest of the Sangre de Cristo Mountains, the Comanche-Venable Loop Trail (USFS Trail 1345) is hard to beat. This is a spectacular hike – lots of granite faces, dark-blue alpine lakes and the famously exposed Phantom Terrace – but you really have to earn it. The 13-mile loop gains over 3600ft in elevation; start with Venable Canyon.

To get here, drive south on Hwy 69 for 3½ miles, then turn off onto County Rd 140 (Schoolfield Rd). Follow the road 4½ miles; when you reach a T, turn left and continue another 2 miles.

South Colony Lakes HIKING
(Jun-Oct) Climbers use South Colony Lakes as a base camp, but the 12,000ft lakes beneath the awe-inspiring trio of Crestone Needle, Crestone Peak and Humboldt Peak also make for an excellent day hike. It's a 4¾-mile round-trip hike from the 4WD trailhead.

To reach the trailhead, drive 4½ miles south of town on Hwy 69. Turn right onto Colfax Lane (signed Music Pass), which will eventually reach a T-junction. Turn right and continue along the dirt road to the 2WD trailhead (parking available). It's another 2.7 miles to the 4WD trailhead.

Music Pass HIKING
(Jun-Oct) This hike traverses the ridge at Music Pass (11,400ft) leading to Sand Creek Lakes on the west side of the range. The area was named by hikers who claimed to hear music made by the wind whistling through the trees. It's a 1½-mile hike to the pass from the 4WD trailhead.

To reach the trailhead, drive 4½ miles south of town on Hwy 69. Turn right onto Colfax Lane (signed Music Pass), which will eventually reach a T-junction. Turn left at the T. The 4WD trailhead is 2½ miles past the 2WD trailhead.

Rainbow Trail HIKING, MOUNTAIN BIKING
This historic trail traverses the eastern slope of the Sangre de Cristo range, stretching over 100 miles all the way from the Continental Divide near Salida to Music Pass south of Westcliffe. It's a multi-use trail in places, open to hikers, horseback riding, mountain biking and ATVs, though there are plenty of solitary sections and it certainly makes for an interesting through hike.

Wherever you go, you'll likely cross it at some point. Check with the Salida ranger office (p233) for various options.

Other Activities

In addition to horseback riding, mountaineering and biking, fishing in the high alpine lakes is another popular pursuit (license required).

Bear Basin Ranch HORSEBACK RIDING
(719-783-2519; www.bearbasinranch.com; 473 County Rd 271; half-day $60, full-day incl lunch $120) Eleven miles east of Westcliffe, this ranch offers horseback rides on its extensive property in the Wet Mountains. All-day and multiday trips into the mountains are also available.

WORTH A TRIP

ORIENT MINE & VALLEY VIEW HOT SPRINGS

This off-the-grid and little-known **hot springs resort** (☎719-256-4315; www.olt.org; 64393 County Rd GG; day/overnight pass $15/30, children under 16yr free; ⊙9am-10pm) is a magical place hidden in the foothills of the Sangres, where geothermal waters cascade down the hillside through a series of natural ponds – certainly among the loveliest hot springs in Colorado. Set on the land of the former Orient Mine and Everson Ranch, Valley View is an ideal spot to recharge the batteries over the course of a weekend.

Now a full-fledged conservation area, you can hike along several trails here (the longest, at 10 miles round-trip, heads up to Garner Pass at 12,700ft), visit the abandoned mining town established in the 1870s or watch thousands of bats exiting the Orient Mine on summer evenings: the former mine is today home to the largest bat colony in Colorado (estimated at 100,000 to 250,000). Male Brazilian free-tailed bats spend each summer in the mine, while females migrate to Carlsbad Caverns in New Mexico. The historic Everson homestead, also part of the conservation area, is currently being renovated as a sustainable and educational ranch.

Lodging options (campsite/dm/cabin $10/15/60;) range from campsites and inexpensive dorm beds to private rooms and cabins that sleep from four to six. To get here, follow County Rd GG 7 miles west from Hwy 17, where it intersects with Hwy 285; follow signs for the Orient Land Trust. Note that the entire area (not just the hot springs) is clothing optional.

Festivals & Events

High Mountain Hay Fever Bluegrass Festival MUSIC
(www.highmountainhayfever.org; ⊙mid-Jul) This town loves bluegrass, and this festival is a chance to see some of the best 'grass heads' in Colorado.

Westcliffe Stampede Rodeo RODEO
(⊙mid-Jul) A rodeo and parade are the featured events at the Custer County Fair.

Jazz in the Sangres MUSIC
(⊙mid-Aug) Young jazz artists perform both day and night at this jazz festival, the culmination of a week-long jazz performance camp that draws students from around Colorado.

Sleeping

Apart from camping, Westcliffe does not have a lot of sleeping options. Do note that the Sangres see a lot of bear activity, and the Forest Service recommends that you take extra precautions down here if you're camping. Abundant open campsites can be found at nearby Middle Taylor Creek SWA and DeWeese SWA, and on local USFS lands. Middle Taylor Creek is about 8 miles northeast of Westcliffe; DeWeese is about 4 miles northeast.

Alvarado Campground CAMPGROUND $
(☎877-444-6777; www.recreation.gov; County Rd 140; campsites $18; ⊙May–mid-Oct;) Up at 9000ft, this campground has 47 reservable sites. Head south from Westcliffe on Hwy 69 for 3½ miles and turn right (west) on Custer County Rd 140 (Schoolfield Rd); it's 7 miles from here. It's located close to the Comanche-Venable Loop Trail.

Lake Creek Campground CAMPGROUND $
(County Rd 198; tent & small RVs $15; ⊙late May–Sep;) This first-come, first-served campground has 11 sites and offers access to the Rainbow Trail north of Westcliffe. To get here, travel 15 miles north on Hwy 69 to Hillside (store and post office), then turn left on Custer County Rd 198; it's 4 miles to the campsites and USFS Trail 300 to Rainbow Lake.

Courtyard Country Inn B&B $$
(☎719-783-9616; www.courtyardcountryinn.com; 410 Main St; d $100-110;) This eclectic, friendly spot features a lovely central courtyard, bedecked with flowers and graced with a variety of birds in spring and summer. The buildings are over a century old (the back rooms are a converted chicken house – nicer than it sounds) and Mo and John make a great continental breakfast with homemade bread and fresh-ground coffee. It's a very welcoming place.

Eating & Entertainment

Sugar and Spice Mountain Bakery BAKERY $
(411 Main St; pastries from $2; 7am-5pm Tue-Sat) This Mennonite bakery has fresh-baked pies, pastries (gluten-free too), bread and quiche. Delish!

Sangrita AMERICAN $$
(719-783-4054; www.sangritarestaurant.com; 212 Main St; lunch $8-10, dinner $13-16; lunch Tue-Sun, dinner Tue-Sat;) Westcliffe's best restaurant is housed inside an adobe-style building. Expect a wide selection of burgers for lunch and finer fare – pecan-crusted chicken, broiled mahi over spinach – for dinner.

Rancher's Roost & Cliff Lanes BOWLING
(www.clifflanes.com; 25 Main St; game $3.50, shoe rental $2.50; 7am-9pm Mon-Fri, 8am-8pm Sat & Sun;) At the west end of Main St, this bowling alley/diner is a good diversion if you're looking for a little Big Lebowski action and reliable diner grub.

Information

Visitor Center (719-783-9163; www.custercountytourism.com; Main St; 9am-6pm Mon-Fri Jun-Sep) The visitor center is located in an old Rio Grande caboose near the west end of Main St.

Getting There & Away

Westcliffe lies at the junctions of Hwys 69 and 96. It's 77 miles southwest of Colorado Springs, 50 miles southwest of Cañon City and 48 miles southeast of Salida.

Crestone

POP 130 / ELEV 7923FT

Despite a population that barely exceeds 100 souls, Crestone is world famous in spiritual circles. A former mining town in the heart of the Sangre de Christo mountains, it has since become an international center of retreat and meditation.

Look around the small grid of streets and you can choose from a buffet of spirituality – there's a Hindu temple and a pair of ashrams, a clutch of Buddhist Zen retreats, a crunchy Carmelite hermitage, a Baptist church, several Tibetan meditation centers and seekers of every stripe.

There are several theories explaining Crestone's status as a powerful spiritual magnet – that it has to do with the energy flow that follows waters off the Continental Divide, or that the mountains themselves call spiritual travelers – but some of the draw likely has to do with Maurice Strong, a former UN undersecretary-general and entrepreneur. Strong planned a large housing development here in the late 1970s, but when it didn't take off he donated plots to various spiritual organizations. Regardless, there's no question about Crestone's setting: the soaring backdrop of 14,000ft peaks is truly stunning.

Activities

Hiking & Backpacking

Two outstanding trails into the high Sangre de Cristo Wilderness Area begin in Crestone's backyard, also providing access to two 14ers (Kit Carson Peak and Challenger Point).

For information about hiking on the west side of the Sangre de Cristo Wilderness Area contact the **Saguache Ranger District** (719-655-2547; 46525 Hwy 114; 8am-4:30pm Mon-Fri) across the valley in Saguache (pronounced 'sah-watch').

South Crestone Lake Trail HIKING
(Jun-Oct) Hikers on the South Crestone Lake Trail travel 4.5 miles to South Crestone Lake, in a cirque beneath Mt Adams (13,931ft). This prime bighorn sheep habitat harbors more than 500 sheep that range between Hermit and Music Passes. There are several campsites on this trail.

Begin from the top of Galena St above the post office and follow the road for a little over 2 miles to the trailhead. An alternate hike from this trailhead is the 9.5 mile hike to Willow Lake (and waterfall), used as a basecamp for those looking to summit Kit Carson and Challenger Point.

North Crestone Trail HIKING
(Jun-Oct) The North Crestone Trail leads to either the North Crestone Lake below Fluted Peak (13,554ft) or you can cross the ridge to the eastern slope over either Comanche or Venable Passes (p335).

From the North Crestone Campground USFS Trail 744 follows the north side of North Crestone Creek for 1.5 miles to a three-way junction: on your right the southernmost trail continues for 3 miles to North Crestone Lake; the middle trail, USFS Trail 746, passes north of Comanche Peak before dropping into the Wet Mountain Valley on USFS Trail 1345; and the northern choice, USFS Trail 747, heads toward Venable Pass.

Spiritual Retreats & Classes

For the most part, it takes extensive advance planning to make a spiritual retreat or stay in Crestone, but a wide spectrum of faiths offer dormitory accommodations and seminars for visitors. Many of the spiritual centers also have drop-in classes, and prayer and meditation services.

Sleeping & Eating

North Crestone Campground CAMPGROUND $
(Alder Terrace Rd; tent sites $10; May-Nov) Thirteen campsites are available about 2 miles north of Crestone, past the town center on Alder Terrace Rd. They're first-come, first-served and fill up in a blink on summer weekends. If you can't get here on a weekday, make sure you research a backup BLM (Bureau of Land Management) option ahead of time or prepare to head into the backcountry.

Sangre de Christo Inn HOTEL $
(719-256-4975; www.sangredecristoinn.com; 116 S Alder St; d $74-84;) The best option in town is this hotel, where monastic rooms come with quilted bedspreads.

Jim & Michelle's Farm Table CAFE $$
(719-937-7800; 121 E Galena Ave; lunch $8-13, dinner $16; 8am-8pm Mon-Sat, to 2pm Sun summer, closed Mon & Tue winter;) This Emmylou Harris–powered cafe sources local ingredients for a veritable cornucopia of healthy, delicious options, from berry-and-brie omelets for breakfast to pasta and gourmet sandwiches for lunch and dinner.

Information

Crestone Area Visitors Agency (866-351-2282; www.crestonevisit.com; 116 S Alder St; hr vary)

Getting There & Away

Crestone is on the east side of the San Luis Valley, about halfway (57 miles) between the Great Sand Dunes to the south and Salida to the north. From Hwy 17, follow Saguache County Rd T 13 miles east to Crestone.

Understand Colorado

Colorado Today

From double-diamond runs to stiff espressos, Colorado is about vigor. Universities and high-tech show the state's industrious side, though even workaholics might call in sick when snow starts falling. It's no wonder that the sunny state attracts so many East Coasters and Californians. Latinos also have answered the call to shore up a huge hospitality industry. And while much of the state is considered conservative, there is common ground in everyone's mad love for the outdoors and an inspiring and friendly can-do ethos.

Best in Print

On the Road (Jack Kerouac) The Denver doldrums and the origins of road-tripper culture.
House of Rain (Craig Childs) Tracks the Anasazi in the Southwest.
Plainsong (Kent Haruf) Examines a Colorado farming community.

Best on Film

Butch Cassidy & the Sundance Kid (1969) The seminal cliff-jumping scene was shot on the Durango & Silverton Narrow Gauge Railroad.
True Grit (1969) Set in Arkansas but filmed in the San Juan Mountains.
The Shining (1980) Inspired by the Stanley Hotel in Estes Park.
Dear Eleanor (2014) Leonardo DiCaprio produced this Sundance flick, which was filmed on the Front Range.

Etiquette

Do dress like a Tour de France competitor on casual training rides about town.
Don't try to keep up with active locals. They're already acclimatised.
Do drink lots of water, or the high altitude and the high-gravity beers will do you in.
Don't compare anything to California. Sore spot.

The Grass Is Greener

Colorado voted to legalize the recreational use of marijuana in November 2012, and became the first jurisdiction in the world (alongside Washington state) to do so. Attitudes toward ganja had been lightening up around the country for some time, but this trailblazing act failed to take into account one detail: marijuana is still illegal on a national level.

But the times they are a changin', and US attorney general Eric Holder recently decided not to block the law. This approach may be the wave of the future, though it isn't as hands off as it appears. The feds seem to be betting that taxing and tightly regulating legal pot growing will be more efficient in the long run than chasing and prosecuting growers and small-time dealers. It's also argued that creating a legal system will help keep it out of the hands of kids.

That's not to say that a future conservative administration would be so lenient. But the coming years will prove an interesting social experiment, so many years after John Denver's homage to the Rocky Mountain high.

The Young & the Restless

Once a mining, ranching and farming stronghold, today's Colorado is a young state getting younger, with 24% of the 5.2 million residents under the age of 18.

Most live in and around Denver. Development in Denver suburbs on what was farmland fueled real estate and technology booms. Some of those jobs were lost in tech busts in the late 1990s and early 2000s, but the area weathered the storm. Growth not only sparked suburban sprawl but also urban gentrification.

Denver's once blighted LoDo neighborhood is a poster child for urban revitalization, with hip residential lofts and dozens of bars and restaurants. Young college grads flock here from across the US, with an eye toward pairing an outdoor, weekend-warrior lifestyle with a high-paying tech gig.

Another industry has gripped northern Colorado, and we aren't talking about the marijuana industry, although that's growing, too. Known as the Colorado Clean Energy Cluster, there are now 32 clean-energy companies working together to promote and produce green energy in the Denver–Boulder area. In 2013, Colorado was ranked among the top states for business by CNBC.

Not everyone is happy about the direction Colorado is taking. In 2013, representatives from eight counties in northern Colorado started a movement to secede from the rest of the state, citing their dissatisfaction with the growing urban-rural divide.

Red State, Blue State

Politically, Colorado is a mixed bag. There's a longstanding tendency of the state to vote Republican. Its conservative streak is rooted in an evangelical base in Colorado Springs and ranching and mining interests throughout the state.

But there are plenty of progressives here too, particularly in Denver, Boulder and throughout the Front Range. This is how Colorado managed to vote for Obama twice. In 2013, the state approved gay civil unions. Then there's current Colorado governor John Hickenlooper, a Democrat and former geologist turned entrepreneur who helped transform Denver's LoDo. A Quaker, he is beloved by Colorado progressives, and has promoted initiatives such as gun control, legalizing marijuana and a sustainable development program called Greenprint Denver.

But liberalism has its limits here too. Guns are a hot-button issue. After lone gunman James Holmes killed 12 moviegoers in an Aurora movie theater shooting on July 20, 2012, new stringent state gun laws were passed. But gun advocates lobbied hard against restrictions and, in September 2013, two Democratic Colorado state legislators were recalled for supporting the laws.

POPULATION: **5,188,000**

AREA: **104,185 SQ MILES**

UNEMPLOYMENT: **7%**

NUMBER OF STATE WILDLIFE AREAS: **222**

PEAKS OVER 14,000FT: **54**

if Colorado were 100 people

70 would be White
20 would be Hispanic
4 would be African American
1 would be Native American
3 would be Asian
2 would be other

belief systems

(% of population)

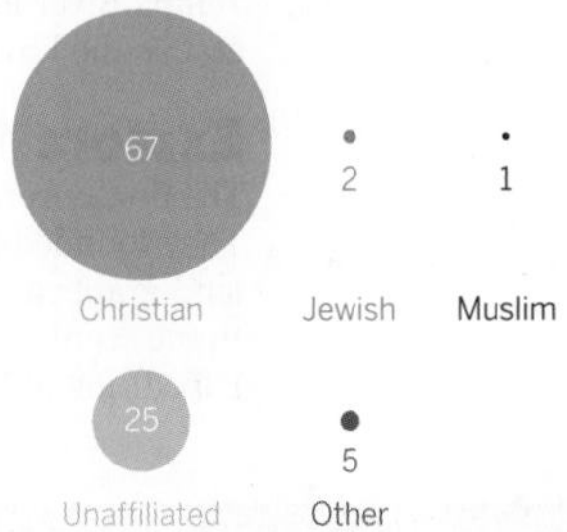

population per sq mile

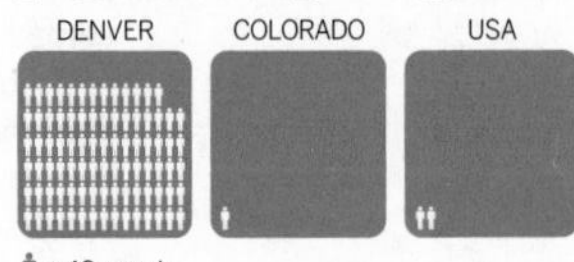

History

Colorado's history is written in petroglyphs, gold dust and ski tracks. A story about the making of today's United States, it's also a parable about European domination of the New World. Ambitious adventurers and salespeople, colonizing politicians and warriors intermingled and spread slowly across Colorado, overtaking the domain of Native Americans whose complex cultures had survived countless generations at the time of first contact.

Colorado has around 500 ghost towns, a legacy of the boom-bust cycle of the gold- and silver-mining days.

Pre-America

Late Paleo-Indian artifacts of the Cody Cultural Complex indicate that inhabitants relied on hunting modern bison, while around 7500 years ago some peoples switched to hunting smaller game – a likely indicator of human population pressure on the declining bison. Petroglyphs near Dinosaur National Monument date back as far as 499 BC, and Colorado has over 56,000 prehistoric sites dating as far back as 12,000 BC.

The most complex societies in North American antiquity, however, were the agricultural pueblos of the Colorado Plateau, where cliff dwellers left behind impressive ruins in areas like Mesa Verde. Today, Mesa Verde National Park is a highlight of a visit to the state, offering the hands-on experience of entering cliff dwellings and joining guided ranger visits.

Many Native American groups occupied the Rocky Mountain region at the time of European contact. The Utes consisted of six eastern bands in Colorado, territory which stretched from the Uinta Mountains and the Yampa River in the north to the San Juan River in the south, and as far east as the Front Range.

Exploration & Settlement

The first European explorers were Spaniards moving north from Mexico. They founded Santa Fe at the end of the 16th century, and established land grants as far north as the Arkansas River in present-day Colorado. In the search for overland routes to California, the Domínguez-Escalante Expedition of 1775–76 explored the Colorado Plateau.

TIMELINE

AD 100

The region's dominant indigenous cultures emerge. The Hohokam settle in the desert, the Mogollon dwell in the mountains and valleys, and Ancestral Puebloans build cliff dwellings around the Four Corners.

1300s

One of history's most enduring unsolved mysteries occurs when the entire civilization of Ancestral Puebloans living in Mesa Verde abandons this sophisticated city of cliff dwellings.

1775–6

Spanish missionaries Francisco Atanasio Domínguez and Silvestre Vélez de Escalante lead an expedition through the Colorado Plateau in search of overland routes to California.

Early 18th-century French explorers and fur traders converged on the northern plains from eastern Canada, but by the early 19th century the Spanish had moved throughout the western half of present-day Colorado, the southwestern corner of Wyoming and even shared, at least formally, occupation of parts of Montana with the British, who had established trading posts. Virtually all of New Mexico, Arizona, California, Utah and Nevada were under Spanish authority.

In 1803, the USA acquired the French territorial claim known as the Louisiana Purchase. It included the coveted port of New Orleans, virtually all of present-day Montana, three-quarters of Wyoming and the eastern half of Colorado. Then president Thomas Jefferson invited army captain Meriwether Lewis to command an exploratory expedition. Lewis invited colleague William Clark to serve as co-commander.

Lewis and Clark's Corps of Discovery set forth to benefit American commerce by seeking a 'Northwest Passage' to the Pacific Ocean. Meanwhile, the expedition managed to make serious scientific observations on flora, fauna, climate and the inhabitants of the region.

Lewis and Clark's was the most successful of early US expeditions to the west; others ended in disaster. After a foray into Colorado in 1806–07, Zebulon Pike was arrested in New Mexico by Spanish police. Pike never climbed the famous peak that bears his name.

In 1839, journalist John L O'Sullivan suggested in his essay 'Manifest Destiny' that it was white America's destiny to own the American continent from coast to coast and tip to tip. Inevitably manifest destiny became US policy under then president James Polk. This in turn spiked westward settlement and caused inevitable violent clashes with both Mexico – which owned southern Colorado – and native peoples. The Mexican–American War raged in the mid-1840s, and by its end Charles Bent, appointed first governor of New Mexico, had been assassinated by Pueblo Indians in Taos, and his brother William was married to a Cheyenne woman in Colorado. The less-publicized Indian Wars were the euphemism for the violent subjugation of Colorado's native people by the Colorado Volunteers. The exclamation point to this process was the 1864 Sand Creek Massacre (p323).

The discovery of gold in 1859 brought more miners and pioneers, among them Barney Ford, an escaped slave and would-be millionaire. Not long after the Pony Express blazed the Overland Trail through the Pawnee Grassland to deliver the US mail, Confederate families came this way post–Civil War, planting sugar beets in northeast Colorado.

Historic Sites

- *Buffalo Bill Museum & Grave, Golden*
- *Overland Trail, Sterling*
- *Santa Fe Trail, Timpas & the Comanche National Grassland*
- *Cliff Palace, Mesa Verde National Park*
- *Durango & Silverton Narrow Gauge Railroad, Durango and Silverton*
- *Pikes Peak Hwy, near Colorado Springs*
- *Cripple Creek & Victor Narrow Gauge Railroad, Cripple Creek*
- *Ouray Mule Carriage Co, Ouray*

1803

US President Thomas Jefferson commissions Lewis and Clark to explore the western interior – the first US overland expedition to the Pacific Coast and back.

1821

After 11 years of war, Mexico gains independence from Spain. The US acknowledges Mexico's hegemony over most of the West, including three-quarters of Colorado.

1846–8

The Mexican–American War is spurred by the United States' recent annexation of Texas; Mexicans know the event as the First US Intervention in Mexico.

1849

Regular stagecoach service starts along the Santa Fe Trail. The 900-mile trail will serve as the country's main freight route for the next 60 years, until the railway finally makes it to town.

Fur Trade & Emigrant Trails

In the early 1800s fur traders spread across the Rockies, trading with Native Americans and living rough lives on the frontier. They came to know the Rockies backcountry better than any other Europeans.

The Santa Fe Trail led west through hostile country from Missouri through Kansas and Colorado. The trail was launched in the early 1830s. By 1833 the brothers William and George Bent had built a fort that was an oasis for pioneers traveling on the trail.

The Denver Mint struck and minted its first gold and silver coins on February 1, 1906. It is the largest producer of coins in the world. The mint was robbed of $200,000 in broad daylight on 18 December, 1922.

Even into the 20th century, hundreds of thousands of emigrants followed the Oregon Trail across the Continental Divide to South Pass, where they split up to reach various destinations. The Mormons came fleeing persecution in New York and the Midwest. In the late 1860s, completion of the Transcontinental Railroad across southern Wyoming slowed the inexorable march of wagon trains.

Water & Western Development

Americans began to think of occupying the area between the coasts. The lingering image of the Great American Desert, a myth propagated by explorers such as Pike and Long, had deterred agricultural settlers and urban development.

Water was a limiting factor as cities such as Denver began to spring up at the base of the Front Range. Utopians such as Horace Greeley, who saw the Homestead Act of 1862 as the key to agrarian prosperity, planned agricultural experiments on the nearby plains. This act envisioned the creation of 160-acre family farms to create a rural democracy on the Western frontier.

FATE OF THE NATIVE AMERICANS

The US government signed treaties to defuse Native American objections to expanding settlement. Huge reservations and rations were an attempt to compensate Native Americans for the loss of hunting territory. Under pressure from miners and other emigrants, the federal government continually reduced the size of the reservations, shifting many to less desirable areas.

Ute territorial sovereignty survived a bit longer than that of other Native Americans in the region, but with the influx of silver miners west of the Continental Divide in the 1870s, Chief Ouray had little option but to sign treaties relinquishing traditional lands.

In 1879, the White River Band of Utes attacked federal troops and White River Indian agent Nathan Meeker and his family near the present-day town of Meeker. All Utes suffered vicious American reprisals. By 1881, Utes not removed to forsaken lands in Utah were left with a narrow 15-mile-wide plateau in southwestern Colorado.

1858

General William H Larimer pegs out a square-mile plot of land, establishing the settlement that will grow into present-day Denver, after gold is discovered nearby.

1864

Colonel John Chivington leads 700 troops and militia in the infamous Sand Creek Massacre. The heads of Arapaho victims are paraded through today's LoDo district in grisly celebration.

1870

Two railroads reach Denver: the Denver Pacific Railroad connects with the Union Pacific's transcontinental line, and the Kansas Pacific arrives from Kansas City.

1876

Colorado is granted statehood, becoming the 38th state of the Union. This takes place 28 days after the US Centennial, earning Colorado its 'Centennial State' moniker.

Government agents encouraged settlement and development in their assessments of the region, but differed on how to bring these changes about. Two of the major figures were Frederick V Hayden of the United States Geological Survey (USGS) and John Wesley Powell, first of the Smithsonian Institute and later of the USGS. Hayden, who had surveyed the Yellowstone River area and played a major role in having it declared a national park, was so eager to promote the West that he exaggerated the region's agricultural potential.

Powell, a great figure in American history, made a more perceptive assessment of the potential and limitations of the region. Famous as the first man to descend the Colorado River through the Grand Canyon, Powell knew the region's salient feature was aridity and that its limited water supply depended on the snowpack that fell in the Rockies. The 160-acre ideal of the Homestead Act was inappropriate for the West. His masterful *Report on the Lands of the Arid Regions of the United States* challenged the tendency toward exploiting the region's minerals, pastures and forests, and proposed distributing land according to its suitability for irrigation.

Powell recommended dams and canals to create an integrated, federally sponsored irrigation system administered by democratically elected cooperatives. Unfortunately, his vision collided with the interests of influential cattle barons. Nor did it appeal to real-estate speculators. These interests united to undermine Powell's blueprint; what survived was the idea that water development was essential to the West.

Twentieth-century development took the form of megaprojects, such as the Glen Canyon Dam on the Colorado River, and water transfers from Colorado's Western Slope to the Front Range and the plains via a tunnel under the Continental Divide. These, in turn, provided subsidized water for large-scale irrigators and electrical power for users far from their source.

Statehood

American expansion in the West spread to Colorado with the discovery of gold in the mountains west of Denver in 1859. In 1861, the boundaries of Colorado Territory were defined, and President Lincoln appointed William Gilpin the first governor.

In 1870 two sets of railroad tracks reached Denver, ending Colorado's isolation. The Denver Pacific Railroad connected Denver with the Union Pacific's transcontinental line at Cheyenne, WY, and the Kansas Pacific arrived from Kansas City, MO. That same year, General William Palmer began planning the Denver & Rio Grande Railroad's narrow-gauge tracks into the mountain mining camps. The mining emphasis shifted from

WOMEN'S SUFFRAGE

On November 7, 1893, Colorado became the first US state – and one of the first places in the world – to adopt an amendment granting women the right to vote.

1879

Major Thornburg and his officers are killed in a Ute ambush, as are Indian agent Nathan Meeker and his 10 staff. The women and children are taken hostage. This becomes known as the Meeker Massacre.

1917

William F 'Buffalo Bill' Cody dies and is buried at Mt Lookout, overlooking Denver. Today you can visit the Buffalo Bill Museum & Grave from Golden.

ZU_09/GETTY IMAGES ©

➡ Buffalo Bill

1998–9

The Denver Broncos beat the Green Bay Packers and the following year the Atlanta Falcons to win back-to-back Super Bowls. Denver, and the rest of Colorado, is ecstatic.

gold to silver during the 1870s as mountain smelter sites, like Leadville and Aspen, developed into thriving population centers almost overnight.

National political expedience led to Colorado statehood in 1876, the centennial of US independence.

Museums & Stately Buildings

- *Black American West Museum & Heritage Center, Denver*
- *Brown Palace Hotel, Denver*
- *Colorado State Capitol, Denver*
- *Byers-Evans House Museum, Denver*
- *History Colorado Center, Denver*
- *Stanley Hotel, Estes Park*
- *Colorado Springs Fine Arts Center, Colorado Springs*
- *Wheeler Opera House, Aspen*
- *Trinidad History Museum, Trinidad*
- *Barney Ford Museum, Breckenridge*
- *Broadmoor, Colorado Springs*
- *Strater Hotel, Durango*

Post-WWII

From its earliest days the West was the country's most urbanized region; when Colorado became a state in 1876, more than a third of its residents lived in Denver. In part, urbanization was a function of the tourist economy, as Americans, who had flocked to the national parks during the economic boom after WWII, began to appreciate the Rockies as a place to live rather than just to visit. The federal government played a role by providing employment, thanks in large part to investment in Cold War military installations such as NORAD (North American Aerospace Defense Command), a facility near Colorado Springs. People relocated to remote towns such as Telluride as communications decentralized some sectors of the economy.

Increasingly, well-educated locals and visitors in the late 1960s and early '70s expressed environmental concerns. Military facilities, such as the Rocky Mountain National Arsenal near Colorado Springs and the Rocky Flats nuclear weapons facility near Denver, came under attack by activists concerned with environmental contamination, and were declared priority cleanup sites under the federal Environmental Protection Agency's Superfund program.

Tourism is now an economic mainstay in the Rockies. The industry blossomed in the post-WWII economic boom, when veterans of the 10th Mountain Division arrived home from war and dreamed up a whole new industry: they built the state's first ski lift out of spare parts and went on to help open ski resorts in Loveland, Arapahoe Basin and eventually Vail and Aspen. While the region's natural attractions have drawn visitors since the 1870s, up until WWII it was mostly only wealthy travelers who saw the backcountry. But post-war prosperity and the improvement of roads brought larger numbers of middle-class tourists.

1999

Students Eric Harris and Dylan Klebold kill 12 students and one teacher before committing suicide at Colombine High School, near Denver.

2000

Coloradans vote for Amendment 20 in the state election, which provides for the dispensing of cannabis to registered patients. A proliferation of medical marijuana clinics ensues over the next decade.

2010

Fires burn for 11 days near Boulder causing mass evacuations and property damage. Over 1000 firefighters are deployed, and 7000 acres and 169 houses are burnt.

2013

The 2013 Colorado Floods result from massive rainfall between September 9 and 12. Over $1 billion of damage was done to the Front Range and eight people died.

Way of Life

This place has always attracted extremes. Yes, Colorado has brought the world both the guttural rants of Hunter S Thompson and Christian activist group Focus on the Family, a strong opponent of same-sex marriage. Yet this diversity is nothing new. Long ago, escaped slaves and beat-down Confederates picked up the pieces after the Civil War; later right-wing militias were created alongside ecoterrorist plots. A symbol of freedom, the state has drawn fortune seekers, nature-lovers and naysayers of the status quo.

A place with this many folks pulling in so many directions is bound to have some quirks – witness the Emma Crawford Coffin Races or Frozen Dead Guy Days festival. Yet overall tolerance is a lucky common trait. While voting fluctuates between red and blue, the general character of today's Coloradan is friendly, fortified by sunshine and eager for the great outdoors.

It's no myth. Colorado really does average 300 days of sun annually, and 300,000 people float down Colorado rivers every year.

Land of Pioneers

Colorado likely gets its active, can-do attitude from the number of immigrants who ventured to this vast wilderness in search of a brighter and richer future. In a state littered with deep and crusty characters from its tawdry pioneering past, a handful stand out and paint a picture of the varying influences still at play in Colorado.

It would be difficult to be more hardcore pioneer than Charles and William Bent. The Missouri brothers were as integral to America's westward expansion as anyone. For 16 years, beginning in 1830, Charles led the Santa Fe Trail trade caravans across what was then an extremely hostile and unsettled prairie. William managed their famous Old Fort and some field operations. He forged harmonious relations with neighboring tribes, married a Cheyenne woman and once hid two Cheyenne from a band of armed Comanche. The fort had Spaniards, Mexicans, Americans and Native Americans bartering and mixing, drinking and dancing. The brothers mingled with John C Fremont, escorted the prospectors on their way to California and hired frontier scout Kit Carson.

Don't knock a prison town. Buena Vista and Cañon City both have a groovy, up-and-coming edge. In the mountains, Buena Vista runs cooler and deeper, but historic Cañon City has the Royal Gorge and fabulous dinosaur sites in the area.

Eventually Charles became New Mexico's first American governor, but was assassinated at his Taos home by an angry mob composed mostly of Pueblos before he could take the post. William's son, George, saw a massacre of a different kind. Half Cheyenne, he also married within the tribe and was present at Sand Creek in 1864 when the Colorado Volunteers attacked a village of Cheyenne and Arapaho, a grisly event that would end the 'Indian Wars' and clear the way for further expansion and gold mining on Native American land.

Barney Ford was born a Virginian slave in 1822. When he was 17 he and his mother escaped via the underground railroad. His mother, who had instilled in him the value of an education and taught him to read, died along the way, and he was recaptured and forced to work the Georgia goldfields. Eventually he escaped to Chicago to study. He dreamt of the California gold rush but was waylaid in Nicaragua before finally pursuing his dreams in Breckenridge, right after the first Colorado gold strike. The former Chicago barber eventually opened restaurants and

QUICK GUIDE TO COLORADO SPORTS

As disparate as the many strands of Colorado may seem, everyone here has one thing in common: a palpable, and some might say blind, passion for all things sport. Here are some facts worth knowing:

- If you're watching a local match in a sports bar, everyone – and we do mean everyone – roots for the home team. This isn't one of those places where you can move and maintain past allegiances. Even newbies love their Broncos, Nuggets, Rockies and Avs.
- Quarterback John Elway looms from billboards in the airport, peers down upon the interstate, and smiles and winks from the morning paper. Why? One of America's great quarterbacks, Elway was the only one to lead the Broncos to a Superbowl title, which he did twice, in 1998 and '99.
- Even many noncompetitive cyclists shave their legs. And most claim to have ridden with Ironman Dave Scott. Lance Armstrong is a touchy subject.
- Everyone in Colorado is always in training for...something. It could be a triathlon (known simply as 'tri') where they're gunning for their PB (personal best), prepping for ski season, or a grueling and highly technical 100-mile ride before happy hour.

hotels, funded gold explorations and sold equipment to miners in Denver and Breckenridge. He became the wealthiest man in Breckenridge and was eventually elected to the state legislature.

Spencer Penrose may have been Ford's polar opposite. Rich and Harvard educated, he spurned a cushy bank gig to go adventuring in 1892. He made a killing in gold and copper, and he married late after many dalliances. He was known to ride horses into the lobby of his business rival's hotel to make an offer on the land. After being spurned, he built the best hotel in America, the Broadmoor. He also built the Pikes Peak Hwy and christened it by staging a car race with his buddies. The Pikes Peak International Hill Climb is still in operation. In additon to giving Colorado Springs a zoo and access to Pikes Peak, he helped build and promote Colorado tourism as nobody ever had.

Industry was Mary Harris 'Mother 'Jones' foil when she came to Trinidad to join a particularly contentious miners' strike. She was 82 years old and taking on the Rockefeller family's Colorado Fuel & Iron. The miners, mostly European immigrants, were evicted from company homes and erected a tented camp in Ludlow. Jones bonded with them and led marches through downtown, bringing the national spotlight on Colorado. Eventually she was arrested and forced into 20 days of solitary confinement while the state militia stormed and torched the tented camp, killing three miners, two women and 11 children. The tragedy humiliated the Rockefellers and led to labor law reformation.

ICE PALACE

When Leadville was fat on silver, local bigwigs built a 90ft-high Ice Palace from blocks of ice. It was party central for the 1896 social season.

Extremism in the Rockies

With so many progressives in towns such as Boulder, Denver, Aspen, Crested Butte and Telluride, it's easy to forget that Colorado has a politically radical streak.

At a 1992 meeting in Estes Park, attended by fringe preacher Peter J Peters, Aryan Nations leader Richard Butler, Texas Ku Klux Klan leader Louis Beam and controversial attorney Kirk Lyons, Colorado birthed the right-wing militia movement of the 1990s. Held in response to a botched federal raid at Ruby Ridge, the meeting saw the attendees come up with a solution to stem what they saw as overreaches by government forces: form militias.

Soon there were militias in Montana, Michigan, Indiana and Colorado, where three men were arrested in connection with a pipe bomb in 1997. Their emergence became front-page news when Timothy McVeigh detonated a truck bomb outside the Oklahoma City Federal Building on April 19, 1995, killing 168 people. According to militia watchdogs, the movement waned after the bombing and subsequent Colorado arrests, although activity has resurfaced in the years since President Barack Obama took office.

But it's the radical left wing that has caused actual physical damage in Colorado. Members of the Earth Liberation Front set fire to Vail chairlifts and a restaurant to protest the expansion of Blue Sky Basin into endangered Canadian lynx habitat. Damages came to $12 million but there were no casualties. Arrests were made and William Rodgers, the man accused of setting the fires, killed himself on the eve of his trial.

Green Sheen

Colorado flies the sustainability flag as a point of fervent local pride. Browse any menu and a litany of local, grass-fed, fair-trade or organic options read like a tedious send-up of *Portlandia*. The EPA (Environmental Protection Agency) recognizes Colorado as having some of the cleanest air and water in the country. It's also a leader in renewable energy, with more LEED-certified buildings than any other state. Colorado College boasts some of these LEED buildings, as well as a permaculture dorm and a conscientious cafeteria: over 40% of the student dining budget goes to locally sourced food.

In the works there's more. The stretch of highway 36 between Denver and Boulder is being revamped to reward alternate transportation, with tolls imposed on single-occupant cars, an express shared-vehicle lane and dedicated bus and bike lanes. The first phase comes in at a cool $312 million. Light-rail transportation from Denver International Airport to the city downtown is also in the works. And not far behind, bike-share programs in Front Range cities will help maintain the state's status as the nation's slimmest.

Bizarre History & Haunted Houses

- *Stanley Hotel, Estes Park*
- *Great Fruitcake Toss, Colorado Springs*
- *Emma Crawford Coffin Races, Colorado Springs*
- *Ullr Fest, Breckenridge*
- *Delaware Hotel, Leadville*
- *Tarabino Inn, Trinidad*
- *Frozen Dead Guy Days, Nederland*

Marijuana Goes Mainstream

With the passing of Amendment 64 in November 2012, Colorado made recreational marijuana legal. But that didn't make it possible. There was a caveat. With marijuana illegal at the federal level, it was unsure how the change would play out. However, in August 2013 the Justice Department decided that it would not challenge state laws on the drug, and instead pursue serious trafficking.

At the time of writing, this news was so new that recreational bud had yet to hit the mainstream market. Essentially the amendment means it will be legal for those of 21 years or older to possess under 1oz (28.35g) or cultivate up to six plants per person for personal use. It may be consumed only within private residences, not in public. Like alcohol, consumption while driving will be regulated.

For dispensaries, which popped up after Colorado legalized medical marijuana back in 2000, the ruling is sure to be a cash cow. But don't expect bud to be sold alongside beer coolers. To keep a low profile with minors, dispensaries have nondescript storefronts, usually away from the prime real estate.

For now, you can stroll the streets of Telluride or Boulder sure of one thing: change is already in the air.

The Arts

More jock than artist, more adventurer than poet, Colorado isn't the most obvious candidate for a flourishing arts scene. But a convergence of key ingredients – transcendent natural beauty, a scrappy history and inspiration – has fostered great performances, literary movements and works of art well worth contemplating. To boot, the state's perfect summer weather has allowed outstanding cultural events such as the Colorado Shakespeare Festival and Aspen Music Festival to take the arts out into the open air.

Top Public Art

- *Dancers, Denver*
- *I See What You Mean, Denver*
- *Stations of the Cross, San Luis*
- *Swetsville Zoo, Fort Collins*
- *Blue Mustang, Denver*

The Mark of Ancient Cultures

The Ancestral Puebloan people lived in sandstone cliff dwellings in the Four Corners region of Colorado. Their striking architecture and handiwork included cylindrical ceremonial kivas and decorated pottery and basketry, all born from utilitarian need.

But their rock and cave paintings are something else entirely. Were they bored classroom doodles that somehow withstood the test of time? Interpretations offered by Native American elders indicate that most have deeper meanings.

On a visit to Petroglyph Point at Mesa Verde National Park, you'll see spirals and palm prints, and human and animal figures. Some help mark time, others hold more spiritual and ritualistic meaning, or display social rank. A petroglyph at Hovenweep National Monument on the Utah border has a well-known solstice marker. Shafts of sunlight strike the spiral differently at the winter and summer solstices.

Pottery, basketry and rock art played a central role in Native American life for hundreds of years. Evidence of Arapahoe, Cheyenne, Apache and Ute artifacts can be viewed in museums across the state. Ute pieces are especially prominent. On display are buffalo-hide paintings, beaded horse bags, rattles and drums made from buffalo rawhide.

To experience ceremonial drumming, chanting and dancing in traditional dress, you'll need to find your way to a powwow. The Southern Ute's annual powwow is held in Ignacio in early September.

An Art World Emerges

Folk art was the way from the days of indigenous freedom right through to the pioneering period. While there was certainly live music, song and dance in saloons that doubled as brothels, there wasn't much of what we would now consider fine art in nascent Colorado. In fact, even as the state grew into a ranching, mining and railroad force in the first half of the 20th century, sophisticated art wasn't part of the equation.

Enter Alice Bemis Taylor, the wife of a powerful mining tycoon. She leaned on her vast connections in the New York art world and, with the help of other wealthy philanthropists, founded the Colorado Springs Fine Arts Center, where Martha Graham danced on stage in its 400-seat theater on opening night. Today the center is still arguably the best museum in Colorado.

But what about iconic Western imagery? The Denver Art Museum, which also has a vast collection of contemporary and global art, as well as the largest Native American art collection in the US, is perhaps most famous for its gallery of cowboy art, including the iconic *Long Jakes, the Rocky Mountain Man* by Charles Deas. The Arthur Roy Mitchell Memorial Museum of Western Art is a decidedly smaller but earnest Western art gallery in Trinidad. Also known as 'the Mitch,' it was built in honor of this local cowboy artist in a late 19th-century department store.

But what about the new West? Public art and the growth of modern art outlets are shaking it up. Our favorite is Denver's newly inaugurated Clyfford Still Museum, featuring the breathtaking works of this major 20th-century abstract impressionist.

Galleries in the West

The most-established and best-connected art scene in Colorado is in Aspen, with a number of galleries tucked between fashion boutiques, perched over courtyard restaurants and occupying entire mini-malls in the historic downtown. Of course, gaudy and clichéd collections cling on like sparkly souvenir shops, but one spot will stand out. The 212 Gallery is among the most forward thinking, bringing a NYC edge to the mountain air.

The fledgling art scenes of Mancos and Pueblo sponsor First Friday art walks in the summer, held on the first Friday of the month.

Jack Kerouac's *On the Road* has more than one scene on Larimer St in Denver. The author's favorite bar was Paul's Place at 2219 Larimer St. There's still a bar, My Brother's Bar, at that address.

Summer Festivals

For the past 60-odd years, the Aspen Music Festival has given this town its artistic gravitas. Some of the best classical musicians from around the world come to perform and learn from the masters of their craft. Students form orchestras led by world-famous conductors and perform at the Wheeler Opera House or the Benedict Music Tent, or in smaller duets, trios, quartets and quintets on Aspen street corners. All told, there are more than 350 classical music events taking place over eight weeks. You can't escape – nor would you want to.

If you're hungry to hear the best music in the sweetest venue, the Benedict is a must. And you don't even have to pay – just unfurl a blanket on the Listening Lawn.

And that's not even the only music festival worth mentioning in Aspen. Jazz Aspen Snowmass is a bi-annual event held at the beginning

THE LITERARY CANON

Colorado's rebellious literary soul was led by the late, great Hunter S Thompson, author of *Fear & Loathing in Las Vegas*. Here's a man who ran for sheriff on the Freak Power Ticket and made his name by hanging with the Hells Angels, heckling Nixon and downing experimental drug cocktails. Eventually he committed suicide and had his ashes blasted out of a canon. His favorite hangout, the tavern in Woody Creek, has become a fan pilgrimage site of sorts.

One of Thompson's inspirations was Jack Kerouac, who also did some time on Colorado's freight trains and downbeat street corners. Another Beat writer (and Pulitzer Prize winner) with a lasting impact is Allen Ginsberg. The author of *Howl* was a founding poet of Jack Kerouac's School of Disembodied Poetics at Naropa University, where Ginsberg taught for more than two decades.

Of course, there's still a mainstream literary scene. Stephen King has set several of his bestsellers in Colorado (*The Stand, The Shining, Misery*), Wallace Stegner's masterpiece *Angle of Repose* is partly set in Leadville, and local Craig Childs has some fantastic books about the Southwest, from hairy wildlife stories in *Animal Dialogues* to the Anasazi in *House of Rain*. Set in eastern Colorado, *Plainsong*, by Kent Haruf, was a finalist in the National Book Award. And then there's good old Louis L'Amour.

COLORADO IN THE MOVIES

➡ **Denver & Around** Set the scene for *Dear Eleanor* (2014), a Sundance film produced by Leonardo DiCaprio.

➡ **Creede** The open range for Johnny Depp's flop *The Lone Ranger* (2013).

➡ **Telluride** Hosted *Darling Companion* (2012), with Diane Keaton and Kevin Kline.

➡ **Boulder** Starred in both *Catch and Release* (2006) with Jennifer Garner and *About Schmidt* (2002) with Jack Nicholson.

➡ **Stanley Hotel** This Estes Park hotel was the setting for Stanley Kubrick's *The Shining* (1980) – another Nicholson gem – though Kubrick filmed in Montana, Oregon and England.

➡ **Durango & Silverton Narrow Gauge Railroad** Bakers Bridge is where Robert Redford and Paul Newman jumped into the river in *Butch Cassidy and the Sundance Kid* (1969). Durango also made a star turn in Renée Zellweger's *Nurse Betty* (2000).

➡ **Silverton** Westerns and silver-screen classics brought Marilyn Monroe, Clark Gable, Anthony Quinn, James Stewart, Janet Leigh and Henry Fonda here.

➡ **Cañon City** The Prospect Heights neighborhood was the defacto Western backlot of film company United Artists; *True Grit* (1969), starring John Wayne, was shot here and in Ridgway.

➡ **Glenwood Springs** The crew of *Mr & Mrs Smith* (2005) stayed at the Hotel Colorado while filming part of the flick.

and end of the summer, featuring jazz masters such as Christian McBride, Nicholas Payton and Natalie Cole in June, and major pop and rock acts such as Wilco around Labor Day. Theatre Aspen is another annual tradition, where Tony-winning romantic comedies and deliciously subversive musicals are staged (mostly in the summer and early autumn) in a gorgeous, tented complex in the heart of Rio Grande Park.

Willie Nelson's seminal album, *Red Headed Stranger* is a concept album about a fugitive Montana cowboy on the run from the law after killing his wife and her lover. Inspired by Colorado's Rocky Mountains, Nelson purportedly wrote the tracks while driving back from a ski weekend.

Of course, summer music festivals aren't exclusive to Aspen. Breckenridge hosts a similar summer-long classical music festival with free concerts along the Blue River, and Telluride hosts a bluegrass festival in June that attracts a mix of straight-up bluegrass players, up-and-coming rockers and global icons. It's worth planning your life around. And bluegrass isn't even what put Telluride on the map. That would be the Telluride Film Festival. It's now considered on par with Sundance, featuring indie and edgy domestic and international fare, and attended by Hollywood stars and career-makers. Celebrating its 40th anniversary, the film festival is an iconic international event attracting 4000 cinephiles each September for a sneak peak at innovative new films. The first megahit to come out of it was *Slumdog Millionaire* (2008), and with guests like Salman Rushdie, Stephen Sondheim and Noah Bombach, it has hosted some heavy hitters. Festival-goers on a budget can enjoy free films, open-air cinema and conversations with influential moviemakers. There are also discounted passes to the late show. But if you want to rub elbows with Hollywood elite at the ticketed social events, you'll need to pony up.

Another solid bet is Telluride's Mountainfilm, a Memorial Day festival showcasing excellent outdoor adventure and environmental films sure to whet your appetite for the San Juans, which loom over the town.

Colorado Cuisine

With ranches on both sides of the Rockies that sprawl across spectacular high-country plateaus, this was a place of meat and potatoes, with only the exotic Rocky Mountain oyster to challenge an outsider's palate. Today's mix of old and cutting-edge influences have made Colorado dining much more dynamic. Of course, there's plenty of middle America left on the plate, but there are a lot of happy surprises too.

The Sustainable Table

The most interesting, tasty – and perhaps most overdue – movement in Colorado dining is the general drift toward high-end farm-to-table cuisine. It's been a grass-roots movement inspired by a widening interest and dependency on farmers markets as a whole. From May (at the latest) until early October there are terrific weekly farmers markets in towns such as Denver, Boulder, Aspen, Telluride, Vail and tiny Minturn – and that doesn't even scratch the surface. It was only a matter of time before restaurants embraced the local breadbasket, too.

The 'eat local' ethos is grounded in the philosophy made famous in Michael Pollan's *The Omnivore's Dilemma:* that food loses both nutrients and flavor the further it has to travel. In other words, food is always healthiest and most delicious when mileage is limited. Plus, without huge distances to cover, it's (theoretically) cheaper, and untold pollution linked to freight is mitigated.

The problem for food-producing states such as Colorado has long been that out-of-state demand has trumped local dollars. For years much of the best-quality beef, lamb, pork and vegetables left town. No more. Denver's Root Down, in the chic Highlands area, is one example of a New American farm-to-table restaurant, and the Squeaky Bean is the city's second-best option. In Boulder you can dine at Salt or Kitchen; Vail's Kelly Liken leans heavily on local suppliers.

For the inside skinny on regional growers, markets and restaurants, check out www.ediblecommunities.com, which features food magazines covering Aspen, the Front Range and the San Juan Mountains (which include Telluride).

A FORK IN THE WILDERNESS

One Colorado dining experience could never be replicated in New York or Paris: the wilderness restaurant. In the high country, there is many a hidden gourmet table accessed only by ski trail, a gondola trip, a sleigh ride or hike. Your reward goes far beyond an appetizing plate and a bottle of wine. Picture a summit panorama, a roaring log fire and the true hunger spawned by being out in the fresh mountain air.

Some of our favorites:

- The Tenth (p203)
- Allreds (p260)
- Game Creek Restaurant (p203)
- Beano's Cabin (p208)
- Pine Creek Cookhouse (p226)
- Tennessee Pass Cookhouse (p240)

BREAKFAST BURRITO

Nobody would actually sell these hot missiles in Mexico, but no matter. The breakfast burrito is one Mexican-inspired food group mastered far and wide here. It's served in diners and Jewish delis in Denver, in ski-punk coffee shops and straight from a bus in Leadville. Packed with protein (eggs, cheese, beans), fresh veggies and hot salsa, rolled to go in paper and foil, it may be the perfect breakfast for those on the go. Smuggle it onto the gondola, grind it in the car, hell, store it in your purse (but not for too long).

The Alt Diet

With the lowest rates of obesity of any state, Coloradans seem to know how to eat. Of course, another factor is their insatiable appetite for activity, though, in research published in the *International Journal of Obesity*, some scientists now speculate that even just living at altitude will make you thinner. Regardless, Colorado is at the cutting edge when it comes to alternative eating.

For visitors, this discerning tendency might make your wait in bakery or deli lines a game of patience. But if you're picky, this might be the place for you. First of all, no one bats an eye at your food allergies or restrictions. It's de rigueur these days to find gluten-free, vegan and vegetarian items on menus in urban and tourist areas, even at the local steakhouse. Many restaurants also nod to the latest food fads, so paleo diet followers and fans of kale will do just fine.

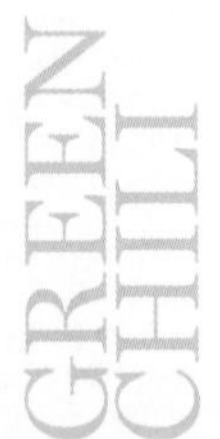

A dish endemic to New Mexico and southern Colorado, green chili is a sauce made from roasted and stewed green and red chilies, cumin, oregano, cilantro (coriander) and chunks of pork. Served hot, it's often poured over burritos, enchiladas and tamales.

You Call This Mexican?

Present-day Colorado borders New Mexico, while a portion of the state once belonged to Old Mexico, which makes it doubly strange that Colorado's Mexican food is mostly underwhelming. However, if you stick around long enough and look hard enough, you can get your fix.

Pueblo is the Hispanic heartland of the state, with half the city on the south side of the Arkansas River, once the official Mexico–America border. Alamosa also has deep Mexican roots, and some ski towns do a surprisingly good job at making a Mexican fix.

Our favorites statewide include Taqueria El Nopal in Glenwood Springs, the Minturn Saloon, Calvillo's in Alamosa, Mirasol Cantina in Winter Park, Telluride's La Cocina de Luz and Lucha Cantina in Georgetown and Breckenridge.

High Hops & Spirits

Colorado has only 2% of the US population, but 8% of its breweries. Today there are over 160 craft breweries, many of them medal winners, and there are more in the works. The Front Range leads the way as the largest market for craft brewing in the US. Colorado also leads the nation in the drinking of draft beer. Call these people overachievers. Homer Simpson would be very happy here indeed.

Real beer aficionados shouldn't miss Denver's Great American Beer Festival, the nation's premier beer event. Held in September or October at the cool Colorado Convention Center, this mammoth three-day festival and competition draws 49,000 people. Unfortunately, tickets sell out almost the instant they go on sale, but you could also check out a number of festivals and dedicated events held around the state at www.coloradobeer.org.

In a state hung up on local ingredients and artisan product, craft distilleries were the logical next step. From garage operations to big names, these businesses are popping up in cities and mountain towns. We're talking about those hand-crafted rums, vodkas, whiskeys, gins and liqueurs that keep cocktail hours interesting.

Bar menus highlight local spirits and many distilleries offer their own tour. Based in Denver, Stranahan's is a small batch distiller that makes only 12 barrels of whiskey per week out of locally grown barley. Another one to watch is Montanya, a Crested Butte–based rum distiller with a number of awards under its belt (and amazing craft cocktails post-tour). Check out Peach Street Distillers in Palisade if you want to taste amazing Palisade peaches in a bottle.

Colorado Wine Country

Though miners brought grapevines in the 19th century, cultivation was small-scale and adversely affected by Prohibition. The practice was resurrected as recently as the 1960s, when a Denver dentist opened the first Colorado winery using California grapes.

Today there are approximately 100 commercial wineries in the state, with most on the Western Slope. Though the Grand Valley and West Elks near Grand Junction have the largest concentration of vineyards, the area around Cortez and the Front Range are other areas that are developing. Between 4000ft and 7000ft above sea level, these vineyards are among the highest in the world. Sunny days, cool nights and low humidity cultivate what locals call ideal conditions for grapes, though the growing season is markedly shorter than in California.

As a result, faster-ripening varietals – such as Bordeaux, Rhone Valley, Merlot, Syrah and Viognier – do well here. But you will also find Cabernet Sauvignon, Chardonnay and many others.

Top Steaks

Jimmy's, Aspen

Elway's, Denver

Juicy Lucy's Steakhouse, Glenwood Springs

Sweet Basil, Vail

Blue Star, Colorado Springs

Briar Rose, Breckenridge

Happy-Hour Dining

Those coming from out of state might not suspect how seriously Coloradans take their happy hour. Indeed, for those who want to beat the bluebirds the next morning to ride 50 miles before work, the only option for socializing is to do it early. The tradition is savored by students, professionals and everyone in between.

Because happy hour is so popular, restaurants compete fiercely and offer incredible deals. Nowhere is this more apparent than in Colorado's fine-dining establishments, which may be out of reach for many during dinner hour, but offer incredible small-plate deals during happy hour that are cheaper than the local pizzeria – and far more lively.

CRUISING THE VINEYARDS

The main destination for Colorado wine country touring is the area around Grand Junction and Palisade (p299). Blue sky, red-rock country, this fledgling vineyard area has a homespun, desert feel that's a stark contrast to the green hills of Sonoma. Here's how to start:

- Visit www.coloradowine.com to find out about upcoming festivals or special events.
- Download the agrotourism brochure and map at the Palisade Chamber of Commerce website (www.palisadecoc.com)– it's a handy guide to keep with you in the car.
- Mix it up – because how much wine tasting can you actually do in a day? Visit lavender farms and alpaca refuges interspersed with vineyards on the dusty backroads of Palisade.
- Consider a do-it-yourself tour by bicycle.
- Dine at top-notch restaurants with Colorado wine lists and knowledgeable servers to research some favorites to visit in person. We like Boulder's Salt, Grand Junction's 626 on Rood and Inari's A Palisade Bistro.

Limited, discounted happy-hour menus are offered in pubs and restaurants between around 3:30pm and 6pm (sometimes until 7pm). Go on the early end to get a table. Check restaurant websites for details. Few offer weekend deals, though some spots offer late-night happy hours from 10pm until close during the week.

In Denver we love happy hour at Steuben's. Old Boulder standbys the Med and Jax have competition from Salt and Cafe Aion. You will also find a thriving tradition in every ski town, pub and brewhouse in the state.

Wildlife & the Land

Colorado is a quilt of arid canyons and mesas, with vast unbroken plains and a burly Rocky Mountain backbone. Much of this extraordinary landscape enjoys some level of protection and management by local, state and federal agencies, but industry has had its say, too. In the early years mining took its toll. Today oil and gas development via the practice of fracking has become a point of contention for public health. The other major issue is that we may be loving Colorado to death, as population growth and ski-resort developments encroach on natural habitats.

Geology

Tectonic shifts and volcanic activity known as the Laramide Revolution shook, folded and molded the Colorado landscape, where granite peaks rise nearly 10,000ft above adjacent plains. Colorado's highest point is 14,433ft Mt Elbert. Behind the Front Range lie several scattered mountain ranges and broad plateaus; their most notable geologic feature is the spectacular Rocky Mountain Trench, a fault valley 1100 miles long.

Glaciers also shaped the land. The Laurentide Ice Sheet left deep sediments as it receded into the Arctic during the warming of the Quaternary period. A cordilleran glacier system formed at higher altitudes in the Rockies, leaving moraines, lakes, cirques and jagged alpine landforms as they melted. Their melting also formed massive rivers that eroded and shaped the state's spectacular canyons on the Colorado Plateau to the southwest.

Conservation plays an important role in Colorado's future. Contact the Nature Conservancy (www.nature.org) for information on current issues and volunteer opportunities. To help out in Colorado parks, contact the individual park offices.

Dinosaurs

Although dinosaurs dominated the planet for over 100 million years, only a few places have the proper geological and climatic conditions to preserve their skeletons as fossils and their tracks as permanent evolutionary place holders. Colorado is near the top of that list. If you or your loved ones are dinophiles, you've come to the right state.

Back in the *really* olden days – like during the Jurassic (208 to 144 million years ago) and Cretaceous (144 to 65 million years ago) periods – Colorado was a decidedly different place. The Rockies hadn't yet risen and Pangea had only recently split (what's a million years?), meaning present-day Colorado was close to the equator.

Most, if not all, of the sites where fossilized dinosaur bones were found en masse are thought to have been in or near a floodplain. These areas were important water sources during wet season, but could be bone dry in dry season. Often dinosaurs would migrate for miles and days and weeks in search of water. If they arrived at the floodplain at the wrong time of year, many simply died. Winds covered their bodies in layers of dust, and later floods further coated their bones in mud. It takes many thousands of layers of dust and mud and approximately 12,000 years for these bones to become fossils. It also takes a pressurized environment, which is why layers of water over the earth is a key (but not vital) ingredient to fossilization.

BEST DINOSAUR SITES

Before embarking on your dino-tracking tour, make sure to stop by the Denver Museum of Nature & Science (p67). A good primer for what you'll see in the field, the prehistoric wing has the most complete *Stegosaurus* skeleton discovered. Excellent field sites include the following:

➡ **Dinosaur National Monument** (p163) The quintessential stop for dinophiles of all ages is in northern Colorado; the visitor center is set in a quarry with views of over 1500 prehistoric bones embedded in the cliff face.

➡ **Picketwire Dinosaur Tracksite** (p323) The largest documented site of its kind in North America, there are as many as 1300 visible *Allosaurus* and *Apatosaurus* tracks, left behind as they migrated along the muddy shoreline of a large prehistoric lake in the state's southeast.

➡ **Garden Park Fossil Area** (p313) Also in the southeast, this is one of Colorado's largest Jurassic graveyards. It was the stage for the so-called Bone Wars, an academic battle to discover new dinosaur species.

➡ **Dinosaur Ridge** (p99) Kids love the footprints and fossils; it's the closest dinosaur option to Denver.

With time and pressure the porous bones begin to absorb the minerals from the dust and stone, which replace the original cell structure of the bones, turning them into fossils.

Flora

Colorado's vegetation is closely linked to climate, which in turn depends on both elevation and rainfall. Vegetation at altitude can still vary depending upon exposure and the availability of water. That's why the San Juans and Spanish Peaks can look so different in places from the Maroon Bells and Rocky Mountain National Park.

Sparse piñon-juniper forests cover the Rockies' slopes from about 4000ft to 6000ft, while ponderosa pines indicate the montane zone between 6000ft and 9000ft, where deciduous alders, luscious white-barked aspens (their lime-green foliage turns gold in fall), willows and the distinctive blue spruce flourish in damper areas. In the subalpine zone, above 9000ft, Engelmann spruce largely replace pine (though some stands of lodgepoles grow higher), while colorful wildflowers such as columbine, marsh marigold and primrose colonize open spaces. In the alpine zone above 11,500ft, alpine meadows and tundra supplant stunted trees, which can grow only in sheltered, southern exposures.

East of the Rockies, the Great Plains are an immense grassland of short and tall grasses, interrupted by dense gallery forests of willows and cottonwoods along the major rivers. The best example of intact savanna is found in the Pawnee National Grassland, where the Pawnee Buttes loom. A good example of eastern Colorado's riparian (riverbank) foliage is found along the Arkansas River near Bent's Old Fort on the Santa Fe Trail. Those arid zones closest to the Rockies consist of shorter species such as wheatgrass, grama and buffalo grass, which grow no higher than about 3ft.

SPANISH PEAKS

The Spanish Peaks, in southern Colorado near La Veta, are not part of the Rocky Mountains, but rather extinct volcanoes.

Wildlife

Colorado wildlife correlates in part (but not completely) to elevation and climate, and the number of animals, especially that of the more mobile ones, varies seasonally. In the alpine zones, for instance, small rodents such as pikas inhabit rockfalls throughout the year, but larger mammals such as Rocky Mountain elk and bighorn sheep are present only in summer.

The Great Plains have their own singular fauna, such as the swift pronghorn antelope and prairie dogs. The swift pronghorn grazes short-grass plains nearest the mountains, while the prairie dog is neither a prairie-dweller nor a dog: related to the squirrel, it lives in sprawling burrows known as prairie dog 'towns.' Species such as mule deer and coyotes range over a variety of zones from the plains to the peaks. The solitary, lumbering moose prefers riparian zones. If luck is on your side, you'll see them wading in lakes and trudging through wetlands in the Kawuneeche Valley in Rocky Mountain National Park.

The most famous animal of the Colorado plains was, of course, the magnificent buffalo or bison that grazed the prairies in enormous herds until its near extinction. The bison survives in limited numbers in Wyoming, but the last-known wild Colorado resident was killed in the South Park area in 1897. There are still bison in Colorado, but they're not wild. They're livestock raised for meat.

Best Wildlife Viewing

- *Weminuche Wilderness Area*
- *Rocky Mountain National Park*
- *Black Canyon of the Gunnison National Park*
- *Arapahoe National Wildlife Refuge*
- *Maroon Bells Wilderness*

Bears

The black bear is probably the most notorious animal in the Rockies. Despite the name, its fur can have a honey or cinnamon tint, its muzzle can be tan, and it can even have white spots on its chest. Adult males weigh from 275lb to 450lb; females weigh 175lb to 250lb. They measure 3ft high on all fours and can be over 5ft when standing on their hind legs. The largest populations of black bears live in areas where aspen trees propagate, and near open areas of chokecherry and serviceberry bushes. Their range can stretch to 250 sq miles.

The grizzly bear, America's largest meat eater, is classified as an endangered species in Colorado, but it is almost certainly gone from the state. The last documented grizzly in Colorado was killed in 1979.

Bighorn Sheep

Rocky Mountain National Park is a special place: 'Bighorn Crossing Zone' is a sign you're unlikely to encounter elsewhere. From late spring through summer, three or four volunteers and an equal number of rangers provide traffic control on US 34 at Sheep Lakes Information Station, 2 miles west of the Fall River Entrance Station. Groups of up to 60 sheep – typically ewes and lambs – move from the moraine ridge north of the highway across the road to Sheep Lakes in Horseshoe Park. Unlike the big under-curving horns on mature rams, ewes grow swept-back crescent-shaped horns that reach only about 10in in length. The Sheep Lakes are evaporative ponds ringed with tasty salt deposits that attract the ewes in the morning and early afternoon after lambing in May and June. In August they rejoin the rams in the Mummy Range.

To see bighorn sheep on rocky ledges, you'll need to hike or backpack. The estimated 200 animals in the Horseshoe Park herd live permanently in the Mummy Range. On the west side, an equally large herd inhabits the volcanic cliffs of the Never Summer Mountains. A smaller herd can be seen along the Continental Divide at a distance from the rim of the crater near Milner Pass. Three miles west of the Alpine Visitors Center on Trail Ridge Rd, Crater Trail follows a steep course for 1 mile to the observation point.

State and federal wildlife authorities list seven amphibians, 19 birds, 23 fish, 13 mammals (including lynx, fox and wolf), 10 reptiles and two mollusks as threatened, endangered or Species of Special Concern in Colorado.

Elk

Seeing a herd of North American elk, or *wapiti* (a Native American term meaning white, reference to the animal's white tail and rump), grazing in their natural setting is unforgettable. According to National Park Services (NPS) surveys, about 2000 elk winter in the Rocky Mountain National Park's lower elevations, while more than 3000 inhabit the park's lofty terrain during summer months. The summer visitor equipped with

COLORADO'S BEST HOT SPRINGS

From the hidden, all-natural variety that takes a full day's hike to discover to day-use private springs in historic towns, to splashy resorts in the shadow of Collegiate Peaks, you'd do well to sink into riverside bliss.

➡ **Conundrum Hot Springs** (p220) Aspen locals love to hike high into the mountains above town then slip into all-natural hot springs beneath the stars.

➡ **Strawberry Park Hot Springs** (p158) Absolutely the most laid-back hot spring in the state, Strawberry Park Hot Springs is a place to check in and chill out.

➡ **Springs Resort & Spa** (p275) Set beneath the looming San Juans, the Pagosa Springs namesake is an attractive private concession beloved by locals.

➡ **Mt Princeton Hot Springs** (p234) A splashy, sprawling resort, bubbling with hot springs in an idyllic Collegiate Peaks location.

binoculars or a telephoto lens is almost always rewarded by patiently scanning the hillsides and meadows near the Alpine Visitors Center. Traffic jams up as motorists stop to observe these magnificent creatures near the uppermost section of Fall River Rd or Trail Ridge Rd. Visitors are warned by signs and park rangers not to harass, call to or come in contact with the animals.

Mature elk bulls may reach 1100lb; cows weigh up to 600lb. Both have dark necks with light tan bodies. Like bighorn sheep, elk were virtually extinct around Estes Park by 1890, wiped out by hunters. In 1913 and '14, before the establishment of the national park, people from Estes Park brought in 49 elk from Yellowstone. The elk's natural population increase since the establishment of Rocky Mountain National Park is one of the NPS' great successes, directly attributable to the removal of their principal predator: men with guns.

Four species of fox are native to Colorado. Red foxes live in mountain riparian zones, gray foxes like canyons, swift foxes live in the eastern plains and kit foxes live in the western deserts.

Other Mammals

You are likely to encounter mule deer, named for their large mule-like ears, somewhere along your journey as they browse on leaves and twigs from shrubs at sunny lower elevations. Howling coyotes commonly serenade winter campfires – lucky visitors may spy a coyote stalking small rodents. Other large carnivores such as the bobcat and mountain lion are very rarely seen. Small but ferocious long-tailed weasel hunt near their streamside dens at night.

Birds

An astounding 465 bird species have been identified in the state of Colorado. Among them are flycatchers, burrowing owls (federally listed as threatened) and great horned owls, crows, mourning doves, mountain plovers, chickadees, Canadian geese, bluebirds and cranes. The newly classified and unique Gunnison sage grouse, found in the southwest, is listed as a Species of Special Concern and is a candidate to be placed on the federal endangered species list. There are two types of eagle. The more prevalent golden eagle has a wingspan of 7ft and ranges throughout North America. The bald eagle only relatively recently bounced back from near extinction and remains on the endangered species list. At its low point only two or three nesting pairs nested in Colorado, but that number has increased by eight or nine each year, and at last count there were 51 breeding pairs and a stable population of over 800 eagles in the state.

Best Birding

Rocky Mountain National Park

Pawnee National Grassland

Alamosa National Wildlife Refuge

Arapahoe National Wildlife Refuge

Chautauqua Park

Survival Guide

Directory A–Z

Accommodations

Colorado provides a vast array of accommodation options: from pitching a tent under a starlit sky and budget motels to midrange B&Bs, adobe inns and historical hotels to four-star lodgings, luxurious spas and dude ranches. The most comfortable accommodations for the lowest price are usually found in that great American invention, the roadside motel.

B&Bs

Many B&Bs are high-end romantic retreats in restored historic homes run by personable, independent innkeepers who serve gourmet breakfasts. These B&Bs often take pains to evoke a theme – Victorian, rustic and so on – and amenities range from merely comfortable to hopelessly indulgent. Rates start around $120, and the best run to more than $300. Many B&Bs have minimum-stay requirements, and some exclude young children.

European-style B&Bs can be found in Colorado: these may be rooms in someone's home, with plainer furnishings, simpler breakfasts, shared bathrooms and cheaper rates. They often welcome families.

B&Bs can close out of season and reservations are essential, especially for high-end places. To avoid surprises, always ask whether bathrooms are shared or private.

Camping

Camping is the cheapest, and in many ways the most enjoyable, approach to a vacation. Visitors with a car and a tent can take advantage of hundreds of private and public campgrounds and RV (recreational vehicle) parks at prices of $13 to $34 per night. The best resource for camping is www.recreation.gov for all reservable USFS (United States Forest Services) campsites.

Some of the best camping areas are on public lands (national forests, state and national parks...), including **Bureau of Land Management** (BLM; ☎303-239-3600; www.co.blm.gov) lands. Free dispersed camping (meaning you can camp almost anywhere) is permitted in many public backcountry areas. Sometimes you can camp along a dirt road, especially in BLM and national forest areas. In other places, you can backpack your gear into a cleared campsite.

Information and maps are available from ranger stations or BLM offices, and may be posted along the road into the campsite. Sometimes, a free camping permit is required, particularly in national parks.

WASTE & FACILITIES

When camping in an undeveloped area choose a site at least 200ft from water and wash up at camp, not in the stream, using biodegradable soap. Dig a 6in-deep hole to use as a latrine and cover and camouflage it well when leaving the site. Burn toilet paper, unless fires are prohibited. Carry out all trash.

Use a portable charcoal grill or camping stove; don't build new fires. If there

SLEEPING PRICE RANGES

Price indicators relate to the price for a double room. Unless otherwise noted, breakfast is not included, bathrooms are private and lodging is open year-round. Rates generally don't include taxes, which can vary considerably between towns.

Prices displayed generally relate to peak-season charges; these can drop markedly out of season.

- **$** less than $100
- **$$** $100 to $200
- **$$$** more than $200

already is a fire ring, use only dead and downed wood or wood you have carried in yourself. Make sure to leave the campsite as you found it.

Developed areas usually have toilets, drinking water, fire pits (or charcoal grills) and picnic benches. Some don't have drinking water, and some turn the water off out of season. It's always a good idea to take a few gallons of water when camping. These basic campgrounds usually cost about $13 to $18 a night. Some areas have showers or RV hookups and often cost $22 to $34.

RESERVATIONS

National forest and BLM campgrounds are usually less developed, while national park and state park campgrounds are more likely to have greater amenities. The less-developed sites are often on a 'first-come, first-served' basis, so arrive early, preferably during the week, as sites fill up fast on Friday and weekends. More-developed areas may accept or require reservations.

PRIVATE CAMPGROUNDS

Private campgrounds are usually close to towns or nearby. Most are designed for RVs but tents can usually be erected. Camp fees are higher than for public campgrounds. Fees are usually quoted for two people per site, with additional fees for extra people (about $6 per person). Some places charge just per vehicle. Facilities can include hot showers, coin laundry, swimming pool, full RV hookups, a games area, a playground and a convenience store.

ONLINE RESOURCES

Camping USA (www.camping-usa.com) A great resource with more than 12,000 campgrounds in its database, including RV parks, private campgrounds, BLM areas and state and national parks.

Kampgrounds of America (KOA; ☎888-562-0000; www.koa.com; depending on hookups $22-36) A vast national network of private campgrounds. You can purchase the annual directory of KOA campgrounds at any KOA, or by calling.

Recreation.gov (☎877-444-6777, 518-885-3639; www.recreation.gov) Organizes reservations for campsites on federal land.

Dude Ranches

Most visitors to dude ranches today are city-slickers looking for an escape from a fast-paced, high-tech world.

Dude ranches date back to the late 19th century. These days you can find anything from a working-ranch experience (smelly chores and 5am wake-up calls included) to a Western Club Med. Typical week-long visits run from $250 to $600 per person per day, including accommodations, meals, activities and equipment.

While the centerpiece of dude-ranch vacations is horseback riding, many ranches feature swimming pools and have expanded their activity lists to include fly-fishing, hiking, mountain biking, tennis, golf, skeet-shooting and cross-country skiing. Accommodations range from rustic log cabins to cushy suites with whirlpools and cable TV. Meals range from family-style spaghetti dinners to four-course gourmet feasts.

Colorado Dude & Guest Ranch Association (☎866-942-3472; www.coloradoranch.com)

Dude Ranchers' Association (☎307-587-2339, 866-399-2339; www.duderanch.org)

Hostels

Staying in a private double at a hostel can be a great way to save money and still have privacy (although you'll usually have to share a bathroom). Dorm beds allow those in search of the ultimate bargain to sleep cheap under a roof. Dorms cost between $18 and $28, depending on the city and time of year. A private room in a Colorado hostel costs between $38 and $60.

US citizens and residents can join **Hostelling International-USA** (HI-USA; ☎301-495-1240; www.hiusa.org; annual membership adult/child $28/free) by calling and requesting a membership form or by downloading a form from the website. HI-USA doesn't have any hostels in Colorado. However, the HI card may be used for discounts at some local merchants and for local services, including some intercity bus companies.

Hotels

Except for chains, Colorado's hotels are mostly found in cities, and they're generally large and luxurious, except for a few boutique hotels, which tend to be small, understated and lavish. Prices start at around $79 and shoot straight up; ask about discounts and special packages when making reservations. Always check online first when booking a hotel.

Long-Term Rentals

Houses or condominiums can be rented for anywhere from two days to two months. This type of lodging

BOOK YOUR STAY ONLINE

For more accommodations reviews by Lonely Planet authors, check out www.lonelyplanet.com/hotels. You'll find independent reviews, as well as recommendations on the best places to stay. Best of all, you can book online.

is most often found in resort areas and almost always includes kitchens and living rooms.

Several people can lodge for the same price, so long-term rentals can be more economical than motels or hotels on a per-person basis, especially if you can cook your own food. The chambers of commerce in resort towns have information on condominium listings and can give advice on renting.

Also consider some of the corporate housing agencies such as **Avenue West** (Map p64; ☎303-825-7625, 877-944-8283; www.avewest.com; 1440 Market St, Denver) and **Oakwood** (☎877-902-0832; www.oakwood.com; ⌚6:30am-9pm Mon-Fri, 7am-6:30pm Sat & Sun).

Motels

Budget chain motels are prevalent throughout Colorado; in smaller towns they're often the only option. Many motels have at-the-door parking, with exterior room doors. These are convenient, though some folks, especially single women, may prefer the more expensive places with more secure interior corridors.

Advertised prices are referred to as 'rack rates' and are not written in stone. Asking about specials can usually save quite a bit of money. Children are often allowed to stay free with their parents.

Discount Cards

Visitors to Colorado should look into all the standard national and international discount cards. Travelers can find all sorts of ways to shave costs off hotel rooms, meals, rental cars, museum admissions and just about anything else that can be had for a price. Persistence and ingenuity go a long way when it comes to finding deals in Colorado.

Students

- Ask for a discount whenever booking a room, reserving a car or paying an entrance fee.
- Generally receive discounts of 10% or so, but sometimes as much as 50%.
- Consider investing in a **Student Advantage Card** (www.studentadvantage.com) or an **International Student Identity Card** (ISIC; www.isiccard.com).
- Always carry proof of student status.

Youths

- Look into the **International Youth Travel Card** (IYTC; www.isic.org).

Seniors (Over 62)

- Ask for a discount whenever booking a room, reserving a car or paying an entrance fee.
- Generally receive discounts of 10% or so, but sometimes as much as 50%.
- Consider an **America the Beautiful Senior Pass** (http://store.usgs.gov/pass/senior.html; $10 valid for the lifetime of the pass owner) for 50% discounts on fees such as camping on federal recreational lands.
- Always carry proof of age.

Over 50s

- Contact the **American Association of Retired Persons** (☎888-687-2277; www.aarp.org) for travel discounts, typically 10% to 25% off hotels, car rentals, entertainment etc.

Motorists

Card-carrying members of automobile associations are entitled to similar travel discounts. **The American Automobile Association** (AAA; ☎866-625-3601; www.colorado.aaa.com) has reciprocal agreements with several international auto associations, so bring your membership card from home.

Other Discounts

Other people whose status might lead to discounts are US military personnel and veterans, travelers with disabilities, children, business travelers and foreign visitors. These discounts may not always be advertised – it pays to ask.

Discount Coupons

Discount coupons can be found at every tourist locale. They always have restrictions and conditions, so read the fine print. Some are hardly worth the effort, but scour tourist information offices and highway welcome centers for brochures and fliers, and you'll find a few gems. For online hotel coupons, browse **hotelcoupons.com** (www.roomsaver.com).

Food

Rates for main meals in Eating sections:

- **$** less than $10
- **$$** $10 to $20
- **$$$** more than $20

See the Cuisine chapter (p353) for more information on eating in Colorado.

Electricity

Gay & Lesbian Travelers

Colorado is very much a mixed bag for gay and lesbian travelers. In general, cities and college towns have more progressive attitudes. Denver especially has a thriving gay and lesbian scene.

Some other areas in the state are characterized by conservative attitudes and old-school ideas of machismo. The more affluent ski areas and artsy communities seem to be less uptight about same-sex relationships, but there's no mistaking the region for San Francisco.

According to www.epodunk.com, here's how some of Colorado's cities fare on a 'gay index', a comparative score based on the percentage of same-sex households in a state. A score of 100 is the national norm; the higher the number, the more gays and lesbians there are.

- Denver 216
- Boulder 138
- Fort Collins 85
- Colorado Springs 78
- Grand Junction 78

Resources

Good national guidebooks include *Damron Women's Traveller, Damron Men's Travel Guide* and *Damron Accommodations*, with listings of gay-owned or gay-friendly accommodations nationwide. All three are published by the **Damron Company** (☎415-255-0404, 800-462-6654; www.damron.com).

Another good resource is the **Gay & Lesbian Yellow Pages** (☎800-697-2812; www.glyp.com), with 33 national and regional directories.

National resources include the **National Gay & Lesbian Task Force** (☎202-393-5177; www.thetaskforce.org) in Washington, DC, and the **Lambda Legal Defense Fund** (☎Los Angeles 213-382-7600, New York City 212-809-8585; www.lambdalegal.org).

Health

Colorado has an extraordinary range of climates and terrains, from the freezing heights of the Rockies to the searing midsummer heat of the desert tablelands. Because of the high level of hygiene, infectious diseases will not be a significant concern for most travelers, who are unlikely to experience anything worse than a little diarrhea, sunburn or a mild respiratory infection.

Insurance

- The USA offers possibly the finest health care in the world, but it can be prohibitively expensive.
- International travelers should check if their regular policy covers them in the US; if it doesn't, travel insurance is essential.

Vaccinations

No special vaccines are required or recommended for travel to or around the USA. All travelers should be up-to-date on routine immunizations.

Health Care

In general, if you have a medical emergency, the best bet is for you to find the nearest hospital and go to its emergency room. If the problem isn't urgent, you can call a nearby hospital and ask for a referral to a local physician, which is usually cheaper than a trip to the emergency room. Stand-alone, for-profit urgent-care centers can be convenient, but may perform large numbers of expensive tests, even for minor illnesses.

If you're heading to more remote areas of the state, it pays to be aware of the closest emergency medical services. If heading into backcountry areas, stop by the local ranger station or visitors center for information.

Wildlife

Common-sense approaches to animal bites and stings are the most effective.

- Wear boots when hiking to protect from snakes.
- Wear long sleeves and pants to protect from ticks and mosquitoes.
- If you're bitten, don't overreact. Stay calm and seek the relevant treatment.

ANIMAL BITES

- Do not attempt to pet, handle or feed any nondomestic animal. Most animal-related injuries are directly related to a person's attempt to touch or feed the animal.
- Any bite or scratch by a mammal, including bats, should be promptly and thoroughly cleansed with large amounts of soap and water, followed by application of an antiseptic, such as iodine or alcohol.
- Local health authorities should be contacted immediately for possible rabies treatment, regardless of immunization.

➡ It may also be advisable to start an antibiotic; wounds caused by animal bites and scratches frequently become infected.

SNAKE BITES

➡ There are several varieties of venomous snakes in Colorado; these snakes do not cause instantaneous death, and antivenins are available.

➡ Place a light constricting bandage over the bite, keep the wounded part below the level of the heart and move it as little as possible.

➡ Stay calm and get to a medical facility as soon as possible.

➡ Bring the dead snake for identification if you can, but don't risk being bitten again.

➡ Do not use the mythic 'cut an X and suck out the venom' trick.

MOUNTAIN LIONS

Chances of encountering an aggressive mountain lion are extremely small, but as humans encroach on their territory attacks are increasing. Avoid hiking alone in prime mountain-lion habitat and keep children within view. If you encounter one, raise your arms and back away slowly. Speak firmly or shout. If attacked, fight back fiercely.

BEARS

Colorado has black bears, which are smaller than grizzlies and have very few incidences of attacking humans. Still, you should never get between a mother bear and her cubs. If camping, always hang your food, lock it in a bear-proof canister or keep it in a closed car. Make noise (whistling, clapping or chatting) when hiking in bear country so you don't surprise a bear. Don't run if you encounter one – they are fast. Back away slowly and avoid eye contact.

When planning a backpacking trip, make sure you know the park safety regulations. In Rocky Mountain National Park, campers are required to bring a bear-proof canister to store food, trash and toiletries in. If you don't want to buy one, they may usually be rented from camping stores.

Insurance

No matter how long or short your trip, make sure you purchase adequate travel insurance before departure.

Also consider coverage for luggage theft or loss and for trip cancellation. If you already have a home-owner's or renter's policy, see what it will cover and consider getting supplemental insurance to cover the rest. If you've prepaid a large portion of your trip, cancellation insurance is a worthwhile expense. A comprehensive travel insurance policy that covers all these things can cost up to 10% of the total cost of your trip.

If you will be driving, it's essential that you have liability insurance. Car-rental agencies offer insurance that covers damage to the rental vehicle and separate liability insurance, which covers damage to people and other vehicles.

Worldwide travel insurance is available at www.lonelyplanet.com/travel_services. You can buy, extend and claim online anytime – even if you're already on the road.

Internet Access

➡ Internet cafés typically charge $3 to $12 per hour for online access.

➡ Accommodations, cafes, restaurants, bars etc that provide guest computer terminals for going online are identified by the internet icon @; the wi-fi icon indicates that wireless access is available. There may be a fee for either service.

➡ Free or fee-based wi-fi hot spots can be found at major airports; many hotels, motels and cafes; and some tourist information centers, museums, bars and restaurants.

➡ Free public wi-fi is proliferating, and even some state parks are now wi-fi enabled.

➡ To find more public wi-fi hot spots, search www.wififreespot.com or www.jiwire.com.

➡ Public libraries have internet terminals (online time may be limited, advance sign-up required and a nominal fee charged for out-of-network visitors) and free wi-fi access.

Legal Matters

Rights

➡ People arrested for a serious offense in the US have the right to remain silent, to an attorney and to make one phone call. They are presumed innocent until proven guilty.

➡ International visitors who are arrested and don't have a lawyer or family member to help should call their embassy or consulate.

Smoking

➡ Smoking is banned at all workplaces, including bars and restaurants.

➡ Private residences and automobiles are exempt unless used for child day care.

➡ Some hotels/motels and other businesses may have designated smoking rooms or areas.

➡ Local governments may have stricter smoking regulations than the state government.

Drugs

➡ Colorado has state-approved use of marijuana for medicinal purposes and recently legalized

INTERNATIONAL VISITORS

Entering the Region

- Every foreign visitor entering the USA needs a passport valid for at least six months longer than the intended stay.
- Apart from most Canadian citizens and those under the **Visa Waiver Program** (https://esta.cbp.dhs.gov/esta), all visitors need to obtain a visa from a US consulate or embassy abroad.
- For a complete list of US customs regulations, visit the official portal for **US Customs & Border Protection** (www.cbp.gov).

Embassies & Consulates

- There are no foreign embassies or diplomatic representatives in Colorado.
- International travelers who want to contact their home country's embassy while in the US should visit **Embassy.org** (www.embassy.org), which lists contact information for all foreign embassies in Washington, DC. Most countries have a mission to the UN in New York City.

Money

ATMs are widely available. Most businesses accept credit cards.

Post

- No matter how much people like to complain, the **US Postal Service** (USPS; www.usps.com) provides great service for the price.
- Private shippers such as **United Parcel Service** (UPS; ☎800-742-5877; www.ups.com) and **Federal Express** (FedEx; ☎800-463-3339; www.fedex.com) are useful for sending more important or larger items.

Telephone

CALLING CODES

- Country code: ☎1
- Area codes: ☎303, ☎719, ☎720, ☎970
- International access code: ☎011

CELL (MOBILE) PHONES

- You'll need a multiband GSM phone in order to make calls in the USA.
- A prepaid SIM card is usually cheaper than using your home network.
- There are plenty of holes in the coverage; don't assume you'll have reception, particularly when between cities.

Time

- Colorado is on Mountain Standard Time (MST), seven hours behind GMT/UTC.
- Colorado switches to Mountain Daylight Time (or Pacific Daylight Time), one hour later, from the first Sunday of April to the last Saturday of October.

the recreational use of marijuana. Though recreational regulations and distribution have yet to be put into place, the basics are that those 21 and older are allowed to possess under 1oz and consume it in private only.

- Possession of any kind of illicit drug, including cocaine, ecstasy, LSD, heroin, hashish or more than 1oz of cannabis, is a felony potentially punishable by lengthy jail sentences. For foreigners, conviction of any drug offense is grounds for deportation.

Public Holidays

New Year's Day January 1

Martin Luther King Jr Day Third Monday of January

Presidents Day Third Monday of February

Easter March or April

Memorial Day Last Monday of May

Independence Day July 4

Labor Day First Monday of September

Columbus Day Second Monday of October

Veterans Day November 11

Thanksgiving Fourth Thursday of November

Christmas Day December 25

Tourist Information

Colorado Travel & Tourism Authority (800-265-6723; www.colorado.com) Statewide tourism information.

Travelers with Disabilities

Travel within Colorado is getting easier for people with disabilities, but it's still not easy. Public buildings are required by law to be wheelchair accessible and to have appropriate restroom facilities. Public transportation services must be made accessible to all, and telephone companies have to provide relay operators for the hearing impaired. Many banks provide ATM instructions in braille, curb ramps are common, many busy intersections have audible crossing signals, and most chain hotels have suites for guests with disabilities. Still, it's best to call ahead to check.

A number of organizations specialize in the needs of travelers with disabilities:

Adaptive Sports Center (970-349-2296; www.adaptivesports.org; 10 Crested Butte Way, Crested Butte) For travelers with disabilities seeking outdoor adventures.

Mobility International USA (541-343-1284; www.miusa.org)

Society for the Advancement of Travel for the Handicapped (SATH; 212-447-7284; www.sath.org; 347 Fifth Ave, Suite 610, New York)

Volunteering

Opportunities for volunteering in Colorado are plenty and various, and it can be a great way to break up a long trip. Volunteering can also provide truly memorable experiences: you'll get to interact with people, society and the land in ways you never would by just passing through.

There are numerous casual, drop-in volunteering opportunities in the big cities, and you can socialize with locals and help out nonprofit organizations. Check weekly alternative newspapers for calendar listings, or browse the free classified ads online at Craigslist (www.craigslist.org) . The public website www.serve.gov and private websites www.idealist.org and www.volunteermatch.org offer free searchable databases of short- and long-term volunteer opportunities nationwide.

More formal volunteer programs, especially those designed for international travelers, typically charge a hefty fee of $250 to $1000, depending on the length of the program and what amenities are included (eg housing, meals). None cover travel to the USA.

Resources

Habitat for Humanity (800-422-4828; www.habitat.org)

Sierra Club (415-977-5500; www.sierraclub.org)

Volunteers for Peace (802-259-2759; www.vfp.org)

Wilderness Volunteers (928-556-0038; www.wildernessvolunteers.org)

World Wide Opportunities on Organic Farms-USA (WWOOF-USA; 949-715-9500; www.wwoofusa.org)

Work

Seasonal work is possible in national parks and other tourist sites, especially ski areas; for information, contact park concessions or local chambers of commerce. These are usually low-paying service jobs filled by young people (often college students) who are happy to work part of the day so they can play the rest. You can't depend on finding a job just by arriving in May or June and looking around.

Transportation

GETTING THERE & AWAY

Most travelers arrive in Colorado by air or car, with arrivals by bus a distant third. There is also a daily Amtrak train service that pulls into Denver's Union Station.

Flights, tours and rail tickets can be booked online at www.lonelyplanet.com/bookings.

Air

Airports

Denver is the region's main air hub but there are alternatives if you arrive on a domestic flight. Consider landing in a neighboring state and driving into Colorado through the Rocky Mountains. Colorado has dozens of smaller airports throughout the state.

Denver International Airport (DIA; ☎303-342-2000; www.flydenver.com; 8500 Peña Blvd; 📶)

Aspen-Pitkin County Airport (☎970-920-5380; www.aspenairport.com; 233 E Airport Rd; 📶)

Colorado Springs Airport (☎719-550-1900; www.springsgov.com; 7770 Milton E Proby Pkwy; 📶)

Durango-La Plata County Airport (☎970-247-8143; www.flydurango.com; 1000 Airport Rd)

Eagle County Regional Airport (☎970-328-2680; www.flyvail.com; 219 Eldon Wilson Dr) West of Vail.

Grand Junction Regional Airport (Walker Field Airport; ☎970-244-9100; www.gjairport.com; 2828 Walker Field Dr)

Gunnison-Crested Butte Regional Airport (☎970-641-2304; W Rio Grande Ave)

Montrose Regional Airport (☎970-249-3203; www.montroseairport.com; 2100 Airport Rd)

Telluride Regional Airport (☎970-778-5051; www.tellurideairport.com; Last Dollar Rd)

Yampa Valley Airport (County Rd 51A) West of Steamboat Springs.

Airlines

AirTran Airways (☎800-247-8726; www.airtran.com) Airlines handling the main routes in and out of Colorado:

Alaskan Airlines (☎800-252-7522; www.alaskaair.com)

Allegiant Airlines (☎702-505-8888; www.allegiantair.com)

American Airlines (☎800-433-7300; www.aa.com)

Delta (☎800-221-1212; www.delta.com)

Frontier (☎800-432-1359; www.frontierairlines.com)

Jet Blue (☎800-538-2583; www.jetblue.com)

Southwest (☎800-435-9792; www.southwest.com)

United Airlines (☎800-864-8331; www.united.com)

US Airways (☎800-428-4322; www.usairways.com)

Land

Bus

➡ **Greyhound** (www.greyhound.com) runs cross-country buses between San Francisco and New York via Wyoming, Denver and Chicago; and between Los Angeles and New York via Las Vegas, Denver and Chicago.

➡ There are also bus services from other eastern seaboard cities such as Philadelphia and Washington, DC, and southern cities such as Atlanta and Miami.

➡ Fares are relatively high and bargain air fares can undercut buses on long-distance routes. On shorter routes it can be cheaper to rent a car.

➡ Very long-distance bus trips are often available at bargain prices by 'web only fares' from the Greyhound website.

Car & Motorcycle

➡ I-70 runs nearly the entire length of the USA, passing through central Colorado.

➡ I-25 runs north–south from New Mexico through Colorado and ends at a junction with I-90 in northern Wyoming.

Train

- **Amtrak** (☎800-872-7245; www.amtrak.com) provides cross-country passenger services between the West Coast and Chicago. Travelers to or from the East Coast must make connections in Chicago. Amtrak trains service only a few destinations in Colorado besides Denver.
- At the time of writing, Denver's Union Station, which includes Amtrak, was undergoing renovation.
- The daily *California Zephyr* from San Francisco (via Emeryville, CA) passes through Colorado en route to Chicago. In Colorado the train stops at Fort Morgan, Denver's Union Station, Fraser-Winter Park, Granby, Glenwood Springs and Grand Junction.
- The *Southwest Chief* goes from Los Angeles via Albuquerque and the southern Colorado towns of Trinidad, La Junta and Lamar to Kansas City and Chicago.

TICKETS

- Amtrak tickets may be purchased aboard the train without penalty if the station is not open 30 minutes prior to boarding. Rail travel is generally cheaper if you purchase tickets in advance. Roundtrips are the best value, but even these can be as expensive as air fares.
- For further travel assistance, call Amtrak, surf its website or ask your travel agent. Note that most small train stations don't sell tickets. Instead you must book them with Amtrak over the phone or buy online. Some small stations have no porters or other facilities, and trains may stop there only if you have bought a ticket in advance.
- Amtrak offers some good-value USA Rail Passes.
- Children aged between two and 15 years travel for half of the adult fare only when accompanied by an adult. Kids under two are free.
- Seniors aged 62 years and over are entitled to a 15% discount (with some limitations) on adult fares.
- Members of the **American Automobile Association** (AAA; ☎866-625-3601; www.colorado.aaa.com) get 10% discount and students with a Student Advantage or **ISIC card** (ISIC; www.isiccard.com) get 15%. Active military personnel, their spouses and dependents get a 10% discount and Veterans Advantage card holders get 15%.

GETTING AROUND

Colorado has fairly comprehensive coverage by commuter flights, although the cost may deter most travelers. On the ground, public transportation leaves much to be desired, and travelers without their own vehicles need to be patient and flexible to take advantage of the limited possibilities. The most enjoyable way to travel is by car or motorbike.

Air

Colorado has many small commercial airports. All are served by flights out of Denver, and Grand Junction also has flights to and from Salt Lake City, UT. During ski season, resort airports offer direct flights to major cities around the US.

Bicycle

- Cycling is a cheap, convenient, healthy, environmentally sound and, above all, fun way of traveling. In Colorado, because of altitude, distance and heat, it's also a good workout.
- Cycling has increased in popularity so much in recent years that concerns have risen over damage to the environment, especially from unchecked mountain biking. Know your environment and regulations before you ride. Bikes are restricted from entering wilderness areas and some designated trails but may be used in National Park Service (NPS) sites, state parks, national and state forests and Bureau of Land Management (BLM) single-track trails.
- Cyclists should carry at least a gallon of water and refill bottles at every opportunity.
- Airlines accept bicycles as checked luggage; contact them for specific rules.

CLIMATE CHANGE & TRAVEL

Every form of transportation that relies on carbon-based fuel generates CO_2, the main cause of human-induced climate change. Modern travel is dependent on airplanes, which might use less fuel per mile per person than most cars but travel much greater distances. The altitude at which aircraft emit gases (including CO_2) and particles also contributes to their climate change impact. Many websites offer 'carbon calculators' that allow people to estimate the carbon emissions generated by their journey and, for those who wish to do so, to offset the impact of the greenhouse gases emitted with contributions to portfolios of climate-friendly initiatives throughout the world. Lonely Planet offsets the carbon footprint of all staff and author travel.

➡ City and long-haul buses and trains can carry bikes, and in the mountains shuttles are fitted with racks for skis in winter and mountain bikes in summer.

➡ Boulder and Denver have bike-share programs called B-Cycle. Fort Collins offers a **bike library** (Map p144; ☎970-419-1050; www.fcbikelibrary.org; Old Town Sq; ⏲10am-6pm Thu-Sun with seasonal variations).

➡ Rental bicycles are widely available. In Colorado's legendary mountain-biking regions the range of rental options can be bewilderingly comprehensive. Hard-tail mountain bikes rent for around $34 a day while fancy full-suspension rentals go for more like $75.

➡ Bicycles are generally prohibited on interstate highways if there is a frontage road. However, where a suitable frontage road or alternative is lacking, cyclists are permitted on some interstates.

➡ Cyclists are generally treated courteously by motorists.

➡ Colorado currently has no legal requirement for cyclists to wear helmets (but they do reduce the risk of head injury).

Bus

➡ The main bus line in and out of the region is **Greyhound** (www.greyhound.com), with a network of fixed routes and its own terminal in most central cities. It has an excellent safety record, and the buses are comfortable and usually on time.

➡ Regional parts of Colorado are poorly serviced by buses. Exceptions are RTD (Denver, Boulder areas), Summit County's Summit Stage, ECO (Eagle County) and Roaring Fork Transportation, in the Aspen region. Bike racks on buses are the norm, as are ski racks in high country.

➡ Greyhound tickets can be bought over the phone or online with a credit card and mailed if purchased 10 days in advance, or picked up at the terminal with proper identification.

➡ Discounts apply to tickets purchased 14 or 21 days in advance.

➡ All buses are nonsmoking, and reservations are made with ticket purchases only.

Car & Motorcycle

One of the great ways to experience Colorado is to drive its roads and byways. The road conditions are generally very good and it's always rewarding when you point the car down an unknown backroad just to see where it goes. Good maps and road atlases are sold everywhere.

The penchant Coloradans have for monster SUVs and mega motorhomes can be a little intimidating when you're put putting up a steep mountain road in your clapped-out Korean rental car. But fellow drivers are courteous and generous with their friendly conversation at roadside diners and gas stations. 'Where you headed?' is a common opener. Tuning into local radio stations is part of the immersive cultural experience.

Rental

The rental-car market is crowded and competitive, which means you can get some good deals, especially if you hire for a week or more.

With advance reservations for a small car, the daily rate with unlimited mileage is about $30 to $40; typical weekly rates are $150 to $200. Rates for midsize cars may be a tad higher. You can often snag great last-minute deals via the internet. Renting in conjunction with an airplane ticket often yields better rates too. Try with a web consolidator engine.

Ask about any extra surcharges, such as one-way rentals and additional drivers.

Some companies won't rent vehicles to people without a major credit card; others require things such as prepayment or cash deposits. Booking can be secured with a credit card and then paid by cash or debit card.

Car-rental companies always offer extra insurance, but if you're adequately covered under a travel-insurance policy or other then don't be suckered by the compelling sales pitch. Basic liability insurance is required by law and included in the basic rental price. Check with your insurance company regarding any extended coverage.

Many rental agencies stipulate that damage a car suffers while being driven on unpaved roads is not covered by the insurance they offer.

Companies operating in Colorado:

Alamo (☎800-327-9633; www.alamo.com)

Avis (☎800-831-2847; www.avis.com)

Budget (☎800-527-0700; www.budget.com)

Dollar (☎800-800-4000; www.dollar.com)

Enterprise (☎800-325-8007; www.enterprise.com)

Hertz (☎800-654-3131; www.hertz.com)

National (☎800-227-7368; www.nationalcar.com)

Rent-A-Wreck (☎800-944-7501; www.rent-a-wreck.com)

Thrifty (☎800-847-4389; www.thrifty.com)

Drive-Aways

Drive-away agencies find people to transport a car for the owner. This can be a cheap way to get around if you meet eligibility requirements. Applicants need a valid license and a clean driving record. Generally drivers pay for gas and a small refundable deposit. You need to be flexible about dates and destinations. Search for

ROAD DISTANCES (MILES)

	Alamosa	Aspen	Boulder	Colorado Springs	Denver	Dinosaur	Durango	Fort Collins	Grand Junction	Gunnison	La Junta	Steamboat Springs
Aspen	15											
Boulder	260	175										
Colorado Springs	165	155	95									
Denver	235	160	25	70								
Dinosaur	360	180	310	360	295							
Durango	150	245	130	320	340	275						
Fort Collins	295	220	60	320	65	285	400					
Grand Junction	250	130	260	310	245	110	165	305				
Gunnison	120	145	215	170	200	235	170	260	125			
La Junta	145	150	200	105	200	465	295	240	350	225		
Steamboat Springs	260	155	170	225	175	130	355	160	195	240	330	
Vail	175	100	110	160	100	200	290	160	150	160	270	95

drive-away and auto transport companies online.

Legal Matters

- Speed limits on Colorado state highways range from 55mph to 65mph, and go as high as 75mph on I-70. Limits in city CBDs is 25mph and it's 35mph in residential areas. On open mountain highways the speed limit is 40mph.
- Texting from cell phones while driving is prohibited, and drivers under the age of 18 years are prohibited from using cell phones.
- Colorado's highway patrol is famously intolerant of speeding and if you're consistently flouting the speed limit you'll get booked.
- Seat belts are required for the driver and front seat passenger and for all passengers on highways and interstates. On motorcycles, helmets are required for anyone under 18.
- Driving while impaired (DWI) is defined as having a blood-alcohol level of 0.05% or above, and will probably land you in jail and definitely earn you heavy fines.

Safety

- Much of Colorado is open-range country where livestock and deer forage along the highway. Pay attention to the roadside, especially at night.
- During winter months, tire chains may be required. Some roads require chains or 4WD. It's a good idea to keep a set of chains in the trunk.
- Other cold-weather precautions include keeping a sleeping bag, warm clothing, extra food, a windshield ice-scraper, a snow shovel, flares and an extra set of gloves and boots in the trunk for emergencies.
- Colorado doesn't require motorcycle riders over 18 years to wear helmets, but it's highly recommended.
- Weather is a serious factor, especially in winter. For road and travel information and state highway patrol information dial ☎877-315-7623.

Hitchhiking

Hitchhiking is illegal in Colorado. Pedestrians on the highway must walk in the opposite direction of traffic.

Train

Rail service within Colorado is very limited beyond the interstate options.

Tourist trains include the Durango & Silverton Narrow Gauge Railroad in southern Colorado, the Georgetown Loop, the Cumbres & Toltec Scenic Railroad from Antonito to Chama in New Mexico, and the Pikes Peak Cog Railway in Manitou Springs. Although they are tourist trains, the Durango and Cumbres lines allow hikers and anglers access to wilderness areas.

Behind the Scenes

SEND US YOUR FEEDBACK

We love to hear from travelers – your comments keep us on our toes and help make our books better. Our well-traveled team reads every word on what you loved or loathed about this book. Although we cannot reply individually to postal submissions, we always guarantee that your feedback goes straight to the appropriate authors, in time for the next edition. Each person who sends us information is thanked in the next edition – the most useful submissions are rewarded with a selection of digital PDF chapters.

Visit **lonelyplanet.com/contact** to submit your updates and suggestions or to ask for help. Our award-winning website also features inspirational travel stories, news and discussions.

Note: We may edit, reproduce and incorporate your comments in Lonely Planet products such as guidebooks, websites and digital products, so let us know if you don't want your comments reproduced or your name acknowledged. For a copy of our privacy policy visit lonelyplanet.com/privacy.

OUR READERS

Many thanks to the travelers who used the last edition and wrote to us with helpful hints, useful advice and interesting anecdotes: Francesca Barton, Karl Borski, Tim Chladek, Ben Costello, Becky Creighton, Ken Dechman, Charlotte Elich, Chad Fogelberg, Gemma Hartley, Sara Hutton, Becky Jones, Corina Marquardt, Will Marquardt, Molly Mickel, Lindsey Modesitt, John Roberts, Erik Schwartz, John Squire, Nancy Venne

AUTHOR THANKS

Carolyn McCarthy

Thanks to all who made my return to Colorado wonderful. Special thanks to Conan for the keys to his classic Saab. Many thanks also go to Lance and his Ouray friends for the bed and BBQ, Jen in Crested Butte and Dave in Durango. In Boulder, Jessica, Stephanie and Francoise made restaurant research a blast. Rachel Dowd proved an excellent driver, copilot, sandwichmaker and keen observer. Virtual craft beers go out to Chris and Greg for their many contributions, and to the Pitts for a home away from home.

Greg Benchwick

Special thanks to my friend and commissioning editor Suki, as well as my co-authors and the rest of the LP team. A special thanks to Brent Weakley for helping me with the Denver gay bar write-up, and to my sister, Cara, my Mom – we'll just call her Mom – and my big baby girl Violeta for helping me research this book. Your support, companionship and love are bottomless, selfless and truly inspiring.

Christopher Pitts

Huge thanks to co-authors Carolyn and Greg for the tips, connections and all-around sage words of advice – and special thanks to Carolyn in particular for house-sitting not one but two houses in our summer of absence. Thanks also to editor extraordinaire Suki for coordinating the whole project. On the road, big thank yous to Cigdem in Glenwood for the inside scoop on the Roaring Fork Valley, Betsy and her lovely family for a delicious home-cooked meal and the lowdown on Carbondale, and the Brutel famille in Colorado Springs for putting us up for a night (and for the best cakes this side of the Atlantic). And finally, love to my dearest partners in crime: Perrine, Elliot and Céleste.

ACKNOWLEDGMENTS

Climate map data adapted from Peel MC, Finlayson BL & McMahon TA (2007) 'Updated World Map of the Köppen-Geiger Climate Classification', *Hydrology and Earth System Sciences*, 11, 1633¬44.

Cover photograph: Rocky Mountain National Park, Michele Falzone/AWL

THIS BOOK

This 2nd edition of Lonely Planet's *Colorado* guidebook was researched and written by Carolyn McCarthy, Greg Benchwick and Christopher Pitts. The previous edition was written by Nate Cavalieri, Adam Skolnick and Rowan McKinnon.

This guidebook was commissioned in Lonely Planet's Oakland office, and produced by the following:

Commissioning Editor Suki Gear

Coordinating Editors Tracy Whitmey, Simon Williamson

Senior Cartographer Alison Lyall

Assisting Cartographer Rachel Imeson

Book Designer Clara Monitto

Associate Product Directors Sasha Baskett, Angela Tinson

Senior Editors Karyn Noble, Catherine Naghten

Assisting Editors Andrew Bain, Michelle Bennett, Paul Harding, Gabrielle Stefanos

Cover Research Naomi Parker

Thanks to Anita Banh, Penny Cordner, Ryan Evans, Samantha Forge, Larissa Frost, Paula Hardy, Genesys India, Jouve India, Elizabeth Jones, Trent Paton, Martine Power

Index

Map Pages **000**
Photo Pages 000

Map Pages **000**
Photo Pages **000**

H

I

J

K

L

M

Map Pages **000**
Photo Pages **000**

GARFIELD COUNTY
LIBRARIES
2231

Map Legend

Sights

- Beach
- Bird Sanctuary
- Buddhist
- Castle/Palace
- Christian
- Confucian
- Hindu
- Islamic
- Jain
- Jewish
- Monument
- Museum/Gallery/Historic Building
- Ruin
- Sento Hot Baths/Onsen
- Shinto
- Sikh
- Taoist
- Winery/Vineyard
- Zoo/Wildlife Sanctuary
- Other Sight

Activities, Courses & Tours

- Bodysurfing
- Diving
- Canoeing/Kayaking
- Course/Tour
- Skiing
- Snorkeling
- Surfing
- Swimming/Pool
- Walking
- Windsurfing
- Other Activity

Sleeping

- Sleeping
- Camping

Eating

- Eating

Drinking & Nightlife

- Drinking & Nightlife
- Cafe

Entertainment

- Entertainment

Shopping

- Shopping

Information

- Bank
- Embassy/Consulate
- Hospital/Medical
- Internet
- Police
- Post Office
- Telephone
- Toilet
- Tourist Information
- Other Information

Geographic

- Beach
- Hut/Shelter
- Lighthouse
- Lookout
- Mountain/Volcano
- Oasis
- Park
- Pass
- Picnic Area
- Waterfall

Population

- Capital (National)
- Capital (State/Province)
- City/Large Town
- Town/Village

Transport

- Airport
- BART station
- Border crossing
- Boston T station
- Bus
- Cable car/Funicular
- Cycling
- Ferry
- Metro/Muni station
- Monorail
- Parking
- Petrol station
- Subway/SkyTrain station
- Taxi
- Train station/Railway
- Tram
- Underground station
- Other Transport

Note: Not all symbols displayed above appear on the maps in this book

Routes

- Tollway
- Freeway
- Primary
- Secondary
- Tertiary
- Lane
- Unsealed road
- Road under construction
- Plaza/Mall
- Steps
- Tunnel
- Pedestrian overpass
- Walking Tour
- Walking Tour detour
- Path/Walking Trail

Boundaries

- International
- State/Province
- Disputed
- Regional/Suburb
- Marine Park
- Cliff
- Wall

Hydrography

- River, Creek
- Intermittent River
- Canal
- Water
- Dry/Salt/Intermittent Lake
- Reef

Areas

- Airport/Runway
- Beach/Desert
- Cemetery (Christian)
- Cemetery (Other)
- Glacier
- Mudflat
- Park/Forest
- Sight (Building)
- Sportsground
- Swamp/Mangrove

OUR STORY

A beat-up old car, a few dollars in the pocket and a sense of adventure. In 1972 that's all Tony and Maureen Wheeler needed for the trip of a lifetime – across Europe and Asia overland to Australia. It took several months, and at the end – broke but inspired – they sat at their kitchen table writing and stapling together their first travel guide, *Across Asia on the Cheap*. Within a week they'd sold 1500 copies. Lonely Planet was born.

Today, Lonely Planet has offices in Melbourne, London and Oakland, with more than 600 staff and writers. We share Tony's belief that 'a great guidebook should do three things: inform, educate and amuse'.

OUR WRITERS

Carolyn McCarthy

Coordinating Author, Boulder & Around, Mesa Verde & Southwest Colorado

Carolyn fell for the Rockies as an undergraduate at Colorado College, where she hiked, skied, camped and paddled while reading the classics. For this title she sampled mountain distilleries, dodged a wildfire and heard even more Old West ghost stories. Carolyn has contributed to more than 20 Lonely Planet titles, specializing in the American West and Latin America, and has written for *National Geographic, Outside, Lonely Planet Magazine* and other publications. Carolyn also wrote the Plan Your Trip, Understand and Survival Guide chapters for this guidebook.

Greg Benchwick

Denver & Around, Rocky Mountain National Park & Northern Colorado

A Colorado native, Greg's been all over the Centennial State. He taught skiing in Vail, walked through fire pits in campsites across the state and attended journalism school in Boulder. He calls Denver's Highlands home.

Read more about Greg at:
lonelyplanet.com/members/gbenchwick

Christopher Pitts

Vail, Aspen & Central Colorado, Southeast Colorado & the San Luis Valley

Chris first drove west on a family road trip across the country and instantly fell in love with Colorado's star-studded nights. After four years at Colorado College, he decided to move up to Boulder for grad school – but only after mastering Chinese first. Fifteen years, several continents and two kids later, he finally made it to the end of what is normally a 90-minute drive. He currently divides his time between writing, dad-dom and exploring Colorado's wilder corners.

Read more about Christopher at:
lonelyplanet.com/members/christopherpitts

Published by Lonely Planet Publications Pty Ltd
ABN 36 005 607 983
2nd edition – May 2014
ISBN 978 1 74220 559 5

10 9 8 7 6 5 4 3 2 1
Printed in China